Frommer's®

500

places to take your kids before they grow up

2nd Edition

By Holly Hughes & Julie Duchaine

WILEY

Wiley Publishing, Inc.

Contents

Published by:

Wiley Publishing, Inc.

111 River St.
Hoboken, NJ 07030-5774

ISBN 978-0-470-47405-1

Editor: Cate Latting
Production Editor: M. Faunette Johnston
Cartographer: Guy Ruggiero
Photo Editor: Cherie Cincilla
Interior book design: Melissa Auciello-Brogan
Production by Wiley Indianapolis Composition Services

Front cover photo: Hawaii: Child snorkeling, holding pencil urchin.
Back cover photos: Wildlife, Mammal, Marsupial, Koala, Australia, Children visiting Monument Valley; Park ranger made out of building blocks outside Legoland, Billund Denmark, Boy pointing at the Leaning Tower of Pisa, Pisa, Tuscany, Italy.

For information on our other products and services or to obtain technical support, please contact our Customer Care Department within the U.S. at 877/762-2974, outside the U.S. at 317/572-3993 or fax 317/572-4002.

Wiley also publishes its books in a variety of electronic formats. Some content that appears in print may not be available in electronic formats.

Manufactured in the United States of America

5 4 3 2 1

About the Author

Holly Hughes has traveled the globe as an editor and writer. A former executive editor of Fodor's Travel Publications, she edits the annual Best Food Writing anthology and is the author of the bestselling *500 Places for Food & Wine Lovers, 500 Places to See Before They Disappear,* and *Frommer's New York City with Kids.* She has also written fiction for middle graders. New York City makes a convenient jumping-off place for her travels with her three children and husband.

About the Co-Author

Julie Duchaine has been a freelance writer for the past 25 years. Most recently, she contributed to *Frommer's 500 Places to See Before They Disappear* and *Frommer's 500 Places for Food & Wine Lovers.* She lives in Milwaukee.

Acknowledgments

Many thanks to all my fellow parents whose brains I picked for travel suggestions over the past 4 years. You were so generous with your trip memories, I almost felt in some cases as if I had traveled there with you. And to all the other parents who had to listen to my enthusiastic ramblings by the coffee urns at PTA meetings and on the soccer field sidelines—thank you for never letting your eyes glaze over as I raved on and on about yet another far-flung destination they really should visit.

I've also relied on the devoted corps of Frommer's writers to supply me with phone numbers, addresses, and recommendations of their own favorite family destinations. Your descriptions have been invaluable—you're the real experts in your various parts of the world, and I'm beholden to you.

And finally, I have to thank my husband and children, who not only put up with having Mom disappear into her office for hours at a time but who are the best travel companions I could ever ask for.

—Holly Hughes

I would like to thank my co-writer, Holly Hughes for sharing her knowledge and providing helpful suggestions over the course of many long phone calls.

I also owe a debt to my editor, Cate Latting, who kept everything on track and running smoothly.

Finally, I would like to thank the Frommer's writers whose work was invaluable when it came time to supply phone numbers and hotel suggestions. Their work made mine easier, and I am grateful for that.

—Julie Duchaine

An Invitation to the Reader

In researching this book, we discovered many wonderful places. We're sure you'll find others. Please tell us about them, so we can share the information with your fellow travelers in upcoming editions. If you were disappointed with a recommendation, we'd love to know that, too. Please write to:

Frommer's 500 Places to Take Your Kids Before They Grow Up, 2nd Edition
Wiley Publishing, Inc. • 111 River St. • Hoboken, NJ 07030-5774

An Additional Note

Please be advised that travel information is subject to change at any time—and this is especially true of prices. We therefore suggest that you write or call ahead for confirmation when making your travel plans. The authors, editors, and publisher cannot be held responsible for the experiences of readers while traveling. Your safety is important to us, however, so we encourage you to stay alert and be aware of your surroundings. Keep a close eye on cameras, purses, and wallets, all favorite targets of thieves and pickpockets.

Other Great Guides for Your Trip:

Frommer's New York City with Kids
Frommer's Chicago with Kids
Frommer's Las Vegas with Kids
Frommer's San Francisco with Kids
Frommer's Washington, D.C., with Kids
The Unofficial Guide to California with Kids
The Unofficial Guide to Walt Disney World® with Kids

Frommer's Icons

We use four feature icons to help you quickly find the information you're looking for. At the end of each review, look for:

ⓘ Where to get more information

✈ Nearest airport

🚆 Nearest train station

🛏 Recommended kid-friendly hotels

Frommers.com

Now that you have this guidebook to help you plan a great trip, visit our website at www.frommers.com for additional travel information on more than 4,000 destinations. We update features regularly to give you instant access to the most current trip-planning information available. At Frommers.com, you'll find scoops on the best airfares, lodging rates, and car rental bargains. You can even book your travel online through our reliable travel booking partners. Other popular features include:

- Online updates of our most popular guidebooks
- Vacation sweepstakes and contest giveaways
- Newsletters highlighting the hottest travel trends
- Podcasts, interactive maps, and up-to-the-minute events listings
- Opinionated blog entries by Arthur Frommer himself
- Online travel message boards with featured travel discussions

Why These 500 Places?

The obvious question just about everybody asked me when I told them I was writing this book: "Have you been to all 500 places?" I regret to say I haven't—not yet—but I've been to a surprising number of them over the past few years. If not, I've talked to other families who have generously shared their travel memories with me. Immersed in writing this book, at times I almost imagined we had been everyplace. But I have to say, now that it's written, I'm glad we haven't seen it all and done it all yet—we still have a few traveling years ahead of us as a family, and now we've got a thicker file than ever of thrilling trips to look forward to.

Of course, choosing a destination is only part of the challenge. Knowing what it's like to travel with youngsters, I've tried to give you the tools you need to make these trips unforgettable. I've dug up tidbits of history or other background, so you can look like experts when you're leading your children around a site. It's not enough just to go to a place—you've got to imagine how the people of this distant era lived, why one army won this battle and not the other, what makes this park different from that one, which animals thrive where. You do it to keep the kids interested, and then somehow you find yourself having a richer experience of the place, too. Awakening that sense of wonder is what travel is all about, for adults as well as children.

I've also suggested strategies for certain destinations—whether or not to hire a tour guide (some enrich the experience, others bog you down in boring details); whether to drive, walk, or take the tram; whether to dawdle over a museum's every exhibit or zero in on a few key displays. With the proper strategy, you'd be surprised how much even young children can delight in these destinations. Don't sell them short! The payoff is all cumulative—the more your children travel, the more they'll observe and appreciate on further trips, and the more intriguing trips you'll be able to plan.

Of course, you are the experts when it comes to knowing your own family's interests—whether that be history, culture, nature, outdoor adventure—so rather than follow a geographic scheme, I've organized this book in groups of destinations with a similar emphasis, spread around the globe. After a successful trip to one destination, I hope you'll consider planning new trips to others in that category—chances are you'll like them too.

The geographic index in the back will help you match nearby destinations, so you can take in a whole cluster of sights on one vacation.

Hotels

I wish I'd had space to give you full-blown hotel reviews, but you can rely on these choices being the most family-friendly lodgings in the area. Traveling with a family is not cheap, so I tended to recommend moderately priced hotels rather than the most expensive lodgings. (You don't need my help in finding the poshest hotel in town—what's hard to find is the small hotel with no advertising budget.). I also recommend modern, plainly furnished hotels rather than antique-laden B&Bs, which, for all their charm, may not welcome children. The other criteria I look for: kitchenettes, room service, room layouts that accommodate extra beds, TVs in the room, and the trump card, a swimming pool (give us a good pool and my kids will accept almost anything). Price ranges of course are relative. The three price ranges I note—$$$ (expensive), $$ (moderate), and $ (inexpensive)—don't conform to one set of dollar equivalents, but reflect the local market. A $125-per-night motel room in South Dakota would seem expensive, but if you can find something clean and safe at that price in London, snap it up. For fuller descriptions (and other useful travel info), please consult the corresponding Frommer's guides for these destinations. Note that any phone numbers listed are what you'd dial from within that country—to dial from overseas, add the appropriate country code.

Age Ranges

For each destination, I've also indicated an age range for children. When I say "All ages," that means you could bring a baby or young toddler in a stroller and not feel out of place. I'm not saying the 6-month-old would get much out of the experience (!), but at least you could take older siblings there without the baby being a hindrance. In a few cases, I've upped the age range on a destination if it somehow poses challenges handled best by older kids. I admit that these recommended age ranges are subjective—for lack of a more objective test, I've based them on what my own children would have been interested in at what age. My kids have become good travelers over the years. Yours can be too.

They're only young once, so see the world through their eyes—you won't regret it!

1 Awesome Vistas

Humboldt Redwoods State Park.

The Grand Canyon
Where the Earth Splits Open
All Ages • Arizona, USA

Postcards just don't do justice to this classic American panorama—this majestic 277-mile-long canyon of the Colorado River, a primeval gash in the earth's crust of titanic proportions. Gaze down into its depth from the rim and you'll see striated bands of multi-colored rock, a living history of geologic periods unfolding at your feet. Descend into it and you'll pass through no less than four distinct climate zones, as if you began your day in Mexico and ended it in Alaska.

Grand Canyon attracts a staggering number of tourists every year—4.5 to 5 million visitors—many of whom simply view the panorama from the North or South Rim viewpoints and then drive on. While it's awesome indeed to gaze around from the rim, something about that monumental chasm makes me long to just dive in. There are any number of hiking trails, from 7 to 9 miles long; if taking on the river is more your style, check the park website for a list of approved commercial outfitters that run 3- to 18-day rafting trips, which include everything from placid floats to heart-stopping whitewater thrill rides.

Perhaps the most memorable way to explore the Grand Canyon is to pick your way down the steep, narrow trails on the back of an ornery mule. The best options for kids depart from the North Rim and are offered by **Canyon Trail Rides** (© **928/638-9875;** www.canyonrides.com). These rides range from 1-hour scenic rides along the rim to half-day trips (either a longer rim route or one that heads 2,300 feet down the North Kaibab Trail), or full-day trips (either down and up the North Kaibab Trail or, from the South Rim, a 12-mile day trip to Plateau Point). The real classics, though, are 1- or 2-night packages that go to the bottom of the canyon and include sleeping arrangements and simple meals at **Phantom Ranch,** the only lodging available below the rim of the Grand Canyon. These Phantom Ranch trips fill up as soon as reservations are accepted, 23 months in advance (© **888/297-2757**). For possible openings the next day, call the **Bright Angel Transportation Desk** at © **928/638-2631,** ext. 6015. Riders must be at least 4 feet 7 inches tall; pregnant women are not allowed.

A fair number of visitors also buzz overhead in sightseeing planes and helicopters. **Grand Canyon Airlines** (© **866/235-9422** or 928/638-2359; www.grandcanyonairlines.com) is the granddaddy of scenic air tours out here, having been in business since 1927. Plane tours out of Tusayan are also offered by **Air Grand Canyon** (© **800/247-4726** or 928/638-2686; www.airgrandcanyon.com). **Papillon Grand Canyon** (© **888/635-7272,** 702/736-7243, or 928/638-2419; www.papillon.com) operates planes and helicopters, both from the South Rim and from Las Vegas. The truly heart-stopping moment is when you're looking down at the treetops of the Kaibab National Forest, and then you cross the North Rim of the canyon and—whoosh!—the ground drops away suddenly beneath you, an effect more spectacular in person than any IMAX film could ever convey.

ⓘ © **928/638-7888;** www.nps.gov/grca.

✈ Grand Canyon National Park Airport, Tusayan, AZ.

🛏 $$$ **El Tovar Hotel,** South Rim (© **928/638-2631**). $$ **Grand Canyon Lodge,** North Rim (© **928/638-2611**). Reservations for either: © **888/297-2757.**

WHY THEY'LL THANK YOU: Discovering what's in that hole in the ground.

The Redwood Forests of California

All ages • Crescent City, California, USA

It's hard to explain the feeling you get in the old-growth forests of **Redwood National and State Parks.** Everything seems big, misty, and primeval—flowering bushes cover the ground, 10-foot-tall ferns line the creeks, and the smells are rich and musty. It's so Jurassic Park, you half expect to turn the corner and see a dinosaur.

The scientific name for these massive conifers is Sequoia sempervirens, cousins of the giant sequoias (see Sequoia National Park ❸). Sheathed in rough reddish bark, miraculously fire-resistant, their stout straight trunks shoot up 100 feet or more before a canopy of branches begins; they often reach a total height of more than 300 feet. Among the planet's most ancient individuals—the oldest dated coast redwood is more than 2,200 years old—they only grow in temperate rainforests, meaning nowhere but the U.S. Pacific Coast. In 1968, the federal government created Redwood National Park (nowadays combined with three state redwood parks) to protect what's left of this seriously endangered species. The relative isolation of this stretch of coast helped the forests survive intact, but it also makes for a long drive.

The most spectacular display is along the **Avenue of the Giants,** a 33-mile stretch of U.S. 101 through the **Humboldt Redwoods State Park** (© **707/946-2263;** www.humboldtredwoods.org). Environmentalists bemoan the tacky attractions along this route, but youngsters love 'em—from south to north, hollow **Chimney Tree,** where J.R.R. Tolkien's Hobbit is rumored to live; **One-Log House,** a small dwelling built inside a log; and the **Shrine Drive-Thru Tree.** More dignified landmarks include **Founders Grove,** honoring those who started the Save the Redwoods League in 1918; and the 950-year-old **Immortal Tree.** Don't settle for looking at all this out your car window—from many parking areas you can ramble on short loop trails into awesome redwood groves.

The other cluster of parks begins another 100 miles or so farther north, threaded along U.S. Hwy. 101. The most scenic drive parallels 101, along the **Newton B. Drury Scenic Parkway,** passing through redwood groves and meadows where Roosevelt elk graze, and **Coastal Drive,** which has grand views of the Pacific. But again, the truly spine-tingling experience requires getting out and hiking through these soaring perpendicular woods. Pick up a park map to find your way to **Tall Trees Trail,** a 3¼-mile round-trip to a 600-year-old tree often touted as the world's tallest (get a permit at the Redwood Information Center in Orick); the self-guided mile-long **Lady Bird Johnson Grove Loop;** the short, very popular **Fern Canyon Trail;** or, for the littlest hikers, the .25-mile-long **Big Tree Trail,** a paved trail leading to—what else?—a big tree.

ⓘ 1111 Second St. (© **707/464-6101;** www.nps.gov/redw).

✈ Crescent City.

🛏 $ **Curly Redwood Lodge,** 701 Redwood Hwy. S. (U.S. 101), Crescent City (© **707/464-2137;** www.curlyredwood lodge.com). $$$ **Lost Whale Inn,** 3452 Patrick's Point Dr., Trinidad (© **800/677-7859** or 707/677-3425; www.lostwhaleinn. com).

WHY THEY'LL THANK YOU: Seeing the redwoods before they're gone.

Sequoia & Kings Canyon National Parks
Giant Trees of the Sierras
All ages • Visalia & Fresno, California, USA

Only 200 miles by road from often-overrun Yosemite National Park, **Sequoia** and **Kings Canyon** national parks still feel like untrammeled wilderness. Only one road, the Generals Highway, loops through the area, and no road traverses the Sierra here. High-altitude hiking and backpacking are what these parks are really all about; some 700 miles of trails traverse this terrain of snowcapped Sierra Nevada peaks (including Mount Whitney, which at 14,494 ft. is the highest point in the lower 48 states), high-country lakes, and alpine meadows. For families, though, there's one main attraction: **the largest groves of giant sequoias in the Sierra Nevada.**

Sequoia National Park.

Though they are two separate parks, Sequoia and Kings Canyon are contiguous and managed jointly from the park headquarters at Ash Mountain—you hardly know when you're leaving one and entering the other.

Of the 75 or so groves of giant sequoias in the parks, the two most convenient to visit are **Grant Grove** (in Kings Canyon, near the Big Stump park entrance), and **Giant Forest** (in Sequoia, 16 miles from the Ash Mountain entrance). In Grant Grove, a 100-foot walk through the hollow trunk of the **Fallen Monarch** makes a fascinating side trip. The tree has been used for shelter for more than 100 years and is tall enough inside that you can walk through without bending over. In Giant Forest, the awesome **General Sherman Tree** is considered the largest living thing in the world; single branches of this monster are more than 7 feet thick. Other trees in the grove (each of them saddled with such names as General Lee or Lincoln) are nearly as large, creating an overall effect of massive majesty. Giant Grove has some 40 miles of intersecting footpaths to wander; the 6-mile **Trail of the Sequoias** will take you to the grove's far eastern end, where you'll find some of the finest trees.

While Sequoia's raison d'être is those incredible trees, Kings Canyon encompasses the **deepest canyon in the United States:** Drive to Road's End on the Kings Canyon Highway (late May–early Nov) to stand by the banks of the Kings River and stare up at granite walls rising thousands of feet above the river.

ⓘ Ash Mountain entrance, CA 198 from Visalia. Big Stump entrance, 180 from

Fresno, CA (℡ **559/565-3341**; www.nps.gov/seki or www.sequoia-kingscanyon.com).

✈ Fresno-Yosemite, 53 miles.

🛏 $ **Dorst Campground,** in Sequoia, near Giant Forest (℡ **800/365-2267**). $$

Wuksachi Village & Lodge, 64740 Wuksachi Way, Sequoia National Park (℡ **866/807-3598** or 801/559-4930 [international]; www.visitsequoia.com).

WHY THEY'LL THANK YOU: The redwoods' awesome (and even more endangered) cousins.

---

4   Postcard Panoramas

Uluru (Ayers Rock)
Australia's Red Rock Center
Ages 6 & up • Uluru-Kata Tjuta National Park, Northern Territory, Australia

It's a bit of a mystery why people trek from all over the world to gawk at **Ayers Rock.** For its size? Hardly. Nearby Mount Conner is three times as big. For its shape? Probably not. Most folks agree the neighboring Kata Tjuta (the Olgas) is more picturesque. And yet, undeniably, a faint shiver goes up the spine when you gaze on the serene, hulking mass known as Ayers Rock.

People used to believe that **Uluru** (Ayers Rock's proper Aboriginal name) was a meteorite, but we now know it was formed by sediments laid millions of years ago in an inland sea and thrust above ground by geological forces (there's twice as much again underground, it's thought). On photos, it may look like a big smooth blob, but face to face, it's dappled with holes and overhangs, curtains of stone draping its sides, and little coves hiding water holes and Aboriginal rock art, all of it changing color dramatically depending on the slant of the sun. The peak time to visit is sunset, when oranges, peaches, pinks, reds, and then indigo and deep violet creep across its face, as if it were a giant opal. At sunrise, the colors are less dramatic, but many folks enjoy the spectacle of the Rock, unveiled by the dawn to bird song.

Aborigines refer to tourists as *minga*—little ants—because that's what we look like crawling up Uluru, which to them is sacrilege. And yet, despite this, and despite ferocious winds, sheer rock faces, and extreme temperatures, visitors still feel compelled to scramble up the rock, which takes anywhere from 2 to 4 hours; the views from the top are amazing, but is it worth it? There are plenty of other options. The paved 9km (5.6-mile) **Base Walk** circumnavigates Uluru, with time to explore water holes, caves, folds, and overhangs; an easy kilometer (.6-mile) round-trip trail from the Mutitjulu parking lot visits a pretty water hole, with rock art near the Rock's base. On the free daily 90-minute **Mala Walk,** a ranger, who is often an Aborigine, discusses the Dreamtime myths behind Uluru and explains the significance of the rock art and other sites you see. Another peaceful way to see the Rock is on hour-long camelback forays through the red-sand dunes with **Frontier Camel Tours** (℡ 61/8/8950-3030; www.ananguwaai.com.au). If it's aerial views you want, several local companies do scenic flights by light aircraft or helicopter over Uluru and other local landmarks.

With a glorious sunset viewing of Uluru your goal, start your day at **Kata Tjuta** (the Olgas), 50km (31 miles) west of the Rock. Kata Tjuta means "many heads," an apt name for this monolith of 36 momentous red domes bulging out of the earth like turned clay on a potter's wheel. The

Olgas are more important in Dreamtime legend than Uluru, and many modern visitors find they're even more spiritual. Good hikers may do the challenging 7.4km (4.6-mile) **Valley of the Winds** walk among the domes; there's also an easy 2.6km (1.6-mile) **Gorge walk.**

(i) **Uluru-Kata Tjuta Cultural Centre** (℃ **61/8/8956-3138**) or www.central australiantourism.com.

✈ Ayers Rock (Connellan) airport.

🛏 $$$ **Emu Walk Apartments.** $$ **Outback Pioneer Hotel and Lodge.** Both at Yulara Dr., Ayers Rock Resort (℃ **61/2/8296-8010**; www.voyages.com.au).

WHY THEY'LL THANK YOU: Getting in touch with Dreamtime.

Postcard Panoramas 5

Lake Titicaca
Jewel of the Andes
Ages 6 & up • Copacabana, Bolivia & Puno, Peru

Face it: The kids will talk a lot about their upcoming trip to **Lake Titicaca**—they just won't be able to resist saying the name. But that's okay. Once they get there and see this huge deep-blue freshwater lake sitting in its cup of mountain peaks, an awesome 3,600m (11,811 ft.) above sea level, they'll stop snickering.

To locals, measuring the altitude is irrelevant: Lake Titicaca is a mysterious and sacred place. Here, in the midst of the lake, Manca Capac and Mama Ocllo—the Adam and Eve of the Incas—were supposedly born on the **Isla del Sol** (Sun Island), which you can visit on a day trip from the picturesque lakeside town of **Copacabana, Bolivia.** (A 3-hr. bus ride from La Paz, Copacabana is also known for its Moorish-style cathedral, with a deeply venerated miracle-working statue of the Virgin inside.) On Sun Island, you'll visit the ruins of Chinkana, a huge stone labyrinth built as a seminary for Inca priests. The path back to the town of Challapampa passes the sacred rock, shaped like a puma, from which Manco Capac and Mama Ocllo first stepped; farther on, you can look down and see the two huge footprints the sun is said to have made when it

landed on earth to give birth to them. Tours also stop at **Isla de la Luna** (Moon Island), site of an ancient convent where

Lake Titicaca.

the Virgins of the Sun performed ceremonies honoring the sun.

Most local tour packages visit not only the Bolivian shore but also the Peruvian side of the lake, with its main town of **Puno** (a 10-hr. train ride from Cusco). Puno is not nearly as lovely as Copacabana, but the kids will want to come here to take a boat tour to the **Uros islands.** Since the time of the Incas, the local Uros Indians have lived on these tiny floating islands built on soft patches of totora reeds. Walking on the springy islets is truly a strange sensation. Some Uros wait for the tour boats to arrive so they can hawk their handmade textiles and reed-crafted items, but many others keep to their thatched huts, far from the snapping cameras, where they quietly fish and catch birds and continually repair the reed underpinnings of their islets. Full-day trips also include stops at **Taquile** and **Amantani islands,** serene and rustic natural islands with Inca ruins to explore.

Other Andean peoples subscribe to a different myth: that Viracocha, the creator

deity, called up the sun, moon, and stars to rise from icy Lake Titicaca to lighten the dark world. Powerful spirits still live in this amazing sky-high lake, they say. Gliding over the calm blue surface, you may find yourself staring down into the water's cold depths to connect with them. But you don't need to believe in these ancient legends to sense the magic of Lake Titicaca.

(i) **Puna tourist office,** Plaza de Armas (© **51/51/36-5088;** www.peru.info).

✈ Manco Capac, Juliaca, Peru, 45km (28 miles) from Puno.

🛏 $$ **Hotel Rosario del Lago,** Rigoberto Paredes and Av. Costanera, Copacabana, Bolivia (© **591/2/862-2141;** www.hotelrosario.com/lago). $$$ **Sonesta Posada del Inca,** Sesquicentenario 610, Sector Huaje, Puno, Peru (© **800/SONESTA** [766-3782] or 51/51/364-111; www.sonesta.com/laketiticaca).

WHY THEY'LL THANK YOU: Gazing up at a star-spangled sky from the stars' birthplace.

6 Postcard Panoramas

The Cliffs of Moher
Where Ireland Plunges into the Sea
All ages • Lahinch, County Clare, Ireland

Something as spectacular as the **Cliffs of Moher** could never go undiscovered by the tourist throngs. They are County Clare's foremost natural wonder, 213m (700 ft.) high and 8km (5 miles) long, a series of sheer rock faces plummeting to the crashing Atlantic surf below. The views from here are truly panoramic, especially from 19th-century **O'Brien's Tower** at the northern end. On a clear day, you can even glimpse the **Aran Islands** up to the north in Galway Bay.

It's a dramatic place indeed, with the roar of the waves crashing below and the call of circling seagulls. While you may see

daredevils venturing onto a forbidden area of north-facing cliffs, which are only half-heartedly fenced off, the kids won't need to follow their dangerous example to get a great view: There's plenty enough room on the main cliffs, with their well-paved path and lookout points; and the heights are awesome without feeling perilous (and believe me, I'm borderline acrophobic). Because the cliffs jut out into the sea on a headland, you can gaze clearly over the sea to the north, west, and south.

Talk about the middle of nowhere—the Irish country road R478 meanders down from the Burren and Galway, with little

The Cliffs of Moher.

along the roadside and very few cars in sight. Then suddenly you round a curve, and there's an immense parking lot filled with cars and tour buses—that's how you know you've arrived at the Cliffs of Moher. Proximity to Shannon Airport means that this is often a tour group's first stop upon hitting Ireland, so don't be surprised if you see a lot of folks staring out to sea with the glazed eyes of jet lag. There's no admission fee per se, although you'll have to pay to get into the parking lot, and some tacky souvenir stalls are set up along the footpath to the cliffs. Just shepherd the children past it all, and head uphill.

While you're here, don't rush on like the tour groups do—take the opportunity to explore farther along the craggy Clare coastline, where you'll find many off-the-beaten-path delights with such intriguing names as **Pink Cave, Puffing Hole, Intrinsic Bay, Chimney Hill, Elephant's Teeth, Mutton Island, Loop Head,** and **Lover's Leap.** The tour buses won't follow you, that's for sure.

(i) **Clare Ireland Tourism,** R478, 7 miles north of Lahinch (② **353/65/708-1171;** www.county-clare.com).

✈ Shannon International, 48km (30 miles).

⊨ $$ **Aran View House,** Doolin (② **353/65/707-4061;** www.aranview. com; closed Nov–Mar). $$ **Royal Spa Hotel,** Main St., Lisdoonvarna (② **353/ 65/707-4288;** www.royalspahotel.com).

WHY THEY'LL THANK YOU: Nothing between you and America but sea.

The Giant's Causeway
Hero's Footsteps in Black Rock
All ages • Bushmills, Northern Ireland

Often called the eighth wonder of the world, the **Giant's Causeway** is a one-of-a-kind natural rock formation that truly captures the imagination. It doesn't take much effort for children to imagine the striding giant who purportedly left these immense stone footprints in the sea off of Northern Ireland.

A **World Heritage Site,** the Causeway consists of roughly 40,000 tightly packed basalt columns that extend for 5km (3 miles) along the North Antrim coast. The tops of the columns form a dense honeycomb of stepping stones that sprawl outward from the cliff foot and eventually disappear under the sea. They're mostly hexagonal, about 30cm (12 in.) in diameter, and some are as tall as 12m (40 ft.). How did they get there? Scientists estimate that they were formed 60 or 70 million years ago by a series of volcanic eruptions and cooling lava. In the surrounding cliff faces, you can see dark stripes of volcanic basalt interrupting the sheer red rock.

But all that is the scientific explanation. The ancients, on the other hand, believed the rock formation to be the work of giants. Another even more romantic legend claims that the Causeway isn't natural at all, but the handiwork of Finn MacCool, the great Ulster warrior and commander of the king of Ulster's armies, who built it as a highway over the sea to bring his girlfriend from the Isle of Hebrides.

Tourists have come here to marvel over the Causeway since the late 17th century. For many years, visitors were forbidden to walk out onto the stones, or had to pay extra to do so; thankfully today they are open to the public. Watch your footing as you scamper over the uneven surface,

traipsing from stone to stone. You'll spy delicate flowers and mosses growing in the crevices, and all sorts of seabirds nesting in the nearby cliffs.

To reach the causeway, follow the path from the visitor center's parking area. Along the way you'll pass plenty of other extraordinary volcanic rock formations, amphitheaters of stone and striated columns and formations with such fanciful names as **Honeycomb, Wishing Well, Giant's Granny, King** and **His Nobles,** and **Lover's Leap.** From the causeway, a wooden staircase climbs up Benbane Head and travels back along the cliff-top walking path, where you'll get spectacular views of the North Antrim coast.

Train buffs, of course, will want to get there via the charming red narrow-gauge **Giants Causeway and Bushmills Railway** (© **44/28/2073-2844**; www.freewebs.com/giantscausewayrailway), which runs for 2 miles along the coast from the town of Bushmills out to the Causeway; it runs weekends in spring and fall and daily in summer.

ⓘ Causeway Rd./B147 (© **44/28/2073-1855**; www.giantscausewayofficialguide.com).

✈ Belfast, 121km (75 miles).

🚃 Portrush (8 miles) and Coleraine (10 miles).

🛏 $$$ **Bushmills Inn,** 9 Dunluce Rd., Bushmills (© **44/28/2073-2000**; www.bushmills-inn.com). $$ **Marine Hotel,** 1 North St., Ballycastle (© **44/28/2076-2222**; www.marinehotel.net).

WHY THEY'LL THANK YOU: Myths written in monumental stone.

Les Calanches
Going Coastal in Corsica
Ages 4 & up • Corsica, France

L'ile de beauté, **Corsica** is called—"island of beauty"—and rightly so. This mountainous Mediterranean island combines rugged landscapes with stunning vistas of the sea, while native herbs and flowers perfume the air with an unforgettable fragrance. Although Corsica is technically a French possession, the island is in fact much closer to Italy (you can practically swim to Sardinia from Corsica), and everything here seems to have an Italian accent. You're lulled into thinking it's simply a fragment of the Riviera that worked itself loose from the mainland—and then you drive through a landscape that looks as though it fell from Mars: **Les Calanches.**

Ferries from Marseilles arrive at Corsica's main city, **Ajaccio,** a Riviera-like town with palm trees, promenades, and the birthplace of Napoleon Bonaparte. Up the western coast from here, driving or cycling along coastal D81, you curve around a headland to the tranquil village of **Piana,** with its red-tiled roofs rising 440m (1,444 ft.) above the azure sea. But beyond Piana, you enter an altered reality: The granite landscape to either side of the twisting road begins to turn red and become strangely striated and crumpled. The highway seems hacked out of the mountainside, and it zigs and zags crazily to cling to the corrugated rock faces. And so it goes, all the way along the southern end of the Gulf of Porto, from Piana over to Porto.

Les Calanches remind me of the buttes of Monument Valley, but smaller and more eccentric, crabbed like the figures of arthritic old crones. And then, of course, there's that dynamite seaside backdrop setting it off, the hazy blue of the Mediterranean contrasting dramatically with the sharp-focused red rocks. As you drive along, ask the children to try to decide what these oddly shaped boulders remind them of—a rearing stallion? A fire-breathing dragon? A stegosaurus? Patches of green pine scrub, snarls of gray thorn, and bursts of dark red and yellow flowering shrubs decorate the creased red-granite spires here and there, and the shoulder of the road drops with heart-stopping suddenness to the waters below. The road bends so sharply, you can't see beyond the next curve—honk to warn oncoming drivers of your presence before you pull around to the next dizzying view.

Several walking paths have been laid out through this tortured landscape—park your car and get out to take a short scramble over the rocks. (Trail maps are available from the **Piana tourist office,** Place de la Mairie, ℂ **33/4/95-27-84-42**). From Porto, you can go on a boat tour to view the spiky red rocks from the water; contact **Nave Va** (ℂ **33/4/95-21-83-97;** www.naveva.com). And I'm sure I don't need to tell you that sunset is the most glorious time of all to view Les Calanches, especially one of those lingering summer sunsets that the Mediterranean does so well.

ⓘ D81, btw. Piana and Porto (www.corsica.net).

✈ Ajaccio, 74km (46 miles).

🛏 $$ **Hotel Le Porto,** Route de Calvi, Porto (ℂ **33/4/95-26-11-20;** www.hotelleporto.com). $$$ **Les Roches Rouges,** 20115 Piana (ℂ **33/4/95-27-81-81;** www.lesrochesrouges.com).

WHY THEY'LL THANK YOU: Spotting the shapes in the rock piles.

Devil's Tower
Something Strange in Wyoming
All ages • Devil's Tower, Wyoming, USA

I knew my kids would love the scene in *Close Encounters of the Third Kind* when Richard Dreyfuss starts sculpting Devil's Tower out of mashed potatoes. Spielberg sure picked the right natural landing pad for his alien spaceship to make contact with earthlings—there is something otherworldly about this stark monolith rising out of the Wyoming pines and prairies. The Northern Plains Indians called it Bears Lodge, and it has sacred meanings for them too. Even seeing a picture of it is unforgettable, but visiting **Devil's Tower** in person—well, that's more special than you'd imagine.

Time for a geology lesson. Devil's Tower is what's known as an igneous intrusion, meaning that it's a column of rock hardened by molten lava that seeped long ago into a vein of sedimentary rock. A shallow sea once covered this part of the Great Plains, and most of the rock is soft sedimentary stuff like red sandstone and siltstone, with a little shale mixed in. The flat-topped cone that became Devil's Tower used to be under that sea, but once the waters had receded, centuries of erosion gradually wore away the softer rock around the igneous cone, leaving it exposed. Today the cone thrusts 1,267 feet above the surrounding pine trees and prairie grasslands. That flat top no doubt gave Spielberg the idea of an extraterrestrials' spaceport; a parachutist did land on top in 1941, drawing great publicity—especially because he then had to figure out how to get down! Vertical cracks groove the sides of the tower in almost parallel columns, giving it its distinctive furrowed look. It's well-nigh irresistible for climbers, although you must register at the visitor center before attempting to ascend and follow strict regulations about bolts and drills. In deference to the Native American reverence for this sacred place, the park's staff urges climbers to voluntarily forego climbing in June, a month with many religious ceremonies for the local tribes.

For most of us, the best way to experience Devil's Tower is to take the 1.3-mile paved **Tower Trail** that circles around the base. It's very kid-friendly, being mostly flat (after a steep climb at the start), with benches and interpretive stations along the way. Take your time walking so that you can examine this rugged pinnacle from every angle and in different lights. Bring sketchbooks and try to draw its stern majesty. And don't be surprised if the kids start mounding their mashed potatoes at dinner that night, tracing ridges on the sides with their forks . . .

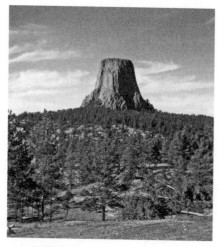
Devil's Tower.

While you're here, kids shouldn't miss the prairie dog towns on the park's east road, where black-tailed prairie dogs scamper about, popping in and out of their subterranean condos. You came out here to see the West—well, this is about as Western as it gets.

ⓘ Off U.S. 14 (✆ **307/467-5283;** www.nps.gov/deto).

✈ Gillette Airport, 40 miles.

🛏 $$ **Alex Johnson Hotel,** 523 6th St., Rapid City (✆ **800/888-2539** or 605/342-1210; www.alexjohnson.com). $$ **Sylvan Lake Lodge,** 24572 U.S. Hwy. 87, Custer (✆ **605/574-2561** or 605/574-4943; www.custerresorts.com).

WHY THEY'LL THANK YOU: An icon of the West with mystical power.

Otherworldly Landscapes **10**

Arches National Park
Sculpted by Nature
All ages • Moab, Utah, USA

More than 2,000 imposing natural stone arches punctuate this sandstone plateau, almost as if it were one gigantic pop-up book. These are natural formations, the result of cycles of freezing and thawing rain and snow that continually dissolve the "glue" that holds together the sand grains of the stone, chipping away at them bit by bit over time. And yet, knowing the scientific process doesn't detract from the marvel of it, a seemingly endless variety of shapes and delicate colors, as if some giant sculptor were deliberately trying to make each arch more fantastic than the one before.

It's a place to let your imagination go wild. Is **Delicate Arch** really so delicate, or would its other nicknames (Old Maids Bloomers or Cowboy Chaps) be more appropriate? And what about those tall spires? You might imagine they're castles, the towering masts of stone sailing ships, or the petrified skyscrapers of some ancient city. Be sure to pick up a map at the visitor center, because half the fun is matching up the formations with the fanciful names that have been given to them. On the 18-mile scenic drive from one end of the park to the other, you'll pass such features as **Park Avenue,** a solid rock "fin" that reminded somebody of the Manhattan skyline; the **La Sal Mountains,** which early explorers thought looked like piles of salt; **Courthouse Towers,** with such monoliths as **Sheep Rock,** the

Hiking in Arches National Park.

Organ, and the **Three Gossips;** and the **Tower of Babel.** A side road leads to the **Windows, Turret Arch,** and the **Cove of Caves,** where erosion is even now slowly making a new arch out of the largest cave. Detour onto **Wolfe Ranch Road** for a brief hike to see a 100-year-old ranch and some **Ute pictographs.**

Along the drive, stop to venture onto the various walking trails, many of them short and easy enough for even young children. A .3-mile walk lets you circle **Balanced Rock,** a 3,000-ton boulder perched on a slowly eroding pedestal; a .5-mile there-and-back trail leads past the **Parade of Elephants** to **Double Arch;** and another .3-mile walk goes to **Sand Dune Arch,** with an irresistible sandy hollow beneath that the kids can play in.

ⓘ U.S. 191 (✆ **435/719-2299;** www.nps.gov/arch).

✈ Grand Junction, CO, 125 miles. Salt Lake City, UT, 230 miles.

🛏 $ **Arch View Camp Park,** U.S. 91 & U.S. 313 (✆ **800/813-6622** or 435/259-7854; www.archviewresort.com). $$ **Bowen Motel,** 169 N. Main St. (✆ **800/874-5439** or 435/259-7132; www.bowenmotel.com).

WHY THEY'LL THANK YOU: Waiting for Balanced Rock to topple.

---

11 **Otherworldly Landscapes**

Going to the Moon
Craters of the Moon National Monument
All ages • Arco, Idaho, USA

Here's one aptly named national park: Bring the children here and they will feel as though they've gone to the moon. Three lava fields, with some 60 distinct lava flows and 25 volcanic cones, cover nearly half a million acres on the Snake River Plain, a haunting black basaltic landscape 60 miles wide with deposits that may lie up to 10,000 feet deep. You may not know the difference between slabby pahoehoe and spiny pahoehoe (hint: they're both types of lava flow), but you'll know that this desolate landscape is one of the strangest sights you'll ever see.

The lava fields at Craters of the Moon were formed as long as 15,000 years ago, though much of it is quite young, formed only 2,000 years ago. At the visitor center, the kids will learn about such weird volcanic features as volcanic bombs (clumps of spewing lava that hardened in the air before falling to rest on the surface), lava tubes (underground tunnels hollowed out by receding flows of molten lava), and tree molds (the shapes of trees encased in lava before they decomposed). They'll learn the difference between steep-sided spatter cones and pock-marked cinder cones. Look for these as you drive the park's 7-mile scenic drive, with various spurs leading to such intriguing features as 700-foot-high **Big Cinder Butte,** one of the world's tallest cinder cones, or the curiously colored **Blue and Green Dragon lava flows.** A half-mile hike will take you through the **Devil's Orchard,** where lava fragments stand like wraiths upon a sea of cinders; another half-mile hike lets you explore several lava tubes such as the **Boy Scout Cave** (bring a flashlight) and the **Indian Tunnel.** Because it is situated along the **Great Rift volcanic zone,** you'll see deep fissures in the earth, collapsed pits and craters, and ridges built by magma oozing upward through old cracks.

This is by no means a dead landscape; if they pay attention, the kids will discover plenty of hardy flora and fauna that has adapted to this environment. Big patches of sagebrush grasslands and islands of grass (kipukas) have sprouted wherever they could find enough soil; on the lacy surfaces of cinder cones, wildflowers, shrubs, and even twisted little limber pines have managed to get a foothold. The mountains at the north end of the park have Douglas fir forests and groves of quaking aspens that look downright lush in contrast. In the daytime, you may see ground squirrels, lizards, chipmunks, and hawks; at dawn and dusk, coyotes, porcupines, and jackrabbits steal forth; and if you were here at night, you'd see wood rats, bobcats, and bats.

(i) Hwy. 20/26/93, near Arco (© **208/527-1300;** www.nps.gov/crmo).

✈ Hailey, 60 miles. Twin Falls, 90 miles.

🛏 $ **Arco Inn,** 540 W. Grand Ave., Arco (© **208/527-3100**). $$ **Best Western Kentwood Lodge,** 180 S. Main St., Ketchum (© **800/805-1001** or 208/726-4114; www.bestwestern.com).

WHY THEY'LL THANK YOU: Discovering life on the moonscape.

Otherworldly Landscapes **12**

Petrified Forest & Painted Desert
Trees of Stone, Stones of Color
All ages • Near Holbrook, Arizona, USA

From the name, the children may expect to see standing trees of stones, leaves and branches and all. Well, a better name for the **Petrified Forest** might be the Petrified Pile of Logs, with its fossilized hunks of ancient trees scattered like kindling across the arid scrubby landscape. But these richly colored petrifactions are plenty impressive close up, and the other half of the park, the **Painted Desert,** more than lives up to its name, in glowing pastel beauty.

Start at the **Rainbow Forest Museum,** the visitor center at the southern entrance to the park, where the displays will teach the kids how those petrified logs got petrified in the first place. These 225-million-year-old conifers date from the late Triassic age, when this area was an equatorial tropical forest. The trees fell, were buried in sediment, and then overlaid with volcanic ash, which gradually deposited silica in the trees that replaced their cells with quartz crystals. This unique set of circumstances left a profusion of these immense fossils in the area, which were sliced up and sold for souvenirs at such a rate that, in 1906, the government stepped in to preserve what was left in this park. A short walking trail behind the visitor center winds around a hillside strewn with logs (4–5 ft. in diameter), giving the children a first chance to examine them up close; across the road, a 1.5-mile loop takes you to **Agate House,** a ruined pueblo fashioned out of colorful petrified wood.

Once you're back in the car, head north on the park's 27-mile scenic road. Several overlooks highlight wonders such as the **Crystal Forest** (unfortunately, tourists pried the quartz and amethyst crystals out of these logs long ago); the **Jasper Forest,** petrified trees with their roots still attached; and **Agate Bridge,** a natural bridge formed by a petrified log. In the hazy blue badlands of the **Blue Mesa,** chunks of petrified wood teeter on mounds of soft clay that are eroding away beneath them. The Teepees are a lovely set of hills striped with different colors. At **Newspaper Rock,** you can gaze upon ancient **Native-American petroglyphs,** with the ruined pueblos of their creators at nearby **Pueblo Parco.**

The Painted Desert.

Across I-40, you'll be fully in the Painted Desert section of the park, where a series of eight overlooks lets you admire the breathtaking desert colors, which were caused by various minerals in the mudstone-and-clay soil—iron, manganese, and others—which oxidized at different rates as they were exposed by erosion. It's a dreamscape of pastels washing over dramatically eroded buttes and mesas, one of nature's best special effects ever.

ⓘ U.S. 180, 20 miles east of Holbrook (✆ **928/524-6228;** www.nps.gov/pefo).

✈ Flagstaff, 90 miles. Phoenix, 180 miles.

🛏 $$$ **La Posada,** 303 N. Second St., Winslow (✆ **928/289-4366;** www.la posada.org). $ **Wigwam Motel,** 811 W. Hopi Dr., Holbrook (✆ **928/524-3048;** www.galerie-kokopelli.com/wigwam).

WHY THEY'LL THANK YOU: If the rock logs don't get them, the Kodachrome mesas will.

13 **Otherworldly Landscapes**

Pinnacles National Monument
Lost Pieces of a Mojave Jigsaw Puzzle
Ages 8 and up • East of Salinas Valley, California, USA

Picture hundreds of towering crags, spires, and hoodoos, ferociously jabbing up out of the rolling brown California hills. The Pinnacles are the world's most dramatic demonstration of plate tectonics, a series of rocky spikes that are actually fragments of a 23-million-year-old volcano in the Mojave Desert that was split in two by the San Andreas Fault. One half of the volcano stayed in the Mojave; this is the other half, carried 195 miles north by shifting geologic plates. Okay, it got a little shattered and jumbled en route; and over the centuries the jagged remains were

further sculpted and scoured by wind and erosion. It's a unique and unforgettable sight.

Those crags and spires beg to be climbed, so it's no surprise that this is one of the most popular weekend climbing spots in central California, with its mild winter climate (spring is also a good time to visit, when wildflowers carpet the chaparral). Located only 80 miles south of San Francisco, the **Pinnacles** get a lot of visitors—some weekends it seems every spire and monolith has a climber clinging to its surface. Most visitors arrive via CA

15

25, at the eastern entrance, where you can get an eyeful of dramatic spires right away, from the **Bear Gulch picnic ground.** For a moderately strenuous half-day hike, take the **Condor Gulch Trail** uphill from the Bear Gulch Nature Center; within 2 miles, you'll be amid clusters of spires, which are much larger up close than they look from the parking lot. Switch to the **High Peaks Trail** to get a dramatic view: the Salinas Valley to your west, the Pinnacles below, and miles of coast to the east. After traversing the high peaks (including stretches of footholds carved in steep rock faces) for about a mile, the trail drops back toward the visitor center via a valley filled with eerie-looking hoodoos.

One intriguing feature of this jumbled rockscape is the talus caves, which are basically narrow stream canyons roofed over with tumbled boulders. Bats love these caves—in fact, **Bear Gulch Cave,** only a short walk from the picnic ground (take the Moses Spring Trail), only allows visitors in half the cave because rare **Townsend's Big-Eared Bats** occupy the other half; it's closed entirely mid-May to mid-July to protect newborn bat babies. If you enter the park from the west, there's a 2-mile loop trail from the Chaparral parking lot to visit **Balconies Cave,** another talus cave. Flashlights are required to explore either cave.

Along with the bats, the Pinnacles—which sit at an intersection of two ecosystems—have an incredible 400 species of **bees** buzzing around their chaparral and grasslands, and half a dozen extremely **rare California condors** were successfully released to the wild here. Keep your eyes open, because you never know what you'll see.

ⓘ **Visitor Center,** off CA 25, at eastern entrance (ⓒ **831/389-4485;** www.nps. gov/pinn).

✈ Monterey Peninsula Airport, 58 miles.

▭ $$ **Casa Munras Garden Hotel,** 700 Munras Ave., Monterey (ⓒ **800/222-2446** or 831/375-2411; www.hotelcasa munras.com). $ **Pinnacles Campground,** off CA 25, near the eastern entrance (ⓒ **877/444-6777;** www.recreation.gov).

WHY THEY'LL THANK YOU: Mountains that migrate.

Otherworldly Landscapes **14**

Hawaii Volcanoes National Park
Where Hot Lava Still Flows
Ages 6 & up • Volcano, Hawaii, USA

Hawaii Volcanoes National Park beats out all the other U.S. national parks on two scores: It has the only tropical rainforest, and it has the only active volcano. Since 1983, the Big Island's **Kilauea volcano** has been erupting regularly, although these are "quiet"' eruptions, with gas escaping slowly instead of exploding violently. Its slow-moving red lava oozes over the landscape, sometimes even over the park roads. The kids may wish they could see volcanic fireworks, but once they're here, feeling the soles of their sneakers getting gummy from the heat below, they'll realize this is spectacular enough.

This is not a tame volcano, not by any means. Over the past 2 decades, some $100 million worth of property has been destroyed by the eruptions, though the lava flow has also added 560 acres of new land. On many days, the lava flows right alongside accessible roads and you can get as close as the heat will allow; sometimes, however, the flow is in underground tubes that spill out miles away.

Near the visitor center, you can get your first look at **Kilauea Caldera,** a 2½-mile-wide, 500-foot-deep pit with wisps of steam rising from it. Going counterclockwise on Crater Rim Road, you'll drive past the **Sulphur Banks,** which smell like rotten eggs, and the **Steam Vents,** fissures where trails of smoke, once molten lava, escape from the inner reaches of the earth. At the **Thomas A. Jaggar Museum,** there's a viewpoint for **Halemaumau Crater,** which is half a mile across but 1,000 feet deep; walk right to the rim to gape at this once-fuming old fire pit, which still gives off fierce heat from its vents. Near the **Iki Crater,** the .5-mile **Devastation Trail** is a sobering look at how a volcanic eruption wreaked havoc in 1959. Another intriguing stop is the **Thurston Lava Tube,** a cool underground hole in a lush forested bowl that somehow escaped the lava flow.

By now you won't be surprised to learn that the volcano goddess, Pele, was an important deity to ancient Hawaiians—you definitely wanted to be on the right side of this lady. At the 15-mile mark down Chain of Craters Road, you can see **Puu Loa,** an ancient site sacred to the Hawaiians, where a .5-mile boardwalk loop trail will show you thousands of mysterious Hawaiian petroglyphs carved in stone.

If the volcano is actively erupting, call the visitor center for directions to the best locations for night viewing—it's quite a sight, watching as the brilliant red lava snakes down the side of the mountain and pours into the cold sea, hissing and steaming ferociously. Of course, the ultimate view is from the sky: **Blue Hawaiian Helicopter** (© **800/745-BLUE** or 808/961-5600; www.bluehawaiian.com) runs several

Desolation Point in Volcanoes National Park.

tours right over the bubbling caldera, for a bird's-eye view you'll never forget.

ⓘ Hawaii Belt Rd. (Hwy. 11; © **808/985-6000;** www.nps.gov/havo).

✈ Hilo, 29 miles.

🛏 $$ **Killauea Lodge,** Old Volcano Rd., off Hwy. 11 (© **808/967-7366;** www.kilauealodge.com). $ **Volcano House,** inside Hawaii Volcanoes National Park (© **808/967-7321;** www.volcanohousehotel.com).

WHY THEY'LL THANK YOU: Red-hot magma.

15

The Monteverde Cloud Forest
A Mountaintop Jungle
Ages 6 & up • Monteverde, Costa Rica

Monteverde means "green mountain," and that's exactly what you'll find at the end of the steep, rutted dirt road that leads to Costa Rica's **Monteverde Biological Cloud Forest Reserve.** Passing through mile after mile of dry, brown pasture, you may wonder if you're in the right place—where's the cloud forest? Well, this land used to be forest, until humans entered the picture. All the more reason to appreciate what has been saved when you finally hit the top of the mountain: a lush, tangled swath of greenery, where orchids and ferns trail from the treetops while monkeys chatter, tree frogs croak, and hummingbirds hum. Walking here in the early-morning mist, with the susurration of leaves and disembodied birdcalls all around, can be an almost out-of-body experience.

Cloud forests are always on mountaintops, where moist, warm air sweeping up the slopes from a nearby ocean condenses swiftly in the higher elevation, forming clouds around the summit. The clouds, in turn, condense moisture on the forest trees, giving rise to an incredible diversity of life forms—Monteverde boasts more than 2,500 plant species, 400 bird species, and 100 different mammal species. Monteverde is no secret, and its main trails are often crowded with ecotourists, all gaping (generally without any luck) to see rare and elusive species such as the quetzal, with its 2-foot-long tail feathers. The density of the cloud forest, however, makes it possible to escape the crowds by branching off the central paths. I suggest booking a guided tour through your hotel, which will also reserve your admission (only 120 people at a time are allowed inside the reserve); the guide will be able to identify far more of the flora and fauna than you could spot on your own.

The option older kids will be dying to try is a canopy tour, where you can zip around harnessed to an overhead cable, going from platform to platform high above the forest floor in the treetops, where two-thirds of the species live. Two good operations are **Sky Trek** (© **506/2645-5238;** www.skytrek.com) and **Selvatura Park** (© **506/2645-5929;** www.selvatura.com), both located outside the reserve, near the town of Santa Elena.

Slightly less crowded than the Monteverde Reserve, but with much the same flora and fauna, the **Santa Elena Cloud Forest Reserve** (© **506/2645-5390;** www.reservasantaelena.org) can be a good alternative; the 3.5km (2.2-mile) **Bajo del Tigre Trail,** in the town of Monteverde, is a great bird-watching option. Other related attractions around Monteverde are the **Butterfly Garden** in Cerro Plano (© **506/2645-5512**), the **Monteverde Serpentarium** (© **506/2645-5238;** www.skytrek.com), the **Frog Pond of Monteverde** (© **506/2645-6320;** www.ranario.com), and the **Bat Jungle** (© **506/2645-5052**).

ⓘ © **506/2645-5112;** www.cct.or.cr or www.monteverdeinfo.com.

✈ Juan Santamaria International, San José, 160km (99 miles).

🛏 $$$ **Hotel El Establo,** adjacent to Monteverde preserve (© **877/623-3198** or 506/2645-5110; www.hotelelestablo.com). $$ **Monteverde Lodge,** 5km (3 miles) outside the reserve, near Santa Elena (© **800/886-2609** in the U.S., or 506/2257-0766 in San José; www.costaricaexpeditions.com).

WHY THEY'LL THANK YOU: Getting your head in the clouds.

Rotorua
Land of Mists
Ages 4 & up • North Island, New Zealand

You'll smell Rotorua long before you see it, a peculiar sulphuric aroma that may provoke a loud "Euww! Who farted?" from the back seat. But then you draw closer, and start to see the steam hissing out of fissures in the landscape, the scattered lakes and waterfalls, the volcano peak of Mount Tarawera in the hazy distance, and—who cares about the smell?

Geothermals are what make Rotorua special, so head first for **Te Puia, Hemo Road** (✆ **64/7/348-9047;** www.nzmaori. co.nz), an ancient site set in a rocky landscape full of mud pools and the prolific **Pohutu Geyser,** which shoots hot water up 16 to 20m (52–66 ft.), 10 to 25 times a day. At its heart is a replica of a Maori village—the population of Rotorua is about one-third Maori (New Zealand's aboriginal peoples), and exhibits of Maori culture are one of the bigger tourism draws here. The other must-do in town is in Ngongotaha, a suburb halfway up Lake Rotorua's western shore: **Skyline Skyrides, Fairy Springs Road** (✆ **64/7/347-0027;** www.skylinesky rides.co.nz) hauls you on a gondola up **Mount Ngongotaha,** then offers all sorts of thrilling ways to descend, from a chairlift to a bone-rattling luge track.

There are more geothermal sites south of town, a whole valley of steamy activity: I'd choose **Wai-o-Tapu** (✆ **64/7/366-6333;** www.geyserland.co.nz), a half-hour drive south on Hwy. 5, where you can see the **Lady Knox Geyser** (she erupts daily at 10:15am) and all sorts of intriguing pools, from the beautiful **Champagne Pool** to the arsenic-tinted **Devil's Bath** to New Zealand's largest bubbling mud pool.

The small village of **Te Wairoa,** or **Buried Village,** on Tarawera Road (✆ **64/7/362-8287;** www.buriedvillage.co.nz), is Rotorua's version of Pompeii, an excavated townscape dug out of the lava that destroyed it when Mount Tarawera erupted in 1886. Lots of artifacts discovered in the excavations are displayed at the museum on-site, but what'll really bring this place alive for the kids is going from one excavated dwelling to another on a meandering pathway along a stream.

Since the 19th century, tourists have been coming to "take the waters" in the geothermal spas and springs. The elegantly restored **Art Deco Blue Baths,** in Government Gardens, now includes the **Rotorua Museum** (Queens Dr.; ✆ **64/7/ 349-4350;** www.rotoruamuseum.co.nz), where a multimedia cinema re-creates the experience of a volcanic eruption. The **Polynesian Spa,** Hinemoa Street (✆ **64/7/ 348-1328;** www.polynesianspa.co.nz), has lots of luxury soaking experiences, including a Family Spa section, where kids

Hell's Gate in Rotorua.

19

can frolic in the warm freshwater pool while adults relax in two adjacent hot mineral pools.

ⓘ **I-Site information center,** 1167 Fenton St. (ⓒ **63/7/348-5179**; www.rotorua.co.nz).

✈ Rotorua.

🛏 $$$ **Peppers on the Point,** 214 Kawaha Point Rd., (ⓒ **64/7/348-4868**; www.peppers.co.nz). $$ **Rydges Rotoua,** 272 Fenton St. (ⓒ **800/446-187** in New Zealand, 1300/857-922 in Australia, or 61/2/9261-4929; www.rydges.com).

WHY THEY'LL THANK YOU: Like one giant hot tub.

Otherworldly Landscapes · 17

The Burren
Ireland's Moonscape
All ages • County Clare, Ireland

In the heart of Ireland's green and rural County Clare lies an amazing landscape of rock and stony outcroppings, a limestone weirdness that looks as if you have just stepped onto the moon. It's called the **Burren,** from the Irish word *boirreann,* which means "a rocky place." What an understatement.

This strange 260 sq. km (100-sq.-mile) region of naked carboniferous limestone once lay under a prehistoric tropical sea; over the next 300 million years, decaying shells and sediment hardened into rock, thrust to the surface, and lay exposed to pelting Irish rains and scouring winds. Today you can drive around and gaze over massive sheets of rock, jagged boulders, caves, and potholes, punctuated with tiny lakes and streams as well as ancient Stone Age burial monuments. Get out of your car to explore, though, and you'll see that it's not all just rocks: Something is always in bloom, even in winter, from fern and moss to orchids, rock roses, milkwort, wild thyme, geraniums, violets, and fuchsia. The Burren is also famous for its butterflies, which thrive on the rare flora. The pine marten, stoat, and badger, rare in the rest of Ireland, are common here.

A good place to begin your exploration is at the **Burren Exposure** (ⓒ **353/65/707-7277**) on Galway Road 4km (2½ miles)

north of the Galway Bay village of Ballyvaughan. This 35-minute multimedia exhibition tells you all you need to know about the extraordinary natural wonders and historical legacy of the Burren. If you're coming from the south or west, however, get your introduction in the historic village of **Kilfenora** at the **Burren Centre,** R476 (ⓒ **353/65/708-8030**), which has landscape models, displays on flora and fauna, and an audiovisual "walk through time."

Drive along corkscrewing R480, between Corofin and Ballyvaughan, through the heart of the landscape, or better yet, hike a portion of the 26-mile **Burren Way** footpath, signposted from Ballyvaughan to Liscannor, near the **Cliffs of Moher** ⑥. A wide swath of the area bordered by Corofin, Lahinch, Lisdoonvarna, Ballyvaughn, and Boston has been designated the **Burren National Park;** it has no official entrance, so find a place to park and begin rambling around the limestone terraces and shale uplands. The area is particularly rich in archaeological remains from the Neolithic through the medieval periods—dolmens and wedge tombs (approx. 120), ring forts (500), round towers, ancient churches, high crosses, monasteries, and holy wells are all noteworthy. It's an eerily different sort of place that the kids will remember forever.

ⓘ **Clare Ireland Tourism** (ⓒ **800/369-87412;** www.county-clare.com).

✈ Shannon International, 50 km (31 miles)

🛏 $$ **Royal Spa Hotel,** Main St., Lisdoonvarna (ⓒ **353/65/707-4288;** www.royalspahotel.com). $$ **Temple Gate Hotel,** The Square, Ennis (ⓒ **353/65/682-3300;** www.templegatehotel.com).

WHY THEY'LL THANK YOU: A trip to the moon without a rocket.

Volcanoes of the Auvergne

Ages 6 & up • Montlosier, Aydat, France

When you think of France, you may not automatically think volcanoes. Yet in one 385,000-hectare (950,000-acre) region, no fewer than 90 extinct volcanic cones—known in French as *puys*—rise dramatically and eerily above the pine forests. Their symmetrical shapes, formed over centuries of successive eruption and cooling, are cloaked with the vivid green grass of the region; peat bogs and lakes, formed by glaciers, are tucked in between. The peaceful rural calm of this region, where few tourists venture, seems at odds with the violent geological activity that blasted craters out of the mountaintops 5,000 to 6,000 years ago; nowadays villages and farms are interspersed with the volcanoes, where farmers tend the cows and goats responsible for the Auvergne's luscious cheeses.

The highest and oldest peak, **Puy-de-Dôme,** has been used as a worship site since prehistoric times by the Gauls and the Romans. In 1648, Pascal used this mountaintop to prove Torricelli's hypothesis that altitude affects atmospheric pressure; in 1911, aviator Eugène Renaux landed here after a nonstop flight from Paris in just over 5 hours. There's a handy shuttle bus up the treacherously winding road to the summit, where on a clear day you'll have a panoramic view as far east as Mont Blanc.

Les Puys (also known as Monts Dômes) are a minichain of 112 extinct volcanoes (some capped with craters, some with rounded peaks) packed densely into an area 4km (2½ miles) wide by 31km (19 miles) long. Each dome is different: Some were built up by slow extrusions of rock; others were the source of vast lava flows. This rectangle of extinct volcanoes traces one of the most potentially unstable tectonic areas in France, the San Andreas Fault of the French mainland.

This is a fantastic area for hiking and biking. The hills may look dramatic, but they're gentle; and the quiet country roads and footpaths through the park have little or no traffic, yet you're never far from civilization. Throughout the region, even in the simple farmhouses, look for blocks of black stone formed by ancient volcanic deposits, with roofs of overlapping tiles of dark gray volcanic schist. (You'll find a prime example, the Romanesque Eglise Notre-Dame-de-Paris, in the Auvergne's capital, Clermont-Ferrand.) It's just another way in which the bizarre beauty of the old volcanoes has been tamed and embraced by the people of the Auvergne.

ⓘ **Visitor center,** Montlosier (ⓒ **33/4/73-65-64-26;** www.parc-volcans-auvergne.com).

✈ Clermont-Aulnat, 4km (2½ miles).

📖 $$ **Hotel Le Kyriad,** 51 rue Bonna-baud, Clermont (📞 **33/4/73-93-59-69;** www.hotel-kyriadcentreclermont.com). $$$ **Mercure Clermont Ferrand Centre,** 82 bd. François-Mitterrand, Clermont (📞 **33/4/73-34-46-46;** www.mercure.com).

WHY THEY'LL THANK YOU: Dead volcanoes, like slumbering green giants.

Blyde River Canyon
Great Green Gorge
Ages 4 & up • Graskop to Blydepoort, Mpumalanga, South Africa

If your mental picture of a canyon is an arid sandstone gorge (as in, say, the Grand Canyon or Mexico's Copper Canyon), South Africa's immense **Blyde River Canyon** will turn your head around. It's a land of heavy mists and high rainfall, precipitated by hot air rising over the canyon wall, giving the upper plateau lush grasslands,

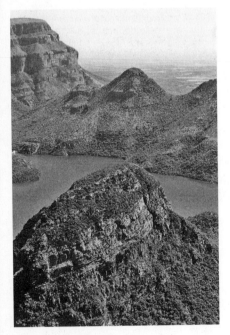

Blyde River Canyon.

the riverbanks dense dark forests, and in between them, pockets of subtropical rainforests tucked into the creases of the ravines. Each level has its own wildlife, too: mountain reedbuck up on the escarpment, hyrax on the canyon walls, hippos and crocodiles in the Blyde Dam, and impala, kudu, blue wildebeest, waterbuck, and zebra on the Lowveld plain near the canyon's mouth. If you're going from Pretoria to the Kruger National Park, take an extra day to drive along R532—the **Panorama Route,** as it's called for obvious reasons.

The starting point is the town of Graskop, where you head north on R532, though almost immediately you'll loop east onto R534 to stop at **God's Window,** your first amazing vista of the whole 33km (21-mile) canyon. Back on R532, head north to see **Berlin Falls,** a crystalline 48m (157-ft.) cascade. Farther north on R532 in Mpumalanga, where the Blyde River meets the Treur River, you'll have to pay an entrance fee to gape at **Bourke's Luck Potholes** (📞 **27/13/761-6019**), one of South Africa's most photographed sights: bizarre swirly holes scooped deeply out of the rock, with mysterious dark pools of water inside. The lichen walking trail here is easy and good for children. A few miles farther, the **Three Rondawels** is an amazing outlook above a heart-stopping sheer drop down to the Blyde River some 1,600m (5,250 ft.) below. The name refers to three massive spiral outcrops, topped with green hats, across from the view-point—I like the other name for them, the **Three Sisters,** because they look like hoop-skirted old biddies to me.

Near the Blydepoort Dam, turn east on R531 for two great options for exploring the landscape: a spectacularly scenic 90-minute boat ride on the Blyde Dam, run by **Blyde Canyon Adventure Centre** (℡ **27/15/795-5961;** look for the turnoff from R531 to Aventura Swadini resort); or, north on R40, the **Hoedspruit Endan-gered Species Centre** (℡ **27/15/793-1633**), where you can take a 90-minute drive through a plains preserve to spot cheetahs, wild dogs, rhino, and various bird species. Head back to Graskop on the

R40, then the R533; the total drive is only 159km (99 miles), but oh, what a ride.

ⓘ **Graskop Information,** Spar Centre, Pilgrim's Way, Graskop.

✈ Hoedspruit.

🛏 $$ **Royal Hotel,** Pilgrim's Rest (℡ **27/13/768-1100;** www.pilgrimsrest.org.za). $$ **Rissington Inn,** off R40, Hazyview (℡ **27/13/737-7700;** www.rissington. co.za).

TOUR: Blyde River Safaris (℡ **27/13/767-1833;** www.wildadventures.co.za).

WHY THEY'LL THANK YOU: That view at the Three Rondavels.

20 Falling Waters

Niagara Falls
The Big Spill
All ages • New York, USA & Ontario, Canada

Everyone's seen a Kodachrome photo of **Niagara Falls,** that stupendous curve of cascading water that lies between the United States and Canada. It's one of those sites, however, to which postcards will never do justice: To stand on a viewing platform and see, really see, how big it is, to hear the thunder of falling water, to feel the mist spritzing your face and the earth shaking under your feet, is another thing altogether. Kids don't understand how amazing it is until they're actually there.

There are actually two waterfalls here, both of them doozies: the **American Falls** and **Horseshoe Falls.** Both are around 175 feet high, although Horseshoe Falls, at 2,500 feet wide, is more than twice as wide as its sibling. The Canadian shore has the real panoramic view; both falls can be seen from the American side, but not together (Prospect Point for the American Falls, Terrapin Point for Horseshoe Falls). The Canadian side tends to have better hotels and more attractions, as well. No

matter where you stay, you can easily visit both, by crossing the **Rainbow Bridge,** preferably on foot—it's only the length of a couple city blocks. Bring a passport (or a driver's license and original birth certifi-cate; you'll need birth certificates for the kids as well).

On the U.S. shore, head for **Niagara Falls State Park** (℡ **716/278-1796;** www. niagarafallsstatepark.com) to explore the falls: An **Observation Tower** overlooks the river, and the **Cave of the Winds tour** (Apr–Oct; ℡ **716/278-1730**) takes you by elevator down onto boardwalks, where you can walk around the base of the American Falls. Canada's 775-foot-high **Skylon Tower,** 5200 Robinson St. (℡ **905/356-2651;** www.skylon.com), has a revolving restaurant on top, and the **Journey Behind the Falls** (℡ **905/354-1551;** www.niagaraparks.com), allows you to descend via elevator to tunnels punctuated with portholes that look out through the blur of water right behind

Niagara Falls.

Horseshoe Falls. The coolest way to see the falls, of course, is the classic *Maid of the Mist* boat ride (Apr–Oct; © **716/284-8897;** www.maidofthemist.com), which plays no favorites; it departs from either shore. You'll chug upriver toward the American and Horseshoe Falls, sailing right up the base of both (don't worry, blue slickers are provided to keep you dry).

Want more of an adrenaline rush? Book a 10-minute helicopter ride over the cascades with **Niagara Helicopters** (© **905/357-5672;** www.niagarahelicopters.com) or **Rainbow Air** (© **716/284-2800;** www.rainbowairinc.com), or crash through the white waters of the Niagara gorge with **Whirlpool Jet Boat Tours** (Apr–Oct; © **888/438-4444** in the U.S., or 905/468-4800 in Canada; www.whirlpooljet.com). This being a major tourist destination, there's a ton of other attractions around, from historic old forts and botanical gardens to aquariums and amusement parks. But over-developed as it may be, the spectacular Falls are still there.

ⓘ U.S. (© **877/FALLSUS** [325-5787] or 716/282-8992; www.niagara-usa.com). Canada (© **800/563-2557;** www.niagara fallstourism.com).

✈ Buffalo Niagara International Airport, 34km (21 miles).

🏨 $$ **Courtyard by Marriott,** 5950 Victoria Ave., Niagara Falls, Ontario, Canada (© **800/771-1123** or 905/358-3083; www.nfcourtyard.com). $$$ **Red Coach Inn,** 2 Buffalo Ave., Niagara Falls, NY, USA (© **866/719-2070** or 716/282-1459; www.redcoach.com).

BEST TIME: May–Oct.

WHY THEY'LL THANK YOU: Roaring water, mist, and rainbows galore.

Victoria Falls

Shades of Stanley & Livingstone

Ages 6 & up • Livingstone, Zambia, or Victoria Falls, Zimbabwe

In 1855, British explorer David Livingstone first gazed in wonder upon these spectacular falls and promptly named them for his Queen. But their local name, Mosi-Oa-Tunya—literally, "the smoke that thunders"—is more apt. When, on a clear day, more than 9 million liters of the Zambezi River crash down into the Batoka Gorge, the veil of roaring spray can be seen from up to 80km (50 miles) away. Straddling the border between Zimbabwe and Zambia, **Victoria Falls** are the world's largest, spanning almost 2km (1¼ miles) and dropping some 100m (328 ft.), twice the height of Niagara Falls. A sight this tremendous can't help but be Africa's number-one tourist destination.

Nourished by perpetual spray, a rainforest flourishes on the southern cliff opposite the falls, protected by the **Victoria Falls National Park.** This is the best vantage point for viewing the falls, and getting drenched is all part of the experience (rent raincoats or umbrellas at the park entrance). You don't need a guide, though many hopefuls stand near the entrances angling for business; a clearly marked trail runs through the lush and fecund rainforest, with side trails leading to good overlooks of the falls. Head down the steep stairs to **Cataract View** to see **Devil's Cataract;** the final viewpoint, nearest the **Victoria Falls Bridge,** is called **Danger Point,** where you can perch on a cliff edge and peer down into the abyss. When the moon is full, the park stays open later so that visitors can marvel at the lunar rainbow reflecting off the mist.

While the Zimbabwe side of the falls has many more scenic overviews, during high water (Apr–June), when the view is less obscured by spray, you may want to cross over to the Zambian side (just purchase a visa at the bridge) for a spectacular panorama of the main gorge and **Eastern Cataract.** You can also walk (or scramble, rather) along the Zambian lip of the gorge to a viewpoint called **Knife Edge,** to stand suspended above the churning waters of **Boiling Pot.** *Warning:* There are no fences on this side of the river. For some kids, that will just add to the thrill.

ⓘ **Zimbabwe Tourism** (www.zimbabwe tourism.co.zw) or Zambia Tourism (www. zambiatourism.com).

✈ Livingstone, Zambia side. Victoria Falls International, Zimbabwe side.

🛏 $$$ **Ilala Lodge,** 411 Livingstone Way, Victoria Falls, Zimbabwe (✆ 263/13/ 44737; www.ilalalodge.com). $$$ **Victoria Falls Safari Lodge,** Squire Cummings Rd., Victoria Falls, Zimbabwe (✆ 263/13/ 43201; www.vfsl.com).

TOUR: Safari Par Excellence (✆ 27/11/ 888-4037; www.safpar.com). **Victoria Falls Tours** (✆ 27/31/765-4446; www. vicfallstours.com).

WHY THEY'LL THANK YOU: Getting all wet.

Iguazú Falls
Spilling through the Jungle
Ages 6 & up • Puerto Iguazú, Argentina

It's not just one spectacular waterfall but a whole series of them, 275 in all, plunging step by step through an incredibly lush jungle canyon. While **Iguazú Falls** doesn't offer one single knock-'em-dead postcard panorama, exploring this rippling sequence of individual falls can be mesmerizing in its own way—in fact, it will engage some children for hours as they hurry ahead, treasure-hunt style, to find the next one, and the next one, and the next . . .

Like Victoria Falls and Niagara Falls, Iguazú Falls sits on the border between two countries, in this case Brazil and Argentina, though the main park is on the Argentina side. Next to the visitor entrance, there's an excellent new interpretation center full of displays about the park's history, flora, and fauna. Past that,

you'll find the starting station for an open-sided train that trundles to the trail heads for the two well-signposted walking trails, the **Upper** and **Lower Circuits.**

The 1km (.6-mile) **Upper Circuit** winds its way along the top of the canyon, where you can walk right to the edges of at least five waterfalls and look over as they drop as much as 60m (197 ft.) to the next stage of the river below. But the best views are along the 1.8km-long (1-mile) **Lower Circuit,** where you'll walk past the feet of nine magnificent waterfalls (the kids may want to keep a checklist), crashing down before you in walls of silvery spray. The most awesome of all the falls is on this route, the furious avalanche of water and spray known as **Garganta del Diable** (Devil's Throat), which is also the final stop for the park train. Along the Lower Circuit,

The lush Iguazú Falls.

you can catch a free boat over to **San Martín Island,** where you'll be literally surrounded by an arch of waterfalls. Combining the two circuits, exploring the cascades will take about 4 hours—it's not so much the distance you'll walk but the many times you'll want to stop and gasp at the views.

While you're here, don't make it all about the waterfalls; the surrounding jungle is just as amazing. The park's system of elevated footbridges and catwalks takes you right up into the dense tree canopy, for a great view of orchids, butterflies, tree frogs, lizards, parrots, parakeets, and brown capuchin monkeys. That's just the short list—within the national park live 200 species of trees, 448 bird species, 71 kinds of mammals, 36 types of reptiles, 20 species of amphibians, and more than 250 kinds of butterflies. Though you'll see a fair bit just on the Upper and Lower circuit trails, a tour with an experienced jungle guide is something too fascinating to pass up. The main local operator, **Iguazú Jungle Explorer** (✆ **54/3757/421-696;** www. iguazujungleexplorer.com), offers a variety of surprisingly inexpensive options.

ⓘ www.iguazuargentina.com.

✈ Cataratas del Iguazú.

🛏 $$ **Hotel Saint George,** Av. Córdoba 148 (✆ **54/3757/420-633;** www. hotelsaintgeorge.com.ar). $$$ **Sheraton Iguazú Resort,** Parque Nacional Iguazú (✆ **0800/888-3535** or 54/3757/491-800; www.sheraton.com).

WHY THEY'LL THANK YOU: Water, water everywhere.

---

23 Falling Waters

Angel Falls

A Strand of Crystal from the Sky

Ages 12 & up • Canaima, Venezuela

In the wilds of southern Venezuela stands the world's tallest waterfall—a silvery wonder with one uninterrupted drop of 807m (2,648 ft.) and a total drop of 979m (3,212 ft.), which adds up to twice the height of the Empire State Building, or 15 times as high as Niagara Falls. **Angel Falls** isn't just some sight you tack on to another nearby destination—there is no other nearby destination, except for Venezuela's largest national park, a wilderness known as **Canaima National Park.** So once you decide to come here, do the kids a favor and make sure you get the full amazing experience.

This region is so wild, there are just about no roads—people get around primarily in motorized dugout canoes called *curiaras.* As a result, most tourists only see the falls out of the window of their airplane as they approach Canaima, and they're often disappointed—Angel Falls is located up a steep canyon that can easily be socked in with clouds, especially in the rainy season. Even when the falls are visible, you'll get only a fleeting glimpse.

If you really want to see the falls, then, go there by river. One-day excursions involve heading upstream through rapids and canyons for about 4 hours, then finishing off with an hour-long uphill hike through tropical forest to reach the pools at the foot of the falls. The hike is strenuous and can be muddy, but your reward at the top is plunging right into those deliciously refreshing jungle pools. And because it was such an arduous trek to get here, you won't have to battle mobs of photo-snapping bus tourists—you'll have that breathtaking view of Angel Falls practically to yourselves.

Super City Views

Help your kids make sense of these bewildering cities you're visiting—find some high-up spot where they can get a bird's-eye view. Maybe you offer that Big Picture panorama to orient them at the start of your visit; maybe you save it for the end of your trip, so they can identify sights they've already seen. Either way, once they've seen it from on high, they'll feel like they *own* that city.

㉔ Domkirche St. Stephans, Vienna, Austria The best place to view mellow Vienna is still from the tower of its great 14th-century Gothic cathedral. Affectionately called Alter Steffl (Old Steve), the South Tower's needlelike spire rises 135m (450 ft.) above Vienna, a focal point of the city's skyline. Built between 1350 and 1433, it was the main lookout for the walled medieval city; you can climb 343 steps to reach the watchmen's room, which offers spectacular views all the way to the Vienna Woods (not to mention a glimpse of the cathedral's colorful tiled roof). There's an elevator in the stumpy North Tower, which was never properly finished; it now contains the church's massive bells. See Prater ㊽. *Stephansplatz 1. www.st.stephan.at.*

㉕ Eiffel Tower, Paris, France Built in 1889 for the centenary of the French Revolution, this skyward swoop of iron gridwork swiftly became the symbol of modern France. At 317m (1,040 ft.), it can be seen over the rooftops for miles, but don't stop there—take an elevator up, at least to the second landing, for a panoramic view. From that height you can gaze in all directions, picking out other postcard sights like the Arc de Triomphe, the Gothic cathedral of Notre Dame, the formal gardens of the nearby Jardin des Tuileries,

The Eiffel Tower.

the exotic white basilica of Sacré-Coeur on a distant Montmartre hilltop, and above all the loopy course of the Seine as it divides Right Bank from Left Bank. See Catacombs ㊏, Pont Neuf �91, Cité des Sciences et de l'Industrie ㉘, Notre Dame ㉞, Louvre ㉞, Paris Opera ㉞, Fontainebleau ㉞, and Versailles ㉞. *5 Av. Anatole France, Champs de Mars. ℂ 33/1/44-11-23-23; www.tour-eiffel.fr.*

㉖ Victoria Peak, Hong Kong An 8-minute ride on the Peak tram—the world's steepest funicular railway—whisks you to the top of Victoria Peak, where there are spectacular views of bustling Hong Kong Harbour. The Peak Tower has a viewing terrace, as well as the obligatory set of tourist traps—a Madame Tussaud's, Ripley's Believe It or Not!, and the motion-simulator theater Peak Explorer. Don't leave without walking around the lush cliffside footpaths. Victoria Peak is an exclusive residential enclave, where the expat British vibe is still strong. Another option: From Des Vouex Road and Queen Victoria Street, you can take a zigzagging series of escalators to the Mid-Levels of Victoria Peak; it takes 20 minutes to go up, but be prepared to walk back down! *ℂ 852/2522-0922; www.thepeak.com.hk.*

㉗ Empire State Building/Top of the Rock, New York City   Crowded onto its narrow island, Manhattan grew up, not out—so to view its spectacular cityscape, you'll have to go high. In Midtown, the most famous view is from the Art Deco Empire State Building; you'll be 102 stories up, right among the skyscraper tops. But I prefer the sleeker deck 70 stories up at Top of the Rock, atop 30 Rockefeller Center. Both offer open-air terraces, for those who dare; and they're open at night, so you can be dazzled by the bright lights of the big city. See Central Park ㊳, Brooklyn Bridge �995, American Museum of Natural History ㉒, Bronx Zoo ㉗, Statue of Liberty ㉒, *Intrepid* ㉕, Metropolitan Museum ㉝, American Museum of the Moving Image ㉞, and Cyclone ㊼. *Empire State Building: Fifth Ave. & 34th St. ② 212/736-3100; www.esbnyc.com. Top of the Rock: 50th St., btw. Fifth & Sixth aves. ② 212/698-2000; www.topoftherocknyc.com.*

㉘ Washington Monument, Washington, D.C.   The world's tallest freestanding work of masonry, the Washington Monument lies at the west end of the National Mall—a perfect vantage point to admire the elegant geometric layout Pierre L'Enfant designed in 1791 for America's new capital. Because D.C.'s zoning prohibits any building taller than the Capitol dome, nothing obstructs the 360-degree view from the top. Due north is the White House; due east stretches the National Mall, ending in the white dome of the Capitol; due west is the Lincoln Memorial; and due south is the Jefferson Memorial and the Tidal Basin. See National Museum of Natural History ㉗, Air & Space Museum ㉗, National Museum of the American Indian ㉑, and the International Spy Museum ㉒. *15th St. & Madison Dr. NW (on the National Mall btw. the U.S. Capitol and the Lincoln Memorial). ② 202/426-6841; www.nps.gov/wamo.*

㉙ Space Needle, Seattle, Washington   Built for Seattle's 1962 World's Fair, this towering landmark (605 ft. tall) still has a futuristic vibe. A flying-saucer-like deck set near the top contains a roomy Observation Deck and the SkyCity restaurant, the oldest revolving restaurant in the world (and the food's pretty darn good, too). Low-lying Seattle doesn't have as many architectural points of interest to spot as some cities do, but the distant views of sparkling Puget Sound, the Olympic Mountains, and even the Cascade Range, are thrilling. See Seattle-Victoria Ferry ㊻ and Experience Music Project (EMP) ㊵. *400 Broad St. ② 206/905-2100; www.spaceneedle.com.*

㉚ CN Tower, Toronto, Ontario   Opened in 1976, this slender 553m (1,815-ft.) tall concrete spike is the tallest freestanding structure in the world, a gargantuan communications antenna with glass-walled elevators zipping up and down its stem. The first stop is the 346m-high (1,136-ft.) Look Out level; young daredevils will run right away down one level to the Glass Floor, where you can look straight down to the sidewalk, over a thousand feet below. Even higher up is the world's highest public observation gallery, the Skypod, where you can usually see all the way to Niagara Falls. The tower's attractions include an IMAX theater and revolving restaurant. See International Hockey Hall of Fame ㊽. *301 Front St. W. ② 416/868-6937; www.cntower.ca.*

Almost all visitors come here as part of a package tour, which will include accommodations, airfare, local guide services, the works. Try **Lost World Adventures** (© **800/999-0558** in the U.S., or 58/212/577-0303 in Caracas; www.lostworld adventures.com), or book your excursion directly through one of the lodges listed below.

✈ Canaima.

🛏 $$ **Jungle Rudy Campamento,** Parque Nacional Canaima (© **58/286/962-2359** in Canaima, 58/212/693-0618 in Caracas; www.junglerudy.com). $$ **Campamento Parakaupa,** Parque Nacional Canaima (© **58/286/961-4963;** www.parakaupa.com.ve).

BEST TIME: It's a trade-off—the river waters are highest during the rainy season, in Aug and Sept, but although this feeds the falls with abundant water, expect frequent rainfall. June and July will be less wet. From Jan to May, the river level is too low to visit the falls by boat at all, although flyovers are still possible.

WHY THEY'LL THANK YOU: Getting there like Indiana Jones.

2 Exploring the Scenery

Going-to-the-Sun Road in Montana.

The Skyline Drive & Blue Ridge Parkway
Driving the Appalachians
All ages • Virginia, North Carolina & Tennessee, USA

Anchored at either end by national parks— Shenandoah National Park at one end, Great Smoky Mountains National Park at the other—this 574-mile stretch of Appalachian mountain-crest highway is stunning any time of year. In May, wildflowers bloom along with dogwood and mountain laurel, and in summer these mountain reaches stay refreshingly cool and green. We drove it in early fall, missing the vivid foliage of mid- to late October but experiencing an amazing sight: a blizzard of monarch butterflies stubbornly plowing into oncoming traffic, refusing to veer off of their hard-wired migration route. In the winter, whenever snow and ice close some parts of the parkway, you can even cross-country ski here.

Tell the kids that all those trees releasing hydrocarbons into the atmosphere create the mountains' distinctive haze— blue along the Blue Ridge, slightly grayer (and therefore "smoky") in the Smoky Mountains. Both parkways are signposted with mile markers, which makes counting down the distances fun for kids, and there are walking trails marked continually (look for signs bearing a rifle-and–powder horn symbol). We also played Spot the Scenic Overlook, keeping watch for the next pull-off area where we could jump out and really drink in those hill-and-valley vistas. Another thing to do is to count the tunnels—there's only one in Virginia but 26 in North Carolina, most of them in the hilly section below Asheville.

The 105-mile **Skyline Drive**, which has an entry fee, begins at Front Royal, Virginia, and slices southwest through long, skinny **Shenandoah National Park**. Around Waynesboro, the road's name changes to the Blue Ridge Parkway (469 miles in total), and the surrounding greenery becomes the **Jefferson National Forest**. You'll cross the border into North Carolina and roll through the **Pisgah National Forest** (my kids love that name), reaching higher elevations as you angle west past Asheville to the **Great Smoky Mountains** park, which spills west into Tennessee.

You can take a break at several sites en route: At the Blue Ridge Parkway milepost 5.8, **Humpback Rocks,** the **Mountain Farm trail** meanders through a cluster of 19th-century farm buildings; at milepost 85.9, the **Peaks of Otter,** a loop trail leads to the rural **Johnson Farm;** milepost 176.2 accesses picturesque **Mabry Mill,** along with a blacksmith shop, wheelwright's shop, and whiskey still; **Puckett Cabi** (milepost 189.9) was the home of a busy 19th-century mountain midwife; the **Jesse Brown Farmstead** (milepost 272.5) consists of a cabin, spring house, and a Baptist church. At milepost 294.2, **Moses H. Cone Memorial Park** offers a turn-of-the-20th-century manor house. Because your drive should take at least 2 days, overnight in Boone, North Carolina, where the **Hickory Ridge Homestead Museum** (© **828/264-2120;** www.horninthewest. com/museum.htm) is a re-created 1780 log cabin farmstead with costumed interpreters.

ⓘ **Shenandoah National Park** (© **540/ 999-3500;** www.nps.gov/shen). **Blue Ridge Pkwy.** (© **828/271-4779;** www. nps.gov/blri).

🛏 $$ **Holiday Inn Express,** 1943 Blowing Rock Rd., Boone (© **800/HOLIDAY** [465-4329] or 828/264-2451; www. ichotelsgroup.com).

WHY THEY'LL THANK YOU: Backwoods trails and the Daniel Boone vibe.

The Cabot Trail
North America's Highland Wilds
All ages • Nova Scotia, Canada

Nova Scotia is Latin for "New Scotland," and the name really fits blustery, craggy Cape Breton Island. The Scots who settled this part of Canada were generally Highlanders who'd rebelled against the English Crown, and I like to think that they immediately felt at home on these isolated uplands. Cape Breton Island National Park is a starkly beautiful wilderness with a split personality: In the interior rises a melancholy plateau of wind-stunted evergreens, bogs, and barrens, a fitting home for druids or trolls; around the edges, the mountains tumble suddenly to the sea in a dramatic coastline seascape of ravines and ragged, rust-colored cliffs. The Scottish Highlands don't have a scenic coastal highway, but the North American version does: the **Cabot Trail,** a 300km (185-mile) loop built in 1939 to take advantage of those astounding sea views.

You'll get onto the roadway at Baddeck, a New England-y town where Alexander Graham Bell spent his summers (there's a good exhibit on his life and work on Chebucto St.), but things get more rugged as you swing north toward the park. The gateway to the park is the Acadian town of Chéticamp, the most French-speaking part of the island—notice the French names on local shops and restaurants—where the visitor center has some good natural history displays and a large-scale relief map to give the kids a geographic idea of where they're going.

The Cabot Trail circuit should take 6 to 8 hours to drive. Don't expect to make good time; the road has lots of brake-testing steep climbs and whooshing descents, and you'll also want to stop at many pullouts. The most gorgeous stretch is the 44km (27 miles) from Chéticamp to Pleasant Bay, along the western coast. You'll lose the water views for a time after Pleasant Bay, as you cut across the headlands to Cape North, where English explorer John Cabot first set foot on the North American continent (although some Newfoundlanders claim he first landed in Newfoundland). Going down the eastern coast, you'll pass through a series of towns with Scottish names—Ingonish Centre, Ingonish Ferry, South Ingonish Harbour—and then make a precipitous climb to the promontory of Cape Smokey, where panoramic views explode on every side.

Stop and stretch your legs on some of the hiking trails that head inland from the road. The best ones for kids are the half-mile-long **Bog Trail,** which follows a boardwalk into the gnarled bogs of the tableland, and the half-mile **Lone Shieling loop,** which enters a verdant hardwood forest that includes 350-year-old sugar

Cape Breton Island, Nova Scotia.

maples; a re-creation of a Scottish crofter's hut is a highlight of the trail. An 11km (6.8-mile) trail leads along the bluffs of **Cape Smokey;** even if you don't go all the way to the tip, it's worth walking partway just to feel the headland winds and taste the salt air.

(i) **Cape Breton Highlands National Park** (© **902/224-2306**; www.pc.gc.ca).

✈ Halifax, 282km (175 miles).

🛏 $ **Cape Breton Highlands Bungalows,** Cabot Trail, Ingonish Beach (© **888/469-4816** or 902/285-2000). $$ **Inverary Resort,** Shore Rd., Baddeck (© **800/565-5660** or 902/295-3500; www.inverary resort.com).

WHY THEY'LL THANK YOU: Scotland via French-speaking Canada.

Drives **33**

Going-to-the-Sun Road
Soaring through Big Sky Montana
All ages • West Glacier, Montana, USA

When the Ice Age ended millennia ago, receding glaciers revealed a stunning valley they'd carelessly gouged out of what is now the state of Montana and lower Alberta, Canada. Majestic mountain crags loom on either side, their crevices hiding lakes and ponds that are really just melted glacial leftovers. The glaciers are still receding, in fact (the effect of global warming, some say); often in winter, avalanches heap over the scenic 50-mile road that bisects this valley. Climbing some 3,400 feet in a mere 32 miles, this breathtaking drive truly lives up to its poetical name: the **Going-to-the-Sun Road.**

The drive begins at West Glacier, the park entrance that meets U.S. Hwy. 2 near Columbia Falls, Montana. The first stretch of road traces the southeast shore of **Lake McDonald,** the park's largest lake, with postcardlike panoramas of shimmering water backed by verdant mountains. Across from the Avalanche Campground ranger station, look for the marker for the **Trail of the Cedars,** a level quarter-mile nature boardwalk. Back on the road, you keep winding up into the mountains, getting a bird's-eye view of the surrounding peaks—be careful about looking out the car's side windows, because some of those drops are dizzying.

There are three landmarks along this middle section: **The Loop,** an excellent vantage point for **Heaven's Peak; Bird Woman Falls Overlook,** where you can gaze across a sweeping valley to a waterfall; and, most kids' favorite, the **Weeping Wall,** a wall of rock that does, in fact, weep groundwater profusely. At the 32-mile mark, Logan Pass has a visitor center, open summers only, that sits right on top of the **Continental Divide**—which, as you no doubt remember from geography class, is the ridge of the Rockies from which all rivers flow either east or west. Downhill (east) from here is the turnout for **Jackson Glacier,** the most easily recognizable glacier in the entire park, followed by trail heads for short wildlife-viewing hikes to **Sunrift Gorge** and **Sun Point.** At the east end lies the St. Mary visitor center. If you'd rather not retrace the park road, complete the loop clockwise another 57 miles by following U.S. 2 south, west, and then north along park borders back to West Glacier. Along the way, the Two Medicine park entrance offers another fun short trail, the **Running Eagle Falls trail** (trail head 1 mile west of the entrance), a one-third mile stroll through dense forest to a large, noisy waterfall.

The whole loop can be done in 1 day, with plenty of time for picnics, short hikes, and pulling off-road to enjoy the jaw-dropping vistas; there are even free shuttle buses that will take you on various sections of the road so you can enjoy the views without having to drive. To get the full effect, journey across the Going-to-the-Sun Road before 8:30am; you'll be astounded by the masterful job Mother Nature does of painting her mountains.

(i) **Glacier National Park** ((C) **406/888-7800;** www.nps.gov/glac).

✈ Kalispell, 29 miles.

🛏 $$ **Glacier Campground,** 12070 U.S. 2 ((C) **888/387-5689** or 406/387-5689; www.glaciercampground.com). $$$ **Lake McDonald Lodge,** on Lake McDonald ((C) **406/892-2525;** www.glacierparkinc.com).

BEST TIME: Early June to mid-Oct.

WHY THEY'LL THANK YOU: Straddling the Continental Divide.

34 Drives

Columbia Icefields Parkway

Back to the Ice Age

Ages 4 & up • Alberta, Canada

Children who loved the animated *Ice Age* films will look around this natural wonder and feel as if they're back in the movies all over again. Spreading over the eastern face of the Canadian Rockies, it's the world's largest nonpolar ice cap, a massive dome of glacial ice and snow straddling the top of the North American continent. The drive to get here is equally spectacular: The 286km (178-mile) **Icefields Parkway,** a majestic stretch of highway between Banff and Jasper national parks, which climbs through deep river valleys, beneath soaring, glacier-notched mountains, and past dozens of hornlike peaks shrouded with permanent snowcaps.

The Icefields Parkway can be driven in 3 hours, but plan on a full day so you can enjoy scenic stops en route. Heading north from Lake Louise, you'll see **Bow Lake** at the foot of **Crowfoot Glacier;** farther north, a short hike from the road takes you to startlingly blue-green **Peyto Lake,** vividly colored by minerals dissolved in the glaciers, and, then, after a dramatic incline, to 3,490m (11,450 ft.) **Mount Athabasca** at Sunwapta Pass. The ice tendrils of the

Columbia Icefields creep close to the road here, though it's only a glimpse of the massive amounts of century-old ice and snow tucked in around these peaks, covering 518 sq. km (200 sq. miles) and lying up to 760m (2,493 ft.) thick in some spots.

Columbia Icefields.

At the Columbia Icefields Centre lodge, you'll find a restaurant, an information center, and the ticket office for **Brewster Snocoach Tours** (☎ **403/762-6700;** www.brewster.ca), where you can book a 90-minute ride onto the surface of the glacier in a specially designed bus with balloon tires. The tour gives you an opportunity to hike on the glacier, but make sure the kids walk carefully—a tumble into a crevasse can easily break a leg.

After that, the road begins to plunge downward into the Athabasca River valley, and the rivers have to plunge downward too, which means—hooray!—waterfalls. The best one to visit is **Athabasca Falls,** where you can walk on a mist-covered bridge over the chasm and follow walking trails to other scenic overlooks. The road rolls on past mountain meadows and lakes until it reaches the town of Jasper.

For a true luxury experience, you could always splurge on a round-trip train journey from Vancouver via the sleek blue-and-white **Rocky Mountaineer** (☎ **877/460-3200;** www.rockymountaineer.com), which includes a motorcoach spin along the Icefields Parkway as part of its dazzling tour through the high passes of the Rockies. However you get here, keep an eye out for bighorn sheep, mountain goats, elks, and maybe even mama black bears with their cubs. Don't try to get close to them though, and by no means try to feed them. Unlike animated animals, these can be dangerous!

ⓘ **Information center,** Hwy. 93N, Sunwapta Pass (☎ 877/423-7433 or 403/762-6700; www.columbiaicefield.com).

✈ Calgary, 257km (160 miles).

🚆 Jasper.

🛏 $$ **Becker's Chalets,** Hwy. 93S, Jasper (☎ **780/852-3779;** www.beckerschalets.com). $$$ **Glacier View Inn,** Sunwapta Pass (☎ **877/423-7433;** www.explorerockies.com/columbia-icefield/hotel.aspx).

BEST TIME: Open Apr–Oct.

WHY THEY'LL THANK YOU: Going back to the Ice Age.

Drives **35**

Haleakala Crater Road

Volcano Touring in Hawaii

All ages • Maui, Hawaii, USA

If you really want to be dull, it's called Hwy. 378, and on the map it's such a wiggly line that you wonder what the road engineers were smoking when they laid it out. But when you drive the **Haleakala Crater Road,** you understand immediately: Every wiggle in that road is another steep switchback curve climbing up, up, up, right to the summit of the world's largest dormant volcano. It may take you over an hour to cover these 20 miles, with the weather changing every few miles as you pass through different climate zones. You'll run into patches of fog that turn out to be not fog at all, but drive-through cumulus clouds. Look out the window and you may see rare black-faced Hawaiian geese flying right beside you. By the time you get to the top, the crater—a black hole so big it could hold Manhattan—is almost beside the point.

And then you get to drive back down (in low gear, please!).

Many visitors time their visits to Haleakala for sunrise or sunset, when the sun gilds the lunarlike landscape with colors so fiery that you can almost imagine that the lava beds have heated up again.

Haleakala does mean House of the Sun, after all, and when you see the sun rise up out of the ocean, it's awe-inspiring. With kids in the car, though, I hesitate to drive those curves in predawn or postdusk darkness. Besides, daylight lets them enjoy the views along the way, which can extend as far as 100 miles on a clear day. There are three scenic overlooks en route to the summit, essential stops not only for the views but to let the kids pop their ears and adjust to the thin air. At **Leleiwi Overlook,** about halfway up, you get your first full panorama of the crater above. When the clouds are low and the sun's in the right place, you can see your own shadows, ringed with a rainbow, reflected on the surface of the clouds below—a rare phenomenon indeed. Shortly before the summit, the Haleakala Visitor Center has great views of the moonlike volcanic landscape. But it's still a few miles to **Puu Ulaula Overlook,** where the **Haleakala Observatories** are located, 10,023 feet high. Often you can see all the way to the Big Island from here (look for the snow-capped peak of Mauna Kea). On your way back down, stop at the **Kalahaku Over-**look to admire the only-in-Hawaii silversword plant, with its spiky silver spears and tiny purple flowers.

If your kids are older, several local operators will take you up the volcano in a van and then give you mountain bikes to coast down the winding road; try **Maui Downhill** (© 800/535-BIKE [2453] or 808/871-2155; www.mauidownhill.com) or **Maui Mountain Cruisers** (© 800/232-6284; www.mauimountaincruisers.com).

ⓘ **Haleakala National Park,** Hwy. 37 to 377 to 378 (© **808/572-4400;** www.nps.gov/hale).

✈ Kahului, 37 miles.

🛏 $$ **Banyan Retreat Center,** 3265 Baldwin Ave., Makawao (© **808/572-8482;** www.hawaii-mauirentals.com). $$ **Hale Ho'okipa Inn Makawao,** 32 Pakani Place, Makawao (© **877/572-6698** or 808/572-6698; www.maui-bed-and-breakfast.com).

WHY THEY'LL THANK YOU: Driving through the clouds.

---

36 Drives

The Ring of Kerry
Ireland's Wide Green West

All ages • County Kerry, Ireland

Ireland's greatest tourism cliché is the **Ring of Kerry,** a 177km (110-mile) route around the Iveragh Peninsula, where scores of tour buses thunder every day in summer. But taking your own car makes all the difference: Follow the road clockwise (the buses go counterclockwise) and you'll have the road less traveled, with room to enjoy the postcard-perfect seacoast views that made the Ring a tourist draw in the first place.

Without stops, the circuit takes 4 hours; plan for twice that so you can stop and explore, not just snap photos out your window. Driving south from tourist-choked Killarney on N71, you'll enter spectacular **Killarney National Park,** where the mountain scenery has an almost Wild West grandeur. From the road, you gaze north over the memorably named range of **Macgillycuddy's Reeks;** Ireland's tallest mountain, **Carrantuohill,** at 1,041m (3,415 ft.), crops up in the distance. Stop to savor it at **Ladies View,** a scenic overlook, where Queen Victoria's ladies-in-waiting raved about the panorama on a royal vacation (thus launching Kerry's tourism industry). Detour south to Kenmare, a neat little town on Kenmare Bay, where a Bronze Age stone circle stands intact around a dolmen tomb. At Kenmare Pier, from May to October, **Sea-Fari Cruises** (© **353/64/42059;** www.seafariireland. com), runs 2-hour excursions to spot dolphins, sea otters, gray seals, and herons.

Wind on down the coast to **Sneem,** Ireland's most colorful village, literally—the kids will be delighted to see all the houses painted in vibrant shades of blue, pink, yellow, purple, and orange. A few miles past Sneem, signs point to **Staigue Fort,** 3km (1¾ miles) off N70 on a narrow one-track road. A huge hit with my youngsters, this circular fort was built around 1000 B.C. of unmortared rough stones, big enough to shelter an entire Iron Age clan. At the western end of the peninsula, Waterville is an improbably Mediterranean-looking resort town, where Charlie Chaplin often summered; there's a super beach here, a good (if windy) spot for a picnic. Detour from the main road to Portmagee, where a bridge leads to **Valentia Island** and **The Skellig Experience** (© **353/66/947-6306;** www.skellig experience.com; Mar–Nov only). Its displays and audiovisuals delve into local birds and plant life, in particular those of the two tiny offshore islands known as the **Skellig Rocks.** These are **Skellig Michael,** a rock pinnacle towering over the sea, where medieval monks built an isolated monastery; and neighboring **Little Skellig,**

where vast flocks of gannets and other seabirds nest in summer. Cruises out to the Skelligs are available from Valentia.

Continue on N70, with Dingle Bay on your right. On this north side of the peninsula, open bog land constantly comes into view, a terrain formed thousands of years ago from decayed trees. The atmospheric **Kerry Bog Village Museum,** in Ballycleave (© **353/66/976-9184;** www.kerry bogvillage.ie), was our favorite stop: a cluster of thatched-roof cottages showing what life was like in Kerry in the early 1800s, from the blacksmith's forge to the roof-thatcher's dwelling to the turf-cutter's house (for centuries local residents have dug up the peaty turf to burn in their fireplaces). The life behind the postcard views—that's what we were after, and we got it.

ⓘ **Killarney Tourist Office,** Beech Rd., Killarney (© **353/64/31633;** www.killarney online.ie).

✈ Kerry County Airport.

🚆 Killarney Railway Station.

🛏 $$ **Derrynane Hotel,** off N71, Caherdaniel (© **800/528-1234** or 353/66/ 947-5136; www.derrynane.com). $$ **Earls Court House,** Woodlawn Junction, Muckross Rd., Killarney (© **353/64/663-4009;** www.killarney-earlscourt.ie).

WHY THEY'LL THANK YOU: Kodachrome views, Celtic history.

Drives **37**

The Amalfi Drive
A Mediterranean Thrill Ride
All ages • Sorrento to Ravello, Italy

Hugging the coast of the Gulf of Salerno, Italy's **Amalfi Drive** (Rte. 163) is the most beautiful and probably most treacherous seaside highway in the world, a heart-hammering series of narrow hairpin turns you'll share with reckless Italian drivers. There are few roadside railings as you follow the edge of a clifftop plunging straight down to a boulder-strewn coast. If you

The Amalfi Drive.

The first 24km (15 miles) of the drive swing around the tip of a rocky peninsula, with Capri lying out to sea on your right, to Positano, a Moorish-style town with a hillside cascade of pink and white villas. If you skipped Capri's Blue Grotto, make up for it by visiting the **Emerald Grotto** 13km (8 miles) east of Positano. From the coastal road, you take an elevator down to this eerie cavern, and then ride a boat past underwater rock formations saturated with dazzling colored light.

The next town, 5km (3 miles) farther east, is Amalfi, an important seafaring republic in the Dark Ages and today a posh beach resort. If you need a break, stop in at the cloisters behind its cathedral, with whitewashed Moorish-style arches and mosaic fragments. Heading east from Amalfi, you negotiate a wickedly curving stretch of road cutting through vine-draped hills that hem in the ominously named **Valley of the Dragon.** After 6km (3¾ miles) of this, you'll land in Ravello, a cliffside retreat for writers from Boccaccio to D. H. Lawrence to Gore Vidal. A few miles past Ravello, at Vietri dul Mare, you can turn (with relief) onto the A3 highway, which cuts back towards Naples on a considerably tamer inland route. You made it!

want to leave the driving to someone else, take the blue SITA public bus that runs between Sorrento and Salerno.

The drive begins in Sorrento, a luxury resort perched on high cliffs overlooking the bay of Naples. Shops along Sorrento's cobbled alleys and flower-ringed plazas sell exquisite items of embroidery, lace, cameos, and marquetry, which will probably bore the kids silly: Instead, take a 45-minute hydrofoil trip to the island of **Capri** to see the **Grotta Azzurra** (Blue Grotto), a spectacular cavern where light refracted from an opening under the water turns everything a dramatic Mediterranean cerulean blue. The beautiful lighting will amaze the kids (although the way passengers are hustled in and out of their rowboats spoils the experience somewhat).

ⓘ **Sorrento tourist office,** Via Luigi de Maio 35, Sorrento (ⓒ **39/81/807-4033;** www.sorrentotourism.com).

✈ Sorrento, 1 hr. from Naples.

🛏 $$$ **Hotel Bristol,** Via Capo 10, Sorrento (ⓒ **39/81/878-4522;** www.bristol sorrento.com). $$ **Hotel Grand Excelsior,** Via Papa Leone X, Amalfi (ⓒ **39/89/83-00-15;** www.excelsior-hotel.it).

WHY THEY'LL THANK YOU: Seat belts are a good thing.

The Great Ocean Road

Awesome Aussie Wonder

All ages • Torquay to Warrnambool, Victoria, Australia

There's no question that coastal roads pack a scenic wallop, but even among coastal roads, the **Great Ocean Road** stands out. If you want the kids to understand Australia's raw power, this drive is essential. Running along the southern coast for 106km (66 miles), it offers the expected sheer cliffs, sea vistas, and beaches, but then there's the Aussie difference: patches of lush rainforest and some incredible rock formations created by the pounding seas of the Southern Ocean.

Some tour operators offer 1-day loops from Melbourne, but it makes a lot more sense to rent your own car and take a leisurely 2 days. Where you stop, of course, depends on the kids' special interests. We associate Australia with surfers, and the eastern section of the drive, starting with

Torquay, home of world-famous Bells Beach, is called the Surf Coast. The **Surfworld Museum,** in Surf City Plaza on Beach Road (© **61/3/5261-4606;** www. surfworld.org.au), has interactive exhibits on surfboard design and surfing history and video of the world's best surfers. In Lorne, another surfing town, stop at the **Ozone Milk Bar** on Mount Joy Parade, a classic Australian milk bar—a kind of down-market cafe that sells everything from shakes and pies to newspapers. From Lorne to Apollo Bay is a thrilling stretch of road, as the pavement narrows and twists along a cliff edge. The **Angahook-Lorne State Park** along here has many marked rainforest walks; about 13km (8 miles) past Apollo Bay, just off the main road, you can stroll on the **Maits Rest Rainforest Boardwalk.** The road

Along Australia's Great Ocean Road.

cuts inland through the **Otway National Forest**; past **Beauchamp Falls,** head south on an unpaved road for 15km (9¹/₃ miles) to the windswept headland and the historic **Cape Otway Lighthouse,** built by convicts in 1848. Five kilometers (3 miles) southwest of the old timber town of Lavers Hill, small **Melba Gully State Park** lets you walk on trails through rainforest ferns to find one of the last **giant gum trees,** some 27m (89 ft.) in circumference; it's thought to be over 300 years old. By now you're on the **Shipwreck Coast,** so named because there were some 80 wrecks along here in just 40 years. You'll reach the water's edge again just past Princetown, where you can see what a treacherous shore this is: Along a 27km (17-mile) stretch through **Port Campbell National Park** are the **Twelve Apostles,** a series of rock pillars standing just offshore; the **Blowhole,** which throws up huge sprays of water; the **Grotto,** intricately carved by the waves;

London Bridge, which looked like the real thing until the center crashed into the sea in 1990; and the **Loch Ard Gorge.** The scenic road ends in Warrnambool, another of those evocative Australian names. There's a faster road back to Melbourne from here—faster, but not nearly so much fun.

ⓘ **Great Ocean Road Visitors Centre,** Stead Park, Princes Hwy., Geelong (ⓒ **61/ 3/5275 5797;** www.greatoceanrd.org.au).

✈ Melbourne, 93km (58 miles).

⊨ $$ **Great Ocean Road Cottages,** 10 Erskine Ave., Lorne (ⓒ **61/3/5289-1070;** www.greatoceanroadcottages.com). $ **Macka's Farm,** 2310 Princetown Rd., Princetown (ⓒ **61/3/5598-8261;** www.mackasfarm.com.au).

WHY THEY'LL THANK YOU: Surfing and shipwrecks.

---

39 Train Rides

Durango & Silverton Narrow Gauge Railroad
Classic Steam Train
All ages • Durango, Colorado, USA

Ever since it was built in 1882, this little train has been puffing along the Rio de las Animas Perdidas (that's Spanish for the River of Lost Souls, a haunting name indeed), traveling 45 miles through the mountains and San Juan National Forest to the town of Silverton and back. When it was first built, Silverton was, as its name suggests, a silver-mining town, and the train's business was to bring precious ore back down to the railroad hub of Durango. When the United States went on the gold standard in 1893, the price of silver dropped dramatically, throwing this region's economy into a tailspin. Many local railroads went belly up, but this one

survived because of its incredible scenic views. Nowadays, it's tourists that trundle along those tracks, in strings of restored gold-colored Victorian-era coaches.

Traveling at around 18 mph, you'll climb 3,000 feet, past relics of the area's mining and railroading activities; elevations en route range from 8,000 feet at the passes to 14,000 feet on the peaks you'll see from the train windows. White puffs of smoke trail from its coal-powered steam locomotives—a fireman shovels about 6 tons of coal per day to power these locomotives. If you look at the tracks, they're only 3 feet apart (standard train tracks are 4 ft., 8¹/₂ in. wide), which makes it easier to navigate

The Durango & Silverton Narrow Gauge Railroad.

sharp mountain curves. In this train's case, however, the narrower tracks also meant workers had fewer inches to cut out of the sheer granite cliff face of the Animas Gorge. Good thing, too—it was already such a risky job that the railroad's president, William Palmer, constructed the route in secret, fearing that the directors of the Denver & Rio Grande Railroad would veto the plan before he could safely complete it.

This is a full-day excursion—it takes 3¹/₂ hours to ride from Durango to Silverton, you're given 2 hours to poke around picturesque Victorian-era Silverton, and then it's another 3¹/₂ hours back down to Durango. (Before getting on the train in Durango, you could also spend half an hour or so in the attached **Durango & Silverton railroad museum,** right beside the train depot.) You'll have a couple of hours to explore Silverton before the return trip; one fun thing to do is to visit the **Old Hundred Gold Mine** (ⓒ **800/872-3009** or 970/387-5444; www.minetour.com) in

Cunningham Pass, just outside of Silverton. The tour takes you a third of a mile deep into **Galena Mountain** on an electric mine car, where miners demonstrate historic mining equipment and techniques. There's also gold panning, and box lunches are included in the deal.

The views are even more spectacular on the ride back. In fact, the stretch of Hwy. 550 that parallels the train tracks is called the **Million-Dollar Highway,** not only because it was so expensive to build, but also because you'll get million-dollar Rocky Mountain views all the way home.

ⓘ 479 Main Ave. (ⓒ **800/872-4607** or 970/247-2733; www.durangotrain.com).

✈ Durango/La Plata, 14 miles.

⊨ $$ **The Strater Hotel,** 699 Main Ave., Durango (ⓒ **800/247-4431;** www.strater.com).

WHY THEY'LL THANK YOU: Clinging to the cliff face.

Chihuahua al Pacífico Railway
Climbing through the Copper Canyon
Ages 8 & up • Los Mochis to Chihuahua, Mexico

If you rode straight through, it would take 15 hours to cross Mexico's rugged Sierra Madre range via the **Chihuahua al Pacífico Railway.** After all, you have to climb from coastal Los Mochis, near the Sea of Cortez, up nearly 2,425m (7,956 ft.) northeast along the rim of the fabled **Copper Canyon** before descending to the city of Chihuahua, a trip of 644km (400 miles), with 86 tunnels and 39 bridges. You pass through some of Mexico's most magnificent scenery—thick pine forests, jagged peaks, and shadowy canyons—but it would all be a blur to the kids.

Instead, spread the trip out over 5 days; stay overnight in various towns en route, where your hotels can arrange side trips—horseback riding, hiking, or jeep rides to caves, waterfalls, old missions, Tarahumara Indian settlements, or quaint mining towns hidden in the many tributary canyons. The Copper Canyon is so big, it could engulf four Grand Canyons—why whiz through it in a single day?

I recommend starting at the western end, Los Mochis, where the train leaves at the eyelid-propping hour of 6am. Take a snooze until the first stop, cobblestoned colonial **El Fuerte,** on the coastal plain before the foothills of the Sierra Madre. Beyond El Fuerte, you enter the most dramatic part of the train ride, snaking steeply up the Pacific Palisade to **Bahuichivo,** the first stop in canyon country. If you overnight here, you'll stay in Cerocahui, built around a sweet-looking mission church. It's little more than unpaved streets and 100 or so houses, but it has a stunning view of the mountains; and several excursions make this a good overnight choice. Take the train onward to Barrancas and then, 3km (1¾ miles) farther, **El Divisadero,** the same Continental Divide you can straddle up in Montana (see "Going-to-the-Sun Road" **33**). A 20-minute stop allows passengers to walk to a lookout to gape at the most breathtaking panorama of the canyon along the whole train route. The next-to-last stop is at **Creel** (rhymes with "feel"), a rustic logging town with access to lots of fabulous side trips.

You must buy tickets for a particular date, point of departure, and destination, so design an itinerary to book in advance or sign up for a packaged tour (several leave from El Paso or Tucson; **Sierra Madre Express** in Tucson [✆ 520/394-2414; www.sierramadreexpress.com] does a 1-week tour that runs its own deluxe trains through the canyon). Just don't expect trains to stick to the official timetable—they won't. Take it in stride and the kids will too.

ⓘ **Mexico's Copper Canyon** (✆ 800/896-8196; www.mexicoscoppercanyon.com).

✈ Los Mochis and Chihuahua.

🛏 $$$ **Hotel Mirador,** El Divisadero (✆ 888/528-8401 in the U.S., or 52/635/578-3020; www.hotelmirador.com). $$ **Hotel Posada del Hidalgo,** Hidalgo 101, El Fuerte (✆ 888/528-8401 in the U.S. or 52/698//893-1194; www.hotelposadadelhidalgo.com). $ **Parador de la Montaña,** Av. López Mateos s/n, Creel (✆ 52/614/415-5408 or 52/635/456-0023; www.hotelparadorcreel.com). $$ **Paraíso del Oso,** Cerocahui (✆ 52/614/421-3372 in Chihuahua; www.mexicohorse.com).

WHY THEY'LL THANK YOU: Going deep into the canyons.

The Mountain Railways of North Wales
Vintage Excursions up the Welsh Peaks
All ages • Llanberis & Porthmadog, North Wales

Lacing around the mountains of North Wales are a number of intriguing little 19th-century railways, built by ingenious engineers to haul the "gray gold"—slate—out of that rugged terrain to be shipped all over the world. It's amazing how many of these charming vintage railways have been preserved in a relatively tiny corner of the country. Your children can get their Thomas the Tank Engine fix on any of six different trains—why not do them all?

You may want to start in the coastal village of Tywyn, where the **Narrow Gauge Railway Museum** has been set up in the tidy red-brick station of the Talyllyn Railway (© **44/1654/710-472;** www.talyllyn.co.uk). From there, a cheery vintage train steams 12km (7¼ miles) up to Abergynolwyn, with five stations en route leading to waterfalls and mountain walking trails. Then head inland to the mountain town of Bala, where the **Bala Lake Railway** (© **44/1678/540-666;** www.bala-lake-railway.co.uk) runs for 7km (4⅓ miles) along glacial **Llyn Tegid** (Bala Lake), mirroring the mountains. Another excellent base is Llanberis, nestling between Lake Padarn and Lake Peris, which has not one but two vintage railways. The **Snowdon Mountain Railway** (© **44/8717/200-033;** www.snowdonrailway.co.uk) runs 7.5km (4⅔ miles) from Llanberis to within a few yards of the top of the Snowdon peak at about 1,085m (3,560 ft.). The only rack-and-pinion train in Britain, it is also the steepest train ride (lasting 1 hr. each way), and the view from the top platform, where the train stops, is one of the most panoramic in the country—it's possible to see some 160km (100 miles) into Ireland on a clear day. Younger children may prefer the tamer **Llanberis Lake Railway** (© **44/1286/870-549;** www.lake-railway.co.uk), which chugs 8km (5 miles) along the dreamy shore of Lake Padarn (1 hr. round-trip). Head west to the coastal town of Porthmadog and the **Ffestiniog Railway** (© **44/1766/516-000;** www.festrail.co.uk), a steep and twisting 22km-long (14-mile) narrow-gauge railway with steam locomotives. It's the only link between the two main train lines in North Wales, so many regular passengers use it as well as tourists. Its endpoint is Blaenau Ffestiniog, a slate-mining village up in the mountains, its surrounding rock face dramatically ravaged by slate quarrying. From the coastal town of Caenarfon, site of a splendid castle ruin and an excavated Roman fort, the **Welsh Highland Railway,** run by the same company, chugs 13km (8 miles) or so uphill into Rhyd Ddu, where walkers can reach hiking trails up Snowdon.

ⓘ **Llanberis Tourist Information Office,** 41B High St. (© **44/1286/870-765;** www.llanberis.org).

🚃 Bangor, 14km (8¾ miles) north of Llanberis.

🛏 $$ **The Legacy Royal Victoria Hotel,** Llanberis (© **44/8708/329-903;** www.legacy-hotels.co.uk).

BEST TIME: May–Oct.

WHY THEY'LL THANK YOU: The thrill of puffing up sheer mountainsides.

Zermatt to St. Moritz
The Glacier Express
All ages • Switzerland

The name "Express" is a bit misleading—it takes 7½ hours for the **Glacier Express** to get from Zermatt, in the southwestern Swiss Alps, over the Oberalp Pass to St. Moritz in the southeast. Along the way, you'll cross 291 bridges—many trestled high above gorges—and duck through 91 tunnels. But every bit of that time, you'll have your noses pressed to the window glass, gaping at the panoramas of hazy blue peaks and deep valleys, whether mantled in sparkling snow or carpeted in wildflowers. Seven-and-a-half hours may seem too short—even normally restless youngsters will be entranced.

Zermatt, at the base of the Matterhorn (in French, Mont Cervin), still has the atmosphere of a village. Though originally better known for mountain climbing (the Alpine Museum in town details the race to climb the Matterhorn, scaled first in 1865 by Edward Whymper), today it's a full-bore ski resort. In fact, Zermatt gets so much snow every winter that high-altitude skiing continues through the spring and early summer. A bewildering number of cable cars, gondolas, and cog railways ascend various peaks around town; if the kids are game, try a day out on the **Gornergrat,** the highest open-air railway in Europe.

At the other end of the train route lies the ultrafashionable ski resort **St. Moritz,** a magnet for jet-setters, movie stars, tycoons, and aristocrats. It became a winter destination in the mid–19th century, when the first skiers ventured onto its slopes (locals thought they were nuts). Today there are five ski complexes, a bobsled run, curling rinks, even winter golf and horse racing on the frozen lake. In

The Glacier Express.

summer, golf and windsurfing are popular, and of course the spas still operate year-round. Expect chic shopping, posh restaurants, and sky-high prices.

When this track was first laid in 1928, some of the mountain bridges had to be dismantled for blizzards every winter, but, in 1982, a new tunnel through the Furka Mountain enabled the route to stay in operation year-round. There's at least one train a day, with up to four in summer. Coaches are comfortably upholstered, with dining cars and panoramic observation coaches; both first- and second-class service is available, and though it's a pricey trip, substantial discounts are offered for children. Advance reservations are essential.

(i) **The Matterhorn-Gotthard Railway** (© **41/27/927-7777;** www.glacierexpress.ch). **Rail Europe** (© **800/622-8600** in the U.S., 800/361-7245 in Canada; www.raileurope.com).

🚂 Zermatt, narrow-gauge from Visp or Brig, 4 hr. from Geneva. St. Moritz, 2 hr. from Chur.

🛏 $$ **Hotel Riffelberg,** Zermatt-Umgebung (© **41/27/966-6500;** www.zermatt.ch/riffelberg). $$$ **Hotel Waldhaus am See,** Via Dimlej 6, St. Moritz (© **41/81/836-6000;** www.waldhaus-am-see.ch).

WHY THEY'LL THANK YOU: Counting the tunnels and bridges.

Train Rides **43**

The Cumbres & Toltec Scenic Railroad

Mountain Train of the Wild West

All ages • Cumbres, Arizona, to Antonito, New Mexico, USA

Back in the 1880s, the Rocky Mountains were laced with little railroad lines, laid down to haul precious metal ore out of remote mines. Weaving through the San Juan Mountains, zigzagging along the New Mexico–Colorado border, the Cumbres & Toltec narrow-gauge railroad is the most classic example of these vintage lines. Along its 64 miles, it passes through a postcard-perfect mountain landscape of wildflower meadows, rustling stands of pine and aspen, and bristling rocky outcrops. It rumbles through two tunnels, over 100-foot-high trestles, and along the magnificent Toltec Gorge of the Rio de los Pinos. And when it crests at the 10,015-foot Cumbres Pass, you're riding higher than any other passenger train in the States.

The Cumbres & Toltec began service in 1880, making it 2 years older than its sister Denver and Rio Grande branch line, the Durango & Silverton Railroad ㊴. Although

the route doesn't climb quite as steeply as the Durango-Silverton line, its entire course is high country, beginning at nearly 8,000 feet and climbing upward from there. Narrow-gauge lines were better suited to mountain terrain, but there was one glitch: They couldn't interchange trains with standard-gauge lines. Finally the Denver and Rio Grande began the expensive job of converting its narrow-gauge routes in the 1890s. This branch line simply wasn't a candidate for conversion—the silver mines it served had shut down with the collapse of silver's value, and the area was otherwise remote and unpopulated. Traffic dwindled to a trickle by the 1920s, chugging along behind archaic coal-fired steam locomotives, the only engines that still fit on narrow-gauge rails. In 1969 the D&RG abandoned the route and began to rip up its tracks. A band of railroad preservationists scrambled to stop the demolition before the route's most scenic stretch, between Chama, New Mexico, and Antonito, Colorado, was lost forever, and the two states cooperated to open it as a tourist attraction (not to mention a bit of a movie star—it's appeared in films from *The Missouri Breaks* to *Indiana Jones and the Last Crusade*).

Trains leave every morning from both Chama and Antonito, meeting halfway at Osier, Colorado, where you're given an hour to stretch your legs and enjoy a buffet lunch beside Osier's old water tank and stock pens. In the afternoon, you can return by train to your original starting point, or complete the 64-mile trip to the other end of the line, where motorcoaches await to complete the round-trip loop. You can also upgrade your ticket to ride in a luxurious parlor car. All passengers can

sample sitting in the open-air gondola, which the kids shouldn't miss—it's the quintessential wind-in-your-face experience.

ⓘ ✆ **888/CUMBRES** or 505/756-2151; www.cumbrestoltec.com.

✈ Albuquerque, 160 miles. Santa Fe, 91 miles.

🛏 $$ **River Bend Lodge,** 2625 U.S. 64/ 285, Chama, NM (✆ **800/288-1371** or 505/ 756-2264; www.chamariverbendlodge. com).

BEST TIME: Late May to mid-Oct.

WHY THEY'LL THANK YOU: When the whistle blows to shoo a high-country steer off the tracks.

---

44 Train Rides

Kuranda's Scenic Skyways

Ages 4 & up • Cairns to Kuranda & back, Australia

The Queensland coast of Australia has not one but two world-class natural wonders: the Great Barrier Reef and the Wet Tropics Rainforest. From a base at Cairns, one day you can go snorkeling on the coral cays, and the next head inland to the mountain village of Kuranda, an exotic retreat of cool mountain air and mist-wrapped rainforest. Some people drive up the winding 25km (16-mile) mountain road, but why remain earthbound when you can glide with the kids over the rainforest canopy in a cable car?

The **Skyrail Rainforest Cableway** is the world's longest gondola cableway, a 90-minute climb 7.5km (4²/₃ miles) upwards in six-person gondolas. Get an early start, and you'll have fine morning light for photographs, but don't cancel if it's raining—a silvery layer of mist only adds haunting beauty to the panorama. From the Skyrail terminal, in the northern Cairns suburbs (Captain Cook Hwy. at Western Arterial

Rd., Smithfield), the view of the coast as you ascend is breathtaking. Rising over the foothills of the coastal range, watch the lush green of the rainforest take over beneath you; as the foliage gets thicker, you can spot ferns and orchids and the brilliant blue butterflies of the region. There are two stops, at **Red Peak** and **Barron Falls,** where you must change gondolas; take the time to stroll around the boardwalks at the intermediate stations for ground-level views of the rainforest.

Once you're in Kuranda, getting close to nature is very easy. Behind the Heritage markets off Rob Veivers Drive, three delightful wildlife attractions are lined up: **Birdworld** (✆ **61/7/4093-9188;** www. birdworldkuranda.com), **Kuranda Koala Gardens** (✆ **61/7/4093-9953;** www.koala gardens.com), and the outstanding **Australian Butterfly Sanctuary** (8 Rob Veivers Dr., ✆ **61/7/4093-7575;** www. australianbutterflies.com). Fashion tip:

Seeing Queensland by rail.

The butterflies will land on you if you wear pink, red, and other bright colors. If you have time, the 40-hectare (100-acre) **Rainforestation Nature Park,** Kennedy Highway (© **61/7/4085-5008;** www.rainforest.com.au), offers visitors a 45-minute narrated ride into the rainforest on a World War II amphibious Army DUKW, or Duck; you can also see a performance by Aboriginal dancers, throw a boomerang on the Dreamtime Walk, or have a photo taken cuddling a koala in the wildlife park.

In the early afternoon (2 or 3:30pm), be back at the fern-draped Kuranda railroad station to board the **Kuranda Scenic Railway,** which snakes 34km (21 miles) through the magnificent vistas of the **Barron Gorge National Park,** past gorges and waterfalls, and through 15 tunnels back down to Cairns' main rail station on Bunda Street. Two spectacular rides in 1 day—what lucky children!

ⓘ **Skyrail Rainforest Cableway** (© **61/7/4038-1555;** www.skyrail.com.au). Kuranda Scenic Railway (© 61/7/4036-9333; www.ksr.com.au).

✈ Cairns.

🛏 $$$ **Pullman Reef Hotel Casino,** 35–41 Wharf St., Cairns (© **02/8584-8673** in Australia, 800/515-5679 in the U.S. and Canada, 0871/702-9469 in the U.K., or 61/7/4030 8888; www.accorhotels.com). $$ **The Reef Retreat,** 10–14 Harpa St., Palm Cove, Cairns (© **61/7/4059-1744;** www.reefretreat.com.au).

WHY THEY'LL THANK YOU: Seeing the rainforest canopy from above.

45 Train Rides

Blue Mountain Scenic Railway
Getting Hazed in the Eucalyptus Forest
Ages 6 & up • Katoomba, Australia

The kids may have seen taller mountains, but that's beside the point: What makes these bush-shrouded hills north of Sydney so incredibly cool is the dreamlike blue haze that hangs over them, a surreal effect that the kids will love. There's a scientific explanation, of course—it's caused by light striking the droplets of oil that evaporate from the leaves of the ubiquitous eucalyptus trees—but that doesn't stop it from being downright magical.

The best vantage point for experiencing this colorful effect is to get right up in the trees—and there's no better way to do that than by taking the world's steepest railway ride, the famous **Scenic Railway.** From the ticket office in Katoomba at 1 Violet Rd. (✆ **61/2/4780-0200** or 1300/ SKYWAY [759929]; www.scenicworld. com.au), you board a carriage on rails that is lowered 415m (1,362 ft.) into the Jamison Valley at a maximum incline of 52 degrees—breathtakingly steep, and quite a thrill. The trip takes only a few minutes, but there's a glorious panorama of the mountains, with their deep river valleys, craggy cliffs, and dense exotic forests. At the bottom of the railway, get out and follow the trails through magnificent primeval-looking tree ferns. Your return trip can be equally exciting if you take the **Skyway,** a cable car that travels 300m (984 ft.) above the Jamison Valley.

In Katoomba, the gateway to the Blue Mountains, the **Blue Mountains Tourism office,** on Echo Point Road (✆ **1300/653-408** in Australia, or 61/2/4739-6266; www. visitbluemountains.com.au), is an attraction itself, with glass windows overlooking a gum forest, and cockatoos and lorikeets feeding on seed dispensers. **Echo Point** is an excellent spot to see the rock formations known as the **Three Sisters,** probably the Blue Mountains' best-known photo op. But now that you've gotten a taste of being up in the trees, persuade your kids to try a little hiking, Australian-style: bush walking. Head 7km (4½ miles) east from Katoomba to the town of **Wentworth Falls.** Sure, the kids will enjoy the postcard view of these spectacular 281m-high (922-ft.) waterfalls, but don't stop there: Take the **National Pass Walk** to the base of the falls, a superb hike cut into a cliff face with overhanging rock faces on one side and sheer drops on the other. (Walking back up, of course, takes a bit more work.) The mist from the falls makes that trademark Blue Mountain haze only more intense.

For a final thrill, head northwest another 14km (8⅔ miles) to Blackheath, the highest town in the mountains, where the 2-hour **Cliff Walk** from Evans Lookout to Govetts Leap offers great views of both the Three Sisters and their Blackheath siblings, the **Three Brothers.** You'll feel like you're on top of the world.

ⓘ **Blue Mountains Heritage Centre,** Govetts Leap Rd., Blackheath (✆ **61/2/ 4787-8877;** www.npws.nsw.gov.au).

✈ Sydney International, 114km (71 miles).

🛏 $$ **The Carrington Hotel,** 15–47 Katoomba St. (✆ **61/2/4782-1111;** www. thecarrington.com.au). $ **Katoomba Mountain Lodge,** 31 Lurline St. (✆ **61/2/4782-3933;** www.katoombabackpackers.com. au).

WHY THEY'LL THANK YOU: A wild blue yonder.

The Seattle-Victoria Ferry

Sailing the High-Speed Puget Cats

All ages • Seattle, Washington, USA, to Victoria, British Columbia, Canada

Crossing the U.S.-Canada border is generally a fairly routine experience—but not if you sail across it on a high-speed catamaran from Seattle, Washington, to Victoria, British Columbia. The trip takes only 3 hours, just enough time for the kids to roam around the boat, get a bite to eat, and stare out the windows at the gorgeous northwest coast. Exciting as open water is, it soon gets monotonous for children; one of the glories of this trip for kids is that most of the ride is on glacier-carved **Puget Sound,** where land can be viewed on either side, the rugged conifer-mantled highlands of the Olympic Peninsula on one side and the rural Skagit Valley on the other.

You leave from Seattle's busy ferry port, Pier 69, with the futuristic Space Needle lifting its curious head over the downtown Seattle skyline and majestic Mount Rainier

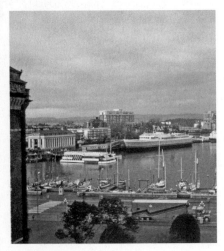

The Seattle-Victoria ferries.

visible to the south, snowcapped even in summer. Working your way past Seattle harbor's sailboat and kayak traffic, you'll enter convoluted Puget Sound, with the mountains of the Olympic Peninsula gradually rearing their peaks on your left. Coming out of Puget Sound near Port Townsend, you'll see the lovely **San Juan Islands** on the right (the same company runs ferries to the San Juans, including some whale-watching excursions). Then it's across the **Strait of Juan de Fuca,** the first stretch of open water on your voyage so far.

On the far side of that strait lies Vancouver—**Vancouver Island,** that is, which is not the same thing as the mainland city of Vancouver. What is on Vancouver Island is British Columbia's capital, **Victoria,** which is like a little slice of Victorian England served up on the northwest coast of North America. Ferry schedules are organized to make a day trip perfectly doable, with plenty of time to explore Victoria before heading back to Seattle. The mild Pacific climate is beautifully suited to horticulture, and Victoria's pride and joy is its rose gardens, particularly the spectacular **Butchart Gardens,** 800 Benvenuto Ave., Brentwood Bay (℗ **250/652-4422;** www. butchartgardens.com). If you can't sell your kids on visiting a garden, there's plenty to see around the charmingly restored Inner Harbour: **Miniature World** in the Fairmont Empress Hotel, 649 Humboldt St. (℗ **250/385-9731;** www. miniatureworld.com), with loads of small-scale dioramas from history and literature, the glass-enclosed views of harbor creatures in the **Pacific Undersea Gardens,** 490 Belleville St. (℗ **250/382-5717;** www. pacificunderseagardens.com), and the **Victoria Butterfly Gardens,** 1461 Benvenuto

Ave., Brentwood Bay (© **250/652-3822;** www.butterflygardens.com), which are exactly what the name says.

(i) **Victoria Clipper Ferries** (© **800/888-2535,** 206/448-5000, or 250/382-8100; www.clippervacations.com).

✈ Seattle-Tacoma International/Victoria International.

🛏 $$ **Admiral Inn,** 257 Belleville St., Victoria (© **888/823-6472;** www.admiral. bc.ca). $$$ **The Edgewater,** Pier 67, 2411 Alaskan Way, Seattle (© **800/624-0670;** www.edgewaterhotel.com).

WHY THEY'LL THANK YOU: Gliding up the fjord in time for tea and scones.

---

47 **Boat Rides**

Cruising the Mighty Mississippi
A River Ride through the Heart of America
All ages • Various locations along the Mississippi River, USA

The Native Americans living on its shores called it the Messipi, or "big river," but in American lore the Mississippi River is so much more. Yes, it is long—at 2,350 miles, it's the third-longest river in the world—but as it surges north to south down the middle of America, it gives this continent a heartbeat that is essentially, uniquely ours. I vividly remember the thrill of crossing it for the first time, at age 13, on a nighttime train, with a momentous feeling of Heading West. To ride its majestic brown waters, for whatever stretch of the river, is to feel connected to West and East and North and South all at once.

Thanks to Mark Twain's depiction of the river in such books as *The Adventures of Tom Sawyer, The Adventures of Huckleberry Finn,* and *Life on the Mississippi,* most Americans envision the Mississippi as a huge, muddy brown river, rolling powerfully between its banks. That's what the river looks like south of St. Louis, in the Missouri area where Twain grew up. But the Mississippi is born much farther north, in Lake Itasca, Minnesota, where it's a much meeker and milder river indeed. After it merges with the Minnesota River at St. Anthony Falls, the Upper Mississippi becomes a more dramatic waterway, cutting its majestic course between steep

river bluffs. That's the section of the river you explore on overnight cruises between the Iowa cities of LeClaire and Dubuque on the **Riverboat** *Twilight* (© **800/331-1467;** www.riverboattwilight.com), or from La Crosse, Wisconsin, either upstream to Winona, Minnesota, or downstream to Dubuque, on the *Julia Belle Swain* **riverboat** (© **800/815-1005;** www.juliabelle. com). Though you'll stay overnight in accommodations on shore, you'll spend your days on the decks of these ornate replica sternwheelers, with lacy white fretwork and fluted smokestacks and the whole banjo-strumming shebang.

In Dubuque, don't miss visiting the **National Mississippi River Museum & Aquarium** (350 E. 3rd St.; © **800/226-3369** or 563/557-9545; www.rivermuseum. com)—it has lots of interactive exhibits to help kids understand the river's flood patterns, geography, and history. If their attention flags, switch over to the connected aquarium to see giant catfish and bayou alligators and other river denizens.

Of course, you can also drive the **Great River Road Scenic Byway,** a national historic highway that follows the river's course for some 3,000 miles through its ten states. Along the way, several river towns offer 1- or 2-hour paddle-wheel cruises to give you a taste of what it feels like to be out on that great river—St. Paul, Minnesota; La Crosse, Wisconsin; St. Louis, Missouri; Memphis, Tennessee; Vicksburg, Mississippi; and New Orleans, Louisiana, all have sightseeing paddle-wheelers. Memphis even has a scale model of the river, constructed in **Mud Island River Park** (125 N. Front St.; © **901/576-7241;**

www.mudisland.com). That'll bring "Ol' Man River" home to the kids for sure.

ⓘ www.experiencemississippiriver.com.

✈ Depends on port of embarkation.

⛴ Included in cruise packages.

WHY THEY'LL THANK YOU: Rolling down the river.

Boat Rides **48**

Scouting Alaska's Inside Passage

Ferries to the Glacier

All ages • Juneau, Alaska, USA

Every summer, boatloads of tourists crowd onto luxury cruise ships to be pampered on their way through Alaska. But that's not my idea of a rugged wilderness experience—not when you can still travel in comfort on the swift, well-outfitted ferries of the Alaska Marine Highway System, with the option of planning your own itinerary to suit your family's interests.

Officially designated an **All-American Road,** the Alaska Marine Highway covers 3,500 nautical miles from Bellingham, Washington, out to the Aleutian Islands. A fleet of sleek blue-hulled ferries steams its entire length, but I think the most interesting segments are those of the **Inside Passage,** that crazy network of inlets and channels around the countless islands of the Alaskan Panhandle. Squeezed between the Canadian Yukon and the Gulf of Alaska, this strip of southeast Alaska—a breathtaking mix of dense green northwest rainforest and pristine white glaciers—stretches 500 miles from Ketchikan to Yakutat.

In the middle is Juneau, Alaska's capital city and where you'll probably arrive by plane. Before leaving Juneau, trundle the kids off to see the **Mendenhall Glacier,** Glacier Spur Road (© **907/789-0097**), where you can stand in front of a wall of blue ice and feel its chilly breath. The two destinations that most interest my kids are in opposite directions from Juneau: **Ketchikan,** a spruced-up logging town, with the world's largest collection of totem poles, that's 17 hours south by ferry; and **Sitka,** an exotic mix of Russian and Tlingit cultures, that's 8³/₄ hours north of Juneau by ferry. The beauty of taking the ferries? Using Juneau as a base and making separate excursions to Ketchikan and Sitka just takes planning. If you schedule it right, you may even be able to hit every town at an hour when the cruise mobs are gone and the locals relaxed.

Spending several hours on these ferries is no problem. These are handsome modern craft, with restaurants, gift shops, and in some cases even movie theaters, not to mention solariums and observation lounges where you can park yourselves to watch the scenic coast roll past. Naturalists often come along for the ride to talk about Alaska's wildlife and geology with passengers; some ships have small video arcades or play areas for toddlers. For overnight journeys, you can reserve two- to four-berth cabins (book several months in advance for summer voyages), although you are also free to roll out your sleeping bags on the comfy reclining seats in the lounges. Hey, that counts as roughing it in my book.

ⓘ **Alaska State Ferry,** 6858 Glacier Hwy. (ⓒ **800/642-0066** or 907/465-3941; www.ferryalaska.com).

✈ Juneau International.

🛏 $$ **The Driftwood Lodge,** 435 Willoughby Ave., Juneau (ⓒ **800/544-2239** or 907/586-2280; www.driftwoodalaska. com). $$$ **Goldbelt Hotel Juneau,** 51 E. Egan Dr., Juneau (ⓒ **888/478-6909** or 907/586-6900; www.goldbelttours.com).

WHY THEY'LL THANK YOU: Waking up to see a glacier slide past your window.

49 Boat Rides

Pirate Cruising in the Caribbean

Ages 6 & up • The Cayman Islands

Ever since Disney's *Pirates of the Caribbean* movies came out, the pirate image has gotten a new lease on life. The fact that no buccaneer ever looked like Johnny Depp's Captain Jack Sparrow is entirely beside the point; I know several 6-year-olds who won't leave the house without their eye patches and cutlasses. Entrepreneurs from Clearwater, Florida, to Bath, Maine, have launched pirate-themed harbor tours, but if you're going to do it, do it the right way: in the warm blue waters of the Caribbean.

The prime site has to be the **Cayman Islands,** which, back in the 17th century, were notorious pirate hangouts (many present-day Caymanites claim to be descendants of the original pirates). Though most visitors come to the Caymans for diving and snorkeling, if you're here with kids, you shouldn't miss the opportunity to take a 2-hour afternoon coastal cruise out of Grand Cayman on the *Jolly Roger,* a rakishly decorated, blue three-masted galleon that is a two-thirds replica of Christopher Columbus's flagship, the *Nina*. (Unlike the original *Nina,* however, this wooden replica has an engine to propel it when there's no wind.) While parents may be happy to lounge back and just enjoy the views of Grand Cayman's palm-fringed white-sand beaches, the kids will be entertained by the troupe of buccaneer actors on board. They perform all the standard pirate shtick, conscripting kids to scamper up the rigging, haul the mainsail, and swab the deck; there's also a swim stop for some snorkeling and splashing about in the Cayman's crystal-clear waters (this may include walking the plank—which looks suspiciously like a diving board off the side of the boat). Tankards of "grog" (fruit juice for the youngsters) are served, naturally. The *Jolly Roger* (which also offers sunset and dinner cruises) departs from the South Terminal in the harbor of George Town, the largest town on this most developed island of the Cayman chain. Next door you'll also find the dock for **Atlantic Submarines** (ⓒ **800/887-8571** in the U.S., or 345/949-7700; www.atlantisadventures.net), which is a great way to explore Grand Cayman's spectacular coral reefs and off-shore shipwrecks, ideal for families with kids too young to go scuba diving.

Every October, Grand Cayman holds a weeklong **Pirate Heritage Festival** (www. piratesweekfestival.com) that's tons of swashbuckling fun—though, with most kids in school that time of year, it degenerates into a rum-soaked adult party. What else would you expect from a pirate convention?

ⓘ **The Jolly Roger** (ⓒ **345/945-SAIL;** www.jollyrogercayman.com).

✈ Grand Cayman.

🛏 $$$ **The Anchorage,** Seven Mile Beach, Grand Cayman (🕿 **800/433-3483** or 345/945-4088; www.theanchorage cayman.com). $$ **The Grand Caymanian,** 278 Crighton Rd., Crystal Harbour, Grand Cayman (🕿 **345/949-3100;** www.grand caymanian.ky).

WHY THEY'LL THANK YOU: Scrambling like monkeys up the rigging.

Boat Rides **50**

Punting on the Cam

Ages 6 & up • Cambridge, East Anglia, England

Punting on the **River Cam** in a wood-built, flat-bottomed boat (which looks somewhat like a Venetian gondola) is a traditional pursuit of students and visitors to Cambridge University, one of England's two venerable universities (see also Oxford). Wafting your way downstream, you pass along the ivy-covered "Backs" of the colleges, their lush gardens sweeping down to the Cam. It's one of the best ways an outsider can glimpse student life at this university, where the illustrious graduates include those such as Isaac Newton, Charles Darwin, and Stephen Hawking.

Cambridge, founded in the early 13th century, is a conglomeration of some 31 colleges. You'll pass the most famous of them as you head downstream: **St. John's,** founded 1511, with its Bridge of Sighs arching over the river; **Trinity College,** founded by King Henry VIII in 1546 and the alma mater of Sir Isaac Newton and Lord Byron; **King's College,** founded 1441, with its exquisite medieval Chapel (be sure to go visit it on foot after punting); and the lovely **Queen's College,** dating from 1448, just before the river splits at Sheep's Green.

Punting on the River Cam.

People sprawl along the banks of the Cam on a summer day to judge and tease you as you maneuver your punt with a pole about 4.5m (15 ft.) long. The river's floor is muddy, and many a student has lost his pole in the riverbed shaded by the willows. If your pole gets stuck, it's better to leave it sticking in the mud instead of risking a plunge into the river.

About 3km (1³/₄ miles) upriver lie the meadows of Grantchester, immortalized by poet Rupert Brooke (the town lies about a mile from the meadows). When the town clock stopped for repairs in 1985, its hands were left frozen "for all time" at 10 minutes to 3, in honor of Brooke's famed sonnet "The Soldier."

Scudamore's Boatyards, Granta Place (✆ **44/1223/359750**), by the Anchor Pub, has been in business since 1910. You rent boats by the hour, and there's a maximum of six persons per punt; the place is open year-round, although March through October is the high season. If you'd rather not attempt punting yourself, you can hire a "chauffeur" for a (hefty) additional fee.

ⓘ **Cambridge Tourist Information Centre,** Wheeler St. (✆ **0871/226-8006** in the U.K., or 44/1223/464732; www.visit cambridge.org).

🚍 Cambridge, 1 hr. from London.

🛏 $$$ **Doubletree by Hilton Cambridge,** Granta Place, Mill Lane (✆ **44/1223/ 259988;** www.doubletreebyhilton.co.uk/ cambridge).

WHY THEY'LL THANK YOU: Rolling, rolling, rolling on the river.

---

51 Boat Rides

Cruising the Fjords
Ages 6 & up • Norway

Say "Norwegian" and what word naturally follows? Most likely it would be "fjord." When most of us picture Scandinavia, our mind's eye is really showing us the distinctively jagged coast of Norway, carved by icebergs into a spectacular series of dramatic furrows and fissures. At some points, in fact, these deep fjords become so narrow that a boat can hardly wedge between the steep mountainsides. Waterfalls spill down their cliffs, brightly painted storybook villages nestle in their creases, rags of mist trail around rocky coves. Gliding up these crystal-clear waters by ship, you'll feel like modern-day Vikings. The scenic city of **Bergen,** a quarter of the way up Norway's coast, is often called the gateway to the fjords; north of here, the coast suddenly fragments and crumbles dramatically into scattered archipelagoes and inlets. Elegantly appointed steamers travel north from Bergen along this breathtaking coast, taking 6 or 7 days to round Scandinavia's northern tip and reach Kirkenes; you can also opt to take a southbound cruise from Kirkenes back down to Bergen—or even better, do the full 12-day round-trip, which times things so that you'll see in the daytime anything you missed while sleeping in your berth on the way up. Though this cruise route is often called "the postal boat" because it's a main source of transport for locals, the ships are definitely luxury cruise vessels, with all the on-board amenities—and you'll pay cruise prices to travel on them. They stop at 34 ports en route, with plenty of time for passengers to hop off for shopping and shore excursions. Among the major stops are **Trondheim,** a city with a remarkably well-preserved timbered medieval district; **Bødo,** the first port north of the Arctic Circle; **Tromsø,** site of the world's northernmost planetarium (see Tromsø ③⓪②); the fishing port of **Hammerfest,** where you may see local Lapps with

Cruising the Norwegian fjords.

their reindeer; and **Honningsvåg,** the world's northernmost village and terminus of the **Midnight Sun Road.** From here you can take an excursion to the stark **Nordskapp plateau,** the "top of Europe," with its dark cliffs dropping precipitously into the Arctic Ocean. Even though you've been traveling in comfort, you'll still feel like ends-of-the-earth explorers, surrounded by the kind of natural beauty they'll remember forever.

ⓘ **Hurtigruten** (boat service) (✆ **866/552-0371** or 212/319-1390, www.hurtigruten.com).

✈ Bergen.

🛏 Sleeping quarters provided on board. $ **Augustin Hotel,** Carl Sundts, Gate 22, Bergen (✆ **47/55/30-40-00;** www.augustin.no). $$ **Quality Hotel Edvard Grieg,** Sandsliåsen 50, Bergen (✆ **47/55/98-00-00;** www.choicehotels.com).

BEST TIME: Summer June to July, when the sun barely sets.

WHY THEY'LL THANK YOU: When you cross the Arctic Circle—and keep on going.

Boat Rides 52

Fiordlands National Park
A Cruise Through Middle-earth
Ages 8 & up • South Island, New Zealand

When it came to those intensely green, mist-shrouded Middle-earth landscapes, the *Lord of the Rings* movies didn't need stage sets or computer animation: Director Peter Jackson simply shot the films in his native New Zealand. The South Island's

Fiordland epitomizes that primeval *Lord of the Rings* look, with plunging waterfalls, pristine lakes, virgin forest, and steep peaks surrounding deep-gouged fjords. It's spectacularly different from such geothermal spots as Rotorua that travelers used to associate with New Zealand.

The entrance off the Tasman Sea to 23km-long (14-mile) Milford Sound is so narrow, Captain Cook missed it completely when he first sailed around New Zealand some 200 years ago. The ancient Maoris knew about it, though; they called it Piopiotahi, and believed it was carved out of the earth by the god Tu Te Raki Whanoa. Base yourself in the lakeside resort town of **Te Anau;** Milford Sound excursions from Te Anau begin with a dramatic 2-hour drive through the Fiordland landscape. While there are many sightseeing cruises available, nature cruises are worth the extra money; they have naturalists on board to point out the most intriguing features of this unique landscape, from the frisky fur seals and rare crested penguins on the rocky shore to the bottlenose dolphins swimming in your wake. Meanwhile, you'll enjoy stunning panoramas of mossy green mountains and mysterious dark waters; the fact that it's usually shrouded in rain and mist just makes it more evocative. **Real Journey's Milford Sound cruises** also include a stop at the **Milford Deep Underwater Observatory** (© **64/3/441-1137;** www.milforddeep.co.nz), where you'll descend over 10m (33 ft.) below the surface to look at a rare black coral reef, swarming with exotic fish, anemones, and sea stars. (Real Journeys also does excursions to the more remote **Doubtful Sound,** a peaceful, rugged spot where you may have the wildlife to yourself.) Another reason for basing yourself in

Te Anau is to follow up your fjord cruise with adventures around the lake country. One of New Zealand's most famous walking trails, the **Milford Track,** heads through the mountains from the lake to the sound (late Oct to mid-Apr only); the full walk takes 4 days, but **Trips & Tramps** offers a couple of guided 1-day samples that are much more doable for kids. Walking along the trail, you can study the striations of its glacially carved rocks, discover delicate alpine wildflowers and mossy hollows, and feel the waterfalls' spray on your skin. Real Journeys can also whip you across the lake on a catamaran to see the **Te Anau Glowworm Caves,** mysterious underground caverns full of fossils, stalactites, and whirlpools—not to mention a grotto where thousands of delicate little glowworms live underground, casting their eerie blue incandescence on the rock walls. The nighttime trip can overwhelm the very young (there are daytime options), but for Middle-earth fans, its ghostly weirdness is perfect.

ⓘ **Fiordlands National Park Visitor Centre** (© **64/3/249-7924**).

✈ Te Anau.

🛏 $ **Amber Court Motel,** 68 Quintin Dr., Te Anau (© **64/3/249-7230;** www.ambercourtteanau.co.nz). $$ **Milford Sound Lodge,** Hwy. 94, Te Anau (© **64/3/249-8071;** www.milfordlodge.com).

TOURS: Real Journeys (© **64/3/249-7416;** www.realjourneys.co.nz). **Trips & Tramps** (© **64/3/249-7081;** www.milfordtourswalks.co.nz).

WHY THEY'LL THANK YOU: On the lookout for Legolas and Frodo.

Crisscrossing Lake Como

All ages • Como, Italy

Back and forth we went, trying to decide which of northern Italy's romantic lakes to visit: Garda? Maggiore? Como? We finally chose **Lake Como** because it's the smallest, only 4km (2½ miles) across at its widest point, with the far shore always visible, and therefore easier for our toddler son to scope out. (It's also closest to Milan, about 48km/30 miles away). I've heard the other two are spectacular, but I don't see how they could out-enchant Lake Como, its shimmering deep-blue waters bordered with flowery gardens and aristocratic villas of soft golden stone. And even though we had a rental car, we soon realized the best way to enjoy Lake Como is to crisscross it on ferries, sitting in the balmy open air with other travelers instead of enclosed in a steel cocoon.

Lake Como is incredibly long and skinny, with its most charming towns clustered midlake. Starting from the town of **Como**

at the southwest tip, we headed north along the western shore 5km (3 miles) to **Cernobbio,** a chic haven dominated by the celebrated **Villa d'Este** (see the hotel recommendation below), originally built in the 16th century. After a stroll in its lush gardens, it was north another half-hour to **Tremezzo,** where the landscaping is surprisingly tropical—citrus trees, palms, cypresses, and magnolias—and as we stood on its panoramic lakeshore, we felt our urban anxieties begin to dissolve. Leaving the car behind, we hopped a ferry to **Bellagio,** a tony resort town as gracious as its Vegas namesake is garish. Clinging to a promontory at the lake's fork, Bellagio has steep cobblestone streets to climb, as well as arcaded shops, smart cafes, and a blossoming lakeside promenade.

Our next ferry took us to picturesque **Varenna,** which still has a certain fishing-village quaintness despite a stock of resort

Lake Como.

hotels. Here we investigated Italy's shortest river, the **Fiumelatte,** a mere 250m (820 ft.) long. It only appears in summer, rushing frothy and milk-white down a rock face to crash into the lake. Leonardo da Vinci once tried to determine the water's source, but neither he—nor anyone else—has ever found it. We boarded another ferry (by this time it was like a game to our son) and crossed back west to **Cadenabbia** to see 19th-century **Villa Carlotta** (✆ **39/344/40405;** www.villacarlotta.it), or at least its gardens, with exotic flowers and banks of rhododendrons and azaleas. (There's a fine art museum, too, but we had a toddler to amuse.) A mile south and we were back at Tremezzo to reclaim our car.

Lake Como is definitely a summertime destination—the boat service operates only Easter to September, and many hotels close November to March. But under a blue sky, when the sun shines and the flowers bloom, it's like heaven on earth.

ⓘ **Gestione Navigazione Laghi** (✆ **39/31/579211;** www.navlaghi.it). **Como tourist office,** Piazza Cavour 17 (✆ **39/31/269712;** www.lakecomo.org).

🚈 Como, 40 min. from Milan.

🛏 $$$ **Grand Hotel Villa d'Este,** Via Regina 40, Cernobbio (**39/31/3481;** www.villadeste.it). $$ **Hotel Du Lac,** Piazza Mazzini 32, Bellagio (✆ **39/31/950320;** www.bellagiohoteldulac.com).

WHY THEY'LL THANK YOU: Hopping a ferry like it was the local bus.

---

54 Boat Rides

Gliding down the Danube
From Vienna to Budapest in Style
All ages • Vienna, Austria, to Budapest, Hungary

Vienna and Budapest are two of Europe's most romantic cities, and two of my personal favorites, so the idea of linking them with a boat trip up the beautiful blue Danube was impossible to resist. Though the Danube doesn't have the majestic Wagnerian chasms and castles of the Rhine, I love the way it waltzes sweetly through green forests and farmlands, through eastern Austria, past Bratislava and along the Slovakia/Hungary border, and then down through the lush Hungarian lowlands. The water may be more brown than blue these days, but the Danube is still beautiful.

Vienna and Budapest make a natural pairing: Both have a 19th-century look and pace, great for strolling aimlessly, lingering in coffeehouses (where the pastries are fabulous!), and listening to schmaltzy music. Their grandest churches are both dedicated to St. Stephen—Vienna's Gothic **Domkirche St. Stephan** and Budapest's domed **St. Stephen's Basilica.** Vienna has the **Prater** (home of the Ferris Wheel); Budapest, the zoo and amusement rides in **City Park.** Budapest has medieval **Buda Palace,** Vienna the baroque **Habsburg palace of Schönbrunn.** Budapest still bears traces of its years under Communist rule, but less so than other former Iron Curtain capitals.

River steamers make a day of this journey, leaving Vienna at 7:45am and making stops in **Komaron,** site of a famous Austro-Hungarian fortress, and **Esztergom,** with its massive neoclassical cathedral. You'll arrive in Budapest late that night, ready to find your hotel and set off sightseeing the next morning; you'll board a luxury motorcoach in the late afternoon and return to Vienna before midnight. To give yourselves more time in Budapest, you can also travel via **hydrofoil,** which takes only 5½ hours to get from Vienna to

7 Super City Parks

When they just can't take one more museum, get your kids out into the big city parks, those "green lungs" that help keep city-dwellers sane. While they get all the fidgets out of their system, they may also have a chance to go skating, row a boat, ride a roller coaster, or visit a zoo.

⑤⑤ Hyde Park, London, England   Originally Henry VIII's deer-hunting ground, Hyde Park still looks like a rolling patch of English countryside smack dab in the middle of the city; it's even got boats and a swimming beach along the Serpentine. Kids fly kites or kick around footballs (the round kind, of course), eccentrics rant from soapboxes up at Speakers Corner in the northeastern tip, and you may even see the Queen's cavalry gallop through on their way home from nearby Buckingham palace. In adjoining Kensington Gardens, track down the spritely statue of Peter Pan alongside the Long Water. See Tower Bridge �94, British Museum ⑰⑥, Tower of London ⑲⓪, Imperial War Museum ㉒⑦, Golden Hinde ㉓⑥, Greenwich ㉙⑦, Science & Natural History Museums ㉘①, Hampton Court Palace ㊱⓪, Shakespeare's Globe Theatre ㉟②, Wimbledon ㊽⑧, and the London Eye ㊽⑤. ✆ **44/20/7298-2100;** *www.royalparks.org.uk/parks/hyde_park.*

⑤⑥ Djurgården, Stockholm, Sweden   Just a ferry ride away from Stockholm's medieval quarter, Gamla Stan, this hilly, wooded former deer park (check out the antlers on the gilded deer on the park gates) is now packed with visitor attractions: the magnificent 17th-century warship at Vasamuseet, the 75-acre open-air history park of Skansen, a zoo, and Gröna Lunds Tivoli amusement park, the Swedish version of Denmark's Tivoli Gardens. Cap it off with a leisurely Stockholm Sightseeing cruise around Djurgården's labyrinthine canals. *www.djurgarden.net.*

⑤⑦ Parc Guell, Barcelona, Spain   Perhaps my kids' favorite Barcelona memory is the afternoon we spent wandering the woodland paths of hilltop Parc Guell, stopping to admire the whimsical architectural fantasies of Antoni Gaudí that spring up everywhere. From the toadstool-like gatehouses on, every sinuous staircase, fantastic fountain, and rustic pavilion expresses the childlike fertility of Gaudí's whacked-out imagination. See Sagrada Familia ㉜④. *www.barcelona-tourist-guide.com/en/gaudi/park-guell.html.*

The whimsical Gaudí benches in the Parc Guell.

⑤⑧ Central Park, New York City   The heart of New York for kids is Central Park, an 840-acre island of green between the apartment buildings of the Upper West Side and the Upper East Side, full of playgrounds, ball fields, lakes and ponds, and some of the best skyline views of skyscrapered Midtown. South of 65th Street, you can ride a vintage carousel, visit the Central Park Zoo, and ice-skate in winter at Wollman Rink. Midpark, at 72nd Street, you can go boating on the Lake, rowing past movie-set-perfect Bethesda Terrace and Bow Bridge. Bring a rose to lay on the Imagine mosaic at Strawberry Fields, that ever-popular landscaped tribute to Beatle John Lennon. See Empire State Building **27**, Brooklyn Bridge **95**, American Museum of Natural History **273**, Bronx Zoo **127**, Statue of Liberty **252**, *Intrepid* **241**, Metropolitan Museum of Art **340**, American Museum of the Moving Image **354**, and the Cyclone **487**. *℘ 212/310-6600; www.centralparknyc.org.*

59 Boston Common, Boston, Massachusetts   The oldest public park in the United States, tree-strewn Boston Common slopes confidently down from the prim mansions of Beacon Hill to the skyscrapers of downtown, overlooked by the gold dome of the Statehouse. In colonial days, it was at various times a public cow pasture, gallows site, and British army encampment; today it bustles with picnickers, Frisbee and softball games, kite flyers, and busking musicians. The Frog Pond, where there really were frogs at one time, makes a pleasant spot to splash around in the summer and skate in the winter. Adjacent to it, the more formal Public Garden features swan boat rides on a picturesque pond; youngsters will beg to climb on the bronze *Make Way for Ducklings* statues. See Black Heritage Trail **266**, New England Aquarium **116**, Lexington **219**, Orchard House **380**, Old Ironsides **239**, and Fenway Park **453**. *Bounded by Tremont, Beacon, Charles, Park and Boylston Streets. ℘ 617/357-8300; www.city ofboston.gov/FreedomTrail/bostoncommon.asp.*

60 Stanley Park, Vancouver, British Columbia   Despite major damage from a 2006 windstorm, this amazing 405-hectare (1,000-acre) rainforest on a peninsula near downtown is still one of Vancouver's must-see attractions. Kids love to gape at the immense totem poles at Brockton Point, to get wet at the Spray Park near Lumberman's Arch, to bike or skate along the magnificent long seawall, or ride on the miniature railway next to the Stanley Park Children's Farm petting zoo—and of course visit the great Vancouver Aquarium **120**. See the First Nations museums **265**. *North foot of Georgia St. ℘ 604/257-8400; http://vancouver.ca/parks/parks/stanley/.*

61 Ueno Park, Tokyo, Japan   Best known for its blizzard of cherry blossoms in spring, this sprawling park in northeast Tokyo occupies the grounds of a famous old temple complex. Devote an entire day to this park, which is now quite a museum mecca. Check out old kimonos and samurai armor at the Tokyo National Museum; dig the dinosaurs and dioramas at Ueno's National Science Museum; commune with the animals at the small Ueno Park Zoo; birdwatch around the huge Shinobazu lotus pond; and for a dose of history, stop by the 17th-century Toshugu Shrine and Kiyomizu Kannon-do Temple, its steps covered with dolls offered to the goddess of child-raising. See Edo-Tokyo **70**, National Museum of Emerging Science **293**, and the Ghibli Museum **356**. *Next to Ueno Station.*

The cherry blossoms of Ueno Park.

Budapest or vice versa; you can opt to take the train back that night, which gives you an extra 3 hours for sightseeing in Budapest. There are three downsides to the hydrofoil option: The spray raised by the boat's jets obscures some details of the scenery, there are no sightseeing stops along the way, and it runs only April through October. But still.

Another (considerably cheaper) option is just to do the Hungarian section of the river, departing from and returning to Budapest. This particularly scenic stretch of the river, called the **Danube Bend,** is overlooked by tall forested hills; there's a dramatic horseshoe bend at Visegrád, known as the Elbow of the Danube, and stops can be made at several charming riverside towns. Leisurely boat rides up the Danube bend are run April through September by **MAHART,** the state shipping company (✆ **36/1/484-4000;** www.mahartpassnave.hu). From Budapest to Esztergom takes 5 hours.

ⓘ **DDSG Blue Danube Shipping Co.,** Handelskai 265, Vienna (✆ **43/1/58880;** www.ddsg-blue-danube.at).

✈ Vienna International/Ferihegy Budapest.

🛏 $$ **Hotel Erzsébet,** V. Károlyi Mihály u. 11–15, Budapest (✆ **36/1/889-3700;** www.danubiushotels.com/en/hotels/erzsebet). $$ **Hotel-Pension Suzanne,** Walfischgasse 4, Vienna (✆ **43/1/513-2507;** www.pension-suzanne.at).

WHY THEY'LL THANK YOU: A dreamy glide into Europe's old-fashioned heart.

Boat Rides **62**

Riverboating up the Amazon
Songs of the Rainforest
Ages 8 & up • from Manaus, Brazil

If your kids are like mine, they've raised money in school for saving the rainforest—but do they really know what it is that they're saving? Before they grow up, at least once they should encounter the world's biggest forest, this amazing tropical wilderness that accompanies the world's largest river on its mighty course through Brazil to the Atlantic Ocean. Indeed it is endangered, indeed we ought to save it—and, properly inspired, your children and mine can do it.

Thanks to the rise in ecotourism, rainforest outings are much more accessible than they used to be. The usual starting point for visiting the Amazon basin is **Manaus,** the largest city in the region, located on the shores of the Rio Negro. Numerous operators run boat trips out of Manaus, usually on a double-decked riverboat that serves as your home base. These package tours generally include certain common elements: nature-spotting excursions in canoes up the smaller channels, sunset and sunrise tours, wildlife-watching walks under the leafy canopy of the rainforest, caiman spotting, piranha fishing, and a visit to a caboclo (river peasant) settlement with houses built on stilts. But when you're not on an excursion, you're moving on the wide brown river, its green shores slipping away to either side. There is always something to see, even if it's just the vastness of the river itself. **Viverde** (✆ **55/92/3248-9988;** www.viverde.com.br), a local travel company, handles a range of tours; **Amazon Clipper Cruises** (✆ **55/92/3656-1246;** www.amazonclipper.com.br) has three old-style Amazon riverboats that make regular 3- and 4-day trips; **Swallows and Amazons** (✆ 55/92/3622-1246; www.swallowsandamazonstours.

com) runs a variety of adventure-tour itineraries on traditional wooden riverboats.

The most amazing thing to see around Manaus is the **Meeting of the Waters** (Encontra das Aguas), where the dark, slow waters of the Rio Negro meet the fast, muddy brown waters of the Rio Solimões. Because of differences in velocity, temperature, and salinity, the two rivers don't immediately blend but carry on side by side for miles. If the boat trip you're signed up for doesn't pass through this phenomenal juncture, try booking a flight-seeing tour over it—and actually, come to think of it, that's the best way to see how its contrasting colors gradually mix and mingle, from up on high.

ⓘ **Manaus Tourist Center Tourist Service Center,** Av. Sete de Setembro 384 (𝄞 **55/92/3622-4948;** www.manaus.am. gov.br).

✈ Eduardo Gomes (Manaus).

🛏 $$$ **Hotel Tropical de Manaus,** Av. Coronel Texeira 1320, Ponta Negra, Manaus, (𝄞 **55/92/2123-5000;** www. tropicalhotel.com.br). $$ **Novotel Manaus,** Av. Mandii 4, Manaus (𝄞 **55/92/2123-1211;** www.novotel.com).

WHY THEY'LL THANK YOU: Either the piranhas or the parrots—depends on the kid.

3 Weird & Wonderful

The Corn Palace in Mitchell, South Dakota.

The Catacombs of Rome

Ages 10 & up • Rome, Italy

Of all the roads that led to Rome, Via Appia Antica (built in 312 B.C.) was the most famous, stretching from Rome to the seaport of Brindisi, where rich cargoes from Greece and the East flowed into the Empire. Along the road's initial section in Rome, patrician Romans erected great monuments and family tombs. Beneath the surface, however, was another story. Beginning in the 2nd century A.D., early Christians carved miles of narrow tunnels out of the soft tufa stone, using them both as burial places and as refuges for celebrating rites during spates of persecution. Today visitors can wander, guided by a priest or monk, through mile upon mile of musty tunnel, past burial niches gouged into walls—long shelves that held two to three bodies each. The dank, dark grottoes are creepily fascinating, but more than that, they are a powerful reminder that even Christianity was once an outlaw sect.

Just outside the city walls, as many as 50 catacombs were dug out over 300 years; together they contain some 20 million graves. If these tunnels were straightened and laid end to end, they'd be as long as Italy itself. Perhaps the most popular are the extensive **Catacombs of St. Callixtus,** the first cemetery of the Christian community of Rome, stretching for nearly 19km (12 miles) on five levels, about 20m (65 ft.) underground. Sepulchral chambers and almost half a million tombs of early Christians are decorated with paintings, sculptures, and epigraphs (look

for such repeated symbols as the fish, anchor, and dove). Sixteen popes from the 3rd century are buried here, along with St. Cecilia, early Christian martyr and patron of sacred music. The bodies of Sts. Peter and Paul, not to mention that of St. Sebastian, were at one time buried in the **Catacombs of St. Sebastian,** where the tunnels and mausoleums are full of mosaics and graffiti from centuries even before the time of Constantine. But kids may prefer the shorter and more dramatic tours of the **Catacombs of St. Domitilla,** the only catacombs where you'll still see bones in the tomb niches. Entering through a sunken 4th-century church adds a touch of mystery, too.

ⓘ **Catacombs of St. Callixtus,** Via Appia Antica 170 ([tel **39/6/51301580;** closed Feb). **Catacombs of St. Sebastian,** Via Appia Antica 136 (*©* **39/6/7850350;** closed mid-Nov to mid-Dec). **Catacombs of St. Domitilla,** Via d. Sette Chiese 280 (*©* **39/6/5110342;** closed Jan).

✈ Leonardo da Vinci International Airport.

🛏 $$$ **Hotel de Russie,** Via del Babuino 9 (*©* **800/323-7500** in North America, or 39/6-328881; www.roccofortehotels.com). $ **Hotel Grifo,** Via del Boschetto 144 (*©* **39/ 6-4871395**).

WHY THEY'LL THANK YOU: Hide-and-seek.

The Beehive Houses of Apulia, Italy

All ages • Alberobello, Italy

Nobody else ever built homes quite like these—beehive-shaped cottages with whitewashed limestone walls and conical fieldstone roofs. If you saw just one you might think it was some modern architect's fantasy, but when you see several dotting the rugged Apulian landscape, or entire neighborhoods—as in the town of **Alberobello,** which has some 1,000 of these houses—you really sit up and take notice. Known as *trulli,* they're like something out of a storybook, and children are instinctively attracted to such curvy, cozy dwellings.

Apulia, the high heel of Italy's boot, is a land of gritty survivors, invaded over the years by everyone from ancient Greeks to Goths, Byzantines, Saracen pirates, and Turks. *Trulli* were built as early as the 13th century, by peasants scavenging whatever materials came easily to hand. What's amazing, when you take a close look, is the craftsmanship involved: The stones fit together in such a way that not a speck of mortar was needed. This allowed medieval peasants to dismantle the structures quickly if a king came to inspect the district. For such provisional dwellings, they sure have lasted a long time.

Trulli-packed **Alberobello** is Italy's most fantastical village, but it can be a tourist trap, with tacky souvenirs on sale everywhere, even in converted *trulli* (the kids may pester you to buy a cunning miniature model, crafted in the same type of stone). From Alberobello's main square, Piazza del Popolo, turn left on Largo Martellotta, which will take you to the edge of the *trulli* neighborhood, a maze of curving cobbled lanes with the round houses on every side. There's no danger of missing it, as hordes of day-trippers descend on Alberobello every day to gawk at the structures. The best-known is the *trullo sovrano* (sovereign *trullo*) at Piazza Sacramento, 15m (49 ft.) tall, the only true two-story *trulli.* It is, however, a 19th-century creation, built as headquarters for a religious confraternity and Carbonari sect. To experience *trulli* living, you might want to book a night at the **Hotel Dei Trulli** (see the hotel recommended below), a cluster of 19 *trulli,* each its own mini-apartment of one, two, or three cones wedged together.

(i) **Tourist office,** Piazza Ferdinando IV (② **39/80/4325171**).

Alberobello, 1¾ hr. from Bari.

$$ Hotel Dei Trulli, Via Cadore 32 (② **39/80/4323555;** www.hoteldeitrulli.it).

WHY THEY'LL THANK YOU: Snug homes to curl up in.

Coober Pedy
Going Underground
All ages • Australia

The Wild West spirit of Australia's interior is something kids naturally respond to—but Coober Pedy has something the Wild West never had: hotels and houses where you can sleep underground. Early 20th-century settlers in this colorful opal-mining town found a unique solution to the harsh heat and dust of Outback existence: Live underground, in the holes left by earlier miners of the sun-bleached mullock heaps of mining waste. Even the hotels and restaurants here are mostly underground. Coober Pedy is home to more than 3,500 people from 44 nations, the majority working and living underground. Many succumb to "opal fever," the compulsion to keep digging for the valuable stone, the first of which was found in 1915. Digging began in earnest 2 years later, when the Trans Continental Railway was completed.

The town got its name from the Aboriginal words *kupa pita,* which translates to "white man's burrow," appropriate when you consider the abundance of holes left by early miners, many of them soldiers returning from World War I. Conditions were harsh, and the area went through a series of bust and boom times. Today, it is the largest supplier of opals in the world and has a thriving tourist industry.

A must-see attraction is the **Serbian Orthodox Church,** featuring wall carvings, a high "ballroom" ceiling and stained glass windows. You may also want to visit **Saint Peter and Paul's Catholic Church,** the first underground church in town, and possibly the world. Of course, no trip to the opal capital of the world would be complete without a visit to the **Umoona Opal Mine & Museum** where daily tours

Coober Pedy.

provide historical information as you explore an underground home, an on-site mine, an **Aboriginal Interpretive Centre** along with a dazzling array of gorgeous opals (www.umoonaopalmine.com.au).

Although the town is known for its underground structures, at its center there are lots of outdoor buildings, including restaurants, service businesses, and surprise of surprises—opal shops. It should be noted that while the hotels and hostels have above ground entrances, the rooms themselves are usually underground.

Just 20 miles away are **The Breakaways,** where you'll find stunning views of desert scenery from flat-topped mesas to the stony gibber deserts. Despite the harshness of the area, it is rich in flora and fauna. The formation of the area is due to the evaporation of a vast sea 70 million years ago. It is considered one of Outback South Australia's most breathtaking natural attractions. Guided bus tours are available through **Radeka's Desert Breakaway Tour,** 1 Oliver St., Coober Pedy (✆ **61/8/ 8672-5223**). Guides are experienced opal miners who explain the history of the area and the town.

At the end of the day, kids will be delighted at the prospect of sleeping underground—you may not even have to prod them to go to bed.

ⓘ **The Coober Pedy Tourist Information Center,** Hutchison St., Coober Pedy (✆ **1800/637-076** in Australia, or 61/8/ 8672-5298; www.cooberpedy.sa.gov.au/ site/page.cfm?u=191).

✈ **Regional Express** flies to Cobber Pedy from Adelaide.

🛏 $ **Radeka's Downunder Motel,** 1 Oliver St. (✆ **61/8/8672-5223**; www. radekadownunder.com.au). The **Comfort Inn Coober Pedy Experience Motel,** Crowders Gully Rd. (✆ **61/8/8672-5777**; www.cooberpedyexperience.com.au).

WHY THEY'LL THANK YOU: This place gives a new meaning to the term "down under."

Atmospheric Places to Explore 66

Under the Sidewalks of Paris
Touring the Sewers & the Catacombs
Ages 8 & up (Sewers); 10 & up (Catacombs) • Paris, France

Paris may be the City of Light, but it has its dark side too, and nothing is more gruesome than these two underground attractions. For older kids with a well-developed Goth sensibility—or at least a gross-out sense of humor—descending into the sewers and the catacombs of Paris will be an unforgettable memory.

Immortalized by Victor Hugo in Jean Valjean's thrilling subterranean escape in *Les Misérables,* the **Parisian sewer system** was begun in 1370, replacing the foul street-level open sewers that had done so much to help the Black Death decimate the population. In the early 1800s, extensive tunnels began to be bored beneath the cobblestone streets, a process accelerated when the Industrial Revolution brought mass-produced iron pipes and power-operated digging tools. Famous French city planner Baron Haussman designed a state-of-the-art system for channeling drinking water separately from sewage (now *there's* a valuable concept) and it's been growing ever since. Today Paris has 2,093km (1,300 miles) of meticulously laid-out tunnels bearing water mains, pipes, cables, and pneumatic tubes, such an

The catacombs of Paris.

impressive engineering accomplishment that the kids will forget all they wanted to see was a tunnel of poop.

Tours of **Les Egouts** (the sewers) begin at Pont de l'Alma on the Left Bank, where a stairway leads into the nether regions of the city; it's incredibly popular, and there's often a half-hour wait. Although most of the tour involves a film and exhibits, eventually you'll be led down for a brief foray into the echoing maze itself (which is in fact well-lit and not nearly as stinky as you may have anticipated).

If the sewers are not quite as gross as the kids hoped, never fear, the **catacombs** will live up to expectations. Not as ancient as the Catacombs of Rome, those of Paris date from the eve of the French Revolution, when, in 1785, city officials decided to convert a set of abandoned medieval quarries near Montparnasse—some 1,000 yards (3,000 ft.) of subterranean tunnels—into a burial space to relieve the overcrowded cemeteries. The remains of seven million persons were subsequently moved here, and in 1810 they were opened to the public, with ghoulishly arranged piles of bones touted as an "empire of the dead." After a brief vogue, in 1830 the prefect of Paris closed down the whole operation,

calling it obscene and indecent, and there the bones rotted until World War II, when French Resistance forces literally went underground to use the catacombs as their secret headquarters.

You enter the catacombs through a couple of narrow stone passages, electric-lit but still spooky. I found myself wondering what those 18th-century workers felt as they systematically piled femur bones in tidy shoulder-high stacks, and then artfully displayed skulls on top.

ⓘ **Sewers,** Pont de l'Alma on the Left Bank (✆ **33/1-53-68-27-82**). **Catacombs,** 1 place Denfert-Rochereau (✆ **33/1-43-22-47-63**; www.carnavalet.paris.fr).

🛏 $$$ **Hotel de Fleurie,** 32–34 rue Grégoire-de-Tours (✆ **33/1-53-73-70-00**; www.hotel-de-fleurie.tm.fr). $$ **Residence Lord Byron,** 5 rue de Chateaubriand (✆ **33/1-43-59-89-98**; www.escapade-paris.com).

BEST TIME: Sewers closed Nov–Apr.

WHY THEY'LL THANK YOU: If they're not creeped out by this, nothing will get them.

Buda Castle's Labyrinth

The Great Maze

Age 8 & up • Budapest, Hungary

Spanning the Danube, the twin cities of Buda and Pest—united in 1873 into one capital named Budapest—survived World War II and the Iron Curtain with a surprising amount of their charm intact. Hungary's medieval greatness is still embodied in Buda Palace, rising above old Buda on Castle Hill, which today contains three museums—the **Hungarian National Gallery,** the **Ludwig Museum of Contemporary Art,** and **Budpesti Történeti Museum** (Budapest History Museum). But it's what lies beneath the castle that I find most fascinating—a 10km (6¼-mile) network of tunnels, snaking underneath the cobblestone streets of the Castle District.

These began as natural caves, hollowed out by hot springs in the porous tufa rock of Castle Hill; people lived here way back in prehistoric times. It wasn't until the

Middle Ages, however—perhaps as early as the 11th century—that underground passages were cut to connect the caves in a vast labyrinth. Many of the houses on Castle Hill apparently had their own private entrances into this interconnected maze, which provided them with wells, storage cellars, and possibly a secret escape route for the king. In World War II, it became a rambling bomb shelter; during the Cold War years, the Soviet-controlled Hungarian communist government turned it into a secret military installation.

Since the fall of the Soviet empire, various efforts have been made to transform this hideaway into a tourist attraction. This latest incarnation presents the labyrinth as a walk through Hungarian history. After a cave filled with copies of famous prehistoric cave paintings, a series of stage-lit

Buda Castle's Labyrinth.

sculptural displays in successive caves represent: ancient shamans; the Magic Deer that was the totem of the nomadic Magyar people; the invading Huns; St. Stephen (who established the first Christian kingdom here in 1000); the invading Tartars, in 1241; the Renaissance leader, King Mathias, who set up his court in 1485; and the invading Ottomans in 1526. These somewhat abstract sculptures, carved out of soft golden tufa stone, are a lot less hokey than the wax museum that was previously installed down here. It's not long on historical detail, but it is an effectively poetic evocation of the dramatic sweep of Hungary's past.

For those who aren't afraid of the dark, there's also a **"Personal Labyrinth,"** a maze of unlit tunnels that visitors can wander around in the dark (although bringing your own flashlight to explore this section is perfectly okay).

ⓘ **Uri utca,** 9 (✆ **36/1/212-0207;** www. labirintus.com).

✈ Ferihegy International.

🛏 $$ **Hotel Erzsébet,** V. Károlyi Mihály u. 11–15 (✆ **36/1/889-3700;** www.danubius group.com). $$ **Hotel Papillon,** II. Rózsahegy u. 3-B (✆ **36/1/212-4750**).

WHY THEY'LL THANK YOU: Underground through the ages.

The Mysterious Souk of Marrakesh
Ages 10 & up • Marrakesh, Morocco

If creature comforts are high on your list of travel requirements, don't bother coming to Marrakesh. If, however, you like to sample the exotic and have a bit of adventure, take the Marrakesh Express right now.

This Moroccan city of half a million people is dirty, noisy, smoggy, and smelly, and a continual whirl of activity. Marrakesh has always been a trading city, ever since this date-palm oasis at the foot of the Atlas Mountains first became a crossroads for North African caravans, and so perhaps it makes sense that the heart of the city is its market—or souk, as they say in Morocco. Find your way first to **Djemaa El Fna Square,** the huge teeming plaza that is the center of activity in Marrakesh, with its throngs of food stalls, snake charmers, fortunetellers, jugglers, henna painters, and all sorts of charlatans trying to snare a few coins from tourists. (Let the kids watch, but do not be intimidated into paying for anything you haven't bought.) The

souk is a rabbit-warren of narrow streets leading off the north side of the square, a maze of tin-roofed alleys lined with stalls. You'll see rug merchants hanging their carpets on the walls of adjacent buildings; legume and spice sellers piling their goods, from orange lentils to dusty green mint to golden saffron, on thin blankets right on the pavements; and mounds of marinated olives, dates, and chickpeas gleaming in bowls. Brass pots, ceramics, caftans, slippers, leather goods, and fabrics are displayed in a jumble of stalls, while some smaller vendors simply squat on the ground, with their merchandise at their feet. At the northern end of the souk, the **workshops** of various craftsmen are open, where the kids may watch them do their leather tooling or slipper embroidering. (Try to avoid the Rahba Kedima section if you don't want to see dead animals or be pestered to buy love potions.)

The souk of Marrakesh.

Expect to be dogged by young men offering to be your guides (don't accept—you can't really get lost in this bazaar, only a square kilometer [¹/₃ sq. miles] in area). Expect to bargain vociferously (start out by offering one-third of the price first quoted to you), using lots of hand gestures, for any item you're interested in buying, and accept that you won't be paying the same price as a local would. Better yet, don't touch any wares, keep strolling, and don't make eye contact with vendors. You're not really here to purchase anything, but to soak up the atmosphere. Make sure you don't get separated from the kids; hold their hands casually, looking as nonchalant as you can. Your clothes will mark you as a tourist, but your body language will mark you as an intrepid one.

ⓘ **Tourist office,** Angle 31 rue Oued Fès et ave. Abtal (✆ **212/37/681-531;** www.tourism-in-morocco.com).

✈ Marrakesh.

🛏 $$$ **Le Meridien N'Fis,** ave. Mohammed VI (✆ **212/24/339-400;** www.starwoodhotels.com).

WHY THEY'LL THANK YOU: A truly bizarre bazaar.

The Taj Mahal

A Love Poem in Stone

Ages 6 & up • Agra, India

Nothing can prepare you for the beauty of the **Taj Mahal.** Yes, you've seen it a million times, on travel posters, in coffee-table books, even on the "It's a Small World" ride at Disneyland. You think you know that graceful center dome, the symmetrical white marble building with its pointed arches, the four punctuating minarets, the serene reflecting pool—but you cannot imagine how intricate it really is, how ethereal. Children generally assume it's a palace, until they learn the eerie truth: It's an over-the-top mausoleum.

Children always like a sight with a good story, and there's none better than the story behind the Taj. It was built by the grieving Shah Jahan, the fifth emperor of the powerful Mughal dynasty, to fulfill a deathbed promise to his favorite wife, whom he called Mumtaz Mahal ("Elect of the Palace"). He placed it beside the Yamuna River (where flooding is always a danger), next to the bustling market of the Tajganj, where it is said he first saw Mumtaz selling jewels in a market stall. Work started in 1641, and it took 20,000 laborers 22 years to complete. When Shah Jahan himself died, his cenotaph was placed beside his beloved Mumtaz's, somewhat spoiling the perfect original symmetry of the mausoleum chamber.

A red-sandstone gatehouse divides the Taj Mahal's tranquil gardens from the crowded city outside. What I always thought of as a sugar-cube white building is in fact a bejeweled box, with exquisite detailing covering the marble inside and out—a technique called **pietra dura,** which came from either Italy or Persia, depending on which scholar you read. As you stroll around, study these intricately carved floral bouquets, inlaid with

The Taj Mahal.

precious stones—agate, jasper, malachite, turquoise, tiger's-eye, lapis lazuli, coral, carnelian. Notice how the panels of **calligraphy,** inlaid with black marble, are designed to get bigger the higher they are placed, so the letters all appear the same size to a beholder on the ground level. Past the central pool rises the arched octagonal building containing the tombs, its white dome ringed by four minidomes. Inside, the two tombs are surrounded by delicate filigreed screens carved from a single piece of marble. Two red mosques flank the mausoleum on either side, one of them required by the Muslim faith, the other a "dummy" built for the sheer love of symmetry.

Open from dawn to dusk, the Taj changes color depending on the time of day. There used to be nighttime hours for visiting by moonlight, no doubt the most shimmering hour of all. But even at high noon, the Taj Mahal will not disappoint you, not any of you.

(i) **Tajganj** (📞 **91/562/233-0496;** closed Mon).

✈ Agra, 35 min. flight from Delhi.

🛏 $$ **Jaypee Palace Hotel,** Fatehabad Rd. (📞 **91/562/233-0800;** www.jaypeehotels.com). $$$ **WelcomHotel Mughal Sheraton,** 194 Fatehabad Rd., Taj Ganj (📞 **91/562/233-1701;** www.welcomgroup.com).

WHY THEY'LL THANK YOU: An eternal symbol of love.

Edo-Tokyo Museum
The Heritage of Old Japan
All ages • Tokyo & Koganei City, Japan

Tokyo is unfortunately short on architectural heritage—between the 19th-century mania for Westernization, the 1923 Great Kanto Earthquake, and World War II air raids, few traditional Japanese buildings have survived. Enter the **Edo-Tokyo Museum** (Edo-Tokyo Hakubutsukan), a city government project to create a **3-D timeline of Tokyo** from its humble beginnings in 1590 to the era of the first shogun to the 1964 Tokyo Olympics. It was an ambitious plan indeed—and a huge success.

The main facility—and the easiest to get to—is on two floors of a spaceshiplike building near Asakusa. Starting on the sixth floor, you'll walk over a replica of Nihombashi Bridge, the starting point for all roads leading out of old Edo. Some of the exhibits are scale models, others life-size re-creations of such buildings as a late-Edo longhouse (cramped quarters for the commoners), a Kabuki playhouse, an 1870 newspaper office. As you move from the Edo Period displays to the modern era, you'll notice the creeping influence of Western architecture—there's even a Ford Model-A taxi parked in front of a house, from the days when Japan had no auto industry. One of the most intriguing rooms shows life during the World War II air raids, with taped windowpanes and blackout shades on the light fixtures.

As a fan of historic re-creations, though, I much prefer the outdoor half of this museum, even though it's out in Koganei, a half-hour's train ride from Shinjuku. This **open-air architectural park** is a vivid portrayal of the evolution of Tokyo. Some 30 original structures, many of them weathered by age, were moved here from around Japan and placed on small streets in chronological order. You can go inside and prowl around, comparing the 1742 thatched-roof farmhouse with its tatami floors and central fire pit with the modern kitchen of a 1920s-era home. You'll visit a 1929 bathhouse, all its tiles and faucets gleaming; an early Meiji tailor's shop; a 1933 store, where bottles of soy sauce and sake line the shelves; and a bright yellow 1960s streetcar waiting at its stop.

If the kids enjoy the Edo-Tokyo, you might also try the **Fukagawa Edo Museum,** 1–3–28 Shirakawa, Koto-ku (© **81/3/3630-8625**), a hangarlike building with 11 full-scale replicas of traditional houses, vegetable and rice shops, a fish store, two inns, a fire watchtower, and tenement homes, re-creating an actual 19th-century neighborhood. The village even changes with the seasons—the trees sprout cherry blossoms in spring—and, every 45 minutes or so, undergoes a day's cycle from morning (roosters crow, lights brighten) to

night (the sun sets, the retractable roof closes to make everything dark).

ⓘ **Edo-Tokyo Museum,** 1–4–1 Yokoami, Sumida-ku, Tokyo (© **81/3/3626-9974;** www.edo-tokyo-museum.or.jp). **Open Air Architectural Museum,** 3–7–1 Sakura-cho, Koganei City (© **81/2/388-3300**).

✈ Narita International, 63km (39 miles).

🛏 $$$ **Imperial Hotel,** 1–1–1 Uchisaiwaicho, Chiyoda-ku (© **800/223-6800** in the U.S. and Canada, or 81/3/3504-1111; www.imperialhotel.co.jp). $ **Sakura Ryokan,** 2–6–2 Iriya, Taito-ku (© **81/03/3876-8118;** www.sakura-ryokan.com).

WHY THEY'LL THANK YOU: Seeing what all those skyscrapers replaced.

Escape to Alcatraz
America's Most Famous Prison
Ages 8 & up • San Francisco, California, USA

What do you do with the most notorious hardened criminals in the federal prison system? In 1934, at the height of the gangster era, the government had a brainstorm: Wall them up in a converted military fort on an island in San Francisco Bay surrounded by sheer cliffs, frigid waters, and treacherous currents. Just let them *try* to escape from there. Thus was the **Alcatraz Island federal penitentiary** born, a maximum-security prison whose infamous inmates included Al Capone, "Machine Gun" Kelly, and Robert Stroud (the Birdman). You may recognize its impregnable profile, lit by an ominous domed beacon tower, from such movies as *The Birdman of Alcatraz, Escape from Alcatraz,* and *The Rock;* it hasn't held a prisoner since 1963, but the vibe is still eerie—and therefore irresistible to youngsters.

These days it's harder to get into **Alcatraz** than it is to get out of it, thanks to the popularity of National Park Service tours to the island; call at least a month in advance to reserve tickets. You'll take a ferry from Fisherman's Wharf and explore the famous prison with a slide show and audio tour, which includes fascinating stories told by former guards and inmates. As you listen to the audio narration and the grim anecdotes delivered by park rangers, you get a chilling sense of what it was like to be isolated in the middle of the bay—with winds blustering through the barred windows and armed guards pacing the gun galley—yet so achingly close to the beautiful city of San Francisco.

By declaring Alcatraz to be "inescapable," the government was almost daring prisoners to break out. Officially, no one

The cell of Robert Stroud, aka the "Birdman of Alcatraz."

ever did, although there were 14 audacious attempts over the years: 23 fugitives were caught, 6 were shot, 2 drowned, and 5 others were missing and presumed drowned.

The ferry ride across the bay is fun, but you'll want to wear jackets, even in summer—and wear comfortable shoes, because there are many stairs to climb. Older kids who want to ratchet up the tour's already-somber tone may opt for the spooky "Alcatraz After Hours" tour. Hey, if you're going for creepy, you might as well go all the way.

(i) Pier 41, at Fisherman's Wharf (© **415/ 773-1188** for info, 415/705-5555 for reservations; www.nps.gov/alcatraz).

✈ San Francisco International Airport.

🛏 $$$ **The Argonaut,** 495 Jefferson St. (© **866/415-0704** or 415/563-0800; www. argonauthotel.com). $$ **Cartwright Hotel,** 524 Sutter St. (© **800/227-3844** or 415/421-2865; www.cartwrighthotel.com).

WHY THEY'LL THANK YOU: Appreciating the sweet taste of freedom.

A Touch of Kitsch 72

Stone Mountain National Park
Bigger Than Life and Then Some
All ages • Stone Mountain, Georgia, USA

Mount Rushmore? A mere pipsqueak compared to this massive memorial to heroes of the Confederacy. It's the world's largest sculpture, and any Northerner who thinks the South lost the Civil War may find this Deep South rewriting of history a mite unsettling—but hey, if General Sherman had mercilessly burned and pillaged your hometown, you'd be pretty slow to forgive, too.

Mount Rushmore's sculptor, Gutzon Borglum, actually began with this sculpture back in 1923, but, after 10 years, the

project soured and he went out to South Dakota, where he could do things his way. It wasn't until 1963, when the state purchased the mountain and its lovely woodland surroundings for a park, that work resumed under Walter Kirtland Hancock and Roy Faulkner. The memorial was finally completed in 1970. Standing 90 feet high and 190 feet wide, hewn in bas-relief out of the side of a gray granite mountain, it depicts Confederate leaders **Jefferson Davis** (President of the breakaway Confederate States of America), **Robert E.**

Lee (top general of the South's armies), and **Stonewall Jackson** (a beloved general who died at Chancellorsville in 1863) galloping on horseback throughout eternity. At the on-site museum, the kids can stand next to replicas of various features from the statue and understand how truly enormous those figures are. The best view of the sculpture is from below, but you can climb a walking trail up its moss-covered slopes, especially lovely in spring when they're blanketed in wildflowers, or take the narrated tram ride to the top.

A highlight at Stone Mountain is **Lasershow,** a spectacular display of laser lights and fireworks with animation and music, every summer night at 9:30pm. And unlike Mount Rushmore, which sits in the middle of badlands, Stone Mountain is surrounded by a host of other park attractions that are tremendously appealing to kids: the **Stone Mountain Scenic Railroad,** which chugs around the 5-mile base of Stone Mountain; the *Scarlett O'Hara,* a paddle-wheel riverboat that cruises 363-acre Stone Mountain Lake; and the **Antique Auto & Music**

Museum, a jumble of old radios, jukeboxes, nickelodeons, Lionel trains, carousel horses, and classic cars. The 19-building **Antebellum Plantation** is a major sightseeing attraction in itself, displaying an authentic 1830s country store, clapboard slave cabins, a smokehouse, a doctor's office, and three restored homes, from the 1790s, 1845, and 1850. And yes, there are also minigolf, a lakefront beach with water slides, 20 acres of wildlife trails, bicycle rentals, and even a petting zoo.

(i) U.S. Hwy. 78 E. ((C) **800/317-2006;** www. stonemountainpark.com).

✈ Atlanta.

⊨ $$$ **The Georgian Terrace Hotel,** 659 Peachtree St., Atlanta ((C) **800/651-2316** or 404/897-1991; www.thegeorgian terrace.com). $$ **Marriott Stone Mountain Park Inn,** 1058 Robert E. Lee Dr. ((C) **770/469-3311;** www.marriott.com).

WHY THEY'LL THANK YOU: Getting in touch with Dixie pride.

---

73 A Touch of Kitsch

Coral Castle
One Big Florida Roadside Souvenir
All ages • Homestead, Florida, USA

There's plenty of competition, but **Coral Castle** is probably the strangest attraction in Florida. Hewn by one solitary folk artist out of some 1,100 tons of pastel-tinted coral rock, this prehistoric-looking roofless "castle" harks back to an earlier age of Florida tourism—a time when the weirder and wackier a roadside attraction was, the better.

Like all such curiosities, this one has a story behind it. In 1923, a Latvian immigrant named Edward Leedskalnin—suffering from unrequited love for his 16-year-old fiancée, Agnes Scuffs, who had left him at the altar—moved to South Miami, after

having knocked around Canada, California, and Texas for a few lonely years. He spent the next 28 years of his life carving huge boulders of coral rock into this collection of outdoor sculptures, including such odd features as a moon fountain, a rocking chair, a table shaped like a heart, and another table shaped like the state of Florida. He began the thing in Florida City, his first home in the Miami area, but later spent 3 years moving the gigantic work-in-progress to his new home in Homestead, using a friend's tractor to haul it on his small trailer. In 1940, he erected a coral-rock wall around it and began charging visitors 10¢ to see it.

You don't come to see the Coral Castle so much for the artistic quality—in fact, the carving is blocky and crude—as for the mystery of it. It seems impossible that Edward Leedskalnin, who was only 5 feet tall and weighed no more than 100 pounds, could have done all this, using only tools he'd made himself from junk parts. Scores of affidavits on display from neighbors swear it happened . . . although nobody ever actually saw Ed working on it. Ed himself, being from a family of stone masons in Latvia, claimed that he worked at night using secret techniques passed down through the ages, the same techniques that allowed slaves to build the Great Pyramids. Hmmm.

ⓘ 28655 S. Dixie Hwy. (✆ **305/248-6345;** www.coralcastle.com).

✈ Miami International, 40 miles.

🛏 $$ **Indian Creek Hotel,** 2727 Indian Creek Dr., Miami Beach (✆ **800/491-2772** or 305/531-2727; www.indiancreekhotel. com). $$$ **Sonesta Beach Resort Key Biscayne,** 350 Ocean Dr., Key Biscayne (✆ **800/SONESTA** [766-3782] or 305/361-2021).

WHY THEY'LL THANK YOU: Deciding whether or not this was a hoax.

A Touch of Kitsch **74**

New Orleans
Aboveground Cemeteries
Ages 8 & up • New Orleans, Louisiana, USA

For some people, it took a hurricane for them to realize they should have visited New Orleans. Here was a true original among American cities, a place where people danced with parasols at funerals, ate beignets and po' boys, believed in voodoo and vampires, and threw plastic beads off parade floats. Despite its raunchy Bourbon Street reputation, it was always a great family destination. And Hurricane Katrina and the flooding that followed *nearly wiped it off the face of the earth.*

Luckily, the reports of New Orleans's demise were premature: Though damaged, New Orleans is still very much with us, and open again for business. One of the city's most emblematic destinations was safe from the floods by design—the aboveground cemeteries were created to keep graves from being flooded and spare residents from the unpleasant sight of bodies surfacing to ground level. The famous vaults of New Orleans were inspired by the Père Lachaise cemetery in Paris, where all of the crypts are designed to look like buildings. The New Orleans sites have been called "cities of the dead," where rows of buildings house the dead along neat lanes. Some of the wealthier families could afford more ornate crypts, gated with decorative iron fences. The earliest cemetery was **St. Louis no. 1,** 3421 Esplanade Ave., established in 1789 where the graves are more haphazard and less typical. The lack of order was due to high demand; there were cholera and fever epidemics making a practical cemetery imperative. The city worked hard to keep up with demand, and soon the cemeteries were incorporated as an integral part of the city. Two adjacent cemeteries are located at the same address in the French quarter: **St. Louis no. 2,** which shares a phone with no. 1 at: (✆ **504/482-5065**) and **St. Louis no. 3,** which may be reached at (✆ **504/486-6331**). All three cemeteries share an aura of creepiness that comes from crumbling tombs and twisting paths.

The crypts themselves are models of efficiency: The sweltering Delta heat and humidity create the conditions conducive to a natural cremation. As bodies are reduced to bone, they are pushed back and the remainders of the coffins are discarded to create room for other coffins. It is common to see dozens of names on a single crypt.

The "cities" have long been associated with voodoo rituals, many revolving around famous voodoo queen Marie Laveau. Laveau was born in the late 18th century, and became such a powerful figure that she was known as the "Pope of Voodoo" by the early 1830s. She is still respected by believers today. You'll find her grave at St. Louis no. 1. Voodoo practices themselves are a fascinating blend of West African and Catholic rituals, many still in practice.

Tourists are warned against visiting the famed cities of the dead alone, and not just because they are creepy. Many of them are in rough neighborhoods, and pose as magnets for muggers. The safest and best way to explore the cemeteries is to join a tour group, where you'll find safety in numbers and some great historical lore to boot. Visitors are also asked to refrain from making marks on the graves, a ritual that many believe to be a bona-fide voodoo ritual. It is, in fact, a hoax, which ultimately causes damage to the old stones. There are many tour groups operating in the city, including **Save Our Cemeteries, Inc.** (✆ **888/721-7493** or 504/525-3377; www.saveourcemeteries.org) and **Haunted History Tours** (✆ **504/861-2727;** www.hauntedhistorytours.com).

ⓘ **Tourist office,** 2020 St. Charles Ave. (✆ **800/672-6124** or 504/566-5011; www.neworleanscvb.com).

✈ Louis Armstrong New Orleans International, 15 miles.

🛏 $$ **Hotel Monteleone,** 214 Rue Royale (✆ **800/535-9595** or 504/523-3341; www.hotelmonteleone.com). $$$ **Omni Royal Orleans,** 621 St. Louis St. (✆ **504/529-5333;** www.omniroyalorleans.com).

WHY THEY'LL THANK YOU: Visiting the grave of Marie Leveau.

---

75 **A Touch of Kitsch**

Paul Bunyan
A North Woods Odyssey
All ages • Bemidji, Minnesota, USA

As a friend of mine from St. Paul pointed out, it seems that every town in Minnesota's beautiful lake-dotted center has some plaster animal on a pole outside of town—a rainbow trout, a beaver, a moose—to proclaim itself to visitors. But why mess around with a mere animal when you could have the North Woods's most enduring legend—the King of the Lumberjacks, Paul Bunyan, and his big blue ox, Babe?

You really know you've hit the North Woods when you arrive in **Brainerd,** Minnesota, and see the new 11¹/₂-foot-tall fiberglass Paul Bunyan statue beside the tourist information stand on Hwy. 371 just south of town. It's too realistic for my taste; the town commissioned this statue when it couldn't acquire the much larger seated Paul Bunyan figure from the now-defunct Paul Bunyan Center. That statue wound up at **This Old Farm,** 17553 Hwy. 18, Brainerd (✆ **218/764-2524**), a delightful mishmash of attractions including a restored 1940s farm, a corn maze, an arcade (where Paul sits), and a small ho-hum amusement park.

Some 70 miles farther upstate, in the town of **Akeley,** on Main Street, you'll find the next Paul Bunyan statue, a really big one—he'd be 25 feet tall if he stood up. Instead he crouches down, resting his axe beside him, with his hand cupped to hold tourists for photo ops. The black beard on this one is seriously impressive. Beside the statue is the Paul Bunyan Historical Museum, which has nothing to do with Paul Bunyan but recounts the area's logging history.

Forty miles north, you come to **Bemidji,** where the granddaddy of all Paul Bunyan statues stands downtown, next to the tourist office, on the pine-edged shore of Lake Bemidji. Eastman Kodak once named this America's second-most-photographed roadside icon, a classic piece of Americana erected in 1937 by the Bemidji chamber of commerce. This rather crude Paul Bunyan figure (instead of a beard, he has a Snidely Whiplash–like handlebar mustache) stands 18 feet high and weighs 2¹/₂ tons. Next to him is his companion,

Babe the Blue Ox, who weighs in at 5 tons. The site chosen for the statues is purportedly Bunyan's actual birthplace (yeah, sure, tell us another). Other legends claim that Lake Bemidji itself was created by one of Paul's footprints. There's also a **Paul Bunyan Amusement Park** beside the statues, and south of town is the **Paul Bunyan Animal Land,** 3857 Animal Land Dr. (✆ **218/759-1533**), a small petting zoo. It might as well cash in on the name—everybody else up here does!

ⓘ **Visit Bemidji** ✆ **218/759-0164;** www.visitbemidji.com.

✈ Grand Forks, ND, 113 miles.

⊨ $$ **AmericInn,** 1200 Paul Bunyan Dr. NW (✆ **800/634-3444** or 218/751-3000). $$$ **Hampton Inn,** 1019 Paul Bunyan Dr. S. (✆ **800/HAMPTON** [426-7866] or 218/751-3600; www.hamptoninn.com).

WHY THEY'LL THANK YOU: A tall man to match the tall tales.

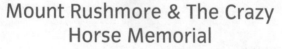

A Touch of Kitsch   76

Mount Rushmore & The Crazy Horse Memorial

All ages • Keystone & Custer, South Dakota, USA

When you think about it, **Mount Rushmore** is one of the oddest monuments ever: Gigantic chiseled faces of four Presidents—why four? Why those four (Washington, Jefferson, Lincoln, and ... Theodore Roosevelt?)? And why in the South Dakota badlands, miles away from most U.S. citizens? But crazy as it is, darned if another group didn't raise money to carve another mountain nearby with an even bigger sculpture, depicting American Indian chief **Crazy Horse.**

Mount Rushmore was the passion of one individual: Gutzon Borglum, a Danish-American sculptor from Idaho, who was hired by South Dakota to make a memorial

to draw visitors to the Black Hills. Borglum—who had previously been hired to carve Stone Mountain in Georgia, until negotiations broke down—chose this peak because it was hard granite, the highest in the area, and it faced southeast, where it would catch good daytime light. He also picked which Presidents to portray: Teddy Roosevelt made the cut because he'd lived in South Dakota and was a conservationist (also because Borglum had already done a bust of T.R. for the U.S. Capitol). The project was conceived in 1923; sculpting began in 1927 and puttered along through the Depression. Washington was unveiled in 1934,

Mount Rushmore.

Jefferson in 1936, Lincoln in 1937, and Roosevelt in 1939. Borglum died in 1941, and though his son Lincoln continued for 7 months, the work halted for good when the U.S. entered World War II.

Visit the **museum** under the amphitheater to learn about Borglum's innovative engineering. A 1-mile **Presidential Trail** leads to viewing terraces at the base of the mountain; take a guided tour so the kids can learn all the curious history. It's great to catch Mount Rushmore by the dawn's early light, or at least as soon as the park opens at 8am. In summer, a nightly lighting ceremony at 9pm (8pm in Sept) makes another splendid viewing op.

To many Native Americans, Mount Rushmore is a sacrilege, an intrusion on sacred landscapes, so the Lakota tribe initiated their own project 17 miles away, hiring sculptor Korczak Ziolkowski, who'd briefly worked with Borglum on Mount Rushmore. He began to hew the image of Chief Crazy Horse astride a thundering stallion in 1948; 50 years later—16 years after Ziolkowski himself had died—only the chief's nine-story-high face was completed. Millions of tons of rock have been blasted from the mountain face, though,

and even kids should be able to trace the form emerging from the granite; nightly laser shows in summer project the finished design onto the rough-hewn rock. When finished, Crazy Horse will be so big that all four heads on Mount Rushmore can fit inside it—641 feet long and 563 feet high. At the base of the mountain, the **Indian Museum of North America** focuses on the tribal history of numerous Native American cultures.

ⓘ **Mount Rushmore National Memorial,** Mt. Rushmore Rd., Keystone (ⓒ **605/ 574-2523;** www.nps.gov/moru). **Crazy Horse Memorial,** U.S. 385, north of Custer (ⓒ **605/673-4681;** www.crazy horse.org).

✈ Rapid City, 35 miles.

🛏 $$ **Alex Johnson Hotel,** 523 6th St., Rapid City (ⓒ **800/888-2539** or 605/ 342-1210; www.alexjohnson.com). $$ **Sylvan Lake Lodge,** S. Dak. 87 & S. Dak. 89 (ⓒ **605/574-2561;** www.custerresorts. com).

WHY THEY'LL THANK YOU: Giant statues for American giants.

The Corn Palace
Harvest Gone Wild
All ages • Mitchell, South Dakota, USA

On that classic coast-to-coast See-America-First drive in the family truckster, once you hit the Great Plains things begin to seem a little slow—it's just such a long way between cities. That's the appeal of **The Corn Palace,** sitting squarely on South Dakota's long east–west stretch of I-90. You have to get off the road somewhere, and when you do, it might as well be somewhere that makes you blink your eyes in wonder.

Turning onto Mitchell's main street downtown, you can't miss the Corn Palace, a gaudy, multicolor riot of onion domes and turrets. It was originally built in 1921 as the main exposition hall for this agricultural market town, but in a way the Corn Palace is built new every year. Every spring, a different artist announces a theme and sets to work, creating a set of **murals** to cover the outside of the Corn Palace—murals made out of *corn*. Yes, that's right, kernels and husks of real corn are applied to the facade, a custom that goes back to the 1890s when the first Corn Palace was opened. Actually, it still seems bizarre, no matter how long they've been doing it. But that's why the Corn Palace looks as though it's made out of corn, though underneath the building is mere reinforced concrete.

Concerts, stage shows, and sports events take place in and out of the hall, and still the artists work to complete their design, using thousands of bushels of native South Dakota corn, grain, and grasses. Come here in the summer and you'll still see a work in progress.

If you are visiting the Corn Palace in July, considering treating your kids to an authentic rodeo. The **Corn Palace Stampede Rodeo** is a 4-day event featuring top-notch competitors. There are tons of activities for kids of all ages. To learn more, check out their website at www.cornpalacestampede.com.

(i) 604 N. Main St. ((©) **866/273-CORN;** www.cornpalace.org).

✈ Rapid City, 35 miles.

⊨ $$ **Days Inn,** 15–6 S. Burr ((©) **800/329-7466** or 605/996-6208; www.daysinn.com).

WHY THEY'LL THANK YOU: It's beyond corny.

Wall Drug
The Power of Advertising
All ages • Wall, South Dakota, USA

At the other end of South Dakota's I-90 corridor from the Corn Palace, Wall Drug is a one-of-a-kind phenomenon—a wayside stop that just kept growing and growing. It all began in the Depression, when nearby Mount Rushmore was still under scaffolding, years away from attracting travelers to this middle-of-nowhere burg. Desperate for business, Wall Drug's owners, Ted and Dorothy Hustead, put up signs on the highway advertising free ice water to thirsty travelers. Motorists poured in.

Now convinced of the power of advertising, the Husteads planted more and more billboards, until they even began to appear in foreign countries. The Highway Beautification Act of the 1960s severely limited Wall Drug's billboard campaign, but still the tourists came; and over the years the Husteads (who still own the place, though it's now in the hands of the third generation) have added more and more popular features to draw them in.

Some 20,000 people a day, it's estimated, pull off the road to mill around this shambling low-slung complex, so extensive that it scarcely seems like a drugstore anymore. (There is a replica of the original small pharmacy inside, however.) Along with a "mall" of 26 little shops, Wall Drug has a restaurant, a vast postcard store, a gallery selling Western art, displays of Native American artifacts, a mechanical

diorama of an American Indian village, and a mocked-up Main Street of a Western town. But wait! There's more! Animated figures tucked into every available niche "speak" to the customers, including a roaring T-Rex. Out in the backyard stand king-size plaster figures of a bucking bronco, a rabbit, and the mythical jackalope, and an 80-foot-long green brontosaurus statue benignly casts its shade over the children's play area.

Nothing defines "tourist trap" better than Wall Drug. That's why you must visit.

ⓘ 510 N. Main St. (✆ **605/279-2175;** www.walldrug.com).

✈ Rapid City.

✈ ⊨ $$ **Alex Johnson Hotel,** 523 6th St., Rapid City (✆ **800/888-2539** or 605/342-1210; www.alexjohnson.com). $$ **Sylvan Lake Lodge,** S. Dak. 87 & S. Dak. 89 (✆ **605/574-2561;** www.custerresorts. com).

WHY THEY'LL THANK YOU: Classic roadside Americana.

---

79   A Touch of Kitsch

Wigwam Motels KY/AZ/CA
Teepee Time
All ages • Kentucky, Arizona & California, USA

Frank Redford was fascinated with Indians—so much so that he decided to build a chain of wigwam-shaped motor courts across America. True, the shape he actually used for his tiny tourist cabins wasn't a wigwam at all, it was a teepee, but that was a minor detail to a visionary like Redford.

Like many other such establishments built in the dawn of the automobile travel age, the 1930s and 1940s, Redford's **Wigwam Villages** offered overnight guests privacy with tiny separate lodgings, marked by kitschy themes that emphasized the character of the region. In the

end, only seven Wigwam Villages were built, but cramped and quirky as they are, they have so much character that three remain perfectly preserved today.

Redford's first village went up in 1934 near Horse City, Kentucky, built to house his collection of Native American relics. Intrigued (obsessed, frankly) with his idea, he patented the design in 1937, closed the small Horse City site, and built a larger Wigwam Village in Cave City, near the popular tourist attraction of Mammoth Cave. Later branches went up in 1940 in New Orleans (closed in 1954) and Bessemer, Alabama

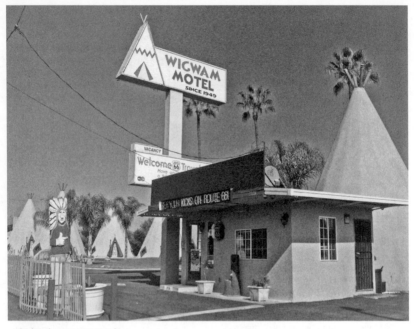

The kitschy Wigwam Motels.

(closed in 1964); after the war, in the late 1940s, three more went up, one in Orlando (the largest of the chain, razed in 1974) and two more, surviving along Rte. 66, the United States' main east–west highway in the pre-interstate era, known for its wacky themed restaurants, motels, and gas stations.

The concept was fairly standard: 15 to 20 white stucco teepees, 30 feet tall, decorated with red zig-zag stripes. Somehow a tiny bathroom was squeezed into the cone-shaped huts, and diamond-shaped windows were discreetly spaced around the base (real teepees, of course, don't have windows). The original exterior design also featured red swastikas, a traditional Indian motif, but when that symbol became associated with Nazi Germany in the late 1930s, the swastikas were painted over. A 50-foot-tall teepee contains the motel office/gift shop/restaurant; guest teepees are clustered around a central court (the California one has a kidney-shaped swimming pool).

The California and Kentucky motels have been updated with satellite TV and Internet access, but the Arizona branch—run by the same family that's owned it since the late 1940s—doesn't even have phones in the rooms. Both the Kentucky and Arizona Wigwam Villages still boast the original 1930s-vintage cane-and-hickory lodgepole-style furnishings.

Be sure to reserve well in advance if you want to stay in these teepee lodgings. The rooms may be tiny and inconvenient, the kitschy Indian theme politically incorrect, but as nostalgic artifacts they can't be beat, and they're very much in demand.

✈ Louisville, KY; Flagstaff, AZ; San Bernardino, CA.

🛏 $ **Wigwam Village Motel,** 601 N. Dixie Hwy., Cave City, KY (© **270/773-3381;** www.wigwamvillage.com). $ **Wigwam Village Motel,** 811 W. Hopi Dr.,

Holbrook, AZ (℃ **928/524-3048;** www.wigwam-motel-arizona.com). $ **Wigwam Motel,** 2728 W. Foothill Blvd., Rialto, CA (℃ **909/875-3005;** www.wigwammotel.com).

WHY THEY'LL THANK YOU: Waking up in a teepee.

80 A Touch of Kitsch

Watts Tower
One Man's Mania
Ages 6 & up • Los Angeles, California, USA

The only reason most tourists venture into this gritty inner-city neighborhood is to view **Watts Towers,** the largest piece of folk art created by a single person. That person was Simon Rodia, an immigrant Italian tile setter who, for 33 years, worked patiently in his spare time on this quixotic project. Nine intricate cement-and-steel structures gradually rose to the sky from the tiny yard of his cottage by the streetcar tracks. They startle the eye and disturb the mind—which is why kids love them.

Rodia began the towers—which he himself called Nuestro Pueblo, or Our Town—sometime in the early 1920s. As the years passed and the surrounding area deteriorated, the childless bachelor grew more and more reclusive, compulsively devoting himself to the art project. Neighbor children threw rocks over the surrounding wall, and during World War II it was even rumored that the towers might be transmission antennae for sending secret information to the Japanese. Rodia abruptly quit the project and moved out in 1954, offhandedly leaving his cottage—and the towers in its yard—to a neighbor. After changing hands several times, they were "discovered" by art lovers and opened to the public in 1960. Rodia claimed to have lost all interest in this creation that had once so consumed him, and he would not give interviews, except to say, "I had in mind to do something big and I did it." We'll never know what inspired him to undertake this extraordinary effort.

Though Rodia had no engineering degrees and used the simplest of tools, he was a skilled craftsman with an old-world pride in his handiwork, and the towers are surprisingly strong (they survived the 1994 Northridge Earthquake with very little damage). They are topped with futuristic-looking spires, skeletal webs of interlaced steel. The tallest is 99 feet high. They are all encrusted with a zany profusion of brightly colored mosaics, created out of anything that came to hand—bottles, seashells, cups, plates, pottery, ceramic tiles, you name it. Ask the kids to look for chips of green glass (which came from old 7-Up bottles) and blue glass (from Milk of Magnesia bottles). Rodia's day job was at the legendary Malibu Potteries, so it seems likely that many fragments of valuable Malibu tile are embedded in the Towers. A few other fanciful structures, such as a gazebo and a birdbath, are placed around the towers. **Tours** are offered every half-hour on a first-come, first-served basis.

ⓘ 1727 E. 107th St. (℃ **213/847-4646**).

🛏 $$ **Beverly Garland's Holiday Inn,** 4222 Vineland Ave., North Hollywood (℃ **800/BEVERLY** or 818/980-8000; www.beverlygarland.com). $$ **Roosevelt Hotel,** 7000 Hollywood Blvd., Hollywood (℃ **800/950-7667** or 323/466-7000; www.hollywoodroosevelt.com).

WHY THEY'LL THANK YOU: Seeing what 33 years can produce.

Winchester Mystery House
Monument to Paranoia
Ages 4 & up • San Jose, California, USA

Truth can be stranger than fiction, and no theme-park attraction could be any stranger than this actual house in San Jose, an hour's drive south of San Francisco. This quirky mansion, set in acres of meticulous gardens, was obviously the handiwork of a madwoman. Walking through it on any of the various guided tours, you'll be astonished at its weird mix of luxury, good taste, and utter craziness.

Begun in 1884, the **Winchester Mystery House** is the legacy of Sarah L. Winchester, a 44-year-old widow. Her husband was the son of the famous rifle manufacturer Oliver Winchester, maker of the fabulously successful Winchester repeater rifle—sometimes called the "Gun That Won the West." After both her husband and her baby daughter died, the disconsolate Mrs. Winchester consulted with a seer, who proclaimed that the family lay under a special curse—targeted by the unhappy spirits of people who had been killed with Winchester rifles. Gullible Mrs. Winchester bought the idea, and that's when her personal tragedy took a peculiar twist. The medium told her those unquiet souls could be appeased by only one thing: perpetual construction on the Winchester mansion. (Makes you wonder if she got a kickback from the contractor.) Convinced that she'd live as long as building continued, Mrs. Winchester—who happened to have a fortune to spend on this scheme—went through most of her $20-million inheritance over the next 38 years, as construction work went on 24 hours a day, 7 days a week, 365 days a year.

As you can probably guess, this is no ordinary home. With **160 rooms,** it

The Winchester Mystery House.

sprawls across half a dozen acres, a red-roofed Victorian mansion with extra turrets and gables sprouting randomly. There was never any master blueprint; Sarah Winchester herself designed the additions, often drawing them on a scrap of paper or a tablecloth whenever a new idea seized her. It has some 40 bedrooms, 47 fireplaces, and 5 kitchens, and a number of high-tech features for its time—elevators, forced-air heating, and gas light fixtures that could be turned on with the press of a button. Her favorite flower was the daisy, and it's fun to look for the **daisy motif** repeated in room after room.

Still, what kids undoubtedly remember most are the many disturbing features: a staircase leading nowhere, a Tiffany window with a spider-web design, a window in the floor, and doors that open onto blank walls. Superstitious Mrs. Winchester harped on the number 13, hoping thereby to confound the vengeful spirits—there are 13 bathrooms, 13 windows and doors in the old sewing room, 13 palms lining the main driveway, 13 hooks in the séance room, and chandeliers with 13 lights. Did the perpetual renovation plan work? Well, eventually Sarah Winchester did die, but not until the ripe old age of 82—with the house still unfinished, of course.

ⓘ 525 S. Winchester Blvd. (I-280 at Hwy. 17; ✆ **408/247-2101;** www.winchester mysteryhouse.com).

✈ San Francisco International Airport, 45 miles.

🛏 $$$ **The Argonaut,** 495 Jefferson St. (✆ **866/415-0704** or 415/563-0800; www.argonauthotel.com). $$ **Larkspur Hotel,** 524 Sutter St. (✆ **800/919-9779** or 415/421-2865; www.larkspurhotelunion square.com).

WHY THEY'LL THANK YOU: Realizing that even grown-ups get out of control sometimes.

---

82 A Touch of Kitsch

Madame Tussaud's & the London Dungeon

Ages 10 & up • London, England

Say you've spent a day or two trooping the kids through London's many cultural and historical attractions. They are growing antsy for something fun, and, being children, what could be more fun than exploring two of the city's most morbid destinations: **Madame Tussaud's** and the **London Dungeon.**

Madame Tussaud's offers more than mere wax effigies. The exhibits include panoramas, stage settings, and rides, along with a constantly updated collection of startlingly realistic figures of people as disparate as Princess Diana, Amy Winehouse, and J.F.K. Although branches of the famous wax museum are all over the world, the London branch prides itself on painstaking realism: Models are taken from real life, rather than pictures. This tradition began when Tussaud started making effigies in France, at the court of Versailles. She is famous for taking death masks from guillotined heads, including those of Louis XVI and Marie Antoinette. These, of course, are part of the exhibit. She moved from Paris to establish the London branch in 1802. Her work became so acclaimed that getting an invitation to sit for a "portrait" was the mark that you had really made it, and today being represented at her house is still a mark of fame, or, in some cases, infamy.

Older children will relish the famous **Chamber of Horrors,** a repository of murder weapons and creepy figures lurking in the shadows. Here you'll find Jack the Ripper as you walk down a re-created Victorian street. For those kids (and adults) wanting less ghoulish entertainment, there is **"The Spirit of London,"** a musical ride that takes visitors through 400 years of London's history, employing animatronic figures that move and speak. (Creepy enough when you think of it. In fact, it should be noted that the effigies can be disturbing to young children.) Tickets are pricey, but there is a discount for kids. Avoid long lines by calling ahead to reserve a ticket, or buy a package ticket that also includes the London Dungeon (www.thedungeons.com/en/admission-prices.html#london).

It must be said that the London Dungeon is not for the faint of heart or small children. Like Madame Tussaud's, it features London's most famous serial killer with **"The Jack the Ripper Experience,"** an elaborate special effects exhibit that allows visitors to retrace the steps of Jack himself. The Dungeon was originally established to depict the horrors of the Middle Ages. To that end, you'll find tableaus featuring torture, murder, and the plague. The current incarnation is a far cry from the attraction I visited in 1980, when the show was limited to wax figures and caged rats. Since then, it's upped the ante with rides including **"Extremis: Drop Ride to Doom,"** an adrenalin inducing experience you'll endure at the hands of "the hangman," a costumed actor. It further strays from historical accuracy by featuring the diabolical, but debatably fictitious **Sweeny Todd,** but if your kids are having this much fun, who's to quibble? Hours vary depending on the time of year, so call ahead for times.

ⓘ **Madame Tussaud's,** Marylebone Rd., London (✆ **44/870/999-0046;** www.madametussauds.com); **The London Dungeon,** 28–34 Tooley St., SE1 (✆ **44/20/7430-7221;** www.thedungeons.com).

✈ Heathrow.

🛏 $$$ **London Bridge Hotel,** 8–18 London Bridge St. 9 (✆ **44/20/7855-2200;** www.londonbridgehotel.com). $$ **Vicarage Private Hotel,** 10 Vicarage Gate, South Kensington (✆ **44/20/7229-4030;** www.londonvicaragehotel.com).

WHY THEY'LL THANK YOU: Telling friends that they've walked in the steps of the Ripper.

A Touch of Kitsch　83

Santa's Village
Where St. Nick Gets His Reindeer
Ages 4 & up • Lapland, Finland

While there are Santa Claus–themed attractions around the world—many of them open year-round—when you think about it, it's obvious that this must be the real one. It's on the Arctic Circle, and Mr. and Mrs. Claus, as well as their elves, need to live at least that far north. And where else do reindeer come from if not from Lapland?

Whatever you call him, Santa Claus or Father Christmas or St. Nicholas or Kris Kringle, the jolly man in the red suit appears in his grotto, **Santa's Office,** daily year-round, and "elves" at the **post office** across the way stamp letters with an authentic postmark. Even older children who don't "believe" anymore can find the low-key charm in this quaint-looking Finnish theme park (though it is certainly sophisticated enough to attract half a million visitors a year). **Santa House** (✆ **16/356-15-13**), set in a traditional Lapp log house, offers a historical exhibit about how various nations' Yuletide traditions developed. The nearby **Napipiri Reindeer Park** has a herd of 30 to 50 reindeer browsing around its corral; in winter they pull sleigh rides, and in the summer you can see spindly-legged calves tottering around the corral. Another kilometer south is **Santa Park** (© **16/333-000;** www.santapark.com), the only part of the development that gets a mite too cute—inside a glamorous stage-set "cave," children can join the elves in baking or toy making, sit on Santa's lap, and watch a film or a show, all for an extra admission fee.

Although winter seems at first the obvious time to go see Santa's Village, remember that this Arctic Circle region is dark continually during the winter (though brightly lit!). Even the Northern Lights—which don't appear as often here as they do at Tromsø—may not be compensation enough. In summer, however, the sun shines around the clock, and Santa will still be here.

ⓘ Hwy. 4, 8km (5 miles) north of Rovaniemi (© **16/356-20-96;** www.santaclaus village.info).

✈ Rovaniemi.

🛏 $$$ **Lapland Hotels Sky Ounasvaara,** Ounasvaara (© **16/335-33-11;** www.laplandhotels.com).

WHY THEY'LL THANK YOU: Whether or not they believe, the charm of the story wins through.

---

84 A Touch of Kitsch

Portmeirion
The Prisoner's Village
Ages 6 & up • Portmeirion, Wales

As longtime fans of the cult British television series *The Prisoner,* my husband and I were determined to squeeze in a visit to this resort town on North Wales' western coast where the series was filmed back in the late 1960s. The question was, would our kids—who'd only seen a few *Prisoner* episodes on DVD—be as thrilled by it as we were?

The answer was a resounding yes. Despite a constant gray drizzle on the summer day we were there (frankly, pretty typical weather for North Wales), they immediately tuned into the charm of this Mediterranean-style vacation village. Pastel Palladian villas, Arts and Crafts cottages, and an Art Deco hotel are set amid flower-filled terraces, sloping lawns, and mature woods of yew, oaks, and rhododendrons. Every perspective seems engineered with an artist's eye; statues and fountains are tucked like surprises into nooks and crannies; sloping stone-paved lanes and rippling steps negotiate the steep coastal shelf; and the contrast between green lawn and silver sea is inexplicably invigorating. Under those brooding Welsh skies, it may not look quite as much like Italy as its founder Clough Williams-Ellis hoped, but its cunning design still works.

Constructed from 1925 to 1973, **Portmeirion** was originally developed to embody Clough-Ellis's utopian theories on harmonizing architecture with nature. In many ways, he was like a Welsh version of Frank Lloyd Wright, and in 1971, he was knighted for services to architecture and the environment. He had already envisioned a tightly grouped costal village before he found a site, and although he later suggested that it was unplanned, there are drawings and models to suggest that he had been designing a place like Portmeirion for some time.

In its early years, the resort's guests included many artists, writers, and social thinkers. It still has a faintly Disney-esque air of manufactured reality, but that just makes its screen turn in *The Prisoner* as a sinister futuristic compound—ominously known only as The Village—all the more believable. Clearly *Prisoner* fans are a big part of Portmeirion's tourist base—there's even a shop on the property where you can buy memorabilia from the series. Prisoner star Patrick McGoohan passed away in January of 2009, but his memory lives on.

ⓘ ✆ **44/1766/770000;** www.portmeirion-village.com.

🚂 Porthmadog.

🛏 $$$ **The Hotel Portmeirion and Castell Durdraeth,** Gwynedd, LL48 6ER (✆ **44/1766/770000**). $$ **The Legacy Royal Victoria Hotel,** Llanberis (✆ **44/870/832/9903;** www.legacy-hotels.co.uk).

WHY THEY'LL THANK YOU: The Mediterranean meets Wales.

A Touch of Kitsch **85**

Hundertwasser's Architecture Run Riot

Ages 6 & up • Vienna, Bad Blumau & Bärnbach, Austria

Imagine this: trees bubbling out of rooftops, tilting floors, mad yellow and white towers topped with onion domes, colorful facades jigsawed with black outlines, patches of mosaic seeming to sprout organically from the corners of windows. It's the sort of architecture your own kids might dream up on a sugar high, if you gave them a shovel, a bucket of Legos, permanent markers, and a blowtorch. But in this case, the child was artist Friedensreich Hundertwasser (a name he invented, meaning "Peace-Kingdom Hundred-Waters"), Austria's version of Antoni Gaudí (see "Gaudí Days in Barcelona" ❸❷❹). In just 2 days, you could easily see all three major buildings in Austria designed by this brilliant, eccentric architect: **Hundertwasser Haus** in Vienna, the spa at **Bad Blumau,** and the **Hundertwasserkirche** in Bärnbach.

Hundertwasser Haus is a low-income housing project in a run-down district of Vienna; you can only see it from the outside, but the whacked-out exterior definitely stands out on this drab working-class street—all the irregular windows, sudden eruptions of color and mosaic, and rambling black lines crisscrossing the facade.

Hundertwasser—who considered straight lines and right angles to be "the devil's tools"—reportedly designed this building for free, just so that nothing ugly would be built in its place.

A 90-minute drive south of Vienna is the spa hotel at **Bad Blumau** in Styria, a region of Austria known for its hot springs. Offbeat as it looks, this is in fact a working spa, and a fairly upscale one, with New Age-y therapies, saunas, and thermal pools. Hundertwasser's love of nature really kicks into high gear here, with grass-covered roofs, curving pools, and gardens, the property erupting with joyous bright pavilions, bridges, and pergolas. Inside you can see how Hundertwasser's ideas extended to interior design, and you can even spend the night—the guest rooms are comfortable, though the suites have about the only level floors in the place ("an uneven floor is a melody to the feet," Hundertwasser once wrote).

In 1987, in a coal town southwest of Graz, named Bärnbach (about a 90-min. drive from Bad Blumau), Hundertwasser renovated the 1948 St. Barbara's church, turning it into the stunning **Hundertwasserkirche.** He blithely stuck a gold onion dome on its clock tower and ornamented the modest white plaster exterior with bold mosaics of major religious symbols, not just of Christianity but of all world religions. Go inside to see the huge mosaic crucifix and, best of all, a glowing window with a stained-glass spiral. No matter your faith, it's a religious experience.

ⓘ **Hundertwasser House,** Löwengasse and Kegelgasse 3, Vienna (www.hundert wasserhaus.at/HwH/en_main.htm). **Bad**

Blumau, A8283 Bad Blumau (www. blumau.com). **Hundertwasserkirche,** Tiberstrasse 15, Bärnbach (www.baern bach.at).

✈ Vienna.

🛏 $$$ **Rogner-Bad Blumau Spa & Hotel,** A8283 Bad Blumau (📞 **43/ 3383/5100-808**; www.blumau.com).

WHY THEY'LL THANK YOU: An artistic vision kids will understand.

---

86 A Touch of Kitsch

The Wasserspiele
A Bishop & His Bad Jokes
All ages • Hellbrunn, Austria

Just 20 minutes southeast of Salzburg, the square yellow baroque palace of **Schloss Hellbrunn** was built as a summer retreat for the Prince-Archbishop of Salzburg back in the early 17th century. Being the Prince-Archbishop of Salzburg was a very important job—and certainly Markus Sittikus was an adept politician and power broker. But after a walk through the gardens of Hellbrunn, we will forever think of him as one of history's most incorrigible practical jokers.

We hurried through the audioguide tour of the 18th-century interior, keen to get on to the **palace garden,** one of the oldest baroque formal gardens in Europe. A tour guide leads the garden tours, for reasons that soon became clear: You need a human being to push buttons to activate the water-powered automata and so-called "water jokes." These were high-tech status symbols in the early 17th century, but only Hellbrunn's have survived.

Passing through the gardens, you'll see water-powered mechanical scenes set in small grottoes, and a truly remarkable mechanical theater of an entire baroque city, with some 250 moving figures. There's a grotto where the walls, ceiling, and even floors are covered with seashells; in the **Neptune Grotto** an immense

leering mask sticks out his tongue repeatedly at you. And just when you least expect it, you get drawn into the action. Lean over to peer closer at a statue in a grotto? You get a spurt of water in your eye. Walk down a staircase between a pair of stately stone urns? You get pelted with spray from both sides. There's even a stone dining table set out in the garden where all but one of the stone seats are rigged with a water jet; sitting safely upon the blank seat, the Prince-Archbishop could nod to a servant and have a spurt of water sent up the backside of any guest he chose to torment. Fooled again!

ⓘ Fürstenweg 37 (📞 **43/662/8203720**; www.hellbrunn.at).

✈ Salzburg-Mozart Regional.

🛏 $ **Altstadthotel Wolf-Dietrich,** Wolf-Dietrich-Strasse 7 (📞 **43/662/871275**; www.salzburg-hotel.at). $$ **Hotel Mozart,** Franz-Josef-Strasse 27 (📞 **43/662/872274**; www.hotel-mozart.at).

BEST TIME: Closed Nov–Mar.

WHY THEY'LL THANK YOU: The 17th-century palace; the timeless sense of humor.

87

Museo de los Momias
A Mexican Day of the Dead
Ages 12 & up • Guanajuato, Mexico

My children's favorite Hispanic holiday—in fact, one of their favorite holidays of all—is the Dios de los Muertos, or Day of the Dead, Mexico's ghoulish version of Halloween. Well, it's Day of the Dead every day at the **Museo de los Momias,** where real human mummies are displayed in glass cases. It's not for the squeamish, and it's the only graveyard I know of that has souvenir stands, selling skulls made out of sugar and tiny effigies of the mummies.

Over the course of a century, from 1865 to 1985, corpses were taken out of the ground in this *panteón* (cemetery) to make room for newcomers, a typical custom in Mexico where graveyards have limited space. What to do with them? Put them on display, of course. At least that's the solution reached here in the beautiful regional city of Guanajuato, where a unique combination of dryness and the earth's gases and minerals in the town's municipal cemetery halted the decomposition of the bodies that were dug up. The mummies are propped up or laid out in their display cases, some of them still wearing the rags of their centuries-old clothing—they

almost seem to be grinning, choking, or staring out of their hollow eye sockets, their long teeth clenched in a rictus of life beyond the grave. If you speak Spanish well enough to follow the tour guides' macabre stories, you'll learn creepy stories about the fates of some of the deceased. Are they true? Who knows? But there's no mistaking the pregnant woman with her collapsed stomach, and there are way too many babies here for my taste. Don't come here unless you've got a decided taste for the gruesome—and even so, be prepared to have nightmares.

ⓘ Esplanada del Pantéon (✆ **52/473/732-0639**).

✈ Léon-Guanajuato, 27km (17 miles).

🛏 $$ **Méson de los Poetas,** Positos 35 (✆ **52/473/732-6657** or 52/473/732-0705; www.mexonline.com/poetas.htm). $$$ **Parador San Javier,** Plaza Aldama 92 (✆ **52/473/732-2222** or 52/473/732-0626).

WHY THEY'LL THANK YOU: Uncovering secrets of the graves.

88

Howe Caverns & Secret Caverns
The Story of the Dueling Caves
Ages 6 & up • Upstate New York, USA

The closer we got to **Howe Caverns,** the vintage upstate New York tourist attraction, the more billboards for it we passed—"Visit Beautiful Howe Caverns, only 6 miles

away!"—nostalgic throwbacks to an earlier era of roadside advertising. And a few yards past every Howe Caverns sign stood another more gaudy sign, hand-painted in

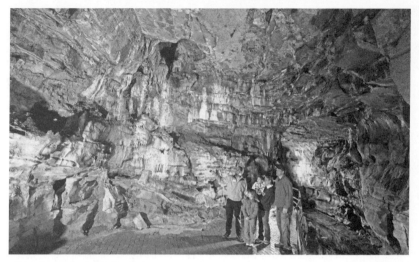

Howe Caverns in upstate New York.

a psychedelic style reminiscent of Grateful Dead album covers, luring visitors instead to **Secret Caverns.** Naturally, we had to visit both.

Howe Caverns is the granddaddy of American underground attractions—discovered in 1842 by farmer Lester Howe, it really took off in 1929, when walkways, lighting, and elevators were installed, and it still has a sweet, wholesome sort of Depression-era charm. While caves such as Mammoth Cave and Carlsbad Caverns are bigger and more spectacular, Howe Caverns doesn't try to gussy things up with laser lights and animatronics—you're underground, it's chilly and damp and echo-y, it's gosh-darn spooky, and that's enough. Eighty-minute **guided tours** lead you through its various chambers, including a **wedding chamber** (yes, many couples have chosen this spot to tie the knot) and a quarter-mile boat ride on the underground **Lake of Venus.** Aboveground there are some other touristy activities such as gemstone mining and pony rides, and the on-site restaurant has panoramic views from its big plate-glass windows. My kids thought it was totally cool . . . until we drove on down the road to Secret Caverns.

Secret Caverns is even smaller and more anticlimactic—a long stairway down to one passageway with a 100-foot waterfall. No big deal. The reason to come here is to revel in its roadside kitsch. The extravagant painting and tongue-in-cheek humor of its billboards are a good indication of the wackiness to be found at Secret Caverns. A supersized bat is painted over the entrance, and droll exhibits within include the "mummified remains" of a tour guide and goofy accounts of its 1928 discovery by a pair of cows. The guided tour often devolves into an improv routine, with the guides making up outrageous names for the rock formations they pass (often different names on the way down and back up). It's a fairly bald send-up of Howe Caverns, but then, Howe Caverns gets all the tourists—let Secret Caverns have all the fun.

ⓘ **Howe Caverns,** 255 Discovery Dr., Howes Cave (ⓒ **518/296-8900;** www.howecaverns.com). **Secret Caverns,** off Mammoth Cave, Rte. 7, east of Cobleskill (ⓒ **518/296-8558;** www.secretcaverns.com).

✈ Albany, 35 miles.

🛏 $$ **Howe Caverns Motel,** on the Howe Caverns grounds (ⓒ **518/296-8950**).

WHY THEY'LL THANK YOU: Spelunking with a sense of irony.

Mammoth Cave
Kentucky's Subterranean Supremo
All ages • Cave City or Park City, Kentucky, USA

Growing up in Indiana, I remember driving down back roads past ramshackle barns with fat yellow letters emblazoned on their roofs: See Mammoth Cave. It always beckoned to us kids like some kind of exotic Shangri-La, or maybe the Eighth Wonder of the World, thanks to this old-timey advertising campaign.

In many ways, Mammoth Cave *is* the eighth natural wonder of the world—it's the planet's longest system of caves, stretching for more than 360 underground miles (and that only counts the parts explored so far!) and going as deep as 379 feet below the surface. There's so much to see here that it can't be viewed all at once, so park rangers have developed many **tours,** ranging in duration from half an hour to 6 hours. While one quarter-mile loop is suitable for small children and the elderly, at the other end of the spectrum lies a tour for teens and adults that requires strenuous climbs and crawling through narrow passages. You could do more than one, because there's little overlap—some focus on the geology or biology of the caves, while others explore its history from prehistoric dwellers to 19th-century tourists to tuberculosis patients to present-day environmentalists; others switch off the electric lights and roam the dark caves with kerosene lanterns. Reservations are essential in summer—all the tours book up quickly.

Kentucky is geologically ripe for caves, with a vast subterranean drainage system that bored through its limestone bedrock. Draining water leaves behind not only the stalagmites and stalactites kids learn about in science, but also rippled formations like flowstone and dripstone. Embedded in the walls you'll see fossils—blastoids, crinoids, gastropods—left from the days

when this region was a vast shallow sea. The ceiling soars 192 feet over Mammoth Dome; the floor sinks 105 feet below the walkways in the Bottomless Pit. I loved the fanciful names given to various "chambers," such as **Fat Man's Misery, Giant's Coffin, Frozen Niagara,** and the **Snowball Room.**

We were glad to find that the surface landscape—53,000 acres of lovely hardwood forests—offers loads of other fun activities: hiking, horseback rides, birdwatching, or canoeing along more than 30 miles of river.

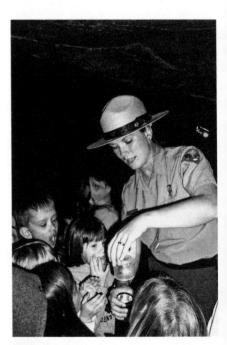

Mammoth Cave.

ⓘ **Visitor Center/Park Headquarters,** South Entrance Rd. (ⓒ **270/758-2328;** www.nps.gov/maca).

✈ Louisville and Nashville are both about 1½ hr. away.

🛏 $$ **Jellystone Park RV/Cabin Resort,** 1002 Mammoth Cave Rd., Cave City (ⓒ **270/773-3840;** www.jellystone mammothcave.com). $$ **Mammoth Cave Hotel,** within the park (ⓒ **270/758-2225;** www.mammothcavehotel.com).

WHY THEY'LL THANK YOU: A whole world underground.

---

90 **Caves**

Carlsbad Caverns
Colossal Underground Refuge
Ages 6 & up • Carlsbad, New Mexico, USA

Native Americans always knew there was a giant cave system snaking around under the porous limestone reef of the Guadalupe Mountains. But white settlers only stumbled upon it a century ago, after noticing vast hordes of bats swarming out of a hole in the ground every summer day at sunset. Some 100 caves lie within today's park, an underground world of pale limestone, where every fantastic and grotesque shape imaginable (and unimaginable) has been sculpted by natural forces—from frozen waterfalls to strands of pearls, soda straws to miniature castles, draperies to ice-cream cones. Above all, what is impressive here is the sheer size of the cave, a constantly cool (56°F/13°C) refuge from the 100°F (38°C) heat outside in the Chihuahuan Desert.

The main cave open to the public, the immense **Carlsbad Cavern,** offers several options. With smaller kids, you may just want to take the elevator from the visitor center down 750 feet to the **Big Room,** which is a pretty understated name for this jaw-dropping rock chamber whose floor covers 14 acres. If you're more ambitious, follow the traditional explorer's route from the historic natural entrance, winding down for a mile into the depths through a series of underground rooms to the same Big Room. A self-guided tour from here runs 1¼ miles over a relatively

level path, taking about an hour. Rangers along the path point out some of the more evocative formations, demonstrating the still-growing dome stalagmites and the daggerlike stalactites jabbing down from the ceiling.

Tours of other sections of Carlsbad Cavern range from the easy **Left Hand Tunnel,** a half-mile lantern tour, to the difficult **Hall of the White Giant** tour, which requires you to crawl long distances, squeeze through tight crevices, and climb up slippery flowstone-lined passages. The 2½-hour tour of **Slaughter Canyon Cave** is a far more strenuous cave hike from a different cave mouth altogether. And if the kids don't like being underground too long, they can still join one of the most popular activities at the caves, a sunset gathering at the natural entrance (May–Oct) to watch a quarter-million Mexican free-tailed bats flap out of the cavern to wheel out over the desert for a night of insect feasting. After all, that's how the *Americanos* found the joint in the first place.

ⓘ 3225 National Parks Hwy. (ⓒ **800/967-CAVE** [2283] or 505/785-2232; www.nps. gov/cave).

✈ El Paso, 150 miles. Cavern City Airport, 23 miles.

7 Famous Bridges

Bridges do more than connect two bits of land—they span centuries of history, ignite the imagination, and inspire with their beauty. Crossing a famous bridge becomes an event, a moment of drama that can crystallize your experience of a city. Natural spots for photo ops, bridges can thrill kids with a panoramic postcard view. Here are seven of the world's greatest bridges, sure to spark vivid family travel memories.

91 Le Pont Neuf, Paris   The city's oldest bridge was erected in 1578, connecting Paris' Right Bank 1st arrondissement with the Left Bank's 6th arrondissement, so just about every visitor walks across it at one time or another. This stone structure was radical for the time: It was not weighed down by houses and its few original shops were removed in a 1606 reconstruction. Featuring one of the world's first pedestrian sidewalks, it remains a popular spot for strolls to this day; offering a dazzling view of **Notre-Dame de Paris 314** in one direction and the **Eiffel Tower 25** in the other. Ask kids to watch for the **statue of Henry IV** on horseback standing at the middle of the bridge. See Under the Sidewalks of Paris **66**, Paris for Art Lovers **336**, and the Paris Opera **344**.

92 The Ponte Vecchio, Florence   Florence owns the bragging rights as fountainhead of the Renaissance, and no landmark is more steeped in history than the Ponte Vecchio. The name means "old bridge," and this triple-arched stone bridge,

Florence's triple-arched Ponte Vecchio.

lined with shops in the medieval custom, dates from 1220. In 1229, the **Palazzo Vecchio** was built at the foot of the bridge. Poet Dante Alighieri lived nearby and crossed the bridge often. See Uffizi Gallery **334**.

93 The Chain Bridge, Budapest   This graceful suspension bridge has played a vital part in the growth of Budapest into a thriving metropolis. In 1849, it became the first permanent bridge across the **Danube**, connecting Buda and Pest into a single city. Designed by William Clark, who also designed the Hammersmith Bridge in London, it replaced a system of pontoon boats that were easily swept away by heavy weather. Blown up by retreating Nazis in World War II, rebuilt after the war, the bridge was a site for demonstrations for independence in 1989, cementing its status as a symbol of liberty. On summer weekends, when it's traffic-free, it's thronged with artists, craftspeople, vendors, and tourists. See Buda Castle's Labyrinth **67**. *www.budapest-tourist-guide.com/chain-bridge.html.*

94 The Tower Bridge, London   Naturally, when they go to London, the kids will ask to see the London Bridge. But what they're really thinking of is this, a graceful drawbridge spanning the Thames with a pair of Gothic-style towers that echo Westminster's spires. However medieval it looks, it was actually built in 1894 next to the **Tower of London 190**; an exhibition inside the bridge commemorates its history.

Remarkably, the engine room still uses its Victorian boilers and steam pumping engine to raise and lower the bridge. Stroll across the walkways to get a stunning view of the loopy course of the Thames. See Hyde Park **55**, Madame Tussaud's & the London Dungeon **82**, London Zoo **131**, the British Museum **176**, the Imperial War Museum **227**, the *Golden Hinde* **236**, the Science & Natural History Museums **281**, Greenwich **297**, Shakespeare's Globe Theatre **352**, Hampton Court **360**, Wimbledon **468**, and the London Eye **485**. © 44/207/357-7935; www.towerbridge.org.uk.

London's Tower Bridge.

95 **The Brooklyn Bridge, New York** As thrilling a sight as this beautiful brown-hued East River bridge is from afar, with its Gothic-style towers and lacy mesh of cables, the view from the bridge is even more thrilling. A boardwalklike pedestrian walkway goes all the way across. One mile long, it should take half an hour to traverse—except you'll be tempted to stop more than once to ooh and ahh at the vision of **Manhattan's skyscrapers** thrusting upward, with the **great harbor** and **Verrazano Bridge** beyond. The bridge took 16 years to build, from 1867 to 1883, becoming the first steel-wire suspension bridge in the world when it opened. See Howe Caverns & Secret Caverns **88**, Bronx Zoo **127**, Statue of Liberty & Ellis Island **252**, Metropolitan Museum of Art **340**.

96 **The Golden Gate Bridge, San Francisco** Warn the kids ahead of time that the Golden Gate Bridge is not golden at all, but a flaming orange. Once past that surprise, though, they cannot fail to be bowled over by this glorious bridge spanning the Pacific Ocean where it meets San Francisco Bay. It's one of those quintessential landmarks, familiar from dozens of movies. Cars roll over it, boats cruise under it, and airplanes buzz overhead, but this bridge is best experienced on foot. Be prepared: The traffic alongside the pedestrian walkway gets pretty noisy, and the bridge vibrates, but if you make it to **Vista Point,** you'll be rewarded with a **breathtaking view.** See Escape to Alcatraz **71**, the Exploratorium **278**, and the Cable Cars of San Francisco **309**. http://goldengatebridge.org/visitors/.

97 **The Sydney Harbour Bridge, Sydney** This mighty steel arch soaring over Sydney Harbour isn't the longest steel arch bridge in the world, but it's the largest, bearing eight lanes of car traffic, two railway lines, a bike lane, and pedestrian walkway. It was opened in 1932, 5 years before the Golden Gate Bridge, and shares in common with that famous bridge the distinction of being a Depression-era public works project. It's the focal point of the classic **Sydney postcard view,** with its high-rise skyline backdrop, the water below bustling with ferries, barges, tall ships and yachts, and the Sydney Opera House looking like a fleet of white sails caught mid-billow over Sydney Cove. See Sydney Aquarium **121**. www.sydney.com.au/bridge.html.

$$ **Best Western Cavern Inn,** 17 Carlsbad Cavern Hwy., White's City (✆ **800/ CAVERNS** [228-3767]; www.bestwestern. com). $$ **Holiday Inn,** 601 S. Canal St.

(✆ **800/HOLIDAY** [465-4329]; www.holiday-inn.com).

WHY THEY'LL THANK YOU: The Big Room.

Caves 98

Cheddar Gorge & Wookey Hole
Where Brits Go Underground
All ages • Cheddar & Wells, England

Say "cheddar" and your kids will think of cheese, and indeed this Somerset village near Bath is the home of cheddar cheese. But it's also an area rich in underground caverns, one of them within **Cheddar Gorge,** the other just outside the nearby cathedral town of Wells. These are hardly undiscovered caverns—they are commercially developed tourist sites, with some cheesy (pardon the pun) special features added—but the caves themselves are impressive; and I for one secretly like the goofy add-ons.

More than a million years old, the **Cheddar Caves** have some spectacular sections, including cathedral-like **Gough's Cave** and **Cox's Cave,** with its calcite sculptures and brilliant colors. The operators have jazzed things up with holograms and optical effects, such as the **Crystal Quest,** a dark walk "fantasy adventure" taking you deep underground. Britain's oldest complete skeleton, 9,000 years old, is gruesomely displayed in the **Cheddar Man exhibit.** Adults and children over 12 years of age who want even more can book an **Adventure Caving** expedition, which is pricey but intriguing; there are also rock-climbing classes. Away from the caves, you can climb 274-step **Jacob's Ladder,** which has been set up as a walking timeline of Earth history. At the top, **Pavey's Lookout Tower** offers grand Somerset views, on some days as far as Wales, and a 5km (3-mile) walking trail lets you explore the **Mendip Hills.**

Ten kilometers (6¼ miles) south of Cheddar, at the source of the Axe River, lies another set of caves with an irresistible name: **Wookey Hole.** It takes 2 hours to tour this extensive set of limestone caverns, which includes an underground lake. Prehistoric people lived down here at least 50,000 years ago; ancient legend maintains that a stony figure in the first chamber is the **Witch of Wookey** turned to stone. Wookey Hole has its share of tacky features such as the **Magical Mirror Maze** and **Pirate Adventure playroom,** but the **Edwardian penny arcade** is worth trying out, a collection of antique game machines that are surprisingly fun to play, even for PlayStation addicts.

ⓘ **Cheddar Gorge** (✆ **44/1/934-742343;** www.cheddarcaves.co.uk). **Wookey Hole** (✆ **44/1/749-672243;** www.wookey.co.uk).

✈ London.

🚆 Bath, 1½ hr. from London.

$$ **The Crown,** Market Place, Wells (✆ **44/1/749-673457;** www.crownatwells. co.uk).

WHY THEY'LL THANK YOU: Cheddar Man and the Witch of Wookey, unforgettably bizarre.

The Caves of Majorca
Journey to the Center of the Earth
Ages 6 & up • Majorca, Spain

The Mediterranean resort island of **Majorca** is a place of sand, sun, and fun, wildly popular with European vacationers and a quick flight from Barcelona, Spain. Part of the Balearic archipelago, tourism has been Majorca's raison d'être for the past couple of centuries, after being popularized by 19th-century artistic types like George Sand, Frederic Chopin, and, later, Robert Graves. In those days, visitors would never dream of coming to Majorca without touring the spectacular caves on its east coast. Two of the most amazing are an easy drive from Palma, Majorca's main town.

Rich in literary associations, **Cuevas de Artà** are said to be the inspiration for Jules Verne's 1864 tale *Journey to the Center of the Earth*. (Verne may have heard or read about the caves; it is not known if he ever actually visited them.) Formed by seawater erosion, the caves are about 32m (105 ft.) above sea level, and some chambers rise about 46m (151 ft.). In the entrance vestibule, notice the walls blackened by torches used to light the caves for tourists in the 1800s. The **Reina de las Columnas** (Queen of the Columns) rises about 22m (72 ft.) and is followed by a set of rooms named after the sections of Dante Alighieri's *Divine Comedy*: a grim, forbidding cavern called "Inferno," then a field of stalagmites and stalactites (the "Purgatory Rooms"), which eventually lead to "Paradise." The stairs in the cave were built for Isabella II for her 1860 visit; in time, such celebrities as Sarah Bernhardt, Alexandre Dumas, and Victor Hugo arrived for the tour.

The roof appears to glitter with endless icicles at **Cuevas del Drach** (Caves of the Dragon), a short drive from Cuevas de Artà. These Dragon Caves contain five subterranean lakes, including **Martel Lake,** 176m long (577 ft.), the largest underground lake in the world. It was named after E. A. Martel, the French speleologist who charted the then-mysterious caves in 1896. Boating on the lake, you can look up at the intricate formations and marvel anew.

ⓘ **Cuevas del Drach,** Porto Cristo (ⓒ **34/971-182-07-53**). **Cuevas de Artà,** Platja de Cañamel (ⓒ **34/971-841-293**).

✈ Palma de Majorca, 8km (5 miles).

🛏 $$ **Hotel Bonsol,** Paseo de Illetas 30, Illetas (ⓒ **34/971-140-2111; www.mallorcaonline.com). $$$ Hotel Villa Hermosa,** Carretera Felantix-Portocolom Km 6, Felantix (ⓒ **34/971-182-4960;** www.hotel-villahermosa.com).

WHY THEY'LL THANK YOU: Leaving the sun-worshipping hordes behind.

4 Walk with the Animals

Giraffe and its baby at the San Diego Zoo

Assateague
Island of the Wild Ponies
All ages • Assateague Island, Virginia, USA

Misty of Chincoteague is one of those books my daughter loved reading as much as I did—it's practically required reading for any girl in her Horse Phase. As every Misty lover knows, the book is about a **Chincoteague pony,** and the place you go to see Chincoteague ponies is . . . **Assateague Island.** Chincoteague comes into the picture because it's the neighboring island, sheltered from the ocean by the outlying barrier island of Assateague; every year in July, Chincoteague townsfolk row over to uninhabited Assateague, round up the wild ponies that live there, make them swim across the narrow channel separating the two islands, and sell the new foals to raise money for the local fire department. Everybody *knows that,* Mom.

The good news is that you don't have to be a pony-crazed girl to enjoy a trip to Chincoteague and Assateague. Like most of this region of Maryland and Virginia, known as the Eastern Shore, it's a tranquil, wind-ruffled shore land with a lot of wildlife refuges and weather-beaten charm. You can drive right onto Chincoteague, an old fishing village that was settled by the English in the late 1600s, and from there take another causeway to Assateague, which was settled by wild horses at about the same time. Legend has it that the ponies' ancestors swam ashore from a shipwrecked Spanish galleon, but more likely they were put there by the English settlers as a natural corral. Go early in the day, because there's a quota for how many cars can be on Assateague at one time. You'll have to wait until 3pm to be allowed to drive onto the paved 4½-mile **Wildlife Drive,** which runs through the

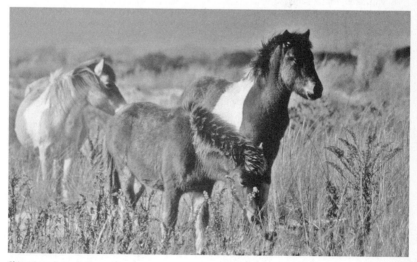

Chincoteague ponies.

marshes and is the best place to see these shaggy, sturdy little horses. (Earlier in the day, you can walk or bicycle around this flat, easy loop to your heart's content; narrated bus tours run all day.) Besides the ponies, there are an amazing number of birds to spot, and at the end of the main road lies a splendid unspoiled beach—the **Assateague National Seashore**—which has bathhouses and lifeguards and a visitor center. If you're into shell collecting, the southern spit of land called Tom's Cove yields pails full.

Back in Chincoteague, there's one more must-do for pony lovers: taking a ride at the **Chincoteague Pony Centre**, 6417 Carriage Dr. (© **757/336-2776**; http://chincoteague.com/ponycentre/pony).

Who knows—the pony you ride might be one of Misty's many descendants!

ⓘ **Assateague Island National Seashore** © **757/336-3696**; www.nps.gov/asis.

✈ Norfolk, 83 miles.

🛏 $$$ **Island Motor Inn Resort,** 4391 N. Main St., Chincoteague (© **757/336-3141;** www.islandmotorinn). $$ **Refuge Inn,** 7058 Maddox Blvd., Chincoteague (© **888/868-6404** or 757/336-5511; www.refugeinn.com).

WHY THEY'LL THANK YOU: Wild horses couldn't drag us away.

In the Wild 101

Crystal River
The Real Mermaids
Ages 4 & up • Crystal River & Homosassa Springs, Florida, USA

Manatees, which early sailors may have mistaken for mermaids, love to spend their winters around the clear, warm waters of Florida's west coast, heading inland along spring-fed rivers where the temperature is generally a steady 72°F. On average, these gentle sea mammals are about 10 feet long and 1,200 pounds—their closest living relatives are elephants—and they move too slowly to get out of the way of boats; injuries due to speedboat collisions are one of the main reasons they are an endangered species. Their prime spot is in the protected warm-water natural springs of King Bay in the **Crystal River National Wildlife Refuge,** which was created especially to protect the few remaining West Indian manatees (a quarter of America's manatee population winters in this one refuge). Several local operators lead daily boat tours out into the manatees' favorite waters to let human swimmers interact with these

endearingly ugly creatures. One of the largest is **American Pro Dive,** 821 SE U.S. 19, Crystal River (© **800/291-3483** or 352/563-0041; www.americanprodiving.com). The refuge is reachable only by boat, so a guided excursion is almost essential. American Pro Dive also runs manatee swims from November to April, 7 miles south of Crystal River in the **Homosassa Springs Wildlife State Park,** where the waters are only 4 feet deep and thus reassuring even for young, inexperienced swimmers. The trusting manatees, who are absurdly nearsighted, come close enough for you to pet their sleek gray-brown skin and feel the whiskers on their droopy snouts. Tours begin early, at 7am, when the manatees are around in greatest numbers; you'll be back at the dock by late morning.

After your face-to-face manatee encounter, you may also want to go underwater in a floating observatory in Homosassa

Springs Wildlife State Park, where you can watch manatees in action, with thousands of fresh- and saltwater fish darting around them. As you'll notice through the observation glass, this is a rehabilitation facility that nurses manatees that have been injured by boat propellers; the sight of their scarred bodies, missing fins, and truncated tails is a sad reminder of the threat of their extinction.

ⓘ **Crystal River** (ℂ **352/563-2088;** www. fws.gov/crystalriver). **Homosassa Springs,** 4150 S. Suncoast Blvd. (ℂ **352/628-5343;** www.floridastateparks.org/homosassa springs).

✈ Tampa International, 70 miles.

╞═ $$ **Best Western Crystal River Resort,** 614 NW U.S. 19, Crystal River (ℂ **800/435-4409;** www.crystalriver resort.com). $$$ **Plantation Inn,** 9301 W. Fort Island Trail, Crystal River (ℂ **352/795-4211;** www.plantationinn.com).

WHY THEY'LL THANK YOU: Save these gentle giants.

---

102 In the Wild

Whale-Watching in Quebec
Ages 4 & up • Baie-St-Catherine & Tadoussac, Quebec, Canada

You expect whale-watching cruises out in the ocean—around Cape Cod, for example, or the California coast, or up in Washington State's San Juan Islands. But whale-watching on a river? Well, you can see whales, and plenty of them, on the **St. Lawrence River** north of Quebec City, where the river widens considerably on its way to becoming the Gulf of St. Lawrence; in fact it's one of the world's best whale-watching sites. The relatively small beluga and minke whales live in these teeming blue waters

Whale-watching in Quebec.

year-round, and from late June through September, larger migratory species like finback and blue whales join them, making sometimes as many as 500 whales swimming around at a time. Ferries from St-Simeon to Rivière-du-Loup sometimes get treated to the sight of one of these majestic sea mammals, but you don't want to disappoint the kids—book a proper whale-watching cruise.

Half a dozen operators run such cruises out of the towns of Baie-St-Catherine (on the north side of the river, near the Saguenay's estuary) and Tadoussac (on the south side of the river). The entire purpose of these cruises is to observe whales, so they will alter their route based on where the whales happen to be that day, and even offer a guarantee that you will sight a whale. Most cruises last 2 to 3 hours, so it's possible to do as a day trip from Quebec. Two leading whale-watch operators are **Croisières AML** (✆ **800/ 563-4643** or 418/692-2634; www.croisieres aml.com) and **Famille Dufour Croisières** (✆ **800/463-5250** or 418/692-0222; www. dufour.ca); both of them operate large catamarans or cruisers that carry up to 500 passengers, with snack bars, inside seating, onboard naturalists, and underwater cameras so you can see what's going on underneath the fluke-flipping surface.

However, Croisières AML has another, more adventurous option for those so inclined: agile little 10-to-25-passenger powered inflatables, called **Zodiacs,** where you're really out on the water, wearing life jackets and waterproof overalls and extra sweaters. The big ships just aren't as maneuverable as the Zodiacs, which can zip in closer to the whales as they playfully roll, spout, and breach in the chilly Canadian waters. It's all a matter of taste, but personally I'd give up the creature comforts to get closer to the whale.

ⓘ **Quebec Visitor Information** (✆ **877/ 266-5687** or 514/873-2015; www.tourisme. gouv.qc.ca).

✈ Jean-Lesage International, Quebec City, 185km (115 miles).

🛏 $$$ **Château Mont Sainte-Anne,** 500 bd. Beau-Pré, Beaupré (✆ **888/824- 2832** or 418/827-5211; www.chateaumont sainteanne.com). $$$ **Fairmont Le Manoir Richelieu,** 181 rue Richelieu, La Malbaie (✆ **800/441-1414** or 418/665-3703; www.fairmont.com).

WHY THEY'LL THANK YOU: Looking these ocean giants in the eye.

In the Wild **103**

Aransas National Wildlife Refuge
Where Whooping Cranes Whoop It Up
Ages 4 & up • Austwell, Texas, USA

In 1941, there were only 15 whooping cranes left—an entire species, reduced to just 15 *birds,* one small flock in this shoreline nesting ground along Texas's Gulf Coast. Today, thanks to a dedicated team of conservationists, their numbers are slowly growing, but this Texas flock is still the only natural population in the world, numbering just over 200 birds. It's an

amazingly rich habitat for birds in general, but the Cinderella story of the whooping crane is what will grab the kids.

Whooping cranes are North America's largest birds, with a wingspan of 7 feet; an adult male stands 5 feet high. With the luxurious long legs and throat typical of shore birds, they have especially elegant plumage—solid white, with just a touch of black on the wingtips and around the eyes, like an artful dab of mascara, and a dashing red cap on the top of the head. The cranes migrate some 2,400 miles up to the North-west Territories of Canada in the summer, but they faithfully return here every year from November through April, where they feed on blue crabs, crayfish, frogs, and wolfberries. Beginning in late winter, you may see their distinctive courtship ritual, a dance that includes whooping, wing flapping, head bowing, and leaps into the air.

A 16-mile paved loop road allows you to drive through a variety of habitats at the refuge; get out of the car to climb the 40-foot **observation tower** or to stroll the **boardwalk** that leads through a salt marsh to the coast. Nine short walking trails are laid out, all between .3 and 1.25 miles. Among the species you may see, besides birds, are American alligators, turtles, lizards, javelinas, wild boars, nine-banded armadillos, raccoons, white-tailed deer, and numerous snake species (only a couple of them poisonous). The excellent visitor center has plenty of exhibits; you can rent binoculars here.

To be sure of seeing whooping cranes, book a guided tour, which will cruise the shoreline in a shallow-draft boat past the birds' most popular waters. Call the **Rockport Chamber of Commerce** (⊘ **800/826-6441** or 361/729-6445; www.rockport-fulton.org) for a list of operators. Most of them start out not from the refuge but from a dock in the nearby town of Fulton; tours last 3 to 4 hours.

ⓘ **U.S. Fish and Wildlife Service,** FM 2040 (⊘ **361/286-3559;** http://southwest.fws.gov/refuges).

✈ Corpus Christi, 50 miles.

🛏 $$$ **The Lighthouse Inn,** 200 S. Fulton Beach Rd., Rockport (⊘ **866/790-8439** or 361/790-8439; www.lighthouse texas.com). $$ **Village Inn Motel,** 503 N. Austin St., Rockport (⊘ **361/729-6370**).

BEST TIME: Nov–Apr.

WHY THEY'LL THANK YOU: Hearing them whoop.

---

104 In the Wild

Custer State Park
Bison on the Prairie
All ages • Custer, South Dakota, USA

As the Beatles once sang, somewhere in the black mining hills of Dakota lives young Rocky Raccoon. But Rocky has a lot of company up here: white-tailed deer, pronghorn antelopes, elk, mule deer, mountain goats, burros, coyotes, prairie dogs, eagles, hawks, and an awesome herd of 1,500 American bison. At Custer State Park, kids can see what the Great Plains once looked like, back in the days when bison filled the land as far as the broad horizon.

A smart place to start is the Wildlife Station visitor center in the southeast corner of the park, where exhibits will acquaint the children with the many species they are likely to see. Then turn out and drive on **Wildlife Loop Road,** an 18-mile circuit through open grasslands and pine-clad hills where those species roam. Early morning and evening are the best times, when the animals are most likely to venture close to the road. Drive slowly, or get out of the car and walk quietly down the short nature trails to get a good look. Just west of the center you'll notice a set of corrals where bison are held after the annual late September roundup, which thins the herd and keeps it healthy (the public is invited to watch the cowboys move 'em out).

The landscape is downright startling along **Needles Highway** in the northwest corner, a 14-mile expedition through spruce forests, meadows fringed with birch and quaking aspen, and giant granite spires that thrust up to the sky. Park the car and walk around—there are several marked trails, and these rock formations are fun to explore, with tunnels you can walk through and a unique shape called the "Needle's Eye." From the northeast corner, **Iron Mountain Road** leads to **Mount Rushmore,** sliding through tunnels that frame the four Rushmore sculptures strikingly as you approach.

Just south of Custer State Park, you can explore **Wind Cave National Park** (© **605/745-4600;** www.nps.gov/wica); of the guided tours, the most fun is the 2-hour Candlelight Tour, where you explore a section of the cave where lighting hasn't been installed. If you're a cave lover and it's summertime, though, definitely head west on U.S. 16 to **Jewel Cave National Monument** (© **605/673-2288;** www.nps.gov/jeca), the third-longest cave in the world, with 133 miles of underground passages charted so far. Eroded by stagnant acidic water rather than underground streams, Jewel Cave has narrow, twisting passages whose walls sparkle with calcite crystals and delicate gypsum deposits.

ⓘ **Custer State Park,** U.S. 16A (© **605/ 255-4515;** www.travelsd.com).

✈ Rapid City, 35 miles.

🛏 $$ **Alex Johnson Hotel,** 523 6th St., Rapid City (© **800/888-2539** or 605/ 342-1210; www.alexjohnson.com). $$ **Sylvan Lake Lodge,** S. Dak. 87 & S. Dak. 89 (© **605/574-2561;** www.custerresorts. com).

WHY THEY'LL THANK YOU: Shaggy bison, outnumbering the people.

In the Wild   105

The Wildlife of Half Moon Bay
Nature Fierce, Nature Fragile
Ages 4 & up • Half Moon Bay, California, USA

Surfers know California's crescent-curved Half Moon Bay as a West Coast surfing mecca; during Prohibition, rumrunners knew its Pillar Point Harbor as a choice smuggling spot. But nature lovers know this coastal area an hour south of San Francisco as a haven for rare wildlife—and not just fleeting glimpses, but long, satisfying views. Mother Nature couldn't have set up a better lab to turn kids on to marine biology.

With younger children, **Fitzgerald Marine Reserve** is the ideal choice. Call ahead to find out when the tide is due to ebb, because low tide reveals an amazing variety of coastal critters clinging to the shallow marine shelf. Perch silently near the shore rocks and wait for shy intertidal animals to emerge from this delicately colored, quiet refuge, with beachy scrub and marshland and Monterey cypress trees. You can touch the hermit crabs, limpets, chiton, sea anemones, sponges, sea stars, and starfish, but don't pick them off their rocks; gulls circle overhead, just waiting to swoop down on an unattached mollusk. If you move a rock, replace it seaweed side up so that the tiny creatures in the vegetation won't be crushed.

Wait until the kids are older to visit **Ano Nuevo State Reserve,** where the main attraction is a primal scene of sex, blood, and pain—namely, the annual mating and birthing of the great elephant seals. These 3-ton marine mammals (one look at their pendulous upper lips and you'll know why they're called elephant seals) live on the open sea for 10 months a year, then come ashore in November, females already pregnant, in such numbers that they carpet the beach. One bull seal protects a harem of females as a few bachelors hang hopefully on the fringes. You can only witness this spectacle on a guided walk, which should be reserved months in advance. It's not a sight for the squeamish: Males clash in often-bloody mating battles, females give birth on the dunes, and they mate frankly on the open sands—all redeemed by the tender sight of mother seals cuddling their young. In March, adults swim back to sea, leaving weaned pups to mature; after April, the youngsters leave too and the beaches are open to the public again. In spring and summer, adults occasionally return to the beach to molt; if you're lucky you'll see some then, but it's nothing like the massed bodies of winter.

If you miss the elephant seals, you can still watch smaller California seals sun themselves year-round at **Seal Cove Beach;** in early spring and fall, look for migrating whales from the bluffs above Princeton-by-the-Sea. Birders know to hunt for rare loons, great blue herons, red-tailed hawks, and brown pelicans. Mother Nature sure outdid herself here.

(i) **Fitzgerald Marine Reserve,** California St., Moss Beach (© **650/728-3584**). **Ano Nuevo State Reserve,** New Year's Creek Rd., Hwy. 1, Pescadero (© **800/444-4445** or 650/879-0227).

✈ San Francisco International, 25 miles.

🛏 $$$ **Beach House Inn,** 4100 N. Cabrillo Hwy. (© **800/315-9366** or 650/728-0220; www.beach-house.com). $$$ **Seal Cove Inn,** 221 Cypress Ave. (© **650/728-4114;** www.sealcoveinn. com).

BEST TIME: Breeding season at the Ano Nuevo State Reserve is Dec–Mar.

WHY THEY'LL THANK YOU: The sea stars and the seals.

---

106 In the Wild

El Yunque
Puerto Rico's Rainforest Gem
All ages • Rio Grande, Puerto Rico

My children have been saving the rainforest for years—what American child hasn't been pelted with this eco-message?—but they had never actually seen one. So they willingly gave up another day at the beach in San Juan to drive west of town to the **El Yunque rainforest.** Within seconds of stepping through its gate, we were enveloped in a lushness so profound, we knew at once that all those school recycling projects had been worth it.

Part of the Caribbean National Forest, El Yunque is the only tropical rainforest in the U.S. National Forest system, a 28,000-acre patch of virgin forest that looks pretty much the way it did when Columbus first sighted Puerto Rico back in 1493. We spent a good hour first in the **El Portal Tropical Forest Center,** with its three pavilions setting forth the four separate forest microclimates that compose the park. The best exhibit of all, though, was simply the bridge leading to the center, set high up near the tree canopy, where we got our first close-up views of the forest's lively birds. At last we hit the walking trails through the forest, and by now we knew what to look for on our hike to the waterfalls, and what to listen for—the distinctive coqui peep of the tiny tree frogs that live here in the millions. We could spot orchids blooming in the treetops, and incredibly tall ferns swaying among the tree trunks. We hiked along the quiet sign-posted trail to **La Mina Falls,** which announced itself through the trees as we drew closer, not only by the roar of tumbling water but also by the unmistakable salsa beat of picnicking families with portable sound systems. On this weekend day, every family in the park, it seemed, was at the falls, sitting waist-deep in deliciously cold water on the slippery, potholed rock shelf below the cascades.

The other trail in the park is longer and steeper: the **El Yunque trail,** which winds upward through forests of sierra palm and palo colorado, before descending into the dwarf forest of **Mount Britton,** which is often shrouded in clouds. There are great views here from various peaks, including **Yunque Rock.**

The weather looked overcast when we started out, and at one point a light rain shower began to spatter upon the canopy, barely enough to get us wet. Somehow, that seemed absolutely perfect. After all, what should you expect in a rainforest if not rain?

ⓘ **El Yunque National Forest,** Rte. 191 (ℂ **787/724-8774;** www.fs.fed.us/r8/caribbean).

✈ San Juan International, 40km (25 miles).

🛏 $$ **Comfort Inn,** Calle Clemenceau 6, San Juan (ℂ **800/858-7407** or 787/721-0170; www.comfortinn.com). $$ **Gallery Inn at Galeria San Juan,** Calle Norzagaray 204, Old San Juan (ℂ **787/722-1808;** www.thegalleryinn.com).

WHY THEY'LL THANK YOU: Hearing the coquis.

In the Wild **107**

The Giant Pandas of Wolong
Pandamonium
All ages • Sichuan, China

Sure, it would be the thrill of a lifetime to glimpse a giant panda in the wild—sighting one of these shy black and white bears in its native bamboo jungle would be a major coup. But just in case that never happens, you and your kids can be sure of seeing giant pandas, and lots of them, at this world famous center in the humid mountain forest of Sichuan—and you'll be helping to support panda preservation in the process. There are actually two separate entities here—**Wolong National Nature Reserve** (Wolong Ziran Bahu Qu) and the attached **Giant Panda Breeding Center** (Daxiongmao Siyang Chang).

Only about 1,590 giant pandas are left in the wild; maybe about 10% of them live in Wolong. The Wolong Nature Reserve is a high tech research facility, founded in 1963, where 60 or 70 pandas at a time are housed and fed in small naturalistic enclosures. Visitors can press right up to the glass and gaze transfixed at panda after panda, from newborn to adults; and the kids will get a kick out of shooting photos with tiny cameras disguised as panda babies. Many of the pandas here were taken from captivity or they were injured; they may never be ready to be returned to the wild. But if they are, they move from the small enclosures into a large open forest, where fences keep other animals out. The pandas in that transition area are still being fed, but they hone their other jungle-living skills.

While the breeding center's success rate on moving pandas back to the wild has been spotty, its real contribution lies in research on panda procreation. Pandas reproduce very slowly—often a female will bear only one child in her entire lifetime—and their young often die in infancy. These issues are the biggest factor in the shrinking panda population, more even than poaching or destruction of habitat.

Once you've finished your visit to the breeding center, you'll probably be drawn into the smaller but similar facility next door, devoted to lesser pandas (red pandas). Then head out into the surrounding reserve, an unspoiled beautiful landscape of yew, beech, and bamboo forests with many excellent hiking trails. Panthers, macaques, golden monkeys, red pandas, white lipped deer, wildebeest, takins, and—you guessed it—giant pandas all live here, though they are rarely seen by the hikers.

To make your panda experience complete, wind up with a visit to the **Panda Museum** in the nearby town of Shawan, a good base for visiting the preserve.

The best time to come? Between 8:30 and 10:30am, when the pandas are fed.

ⓘ **Daxiongmao Siyang Chang** (Giant Panda Breeding Center), Hetao Ping (www.pandasinternational.org).

✈ Chengdu.

🛏 $$ **Panda Inn** (Xiongmao Shanzhuang), Heato Ping, next to the breeding station (✆ **86/837/624-3028**). $$ **Shanzhuang** (Wolong Hotel), in the Wolong Nature Reserve (✆ **86/837/624-6888**).

WHY THEY'LL THANK YOU: Panda feeding time.

---

108 **In the Wild**

Booby Pond Nature Reserve
Red-Footed Boobies & Caribbean Pirates
Ages 8 & up • Little Cayman, the Caribbean

Every evening at twilight, the drama begins. A mass of **red-footed boobies** hovers above the Caribbean Sea offshore, eyeing their enemies, the magnificent **frigate birds.** Marauding pirates who love to steal other birds' food, the huge frigates circle hungrily, stretching their pointed black wings nearly 2.4m (8 ft.) wide. They know the boobies have been out over the ocean all day, filling their crops with food to take back to their chicks nested in the mangrove lagoon. Desperately, the boobies gather in large groups. Suddenly they spiral upward in a column, then wheel and dive like torpedoes toward shore. The magnificent frigate birds dart in to attack. Who will win this battle for survival?

This adventure is played out every evening in nesting season on **Little Cayman Island,** an isolated scrap of coral and sand barely 16km (10 miles) long, flung down in the middle of the Caribbean Sea due south of Cuba. About 5,000 pairs of red-footed boobies—the largest colony of this species in the Western hemisphere—nest every year in the saltwater lagoon of the 83-hectare (204-acre) **Booby Pond Nature Reserve** on Little Cayman. February is peak nesting season for the boobies, who perch in the mangroves and forest trees around the pond. The name alone is irresistible—is it even possible to say "red-footed booby" without laughing?—but the kids will be charmed by these water birds

An inhabitant of the Booby Pond Nature Reserve.

with their strange guttural screeches. The smallest species of booby, they're still good-sized birds, with a wingspan of nearly 1.5m (5 ft.). Adults are either buff-colored or white with dark wingtips and, of course, unmistakably bright red feet.

Take your place on the lookout platforms built around the edges of the pond to witness this twilight battle; there are also telescopes on the veranda of the visitor center, a traditional Caymanian gingerbread bungalow. During the day, other water birds visit the pond as well. Let the kids explore the drylands adjacent to the pond, too, where they may see 1.5m-long (5-ft.) **rock iguanas,** the largest population of these spiny gray-brown lizards in the Caribbean.

ⓘ **Booby Pond Nature Reserve** (www.nationaltrust.org.ky/info/boobypond.html).

✈ Grand Cayman, charter from there to Little Cayman.

🛏 $$$ **The Anchorage,** Seven Mile Beach, Grand Cayman (✆ **800/433-3483** or 345/945-4088; www.theanchoragecayman.com). $$$ **Pirates Point Resort,** Preston Bay, Little Cayman (✆ **345/948-1010;** www.piratespointresort.com).

WHY THEY'LL THANK YOU: The sunset battle.

Sea Turtles on the Costa Rican Coast

Ages 8 & up • Tortuguero, Costa Rica

Christopher Columbus first set foot on this Caribbean shore in 1502, on his fourth and final voyage to the Americas, and promptly named the place Costa Rica, or "Rich Coast." Looking at its dense green jungle, you'll know what he was talking about. Even today, this undeveloped region's greatest richness is its wildlife; nature lovers and ecotourists continue to arrive in ever-greater numbers. And perhaps the most sought-after wildlife experience in Costa Rica is watching giant sea turtles come ashore to lay their eggs.

The top turtle-nesting beach on the Caribbean coast is isolated **Tortuguero**—the very name refers to sea turtles, or *tortugas* in Spanish. It's quite an adventure to get to Tortuguero, which has no roads, only a labyrinthine series of rivers and canals linking it to the port city of Limón, 50 miles away. Gliding on a boat through this dense rainforest populated by howler and spider monkeys, three-toed sloths, toucans, and great green macaws is almost like a minicruise up the Amazon. A number of lodges perch on the hills around the village of Tortuguero; generally visitors book a **package** from a lodge that includes rooms, meals, a boat trip from Limón, a bus from San José, and a guided 2- to 4-hour nighttime visit to the beach to watch sea turtles (the only way

A sea turtle heads for the water in Costa Rica.

the giant leatherback. Considering its great size (up to 2m/6½ ft. long and weighing as much as 454kg/1,000 lb.), the giant leatherback is truly a spectacular turtle to see if you get the chance (Mar–May), but it's more likely that you will spot green turtles. Although they're an endangered species, they arrive in Tortuguero by the thousands during their prime nesting period, July through mid-October. The small **Caribbean Conservation Corporation Visitor Center** in the village has detailed exhibits on local flora and fauna, especially the sea turtles.

(i) **Caribbean Conservation Corporation** (📞 **800/678-7853;** www.cccturtle.org).

✈ San José, 249km (155 miles).

🛏 $$ **Pachira Lodge** (📞 **506/256-7080;** www.pachiralodge.com). $$$ **Tortuga Lodge** (📞 **506/257-0766** in San José, or 📞 506/710-8016 in Tortuguero; www.costaricaexpeditions.com).

WHY THEY'LL THANK YOU: The cycle of life renews itself.

you can get on the beach at night). Four species of turtles nest on this desolate 35km-long (22-mile) stretch of black sand—the green turtle, the hawksbill, the loggerhead, and the world's largest turtle,

---

110 In the Wild

The Galápagos
Nature's Laboratory
Ages 8 & up • Galapagos Islands

The denizens of the **Galápagos Islands** must be the world's most trusting wildlife—and why not, because they've never had to worry about predators? On the Galápagos, you don't have to creep silently behind a bush to observe wildlife: Young sea lions will show off their best moves as you snorkel among them, mockingbirds will peck at your shoelaces, and the blue-footed boobie will perform its famous two-stepped mating dance right under your nose. It isn't easy to get here, nor is it cheap, but it is definitely the wildlife-viewing experience of a lifetime.

An astounding number of unique species thrive on this isolated equatorial Pacific archipelago of 19 small volcanic islands (plus about 40 islets), a fact that led English scientist Charles Darwin—who visited in 1835 as ship's doctor on the *Beagle*—to develop his 1859 theory of evolution. The Galápagos have been famous ever since, though their extreme location discourages mass tourism. That's a good thing. Most of the islands are protected as a national park, and the number of visitors is strictly limited; so you won't battle crowds. There's still a **Darwin**

Sea lions on the Galápagos.

Research Station in Puerto Ayora (© 05/526146) on Santa Cruz, the most populated island, where you can get an up-close view of the gentle giant tortoises that have captured public imagination ever since Darwin first wrote about them. But to see the astonishing variety of rare species that thrive on these islands, you'll need to get on a boat. A **cruise** to the Galápagos is an excellent option—departing from Guayaquil, you'll sleep and dine on the cruise boat and take small dinghies to the islands by day for naturalist-led hikes, climbs, kayak trips, or snorkel outings to the best wildlife viewing spots. (This is definitely an active vacation!) Otherwise, base yourselves on Santa Cruz and book day trips to various islands.

When choosing your itinerary, consider the following islands: Santa Cruz for the tortoises; Santiago, its rocky tide pools home to rare fur sea lions and many beautiful heron species; Española, home to albatrosses and blue-footed boobies; Fernandina, with its vivid marine iguanas and flightless cormorants; Isabela, where Galápagos penguins (the world's only tropical penguins) can be found in underwater caves; Genovesa, where frigate birds puff up their red necks to attract mates and red-footed boobies nest in the mangroves; or San Cristobal, where sandy Cerro Brujo beach is a good place to cavort with California sea lions, red crabs, and lava gulls.

ⓘ **Ecuador Tourist Board,** (© 800/328-2367 in the U.S. and Canada; © 800/328-2659 for international and local; www.tourism@equadortouristboard.com).

✈ Baltra, near Santa Cruz Island.

🛏 $$ **Finch Bay Hotel,** Punta Estrada, Santa Cruz Island (© 593/2/298-8200; www.finchbayhotel.com). $$$ **Royal Palm Hotel,** Via Baltra, Km 18, Santa Cruz Island (© 800/528-6069 in the U.S., or 593/5252-7408; www.royalpalmhotel.net).

CRUISE OPERATORS: $$$ **Ecoventura,** 6404 Blue Lagoon Dr., Miami (© 800/633-7972; www.ecoventura.com/home.aspx). $$$ **KLEIN Tours,** Av. Eloy Alfaro and Caralina Aldaz, Quito, Ecuador (© 888/50-KLEIN in the U.S.; www.kleintours.com).

WHY THEY'LL THANK YOU: Seeing the world as Darwin did.

Monarchs of Michoacán

Ages 10 & up • Near Angangueo & Ocampo, Mexico

High in the mountains of northeast Michoacán, you're hiking up a mountain, no doubt fighting for breath in this altitude. Then you arrive in a grove of fir trees—and whatever breath you had left is truly snatched away. It's as if you had stepped into a kaleidoscope, with fragments of obsidian and gold flitting randomly around you. The branches on all sides sway under the weight of *butterflies*, massed millions of **monarch butterflies,** their gossamer wings whispering softly as the wind blows through the forest. This is what you came here to see—but the vision is so much more astonishing than you expected.

The monarchs have been coming here since time immemorial; the ancient Aztecs revered these poisonous black-and-orange butterflies, which they believed were the reborn spirits of fallen warriors, dressed in battle colors. There are actually seven monarch nesting grounds in Michoacán (nesting season lasts from mid-Nov to Mar). Only two, however, are open to the public: **El Rosario** and **Chincua,** both reachable by day trip from the graceful Colonial-era city of Morelia, which is about halfway between Mexico City and Guadalajara. Save the trip for a sunny day if you can—the effect is most dazzling with the benefit of a little sunshine.

It is possible for you to visit the sanctuaries on your own, but a licensed English-speaking guide is a worthwhile investment—they can answer the kids' scientific questions, transport you reliably over the back roads to the sanctuary, and steer you right to the nucleus of the butterfly colony, which constantly shifts around the mountain throughout the season. Guided butterfly excursions take 10 to 12 hours and usually provide lunch. While it varies, the hike through the mountain forest will probably take around an hour each way; it's often a steep walk, so wear sturdy shoes. One option at Chincua is to ride up on **horseback;** a local handler will lead the horse for you (facilities for renting are at the sanctuary gate). English-speaking guides can be contacted through a cooperative called **Mex Mich Guías** (www.mmg. com.mx).

ⓘ **Michoacán** (www.michoacan-travel. com).

✈ Morelia.

🛏 $$ **Best Western Hotel Casino,** Portal Hidalgo 229, Morelia (ℂ **52/ 443/3131-328;** www.hotelcasino.com. mx). $$$ **Villa Montaña,** Patzimba 201, Col. Vista Bella, Morelia (ℂ **52/443/314-0231;** www.villamontana.com.mx).

WHY THEY'LL THANK YOU: That dazzling grove.

---

112 **In the Wild**

The Cape Town Colony
March of the African Penguins
Ages 4 & up • Cape Town, South Africa

It began with two African penguins, who showed up unexpectedly in 1985 on Foxy Beach, just south of Cape Town. They seemed unfazed by the human population close at hand; what they liked was the cluster of large granite boulders sheltering several tiny bays, where they could dig protected burrows in the sand and lay their eggs. The next year, a few more joined them, then more the next year. By now, there are over 2,500 African penguins in the breeding colony at the **Boulder Coastal Park,** which has been turned into a penguin reserve. With commercial fishing banned from False Bay, the nearby waters have plentiful fish for the penguins to eat. Still unfazed by the presence of humans, the penguins call the beach their own, but they'll let you share it with them. Heck, they'll even let you swim in "their" waters.

It's an experience not to be missed. African penguins return year after year to this haven, where they breed and nest from March through August. (Remember, in South Africa, that Aug is winter, though

The penguins at Boulder Coastal Park.

A fence keeps humans away from the penguins' nesting area, but the penguins go wherever they like, including onto the adjoining public beach. The time to come is the late afternoon, when the seabirds have finished their day of ocean fish catching and return home to disgorge partially digested fish (yum, yum) into the mouths of their chicks. If you're out in the water, you can feel them whiz right past you, swimming at speeds up to 24kmph (15 mph). After watching how awkwardly they waddle on land, it's amazing to sense their grace and power in the sea. Having finished their day's business, they may bask on the beach right near you, but cute as they look, don't let your kids chase the penguins. They have a right to be left alone—it's their beach, after all.

it never gets all that cold.) You can view them from a raised boardwalk overlooking Foxy Beach, observing their comical interactions as they defend their tiny bits of territory on the crowded rocks. Depending on the time of year you're there, you may be able to spot eggs in nests, tucked beneath beach vegetation or buried in the sand, or you'll see newly hatched chicks, still covered with fluffy gray down. Older penguin babies have blue-gray backs and white stomachs, in contrast to the adults' black and white with a black stripe across their chests. Even the tallest adults are only about 50cm (20 in.) tall.

ⓘ **Simon's Town** (ⓒ **27/21/701-8692**; www.cpnp.co.za).

✈ Cape Town International.

🛏 $$ **British Hotel Apartments,** 90 St. George's St., Simon's Town (ⓒ **27/21/786-2214**; www.britishhotelapartments.co.za). $$ **De Waterkant Village,** 1 Loader St., De Waterkant (ⓒ **27/21/437-9707**; www.dewaterkant.com).

WHY THEY'LL THANK YOU: Feeling the whoosh of a penguin's depth-dive.

In the Wild **113**

On Safari in Kruger National Park
Nature Red in Tooth & Claw
Ages 10 & up • Mpumaplanga, South Africa

Safari veterans boast of seeing the Big Five: lion, leopard, rhino, elephant, and buffalo. The kids will certainly have something to brag about at school after you visit vast **Kruger National Park** in South Africa, where many safari-goers spot four of the Big Five in 1 day (leopards are the most elusive). But going into the African bush is about so much more than spotting big game: Take a few days to explore this land, sensing the rhythms of its day from the first hungry stirrings to midday naps to twilight watering stops to nocturnal skitters and rustles. The graceful gallop of an antelope, the scuttling of a beetle, the wheeling flap of a heron (or vulture!), all have their own fascination once you're attuned to the African savanna.

Even from the safety of a Jeep, seeing a lion on Safari in Kruger is a thrill.

Kruger covers 2.5 million hectares (6.2 million acres) from the Crocodile River in the north to the Limpopo River in the south, encompassing 16 distinct eco-zones—though as you drive through, it may all look the same, a rolling plain covered with a large shrublike tree called mopani. You can drive the park roads by yourself—driving slowly, peering for animals that blend into the landscape, waiting patiently at the rivers and water holes that attract wildlife—but you're only allowed to get out at designated rest stops. Binoculars and cameras are a must. To increase your number of sightings, also book at least one **guided game drive,** led by experienced rangers in vehicles that seat from 10 to 46 people; the sunrise and early-morning drives usually offer the most animal encounters. It's surprising how close you may be able to get to the animals, who apparently don't associate the smell of gasoline with humans. To let the kids get a more intimate feel for the bush environment, also book a morning walk, a 3- to 4-hour tramp where you won't see as much big game (in fact you'll hope you don't encounter anything too aggressive) but you will get closer to the trees, insects, and small animals, all part of the circle of life. Guided drives and walks are booked directly from rest camps, the lodgings offered within the park, which are hardly swanky—often tents or round thatched huts—but have an authentic safari flavor to them.

Flanking the park, there are also several private game reserves, wildly expensive once-in-a-lifetime experiences where you'll stay in luxury lodges, dine on gourmet cuisine, and be driven off-road in a Jeep by your own expert tracker and ranger. Many of them won't even accept children under 12; two child-friendly options are **Umlani Bushcamp** (www.umlani.com) and **Sabi Sabi,** P.O. Box 52665, Saxonwold 2132 (✆ **27/11/447-7172;** www.sabisabi.com).

✈ Kruger-Mpumaplanga International (near Hazyview). Eastgate (near Hoedspruit). Kruger Park Gateway (at Phalaborwa).

🛏 **Olifants** and **Lower Sabie** rest camps, apply through **South African National Parks,** P.O. Box 787, 643 Leyds St., Muckleneuk, Pretoria (✆ **27/12/426-5000;** www.sanparks.org).

WHY THEY'LL THANK YOU: The drama of the watering hole at sunset.

Foula
Scotland's Bird Island
Ages 8 & up • Shetland Islands, Scotland

In local dialect, foula means "bird island"—and no name could be more fitting. **Foula** is tiny—only 5km wide by 8km long (3×5 miles)—and geologically rugged, with five high peaks and towering sea cliffs, one of them Britain's second-highest cliff face, the Kame, 372m (1,220 ft.) high. Mostly treeless moors and marshes, it looks inhospitable, despite a profusion of wildflowers in midsummer. But it's exactly the sort of place you'd want to live if you were a **great skua,** and not surprisingly about 3,000 pairs of them, the world's largest colony, nest here on the sheer face of the Kame. Locally known as "bonxie," these fierce seagulls are the mortal enemies of Arctic skuas, perennially fighting them for territory. The rock-climbing prowess of locals who go in search of gulls' eggs is the stuff of Shetland legend.

Foula isn't all about skuas; uncountable numbers of other birds haunt the isle too: kittiwakes, puffins, guillemots, razorbills, gannets, and red-throated divers, as well as grey heron, whooper swans, kestrels, golden eagles, ravens . . . the list goes on and on. Grey seals cavort onshore; killer whales swim offshore, and harbor porpoises playfully follow the ferryboat. Shetland ponies and the hardy local sheep roam freely on the bleak moors.

Sheep vastly outnumber humans on Foula; the population hovers at around 40 people, most of them crofters. With an instinct for survival, they built their own airstrip in the 1970s so that they wouldn't be dependent on the ferry anymore. Until the beginning of the 19th century, Old Norse was the language spoken, for although long-ago politics made the islands Scottish territory, they are much closer in spirit to Scandinavia.

Scotland's Shetland Islands are remote already—even the Orkneys are closer to the mainland. But once you've taken a plane or car ferry from Aberdeen to the main Shetland island—called, of course, Mainland—you'll have to take another plane or the weekly mail boat to far-flung Foula, 43km (27 miles) west of Mainland. Your best bet for visiting Foula may be on a daylong trip with **Cycharters Ltd.** (© **44/1595/693434**), which cruises past the bird cliffs so you can view them from the water. But if you're passionate about birds, this is a trip well worth the effort.

ⓘ **Visit Shetland** (www.visitshetland.com).

✈ Foula has 3 flights a week, summer months only, from Sumburgh airport on Mainland.

🛏 Contact Mrs. Marion Taylor, Leraback, Foula (© **44/1595/753226**).

WHY THEY'LL THANK YOU: Totally for the birds.

Vestmannaeyjar's Great Puffin Rescue

Ages 6 & up • Heimaey, Vestmannaeyjar, Iceland

Every August in the Westmann Islands off the south coast of Iceland, a peculiar ritual takes place. After a summer of midnight sun, darkness is just beginning to return to the nighttime skies. And up on the sea cliffs, adult members of the world's largest Atlantic puffin colony—who have been dutifully feeding their babies tucked away in clifftop burrows—suddenly stop bringing food. The curious young pufflings poke their colorful curved beaks and white faces out of their holes. Gathering the strength in their black wings, these penguinlike seabirds take to the skies to begin feeding themselves. Though they have never seen the night before, they instinctively know how to fly in the dark, navigating by the moon.

And then they soar over Heimaey, the largest town in the Westman Islands. Confused by the city lights, the young birds get thrown off course. They waver; they crash into buildings. They fall to the pavement, stunned.

That's when the children of Heimaey jump into action. Allowed to stay up late in August just for this rescue work, they gently scoop up the dazed pufflings—chubby little creatures not quite 25cm (10 in.) tall, with webbed red feet—and carry them home in cardboard boxes to watch over them. Some kids may rescue as many as 10 a night. In the morning, they gather at the sea's edge, lift up the pufflings' glossy bodies, and fling them into the sky. Recovered, the pufflings flap their wings and head out over the open sea, where they will live for the next 2 years. Come here in August and your children can join in this thrilling rescue, a night they'll never forget.

From April through August, some 8 to 10 million puffins—60% of the world's total of this species—nest in the rugged volcanic Westmann Islands (in Icelandic, Vestmannaeyjar); the rest of the year they live out on the open ocean. On a 90-minute boat tour around Heimaey Island conducted by **Viking Tours** (© **354/488-4884;** www.boattours.is), you can study the puffin-inhabited cliffs through binoculars, watching the adult puffins (who mate for life and use the same burrows year after year) disgorge fish from their thick multicolored beaks to feed their young.

In town, also visit the local **Natural History Museum,** Heiðarvegur 12 (© **354/481-1997**), which has a fascinating little aquarium and several exhibits about the local seabirds. Just don't point out to the kids that the menus of local restaurants often feature a tasty dish called *lundi*—the Icelandic word for "puffin."

ⓘ www.icetourist.is.

✈ Heimaey.

🛏 $$ **Hotel Eyjar,** Bárustíg 2 (© **354/481-3636** or 354/895-8350; www.hotel eyjar.eyjar.is).

WHY THEY'LL THANK YOU: The rescue mission.

7 Fantastic Aquariums

Public aquariums are a wonderful place for kids to learn, and many provide educational opportunities for young visitors. Although learning is the aim, kids will also take away the memory of coming nose to nose with a toothy shark or some fanciful creature that will delight and awe. Most major cities have aquariums, so it's easy to make this a highlight of your family trip. Here are seven outstanding choices:

116 The New England Aquarium, Boston   Kids will marvel at the New England Aquarium's centerpiece, a four-story, **200,000-gallon Giant Ocean Tank.** A spiral ramp encircles the tank, which contains a replica of a **Caribbean coral reef,** its tropical colors glowing like neon in the low light of the aquarium's cool interior. An assortment of sea creatures coexists amazingly well in the tank. Part of the reason for that might be that scuba divers subvert the food chain by **feeding the sharks** twice a day. Your kids will want to press their noses against the glass to see the divers doing this as sea turtles glide by. See Boston Commons **59**, Lexington & Concord **219**, *Old Ironsides* **239**, Black Heritage Trail **266**, Orchard House **380**, and Fenway Park **453**. *Central Wharf.* © **617/973-5200;** *www. neaq.org.*

117 Shedd Aquarium, Chicago   The setting is magnificent to start with—a Beaux Arts–style marble octagon right on the shore of Lake Michigan. But the Shedd is enormous, and in this case size does matter. Thousands of fish, reptiles, amphibians, and marine mammals inhabit this lakeside palace, all gorgeously displayed. The centerpiece is a **90,000-gallon circular tank** in the central rotunda, where vividly colored fish, sharks, and stingrays swirl in an immense replica of a coral reef. An underwater camera and audio system pipe close-up views and sound effects out to eager crowds. See Field Museum **274**, Museum of Science and Industry **277**, the Art Institute of Chicago **341**, and Wrigley Field **454**. *1200 South Lake Shore Dr.* © **312/939-2438;** *www.sheddaquarium.org.*

118 The Georgia Aquarium, Atlanta   The world's largest aquarium is cleverly divided into galleries that represent marine environments as varied as cold ocean waters to warm coral reefs. Here, it's possible to travel through representations of all the regions of the world in a single afternoon. The **Kids Corner** offers a variety of fun activities that children can enjoy on-site or after their visit. Strategically placed webcams allow kids to get a close up view of the aquarium's many residents, including sharks and manta rays. A highlight is its popular **Beluga Whale Webcam.** See Stone Mountain National Park **72** and Dr. King's Legacy **268**. *225 Baker St. NW.* © **404/581-4000;** *www.georgiaaquarium.org.*

119 Monterey Bay Aquarium, Monterey   Yes, it's huge, with more than 350,000 marine animals and plants on display, and it has two truly awesome big tanks—the million-gallon **Outer Bay tank,** populated by yellowfin tuna, large green sea turtles, barracuda, sharks, giant ocean sunfish, and schools of bonito; and the three-story **Kelp Forest** with its stunning view of leopard sharks and other sea creatures. But what is truly striking is how this facility's displays highlight the sheer beauty of sea creatures—the feathery flutter of jellyfish, the supple grace of rays, the quicksilver flash of anchovies, sardines, and mackerel swimming in massive schools (www.monterybayaquarium. com). *886 Cannery Row. © **831/648-4800**; www.monterey bayaquarium.org.*

Jellies at the Monterey Bay Aquarium.

⑫ Vancouver Aquarium, Vancouver This aquarium has been designed to be as hands-on as possible for children; rocklike stoops are provided for small folks to get a better view into fish tanks. Regal angelfish glide through a re-creation of an **Indonesian coral reef;** blacktip sharks scour the waters of the **Tropical Gallery.** The **Pacific Canada** exhibit is dedicated to indigenous sea life. The stroll-through **Amazon Gallery** is another standout. On the outside terrace, kids can delight at the antics of seals, sea otters, and beluga whales. *845 Avison Way. © **604/659-3474**; www.vanaqua.org.*

⑫ Sydney Aquarium, Sydney For kids, it's a no-brainer: Any child who's seen *Finding Nemo* knows that Sydney Harbour is an important place for fish. Still, this aquarium is even better than you'd expect. The route through its exhibits deals with four native Australian aquatic habitats, and right away, in the **Southern Rivers rooms,** the kids will see something truly exotic—what may be their first **platypus.** Perhaps the most appealing part of the aquarium is the display of perky little **fairy penguins** and the huge walk-through tank of big-eyed **fur seals** and **sea lions,** cavorting all around you. See Sydney Harbour Bridge �97 and Powerhouse Museum ㉘. *Aquarium Pier (right next to Sydney Wildlife World). © **61/2/8251-7800**; www.sydneyaquarium.com.au.*

A fairy penguin at the Sydney Aquarium.

⑫ Kaiyukan Aquarium, Osaka If the word "aquarium" simply means tank full of fish, then Osaka's immense waterfront attraction needs another name. After entering through a dramatic **glass tunnel** where colorful fish swim all around you, you are treated to videos of erupting volcanoes and begin a journey down a spiraling corridor into a **Japanese forest.** As you pass through the habitats along the spiral, pieces begin to fit together. The entire Pacific Rim is encircled by volcanic activity, a so-called "Ring of Fire." But along with the Ring of Fire comes a Ring of Life. Your kids will love gazing into all 14 different **Pacific Rim habitats,** which include mammals as well as sea life. *1-1-10 Kaigan-dori. © **81-6-6576-5501**; www.kaiyukan.com.*

Stewart Island, New Zealand

Ages 8 & up • Stewart Island, New Zealand

New Zealanders lover their national bird, the kiwi; they even proudly refer to themselves as "kiwis" from time to time. So where do you go to see these funny flightless brown birds? The premier place is New Zealand's third-largest island, lying just south of the South Island, which provides a haven for this beloved dwindling species. The island offers refuge from predators that populate the mainland, and because it is practically deserted, (only 1% of it is inhabited) visitors are afforded an opportunity to see the birds in their natural habitat. **Stewart Island** is just across a narrow straight from South Island, with a wonderful temperate climate and so much wildlife that you won't believe it.

Hiking, kayaking, and diving are the main forms of entertainment on this rough and ready island, and there is plenty of wildlife to enjoy here, including outstanding bird-watching. With so much natural habitat, you can easily view uniquely New Zealand species such as the kaka, tui, weka, kereru, and korimako. Frequent sightings of the famously shy kiwi are the icing on the cake. All it takes is a little extra effort, like booking a nighttime kiwi-spotting boat tour with **Bravo Adventure Cruises** (© **64/3/219-1144**). Though kiwis are not always a nocturnal species, they have often become so to avoid predators. Taking only 15 passengers at a time, so as to not spook the kiwis, these 3-hour tours involve prowling the length of the remote **Ocean Beach** with flashlights. The plump, spiky feathered kiwis can be found poking around the washed-up kelp, sniffing out food like sand hopper, with the nostrils located at the end of their long pointed beaks. Darting and skittering in their ungainly, comical way, the kiwis take a little patience to see, but they're worth it.

Technically, Stewart Island's kiwi is its own species, slightly different from the spotted kiwis and the brown kiwis found on the North and South islands; the Stewart Island kiwi has larger legs, a longer beak, and slightly lighter colored plumage. Kiwis on these islands are threatened by human settlement and predators, making Stewart Island a veritable haven.

Hikers in your group can enjoy 155 miles of walking tracks, including tramps that can take 10 or 20 minutes to 3-day treks, where you can rest at the end of the day at a hut along the course. Experienced guides provide background and island history. Shorter walks may be more suitable if you are traveling with younger children and there are a few that are sure to delight the entire family, including a 10-minute hike through a fuchsia forest to **Maori Beach,** which offers birds, bush, and beaches.

ⓘ **The Stewart Island Visitor and Information Centre,** 12 Elgin Terrace © **64/3/219-1400;** www.stewartisland. co.nz).

✈ Stewart Island (service from Invercargill, South Island).

🛏 $$$ **Port of Call,** Leask Bay Rd. (© **64/3/219-1394;** www.portofcall.co. nz). $ **South Sea Hotel,** Elgin Terrace, Oban (© **64/3/219-1059;** www.stewart-island.co.nz).

WHY THEY'LL THANK YOU: Glimpsing the elusive kiwi.

Dolphin Discovery Centre
A Dolphin Float in West Australia
Ages 6 & up • Bunbury, Australia

Just 2¹/₂ hours down the scenic Old Coast Road from Perth is one of Australia's best-kept secrets: a bay where wild dolphins cruise into shallow waters to hang out with humans. No, this isn't the much-more-famous Monkey Mia Resort, which is a full day's drive north of Perth on the semideserted northwest coast. Dolphins swim to shore there, too, but there are often busloads of tourists waiting for them, strictly supervised and lined up like statues on the beach. At the **Dolphin Discovery Centre,** however, there's usually just a small and laid-back gang of visitors, who get to wade into the water and actually float with the dolphins.

There is a catch: Those sleek gray bottlenose dolphins only show up at Bunbury about two-thirds of the time (at Monkey Mia they show up pretty much every day). However, I think it's worth the gamble to get a less crowded, more natural interaction with these fascinating cetaceans. Mornings are prime time for encountering dolphins, and they visit much more often in the summers (Nov–Apr, this being the Southern Hemisphere), less often in winter. An "interaction zone" has been marked off on the flat sandy beach in front of the discovery center, which has a cafe and a good little eco-display on the life cycle of the dolphin. (There are loggerhead turtles in the aquariums here, too.) The water is only waist-deep, so even young children can touch bottom. Volunteer guides in red shirts stand out in the water with you to make sure everybody is safe and respectful.

Just to make sure the kids aren't too let down if the dolphins don't show, also book a 90-minute dolphin-watch cruise from **Naturaliste Charters** (✆ **61/1300/361-351** or 61/8/9755-2276; no children under 4 years old). After all, there are about a hundred bottlenoses living in Koombana Bay, so once you get farther out from shore, your chances of at least seeing dolphins is high. From November to April, the center runs 2-hour boat tours out into the deeper waters for stronger swimmers (ages 8 and over) to swim around near the dolphins. If they won't come to us, we'll go to them.

ⓘ Koombana Dr. (✆ **61/8/9791-3088;** www.dolphindiscovery.com.au).

✈ Perth, 241km (150 miles).

🛏 $$ **Abbey Beach Resort,** Busselton (✆ **61/8/9755-4600;** www.abbeybeach. com.au). $$ **Sanctuary Golf Resort,** Old Coast Rd., Bunbury (✆ **61/8/9725-2777;** www.sanctuaryresort.com.au).

WHY THEY'LL THANK YOU: Dolphins whooshing past you.

7 Great Zoos

Almost all kids are nuts for animals, whether cuddly or savage, and a zoo lets them see several species in one day, with a little education snuck in. Most major zoos have a headliner species, such as giant pandas or gorillas, but don't expect kids to stay focused on one species; they may go home with a new favorite.

125 The San Diego Zoo, California For most people, the highlight of this zoo is seeing the **giant pandas,** but it's also known for its vast array of species, including such rarities as the **Buerger's tree kangaroos** of New Guinea, **long billed kiwis** from New Zealand, **Przewalski's horses** from Mongolia, **lowland gorillas** from Africa, and **giant tortoises** from the Galapagos, all in naturalistic settings. In fact, the San Diego Zoo is the first zoo in the U.S. to separate animals from humans with moats instead of bars, and has long been active in conservation efforts around the world as well as breeding programs for endangered species, including those beguiling black and white bears. See Old Town State Historic Park **248**, California Mission Trail **249**. *2920 Zoo Drive.*

A giant panda at the San Diego Zoo.

619/ 231-1515; www.sandiegozoo.org.

126 The Cincinnati Zoo, Ohio While most major zoos are active in conservation efforts, the Cincinnati Zoo is the one that really gets the point across to kids. Every one of its exhibits demonstrates the delicate balance of an ecosphere, the entwined roles of predator and prey, and the interplay between plant and animal life. An old Taj Mahal–inspired **elephant house** has been redesigned to show how dwindling habitats can effect supersized species such as the **Asian elephant,** the **giraffe,** and the **okapi.** One of the most popular parts of the children's zoo is the nursery, where kids crowd around to see the newest **zoo babies** being hand fed by the zoo staff. See National Underground Railroad Freedom Center **267**. *3400 Vine St.* *513/281-4700; www.cincinnatizoo.org.*

127 The Bronx Zoo, New York The Big Kahuna of New York City's wildlife parks, the 265-acre Bronx Zoo is home to more than 4,000 animals from **Siberian tigers** and **snow lions** to its star attractions living in the **Congo Gorilla Forest** and the **Butterfly Zone**—both of them fascinating. As befits its status as flagship zoo of the Wildlife Conservation Society, the exhibits are extremely humane, outdoors if possible, in large environments re-creating the species' native habitats. This does mean that there are often long walks between exhibits, but strollers are available. Don't miss the narrated **Bengali Express** monorail, which somehow convinces children that they've taken a 20-minute trip to the wilds of West Asia. See Howe Caverns & Secret Caverns **88**, Brooklyn Bridge **95**, Statue of Liberty & Ellis Island **252**, and Metropolitan Museum of Art **340**. *2300 Southern Blvd.* *718/220-5100; www.bronxzoo.com.*

128 Toronto Zoo, Canada You want big? Then come to the zoo in Toronto that meanders over more than 287 hectares (709 acres). Opened in 1974, the zoo never had to shoehorn naturalistic environments designed for cages and pens. Animals here have room to roam, and over 5,000 animals live here. Popular exhibits include **The African Savanna,** the **Gorilla Forest,** the **Grizzly Bear Trail,** and the **Australasia section** featuring **kangaroo, kookaburra, Komodo dragon, wombat wallaby,** and **emu.** Another thing that makes the zoo special is the **kid's zone,** which is divided into biomes—the prairie and a wetland—and ends up at a kids-only **water park.** See CN Tower ③⓪ and the International Hockey Hall of Fame ④⑥③. *361 Old Finch Ave.* ✆ *416/392-5929; www.torontozoo.com.*

Two gorillas at the Toronto Zoo.

⑫⑨ **Berlin Zoo, Germany** Like most of East Germany, the Berlin Zoo has a phoenixlike history, all about rising from the ashes of World War II and the post-war division. It's Germany's oldest zoo, dating from 1844, and you distinctly feel that you are in an old world–style zoo, not a simulated safari or jungle. Many historic animal buildings have been retained, their varied architectural styles giving the impression of embarking on a round-the-world journey. The zoo is home to 1,500 species, grouped by species similarities rather than the more usual choice of ecosystem niches, so you'll see a **North American wolf** next to **African wild dogs** and **American bison** next to **Asian buffalos.** See Jewish Museum Berlin ②③① and Berlin Wall ②③④. ✆ *49/30/25 40 10; www.zoo-berlin.de/en.html.*

⑬⓪ **Schonbrunn Zoo, Austria** The world's oldest zoo is a sweet little gem set in the formal gardens of **Schonbrunn Palace.** This was the summer palace during the reign of Empress Maria Theresia; in 1752 her husband set up a royal menagerie where Maria Theresia liked to have breakfast with her children. It had become sadly behind the times before it was taken over by new management. Recently redesigned, it is now home to 700 species and boasts naturalistic environments, breeding programs, and ecosystem displays. Perhaps the most impressive of the exhibits is the **Borneo rainforest** where there's a periodic stage-set storm complete with pelting rain, thunder, lightning, and fog. See Summer Bobsledding in the Austrian Alps ④⑦⑥. *Maxingstrasse 13 B.* ✆ *43/1/877-92-94; www.zoovienna.at/e/index.html.*

⑬① **The London Zoo, England** The world's first scientific zoo was founded in 1826, primarily as a laboratory for study and conservation efforts, attracting visitors like Charles Darwin, who was especially taken with the zoo's orangutan, the first ever seen in Europe. It was opened to the public a few years later and now occupies 36 acres of Royal Park, just two miles from the center of London. The zoo features modern naturalistic environments, and its innovative **children's zoo** includes **treetop walkways** and **underground tunnels,** making it a dynamic **interactive experience** the kids won't forget. See Hyde Park ⑤⑤, Madame Tussaud's & the London Dungeon ⑧②, the British Museum ①⑦⑥, the Imperial War Museum ②②⑦, the *Golden Hinde* ②③⑥, the Science & Natural History Museums ②⑧①, Greenwich ②⑨⑦, Shakespeare's Globe Theatre ③⑤②, Hampton Court ③⑥⓪, Wimbledon ④⑥⑧, and the London Eye ④⑧⑤. *Regent's Park.* ✆ *44/20/7722-3333; www.zsl.org.*

WALK WITH THE ANIMALS

Kangaroo Island
Unspoiled Australian Ecosystem
All ages • South Australia

When kids think of Australia, what do they think of? Koalas and kangaroos. And sure, they're on display at wildlife parks and attractions all over Oz. But if you really want to see these iconic Australian marsupials in the wild, there's no place better than **Kangaroo Island,** just across the strait from Adelaide. Spend a few days here with the right guide and you can walk among sea lions, spot playful New Zealand fur seals, creep through the bush on the trail of wallabies or kangaroos, pick out clumps of koalas hanging sleepily on branches overhead—the list goes on and on.

Kangaroo Island has somehow managed to preserve its unique Australian ecosystem. No foxes or rabbits were ever introduced to prey on the native inhabitants; the island was also never colonized by the dingo (Australia's "native" dog, which probably was introduced from Asia some 4,000 years ago). About one-third of the island is unspoiled national park, with most of the rest devoted to sheep farms. Of the many preserves on the island, kids will score the most wildlife sightings at **Flinders Chase National Park** on the western end of the island. Birders have recorded at least 243 species here; koalas are so common they're almost falling out of the trees (in fact, the government has had to take steps to reduce the koala population). Kangaroos, wallabies, and brush-tailed possums are so tame and numerous that a barrier was erected around the Rocky River Campground to stop them from carrying away picnickers' sandwiches. Platypuses have been seen, too, but they're elusive—you might need to wait next to a stream in the dark for a few hours. At Cape du Couedic, the southern tip of the park, the hollowed-out limestone promontory called **Admiral's Arch**

is home to a colony of some 4,000 New Zealand fur seals that frolic in the rock pools and nap on the rocks.

Rangers at **Seal Bay Conservation Park** (✆ **61/8/8559-4207**), midway along the southern coast, lead guided tours along boardwalks through the dunes to a beach where you can walk through a colony of Australian sea lions. Up on the north coast, Lathami Conservation Park, just east of Stokes Bay, is a wonderful place to see wallabies in the wild—just dip under the low canopy of casuarina pines and walk silently, keeping your eyes peeled. If you want to see penguins—tiny ones that stand about 30cm (1 ft.) high—the **National Parks & Wildlife South**

It's hard to miss seeing koalas on Kangaroo Island.

Australia conducts tours of their colonies around Nepean Bay at both Kingscote and Penneshaw (© **61/8/8553-2381**).

ⓘ Howard Dr., Penneshaw, Kangaroo Island (© **61/8/8553-1185;** www.tour kangarooisland.com.au).

✈ Kangaroo Island, 25-min. flight from Adelaide.

FERRY: Ferry Port: Penneshaw, 40 min. from Cape Jervis.

🛏 $$ **Kangaroo Island Lodge,** Scenic Rd., American River (© **61/8/8553-7053;** www.kilodge.com.au). $$$ **Ozone Seafront Hotel,** The Foreshore, Kingscote (© **61/8/8553-2011;** www.ozonehotel.com).

WHY THEY'LL THANK YOU: Koala cuteness to the max.

133 In the Wild

Mission Beach
Make Way for Cassowaries
Ages 8 & up • Australia

Somehow, the folks of **Mission Beach, Australia** have managed to keep their town off of the tourist radar—quite a feat, considering they're only an hour's boat ride from the Great Barrier Reef. When you take the Mission Beach turnoff from the Bruce Highway, at first you seem to be in the middle of nowhere. Dense tangled vine forests almost hide the town from view until you round the corner to Mission Beach Proper, an appealing collection of shops, restaurants, and hotels. For kids, though, the highlight of their visit will probably be the chance to see a **cassowary,** Australia's largest land creature.

If Mission Beach weren't so laid back, the cassowaries wouldn't have stayed here. After all, these highly endangered 1.8m tall (6-ft.) birds abandoned areas like the Mabi Forest inland—a significant loss to those forests, as roaming cassowaries disperse an extraordinary amount of seeds in their excrement. Scientists reckon only about 900 southern cassowaries remain in the Wet Tropics, but about 100 of these ostrich-like black birds live in the last patches of rainforest around Mission Beach, which is actually a cluster of four small towns strung along an 18km (11-mile) beach. It's a surprisingly diverse habitat, with half the world's remaining licuala fan palms, six

ancient flowering plant families, and 60% of all Australia's butterflies.

Though they mostly keep to the forests, cassowaries have been known to stroll right through town, cruising for the fallen and low hanging fruit that are the staple of their diet. (Being flightless, they can't forage any higher than that.) The kids will be astonished by these spectacularly bizarre-looking birds, with a peacock blue neck, long red wattles, and a stiff blue casque that may remind them of an Aztec chieftain's headdress. Despite their stately walk, however, they're aggressive creatures with enormous claws. Warn the children never to approach or try to feed one, and tell them that if they do accidentally disturb a cassowary to back off slowly and hide behind a tree.

Even in conservation-minded Mission Beach, cassowaries have lost 50% of their critical habitat in the last decade. And living around humans isn't really healthy for them. Between dog attacks, car accidents, and the temptations of unsuitable snacks from foolhardy humans, they're at a disadvantage. Still, Mission Beach promotes itself as cassowary capital of the world, and great local efforts have been made to protect these spectacular rare birds. Check out the wildlife displays at the **C4**

125

Environment Center in town, then explore the cassowary territory on the 8km (5-mile) **Licata Fan Palm Trail,** which starts at a parking lot on the Mission Beach-Tully Road. There's even a "follow the cassowary footprints" trail for the kids. Sightings aren't guaranteed, but if the kids are patient they may well score a glimpse of this exotic flightless bird.

ⓘ **Mission Beach Information Centre,** Wongaling Shopping Centre, Mission Beach (✆ **61/7/4068-8699;** www.mission beachinfo.com).

✈ Cairns.

🛏 $$$ **The Horizon,** Explorer Dr., Mission Beach (✆ **1800/079-090** or 61/ 7/4068-8154; www.thehorizon.com.au). **Mackays,** 7 Porter Promenade, Mission Beach (✆ **61/7/4068-7212;** www.mackas missionbeach.com).

WHY THEY'LL THANK YOU: A big bird that isn't yellow.

5 Lost in the Mists of Time

Cliff Dwellings at Mesa Verde

Fossils **134**

Dinosaur Valley
In the Tracks of the Dinosaurs
All ages • Glen Rose, Texas, USA

Even the very youngest dinosaur lovers—and aren't preschoolers the biggest dinosaur fans there are?—can interpret the fossil record left in stone at Dinosaur Valley: The huge footprints in the rocks here are so unmistakable, it's easy to picture the prehistoric theropods and sauropods who made them 110 million years ago.

You'll find the prints beside the Paluxy River, a branch of the Brazos, which winds through this shady, lovely 1,500-acre park in Texas, about an hour's drive southwest of Fort Worth. Late summer, when the river is low, is the best time to come. You can discern the footprints best when the rock is just slightly underwater, with the wetness darkening it. (Bring a whisk broom with you to clear any debris.) It's strikingly evident that two different types of dinosaurs walked in the moist limy mud that formed this rock. Many of the footprints (typically 15–25 in. long) show three toes and sharp claws, indicating a meat-eating dinosaur called *Acrocanthosaurus*. This guy stood 20 to 30 feet tall and walked on two legs. The even larger footprints (some more than 3¼ ft. long) were made by long-necked plant-eating dinosaurs, your basic sauropods (nicknamed **"brontosaurs"**). The kids can tell its front tracks from its back ones: The front feet were round with peglike toes, like elephants' feet, while the back ones had large claws angling rearward. Most likely these were left by a 30- to 50-foot-long dinosaur named *Pleurocoelus*.

The tracks can easily be seen at two spots in the park: The main site is across the northwest parking lot and down some stone steps to the river; upstream is the Blue Hole, a sinkhole with many more brontosaur tracks (it's also a great place for swimming, so bring your suits). The kids will have no trouble imagining a scenario of the carnivorous Acrocanthosaurus stalking the gentle, slow-moving Pleurocoelus (originally a slab of tracks showed the meat-eater ambushing the plant-eater—to see that slab today, unfortunately, you'd need to be in New York City at the American Museum of Natural History). But what's still here is graphic evidence indeed.

The **visitor center** has replicas, foot skeletons, murals, and diagrams to help kids visualize the dinosaurs. What's more, outdoors stand two immense fiberglass models, one of a brown T-Rex and the other of a green Apatosaurus—relics of the Dinosaur World exhibit at the 1964 New York World's Fair. Built by the Sinclair Oil Company (remember the old Sinclair gas station sign with its green brontosaurus?), these models are historic artifacts in their own right. Scientists still argue over what the head of the Apatosaurus should look like, but hey, we're all still learning.

ⓘ ℂ **254/897-4588;** www.tpwd.state.tx.us/park/dinosaur.

✈ Dallas–Fort Worth International, 75 miles.

🛏 $ **Residence Inn Fort Worth University,** 1701 S. University Dr., Ft. Worth (ℂ **817/870-1011;** www.marriott.com/hotels/travel/dfwrp). $$$ **Stockyards Hotel,** 109 W. Exchange Ave., Ft. Worth (ℂ **800/423-8471** or 817/625-6427; www.stockyardshotel.com).

WHY THEY'LL THANK YOU: Dinosaurs walked here.

Agate Fossil Beds
A Ranch Full of Old Bones
Ages 4 & up • Harrison, Nebraska, USA

They were a young courting couple, Kate Graham and James Cook, strolling on the buttes above the Niobara River on Kate's family's ranch in northwestern Nebraska in 1878. Young James had knocked around a bit as a sailor, a scout, a trapper, but like many frontiersmen he was a keen observer. Looking down, he noticed a peculiar glitter on a bone fragment by his feet; he picked it up and discovered it was a petrified animal leg bone, with tiny calcite crystals in the marrow cavity. By a stroke of luck, Cook had recently befriended a Yale University paleontologist roaming the West in search of fossils, and the ever-curious Cook had learned much about that exciting new science from the professor (or "Man-That-Picks-Up-Bones," as Cook's friend Red Cloud, the Lakota Sioux leader, called him). Cook was just the man to sense that bone was something special.

It took over 30 years for James Cook to persuade paleontologists to study this isolated land—which he and Kate, after marrying, took over and named **Agate Springs Ranch.** But from 1909 on, the pair of high conical hills overlooking the river and grasslands became a beehive of activity. No fewer than six quarries were dug and combed through by scientists from several major universities; I can just imagine the fierce competition, each team of scientists protecting its own fossil trove. This is the world's best fossil deposit from the **Early Miocene Epoch,** filling in the missing links of many species from 20 million years ago—carnivorous beardogs, land beavers, the piglike Dinohyus, the gazelle-camel Stenomylus, and the short

rhinoceros Menoceras. It tells the story of a severe drought hitting this savanna, and mammals converging upon the few last drinking holes to eventually die, leaving their bones in the soft sedimentary soil. Natural history museums all over the world are indebted to Agate Springs for the rare fossils unearthed here.

The visitor center has some dramatic **reconstructed skeletons** of those early mammals; kids can get a good sense of the process of paleontology from looking at a massive slab of stone with bones still embedded in it. There's also a fine exhibit of **Native American artifacts** given to James Cook over his years of friendship with local tribes. Computer touch-screens show you points of interests to look for when you go out on the park's two easy walking trails to various quarries. You can also see the Bone Cabin, where paleontologists worked and stayed with the Cooks' son Harold, who himself became a paleontologist—growing up here, how could he become anything else?

ⓘ 301 River Rd., at Hwy. 29 (© **308/668-2211;** www.nps.gov/agfo).

✈ Western Nebraska Regional, 50 miles.

🛏 $$ **Candlelight Inn,** E. Hwy. 26, Scottsbluff (© **800/424-2305** or 308/635-3751; www.candlelightscottsbluff.com). $$ **Hampton Inn Suites,** 301 W. Hwy. 26, Scottsbluff (© **800/HAMPTON** [426-7866] or 308/635-5200; www.hamptoninn.com).

WHY THEY'LL THANK YOU: Seeing where the fossils came from.

129

Ghost Ranch
Haunted by Dinosaurs
Ages 4 & up • Abiquiu, New Mexico, USA

You want old dinosaurs? Try 215 million years old. You want complete skeletons? Ghost Ranch has those too, and in abundance. When an exposed cliff face on this dude ranch in northern New Mexico first yielded its fossil secrets in the late 1940s, the world of paleontology was turned upside down: Here, embedded in mudstone, was a mass grave of nimble two-legged Triassic carnivores named *Coelophysis*—hundreds of them, and not just bones but compete intact skeletons. Now *that's* a paleontologist's dream come true.

Ghost Ranch isn't a dude ranch anymore, but an education and retreat center set in a stunning Southwest landscape of colorful cliffs and eroded red hills. The adobe **dinosaur museum** on the grounds may be small but it's fabulous for kids. Its centerpiece is an 8-ton block of mudstone removed from that cliff, embedded with more than a thousand Coelophysis fossils; the children can inspect the fossil hoard at very close range and watch a paleontologist removing bones from the rock. This is still cutting-edge work: A **crocodilian skeleton** removed from Ghost Ranch slabs as recently as 2005 turned out to be an entirely new species, a 6-foot-long, two-legged reptile with tiny arms, a long neck, huge eyes, and a birdlike beak. (If any kids drew something that weird, you'd be tempted to tell them they were just making it up.) Other fossils on display include bones from the 100-foot-long **Seimosaurus** and the crocodilelike **Hesperosuchus,** two other early reptilians

that were soon to be rendered extinct by the hollow-boned Coelophysis and its descendants.

Once you're done with the museum, don't pass up the chance to hike around the buttes and mesas: A **walking trail** leads from the museum to a steep hill where many more Coelophysis skeletons were unearthed.

Visitors can drop in just to view the exhibits or can reserve slots in **paleontology workshops** at Ghost Ranch, some of which are designed specifically for parents and children or grandparents and grandchildren; there are also weeklong courses, more or less summer camps for the whole family (parents get their own activity program) utilizing the ranch's art studios, ropes courses, lake, hiking trails, and horseback riding. Semirustic lodging is available on-site, although in July and August it's usually filled with course participants.

ⓘ On U.S. 84, 14 miles north of Abiquiu (© **800/821-5145** or 505/685-4333; www.ghostranch.org).

✈ Santa Fe Municipal, 60 miles. Albuquerque, 120 miles.

🛏 $$ **El Rey Inn,** 1862 Cerrillos Rd. (© **800/521-1349** or 505/982-1931; www.elreyinnsantafe.com). $$ **Old Santa Fe Inn,** 320 Galisteo St. (© **800/734-9910** or 505/995-0800; www.oldsantafeinn.com).

WHY THEY'LL THANK YOU: Fossil finders still at work.

La Brea Tar Pits
Oozing Ancient History
Ages 5 & up • Los Angeles, California, USA

An odorous swamp of gooey asphalt oozes to the earth's surface in the middle of Los Angeles. No, it's not a low-budget horror-movie set—it's the La Brea Tar Pits, a bizarre primal pool on Museum Row where hot tar has been seeping to the surface from a subterranean oil field for more than 40,000 years. It's an incongruous sight in the middle of built-up Los Angeles; in this grassy patch of Hancock Park, you can walk right up to the abandoned asphalt quarry's slick black pool of oily water, inhaling its acrid scent and watching bubbles of methane gas bloop to the steamy surface. Suddenly the high-rise office towers of Wilshire and Fairfax boulevards seem to recede, and you can imagine a distant past when mammoths and saber-tooth cats prowled this fern-shaded landscape.

The **bubbling pools** have tempted thirsty animals throughout history—with fatal consequences. Nearly 400 species of mammals, birds, amphibians, and fish, many of them now extinct, walked, crawled, landed, swam, or slithered into the sticky sludge, got stuck in the worst way, and stayed forever. For many years, their fossilized bones were pried out of hardened asphalt by the pit's owners, who were too busy extracting commercial tar to care about them. But, because paleontology came of age in the early 20th century, in 1906, scientists began to study this prehistoric trove. Some 100 tons of **fossils** were eventually removed—ground sloths, giant vultures, mastodons, camels, bears, native lions, dire wolves, lizards, and relatives of today's super-rats—the world's largest collection of Ice Age remains.

Today those entombed specimens are displayed at the adjacent **Page Museum.** Some 30 complete skeletons, along with assorted skulls and other bones, are handsomely mounted with in-depth explanations;

there are also a few animatronic figures flailing about, though nothing that would terrify young children. Advise them not to expect dinosaurs—these fossils are all from the Ice Age, but in fact those are even rarer than dinosaur fossils. Until we came here, I never knew that there were native horses in prehistoric North America (they became extinct long before the conquistadors arrived with their European horses). Archaeological work is ongoing; you can watch as scientists clean, identify, and catalog new finds in the Paleontology Laboratory.

This quarry has always been open to the public, and thankfully it hasn't been walled off and overcommercialized (the kitschy figures of struggling mastodons set outdoor in the pits are time-warp quaint). Poking around the park, I felt as much connected to the 1950s, when I first visited California, as I did to the Ice Age. Somehow in all my trips to L.A., I had never before made time for the La Brea Tar Pits. And now, at last, I was here, and it was so much cooler than the glitzy theme parks and Hollywood Boulevard attractions. I was thankful to be able to introduce it to my kids.

(i) 5801 Wilshire Blvd. (✆ **323/934-PAGE;** www.tarpits.org).

✈ Los Angeles International.

🛏 $$ **Beverly Garland's Holiday Inn,** 4222 Vineland Ave., North Hollywood (✆ **800/BEVERLY** [238-3759] or 818/980-8000; www.beverlygarland.com). $$ **Roosevelt Hotel,** Hollywood, 7000 Hollywood Blvd. (✆ **800/950-7667** or 323/466-7000; www.hollywoodroosevelt.com).

WHY THEY'LL THANK YOU: Mastodons checked in, but they never checked out.

The Jurassic Coast
Dinosaurs in Devonshire
All ages • Exmouth to Lulworth, England

You've heard of Jurassic Park; well, here's the Jurassic Coast, a 153km (95-mile) stretch of English coastline in East Devon and Dorset that is so rich in fossils and dinosaur footprints, it's been named a World Heritage Site. Beachgoers normally seek out fine, soft sand, but in this area the prime spots are rocky shingle beaches, where fossils wash right up at your feet.

Passing along the coast, point out to the kids the changing color of the cliff faces: Red cliffs have no fossils, being from the Triassic period, when this area was desert; darker gray cliffs are from the swampy Jurassic Age, perfect for dinosaurs; white chalk cliffs were formed underwater in the Cretaceous era and have marine fossils, mostly ammonites.

A good base is **Lyme Regis,** a charming sea resort. In 1810, 11-year-old Mary Anning discovered an articulated ichthyosaur skeleton here, and went on to become one of the first professional fossilists. You'll learn more about Anning and local

geology at the **Lyme Regis Philpot Museum,** Bridge Street (✆ **44/1297/ 443370;** www.lymeregismuseum.co.uk), in an Edwardian brick building on the site of Mary Anning's girlhood home. Don't miss the Dinosaur Poo Table, inlaid with coprolites (fossilized dino spoor). At **Dinosaurland,** Coombe Street (✆ **44/ 1297/443541;** www.dinosaurland.co.uk), in a church where Anning was baptized, you can view an enormous collection of fossils and consult a map to find local fossil-hunting sites—such as nearby **Monmouth Beach,** where a huge stretch of rocks is embedded with ammonites. The lovely beach at **Seatown,** farther west of Lyme Regis, is also great for fossil collecting.

Even better for fossil hunters is the beach at **Charmouth,** just east of Lyme Regis. As fossil-bearing rocks fall into the sea here, the waves break them up, exposing the fossils; the rocks then wash ashore at low tide, ready for the picking. At the **Charmouth Heritage Coast Centre** (Lower Sea Lane; ✆ **44/1297/560772;** www.charmouth.org), wardens explain what fossils are and how to collect them. Check their schedule for organized fossil-hunting weekends.

East of Swanage, the **Lulworth Cove Heritage Centre** (Main Rd., Lulworth Cove, ✆ **44/1929/400587;** www.lulworth. com/education/heritage_centre.htm) has fascinating displays on the local geology, particularly the picturesque rock arch named Durdle Door and the nearby Purbeck Beds, thick layers of limestone and clay containing many dinosaur footprints. Just east of the cove, a footpath from the Wealden Cliffs leads to the **Fossil Forest,** full of fossilized tree stumps; it's on an Army range but can be visited on weekends.

The Jurassic Coast.

Inland at Dorchester, the **Dinosaur Museum,** Icen Way (🕿 **44/1305/269880;** www.thedinosaurmuseum.com) is full of interactive hands-on displays, including several life-size dinosaur reconstructions.

ⓘ **Jurassic Coast** (www.jurassiccoast. com). **Lyme Regis Tourist Information,** Church St. (🕿 **44/1297/442138;** www. lymeregistourism.co.uk).

🚆 Dorchester (2¹/₂ hr. from London) or Axminster.

🛏 $$ **The Royal Lion Hotel,** Broad St., Lyme Regis (🕿 **44/1297/445622;** www. royallionhotel.com). $ **Portland Bird Observatory,** The Old Lower Light, Portland Bill (🕿 **44/1305/820553;** www. portlandbirdobs.org.uk).

WHY THEY'LL THANK YOU: Fossil hunting with spectacular sea views.

---

139 Fossils

Newark Earthworks
Ancient Observatory
Ages 8 & up • Newark, Ohio, USA

There's always something haunting to me about ancient observatories—the very idea that supposedly primitive peoples could position standing stones or mounds of dirt in perfect alignment with heavenly bodies. The mounds in Newark, Ohio, are even more confounding because they are so huge, big enough to hold four Roman Colosseums and twice as accurate astronomically as Stonehenge. But now here's the kicker: The Newark Earthworks have a golf course on top. Only in America, right?

To be fair, the Moundbuilders Country Club course was built in 1933, long before professors from Earlham College discovered in 1982 how precisely the ancient mounds aligned with the lunar cycle. The existence of the earthworks, however, has been charted since the 1840s. A viewing platform has been built near the golf club's parking lot, but you need to contact the Ohio Historical Society (see numbers later) to arrange to walk around the fairways.

At ground level, the Newark Earthworks appear simply like gentle grassy humps, 3 to 14 feet high; it's only when seen from the air that their geometric precision becomes evident. A huge octagon, spanning 40 acres, is linked with a pair of parallel walls to an adjoining circle that encloses 20 acres; the opening of the octagon lines up perfectly with the moon when it is at the northernmost point of its 18.6-year cycle, and each of the octagon's eight corners aligns with a different significant lunar event in the cycle. It's theorized that the prehistoric Hopewell Indians built these mounds around A.D. 250—perhaps to attract the attention of the moon divinity, or perhaps to predict lunar eclipses. Perhaps they also climbed atop the mounds to view the moonrise (certainly not to hunt for their balls in the rough!).

You can also play explorers and search out other preserved bits of the ancient earthworks around Newark. There's the **Great Circle Earthworks** (455 Hebron Rd., Heath), a ceremonial circle 1,200 feet in diameter set in a park off S.R. 79, between Parkview Drive and Cooper Street; the Great Circle Earthworks Museum has excellent displays including a timeline of Ohio's ancient cultures. The third section is the **Wright Earthwork,** a 50-foot section of mound wall just west of S.R. 79 in Newark, which you view from James Street.

A prehistoric highway beginning at the octagon led southwest to Ohio's other major Hopewell site, 40 miles south of Columbus: **Hopewell Culture National Park** (Rte. 104, Chillicothe; ✆ **740/774-1126;** www.nps.gov/hocu). Otherwise known as Mound City, this immense rectangle of earthen walls encloses a number of burial mounds.

ⓘ 125 N. 33th St. (✆ **800/600-7178** or 740/344-1919; www.ohiohistory.org/places/newarkearthworks).

✈ Columbus (30 miles).

🛏 $$$ **Cherry Valley Lodge,** 2299 Cherry Valley Rd., Newark (✆ **800/788-8008** or 740/788-1200; www.cherryvalleylodge.com). $$ **Courtyard Newark Granville,** 500 Highland Blvd. (✆ **888/236-2427** or 740/344-1800; www.marriott.com).

BEST TIME: Late May to early Sept.

WHY THEY'LL THANK YOU: Discovering the ancient past right underneath our modern feet.

Fossils **140**

Cahokia Mounds
Metropolis of the Ancient Mississippians
Ages 6 & up • Collinsville, Illinois, USA

It was once the biggest city north of Mexico, with somewhere around 20,000 residents—farmers, hunters, craftsmen, traders, priests—at its peak in A.D. 1100–1200. Archaeologists have named them the Mississippians, but we don't know what they called themselves, because they left no writings behind. An air of mystery hangs over this site, just across the Mississippi River from St. Louis. Who were these people and what was their world like? The answers are hauntingly elusive.

Exhibits at the site's visitor center show how archaeologists play detective with the ancient past. The variety of arrowheads dug up, for example, proves that these people were sophisticated enough to trade with tribes as far away as southern Minnesota and the Gulf Coast. Experts gather that the mounds were built by hand, with workers carrying dirt in baskets on their backs from so-called "borrow pits" to the mounds. Ordinary citizens apparently lived in simple houses with pole walls and thatched roofs, but they labored to erect these immense earthen structures—109 still exist, 68 of them in this park—for public ceremonies.

After viewing the center's model of the ancient city, you can take tours of three different sections of the 2,200-acre site—hour-long ranger-led tours, or 30- to 45-minute self-guided walks (maps and audiotapes available) of each area. You certainly can't miss **Monk's Mound,** a four-terraced platform mound that once held the home of the city's ruler; it's the biggest mound in the western hemisphere, covering 16 acres at its base and rising 100 feet. Climb the modern steps to its now-grass-covered flat top, and you gaze over a huge leveled plaza, bounded by the city's 2-mile-long log stockade wall, bits of which have been reconstructed. From this vantage point, the kids can identify several mound shapes—flat-top, conical, ridge-top—which apparently had various purposes. Unlike other cultures, the Mississippians generally did not use mounds for burials, although in a few cases skeletons have been unearthed with all the trappings of a prince or chieftain; other skeletons found are mostly those of young women or men with hands and feet cut off, which suggests they

Monk's Mound at Cahokia Mounds.

were human sacrifices. (Mound 72 was particularly full of sacrificial burials.)

Once archaeologists started to dig, they found something even more amazing: the remains of an astronomical observatory, similar to Stonehenge but built of red cedar logs instead of stones: Woodhenge, the scientists have named it. How did two prehistoric cultures on different continents each get the same idea? And why did this great Mississippian city die? Archaeologists keep on digging, for they still have a lot of questions to answer.

ⓘ 30 Ramey St. (✆ **618/346-5160;** www. cahokiamounds.com).

✈ Lambert-St. Louis International, 22 miles.

🛏 $$ **Drury Inn Union Station,** 201 S. 20th St. (✆ **800/378-7946** or 314/231-3900; www.druryhotels.com). $$$ **Embassy Suites,** 11237 Lone Eagle Dr., Bridgeton (✆ **800/362-2779** or 314-739-8929; embassy suites1.hilton.com).

WHY THEY'LL THANK YOU: Ancient mysteries, right in America's backyard.

---

141 Fossils

Effigy Mounds
Bears & Birds Rising from the Ground
Ages 6 & up • Harper's Ferry, Iowa, USA

The kids can see Indian burial mounds in many parts of the country—but mounds in the shape of animals? That's even cooler, and you'll find them only here, in the upper Mississippi valley.

On the riverside bluffs and flood plains of the upper Mississippi River, where the eastern woodlands give way to the western plains, ancient nomadic hunter-gatherers—as if drawn to the great river—built rock shelters and burial mounds as long ago as 500 B.C. Artifacts displayed in the visitor center—pottery, stone spearheads, clam shells (highly valued by these tribes), and flat stones for grinding corn meal—demonstrate how their culture developed over the centuries. But as they grew more sophisticated, from A.D. 600 to 1300 the Indians of this region had the novel idea to put a little more spin on their mounds, shaping them to resemble their tribal totems—bison, deer, turtles, lizards, but especially bears, eagles, and falcons. Strung along the **walking trails** through this 2,500-acre park, the mounds (there are over 200 of them) are unmistakable.

They may rise only a yard or so above the surrounding ground, but the shapes are well-defined, edged with gravel paths or sprouting taller grass. The biggest one, **Great Bear Mound,** rises 3½ feet and is 70 feet wide at the shoulders and 137 feet long. Some mounds still bear traces of fire pits, where the animal's head or heart or would be, suggesting that their purpose was highly ceremonial. There are three simple conical burial mounds right by the visitor center, but that's just a foretaste; an excellent 2-mile trail from the visitor center leads past 25 mounds, both conical mounds and effigy mounds, on the way to the **Fire Point overlook,** 300 feet above the river, for a truly stunning Mississippi River panorama. A longer hike, 4 miles round-trip from a parking area south on Hwy. 76, takes you to the park's biggest mound cluster, the **Marching Bear group,** which has 10 bears and three bird shapes.

The park is right off the scenic Great River Road in northeastern Iowa, just across the river from Prairie du Chien, Wisconsin. If the kids are eager to see more, **Pikes Peak State Park,** 15316 Great River Rd. (© **563/873-2341**), only 7 miles away in MacGregor, Iowa, has several effigy mounds along its walking trails as well.

ⓘ 151 Hwy. 76 (© **563/873-3491;** www. nps.gov/efmo).

✈ Dubuque, 80 miles.

🛏 $$ **Best Western Bluffview Inn & Suites,** 37268 Hwy. 18, Prairie du Chien, WI (© **800/780-7234** or 608/326-4777; www.bestwestern.com). $$ **Windsor Place Inn,** 1936 Marquette Rd. S., Prairie du Chien, WI (© **608/326-7799;** www. windsorplaceinnpdc.com).

WHY THEY'LL THANK YOU: Earth sculptures they can relate to.

Early Humans **142**

Canyon de Chelly
Hanging Out with the Anasazi
Ages 8 & up • Chinle, Arizona, USA

For nearly 5,000 years, people have made their homes in this spectacular pair of narrow sandstone canyons of remote northeastern Arizona. The Navajos are the most recent guardians of this land; the Ancestral Puebloans (also known as the Anasazi) left their mark too, in the giant rock amphitheaters where they created caves, dwelling rooms, and ceremonial kivas. To explore the canyons is to see centuries unfold.

Ancestral Puebloan civilization reached its zenith between A.D. 1100 and 1300, but evidence suggests that these canyons may have been occupied as early as A.D. 300. In the nooks and crannies of the canyons, you'll see ancient dwellings hollowed into the rock walls and the circular

Canyon de Chelly.

sacred rooms known as kivas; the largest and most impressive ruins are the **White House Ruins** in Canyon du Chelly, which were inhabited between 1040 and 1275. You'll also see ancient tombs—the **Tomb of the Weaver** near the Antelope House ruins, and the **Mummy Caves,** both appropriately enough in Canyon del Muerto, or the Canyon of the Dead.

While most tourists simply drive along the two scenic drives—the 15-mile North Rim drive, which overlooks Canyon del Muerto, and the 16-mile South Rim drive, which overlooks Canyon de Chelly (pronounced "duh shay")—hire a guide and you can take the kids right down into the canyons, where they can poke around these fascinating ruins. Navajo guides or local tour companies will lead you either on foot or in a four-wheel-drive vehicle. The hike down is fairly demanding, so with kids you'll probably opt to drive—there'll still be a bit of walking to reach the various ruins.

Because you'll be seeing both Navajo and Ancestral Puebloan relics, make sure the kids learn the difference between the two kinds of rock art. Look for dark slick streaks on the canyon walls, created by water seepage reacting with iron oxide—ancestral Puebloans chipped away at this so-called "desert varnish" to expose the lighter-colored rock underneath, forming pictorial designs we now call petroglyphs. Pictographs are similar designs made later by the Navajos, applying colorful paints directly to the sandstone walls to commemorate important tribal events. Urge the kids to take time to decipher the stories told by the rock pictures—they're windows into an ancient way of life.

ⓘ Off Rte. 191 (🕾 **928/674-5500;** www.nps.gov/cach).

✈ Flagstaff, 222 miles.

🛏 $$ **Holiday Inn Canyon de Chelly,** Indian Rte. 7 (🕾 **888/HOLIDAY** [465-4329] or 928/674-5000; www.ichotelsgroup.com). $$ **Thunderbird Lodge** (🕾 **800/679-2473** or 928/674-5841; www.tbirdlodge.com).

WHY THEY'LL THANK YOU: Seeing pictographs and petroglyphs.

Mesa Verde
Ancient Colorado Condos on the Cliffs
Ages 4 & up • West of Cortez, Colorado, USA

Though the kids may come to Mesa Verde National Park thinking that our 21st-century high-rise cities are the ultimate in civilized living, they'll soon learn otherwise—these mysterious ancients had the concept down centuries ago. Over 800 years ago—A.D. 500 to 1300—as the Ancestral Puebloans gave up their nomadic hunter-gatherer lifestyle and began to settle in the canyons and mesas of the American Southwest, they developed their own creative solution to the residential real estate question: Build up, not out.

Start 10 miles north of Cortez, at the **Anasazi Heritage Center,** 27501 Colorado Rte. 184 (℃ **970/882-5600;** www.co.blm.gov/ahc), a fabulous hands-on place for the kids to learn about Ancestral Puebloan culture. Then head down to the park, which you enter via U.S. 160. Stop off first at the **Far View Visitor Center** (15 steep and winding miles from the park entrance) to book ranger-led tours of the park's three must-see sites, Cliff Palace, Balcony House, and Long House.

The largest site, **Cliff Palace,** is just that—a 151-room, four-story apartment house set under the rim of a cliff, with each stepped-back roof forming a penthouse courtyard for the next level up. The 45-room **Balcony House** hangs above Soda Canyon, with stone stairs, log ladders, and narrow crawl spaces. **Long House** stretches across a long alcove in Rock Canyon, with 150 rooms and 21 kivas (subterranean chambers used for ceremonies and meetings) and a large public plaza for community gatherings.

Before or after your guided tour, there are plenty of other dwellings to visit—Mesa Verde is the largest archaeological preserve in the United States, with almost 5,000 archaeological sites. The 6-mile **Mesa Top Loop Road** has 10 stops where you can either view dwellings or walk a short distance to them. The **Chapin Mesa Museum** has dioramas and interpretive displays on Puebloan culture; behind the museum, a paved .3-mile trail leads down to **Spruce Tree House,** a 130-room dwelling set safe and snug inside an 89-foot-deep alcove. Or drive west to less-crowded **Wetherill Mesa,** where a half-mile hike takes you to **Step House;** to its left you'll find three even older homes, pit houses made by earlier Puebloans around A.D. 626. If the kids are seasoned hikers, try the **Petroglyph Point Trail,** which begins just past the Chapin Mesa Museum; it's almost 3 miles long, running along the rim of a stunning canyon to reach an impressive panel of rock art.

ⓘ Off U.S. 160, 10 miles west of Cortez (℃ **970/529-4465;** www.nps.gov/meve).

✈ Durango La Plata County Airport (65 miles).

🛏 $$ **Holiday Inn Express,** 2121 E. Main, Cortez (℃ **888/465-4329** or 970/565-6000; www.ichotelsgroup.com).

WHY THEY'LL THANK YOU: Chutes and Ladders come to life.

Valley of Fire
Ancient Art Gallery
Ages 8 & up • Overton, Nevada, USA

Out here in the desert, 55 miles from Las Vegas, the vistas are awesome—eccentric red rock outcroppings, sand dunes spiked with desert scrub and green creosote bushes—but it's hardly a hospitable place to live. And yet ancient peoples, such as the Ancestral Puebloans and the even earlier prehistoric Basket Makers, were drawn here to etch artwork onto the canyon walls and rock formations. Were they writing history, telling folktales, or creating sacred places to worship? No one knows for sure; maybe it was a little of each. But what I find most awesome about standing here is to sense, down through the centuries, the ineffable human passion to leave some permanent records of their doings, to communicate with eternity.

Two easily accessible sites in this state park display some of the most intriguing petroglyphs found anywhere. The first set is near the west entrance, at **Atlatl Rock,** where a 40-foot-high stairway leads up to an eroded red sandstone formation that looks as if one precariously balanced boulder is about to topple over. The park is full of such arresting formations, but this one shelters a smooth stone face etched quite clearly with pictures of ancient hunting or warfare—the drawings unmistakably depict an *atlatl,* a notched stick used to fling spears in an early precursor of a bow and arrow. Why is this weapon drawn so prominently? Some experts believe it was because this was considered a magic spot for warriors to be healed from spear wounds. The weird thing is that the panel is angled to face east, to catch the sun's rays at sunrise; it's been angled so

precisely that there must have been some ceremonial or religious intent.

Then there's an easy .5-mile loop trail through a small, twisty canyon that's been named **Petroglyph Canyon,** for obvious reasons: It just may be the world's most amazing place to see ancient Puebloan rock art. Panel after panel of slick dark rock along the course of the canyon was etched by these ancient artists with astoundingly expressive figures—big-horned sheep, dancers (try to tell which ones were men and which ones were women), birds, suns. Trail markers point them out, but no one can say for sure what events these pictures narrate. Victory in a war against their neighbors? Celebrations of the end of a drought? Visits from aliens in spaceships? Encourage the kids to interpret the figures for themselves and tell their own versions of the stories. And hope that, at some point, they'll shiver with awe, sensing the spirits of the ancients speaking to us still today.

ⓘ Valley of Fire Rd./Hwy. 169 (✆ **702/397-2088;** www.parks.nv.gov/vf.htm).

✈ McCarran International, Las Vegas (55 miles).

🛏 $$ **Mandalay Bay,** 3950 Las Vegas Blvd. S. (✆ **877/632-7000** or 702/632-7000; www.mandalaybay.com). $$ **MGM Grand,** 3799 Las Vegas Blvd. S. (✆ **800/929-1111** or 702/891-7777; www.mgmgrand.com).

WHY THEY'LL THANK YOU: Telling stories in stone.

Puako Petroglyphs
Hawaiian History Carved in Stone

Ages 6 & up • Big Island, Hawaii

In the ancient Hawaiian language, they call it "mana"—the spiritual force that flows through all creation. Some places in the Hawaiian Islands have a particularly powerful mana, and this was one of them: A shelf of pahoehoe lava rock the size of a football field, hidden in a tangle of forest on the Kohala Coast, overlooking the vast Pacific, where early Hawaiian artists carved a panoply of arresting figures, some 3,000 strong.

In the complicated history of modern Hawaii, all too often native Hawaiian culture was obliterated by white European settlers, but not this time. The developers of the Mauna Lani resort, setting out to design a new golf course for its Orchid hotel, discovered this amazing site in the scrubby woods and respectfully set it aside in its own protected park. It takes about half an hour to hike the winding trail through the tough little trees that sprang up on this hardened lava flow, but when we made that last turn and saw the great sheet of dark jagged rock, etched over and over with a joyous riot of figures . . . I swear my son and I felt the mana wash over us.

These petroglyphs served many functions: as historical record, as a repository of sacred legend, and as beautiful art. The skilled artists who carved these figures followed a strict, highly stylized iconography (don't skip the plaques at the beginning of the trail, where a series of reproduction stones display the significant symbols; kids can make rubbings here). Once you've reached the real petroglyphs, you won't be allowed to walk on the fragile lava rock, but circle around the railing and pick out individual figures: dancers and paddlers, fishermen and chiefs, hundreds of marchers all in a row, and many family groups, probably honoring specific clans. Images from daily life crop up everywhere: fish hooks, spears, poi pounders, outrigger canoes. The best way to see it is on a guided walk, available from the Fairmont Orchid concierge; the guide will point out special figures, including some kites (proof of ancient contact with the Maoris in New Zealand) and the first of the sailing ships that heralded a new era for the islands. Bonus points for whoever can find the single snake in the whole tableau. Come early or late in the day, when the sun's slanting rays hit the carvings in sharp relief.

The Puako Petroglyphs are the island's most spectacular—in fact, this the largest rock art site in the entire Pacific—but there are several others along this coast, the sacred domain of Hawaii's ancient kings. At the Waikoloa Beach Resort, off

Puako petroglyphs.

Hwy. 19 just south of the Mauna Lani, free daily **tours** of the property's petroglyphs leave from the Kings' Shops (© **808/886-8811**). Farther south along Hwy. 19, the **Kona Village Resort** (© 800/367-5290 or **808/325-5555;** www. konavillage.com) offers free tours of its **Kaupulehu Petroglyphs** (reservations required; this tour is ADA accessible). You may also want to head for the other end of the Mauna Lani property, to see the Hawaiian kings' ingenious fish farm: the Kalahuipuaa Fish Ponds, preserved in a suitably royal tropical beachside setting.

(i) Holoholokai Beach Park, off Hwy. 19, in the Mauna Lani Resort, N. Kaniku Dr. (© **808/885-1064**).

✈ Kailua-Kona.

�． $$$ **The Fairmont Orchid,** 1 N. Kaniku Dr., (© **866/540-4474** or 808/885-2000; www.fairmont.com/orchid). $ **Kona Tiki Hotel,** 75-5968 Alii Dr., Kailua-Kona (© **808/329-1425;** www.konatiki.com).

WHY THEY'LL THANK YOU: Feel the mana.

146 Early Humans

The Caves of Lascaux
The Oldest Paintings in the World
Ages 6 & up • Montignac, France

Imagine what went through the minds of those four French boys, hunting for a dog that afternoon in 1940, down in the Dordogne region of France. Innocently crawling into a cave, they looked up to see walls daubed with hundreds of vivid paintings—majestic bulls, wild boars, stags, horses, and deer—astonishingly lifelike figures painted by Stone Age hunters 15,000 to 20,000 years ago.

Opened to the public in 1948, the **Caves at Lascaux** speedily became one of France's major tourist attractions, drawing a quarter of a million visitors annually—and causing such grave atmospheric changes that the precious paintings began deteriorating. The cave closed to the public in 1964, though qualified archaeologists can still apply to visit. But the kids don't have to be disappointed: A short walk downhill from the real caves, **Lascaux II** is an impressive reproduction of the original, molded aboveground in concrete, where some 200 paintings have been faithfully copied. Come early, because only 2,000 visitors are allowed in

per day; from April to October, buy tickets at a kiosk by the Montignac tourist office (see below).

Also in Lascaux, up a hill from the caves, the intriguing site of a prehistoric bear cult has been preserved at **Site Préhistorique du Regourdou** (© **33/5/53-51-81-23**). Alongside the sepulchers and skeletons of a Neanderthal man and several bears, you can watch a pack of quite live semiwild bears roam around a naturalized habitat (off-limits to humans, of course), a charming way to bring visitors closer to their bear-worshipping ancestors.

Three other authentic caves in the area can be visited as well, but be sure to call up to a year ahead for reservations. Along D47, **Grotte de Font-de-Gaume** (1.5km/1 mile outside Les Eyzies) and **Grotte des Combarelles** (17km/11 miles north of Bergerac) feature Stone Age paintings (© **33/5/53-06-86-00** for both); in Rouffignac-Saint-Cernin, Grotte de Rouffignac © **33/5/53-05-41-71;** www.grottede rouffignac.fr), nicknamed the Cave of the Hundred Mammoths, contains nearly half

141

of the existing paintings of wooly mammoths, as well as rare renderings of rhinoceros and ibexes. The **Musée National de la Préhistoire,** in Les Eyzies (✆ **33/5/53-06-45-65;** www.musee-prehistoire-eyzies.fr), displays a hoard of prehistoric artifacts unearthed in local excavations.

ⓘ **La Grotte de Lascaux,** off D706, 2km (1¼ mile) from Montignac (✆ **33/5/53-05-65-65**). **Montignac Office de Tourisme,** place Bertrand-de-Born (✆ **33/5/53-51-82-60;** www.bienvenue-montignac.com). **Les Eyzies Office de Tourisme,** 19 rue de la Préhistoire (✆ **33/5/53-06-97-05;** www.leseyzies.com).

✈ Périgueux-Bassillac, 45km (28 miles).

🚆 Condat-Le-Lardin, 486km (302 miles) from Paris.

🛏 $$$ **Hotel Les Glycines,** Rte. De Périgueux, Les Eyzies-Tayac-Sireuil (✆ **333/5/53-06-97-07;** www.les-glycines-dordogne.com). $$ **Relais du Soleil d'Or,** 16 rue du 4 Septembre, Montignac (✆ **33/5/53-51-80-22;** www.le-soleil-dor.com).

BEST TIME: Mar–Dec.

WHY THEY'LL THANK YOU: Cave men rock.

Altamira Cave
Picassos of Prehistory
Ages 8 & up • Cantabria, Spain

Michelangelo may have painted the ceiling of the Sistine Chapel, but that feat was nothing new—a bunch of nameless artists did the same thing 15,000 years ago, at the end of the Ice Age. In an S-shaped set of caves at Altamira, Spain, instead of the Creation, they depicted bison, boars, and horses, leaping and plunging across the cave ceiling. Whoever these artists were, they created perhaps the most beautiful cave paintings anywhere.

The paintings are almost all in one main room of the cave system, called the **Polychrome Chambers.** Bison are the star players here, with the most stunning section featuring 21 red bison stampeding across the ceiling—you can practically hear them stamp and snort. Using only three colors—ocher, red, and black—these are large-scale pictures, practically life-sized, and executed in meticulous realistic detail, rippling muscles, bristling manes, and all. The paintings were ingeniously positioned to take advantages of natural bulges and furrows in the rock, giving a 3-dimensional realism to the animals. Another unusual feature is eight engraved anthropomorphic figures, various handprints, and hand outlines, almost as if the artists were determined to leave their own signatures.

Although the caves were discovered in 1868, it wasn't until 1879 that a little girl—daughter of the nobleman who owned the land—noticed paintings on the ceilings of the dark cave. Because they were so well preserved, archaeologists insisted they were forgeries; not until 1902 were they authenticated. Over the course of the 20th century, the Altamira caves became so popular with visitors that, inevitably, harmful bacteria were tracked in and damaged these masterpieces. Even more damaging were the walls built in the 1950s to prop up the ceiling of this karst cave, which seemed on the verge of natural collapse: The walls cut off the main chamber, thus irrevocably altering the atmospheric conditions that were responsible for its perfect preservation in the first place. The caves have been repeatedly closed to the public ever since the 1970s; currently there are no visits allowed, but cave officials hope to grant limited access again eventually, so keep checking for updates.

In the 1960s, anticipating such closures—or even total collapse of the cave—a couple of exact replicas were built, one for the Deutsches Museum, another to be displayed in Madrid. In 2001, an even more precise replica was opened a few hundred feet away from the original caves. Called the Altamira Center, it's much more convincing than Lascaux's replica: The ceiling paintings were copied using sophisticated computerized digital-transfer technology that captured every crack, stain, and hollow of the original. Alongside the replica of the cave's main chamber, the museum has set up reconstructions of an archaeological dig, the ancient artist's workshop, and a cave bear's den. Who needs to damage the real thing any further, when all of the incredible artistry lives on here?

ⓘ **Cuevas de Altamira,** Santillana del Mar (✆ **34/942/81-80-05;** http://museo dealtamira.mcu.es).

✈ Santander, 29km (18 miles).

🛏 $$ **Casa del Marqués,** C. Cantón 26 (✆ **34/942/81-88-88;** www.turismo santillanadelmar.com). $ **Casa del Organista,** C. Los Hornos 4 (✆ **34/942/84-03-52;** www.casadelorganista.com).

WHY THEY'LL THANK YOU: Swept up in the red bison stampede.

---

148 Early Humans

Teotihuacán
Ghost City of Ancient Mexico
Ages 8 & up • San Juan Teotihuacán, Mexico

Even the Aztecs were awestruck when they first discovered these haunting ruins, naming them Teotihuacán (pronounced "teh-oh-tee-wa-*khan*"), or "place where gods were born." Gazing out upon the rough stone ruins, an easy day trip northeast from Mexico City, you can see why. Beneath these fragments—three pyramids, sacrificial altars, the remains of a few grand houses—lies the ghost of a great city that once covered 31 sq. km. (12 sq. miles), its temples and palaces painted with brilliant red frescoes.

With a population of 200,000 at its zenith, Teotihuacán was the cultural epicenter of ancient Mesoamerica. Yet today it's one of history's great mysteries, for we know precious little about the people who lived here: what language they spoke, where they came from, or why they abandoned the place around A.D. 700, to vanish without a trace.

About the same time as the Romans were building the Colosseum and the Forum, the Teotihuacán people erected their own **Pyramid of the Sun,** still the third-largest pyramid in the world. Celestial observations were apparently vital to this culture—the movements of the planet Venus determined wars and human sacrifices—and the city was laid out accordingly. Climb 248 steps to the top of the pyramid to see its precision: The front wall of the Pyramid of the Sun is exactly perpendicular to the point on the horizon where the sun sets at the equinoxes, and the rest of the grand buildings lie at right angles to it. The first structure of the pyramid was probably built a century before Christ, and it was topped off with a temple about A.D. 300. When the site was discovered early in the 20th century, though, the temple had disappeared and the pyramid was an overgrown mass of rubble.

As you explore the site, set the kids on a treasure hunt for animal motifs. Walking up the main north–south street, the Calzada de los Muertos (Avenue of the Dead), look for a bit of wall sheltered by a corrugated roof: The fragment of a **jaguar painting** suggests what this street may have looked like with all its original paintings intact. Proceed to the **Pyramid of the Moon;** upon its plaza sits the **Palace of Quetzalpapalotl,** where figures of Quetzal-Mariposa (a mythical bird-butterfly) are painted on walls or carved in pillars; behind it, the **Palace of the Jaguars** has murals and frescoes of jaguars. At the south end of the Avenue of the Dead, in the immense sunken square named the Ciudadela (Citadel), there are the **Feathered Serpent Pyramid** and the **Temple of Quetzalcoatl;** point out to the kids the large serpents' heads jutting out from collars of feathers carved in the stone walls, as well as other feathered serpents carved on the walls.

ⓘ Hwy. 85D or 132D northwest, 48km (30 miles) from Mexico City (✆ **52/59/4956-0276** or 52/59/4956-0052).

✈ Mexico City.

🛏 $$$ **Hotel Four Seasons,** Paseo de la Reforma 500, Mexico City (✆ **800/819-5053** in North America, or 52/55/5230-1818; www.fourseasons.com). $$ **Hotel Imperial,** Paseo de la Reforma 64, Mexico City (✆ **52/55/5705-4911;** www.hotel imperial.com.mx).

WHY THEY'LL THANK YOU: Serpents, jaguars, and butterflies.

Early Humans **149**

England's Standing Stones
Stonehenge & Avebury
Ages 6 & up • Wiltshire, England

One of the world's most mysterious sites, Stonehenge may look instantly familiar to the kids; they've seen it depicted in hundreds of photos and cartoons. But seeing it in person is still awe-inspiring—there's definitely an aura about the place that can't be shrugged off.

No one knows who built it, though scholars have determined that it was first laid out around 3100 B.C. as a circle of upright timbers. Around 2500 B.C. it was rebuilt using 5-ton bluestones floated on rafts from Wales; 2 centuries later, the ancient builders replaced the bluestones with 45-ton Sarsen sandstone blocks. Moving rocks this big is quite a feat; you can still see drag marks in the earth. How did ancient workers stand these rocks on end, much less lift the distinctive crosspieces to place on top?

The biggest mystery, though, is why it was built at all. Archaeologists suggest that because the circle is perfectly aligned with the sun on the summer solstice, it was the site for some sun-worship ceremony.

Over the centuries, many stones fell over or were carted away by farmers, and visitors chipped off bits for souvenirs; immediate access to the stone circle has therefore been cut off to tourists—you'll have to circle around it on a walkway that never gets closer than 15m (50 ft.) to the actual stones. Nevertheless, in its solitary setting on this windswept grassy plain, Stonehenge's silent majesty exerts an eerie power that no visitor can deny. Rent a headset for the audio tour of the site—while the narrators tend to natter on too long, you can condense it for the kids and

Mysterious Stonehenge.

provide them with historical context that will make it seem even cooler.

Only 32km (20 miles) north, there's another set of standing stones that originally was even larger than Stonehenge: Avebury. Some visitors prefer **Avebury,** because it's not overrun with tour buses, and you can walk right up and around the few remaining stones, bristling out of the ground around the edge of the village. Archaeologists estimate it was built around 2400 B.C., a century or so before Stonehenge upgraded from bluestones to the same sarsen stones Avebury used (talk about keeping up with the neighbors). Rather than a celestial observatory, however, Avebury was most likely dedicated to earth goddess worship, celebrating the human cycle of birth, life, and death. (Note the sexually symbolic shape of several stones; there are also funerary groupings in this vast circular earthwork.) More than 100 sarsen stones—nearly a quarter of the original 400 or so—remain from this

vast complex, although they are more worn down than the ones at Stonehenge, and never did have the cross pieces on top. Avebury also has a tiny but significant archaeological museum on-site, the **Alexander Keiller Museum** (High St.; 44/1672/539250), displaying artifacts from Avebury and other nearby prehistoric sites.

ⓘ **Stonehenge,** Junction of A303 and A344/A360, 3.2km (2 miles) west of Amesbury (**44/1980/623108;** www.stonehenge.co.uk). **Avebury,** A361, btw. Swindon and Devizes (**44/1672/539425;** www.avebury-web.co.uk).

🚆 Salisbury, 1½ hr. from London.

🛏 $$$ **Grasmere House,** 70 Harnham Rd., Salisbury (**44/1722/338388;** www.grasmerehotel.com).

WHY THEY'LL THANK YOU: Ancient riddles without answers.

Ancient Stones of the Orkney Islands

Ages 8 & up • The Orkney Islands, Scotland

To visit the Orkney Islands, a sparsely populated archipelago some 6 miles north of the Scottish mainland, is to look at 1,000 years of history. It's virtually an archaeological garden, full of megalithic chambered tombs, stone chambers, and fortified Pict brochs (round stone towers). Don't expect slickly developed tourist sites—often you'll have to ask at a farmhouse for the key to a crumbling cairn, where you can poke around the eerie chambers by yourselves.

On the island called **Mainland,** the best stuff lies in West Mainland, around the town of Stromness. The magnificent chambered cairn of **Maes Howe** (℗ **44/1856/761-606;** book in advance) is a superb achievement of prehistoric architecture, a soaring space constructed from single rock slabs 5.4m (18 ft.) long and 1.2m (4 ft.) wide. The tour guide will show you one perfectly aligned passageway where the sun shines through only at the winter solstice, as well as point out the world's largest collection of Viking rune inscriptions, the work of marauding Norsemen hunting for buried treasure. Set on a bluff by the sea, the Stonehenge-like **Ring of Brodgar** (1560 B.C.) is a circle of some 30 stones surrounded by a deep ditch carved out of solid bedrock; nearby are the remnants of an even older stone circle, the four upright **Stenness Standing Stones.** The remarkable **Unstan Chambered Tomb** (℗ **44/1856/873-191**) is a burial mound, 35m (115 ft.) across, dating from 2500 B.C., with a chamber over 2m (6¹/₂ ft.) high. Of all the island's sites, though, the one the kids won't want to miss is **Skara Brae** (℗ **44/1856/841-815**), Europe's most complete Neolithic village. It's a whole settlement of stone-walled houses joined by covered passages. Last occupied about 2500 B.C., it was amazingly preserved by being buried in sand for

4,500 years. Not only have the outer walls been preserved, but you can even see the built-in stone furnishings—you can almost imagine that the residents have just moved out.

Take a ferry to **Rousay** island, off the northeast coast of Mainland, which has nearly 200 prehistoric monuments. On a stark promontory in its southwest corner broods the now-enclosed Iron Age **Midhowe Broch and Tombs,** a 23m-long (75-ft.) cairn divided into a dozen compartments. When it was excavated in the 1930s, the graves of some two dozen settlers, along with their cattle, were found inside. The other major sight, the nearby **Blackhammer Cairn** (℗ **44/1856/751-360**) is a megalithic burial chamber from the 3rd millennium B.C. Between them is an old Norse grave site, **Westness;** from here there's a marked 1.6km-long (1-mile) archaeological trail past dusty-looking excavations on either side.

On southeast **Sanday Island** is one of the most spectacular chambered cairns in the Orkneys: the **Quoyness Chambered Tomb** (ask for the key at the Lady Village post office), dating from around 2900 B.C., its 4m-high (13-ft.) chamber twice as high as Unstan's. Over on **South Ronaldsay,** the **Tomb of the Eagles** (south of Windwick Bay; ℗ **44/1856/831339**) is a fine chambered tomb from 3000 B.C.

ⓘ **Orkney Islands Travel Centre,** W. Castle St., Kirkwall (℗ **44/1856/872856;** www.visitorkney.com).

✈ Kirkwall Airport, Mainland Orkney. Small airstrip on Sanday.

FERRY: Northlink Ferries (to Orkneys; ℗ **44/845/600-0449;** www.northlinkferries.co.uk). **Orkney Ferries** (inter-island service; ℗ **44/1856/872044;** www.orkneyferries.co.uk).

⊨ $ **The Ferry Inn,** John St., Stromness (☏ **44/1856/850280;** www.ferryinn. com). $$ **Stromness Hotel,** The Pierhead, Stromness (☏ **44/1856/850298;** www. stromnesshotel.com).

TOUR: Orkney Archaeology Tours (☏ **44/ 1856/721450;** www.orkneyarchaeology tours.co.uk).

BEST TIME: May–July, when the midsummer sun remains over the horizon as long as 18¼ hr. a day.

WHY THEY'LL THANK YOU: The intense Indiana Jones vibe.

Newgrange
Mysterious Mound of the Ancient Celts
Ages 6 & up • Slane, County Meath, Ireland

It's older than England's Stonehenge, older even than the Great Pyramids in Egypt. Presiding serenely atop a hill near the Boyne River in Ireland, this **massive burial mound** dates back over 5,000 years—now that's ancient for you.

Newgrange is not only Ireland's best-known prehistoric monument, but it's also one of the archaeological wonders of western Europe, classified as a World Heritage Site by UNESCO. Here are Newgrange's vital statistics: The mound rises 11m (36 ft.) tall and measures approximately 79m (260 ft.) in diameter. Inside, a passage 18m (59 ft.) long leads to a central burial chamber with a cathedral-like ceiling 6m (20 ft.) high. The structure is so huge, it contains 200,000 tons of stone, including a 6-ton capstone; other stones weigh up to 16 tons each. All of this would be impressive enough if it had been erected with modern engineering

techniques, but when you make the children stop and think about what primitive tools were available to Newgrange's architects, they'll really be awed. Huge as the stones are, many of them were laboriously hauled from as far away as County Wicklow and the Mountains of Mourne—without the benefit of modern cranes, trucks, or trains.

Newgrange really is an amazing feat of engineering. Examine the unmortared stone walls closely: Each stone fits so perfectly in the overall pattern that the whole edifice is watertight. And this is no mere utilitarian construction—the passage walls are carved with myriad decorative spirals, diamonds, and concentric circles.

Now here comes the really amazing part: Every year at the winter solstice, sunlight pierces the inner chamber with an orange-toned glow for about 17 minutes

Ireland's prehistoric burial mound, Newgrange.

at dawn, from December 19 to December 23. Special **solstice viewing parties** are chosen by lottery months in advance; inquire at the visitor center.

All tickets are issued at the visitor center; get there early to ensure getting on a **tour** (the last tour is at 4:30pm). Shuttle buses will take you from there to the sites themselves (there is no direct access to the monuments). In summer, the site is extremely popular, so prepare to wait around for a while. Your combination ticket also lets you tour **Knowth,** a slightly more recent megalithic passage tomb (begun in 3000 B.C.) a mile away. Although it's not quite as massive, underneath its grassy mound, Knowth is more complex than Newgrange, with two main burial chambers, 17 satellite tombs, and a wealth of passage-tomb art, including some incredible calendar stones and lunar maps.

ⓘ **Bru na Boinne Visitor Centre,** Donore, (✆ **353/41/988-0300;** www.knowth.com/newgrange.htm).

🚆 Drogheda, 48km (30 miles) from Dublin.

🛏 $$ **Conyngham Arms Hotel,** Main St., Slane (✆ **353/41/988-4444;** www.conynghamarms.com). $ **Lennoxbrook Country House,** N3, Carnaross, near Kells (✆ **353/46/45902**).

WHY THEY'LL THANK YOU: Prehistoric doesn't always mean primitive.

Early Humans 152

The Hill of Tara
Throne of the High Kings
Ages 6 & up • County Meath, Ireland

Ireland is a nation of storytellers, where seemingly every mossy stone and country crossroads has a tale spun about it. But even so, there's no disputing the legendary significance of the Hill of Tara, traditional seat of the High Kings of Ireland.

On first glance, Tara today doesn't look like much—a 90m (300-ft.) high hill dotted with grassy mounds, some ancient pillar stones, and depressions that show where the Iron Age ring fort, Ráith na Ríogh, encircled the brow of the hill. But audiovisuals at the visitor center deconstruct just what those mounds represent, as if peeling away the centuries from this time-hallowed ridge, and a guided tour will make sure the kids note all the details as they explore the landscape. Prominent features include the ring barrow called Teach Chormaic (Cormac's House, referring to the great 3rd-century Celtic king Cormac Mac Airt) and the Forradh, or royal seat. A pale granite standing stone known as the Lia Fáil (Stone of Destiny) stands erect at the center of the Forradh's circular trench—according to legend, this pillar would roar its approval when a worthy king was crowned. The trenches of three other smaller ring forts are nearby, as well as Tara's oldest feature, an excavated passage tomb just to the north: the astronomically aligned Mound of the Hostages, which dates back to 2000 B.C.

The wood timbers of the old royal halls rotted long ago; the last great *feis*—a triennial banquet for princes, poets, priests, and politicians—was held in A.D. 560, after which the rise of Christianity forced ancient Celtic traditions into hiding. But Tara was always more than just one hill—it was the epicenter of Ireland's foremost kingdom, with many other important sites nearby. From Tara's green heights, for example, gaze toward the coast, and, in the distance, you can spot the great burial mound of Newgrange ⑮ and the

Hill of Slane, where St. Patrick readied himself to take on the Irish pagans—which, of course, he needed to do at Tara, Ireland's symbolic heart. Recent construction of the M3 motorway nearby, which has been bitterly protested by preservationists, unearthed several more underground residences that probably belonged to various nobles attached to the High King's court.

Give yourselves a few extra minutes to drink in the airy grandeur of this commanding hilltop—you just may feel the presence of those long-ago kings, haunting their ruined halls.

ⓘ **Hill of Tara,** off the N3, Navan, County Meath (✆ **353/46/902-5903** or 353/41/ 988-0300; www.knowth.com/tara.htm).

✈ Dublin.

🚆 Navan.

🛏 $$ **Conyngham Arms Hotel,** Main St., Slane (✆ **353/41/988-4444;** www. conynghamarms.com). $ **Lennoxbrook Country House,** N3, Carnaross, near Kells (✆ **353/46/45902**).

BEST TIME: Open mid-May to mid-Sept.

WHY THEY'LL THANK YOU: Getting a Celtic high.

153 Early Humans

Dun Aengus
A Ruin & a Riddle in Gaelic Ireland
Ages 6 & up • Inis Mór, Aran Islands, Ireland

On the Aran Islands, the locals are a hardy lot, living in stone cottages, speaking only Gaelic among themselves, and casting out to sea every day in small round currachs made of tarred canvas. In many ways, life here hasn't changed much for centuries—and that's why it's such a time warp experience to take a day trip from modern Galway City to the great **Iron Age fort** of Dún Aengus.

On a clear day, you can see the offshore Aran Islands from both the Cliffs of Moher and the coastline of Connemara. Ferries from Galway land at **Kilronan,** the main town on the island of **Inishmore** (Inis Mór); at the docks you can rent bikes or hail a minivan or, even better, an old-fashioned pony-drawn jaunting cart to get around the island. Follow the tourist traffic 7km (4⅓ miles) west to the island's greatest draw, Dún Aengus (Dún Aonghasa), which sits on a 90m-high (300-ft.) western cliff brooding over the sea. Set against the impossibly green landscape, this rough-piled structure of dark gray stones looks almost as if it had grown organically out of the gray-and-red-blotched rocky headland.

The fort is of great significance—every scholar agrees on that—but what they can't agree on is what that significance is. When you walk up the hill (a 20-min. hike from the visitor center), you pass a zone where sharp stones jut out of the ground, a primitive defensive measure known as a **cheval-de-frise.** Yet the design of the structure—three concentric semicircles opening to the sea—looks more like a theater than a fortress. True, the cliff behind it is so sheer that there would have been no need to fortify that side. (Look over carefully, and hold young children's hands—there's no guardrail.) The walls are certainly defensive, 6m (20 ft.) high in some places, and the thickest is 4.3m (14 ft.) thick. Yet if it was a fort, why are there no dwellings inside, and why is there no provision for bringing in water in case of siege? And within the centermost horseshoe, what is the purpose of that large table rock, almost like a sacrificial altar?

Taking a pony-drawn cart ride to Dún Aengus.

Even more vexing is the question of who built Dún Aengus. It could have been an ancient Celtic tribe called the Fir Bolgs, living a few centuries B.C., or it could have been 8th- or 9th-century Danes. Whoever built it also felt the need to build several such structures nearby—leave the other tourists behind and visit **Dún Dubh-chathair,** 2km (1¼ miles) southwest; **Dún Eochla,** the same distance northwest; and Dún Eoghanacht, 7km (4⅓ miles) west–northwest. Though smaller than Dún Aengus, they have the same primitive power, the same sense of mystery. If only these stones could speak!

(i) (C) **353/99/61008.**

✈ Inis Mór, Galway City, 37km (23 miles) from Rossaveal.

FERRY: Kilronan, 40 min. from Rossaveal.

🛏 $$$ **Harbour Hotel,** New Dock Rd., Galway City ((C) **353/91/569-466;** www.galwayharbourhotel.com). $$ **Kilmurvey House,** coast road, Inis Mór ((C) **353/99/61218;** www.kilmurveyhouse.com).

WHY THEY'LL THANK YOU: Trying to solve the riddle.

Carnac
A Mob of Megaliths
Ages 6 & up • Brittany, France

The French call this rugged stretch of Brittany the Côte Sauvage, or Wild Coast. Winds lash across the pine scrub dunes, and waves crash with fury against the reefs. Such a raw and elemental spot seems the perfect place for a prehistoric site such as Carnac's Field of Megaliths, where some 3,000 great rough stones stand—not in architectural circles like Stonehenge and other stone circles, but marching across the heath in regimented ranks, almost like a rock army.

The word for these stones is *menhirs,* a term taken from the old Breton language—fittingly, because there are more of these monolithic stones in Brittany than any other part of the world. Like their distant clansmen across the Channel, the pre-Celtic Bretons were fond of erecting such tall, tapering stones all over the countryside, whether to mark directions, commemorate a person or event, or provide a focus for religious rites. You'll find a few stones lined up in other sites around Brittany, but nowhere else are so many menhirs so strictly assembled in one place as at Carnac. The worn, lichen-coated gray stones—some as much as 20m (60 ft.) tall—stand lined up enigmatically in three major groupings: the large Ménec, the curving Kermario, and the smaller Kerlescan alignments. Notice how the rows seem to grow taller at the western end, and how the alignments are anchored at the ends with the ruins of either stone circles or small cromlechs (chambered tombs). Gazing at them, kids will readily believe the local legend, which says they're a Roman legion turned to stone by Merlin (the old Bretons told their own version of the King Arthur story).

Scientists date the Carnac stones to 4500–3300 B.C. and theorize that they served as a form of ancestor worship, with each stone marking a burial site. Besides the cromlechs, the fields contain a few *tumuli,* grass-covered mounds of earth heaped over graves. The kids should be able to pick out the largest of these tumuli, Saint-Michel, topped with its white chapel (a replica of the 17th-century original). Then ask them to find the site's largest individual menhir, the Giant, which stands 6.5m (21 ft.) tall. (Hint: Look for it near the Kerlescan alignment.)

To prevent vandalism, the local tourist authorities—amid much controversy—have fenced in the megaliths. You can wander freely among them only between October and March; the rest of the year (Apr–Sept) you'll have to come in with a guided tour. Tours last about an hour, and are usually conducted in French, though guides may add remarks in English if enough English speakers are in the group. Before or after your tour of the fields, you may also want to stop in town to visit the **Musée de Préhistoire** (10 place de la Chapelle; © **33/2/97-52-22-04**), which displays a huge collection of artifacts from the Paleolithic era to the 8th century, including burial objects excavated from the Saint-Michel tumulus.

ⓘ **Office de Tourisme,** 74 av. des Druides (© **33/2/97-52-13-52;** www.carnac.fr).

🚆 Quiberon or Auray.

🛏 $ **Hôtel Lann-Roz,** 36 av. de la Poste (© **33/2/97-52-10-48;** www.lannroz.com). $$$ **Hôtel le Diana,** 21 bd. de la Plage (© **33/2/97-52-05-38;** www.lediana.com).

WHY THEY'LL THANK YOU: An army turned to stone.

Secrets of Ancient Peru
The Nasca Lines
Ages 10 & up • Nazca, Peru

It's amazing enough to see ancient petroglyphs etched onto sandstone canyon walls—but what about geoglyphs, cut into the surface of the earth itself? Sprawling over nearly 1,036 sq. km (400 sq. miles) of the San Jose desert in southern Peru, the Nasca Lines are one of the most mysterious and awe-inspiring of ancient wonders: at least 10,000 lines forming **geometric designs**—trapezoids, zigzags, spirals—with another 300 **plant and animal figures** carved out of the barren earth beside them. And while you can see them from ground level, it wasn't until the age of airplanes that observers saw the pattern as it was meant to be seen—from the air. Which should lead kids to ask the obvious question: Why did the prehistoric creators of these lines draw them?

Experts believe they were constructed by the Nasca (pre-Inca) culture between 300 B.C. and A.D. 700, by removing dark surface stones to expose the pale soil beneath; the darker stones were then laid along the edge to sharpen the contrast. But why? There are lots of competing theories to explain these lines: that they were an astronomical calendar; that they marked out underground sources of water; that they were pointers to direct the divine spirits of the nearby Andes mountains to bring rains to this desert; or perhaps even that they were landing strips for alien spacecraft. (There's no hard science to support that last theory, of course.) The animal shapes represent age-old Andean fertility symbols, particularly those associated with water. But it's still mind-boggling to imagine these ancient people going to all the trouble of designing a pattern they'd never be able to view in its entirety—let alone doing it so accurately.

The Pan-American Highway was built in 1934 right through the Nasca Valley, rudely cutting across some of the biggest figures, just 21km (13 miles) north of the town of Nasca. Driving or hiking through the valley may further damage this fragile landscape, so why not do the responsible thing: See them from the air. Various tour operators offer flyovers in small private planes from the town of Nasca; or you can cut to the chase and book a fairly pricey day trip from Lima offered by **AeroCondor,** Jr. Juan de Arona 781 (© **51/1/614-6000** in Lima, or 51/56/25-6230 in Nasca; www.aerocondor.com.pe). From the window of an airplane, the kids will be able to identify specific shapes—a parrot, a hummingbird, a spider, a condor, a dog, a whale, a monkey—and they're huge: The spider is 50m (164 ft.) long, the monkey 100m (328 ft.) wide. The oddest of all is one humanlike figure with his hand raised in greeting, which almost inevitably has been named "the Astronaut." Cue up the *Twilight Zone* theme. . . .

✈ Lima, 346km (215 miles).

🛏 $$ **Casa Andina,** Jr. Bolognesi 367, Nasca (© **866/447-3270** in North America, 0800/047-0659 in U.K., or 51/56/52-3563; www.casa-andina.com). $$$ **Sonesta Posada del Inca,** Alcanflores 329, Miraflores, Lima (© **800/SONESTA** [766-3782] or 51/1/241-7688; www.sonesta.com/peru_miraflores). $ **Hotel Alegria,** Calle Lima 166, Nasca (© **51/56/522-702;** www.hotelalegria.net).

WHY THEY'LL THANK YOU: Seeing an ancient wonder as its makers never could.

Easter Island
The Big Heads of Rapa Nui
Ages 8 & up • Chile

Though it may be the most remote inhabited place on earth—2,480 miles (4,000 km) off the coast of Chile—Easter Island lives on tourism. And just about every visitor comes here to see the same thing: an enigmatic horde of some 600 immense stone figures hewn from dark volcanic tufa rock.

You can't deny the power of these sculptures. The faces are huge, with jutting brows and square jaws and startling white coral eyeballs. Every statue is strikingly individual, which suggests that they represented specific ancestors rather than gods. They were designed to be mounted

Some of Easter Island's 600 moais.

grandly on ceremonial stone platforms, ringed around the edge of the island.

But these big statues are shrouded in mystery. Fossil evidence suggests that Rapa Nui (the native name, which means "Navel of the World") was once covered with palm trees, which the original islanders may have razed during a frenzy of statue-building—an act that spelled environmental doom for this isolated population. (Trees are being replanted, but it's still a shadeless place.) Because that first population died out, no oral tradition has been passed down to explain why the statues, or *moais*, were built; many were found lying half-finished in an inland quarry, tumbled carelessly on their sides, or abandoned midroute to their pedestals. When the first Europeans visited the islands in 1722, the moais were upright; 50 years later, the next visitors found them knocked over, whether by desperate islanders or by hostile neighbors, we'll never know.

Even more baffling, *how* were such massive sculptures built by such primitive people? Experts assume that the moais were hauled from the quarry to the coast on a wooden sledge atop log rollers—hence the need for cutting down trees. Apparently the eyes weren't added until they were levered upright onto the platforms. Perhaps the islanders thought the eyes gave the moais spiritual power—when the statues were knocked from their platforms, most were toppled face forward, as if to hide the eyes in shame.

Some statues have been re-erected; they stand in an inscrutable row, staring wordlessly over this volcanic blip in the middle of the Pacific. Tourism is now Easter Island's main economic base; there are a handful of basic hotels and restaurants, along with tour guides, watersports operators (the island has some lovely white-sand beaches), and stables for horse trekking. From November through March, a stream of planes from Santiago, full of package tourists, lands on the island's tiny airstrip; cruise ships pull up, disgorging 800 to 900 passengers at a time; private island-hopping charter planes pop in, letting privileged travelers snap a few shots of the moais, then jet off somewhere else. Everyone sees the same sights: a few ancient temples and ceremonial sites, cave paintings and petroglyphs, a lake-filled volcanic crater, but mostly the quarries and moais. The more you stare at them, the grander and more mystical they seem. Who needs any distractions from that?

(i) **Easter Island** (Isla la Pascua; www. netaxs.com/trance/rapanui.html).

✈ Mataveri, Easter Island, 5½ hr. from Santiago.

🛏 $$$ **Posada de Mike Rapu,** Te Miro Oone (© **866/750-6699** in U.S., or 56/2/206-6060 in Santiago; www.explora. com). $$ **Hotel Taura'a,** Atamu Tekema, Hanga Roa (© **56/32/210-0463;** www. tauraahotel.cl).

WHY THEY'LL THANK YOU: The silent statues keep their secrets.

6 The Ancient World

Luxor

The Egyptian Museum
Cairo's Treasure Chest
Ages 6 & up • Cairo, Arab Republic of Egypt

Something about ancient Egyptians really fires the interest of young children—is it the squiggly hieroglyphic writing? The anthropomorphic animals? The wigs and the jewelry and the streamlined elegance of their fashion sense? Who knows, but if you've come to Egypt to see the great desert monuments—and you'd be nuts to bring the kids here without seeing them—an essential first stop is in Cairo, at the world's largest collection of Egyptian antiquities. Some 120,000 pieces of priceless sculpture, painting, bas-relief, pottery, and jewelry have been crammed into two floors of a cavernous, dark, rather ugly neoclassical building. Unlike Western museums, the **Egyptian Museum** doesn't go to any trouble to make exhibits attractive or interesting, let alone interactive—displays are labeled with crumbling yellowed index cards typed in Arabic, French, and appalling English. What you see is what you get. But what you see is spectacular enough to make it all worthwhile.

Take, for example, the upstairs rooms dedicated to the **treasures of Tutankhamun** (14th c. B.C.). The enameled gold funerary mask, a remarkably lifelike and sensitive portrait of the teenage Pharaoh, always has a crowd of admirers around it; his solid-gold innermost coffin, displayed nearby, is a dazzling masterpiece of tasteful, restrained inlay and engraving. There's an extra charge to visit the **Mummy Rooms,** also upstairs, but it may be the highlight of the trip for the children: The remarkably well-preserved remains of Egypt's mightiest rulers exude much more personality than you'd expect. (Tutankhamun, by the way, is not here but rests once again in his Valley of the Kings tomb.) Gazing upon the features of three 19th Dynasty

god-kings—Seti I and his son Ramses II, the notorious oppressors of the Israelites, and Ramses' son Merneptah, the Pharaoh of the Exodus—you get an undeniable impression of regal power and imperiousness, even though they are shriveled and stripped of all their royal paraphernalia.

This enormous, treasure-packed museum is not a place you can race through in an hour or even an afternoon. If you only have 2 hours, see the mummies and Tutankhamun. Take the other galleries at a child's pace, strolling past the glass cases until something catches your eye—something shiny, perhaps, or something very tiny and intricate, or something monumental and awesome. To interpret it all, try to get an **English-language guidebook** at the museum's gift shop, rather than investing in a guided tour (the Museum's tour guides are not really worth the fee).

(i) **Midan al-Tahrir** (© **20/2/579-6974**).

The mask of Tutankhamun.

✈ Cairo International, 19km (12 miles).

🛏 $$ **Ramses Hilton,** 1113 Corniche El-Nil (✆ **800/HILTONS** or 20/2/2577-7444; www.hilton.com). $$$ **Cairo Semiramis,**

Corniche El-Nil (✆ **888-424-6835** or 20/2/2795-7171; www.ichotelsgroup.com).

WHY THEY'LL THANK YOU: Tutankhamun, mummies, animal-headed statues: What kid could ask for more?

---

158 Cradles of Civilization

The Pyramids of Giza
Ancient Wonders in the Desert
Ages 6 & up • Giza (Al-Jizah), Arab Republic of Egypt

There are other pyramids scattered around the north of Egypt, but they're just shabby mounds of adobe compared to the **Pyramids of Giza.** This trio of stupendous tombs was one of the original Seven Wonders of the World—they're the only survivors of that ancient must-see list. And to sweeten the deal on this day trip from Cairo, there's a bonus: The kids can also see a bizarre statue right there guarding the Second Pyramid, a little monument they may know as the **Sphinx.**

Though urban sprawl makes it impossible these days to get the long view of the three Pyramids looming in the distance, up close the thing that staggers you is their size—an estimated 2,300,000 stones in the **Great Pyramid** alone, weighing on average about 2.5 tons apiece (some stones weigh as much as 9 tons). They were built for three Pharaohs of the 4th Dynasty (about 27th c. B.C.): the **Great Pyramid of Cheops,** the slightly smaller **Second Pyramid of Chephren,** and the much smaller **Third Pyramid of Mycerinus.** Miniature pyramids nearby entombed the wives of these kings. The Great Pyramid is about 137m (450 ft.) tall—its missing pinnacle would have added another 9m (30 ft.)—and measures 230m (755 ft.) on each side; the four sides almost perfectly face the points of the compass. Originally the Great and Second pyramids were faced with polished white limestone, though their facades today are jagged

The second Pyramid of Chephren.

from centuries of thievery (you can still see a white bit at the top of the Second Pyramid). The Third Pyramid is faced with red granite. The eternal puzzler, of course, is how they were erected at all, given the primitive technology available. Obviously it took a lot of manpower, or rather slave-power. The Pyramids' shape was chosen to imitate the rays of the sun shining down from its desert zenith—the idea was that the buried king might ascend to heaven using his pyramid as a ramp.

The **Great Sphinx,** Egypt's most mysterious symbol, has been repeatedly buried in sand and dug out again over the 4 millennia of its existence; 20m (66 ft.) tall and about 73m (240 ft.) long, it's a gargantuan likeness of King Chephren himself, dressed up as Harmachis, god of the rising sun. Ancient orange-red paint still clings in places to the battered face, which was vandalized by medieval Muslims. The Sphinx wasn't part of the original plan, but was improvised to get rid of a limestone knoll that blocked the king's view of his pyramid—maybe the most brilliant afterthought of all time. Its soft limestone, however, has required continual restoration over the ages. The royal "artificial beard," however, broke away in ancient times, beyond any hope of restoration (fragments are in the British Museum).

✈ Cairo International, 19km (12 miles).

🛏 $$ **Ramses Hilton,** 1113 Corniche El-Nil (© **800/HILTONS** [445-8667] or 20/2/2577-7444; www.hilton.com). $$$ **Cairo Semiramis,** Corniche El-Nil (© **888-424-6835** or 20/2/2795-7171; www.ic hotelsgroup.com).

WHY THEY'LL THANK YOU: If the Pyramids don't wow them, the Sphinx sure will.

Cradles of Civilization 159

The Valley of the Kings
Royal Tombs beneath the Desert Sands
Ages 8 & up • Across the Nile from Luxor, Arab Republic of Egypt

With all their romantic associations of buried treasure and tomb robbers, the cavernous tombs of the **Valley of the Kings** have been a tourist magnet since Greco-Roman times. After centuries in which successive pharaohs' pyramids were plundered of their treasure, in the 16th century B.C. Tuthmosis I tried a new-and-improved method of royal burial: in underground chambers under a pyramid-shaped mountain across the river from Thebes (modern Luxor). Throughout the 18th, 19th, and 20th dynasties, over 60 personages (mostly royalty) followed Tuthmosis I's lead. In the end, of course, this elaborate necropolis was no more thief-proof than the pyramids (only Tutankhamun's survived intact up to modern times). But while the pharaohs' buried riches are long gone, seeing the intricately decorated walls of these crypts is well worth the long trip up the Nile from Cairo.

Only about a quarter of these tombs are open to the public on a rotating basis.

The rules for touring them are strict: Photography is forbidden (most paintings are widely reproduced anyway), visitors must be quiet and file in one by one, and the kids should be reminded not to touch *anything.* If you're lucky, on the day you visit you may be able to see the small but interesting **tomb of Ramses I,** which has a vivid scene of the pharaoh consorting with hawk- and jackal-headed spirits; the burial chamber of the **tomb of Ramses VI** (12th c. B.C.), where magnificent ceiling paintings depict the stars and other heavenly bodies; or the dazzling quartzite sarcophagus in the **tomb of King Tutankhamun.** Though most of Tut's treasures were moved long ago to the Egyptian Museum in Cairo 157, inside that sarcophagus, under bulletproof glass, lies the gilded coffin that still contains Tut's mummy.

Decorations on the smoothly plastered tomb walls were carved to raise designs out of the surface, and then boldly painted.

Before you enter these narrow, mazelike passageways, ask the kids to imagine working down here, with only a guttering wick lamp to light the wall—it's amazing how much meticulous detail these anonymous artists accomplished under such odds.

While you're here, don't miss the elegant columned **Temple of Hatshepsut,** just across the hill, or the jumbled ruins of the **Temple of Karnak,** with their elaborately incised round columns, just north of Luxor.

ⓘ **Tourist Office,** Nile St., Luxor (ℂ **20/ 95/382215;** www.luxorguide.com).

✈ Luxor International.

🏨 $$ **Hotel El Nakhil,** Gezirat al Baraat, (ℂ **20/95/2313922;** www.el-nakhil.com). $$$ **Hilton Luxor Resort & Spa,** Karnak (ℂ **800/HILTONS** [445-8667] or 20/95/ 2374933; www.hilton.com).

WHY THEY'LL THANK YOU: Where the Pharaohs went to become gods.

Knossos
Daedalus's Ancient Labyrinth
All ages • Iraklion, Crete

Though today it's part of modern Greece, the island of Crete long ago was home to its own powerful Minoan civilization, named after the famous king Minos. In Greek mythology, King Minos's palace at Knossos was notorious for its labyrinth, designed by the ingenious Daedalus and containing a grotesque monster, the Minotaur. Half-bull and half-man, the Minotaur devoured young victims purposely lost in the labyrinth. Finally the hero Theseus navigated the maze safely (with the help of Minos's daughter Ariadne) and slew the Minotaur. To punish Daedalus for revealing the secret to Ariadne, Minos imprisoned Daedalus and his son Icarus in the labyrinth. Daedalus built them wax wings to fly out, but Icarus, like any reckless adolescent, flew too near the sun, melted his wings, and fell to his death. It's a particularly vivid myth for youngsters, and rambling around the haphazardly laid-out ruins of Knossos, they'll feel it come thrillingly to life.

Arriving in Iraklion, Crete's gateway city, it's a good idea to look at the Minoan antiquities in the **Archaeological Museum,** 1 Xanthoudidou (ℂ **30/2810/226-092)**

before heading out to Knossos. These artifacts cover every phase of Crete's checkered history, from the first settlement by humans (around 6000 B.C.) to the emergence of a distinctive Minoan culture (2500 B.C.), the intrusion of Mycenaean Greeks (1500 B.C.), Roman occupation (starting in 67 B.C.), and conquest by Venetians in the 13th century. The original frescoes from Knossos are kept here for preservation (the frescoes now at Knossos are copies).

About 5km (3 miles) south of Iraklion, the **Palace of Knossos** is one of the world's great archaeological sites, the remains of not one but two major palaces from about 2000 to 1250 B.C. This was not just a royal residence but also the Minoans' chief religious ceremonial center, as well as their administrative headquarters. Until archaeologist Arthur Evans began excavations in 1900, little was known about the Minoans, but the wealth of artifacts allowed archaeologists to virtually reconstruct an entire culture.

While many ancient sites present only authentic ruins, Evans took a different approach, using every available clue and remnant to rebuild large parts of the palace—walls, floors, stairs, huge timber-framed windows to let in the Mediterranean sunlight, and wooden columns painted red and black. Copies of the original frescoes brighten the walls; stairways lead tantalizingly to long-gone upper stories. Look for King Minos's **stone throne,** dating from the 15th century B.C., in the throne room, a brilliant **fresco of leaping dolphins** in the queen's apartments, and **pictures of bulls** in numerous friezes and murals. This palace was so luxurious, it even had running water and flush toilets (and we're talking B.C.-era plumbing). For children especially, such aggressive restoration makes it easier to imagine the lives of ancient Minoans, Minotaur and all.

ⓘ Knossos Rd. (✆ **30/2810/231-940**).

✈ Iraklion, 5km (3 miles).

🏨 $$$ **Aquila Atlantis Hotel,** 2 Igias, Iraklion (✆ **30/2810/229-103;** www.theatlantishotel.gr). $$ **Xenia-Helios,** Kokkini Hani (✆ **30/2810/761-502**).

WHY THEY'LL THANK YOU: Getting caught up in the labyrinth.

Cradles of Civilization **161**

The Ruins of Ancient Troy
Where the Iliad Comes to Life
Ages 10 & up • Hisarlik, Turkey

Site of Homer's epic battle between the Trojans and the Greeks, immortalized in *The Iliad,* the ruins of what claims to be ancient Troy aren't very large, or very complete. But to my mind, Troy *should* look like a bereft ruin—wasn't it in flames when the victorious Greeks sailed away?—and it should have a tantalizing air of mystery. Though all you can see today is a hodge-podge of stony debris dug out of a windswept Turkish flood plain, overlooking the Dardanelles, it's still exciting to feel that you've stepped into one of the greatest stories of all time.

Thanks to the dogged archaeology of an obsessed German named Heinrich Schliemann, the foundations of this ancient city—lost for so long that many thought Homer had made it up—were uncovered in the 1870s on the Biga Peninsula of Turkey, where a silted-up bay had once connected to the Scamander River. Schliemann, however, unscrupulously removed significant amounts of treasure for his own personal gain, and some scholars (miffed no doubt by Schliemann's unorthodox behavior) dispute whether this buried city was actually Troy. Still, there's no question there was a major city here—in fact, several major cities: Archaeologists have defined at least nine different layers of construction dating back to 3500 B.C. The seventh layer down is assumed to be Homer's Troy, which evidence shows was destroyed by fire around 1200 B.C. (1184 B.C. is the date traditionally assigned to the events of the *Iliad*). Rebuilt 400 years later, Troy became an important city again during the Roman period—Augustus Caesar, Marcus Aurelius, and Hadrian all slept here.

A **guided tour** is a wise idea—experienced guides will be able to tell the kids a lot more about what they're seeing than you could possibly cull from a guidebook. Half-day tours are available from Çanakkale, or overnight tours from Istanbul (which include a visit to the tragic World War I battlefield of Gallipoli right across the straits). One experienced operator is **Hassle Free Travel Agency,** Cumhuriyet Cad. 61, in the Anzac House in Çanakkale (✆ **90/286/217-5482;** www.anzachouse.com). Archaeologists estimate that the ruins of Troy actually extend 10 times farther than the 165 sq. m (1,776 sq. ft.) they've uncovered so far. A few structures have been reconstructed on the site, including a temple of Athena, a sacrificial altar, a Roman theater, a Senate building, and a graveyard of homeless marble columns. And of course there's a very satisfying model of the **Trojan Horse,** with steps so the kids can climb up inside.

ⓘ Hisarlik-Troia, off Hwy. 17–56, 16km (10 miles) south of Çanakkale.

FERRY: Çanakkale.

🛏 $$$ **Kolin Hotel,** Kepez (ⓒ **90/286/ 218-0808;** www.kolinhotel.com). $$ **Tusan Hotel,** Güzelyali (ⓒ **90/286/232-8746;** www.tusanhotel.com).

WHY THEY'LL THANK YOU: Walking in the steps of Achilles.

The Warriors of Xīān
A Chinese Army of Stone
Ages 6 & up • Bīngmǎyǒng, China

Any child who's ever played with toy soldiers will thrill to this sight: Thousands upon thousands of life-size warriors, an entire army of ancient terra-cotta statues standing at attention in an underground trench, ready to march before their emperor into the afterlife. After The Great Wall **203**), **Qín Shǐ Huáng's tomb** at Bīngmǎyǒng is the sight most Western visitors look forward to seeing when they come to China—and this is one major sight that never disappoints.

The nearby town of Xīān was once the largest, most cosmopolitan city in the world—perfectly located to dominate the Silk Road trading routes, it served as capital of several dynasties, up through the Tang dynasty (A.D. 618–907). The stone soldiers buried at Bīngmǎyǒng, however, date from much earlier, in the 2nd century B.C. The ambitious, totalitarian Qín Shǐ Huáng, the first Emperor of China, was bent on ensuring his place in the afterworld, and so he hired a corps of 700,000 workers (more than twice the number used to build the Great Wall) to do no less than reproduce the entire universe under ground. Historians tell us that his many-chambered **burial complex** covered a full square mile, containing models of palaces,

towers, and buildings. A ceiling was painted with the constellations, and the Yangzi and Yellow rivers flowed in mercury. Whale-oil lamps provided permanent lighting, and automatic crossbows were set up to shoot grave robbers; the rafters were reportedly hung with pearls, jade, and green feathers. There was so much down here that historians of the time don't even mention the soldiers.

The main part of the tomb has not been opened, although most likely it was plundered long ago. Still, if the soldiers are any evidence, the craftsmanship throughout was amazing. In Bīngmǎyǒng's first pit, you'll see 11 passageways with four columns of warriors in each—about **6,000 infantry** lined up, battle ready. Though their bodies were mass-produced from molds, by using interchangeable parts—varying leg or shoulder shapes, which then were posed at different angles—the workmen produced a mind-boggling variety of individual figures. The heads were all handmade, and no two are the same—study their facial features, hairstyles, and headdresses and you'll see a surprising range of ethnic types. Every detail, from the rivets on their armor to the straps on their sandals, has

The terra-cotta warriors of Xiān.

been rendered as realistically as possible. The regular soldiers are 5 feet 11 inches tall; senior officers, laid in pit 3, are a little taller, as befits their rank (one general dug up from pit 2 is nearly 6½ ft. tall).

The sight of these lifelike ranks of terra-cotta men, filling the vast hangarlike exhibit space, is simply astonishing—they go on and on, like a digitally dubbed cast of extras in a blockbuster movie, except these were individually created *by hand*, each one given his own distinctive face. Qín Shǐ Huáng got his wish all right—he'll be eternally remembered for this grandiose mania, and for the stunning artworks that resulted.

ⓘ On the Eastern Route, in Lintong, 35km (22 miles) east of Xiān (✆ **86/29/8391-1961**).

✈ Xiān.

🛏 $$$ **Sheraton Xiān,** Fēnghào Dōng Lù 262 (✆ **86/29/8426-1888;** www.sheraton.com/xian). $$ **Wǔyī Fàndiàn,** Dǒng Dàjiē 351 (✆ **86/29/8768-1098;** www.may-first.com).

WHY THEY'LL THANK YOU: Emperors have toy soldiers too.

The Acropolis
Hilltop Shrine of Ancient Athens
All ages • Athens, Greece

We've all seen it a hundred times on posters and postcards and cardboard coffee cups: the **Acropolis,** that hilltop rising boldly out of Athens with the famous columns of the **Parthenon.** But to actually be here, to walk around its crumbling stones, can be the experience of a lifetime. Ignore the crowds: We found a place to sit, gazed out over modern Athens sprawling below, and took time to muse about all who had been here before us.

For 25 centuries, these marble columns and pediments have floated above the rat race of Athens, glowing beige at dawn, golden at high noon, rose at sunset, ethereal white in the moonlight. Successive waves of invaders took over this sheer rocky outcrop—the Romans made it a brothel, the Christians an Orthodox church, the Turks a mosque and arsenal—and earthquakes and explosions did their part as well. Still, nothing could erase the serene, sacred beauty of the Acropolis.

Though you enter the Acropolis through the Roman-era Beulé Gate, that is merely an entrance to the real entrance—the monumental **Propylaia** arch. Just above the Propylaia, to the right, is the little, beautifully proportioned **Temple of Athena Nike;** to the left is the **Erechtheion,** the tomb of legendary Athenian king Erechtheus. Take time to study its delicate stone carving, especially the female figures (caryatids) holding up its pediments. Ask the children to imagine these buildings and statues painted in their original vivid color schemes—how different that must have looked!

The real star of the show is the **Parthenon,** the great temple dedicated to Athena. Ictinus, the Parthenon's architect, was a master of optical illusions: Big as it is, this temple seems light and graceful, with 46 slender columns (17 on each side, 8 at each end) ranged along the outsides. Its columns and stairs appear straight, yet all are minutely curved, with each exterior column thicker in the middle. The airy look of the Parthenon is also due to the fact that it has no roof—in 1687, Venetian invaders blew it to smithereens. The original sculptures on its triangular pediments portrayed the life of Athena, while battle scenes decorated a frieze above the columns. In the 19th century, however, British ambassador Lord Elgin carted off most of the sculptures to London (see them in the British Museum) for "safekeeping."

In 2007, the **Acropolis Museum** was opened at the base of the sacred mount, to protect indoors as much of the statuary as could safely be transferred. (They've been replaced on the outdoor site by meticulous reproductions.) Artifacts are arranged in chronological order; the climax is a majestic glass gallery displaying the few Parthenon friezes the Greeks still possess. The gallery opens up to a view of the Parthenon on the hill above, and has left gaping spaces where those Elgin

The Acropolis.

Marbles *could* be installed, if ever Great Britain gives them back.

(i) **New Acropolis Museum,** Dionyssiou Areopagitou St. (© **30/210/924-1023;** www.newacropolismuseum.gr).

✈ Athens International, Spata, 27km (17 miles).

🛏 $$ **Athens Cypria,** 5 Diomias (© **30/210/323-8034;** www.athenscypria.com). $$$ **Hilton,** 46 Leoforos Vas. Sofias (© **800/HILTONS** [445-8667] in the U.S., or 30/210/728-1000; www.hilton.com).

WHY THEY'LL THANK YOU: Socrates and Plato walked here.

Classical Capitals **164**

National Archaeological Museum
The Great Hoard of Greek Antiquities
Ages 4 & up • Athens, Greece

If Western civilization was born in ancient Greece, intervening centuries of war and invasion destroyed much of its heritage—or at any rate scattered it, for every new conqueror looted whatever Greek antiquities were available, a cache displayed today in museums around the globe. Still, enough wondrous art and artifacts remained in Greece to fill Athens's rambling **National Archaeological Museum.** If these are the leftovers, just imagine how rich the total collection might have been.

While the **Acropolis** is an open-air shrine to 5th-century Athenian culture, this museum's vast collection ranges all over the Greek isles and across centuries of Greek culture, giving us a great sense of the full sweep of Greek history. Like magpies, we were attracted, of course, to the stunning **Mycenaean Collection,** blazing with gold masks, cups, dishes, and jewelry unearthed from the site of Mycenae by Heinrich Schliemann in 1876. We Trojan War fans stared open-mouthed at the majestic burial mask that Schliemann called the **"Mask of Agamemnon":** archaeologists have pretty much debunked that theory, but even if the mask belonged to an earlier, unknown monarch, it still has a haunting power, and all that gold testifies to the wealth and power that was Mycenae.

But as we passed through the museum's calm white galleries, we began to be more intrigued by the development of sculpture over time. We began with the **Cycladic figurines,** which date from about 2000 B.C., a collection of pale marble figures so simple and yet expressive, they reminded us of modern abstract art, like Henry Moore and Brancusi. With the Archaic period came stiffly posed *kouros* statues, carved from warm-colored stone, intricately detailed and yet less lifelike. By the **Classical period,** however, the Greeks had become such skilled sculptors, they could celebrate idealized physical beauty in bronze. Probably the most awesome example is the 5th-century *Zeus of Artemision,* which many scholars contend is really a statue of Poseidon. Mull over with the kids the crucial question of what this powerful-looking god originally held in his backward-flung hand, ready to hurl—if it was a thunderbolt, then this was Zeus; if it was a trident, Poseidon. In the **Hellenistic period** (323–31 B.C.) the statues finally become vivid individuals, like the coolly self-confident *Youth of Anticythera,* usually identified as Perseus (imagine his outstretched arm holding aloft a trophy head of Medusa), or the riveting statue of a small boy riding jockey on a powerful leaping horse. Before we came here, it was all Greek to us; 1½ hours later, we knew how much more we had to learn.

ⓘ 44 Patission St. (✆ **30/210/821-7724**).

✈ Athens International, Spata, 27km (17 miles).

🛏 $$ **Athens Cypria,** 5 Diomias (✆ **30/210/323-8034;** www.athenscypria.com). $$$ **Hilton,** 46 Leoforos Vas. Sofias (✆ **800/HILTONS** [445-8667] in the U.S., or 30/210/728-1000; www.hilton.com).

WHY THEY'LL THANK YOU: A thunderbolt or a trident—you decide.

165 Classical Capitals

Where the Gods Spoke to the Greeks

Ages 6 & up • Delphi, Greece

The ancient Greeks believed that Delphi, on the slopes of Mount Parnassus, was the center of the world, chosen by Apollo as the home of his most famous oracle. Pilgrims came from throughout the Greek world to ask Apollo's advice, on affairs of state or even small personal matters. The god's advice was often cryptic—"Invade and you will destroy a great empire," King Croesus of Lydia was told when he asked if he should go to war against Persia. So Croesus invaded, and destroyed a great empire—his own.

Delphi, which is close enough to Athens for a long day trip, is one of Greece's loveliest sites, perched above a beautiful plain of olive trees stretching toward the Gulf of Corinth. Maybe it's just my imagination, but a mysterious aura still seems to hang over the ruins. As you enter along the marble Sacred Way, trod by visitors for thousands of years, the centuries seem to unfurl.

Originally the sanctuary was lined with outdoor sculptures; most have been moved inside to the **Delphi Museum.** The star of the museum, with a room to himself, is the 5th-century-B.C. **Charioteer of Delphi,** a larger-than-life bronze figure (his four-horse chariot, sadly, is long lost). Delicate eyelashes shade his enamel-and-stone eyes, and realistic veins stand out in his hands and feet.

The main attraction is the **Sanctuary of Apollo,** immediately beyond and just above the museum. On your way uphill, you'll pass the remains of Roman stoas and a number of Greek treasuries, small templelike buildings that city-states built at Delphi to store riches and artworks dedicated to Apollo (ever vying to outdo their neighbors). Note the countless ancient inscriptions incised on the treasury walls. The public can no longer enter the massive 4th-century-B.C. temple of Apollo, but peer inside where three Pythian priestesses were always on duty, one of them delivering "Apollo's" pronouncements from a room deep within the temple. No one knows for sure how the priestesses, who often spoke in tongues, came up with their predictions—they may have inhaled hallucinatory fumes or chewed mind-altering herbs, such as the laurel leaf sacred to Apollo.

Delphi was also the site of the once-every-4-years Pythian Games, the most famous festival in Greece after the Olympics (see Olympia ❹❻❹), held up a steep hill from the temple at the remarkably well preserved 4th-century-B.C. **theater** and **stadium.**

Follow the Arakova-Delphi road toward the fragmentary ruins of the **Sanctuary of Athena,** who shared the honors here with Apollo. As a writer, I halt midway at the **Castalian Spring,** where legions of poets came to drink in hopes of finding inspiration.

Above are the rose-colored cliffs known as the **Phaedriades** (Bright Ones), which almost magically reflect the sun's rays. It's no longer possible to drink from the springs, but inspiration wells up regardless.

ⓘ **The Sanctuary of Apollo & Delphi Museum** (✆ **30/22650/82-312**).

✈ Athens International, Spata, 200km (125 miles).

🛏 $$$ **Amalia Delphi,** 1 Apollonos St. (off the Delphi-Itea Rd.; ✆ **30/22650/82-101;** www.amalia.gr).

WHY THEY'LL THANK YOU: We have fortune cookies and horoscopes; the Greeks had an oracle.

Classical Capitals

166

In the Footsteps of Alexander the Great

Ages 8 & up • Pella, Vergina & Dion, near Thessaloniki, Greece

Thessaloniki, Greece's second city, is known for its Byzantine churches and atmospheric Turkish quarter, but we came here to explore something more ancient: Alexander the Great country. When it comes to heroes, they don't get much more heroic than Philip of Macedonia and his son Alexander. When Philip was born in 382 B.C., most Greeks thought of Macedonians as a rude northern tribe of barbarians; by 338 B.C., he had conquered all of Greece. Two years later, Philip was dead, leaving his empire to his untested son Alexander, and many wondered how the youth could run Macedonia, let alone Greece. By the time he died at age 33, he was known as Alexander the Great and ruled most of the known world, as far east as India.

Both Philip and Alexander were born in **Pella,** a once-great seaport (now silted up) 40km (25 miles) west of Thessaloniki. On the hilltop north of the archaeological site, you can peer over a wire fence at the ruins of a vast palace complex (closed to the public), birthplace of both Philip and his son Alexander, and also where Aristotle tutored the young Alexander. In Pella's small **museum** (Thessaloniki-Edessa Hwy.; ✆ **30/23820/31-160** or 23820/31-278; closed Sun), look for a mosaic of a lion hunt—some scholars suggest that it depicts an incident in which a friend saved

Alexander from a lion. Compare it to the marble bust of Alexander in the museum and decide for yourself.

Another 20km (12 miles) south in **Vergina,** Philip had another immense **palace,** with a huge inner courtyard, a long colonnaded veranda, and an impressive theater where, walking to a play one fatal day in 336 B.C., he was assassinated. (Some scholars think Alexander was behind the foul deed.) Driving across the rolling plain, you'll see hundreds of **burial mounds.** In 1977, Greek excavators opened the marble gates of an unidentified tomb to find a solid gold ossuary: Inside, a pile of charred bones was still stained royal purple from the cloth in which they had been wrapped. Could it be Philip's tomb? It has never been fully proven, but alongside the bones were gold wreaths, little ivory portraits of Philip and Alexander, and an unmatched pair of bronze shin guards (an early injury had left one of Philip's legs shorter than the other). Inside the town's **Royal Tombs Museum** (✆ **30/23310/92-347**), a passageway leads into an area where the five temple-like tombs, their facades beautifully painted, can be viewed through a protective glass wall.

Some 78km (48 miles) south of Thessaloniki are the ruins of **Dion,** once Macedonia's most important religious sanctuary. Both Philip and Alexander established military camps here. Check out the site's **museum** (℅ **30/23510/53-206**), for models that help you visualize the Dion of Philip and Alexander. It was here that 8-year-old Alexander first saw Bucephalos, a handsome black stallion that neither Philip nor any of his men could tame. Alexander asked if he could try, and, turning Bucephalos so that he could not see his shadow, the boy leaped on his back and galloped away. When the prince returned from his ride, Philip said, "My son, look for a kingdom equal to you. Macedonia is too small." There's a great deal to see at Dion, but leave time to picnic under the shade trees, imagining Alexander, at age 22, mounting Bucephalos and setting off to conquer the world.

ⓘ **Tourist Office,** 136 Tsimiski St., Thessaloniki (℅ **30/2310/221-100;** www.saloniki. org. Also www.macedonian-heritage.gr/museums).

✈ Macedonia International Airport, Thessaloniki.

🚂 Thessaloniki, 6 hr. from Athens.

🛏 $$$ **Electra Palace Hotel,** 9 Aristotelous Sq., Thessaloniki (℅ **30/2310/294-000;** www.electrahotels.gr). $$ **Philippion,** Seich-Sou Park, Thessaloniki (℅ **30/2310/203-320;** www.philippion.gr).

WHY THEY'LL THANK YOU: Where Alexander became great.

---

167 Classical Capitals

The Colosseum
The Arena Rocks

All ages • Rome, Italy

Perhaps no classical Roman ruin evokes the excesses of the late Empire like the **Colosseum.** In A.D. 80, the opening event at this 50,000-seat elliptical arena was a weeks-long bloody combat between gladiators and wild beasts. Later shows kept upping the ante: Vestal Virgins from the temple screamed for blood, ever-more exotic animals were shipped in to satisfy jaded curiosities, the arena floor was flooded for not-so-mock naval battles. Really big events such as chariot races were held at the Circus Maximus, on the other side of the Palatine hill, but today it's a formless heap of ruins. The Colosseum, though—a kid can stand here and really imagine the whole scene.

Over the years, the Colosseum has been damaged by earthquake, stripped of its rich marble facing, and begrimed by exhaust from cars whipping around the vicious traffic circle outside. But to modern eyes, its time-ravaged shell has its own haunted grandeur. While you're waiting in line outside—and you will wait seemingly forever in line, unless you reserved your tickets in advance or you join a private tour (freelance guides constantly scout the lines for business; they're pricey but if the line's long and your kids are getting cranky, it may be worthwhile)—look up and study the taller sections, which have preserved the original four-tiered design. Note how each level has a different style of column, like a textbook illustration of Doric, Ionic, and Corinthian. Once inside, roam around the shattered seating and look down at the center ring where the fighters met either glory or a bloody death. Most of the flooring is gone now, revealing the honeycomb of compartments underneath where elephants, lions, and wild animals waited to be hoisted up onto the arena floor. It's dusty, crumbling, and utterly amazing.

Across from the Colosseum are the **Roman Forums,** the center of Roman life

The Colosseum.

in the days of the Republic, which are still being excavated (if you're lucky, you may see archaeologists at work). Traversed by the Via Sacra (Sacred Way), the vast public ground of the Forum lay between the Palatine and Capitoline hills. When it came to praising Caesar, purchasing a harlot, sacrificing a naked victim, or just hashing over the day's events, the Roman Forum was the place to be. By day, the columns of now-vanished temples and triumphal arches (not to mention the worn stones from which long-forgotten orators spoke) are mere shells overrun with wild grass and weeds. But at night, when the Forum is silent in the moonlight, it isn't difficult to imagine those zoned-out Vestal Virgins still guarding the sacred temple fire.

ⓘ **Colosseo,** Piazzale del Colosseo (✆ **39/ 6/3996-7600;** www.colosseum.net).

✈ Leonardo da Vinci International Airport.

🛏 $$$ **Hotel de Russie,** Via del Babuino 9 (✆ **800/323-7500** in North America, or 39/06-328881; www.romeby. com/derussie/pages/reach.htm). $ **Hotel Grifo,** Via del Boschetto 144 (✆ **39/06- 4871395;** www.hotelgrifo.com).

WHY THEY'LL THANK YOU: *Gladiator* comes to life.

The Pantheon
Glory of the Roman Empire
Ages 6 & up • Rome, Italy

Viewing the battered shell of the Colosseum, the kids will know they're looking at ancient Roman ruins. But the Pantheon? My kids stood inside that perfectly engineered dome and were amazed to learn how long ago it was built. Not only is it wonderfully preserved (converted to a Catholic church in 609 A.D., but it also was spared the ravages of later invaders), this most intact of all ancient Roman buildings also survived simply because it was built so well in the first place.

The Pantheon doesn't tower on a lofty hilltop or preside over a ceremonial plaza; it comes upon you almost by surprise, tucked away amid the buildings of modern Rome. Unlike Rome's "big" sights, you don't have to wait in line to visit, and there are few displays to look at—which made my kids like it even more. **The name means "place for all the gods,"** and that was this temple's original purpose when it was built, in 27 B.C., by Marcus Agrippa. (Like many other buildings, it was reconstructed by that busy architecture maven, Emperor Hadrian, in the 2nd century A.D.) The statues of Roman gods that used to decorate its ring of niches were lost long ago. But while so many shrines proclaim their own importance with monumental flights of steps or endless rows of columns, the Pantheon instead inspires awe with a stunningly simple design: a perfect sphere nestled in a cylinder, exactly as wide as it is tall (for the record, it's 43m/142 ft. in either dimension). It's the scale that makes it extraordinary—up until the 20th century, its massive hemisphere of cast concrete was the biggest pile of concrete ever constructed. Another ribbed dome of ingeniously cantilevered brick was then laid on top and brightly gilded (the gilt wore off long ago).

Inside it's basically one big room, a round domed chamber faced with bands of multicolored marble. Standing in the center of the temple, look straight up and you'll see a round aperture at the top, almost like the pupil of this giant eyeball. It's hard to believe it's actually 5.5m (18 ft.) in diameter—the dome is so high, that oculus looks like a pinhole. While it admits welcome beams of light into the dusky interior, its real purpose was to funnel out the smoke from animal sacrifices that were burned on an altar in the center.

That domed design was so brilliant, it was copied endlessly throughout the Renaissance and again in every classical revival in architectural history, all the way from Michelangelo's cupola of St. Peter's down to Thomas Jefferson's Monticello (just turn over a U.S. nickel to see the same iconic shape). Maybe that's why the kids instantly felt at home here—they've already seen the Pantheon's offspring, all over the world.

ⓘ Piazza della Rotonda (✆ **39/06-68300230**).

✈ Leonardo da Vinci International Airport.

🛏 $$$ **Hotel de Russie,** Via del Babuino 9 (✆ **800/323-7500** in North America, or 39/06-328881; www.romeby.com/derussie/pages/reach.htm). $ **Hotel Grifo,** Via del Boschetto 144 (✆ **39/06-4871395;** www.hotelgrifo.com).

WHY THEY'LL THANK YOU: Built to last.

Under the Volcano
The Buried Town of Pompeii

Ages 8 & up • Pompeii & Ercolano, Italy

Yes, **Pompeii** was the site of a natural disaster when it was buried in volcanic ash and mud after Mount Vesuvius erupted in A.D. 79. But while the kids may pick up a melancholy aura about this ghost city, they'll soon see that Pompeii is exciting not because it was destroyed, but because it was saved—preserved by the very same volcanic debris, exactly it was 2,000 years ago. In other cities, a few large and important classical buildings survived, but Pompeii is an entire town: There's no better place to imagine the daily life of the ancient Roman Empire.

It's only a 45-minute train ride from Naples via the Circumvesuviana railway (get off at the Pompeii Scavi stop). Not every artifact of ancient Pompeii remains on-site: The Pompeiians themselves (those who escaped) returned once the ashes had cooled to grab a few treasures before abandoning the town. The buried city was rediscovered in 1599, and once serious excavation began in the mid–18th century, several of the most precious mosaics and frescoes were taken up to Naples, where you can see them in the **National Archaeological Museum,** Piazza Museo Nazionale 18–19 (© **39/81/440166**). Still, there is plenty left to see in the forlorn, still dilapidated-looking ruined town. Highlights include the **House of the Vettii**'s black-and-red dining room with its frescoes of delicate cupids; the spectacular frescoes in

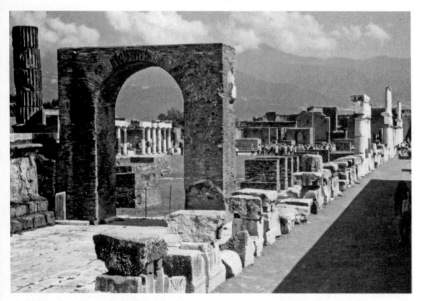

The ruins of Pompeii.

the **House of the Mysteries,** outside the city walls; and the imposing **House of the Faun,** with no fewer than four dining rooms and two spacious peristyle gardens. (Be aware that the Pompeiians had a different attitude toward sex than we do; you may prefer to distract the kids from erotic images in some frescoes and mosaics.) In the center of town is the **forum,** the heart of Pompeiian life, surrounded by a basilica, the Temple of Apollo, the Temple of Jupiter, and the Stabian Thermae (baths), where you'll even see some skeletons. The open-air **Great Theater** could hold 5,000 spectators at its bloodthirsty battles between wild animals and gladiators. The main thing, though, is to walk these paved streets between largely intact buildings and visualize citizens going about their daily routines on that August day, just before an exploding cloud blotted out the sun.

If you're energetic enough, you can also stop at neighboring Herculaneum, buried by the same eruption. **Herculaneum,** one-fourth the size of Pompeii, was found in 1709, but it still hasn't been completely dug out—it was more heavily buried than Pompeii, and being an upper-class resort, its buildings are more complicated and thus harder to unearth. You can get a good idea of how aristocrats lived at the **Casa dei Cervi** (House of the Stags). In the end, the wealthy were smothered under the ash just as permanently as the poor—there's another lesson learned at Pompeii.

ⓘ **Ufficio Scavi di Pompeii,** Via Villa dei Misteri 1, Pompeii (ⓒ **39/81/857-5111**). **Ufficio Scavi di Ercolano,** Corso Resina 1, Ercolano (ⓒ **39/81/857-5347**).

✈ Aeroporto Capodochino, in Naples.

🛏 $$ **Hotel Britannique,** Corso Vittorio Emanuele 133, Naples (ⓒ **39/81/ 7614145;** www.hotelbritannique.it). $$$ **Hotel Excelsior,** Via Partenope 48, Naples (ⓒ **39/81/7640111;** www.excelsior.it).

WHY THEY'LL THANK YOU: Ancient lives trapped in stone.

---

170 Outposts of Empire

Paestum
Where Ancient Greece & Rome Collided
Ages 6 & up • Italy

Magna Graecia is a convenient term for it, a network of settlements founded around the Mediterranean by voyaging ancient Greeks. Who would have thought that so near the luxe resorts of the Amalfi coast, you could wander around a Greek colony founded in 600 B.C.? Abandoned for centuries, the ruins of Paestum began to attract archaeologists in the mid–18th century, shortly after the discovery of Pompeii up the coast. An easy day trip from anywhere in Campania—Naples is 100km (62 miles) northwest, Salerno only 40km (25 miles) away (see the Amalfi Drive 37)—it may be the oldest place the children will ever visit.

What fascinated us most about Paestum is that it's really two ruined cities atop each other. The first was the Greek city of Poseidonia, named after patron god Poseidon. A vigorous trading center, it thrived for 2 centuries as the northernmost Greek colony in Italy, only a few miles from the Etruscan border. Then the Romans took over in 273 B.C., and renamed the city Paestum. Curiously, the Greek ruins are more completely preserved, for even though the Romans rudely set up shop right on top of the Greek town, they could not bring themselves to knock down the three mighty temples of Poseidonia. The Roman remains are less awesome, but they'll give the kids a sense of a living town—the foundation stones of its shop-lined forum, a gymnasium, and an amphitheater.

Even the ancients wrote about the roses of Paestum, which bloom twice a year, splashes of scarlet perfectly complementing the salmon-colored Greek temples. The largest is the **Temple of Neptune,** arguably the best-preserved Greek temple in the world. Much of it is still standing—six columns in front, crowned by a massive entablature, and 14 columns on each side. Built in the 5th century B.C., Neptune's temple is relatively young for Paestum: Both the **Temple of Hera** and the **Temple of Athena** date way back to the 6th century B.C. The Temple of Hera is Italy's oldest Greek temple, and it's surprisingly intact, with nine chunky Doric pillars in front and 18 on the sides. The Temple of Athena (also known as the Temple of Ceres) has 34 stout Doric columns, along with ragged bits of its triangular pediment and a large altar for sacrifices to the gods.

Across from the Temple of Athena, the **National Archaeological Museum of Paestum,** Via Magna Grecia 919 (℃ **39/828/811023**), displays some metopes removed from the Temple of Hera and some fine tomb paintings from the 4th and 5th centuries B.C.; don't miss the beautiful paintings of the Diver's Tomb.

ⓘ **Tourist Office,** Via Magna Grecia 887 (℃ **39/828/811-016;** www.info paestum.it).

🚊 Paestum, 30 min. from Salerno.

🛏 $$ **Strand Hotel Schuhmann,** Via Marittima (℃ **39/828/851-151;** www. hotelschuhmann.com).

WHY THEY'LL THANK YOU: Gigantic columns, all in a row.

Outposts of Empire **171**

Masada

Fortress by the Dead Sea

Ages 8 & up • Israel

Masada is to Israelis what Mount Fuji is to the Japanese—national pride requires every citizen to scale these heights at least once. But like much else in Israel, the meaning of Masada is controversial. Does this mountaintop fortress symbolize raw courage, or does it glorify foolhardy political extremism? Whichever you believe, the kids will still be riveted by Masada's compelling tale of a small garrison that defied the Roman army.

The story begins with King Herod, who built a stout fortress and magnificent palace atop this nearly inaccessible desert plateau on the western shore of the Dead Sea, around 30 B.C. After Herod's death, a small Roman garrison occupied the mount; it was taken over by a band of Jewish zealots during the Jewish revolt in A.D. 66.

Living off the vast stores of food left by Herod, they had more than enough arms with which to defend themselves. Finally, in A.D. 73, 3 years after the fall of Jerusalem, the Romans got fed up with this last pocket of resistance; they built a ramp to scale the rock—in itself a remarkable feat of engineering—and attacked Masada with 10,000 troops, pulling out all the stops: siege engines, flaming torches, rock bombardments, battering rams. It seemed only a question of time until the 900 defenders surrendered. After one brutal night attack set the fortress gates on fire, the Romans, seeing Masada now defenseless, decided to wait until dawn to storm the fort. That final night, the 900 Jewish men, women, and children inside chose to commit mass suicide rather than succumb. The Romans, who had expected to fight their way in, were astonished in the morning by the Jews' lack of resistance—and then, after they discovered the bodies, impressed by their stoic courage.

From the parking lot at the foot of the mount you've got three choices—ride the **cable car** that carries you almost to the summit; **climb** the winding path on the Dead Sea side, which has great views but can take up to an hour; or **drive** to the Arad side and walk up the Romans' great ramp, which takes only 15 to 30 minutes. If you climb, especially in the summer months, be sure to start at the crack of dawn—the heat is murderous by midday.

Masada **excavations** have unearthed perhaps the most exciting ruins in all of Israel: the original palace, synagogue, casement walls, houses, straw bags, plaits of hair, pottery shards, stone vessels, cosmetics, cooking utensils, and important scroll fragments. Walk with the kids around the ruins of the **Roman siege encampments,** a virtual crash course in Roman military field strategy. Evidence of the Jewish defenders' lives includes **ritual baths** *(mikvehs)* used by observant Jews, and some *ostraca* marked with Hebrew names—perhaps the very lots cast by the defenders as they decided who would kill the others rather than let them fall into Roman hands.

ⓘ **Masada National Park,** Dead Sea Hwy. (Rte. 90), 18 km (11 miles) south of Ein Gedi (✆ **972/7/658-4207**).

✈ Jerusalem, 112 km (70 miles).

🛏 $$$ **Golden Tulip Dead Sea,** Ein Bokek (✆ **972/8/668-9444;** www.goldentulipclubdeadsea.com). $ **Massada Youth Hostel,** Masada National Park (✆ **972/8/995-3222;** www.hihostels.com).

WHY THEY'LL THANK YOU: Discussing what you'd have done in their place.

---

172 Outposts of Empire

The Ancient City of Petra
Red Rock Wonder
Ages 8 & up • Wadi Musa, Jordan

You approach it through the Siq, a deep, narrow sandstone gorge winding for a mile through the southern Jordanian desert. You come to the last turning—and there before you, just visible in the gap, is a dramatic columned temple cut *right out of a cliff face.* The fierce desert sun highlights its columns and pediments and mythological figures; you catch your breath in wonder. And that's just the beginning of Petra, a magical desert fortress whose very name means simply "Rock."

Petra sprang up between 400 B.C. and A.D. 100, a Nabataean city set squarely on important caravan routes. As camels laden with incense crossed the Wadi Araba desert, they paid heavy duties to the tax collectors of Petra, whose wealth gave rise to a grand cityscape chiseled out of the living rock. Deep in this natural stronghold, the Nabataeans were conquered by no one, though many tried; not until Red Sea shipping bypassed caravan routes did a diminished Petra finally fall under control of Rome. Its ancient buildings may have been eroded by desert sand and wind, but because they were gouged out of the cliffs rather than free-standing, they haven't toppled like many buildings of similar eras. Their facades' original plaster and paint have worn off, but the city still glows with the natural color of the rose-red rock.

The city really begins at that first famous view from the **Siq of the Khazneh,** or Treasury. (The kids may recognize it from shots in the movie *Indiana Jones and the*

The desert fortress of Petra.

facades completely out of proportion to the small chambers within. Strangely, considering how many of Petra's buildings are tombs, no bodies have ever been found here.

As you explore Petra's various temples and shrines, remember what an international city this trade hub was: Temples built to Nabataean deities were later adapted to Roman gods, and possibly to Christian saints in the Byzantine era. On a summit behind the yellow-sandstone **Temple of Dushara** (one of Petra's few extant free-standing buildings), there's even the remains of a **fort,** built by 12th-century Crusaders. Another climb to the cliff top will take you to the **High Place of Sacrifice,** a circular ceremonial arena set up explicitly for gruesome acts of blood sacrifice—and also killer views of the site and the surrounding desert.

ⓘ **Petra Archaeological Park** (ⓒ **962/3/215-6441;** www.petrapark.com).

✈ Aqaba, 150km (93 miles).

🛏 $$$ **Golden Tulip,** King's Way (ⓒ **962/3/215-6799;** www.goldentulip kingsway.com). $$ **Petra Palace,** Wadi Musa (ⓒ **962/3/215-6723;** www.petra palace.com.jo).

WHY THEY'LL THANK YOU: Desert surprise.

Last Crusade.) Beyond lie the spectacular **royal tombs,** which became more than just burial places—they were 1st-century architectural fantasies, picking up an eclectic mix of elements from such cities as Alexandria and Rome, their ornate

Outposts of Empire **173**

Ephesus
A Bit of Rome in Anatolia
Ages 8 & up • Near Selçuk, Turkey

While the excavations at Troy are worth visiting for their literary value, the ones at Ephesus will simply take your breath away. It's one of the best-preserved ancient cities on the Mediterranean, a once-bustling Roman town that served as the capital of the Asian provinces. Built on the slopes of

Panayir Dagi (Mt. Pion), the archaeological site requires only 1.6km (1 mile) of walking, but it'll take 2 or 3 hours to wander through, there's so much to see—mosaic floors, arched colonnades, roads paved with marble, and layers upon layers of frescoes.

Enter at the Magnesia Gate, at the top of the hill, and you'll walk first through the **Upper Agora,** the official part of town. You'll see temples and monuments and fountains, a town hall, and the Odeon, where the government council met. Sloping away from it is **Curettes Way** (curettes were a class of priests)—point out to the kids the pockmarks on the pavement made by thousands of horses' hoofs over the centuries. You'll pass a **Gate of Hercules** (that's Hercules wearing the skin of the Nemean Lion he slew) and the two-story **Trajan's Fountain** on your way to the **Temple of Hadrian,** with its glorious Corinthian columned porch. Behind it are a grand set of baths the **Baths of Scholastika**. Across Curettes Way is a colonnaded shopping street with a fine mosaic floor; and above it the section that kids will probably enjoy the most: the **Terraced Houses.** This is where the richest citizens of Ephesus lived, and it's a great window into their sophisticated lifestyle—running water, heating systems, private inner courtyards, and a rich decor of mosaics and frescoes. You'll see the **Library of Celsus,** with its fine two-tiered facade and three levels of niches for storing scrolls or books; the **Marble Way** (paved in real marble) leads from there to the **Great Theatre,** a hillside amphitheater that could seat 25,000—St.

Paul delivered sermons here to the Ephesians in the early Christian era. Ephesus was an important Christian center as the religion spread throughout the Empire; Jesus' mother, Mary, lived here after his death, accompanied by St. John. Her house, now a church that's always crowded with pilgrims, is another couple of miles to the southwest in Meryemana.

Make sure you leave enough time to see a few sights in **Selçuk,** the nearby city you'll use as a base: the **Ephesus Museum** at the intersection of Atatürk Cad. and the park, for spectacular statues and friezes removed from the ruins; the ruined **St. John's Basilica** (off of Atatürk Cad.), built by Emperor Justinian over the tomb of St. John; and the forlorn single column that's all that remains of the **Temple of Artemis** (off the road to Kuşadası), once one of the Seven Wonders of the Ancient World.

ⓘ 3 km (1³/₄ miles) south of Selçuk.

✈ Izmir, 80km (50 miles).

🏨 $$ **Hitit Hotel,** Sarapçi Kuyu Mevki P.K. 66 (✆ **90/232/892-6075;** www.hitit hotel.com). $$ **Hotel Kalehan,** Izmir Cad. (✆ **90/232/892-6154;** www.kalehan.com).

WHY THEY'LL THANK YOU: Imagining their daily lives.

---

174 Outposts of Empire

Arles
Roman Ruins in Old Provence
Ages 6 & up • Arles, France

Few places in France wear the marks of Roman occupation as clearly as Arles, on the banks of the Rhone in Provence. Yes, this is where Vincent van Gogh painted *Starry Night* and *Sunflowers* (and cut off his left ear); and yes, this is where Frederick Barbarossa was crowned in 1178 at the church of St-Trophime. But in Arles, where layer upon layer of history overlap, it's fun

to see the Roman past keep popping up—a crumbling column here, an ancient sarcophagus there—not set apart as an archaeological site but incorporated into a living town.

The Greeks founded Arles in the 6th century B.C., but Julius Caesar, that great empire builder, really put it on the map. By the time of Constantine the Great, in A.D.

306, it was the empire's second capital, known as "the little Rome of the Gauls." At the heart of the town, tree-shaded Place du Forum is built over the old **Roman forum**—point out to the kids the two Corinthian columns and fragments from a temple embedded in the facade of the Grand Hotel Nord-Pinus. The courtyard of the **Muséon Arlaten** in the Hôtel du Laval (rue de la République) contains an ancient Roman temple. West of here stands a crumbling stretch of the old **Roman city walls,** as well as two relics from the 1st century, when Augustus was emperor: the semicircular open-air **Théâtre Antique,** rue de la Calade, and the **Amphitheater** (Lés Arènes), rond-point des Arènes. The Amphitheater, an oval arena with two tiers of round arches, is surprisingly intact and still can seat a crowd of almost 25,000 on its worn stone benches; bullfights are held here in summer. Even bigger than the arena was the **Roman circus,** with a circular track so wide that 12 chariots could race side by side. Fragments of the circus are preserved beside the **Musee de l'Arles Antique on** Presqu'île du Cirque Romain (© **33/4/90-18-88-88**), an archaeological trove of exquisitely carved sarcophagi and intricate floor mosaics that supply rich detail for those ruins you've seen outdoors.

Near the river, the **Baths of Constantine** (on rue D. Maisto) were probably the largest baths in Provence, dating from the later days of the Empire (note the use of concrete, a high-tech marvel at the time). Perhaps the most memorable sight is **Les Alyscamps,** rue Pierre-Renaudel, an ancient Roman necropolis that became a Christian burial ground in the 4th century (it was mentioned in Dante's *Inferno*). Though only a few of its empty marble sarcophagi remain on site, this poplar-shaded spot is a favorite refuge for Arlesians.

ⓘ **Arles Office de Tourisme,** bd. des Lices (© **33/4/90-18-41-20;** www.tourisme.ville-arles.fr). **Arles historical society** (© **33/4/90-49-38-20;** www.patrimoine.ville-arles.fr).

🚄 Arles, 4¹/₂ hr. from Paris.

🛏 $$ **Hotel d'Arlatan,** 26 rue du Sauvage (© **33/4/90-93-56-66;** www.hotel-arlatan.fr). $$$ **Hotel Jules Cesar,** 9 bd. des Lices (© **33/4/90-52-52-52;** www.hotel-julescesar.fr).

WHY THEY'LL THANK YOU: A scavenger hunt for tokens of the classical past.

Outposts of Empire **175**

Trier

Mini-Rome on the Mosel

Ages 4 & up • Germany

Its Roman name was Augusta Treverorum, founded under Augustus in 16 B.C. on the site of an ancient Assyrian colony from 2000 B.C.—even in European terms, that's *old.* Soon folks were calling this prosperous provincial capital Roma Secunda, the second Rome. Although the last Roman prefect departed in about A.D. 400, Trier today has an impressive set of monuments from its Roman era, their ancient stones meticulously cleaned and neatly landscaped.

Begin your exploration at the best-preserved Roman structure in all of Germany, the handsome **Porta Nigra,** the last surviving fragment of the great wall that once surrounded Trier. Porta Nigra earned its name—which means "black gate"—in medieval times, when its huge sandstone blocks, assembled without mortar, were blanketed in soot. Kids who like to play war games will admire its cunning design, a secret courtyard between double arches, where armed defenders could surprise would-be invaders. Trier's tourist office is at the old gate; buy a combination ticket here that will cover most of the Roman sights.

Head south through the historic quarter to Basilikaplatz to find the rosy sandstone **Basilica**—today a Protestant church, but originally built as a Roman palace, an imposing symbol of imperial might. The huge nave is believed to have been Emperor Constantine's throne room, a grand affair with two tiers of windows within high-rising arches; it looks even longer than it actually is, an optical illusion created by narrower arches in the center. Most of its interior decoration was destroyed by Frankish invaders in the Dark Ages, but traces of the original wall paintings still cling to the stone, and you can see the hypocaust heating system in its hollow floor. To get an idea of what filled these shells of buildings, stop in the nearby **Rheinisches Landesmuseum,** Weimarer Allee 1 (📞 **49/651/9-77-40**), a treasure house of Roman antiquities—mosaics, frescoes, ceramics, glassware, and funerary monuments.

Just past the nearby Palastgarten park are the remains of a huge complex of **Imperial Baths, Kaiserthermen,** built in the early 4th century under Constantine I.

Though never completed, these were among the largest in the Roman Empire. Wandering around its subterranean labyrinth, we could just imagine ourselves as fastidious Roman subjects, being soaked, scrubbed, and plucked before a feast at the Basilica.

The city's oldest Roman building lies just east of here, beyond the former city walls. Dating back to A.D. 100, the **Amphitheater** could hold an audience of 20,000 on three circles of stone seats, today carpeted with grass. Its acoustics are still impeccable; open-air performances are held here from time to time. Little doors in the arena walls lead to underground chambers where gladiators were imprisoned and wild animals chained before being set loose in the ring—just like in the Colosseum in Rome.

ⓘ **Tourist Information,** An der Porta Nigra (📞 **49/651/97-80-80;** www.trier.de).

🚆 Trier.

🛏 $$ **Hotel Petrisberg,** Sickingenstrasse 11 (📞 **49/651/46-40**). $$$ **Villa Hugel,** Bernhardstrasse 14 (📞 **49/651/ 937-100;** www.hotel-villa-huegel.de).

WHY THEY'LL THANK YOU: Glimpses of a real toga party.

176 Outposts of Empire

The British Museum's World of Treasure
Ages 8 & up • London, England

One of the big perks of having one of the world's most powerful empires is scarfing up treasures from around the world and then building a huge columned museum to show them all off. You could get lost in the grand echoing marble galleries of the British Museum, gazing in wonder at all the Neat Stuff acquired in the name of the Empire. Here are the six coolest things to see:

The Rosetta Stone: Dug up by Napoleon's soldiers while conquering Egypt, this obelisk honoring pharaoh Ptolemy V from 146 B.C. holds a fascinating code, deciphered in 1821 by French scholar Jean-François Champollian. Look at the carved letters covering its surface; they are written in three languages—ancient hieroglyphics at the top, the demotic language used by everyday Egyptians in the

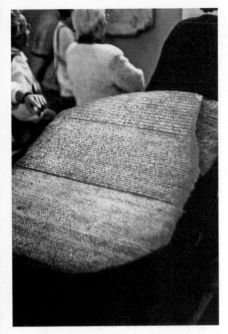

The Rosetta Stone at the British Museum.

middle, and classical Greek at the bottom. The art of reading hieroglyphics had died out centuries earlier, but when they were compared to the same words in demotic Egyptian and Greek, the hieroglyphics were finally deciphered.

The Mummy of Henutmehyt: This gold-encased mummy of an aristocratic woman is one of the most dramatic items in the museum's stellar Egyptian collection. Note the protective wings of the sky-goddess Nut on her coffin case, and in her armpits the watchful eye symbols to ward off danger in the afterlife.

The Elgin Marbles: The British Museum has taken a lot of flak for holding onto these beautiful 5th-century-B.C. Greek artworks, which Greece would very much like back. However, the Brits do have a case. Lord Elgin, the British Ambassador to Constantinople (now Istanbul) in 1801–05, was given permission by the Ottoman Empire to take away bits of ancient statuary in Athens, which was under Turkish rule at the time. The Turks were merely using the Acropolis to store gunpowder, which Lord Elgin thought a shame, so he quietly removed a fair amount of the Parthenon and Erechtheon to preserve them for posterity—and England's still got 'em, a classical case of finders keepers. The centerpiece is a stunning 75m-long (247-ft.) frieze that once decorated the Parthenon, unfolding like a long comic strip starring all your favorite Greek gods and goddess.

Lindow Man: For connoisseurs of the creepy, regard the mummified corpse of a Druid human sacrifice, dating from the 1st century A.D.

Sutton Hoo: Dug up in 1938 in an earthern mound in Suffolk, this funeral hoard of an ancient British warrior-king, heaped in the rotted remains of an old wooden boat, includes a scepter, silver bowls, a gold belt buckle, jeweled shoulder clasps, and a fearsome helmet covered with animal carvings.

The Reading Room: There's nothing classical about this section, except maybe its Parthenon-inspired domed rotunda, now brilliantly incorporated into the central courtyard. Still, there's an incredible intellectual aura still hanging around the original Reading Room of the famous British Library (recently relocated to its own separate site), where scholars and writers as diverse as Mark Twain, Karl Marx, and Oscar Wilde researched and wrote some of their most famous books, thus carrying on the torch of civilization.

ⓘ Great Russell St. (℗ **44/20/7323-8299;** www.thebritishmuseum.ac.uk).

✈ Heathrow.

🛏 $$$ **London Bridge Hotel,** 8–18 London Bridge St. 9 (℗ **44/20/7855-2200;** www.londonbridgehotel.com). $$ **Vicarage Private Hotel,** 10 Vicarage Gate, South Kensington (℗ **44/20/7229-4030;** www.londonvicaragehotel.com).

WHY THEY'LL THANK YOU: It's like one giant time machine.

Hadrian's Wall
Roman Britain Ends Here
Ages 8 & up • Carlisle to Newcastle-upon-Tyne, England

Stretching for 117km (73 miles) across the north of England, from the North Sea to the Irish Sea, Hadrian's Wall marks the line where civilized Britain—that is, the part ruled by Rome—ended and the land of the barbarians began. One of Europe's best Roman ruins, the wall represents the farthest-flung point of the great Roman Empire.

The wall was built in A.D. 122–128 after emperor Hadrian, on an inspection tour of his empire's frontiers, sensed that his British territories were vulnerable to invasion, and ordered legionnaires to build a defensive wall across the island. Sections were originally made of turf, but eventually the whole thing was done in stone, with a fortified "castle" every mile and sentry turrets in between. The wild and forbidding landscape of the Cheviot Hills has always made a pretty effective buffer between England and Scotland, but Hadrian wasn't taking any chances.

The wall exists today as a series of fragments, many of them within **Northumberland National Park.** The most complete section runs for 16km (10 miles) starting west of Housesteads, near Bardon Mill; the lower courses of the wall have been preserved intact, with the rest reconstructed in the 19th century using the original stones. From the wall, there are incomparable views north and south. A good place to start is 29km (18 miles) west of Hexham, at the **Roman Army Museum,** junction A69 and B6318 (© **44/1697/747 485**), where a barracks room depicts living conditions in the Roman army, with realistic life-size figures. A short walk away, you can scale one of the most imposing and high-standing sections of the wall, **Walltown Crags.** From here, working your way east, the fort of **Vindolanda,** 2.5km (1½ miles) off B6318 (© **44/1434/344277;**

www.vindolanda.com), gives you a good idea of daily life in Roman times, re-creating the civilian settlement that lay outside fort walls. The **Housesteads Fort and Museum,** B6318, just north of Bardon Mill (© **44/1434/344363;** www.english-heritage. org.uk), is the most complete Roman fort in Britain, though it's still only partially excavated. Here you can see Britain's only example of a Roman hospital; kids, however, may be more intrigued by the latrines. The more thoroughly excavated **Chesters Roman Fort and Museum,** B6318 from Chollerford (© **44/1434/681379;** www.english-heritage. org.uk), gives kids a good picture of a Roman cavalry fort, built to guard the spot where Hadrian's Wall crossed the river Tyne.

A **footpath** runs along the entire Wall, and many hikers do the whole route, checking out various bits and pieces along the way. With youngsters in tow, however, it may be easier to drive along B6318, which more or less traces the wall, with signposts to major sites. From early May to late September, the Hadrian's Wall **bus service** (© **44/1434/322002**) traces the Wall from Newcastle to Carlisle.

ⓘ www.hadrians-wall.org.

🚆 Hexham or Haltwhistle, 4½ hr. from London.

🛏 $$ **Hadrian Lodge,** Hindshield Moss, above Haydon Bridge, near Hexham (© **44/1434/684-867;** www.hadrianlodge. co.uk). $$$ **Vallum Lodge,** Military Rd. (B6318), near Bardon Mill (© **44/1434/344 248;** www.vallum-lodge.co.uk).

WHY THEY'LL THANK YOU: Not just a line on a map, but a life-size border built in stone.

In Search of Roman Britain

Ages 8 & up • Cirencester, Chedworth & Bath, England

The Romans didn't just breeze into Britain and then go home; they were there for almost 4 centuries, building cities and roads and co-opting local tribal chieftains to administer the Roman way of life. The army pushed as far north as Hadrian's Wall, but this western area, on the edge of the Cotswolds and down into Somerset, was where their culture really took hold.

Begin in **Cirencester,** known as Corinium in Roman days; five roads converged here and it was a major city, second only to Londinium (let the kids guess what that town's called today). The **Corinium Museum** (Park St., Cirencester; ℂ **441285/655611;** www. cotswold.gov.uk/go/museum) houses one of the country's finest collections of archaeological remains from the Roman occupation, including some amazing mosaics. Pottery, artifacts, and provincial Roman sculpture, including figures of Minerva and Mercury,

provide a link with the remote civilization that once flourished here.

From Cirencester, head north about 10km (8 miles) on the A429 to Yanworth, almost to Cheltenham, to **Chedworth Roman Villa** (ℂ **44/1242/890256;** www. nationaltrust.org.uk), the remains of a 4th-century country home excavated in 1864. Set in a lovely wooded valley, this sizable villa—32 rooms, arranged around a central courtyard—was probably the home of a native Briton who had gained a position of authority with the Roman occupiers; some of the beautiful mosaic floors here depict clothing and animals that are definitely British, not Italian. Built around a natural spring, which still bubbles forth in the cistern, the villa had a shrine where native Celts also had worshipped, but the extensive baths show how Roman customs had taken hold. My boys were fascinated by the exposed

The Roman Baths in Bath.

hypocaust, the underground hot-water heating system—much more necessary on a cold English night than it would have been back in Rome. Look at the worn steps, hollowed out by the sandaled feet of the Romans, and you'll get a real sense of these long-ago people.

An hour or so south on the A46 lies the elegant Georgian spa town of **Bath.** Founded in A.D. 75 by the Romans, the **Roman Baths** in Stall St. (© **44/1225/ 477785;** www.romanbaths.co.uk) were dedicated to the goddess Sulis Minerva; in their day, they were an engineering feat. Even today, they're among the finest Roman remains in the country, and are still fed by Bath's famous hot-spring water. The baths' accompanying Temple of Sulis Minerva has been excavated and is now open to view.

The on-site museum displays many interesting objects from Victorian and recent digs (look for the head of Minerva). In the adjoining pump room, you may want to taste the mineral water, but be forewarned—it's hot and tastes horrible.

🚉 Cheltenham, 2¼ hr. from London. Bath, 1½ hr. from London.

🛏 $$ **The Fleece Hotel,** Market Place, Cirencester (© **44/1285/658 507;** www. fleecehotel.co.uk). $$ **Pratt's Hotel,** S. Parade, Bath (© **088/144-9494** in the U.K. or 44/1225/460 441; www.prattshotel. com).

WHY THEY'LL THANK YOU: Amazing that the Roman Empire reached this far.

---

179 Outposts of Empire

Walk through Ancient Ireland
Ages 6 & up • Ferrycarrig, Ireland

Down on the southeast corner of Ireland, County Wexford was ripe territory for invaders—first the Vikings in the 9th century, then the Normans in the 12th century. Whereas western Ireland was mostly able to escape the scrutiny of the English occupiers, Wexford chafed under nearby Britain's grip, and Wexfordmen early on were supporters of an Irish republic. If Dublin is your entry point into Ireland, drive down to Wexford before heading out to the rest of the country—this is the best introduction you could get to the many layers of ancient Irish history.

Set on 15 hectares (36 acres) along the River Slaney, off N11, Irish National Heritage Park is laid out as a trail through many centuries of Ireland's past, with detailed reconstructions from successive periods, ending at the medieval period. Guided tours are included with admission, but you can also walk through it on your own; either way, plan on at least 2 hours.

You'll begin with a **Stone Age campsite,** a domelike tent covered with animal hides, then a later Stone Age settlement with wattle-and-daub huts topped by thatched roofs. The **Bronze Age** is represented by a stone circle, which couldn't have been built without that age's new sharp metal tools. If you tour more of Ireland later, you may see Celtic ruins that correspond to the reconstructions here— for example, the **hilltop ring fort** (such as Staigue Fort on the Ring of Kerry) or the **early Christian monastery** (such as Clonmacnois). The park even displays a **Fulacht Fiadh,** a Celtic version of a barbecue pit, where interpreters occasionally roast meats in the open air. Down by the river, you'll find a Viking house and boatyard with a longboat moored (see Viking Days in Dublin ⓮). The Norman period is represented by a generic lime-washed white **castle,** where a Norman aristocrat might have lived, and an intriguing **crannog,** or artificial island, like those where Irish farm owners lived.

There's nothing Disneyfied or hokey about this place—the costumed interpreters and guides take things seriously. Archaeological purists may sniff at these sites because they're reconstructions, but kids won't care; they'd rather see whole buildings than ruins, and the furnishings that have been added bring them to life.

(i) **Irish National Heritage Park,** Dublin-Rosslare Rd., N11 (✆ **353/53/912-20733;** www.inhp.com).

🚂 Wexford.

🛏 $$$ **Kelly's Resort Hotel,** Rosslare Strand, Rosslare (✆ **353/53/9913-2114;** www.kellys.ie). $$ **McMenamin's Townhouse,** 6 Glena Terrace, Wexford (✆ **353/53/914-6442;** www.wexford-bedandbreakfast.com).

WHY THEY'LL THANK YOU: Blows the dust off ancient times.

New World Marvels 180

Chichén Itzá
Marvel of the Ancient Maya
Ages 6 & up • Near Pisté, Mexico

To me, the best reason for traveling to the Yucatan Peninsula is not to frolic on the beach at Cancun, but to commune with the spirits of the ancient Maya at Chichén Itzá. (And no, it doesn't rhyme with "chicken pizza"; accent the last syllables: chee-*chen* eet-*zah*.) This immense ruined city, raised out of the encroaching jungle, holds an undeniable glamour for kids, a mix of ornate pyramids, celestial imagery, and gory human sacrifice. Just stand at the top of one of its vast plazas and imagine it packed with people during frequent mass rituals—the mind simply boggles.

One of the most important buildings here was **El Caracol** (the Observatory), where astronomers peered through slits in a circular tower to chart the approach of the all-important equinoxes and summer solstice. This celestial obsession is reflected in the design of the magnificent El Castillo pyramid. Four stairways leading up to the central platform each have 91 steps, making a total of 364; add the central platform and you've got 365, equal to the days of the solar year. On either side of each stairway are 9 terraces, equaling 18 on each pyramid face, the same as the number of months in

the Maya calendar. The pyramid is precisely aligned to cast a moving shadow—said to be the spirit of the feathered serpent—on its northern stairway at sunset on the spring and fall equinox, an awesome twice-a-year event to witness.

Elsewhere around the site, kids will find riveting **murals** of 9th-century Mayan customs. In the **Juego de Pelota,** Chichén's main ball court, scenes carved on both walls show figures playing a jai alai–like game in heavy protective padding—spot the kneeling headless player, blood spurting from his neck, while another player calmly holds his head (legend has it that losing players paid with their lives). In the **Temple of Jaguars,** a mural chronicles a battle in a Maya village. In the **Temple of the Skulls,** where sacrificial victims' heads were displayed on poles, carved into the stone are pictures of eagles tearing hearts from human victims; the **Platform of the Eagles** has carved reliefs showing eagles and jaguars clutching human hearts in their talons and claws. Most impressive of all is the **Temple of the Warriors,** named for the carvings of warriors marching along its walls; a figure of the god Chaac-Mool sits at the top of the temple,

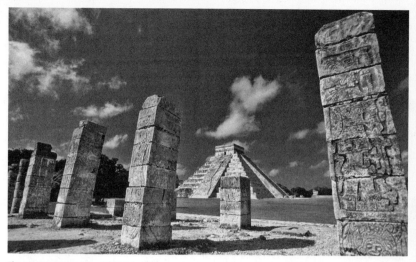

The ancient Mayan ruins at Chichén Itzá.

surrounded by columns carved to look like enormous feathered serpents. At **La Iglesia** (the Church), masks of Chaac decorate two upper stories, but look closely and you'll see other pagan symbols—an armadillo, a crab, a snail, and a tortoise—representing Maya gods.

Scholars quibble over whether Chichén Itzá was always a Maya site or whether it was taken over at one point by the Toltec, but the kids won't care—they'll just scamper up and down the pyramids and romp across the wide-open plazas. Plan to stay

the night if you can—the kids will love the nightly sound-and-light show.

(i) Off Old Hwy. 18 (www.yucatantoday.com or www.mesoweb.com/chichen).

✈ Merida, 121km (75 miles).

🛏 $$$ **Hotel Mayaland,** Zona Arqueológica (© **800/235-4079** or 52/985/851-1503; www.mayaland.com). $ **Dolores Alba,** Hwy. 180 (© **52/985/858-1555;** www.doloresalba.com).

WHY THEY'LL THANK YOU: Human sacrifice and killer ballgames.

181 New World Marvels

Tulum
Walled City of the Maya
Ages 4 & up • Tulum, Mexico

I like to think of Tulum as the beach resort of the Maya—poised on a rocky hill overlooking the turquoise Caribbean, this superbly preserved fortress-city has a

killer location, the best of all the Mayan ruins. Later explorers named it Tulum, from the Maya word for "wall"—it's quite rare for an ancient Mesoamerican city to have walls like this—but the original name was thought to be Zama, which means "dawn." Come here at daybreak, when the sun first kisses the Yucatan coast, and you'll see how perfectly that name fits.

Tulum may have been settled as early as the 6th century A.D., but its heyday was later than Chichén Itzá's, in the 12th to 16th centuries A.D., when Maya civilization in general had begun to decline. Being on the sea made Tulum a natural seaport, and as a trade hub it was able to hang on for 70 years after the Spanish conquest (until diseases brought by the Europeans finally decimated the population). Most of the inhabitants probably lived in wooden huts outside the walls; only governors and priests were important enough to live inside, near the temples. The primary god here seems to have been the **diving god**—ask the kids to look for his curious, almost comical upside-down figure in the building's decorations, usually above doorways.

Tulum is handily within day-trip range of Cancún, a couple of hours south in the neighboring state of Quintana Roo. If you have to make a choice, Tulum may be easier for younger children to comprehend than the more famous Chichén Itzá—it's a smaller and more open site, and the walled fort layout is something they're familiar with. Those incredible views out over the sea are pretty hard to resist, too. There are plenty of intriguing **carvings and reliefs** on these gently eroded gray stone piles, though they're not as gruesome as the ones at earlier Maya sites. Check out the **Temple of the Frescoes,** which depicts the head of the rain god in relief on its cornice—if you pause a slight distance from the building, you can put together an entire face, eyes, nose, mouth, and chin.

The center of interest in Tulum is a hulking stone building above the cliff called the **Castillo,** the tallest building on the site; set like a beacon on that cliff, it has also been called the Lighthouse. A combination temple and fortress (look for the image of the plumed serpent on its upper story), it was once covered with stucco and painted bright red. In fact, the kids can go ahead and imagine the whole town painted bright red, as it once was. That'll bring the ancient Mayans to life for them!

ⓘ **Yucatan Today,** Off Hwy. 307 (www.yucatantoday.com).

✈ Cancún, 129km (80 miles).

🛏 $$ **El Pueblito,** Bulevar Kukulkán Km 17.5, Cancún (© **52/998/881-8800;** www.pueblitohotels.com). $$ **Zamas,** Carretera Punta Allen Km 5, Tulum (© **415/387-9806** in the U.S.; www.zamas.com).

WHY THEY'LL THANK YOU: Painting the town red.

New World Marvels **182**

Tikal

Temples of the Jaguar Clan

Ages 6 & up • Near Flores, Guatemala

Nestled in lush subtropical jungle, where parrots and toucans and monkeys chatter in the canopy overhead, the Mayan ruins of Tikal are the ace in Guatemala's tourist deck. Once ruled by a dynasty known as the Jaguar Clan lords (sounds to me like something out of an anime film), this immense temple complex is a fascinating look into the heart of an ancient culture.

The ancient Mayans weren't only in Mexico—in fact, some historians believe that the center of Mayan civilization was here in the huge El Peten jungle, from about 600 B.C. to A.D. 900. Covering 16 sq.

km (6 sq. miles), the Tikal complex was the ceremonial heart of a city of 100,000 people, who gathered on its plazas for everything from religious rites (often including human sacrifices) to ballgames (where the losers sometimes became human sacrifices).

Though some 3,000 structures remain, the chief ones are half a dozen rectangular pyramids built of gray limestone, which long ago were probably painted a bold red. Notice how precisely cut and mortared the stones are, even though the Mayans had no iron tools. These pyramids go by names the kids will love, like the **Temple of the Masks, the Temple of the Jaguar Priest,** and (my personal favorite) the **Temple of the Double-Headed Serpent,** which, at 65m (212 ft.), was the tallest building in North America all the way up until the late 1800s. It's quite a climb to its top plateau, but as you look out over the rainforest, try to imagine the ancient city, which covered five times the area of what's here today.

For the Mayans, pyramid building was an act of devotion: They sought to exalt their god/kings by setting them on man-made mountains. The exteriors are huge, with broad, steep ceremonial stairways leading solemnly to their peaks, but inside are only small chambers for ceremonial purposes. At public events, kings and nobles were seated grandly atop the pyramids; the acoustics are so perfect that you can speak at a normal volume from Temple I and be heard clearly on Temple II, all the way across the Grand Plaza.

The ancient Mayans were sophisticated mathematicians and astronomers; the section of ruins known as the **Mundo Perdido,** or Lost City (another cool name), seems to have been built for ceremonies based on the Mayans' obsessively detailed calendar. Hundreds of **standing stones** that dot the grounds minutely record historic events and long-dead kings, with either carved pictures or Mayan glyph symbols. They tell the saga of the Jaguar Clan—a riddle from the jungle's ancient past.

(i) **Tikal National Park** (www.tikalpark.com).

✈ Flores, 64km (40 miles).

🛏 $$ **Jaguar Inn,** Tikal National Park (© **502/7926-0002;** www.jaguartikal.com). $$$ **Jungle Lodge** (Posasa de la Selva), Tikal National Park (© 502/7861-0447; www.junglelodge.guate.com).

TOURS: Maya Vacations (© **866/498-5333**; www.mayavacations.com). Grayline Guatemala (© 502/2383-8600; www.graylineguatemala.com).

WHY THEY'LL THANK YOU: Talking from the tops of pyramids.

---

183 New World Marvels

Machu Picchu
Lost City of the Incas
Ages 8 & up • Near Aguas Caliente, Peru

In the 16th century, Spanish conquistadors ravaged most of the fabled cities of the Incas, desperate for their gold. Only Machu Picchu escaped—the Spanish couldn't even find it, snuggled between two peaks cloud-high in the Andes. Of course, no one else could find it either. Abandoned by its own citizens, Machu Picchu lay silent in its mountain fastness, swallowed up by the jungle for 4 centuries. Today the jungle has been cleared away and it's South America's most overrun

Machu Pichu.

too, as you'll see from the famous **Temple of the Sun,** whose windows are perfectly aligned to catch the sun's rays at the winter solstice (which is in June down here) and focus them on the stone at the center of the temple.

Guides, many of whom speak English, can be hired fairly inexpensively on-site, and it is useful to have an expert point out the significant details. Two sights you shouldn't miss are the baffling **Inntihuatana,** or "hitching post of the sun," a ritualistic carved rock that seems to have functioned as some sort of sundial or calendar; and the **Sacred Rock,** perhaps a communal meeting area or performance space. Both of these landmarks were sculpted to resemble specific neighboring peaks—have the kids try to guess which ones.

Getting here is all part of the spiritual journey, according to Inca beliefs, and the classic way to reach Machu Picchu is to hike the **Inca Trail,** the ancient royal highway. From Qorihuayrachina, a 4-day, 43km (27-mile) trek follows winding paths and hand-hewn stone stairs through cloud forest, mountain passes, and dozens of other ruins. With kids, however, you might opt for the 2-day version, beginning at Wiñay Wayna. Both treks arrive at Machu Picchu at dawn—and what a thrill it is to watch the rising sun gild these granite stones row by row. If hiking's not your thing, the train ride from Cusco is plenty spectacular too—stay the night in nearby Agua Calientes and you can still get that brilliant sunrise view.

tourist sight—but even floods of tourists can't diminish the majesty and mystery of this lost city of the Incas.

Scholars don't know why Machu Picchu's residents deserted it—civil war? drought?—and they aren't even certain whether the city was mainly a fortress, a temple complex, a market town, or an astronomical observatory. What they can tell, however, is that its buildings survived remarkably intact—as you walk around, look at how skillfully the stonemasons fitted walls together, and how intricate the decorative stonework was. From **Funerary Rock,** just inside the entrance, you can get an overview of how the Incan love of nature translated into architecture. Steep terraces, gardens, granite and limestone temples, staircases, and aqueducts all are integrated gracefully into the hillsides; the buildings' forms seem to echo the very shape of the mountains. Celestial observations were important to the Incas,

ⓘ ℂ **51/84/22-9297;** www.peru.info.

✈ Cusco, 111km (69 miles).

🚆 Machu Picchu, 4 hrs. from Cusco.

🛏 $$ **Gringo Bill's Hostal,** Calle Colla Raymi 104, Aguas Calientes (ℂ **51/1/84/ 211-406;** www.gringobills.com). $$$ **Inkaterra Machu Pichu,** next to the ruins (ℂ **800/442-5042** in the U.S., 0800/458/7506 in the U.K., or 51/1/610-0400; www.inkaterra.com).

WHY THEY'LL THANK YOU: Sunrise turning the lost city to gold.

7 Positively Medieval

The Alhambra in Granada, Spain.

Viking Days in Dublin

All ages • Ireland

If it hadn't been for Vikings raiding Ireland in A.D. 795, Dublin might still be a quiet river ford with a minor monastery. Compared to the Irish kings, who were hunter-herders holed up in mountain fortresses like the **Hill of Tara 152**, the Vikings were cosmopolitan merchant-politicians who immediately grasped the importance of seaports. Dublin duly became the Viking capital, and 150 years of Viking rule put Ireland squarely on the medieval trade map, making Dublin Ireland's greatest city. No wonder Dubliners have wholeheartedly embraced this chapter of their heritage.

The place to start is at **Dublinia,** St. Michael's Hill, by Christchurch (© **353/1/679-4611;** www.dublinia.ie), a fascinating living history lesson about medieval Dublin. Designed specifically for kids, it's a hands-on sort of place, where youngsters can don bits of armor, sample spices and medicines, write in a scribe's book, put their heads in the stocks (always a crowd pleaser), and tot up cargo values at the wharf—my kids were totally engrossed. The section called Viking World focuses on the Viking era, when Dublin was called Dyflin. Here you can peek inside a reconstructed Viking warship, or be chained up as a slave (Dyflin had one of Europe's biggest slave trading markets). Dublinia's museum displays a selection of artifacts from the National Museum of Ireland's excavation at Wood Quay, site of the original Viking settlement; for a creepy thrill, look at the well-preserved skeleton of a 12th-century Dublin woman. The Viking era ended with the arrival of the Anglo-Normans in 1170, led by a warrior aptly named Strongbow.

Now that you've got a sense of the era, head off on a **Viking & Medieval Dublin iWalk,** which you can download at www.visitdublin.com/iwalks. This free podcast tour leads you around the center of town, scouting for traces of the Viking era, from Fishamble Street to the outlines of an excavated Viking house on Wine Tavern Street. (Listen to the 1½-hr. tour ahead of time and edit it to focus on the areas your kids will be most interested in.)

An almost irresistible add-on is the **Viking Splash Tour,** 64–65 Patrick St. (© **353/1/707-6000;** www.vikingsplash.ie), a 1¼-hour ride around Dublin in a reconditioned World War II amphibious vehicle called a "duck boat." The garrulous driver is dressed like a Norseman, passengers can wear horned helmets if they so choose, and everybody is urged to let out a lusty Viking war cry from time to time. After a drive-by of standard Dublin sights such as Christchurch Cathedral, **Trinity College,** the elegant houses of Merrion Square, and lushly planted St. Stephen's Green, you'll plunge into the Grand Canal Basin for a final 20 minutes on the Liffey. It's pricey, but memorable.

ⓘ **Dublin Tourism Centre,** Suffolk St. (© **353/66/979-2083** or 0850/230-330, www.visitdublin.com).

✈ Dublin.

🛏 $$ The Central Hotel, 1–5 Exchequer St. (© **353/1/679-7302;** www.centralhotel dublin.com). $$$ **Premier Suites Dublin,** 14–18 Lower Leeson St. (© **353/1/638-1111;** www.stephens-hall.com).

WHY THEY'LL THANK YOU: Kids and Vikings, wild kindred spirits.

Jorvik Viking Centre
Ghosts of the Norse Invaders
All ages • York, England

With so many layers of history jostling each other in Great Britain, it's easy to forget that this country was also once a colony of the Vikings—who, far from being bloodthirsty rampagers, were often in fact solid Danish citizens eager to settle in new lands, plant crops, intermarry with the natives, and adopt local religions. Northwest England, just across the sea from their Scandinavian home base, was prime Viking territory, and their legacy is brought vividly to life in York, at the Jorvik Viking Centre.

Before the Viking era, York was a Roman stronghold, but after the legions decamped (around A.D. 400), York lay deserted until 597, when Christian missionaries built a bishop's church here (the basis of today's York Minster) to spearhead the conversion of the Saxons. A civilized center of learning and religion gradually began to evolve. Then suddenly, in 867, the conquest-hungry Vikings abruptly arrived with an invincible army to capture the city, which they named Jorvik (easy to see how that evolved into York). Permanent settlers followed a decade later, and the area soon became its own self-sufficient kingdom, ruled by Viking kings for almost a century, until Eric Bloodaxe (what a name!) was expelled in 954.

When 20th-century archaeologists discovered the **ancient Viking city** of Jorvik deep below modern ground level, it took them 5 years, from 1976 to 1981, to excavate it. As they dug they found 1.8m-high (6-ft.) wooden house walls, fence lines, alleyways, and backyards, along with tens of thousands of buried objects, many of them perfectly preserved in the wet soils. Based on this wealth of evidence, the Jorvik Viking Center is a reconstruction of the old city as it stood in its heyday in 948, meticulously patterned after the excavated town.

Riding in a so-called "time car," you travel back through the ages (stopping briefly in 1067, when Normans sacked the city) to visit a Viking street market, a family's house, and a waterfront where ship chandlers work and a Norwegian ship unloads its cargo. Sounds and even smells are piped in, and the faces of the modeled figures have been reconstructed from individual Viking skulls. At the end, you enter the **Finds Hut,** where thousands of real artifacts are displayed and explained by costumed staff.

While you're here, of course, don't miss visiting the 13th-century **York Minster,** one of the world's most beautiful church buildings, with 100 stained-glass windows.

(i) **Coppergate** (© **44/1904/543-400;** www.jorvik-viking-centre.co.uk).

🚂 York (2 hr. from London).

🛏 $$$ **Park Inn York,** North St. (© **44/1904/459-988;** www.york.parkinn.co.uk). $$ **Beechwood Close Hotel,** 19 Shipton Rd. (© **44/1904/658-378;** www.beechwood-close.co.uk).

WHY THEY'LL THANK YOU: Brings the Dark Ages to light.

Thingvellir
The First Parliament
Ages 8 & up • Thingvellir, Iceland

Long after the democracies of ancient Greece and Rome had been lost to the Dark Ages, the chieftains of one rugged little North Atlantic island got the notion that a nationwide meeting to settle disputes and set laws would be a pretty good idea. In the year 903, they gathered at a central meeting place—a treeless lava plain bordered by a glacial lake and two deep chasms formed by geological faults. The conclave worked so well, they met again the next summer—and the next, and the next, for nearly 900 years.

To stand at ancient Thingvellir, its stark lava hills reflected in the pure chilled waters of Lake Thingvallavatn, is a moving experience indeed. The place name Thingvellir means "parliament plain"; Althing was the name of the parliament (which still meets today in Reykjavik, an hour's drive away). There are few historic buildings here—the 16th-century building for the upper council, or Lögrétta, is long gone, and only an Icelandic flag marks the probable site of the **Law Rock** (Lögberg), where the elected Speaker of the Law announced new rulings and took questions from the floor, so to speak. You can see grass-covered mounds that used to be merchants' booths for the temporary city that sprang up for 2 weeks each summer. You can also see a simple white frame **church** from 1859, the most recent of many at this site, where Althing members worshiped and sometimes met when the weather was harsh. Of course, the first chieftains who met at Thingvellir were pagans, descendants of the Vikings who settled the island (along with a few Irish slaves they picked up on their way). But in the year 1000, with the assembly split between pagans and converted Christians, leaders of the two factions voted on a peaceable compromise: Christianity would prevail but pagans could freely practice their rites. There's proof that democracy works.

This mossy sheltered spot, perched bravely on a craggy volcanic landscape, has the hallowed stillness of a momentous place. I came here on an early July morning, the air hung with the usual sulphur-scented haze of Iceland, and I swear I could hear ghosts whispering. (Okay, maybe it was the nearby waterfalls—I'd just been up all night admiring the midnight sun.) I wish the new **visitor center** had been around then, with its interactive multimedia presentation on Thingvellir's fascinating history. I wish I'd had time to rent an **Icelandic pony** from Skógarhólar farm and ride past old abandoned farmsteads along the timeworn tracks the Althing members rode on their way here. But even so, I was bowled over by Thingvellir. Your family will be too.

ⓘ **Thingvellir National Park,** Selfoss (ℂ 354/482-2660; www.thingvellir.is).

✈ Keflavik International, 96km (60 miles).

⊨ $$ **Hotel Bjork,** Brautarholt 22–24, Reykjavík (ℂ **354/511-3777**; www.bjork hotelreykjavik.com). $$ **Hotel Vik,** Síumúla 19, Reykjavík (ℂ **354/588-5588**; www. hotelvik.is). $ **Nyrthi-Leirar Campground,** next to the Thingvellir information center (ℂ **354/482-2660**).

WHY THEY'LL THANK YOU: The commanding view from the Law Rock.

The Book of Kells
The Most Beautiful Book in the World
Ages 8 & up • Dublin, Ireland

The Book of Kells is a 680-page illuminated manuscript of the four Gospels, hand-lettered by ancient Irish monks around A.D. 800. Okay, so it's one of Ireland's greatest cultural treasures—still, I'd never have expected it would be one of my children's favorite memories of Ireland. But they didn't just like it, they *loved* it.

Much of the credit goes to **Trinity College,** Dublin, which has done a great job of displaying this treasure. Visitors are led through several anterooms meticulously explaining medieval bookmaking techniques, the lives of the anonymous monks who labored over the manuscript, decorative motifs to look for, and the adventure tale of the book's lucky survival over so many centuries. By the time visitors reach a dramatically darkened room with the great glass case displaying the book itself

(curators turn it to a different page every day so that no one page is exposed to light too frequently), the children really get why this book is so important and are prepared to appreciate it—every patient brush stroke of the scribe's lettering, every gold gleam in the dazzling decorative borders, every vivid splash of lapis lazuli blue in the illustrations.

This is the most majestic work of art to survive from the early centuries of Celtic Christianity, and has often been described as "the most beautiful book in the world." Its creators managed to combine new artistic influences from Eastern Christendom with the traditional interlace patterning of Celtic metalwork to produce what Gerald of Wales, a 13th-century chronicler, called "the work not of men, but of angels." For most of the Middle Ages the monastery of

The book of Kells is on display at Trinity College.

Kells, in County Meath, possessed the book. Whether it was originally created in Kells is unknown; some historians think it might have been made in St. Columba's monastery on the Scottish island of Iona, because several monks fled Iona, escaping Viking raids, and wound up in Kells in 807 to found a new center for Celtic Christianity.

I also didn't expect my children to be so fascinated by the library's **Long Room,** with its intricate dark woodworking, busts of famous Irish writers, and tottering shelves of rare books. As for strolling around the 40-acre Trinity College campus, with its cobbled squares, gardens,

quadrangle, and 18th-century buildings—that I expected them to love, and they did.

ⓘ **Old Library,** Trinity College (ⓒ **353/1/896-1661;** www.tcd.ie).

✈ Dublin.

🛏 $$ **The Central Hotel,** 1–5 Exchequer St. (ⓒ **353/1/679-7302;** www.centralhotel dublin.com). $$$ **Premier Suites Dublin,** 14–18 Lower Leeson St. (ⓒ **353/1/638-1111;** www.stephens-hall.com).

WHY THEY'LL THANK YOU: Who knew a book could be this awesome?

Monks, Priests & Pilgrims 188

Santiago de Compostela
Making the Pilgrimage
Ages 4 & up • Spain

All roads in Spain once led to the northwestern city of **Santiago de Compostela,** where the Catholic faithful flocked to visit the **tomb of St. James,** hoping thereby to win a spot in heaven. The pilgrimage route ran from Paris over the Pyrenees and along Spain's northern coast—an enormous distance even by car. (Some hardy souls still make the trek on foot.) Even if you only drive the last section, from Pamplona through León to Santiago de Compostela, you can imagine the joy of weary pilgrims arriving at last in front of this glorious Romanesque cathedral.

It all began in A.D. 813, when priests unearthed what were said to be the remains of St. James (Santiago, in Spanish), the patron saint of Spain. In the 11th century, this huge cathedral was built over his tomb, and a trickle of local pilgrims grew into an international flood. From the Praza do Obradoido, admire its three ornate towers and the wrought-iron enclosed staircase; in an arch inside the middle tower is a statue of St. James, dressed in traditional pilgrim garb (wide-brimmed hat and walking staff),

because he traveled widely around western Europe spreading the gospel. Show the kids the rounded arches, thick walls, and small windows, different from the more familiar pointy Gothic architecture. The west door's **triple-arched front portico** is famous, with sculpted biblical figures representing the Last Judgment. Look for St. James, in the center beneath Christ. The carved column under him bears five grooves worn into the stone by centuries of pilgrims, leaning forward to place their hands on the pillar and knock foreheads with the carved face at the bottom—the likeness of the portico's designer, Maestro Mateo. It's nicknamed—what else?—**Santo dos Croques** (Saint of the Bumps).

In our age of jet travel, it's amazing to recall that most medieval folks spent their entire lives in one village, without TV or newspapers or the Internet to tell them about the rest of the world. The few who took a pilgrimage played a vital role in disseminating European culture. Inside, notice how wide the barrel-vaulted aisles are, built to accommodate hordes of pilgrims. On the altar is a huge golden **mollusk shell** that pilgrims traditionally kissed, as well as a great silver incense burner—the *botufumiero*—which purified the air at night while hundreds of pilgrims slept in the cathedral.

The remains of St. James are in a silver urn in the crypt. Hard as it is to believe, they went missing for almost 300 years, when, in the 16th century, with Sir Francis Drake (see The *Golden Hinde* ❷❸❻) raiding the coast, the church fathers hid them so well that they weren't found again until 1879. To verify their authenticity, a sliver of the skull of St. James was fetched from Italy—and it fit perfectly into the recently discovered skeleton.

ⓘ **Catedral de Santiago,** Praza do Obradoiro (✆ **34/981/58-35-48;** www.catedral desantiago.es).

✈ Santiago de Compostela.

🛏 $ **Hotel Real, Caldereria 49** (✆ **34/ 981/56-92-90;** www.hotelreal.com). $$ **Los Abetos Hotel,** San Lázaro (✆ **34/981/ 55-70-26;** www.hotellosabetos.com).

WHY THEY'LL THANK YOU: Knocking heads with the Saint of the Bumps.

The Leaning Tower of Pisa
Ages 8 & up • Pisa, Italy

How many cardboard pizza boxes carry a picture of the Leaning Tower of Pisa? It may be the most instantly recognizable building in the Western world, with the possible exception of the Eiffel Tower. A grayish-white stack of colonnaded rings with a neat top hat, it has a certain architectural élan, but the thing that really makes it famous—face it—is that rakish tilt, nowadays a whopping 4m (13 ft.) off the perpendicular. If it stood straight, it would be 55m (180 ft.) tall; but it doesn't stand straight. It's famous for *not* standing straight.

Back in 1173, this eight-story freestanding tower was begun as a campanile—or bell tower—for the cathedral at Pisa. Like any medieval city, Pisa was trying to assemble an impressive cathedral complex, mostly to show up its Tuscan rival Florence. But about the time the third story was completed, in 1198, it became obvious that the tower was leaning. The horrified builders discovered that the site they'd chosen wasn't solid rock, as they'd thought, but water-soaked clay. The architect, Bonnano Pisano, disappeared in shame, a few bells were stuck in the third

story, and work halted for decades, while Pisa fought an on-again-off-again war with Florence. After a serious 1284 naval loss against Genoa, a much less powerful Pisa took up the embarrassing project again, completing the tower in 1319. The bells were finally installed in the top in 1350 (although they are no longer rung, for fear the vibrations might rattle the tower). But by then, Pisa had become a minor citystate, finally annexed by Florence in 1392—the final humiliation.

Climbing the 294 steps to the top of the tower isn't nearly as tippy an experience as I expected, but looking at it from the outside, you almost want to hold your breath, it looks so ready to topple over onto the roof of the cathedral next door, like a medieval set of dominoes. Famous as it has become, the tower was originally only a small component of this beautiful Romanesque cathedral complex; make sure to visit the cathedral and the immense Baptistery as well while you're here, and you'll see why it's been nicknamed the Piazza dei Miracoli, or "field of miracles."

For years, annual measurements showed the tower leaning a fraction of an

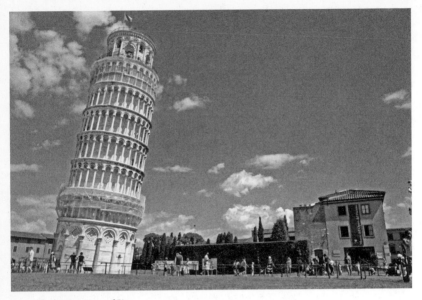

The leaning tower of Pisa.

inch farther every year. Recent restoration sought to arrest the tilt, removing tons of soil from under the foundation and placing lead counterweights at the tower's base. But Pisans staunchly believe the tower will never fall. After all, they point out, several mild earthquakes, not to mention extensive bombing in World War II, have not done the trick. Besides, the Pisa city fathers have no vested interest in making it straight again. It never has been perpendicular, and it never will be. After all these years, this botched building project has turned out to be Pisa's greatest landmark—and the one thing Pisa's got that Florence never will.

ⓘ Piazza del Duomo 17 (✆ **39/50/387-2211**).

✈ Galileo Galilei Airport, Pisa.

🚄 Pisa, 1 hr. from Florence.

🛏 $$ **Royal Victoria,** 12 Lungarno Pacinotti (✆ **39/50/940-111;** www.royal victoria.it).

WHY THEY'LL THANK YOU: Catch me now, I'm falling.

The Tower of London
England's Real-Life Chamber of Horrors
All ages • London, England

This ancient castle just may be the most haunted spot in England. Headless bodies, bodiless heads, phantom soldiers, icy blasts, clanking chains—you name them, the Tower's got them. Every stone of the Tower tells a story, and it's usually a gory one.

This sprawling fortified compound is like its own small city, with a walled moat outside and a spacious grassy keep inside. At the center is the oldest part, the **White Tower,** built by William the Conqueror in 1078 to keep London's native Saxon population in check. For centuries it was a royal residence—one section, fronting on the river, re-creates the era of Edward I, with guides in period costumes and reproduction furnishings including Edward's throne. When James I took over from Elizabeth I in 1608, however, the royal family moved out—understandably, for over the years the Tower had come to be the realm's most important prison. On the walls of the **Beauchamp Tower,** you can still read the last messages scratched by despairing prisoners. According to murky legend, two little princes (the sons and heirs of Edward IV) were murdered by henchmen of Richard III in the so-called **Bloody Tower**—at least, that's the way Shakespeare told it, although some historians differ. In the lower part of the **Bell Tower,** you can tour a white-washed prison cell where it is believed Sir Thomas More lived for the last 14 months of his life. Sir Walter Raleigh spent a whopping 13 years here when he was out of favor with Elizabeth I. Many of these prisoners arrived by boat through the spiked iron portcullis of **Traitor's Gate,** and were publicly executed in the central courtyard on **Tower Green** (an eerie plaque there commemorates the execution of not one but two of King Henry VIII's wives, Anne Boleyn and Catharine Howard, as well as the so-called Nine-Day Queen, Lady Jane Grey).

As a fortress, the Tower also made a great place to store weapons and treasures. The White Tower today holds the **Armouries,** with an impressive display of weaponry and armor. In the **Jewel House,** you'll find the tower's greatest attraction, the **Crown Jewels,** some of the world's most precious stones set into robes, swords, scepters, and crowns. The Imperial State Crown is the most famous crown on earth; made for Victoria in 1837, it's worn today by Queen Elizabeth when she opens Parliament, and it includes the Black Prince's Ruby, worn by Henry V at Agincourt. Prepare to stand in long lines to catch a glimpse of the jewels as you scroll by on moving sidewalks, but the wait is worth it.

One-hour guided **tours** of the entire compound are given every half-hour by the Yeoman Warders (also known as "beef-eaters") in their distinctive red-and-gold uniforms. And oh, yes—don't forget to look for the ravens, six huge, glossy black birds (plus two spares), all registered as official Tower residents. According to legend, the Tower of London will stand as long as the ravens remain—so just to be safe, one wing of each raven is clipped.

ⓘ Tower Hill (📞 **44/20/3166-6000** from overseas, 844/482-7777 from the U.K.; www.hrp.org.uk).

✈ Heathrow (24km/15 miles) or Gatwick (40km/25 miles).

🛏 $$$ **London Bridge Hotel,** 8–18 London Bridge St. (📞 **44/20/7855-2200;** www.londonbridgehotel.com). $$ **Vicarage Private Hotel,** 10 Vicarage Gate, South Kensington (📞 **44/20/7229-4030;** www.londonvicaragehotel.com).

WHY THEY'LL THANK YOU: It's bloody historic.

Warwick Castle
A Noble's Medieval Masterpiece
All ages • Warwick, England

Perched on a rocky cliff above the River Avon, this magnificent 14th-century fortress, the finest medieval castle in England, is surrounded by gardens, lawns, and woodland where peacocks roam freely. It's a mass of thick white crenellated curtain walls punctuated with formidable towers, their slit windows designed for archers to shoot arrows at besiegers—exactly what a child pictures when you say the word "castle." Ethelfleda, daughter of Alfred the Great, built the first significant fortifications here in 914. Two years after the Norman Conquest, William the Conqueror was on the scene, ordering the construction of a motte-and-bailey castle, and his son created the title Earl of Warwick to give to his Norman cronies, the Beaumont/Beauchamp family. Simon de Montfort thoroughly sacked it in the Barons' War of 1264; all that's left of the Norman castle is a steep mound in the garden. The Beauchamps' 14th-century reconstruction is pretty much what you see today. The earls of Warwick were so powerful back then that Richard Neville, earl during the Wars of the Roses, was called "the Kingmaker."

When the castle was granted to Sir Fulke Greville by James I in 1604, he spent £20,000 (a huge sum in those days) converting the existing castle buildings into a luxurious mansion. The staterooms and Great Hall house fine collections of

Warwick Castle.

paintings and furniture, but kids will probably be more interested in the arms and armor (one of the finest collections anywhere), not to mention the dungeon, torture chamber, ghost tower, clock tower, and Guy's tower. The Tussaud company, which now owns the castle, has outfitted the private apartments of Lord Brooke and his family as a carefully reconstructed Royal Weekend House Party of 1898. You'll see **wax portraits** of important figures of the time, including a young Winston Churchill; in the Kenilworth bedroom, a likeness of the Prince of Wales, later King Edward VII, reads a letter; the duchess of Marlborough prepares for her bath in the red bedroom. Among the most lifelike of the figures is a uniformed maid bending over to test the temperature of the water running into a bathtub. Purists may shudder, but I'm in favor of anything that helps children get a picture of how the aristocracy actually lived.

(i) High St., Warwick ((C) **44/870/442-2000;** www.warwick-castle.co.uk).

Warwick, via Stratford-upon-Avon, 2¹/₂ hr. from London.

$$ Hilton Warwick, Warwick Bypass, A429 Stratford Rd. ((C) **800/HILTONS** [445-8667] in the U.S., or 44/1926/499-555; www.hilton.com).

WHY THEY'LL THANK YOU: A textbook castle, just like kids draw them.

192 Castles

Bunratty Castle & Folk Park
Life on the Irish Manor
All ages • Bunratty, County Clare, Ireland

Get off the plane in Shannon, Ireland, and you may be disappointed to drive right onto a stretch of superhighway without a thatched cottage or a single-lane country road in sight. But never fear, traditional Ireland is not far away. In fact, you can get your first taste of it—and a very satisfying first taste at that—just off that highway at Bunratty Castle.

Nestled beside the O'Garney River, Bunratty Castle is Ireland's most complete **medieval castle.** Children may wonder at first what happened to the rest of it—this appears to be just one big tower with a moat, not the sort of walled keep with a grand inner house that they may be familiar with. But in Ireland that other sort of castle belonged to the era of the Norman invaders; by the time Bunratty was built, in 1425, fortified towers were extremely popular among Ireland's wealthy families, built as "safe houses" to protect the inhabitants from their feuding neighbors. Walk across the stout drawbridge and you'll find a carefully restored ancient stronghold, full of authentic furniture, armorial stained glass, tapestries, weapons, and works of art.

On the 8-hectare (20-acre) property surrounding Bunratty Castle, Bunratty Folk Park shows visitors the more plebeian side of Irish life, and my family actually found this much more engrossing. An entire **19th-century Irish village** has been re-created, complete with outlying thatched cottages and farmhouses. The main village street has a school, post office, pub, grocery store, print shop, ice-cream store, and hotel—all open for browsing and shopping. Fresh scones are baked in the cottages, and craftspeople ply such trades as knitting, weaving, candle making, pottery, and photography. Up on a hill (with fabulous views of the countryside) sits the slightly larger home where a family of the minor gentry lived, socially distinct from both the grand folks at the castle and the village people.

At night, the castle's baronial Great Hall serves as a candlelit setting for a 3-hour **medieval banquet.** Guests are seated at long trestle tables, where platters of traditional dishes (made with modern Irish ingredients) are served, to be eaten in strictly medieval use-your-fingers style and washed down with mulled wine, claret, and mugs of the traditional honey-based drink called mead. Hokey, yes, but undeniably fun. As a counterpoint, the Folk Park offers an "at home" evening in a farmhouse cottage, with homey Irish stew and soda bread and trad music played on fiddle, flute, and bodhrán.

ⓘ Limerick-Ennis Rd., N18 (ⓒ **353/61/360-788;** www.shannonheritage.com).

✈ Shannon International Airport, 29km (18 miles).

🛏 $$$ **Dromoland Castle,** N18, Newmarket-on-Fergus (ⓒ **800/346-7007** in the U.S., or 353/61/368-144; www.dromoland.ie). $$ **Lynch Clare Inn Hotel,** Limerick-Ennis Rd., N18, Newmarket-on-Fergus (ⓒ **800/473-8954** or 353/65/682-3000; www.lynchhotels.com).

WHY THEY'LL THANK YOU: From castle to cottage, the whole social spectrum.

At Bunratty Castle & Folk Park.

Castles **193**

The Alhambra
Spanish Castle with a Moorish Heart
Ages 6 & up • Granada, Spain

When you first see the celebrated Calat Alhambra (Red Castle), you may be surprised by its somber exterior, looming on a rocky outcropping above the city of **Granada.** Deep in southern Andalusia, Granada is where Spain's Muslim past is most evident, nowhere more so than at the Alhambra—but you have to cross the threshold to discover the true delights of this Moorish palace.

It was originally built for defensive purposes, that's true, and a portion of the Alcazaba, the original rugged 9th-century fort, still exists inside. But the castle's Moorish occupants gradually transformed this stern fortress into a lavish pleasure palace for the Nasrid princes and their harems. The heart of the old Nasrid palace is the arcaded **Patio de los Leonares** (Court of the Lions), with its immense fountain resting on 12 marble lions—representing the hours of the day, the months of the year, and the signs of the zodiac. Every room around this courtyard tells a story: The **Sala de los Abencerrajes,** with its richly adorned honeycombed ceiling, is where the last emir, Boabdil, staged a banquet for his most powerful rivals, only to have his guards massacre them in mid-dinner. Check out the exquisite ceiling paintings on leather in the **Sala de los Reyes** (Hall of Kings), a great banqueting hall where, legend has it, one sultan beheaded 36 Moorish princes here because he suspected one had seduced his favorite wife. The **Hall of the Mexuar** was once the sultan's main council chamber; Spanish rulers converted it into a Catholic chapel in the 1600s.

To me, this conjunction of Muslim and Spanish culture is the most intriguing thing about the Alhambra. After the Reconquest, in 1526 the Holy Roman Emperor, Charles V, had a new Renaissance palace plunked down in the middle of this Moorish stronghold (apparently the Nasrid palace wasn't grand enough for his royal presence). My favorite part of it is the magnificent circular **two-story courtyard** that is open to the sky.

But there's more outside the Alhambra's walls: **The Generalife,** the sultans' summer retreat, where they used to spend their summers locked away with their harems. As a vacation spot, it's full of beautiful courtyards and gardens; look for the **Escalera del Agua** (Water Staircase); an enclosed Asian garden, **Patio de la Acequia,** with water jets arching over its long central pool; and **Patio de la Sultana,** the secret rendezvous point for Zoraxda, wife of Sultan Abu Hasan, and her lover.

Due to the Alhambra's immense popularity, the government controls the crowds by issuing only a limited number of timed-entrance tickets. Go as early as possible—even if you arrive at 10am you may not be admitted until an afternoon time slot. Even better, book your tickets in advance through **ServiCaixa** (© **34/902/888-001;** www.alhambra-tickets.es). Come here at night, when floodlights bathe the exotic gardens and palaces—it's a sight you'll never forget.

ⓘ **Calle Real de la Alhambra** (© **34/902/441-221;** www.alhambra-patronato.es).

✈ Granada.

🛏 $$ **Hotel Palacio Santa Inés,** Cuesta de Santa Inés 9 (© **34/958/222-362;** www.palaciosantaines.com). $$$ **Parador de Granada,** at the Alhambra (© **34/958/221-440;** www.parador.es).

WHY THEY'LL THANK YOU: A glimpse inside the harem.

Chester
Medieval Walled City
All ages • England

Not all medieval people lived in castles—throughout the era more and more came to live in cities, and there's no better place to see how this new urban lifestyle evolved than in Chester, England. Still beautiful, with its distinctive red sandstone buildings, Chester has been lucky enough to preserve it all—a cathedral, a castle, and a full 3km (1¾ miles) of fortifying city walls, not to mention a half-timbered shopping district. Compact and easy to explore on foot, Chester is the sort of historic town that children immediately get the point of.

Chester's heyday was in the 13th and 14th centuries, when it was a bustling port on the River Dee, and a strong guild system attracted craftsmen and the up-and-coming professional class. When the river eventually silted up and trade evaporated, Chester was left a quiet provincial town with no reason to tear down its medieval structures; even in Georgian and Victorian times, builders continued to copy the black-and-white timbered facades. Visitors can ramble at will on the walkway atop the **city walls,** passing from one towered city gate to another; kids love to run along the balconied second story of **The Rows,** extensive double-tiered Tudor arcades in the center of town where shops still thrive. Only a few steps away on St. Werburgh Street is a glorious **cathedral,** built in 1092 as a Benedictine abbey, with hushed cloisters, a soaring nave, and amazingly inventive woodcarvings in the choir section (my kids could have studied those for hours). Chester even has a town crier—a costumed fellow who materializes at City Cross ringing a hand bell, at noon most summer weekdays, shouting local news and jovially chaffing the crowd, a hokey promotional gimmick that still amuses kids.

Chester's story didn't begin in medieval times; a Roman legion founded the town as a defensive stronghold on the Dee in the 1st century A.D., and many Roman remains have been excavated in the past few years, including an impressively complete **Roman amphitheater.** The original Roman fortress lies buried underneath the city, but its story is told at the **Dewa Roman Experience,** Pierpont Lane, off Bridge Street (© **44/1244/343-407;** www. dewaromanexperience.co.uk), with lots of hands-on exhibits and reconstructions. If you don't mind being stared at, you can even book a walking tour of the town with a guide dressed as a Roman centurion (contact www.romantoursuk.com).

After all this, **Chester Castle,** looming on a bluff over the river, is a letdown; originally built in 1069, when Chester was one of the final strategic spots to fall to William the Conqueror, it fell into decay during the Civil War and was knocked down and completely rebuilt in the early 19th century, with only one original three-story tower still standing. The only tourist attraction inside the castle is a military museum.

ⓘ **Tourist Information,** 2 Vicars Lane (© **44/1244/351-609;** www.chester. com).

🚃 Chester, 4km (2½ miles) from London.

🛏 $$$ **Macdonald New Blossoms Hotel,** St. John's St. (© **44/844/879-9113;** www.macdonaldhotels.co.uk). $$ **The Queen Hotel,** City Rd. (© **44/1244/305-000;** www.bw-queenhotel.co.uk).

WHY THEY'LL THANK YOU: Meandering atop the city walls.

Town & Gown **195**

Oxford University
Great Halls & Secret Gardens
Ages 6 & up • Oxford, England

After the Sorbonne in Paris, Oxford University is the oldest university in the world, and it's still very much alive. Larger than its sister university, Cambridge, and in a more bustling commercial town, Oxford may seem less picturesque—but venture inside its walled colleges and you'll get an idea of how black-gowned scholars have pursued their studies for centuries.

Oxford University.

Originally Oxford was a cluster of separate foundations for monks, and even today its colleges are independent of each other, although they share a common curriculum and examination system. An Oxford student belongs to one college with its own tiny walled campus. He or she lives there, dines there, and studies with an in-house professor called a "tutor" or a "don," preparing for the general university exams. There are some 40 colleges in Oxford today, most of which you can visit (opening times are posted at gatehouses). Here's a quick tour of the best known.

Christ Church on St. Aldate's Street, founded by Henry VIII, has the largest front quadrangle in Oxford, with a big clock tower housing a 9-ton bell (nicknamed Tom) and a grand fishpond. The stairway leading to its dining hall was the basis for the shifting staircases of Hogwarts in the Harry Potter movies. **Balliol** on Broad Street, built of a dour gray stone compared to the warm yellow of most Oxford colleges, is often said to be the most "intellectual" college. **Trinity College** on Broad Street, next to Balliol, is known for its lovely gardens. **New College** on Holywell Street, snuggled in the lee of the old city wall, has Oxford's oldest

quadrangle—despite the name, it's actually one of the oldest colleges, founded in 1379. **Magdalen College** on High Street, pronounced "maudlin," sits on the banks of the Cherwell River and has a huge surrounding park with deer roaming in it. The **Bodleian Library** on Catte Street, which nowadays receives a copy of every book published in Britain, also has many old and rare books. Its centerpiece is a beautiful domed building called the Radcliffe Camera. On the same street, **Hertford College** is most famous for its Bridge of Sighs arching over a side street. Back on Broad Street, you'll pass the **Sheldonian Theatre,** with its crumbling busts of Roman emperors on the fence pillars; students receive their degrees here. Slip into **St. John's** on St. Giles to view its beautiful cloistered quadrangle—and while you're here, stop by the **Eagle and Child** pub at 49 St. Giles, a favorite hangout of Oxford dons C.S. Lewis and J.R.R. Tolkien and their circle.

ⓘ **Tourist Information,** 15–16 Broad St. (ⓒ **44/1865/252-200;** www.visitoxford. org).

🚌 Oxford, 1½ hr. from London.

Town & Gown 196

🛏 $$ **Eastgate Townhouse,** 23 Merton St. (ⓒ **44/1189/711-400;** www.eastgate-hotel.com). $ **Victoria House Hotel,** 29 George St. (ⓒ **44/1865/727-400;** www.victoriahouse-hotel.co.uk).

WHY THEY'LL THANK YOU: Book learning rules.

Bruges
City of Guilds
All ages • Belgium

Let other cities boast palaces and cathedrals—the Flemish town of Bruges shows off guildhalls, exchanges, warehouses, and the homes of wealthy merchants. In the 15th century, Bruges was a center for the Hanseatic league, a confederation of merchant cities that knit Europe together in trade, and it became one of the wealthiest cities in medieval Europe. It's still a fairy-tale mixture of gabled houses, magnificent squares, narrow cobblestone streets, and meandering canals full of swans.

Every quarter-hour, a magnificent 47-bell carillon peals out from the **Belfry** on the **Markt** (Market Square)—between rings, we hurried to the top (366 steps) for a panoramic overview of the surrounding countryside. The attached **Market Halls** were the heart of Bruges's commerce from the 13th to the 16th centuries. Things didn't always run smoothly, as we learned from the sculpture in the center of the Markt, depicting butcher Jan Breydel and weaver Pieter de Coninck, who led a 1302 uprising against the rich merchants and nobles who dominated the city's trade guilds. A few steps away is another public square, the Burg, site of the Gothic **Stadhuis** (Town Hall), built in the late 1300s, which makes it the oldest town hall in Belgium. Upstairs, in the ornate **Gothic Room,** we pored over wall murals depicting Bruges's history. Across the Burg, the 18th-century **Palace of the Liberty of Bruges,** a former courtroom and administrative center, also has a great room: the **Renaissance Hall,** which has been restored to its original 16th-century condition—on the oak chimney piece, we grinned at the figures of various European monarchs, an open bit of flattery from Bruges's shrewd merchants.

To see how these merchants lived, stop by the **Gruuthuse Museum,** Dijver 17, the fancy Gothic mansion of Flemish nobleman and herb merchant Lodewijk Van

The Renaissance Hall in Bruges.

Gruuthuse. At the other end of the economic spectrum, the **Stedelijk Museum voor Volksunde,** Balstraat 43, occupies the low whitewashed houses of the former Shoemakers Guild Almshouse, or charity home. Various rooms show daily life from times gone by—a primary school, a cooper's workshop, a spice store. As a city of craft guilds, Bruges shows off two of its top crafts at the **Kantcentrum** (Lace Center), Peperstraat 3A, and **Diamantmuseum** (Diamond Museum), Katelijnestraat 43B. We ended up at the most tranquil spot in Bruges, the **Begijnhof** on Wijngaardstraat, a retreat for religious women founded in 1245. Benedictine nuns live now in this cluster of 17th-century white-washed houses, where you can step inside the courtyard and almost breathe the air of another century.

ⓘ **Toerisme Brugge,** t' Zand 34, in the Concertgebouw (✆ **32/50/44-46-46;** www.brugge.be).

🚃 Bruges, 1 hr. from Brussels.

🛏 $$ **Hotel Erasmus,** Wollestraat 35 (✆ **32/50/33-57-81;** www.hotelerasmus.com). $$$ **Oud Huis Amsterdam,** Spiegelrei 3 (✆ **32/50/34-18-10;** www.oha.be).

WHY THEY'LL THANK YOU: The swans on the canals.

197 Town & Gown

San Gimignano
Medieval Skyscraper City
All ages • Italy

The fortresslike walled town of San Gimignano rises proudly out of the Tuscan plain, its 13 noble towers giving it a "skyscraper" skyline. Just imagine what it was like in its heyday, in the 13th and 14th centuries, when there were as many as 72 towers. My middle son, the *Lord of the Rings* fan, pictures Minas Tirith, in Middle Earth, as looking a lot like San Gimignano, and he's pretty much right.

Bound inside its walls, the tiny town is like a medieval stage set, remarkably unchanged since the days when it was a prosperous player in Tuscany's turbulent Guelph/Ghibelline politics. The heart of San Gimignano is a connected pair of large paved squares, the **Piazza della Cisterna** (named for the 13th-c. cistern in the middle), and the **Piazza del Duomo,** a beautiful composition of medieval towers and palaces. San Gimignano's **Duomo** (technically no longer a cathedral but a "collegiata" since the town's prestige dwindled) may look plain and austere, but that's just because its 12th-century facade was never finished. Inside you'll be dazzled by tiger-striped arches, a galaxy of gold stars, and loads of frescoes retelling Bible stories—look for *Noah with the Animals* and a particularly gruesome *Last Judgment,* which shocked churchgoers with its distorted and suffering nudes. In the Chapel of Santa Fina, the life story of a local girl, Fina, the town's patron saint, is told in frescoes by Domenico Ghirlandaio, Michelangelo's fresco teacher.

Also on the square, the town hall, **Palazzo del Popolo,** Piazza del Duomo 1, was designed in the 13th century; the civic museum inside preserves a room where the great poet Dante Alighieri made an impassioned pro-Ghibelline speech in 1300, when he was Florence's ambassador to San Gimignano. (Two years later, his faction fell from power and he was exiled forever from Florence.) Climb the palazzo's **Torre Grossa,** the town's tallest tower (about 53m/174 ft. high), for a fabulous bird's-eye view of the Tuscan countryside.

San Gimignano's towers.

It's tempting to idealize the past, but the Middle Ages was a time of cruel politics, as the kids will realize after visiting the **Museo della Tortura** (Torture Museum), Via San Giovanni 15 (© **39/577/940-526;** www.museodellatortura.com). In this slightly cheesy Tuscan chamber of horrors, you'll see items such as cast-iron chastity belts and the garrote, that horror of the Inquisition trials of the 1400s. If that's a little too strong for your kids, check out the archaeological exhibits in the old Santa Fina hospital, the **Spezeria di Santa Fina,** Via Folgore 11—the Etruscan artifacts on the first floor may bore them, but the re-creation of a medieval pharmacy upstairs is intriguing. Whatever you do, take time to slip away from the tourist crowds into a quiet courtyard or church to get a sense of this isolated town's ageless spirit. Even better, stay here overnight, when the day-trippers are gone and San Gimignano becomes its quiet medieval self again.

ⓘ **Tourist Information,** Piazza del Duomo 1 (© **39/577/940-008;** www.sangimignano.com).

🚃 Pisa Centrale station, 80–90 min. from Florence, 100–110 min. from Siena.

🛏 $$ **Hotel La Cisterna,** Piazza Cisterna 23–24 (© **39/577/940-328;** www.hotelcisterna.it). $$ **Hotel Leon Bianco,** Piazza Cisterna 8 (© **39/577/941-294;** www.leonbianco.com).

WHY THEY'LL THANK YOU: A Tuscan time warp.

Town & Gown **198**

Heidelberg's Royal Ruins
Ages 10 & up • Germany

Situated in the picturesque Neckar Valley, Heidelberg is one of the few German cities that wasn't leveled by air raids in World War II. As a university town, it also escaped being overtaken by heavy industry. Sometimes it's hard to get a handle on Germany's medieval history, but here in the compact **Altstadt** (Old City) of Heidelberg, we suddenly felt in touch with the late Middle Ages and early Renaissance of Germany.

As in most medieval cities, all things radiate from the **Marktplatz,** which is still filled on market days with stalls selling fresh flowers, fruit, and vegetables. And, typically, here sits the **Rathaus** (city hall) at one end, the main church—the late-Gothic **Heiliggeeistkirche,** built around 1400—at the other. A few steps north, we walked through the turreted baroque Bridge Gate onto the arched **Alte Brücke** (Old Bridge) to get a sweet view up and

Heidelberg's Alte Brücke and Castle.

down the Neckar. Then it was back to the narrow pedestrian-only Hauptstrasse, lined with quaint shops, to go west through the university quarter. Knowing that Heidelberg University was founded as a monastic institution in 1386, we were vaguely disappointed that most of the buildings are more recent, but you can still get a glimpse of the past here and there—look for the baroque palace at Hauptstrasse 97 (now the **Krupfälzisches Museum,** full of paintings and sculpture) and the highly ornamented late Renaissance townhouse at Hauptstrasse 178, called Zum Ritter Sankt Georg after the sculpture of Saint George that crowns its roofline. To get a sense of student life in the old days, stop by the old Studentenkarzer, Augustinergasse 2, a jail where unruly students were locked up, its walls and ceilings covered with graffiti and drawings.

To reach the huge red-sandstone **Heidelberg Castle,** perched high above the Altstadt, there are two routes uphill; we chose the steeper route, a punishing half-hour climb. The castle is a dignified ruin today, but even so it's one of the finest Gothic-Renaissance castles in Germany. The stern palace of Friedrich IV, built 1601–07, is the least damaged section; its rooms are almost completely restored, including a portrait gallery

of German princes and kings since the time of Charlemagne. In the cellars of the castle, the kids may gape at the Great Cask, a barrel-like monstrosity built in 1751 that can hold more than 208,000 liters of wine.

Finish up with a scenic walk where the university's professors and poets traditionally strolled to discuss weighty matters—the **Philosopher's Walk.** Cross the river on the Theodor Heuss Bridge and turn right onto Philosopherenweg—as it climbs the hill on the north bank, you'll get a fabulous vista of the town and the valley. Who knows what deep thoughts it might inspire?

(i) **Tourist Information,** in the Rathaus, Marktplatz (© **49/6221/14220**; www.cvb-heidelberg.de).

✈ Frankfurt, 70km (44 miles).

🛏 $$$ **Heidelberg Marriott Renaissance Hotel,** Vangerowstrasse 16 (© **800/228-9290** in North America, or 49/6221/9080; www.marriott.com). $$ **Parkhotel Atlantic Schlosshotel,** Schloss-Wolfsbrunnen-Weg 23 (© **49/6221/60420**; www.parkhotel-atlantic.de).

WHY THEY'LL THANK YOU: The student jail and the giant wine cask—is there a connection?

Swiss Open-Air Museum
Walk into an Alpine Panorama

All ages • Ballenberg, near Brienz, Switzerland

Tucked into the German part of the Swiss Alps—the Bernese Oberland—the Swiss Open-Air Museum looks like a scene out of *Heidi,* with clusters of typical old farm buildings, tiny Alpine settlements, and gardens and fields being cultivated with traditional agricultural methods. It's a sprawling site, covering more than 809 hectares (2,000 acres)—prepare to do a lot of walking—set up like a mini-Switzerland, with 13 different geographic groupings from the Jura to the Valais. Fringed with stands of dark pine and wildflower-spangled meadows, it's a charming slice of Swiss village life where kids can scamper and roam around in the fresh Alpine air.

The oldest building here is a rough timber farmhouse from 1336. Yes, of course you'll see brown wooden chalets with tiny-paned windows and window boxes of red geraniums, your classic Alpine homes straight off a jigsaw puzzle, but there are many surprising variations. Look out for the house from Ostermundigen, with its fanciful Baroque roofline, the wooden facade painted gray to look like expensive stone. As you wander around (I'd plan for at least 3 hr. to see it all), ask the kids to note the different roof materials, from thatch to wood shingles to tiles, and to compare the half-timbered homes to weathered brown frame-and-plank construction, with white plaster walls appearing in some of the newer homes (if you can call the 17th c. new!). Notice how efficiently these Swiss ancestors made their homes play multiple roles, tucking in a threshing floor or a weaving cellar and

attaching a barn (no doubt it was easier to milk the cows on a winter morning that way).

Children are also delighted to discover how many **farm animals** live on-site, some 250 of them—everything from bees and hens to pigs and horses, including a few nearly extinct breeds of goats and cattle, many of which the kids can pet. **Craft demonstrations** are scatted among the hamlets, showing not only common domestic skills like cheese making, bread baking, spinning, and weaving, but also more specialized skills such as bobbin lace making and the woodcarving for which this region is famous. Don't miss the **Oberentfelden house,** where every historic object is purposely laid out for kids to touch.

It's a handy day trip from Interlaken, past the resorts of Lake Brienz. Guided tours are available, for an extra fee (reserve ahead), but they aren't necessary—just roaming around is all the fun you'll need.

ⓘ ⓒ **41/33/952-1030;** www.ballenberg.ch.

🚌 Brienz, 17km (11 miles) from Interlaken.

🛏 $ **The Swiss Inn,** Général Guisanstrasse 23, Interlaken (ⓒ **41/33/822-3626;** www.swiss-inn.com). $$$ **Victoria-Jungfrau Grand Hotel,** Höheweg 41, Interlaken (ⓒ **800/223-6800** or 41/33/828-2828; www.victoria-jungfrau.ch).

WHY THEY'LL THANK YOU: Petting the goats.

The Jewish Quarter of Prague

Ages 8 & up • Czech Republic

The history of Czech Jews is not a happy one—massacred by Crusaders in the 11th century, walled up in a ghetto in the 13th century, enduring a massive 1389 pogrom, forced to wear identifying caps or yellow stars of David. Even after Austrian emperor Josef I relaxed the prohibitions against them, in 1781, it turned out badly—once all the prosperous Jews were free to move out, the ghetto became such a slum it had to be razed in the 1890s, with only a few historic buildings preserved. The Nazi occupation and World War II literally decimated Prague's Jewish population, reducing it from 56,000 to about 5,000 or 6,000. And yet the Jewish quarter—**Josefov,** the northwest sector of Prague's beautiful Old Town—survived, and today it's one of Prague's most popular tourist draws. Even if you have no Jewish ancestors, it's an inspiring place to visit.

Most of Prague's ancient Judaica was destroyed by the Nazis during World War II, except for what the Germans salvaged—thousands of objects such as Torah covers, books, and silver—to install in an "exotic museum of an extinct race." At long last the Jewish community retrieved their artifacts and set up the **Jewish Museum,** U Starého hřbitova 3a (© **420/ 221/317-191;** www.jewishmuseum.cz). Sign up here for an English-language guided tour of the various sites where the collection is displayed. You'll begin with the **Old Jewish Cemetery** (U Starého hřbitova 3A), dating from the mid–15th century. It's one of the world's most crowded cemeteries, a jumble of gray tombstones marking more than 20,000 graves. Local governments of the time forbade Jews to bury their dead anywhere else, so they resourcefully dug graves deep enough to hold 12 bodies vertically.

The tightly packed gravestones in Prague's Old Jewish Cemetery.

207

Brace yourself before entering the adjoining **Ceremonial Hall**—it displays heartwrenching drawings by children held at the nearby Terezín concentration camp in World War II.

Europe's oldest Jewish house of worship, the **Staronová Synagoga** (Old-New Synagogue), Červená 3, got its name when built in 1270 to distinguish it from an older one that's long gone. Jews have prayed in this vaulted Gothic sanctuary continually for more than 700 years, except for 1941–45, during the Nazi occupation. Czech writer Franz Kafka had his bar mitzvah here. Kids are fascinated by the pink rococo **Jewish Town Hall** (Židovská Radnice) for one feature: the clock face on its north side, which has Hebrew figures instead of numbers, and hands that run counterclockwise, just as Hebrew writing is read right to left. Another lovely old synagogue, the **Maisel Synagogue,** Maiselova 10, is a major exhibit space for the museum, while the 15th-century **Pinkas Synagogue** has been set up as an affecting memorial to the Czech Jews killed by the Nazis. It's stark and simple—just 77,297 names inscribed around its walls—but that's enough to send chills up your spine.

ⓘ **Tourist Information,** main railway station or old Town Hall, Rytírská St. 31 (✆ **420/12-444;** www.prague-info.cz).

✈ Ruzynê Airport, Prague.

⊨ $ **Hotel Cloister Inn,** 14 Konviktská (✆ **420/224/211-020;** www.cloister-inn.cz). $$$ **Hotel Ungelt,** Stupartská 7 (✆ **420/224/ 745-900;** www.ungelt.cz).

WHY THEY'LL THANK YOU: The ghetto survived, against all odds.

Old Town Ceský Krumlov
Watching the River Flow
Ages 8 & up • Ceský Krumlov, Czech Republic

Under the Communist regime, this part of Czechoslovakia had little money to spare for "development." Who knew that that would turn out to be Ceský's Krumlov's saving grace? No glass-and-steel monstrosities spoil the architectural beauty of what is now Bohemia's tourism jewel.

Since the fall of communism in 1989, the Czech government has invested heavily in sprucing up historic Ceský Krumlov, a near-perfect assemblage of medieval and Renaissance-era townhouses, set in a horseshoe bend of the river Vltava. It's now jam-packed every summer, especially at the summer solstice for the Slavnost Petilisté Ruze (Festival of the Five-Petaled Rose), when townfolk dress up in Renaissance costume and the streets are full of living chess games, music, plays, and staged duels.

The town's historic castle—the second biggest in Bohemia—dominates the town from its dramatic rocky hill across the river. **Ceský Krumlov Château** (open Apr–Oct, by guided tour only) is a suitably grand gray stone castle packed with ancestral portraits and heavy tapestries where the powerful Rozmbeck family presided over the town's medieval heyday. Later, the prominent Schwarzenberg family ruled this roost (along with the brown bears that traditionally live in the moat— the kids will love that touch). Though it was founded in the 13th century, a 16th-century makeover is responsible for the present exterior; inside are some stunning baroque and rococo interiors. The lavish decorative details may be lost on the kids, but it's worth taking the tour just to wander through this classic castle.

Cross the wooden bridge to Krumlov's low-lying Inner Town and you'll discover what tourists really fall in love with—the harmony of the old quarter's red roofs, gabled housefronts in a range of colors, and narrow medieval streets (let the kids pore over the town model at the **Okresní Muzeum,** Horní Ulice 152). The cobblestoned, traffic-free Inner Town contains many charming buildings, such as the late Gothic **St. Vitus Cathedral** (great views from its tower), the **Radnice (Town Hall),** at Námestí Svornosti 1, with Gothic arcades and Renaissance vaulting, and the **Hotel Ruze** (Horní 154), a 16th-century amalgamation of Gothic, Renaissance, and rococo influences. As you wander closer to the river, point out to the kids the high-water marks that still mark some of the quirky bank-side houses, reminders of the 2002 floods that nearly wiped out Cesky's Inner Town. In the Middle Ages, towns mostly flourished on riverbanks, close to trade routes. Now, due to deforestation and climate change, Europe's rivers are on the rise. Ceský Krumlov has been spared destruction so many times—will nature finally take its toll?

ⓘ **Tourist Information,** Náměstí Svornosti 2 (☎ **420/380/704-621;** www.ckrumlov.cz).

✈ Prague (2 hrs.).

🛏 $$$ **Hotel Ruze,** Horní 154 (☎ **420/380/772-100;** www.hotelruze.cz).$ **Pension Na louzi,** Kájovská 66 (☎ **420/380/711-280;** www.nalouzi.cz).

WHY THEY'LL THANK YOU: The bears in the moat.

---

202 Town & Gown

Kyoto
City of Samurai & Shoguns
Ages 6 & up • Japan

Tokyo is an exciting big city, but if you really want to say you've been to Japan, visit Kyoto. The capital of Japan from 794 to 1868, it is like a treasure box of history, so precious that during World War II, Allied bombers intentionally spared it from destruction. When you're in Tokyo, it's easy to overlook Japan's rich medieval heritage; when you're in Kyoto, it's impossible to forget.

Take its temples, for example. **Ryoanji Temple** (Goryoshita-cho) contains Japan's most famous Zen rock garden, laid out in the late 15th century—15 pristine rocks, set in waves of raked white pebbles. Then there's the awe-inspiring view at **Kiyomizu Temple,** with its grand wooden veranda hanging over a cliff overlooking Kyoto. Founded in 798, it was rebuilt in 1633 without a single nail. Its grounds are stunning during cherry-blossom season and when the maples turn color in fall. **Sanjusangendo Hall** (Shichijo Dori) is an overwhelming sight: 1,001 life-size cypress statues of the thousand-handed goddess Kannon, standing row upon row in the longest wooden building in Japan. (Each Kannon only has 40 arms, but supposedly each hand has the power to save 25 worlds.)

In medieval Japan, feudal lords known as shoguns ruled the nation from Kyoto. The **Temple of the Golden Pavilion** (Kinkakuji-cho), built in the 1390s for Shogun Ashikaga Yoshimitsu, has a shamelessly luxurious three-story pavilion covered in gold leaf (and this at a time of famine, earthquakes, and plague). His grandson died in 1482 before completing

The Kiyomizu Temple.

its sequel, the **Temple of the Silver Pavilion** (Ginkakuji-cho)—ask the kids to imagine this beautiful wooden villa coated with silver as originally planned. Shogun Ieyasu Tokugawa built the moated **Nijo Castle** (Horikawa Dori and Nijo Dori) in 1603, an elegantly understated palace of Japanese cypress, with delicate transom woodcarvings and exquisitely painted sliding doors. All the doors on the outside walls can be removed in summer, a sort of medieval air-conditioning. One of the paranoid shogun's security measures was the "nightingale floors," special floorboards designed to creak so that sentries could hear enemies sneaking in.

Though not an authentic historic site, at **Kyoto Studio Park Toei Uzumasa** (10 Higashi-Hachigaokacho, Uzumasa, Ukyo-ku; ℂ **81/75/864-7716**), one of Japan's three major film studios, you can walk around Feudal-era "village" sets lined with samurai houses and old-time shops. Besides the daily Ninja shows, kids can enjoy a special-effects show, a haunted house, a games arcade, and indoor rides.

ⓘ **Tourist Information,** Karasuma Dori (ℂ **81/75/343-6655;** www.city.kyoto.jp).

🚄 Kyoto, 2½ hr. from Tokyo by bullet train, 75 min. from Kansai International outside Osaka.

🛏 $$ **ANA Hotel Kyoto,** Nijojo-mae, Horikawa Dori, Nakagyo-ku (ℂ **800/993-3563** in North America, or 81/75/231-1155; www.ichotelsgroup.com). $$$ **The Westin Miyako,** Sanjo, Keage, Higashi-yama-ku (ℂ **800/WESTIN-1** [937-8461] in North America, or 81/75/771-7111; www.westinmiyako-kyoto.com).

WHY THEY'LL THANK YOU: Shogun showplaces.

The Great Wall of China

Ages 6 & up • Beijing to the Gobi Desert

The first question everyone will ask when you get back from China is whether you saw the Great Wall. Maybe it isn't so big you can see it from outer space, but it is still a mind-boggling edifice. To hike along its broad walkways, climbing flights of stairs as the wall zigzags over pleated green mountains, is to feel in touch with the ages. Talk about fortresses—here's a wall so big, it turned the entire country into a fortress.

The Great Wall deserves its name—it is as much as 10,000km (6,214 miles) long when you put together all the fragments. Standing 6m (20 ft.) wide at the base and between 6 and 9m (20–30 ft.) high, it is wide enough for five horses to ride abreast along the ramparts. Its origins lie way back in the Warring States Period (453–221 B.C.), when rival kingdoms built defensive walls against their enemies; over the centuries subsequent emperors connected the various bits and added more to keep out Huns and Mongols and other invaders. The Wall begins east of Beijing at Shan Hai Guan, on the coast of the Bó Hai Sea, and runs west to the Gobi Desert. The chief portion, however—the part most tourists visit, an easy day trip from Beijing—is clearly medieval, reconstructed during the Ming dynasty (1368–1644), with high slotted battlements (*duo kou*) on the outer wall, level parapets on the inner, and stout stone watchtowers every 70m (230 ft.). While the older sections of the wall were built of rammed earth, the Ming rebuilt this section with stone and brick. The most popular, and most developed, section is at **Bādálǐng,** only 70km (44 miles) northwest of the city, where you'll find a museum, theater, restaurants, souvenir stands, even a cable car. Its dramatic setting in a steep forested

The Great Wall of China.

mountain range means you'll have tremendous views, but you'll have to hike past the tourist crowds to get there. Even closer to Beijing—a relatively easy taxi ride from the city center—is the recently restored section at **Juyong Guan,** 59km (37 miles) northwest of the city, which is often less crowded than **Bādáling.** Be sure to check out the impressive Buddhist **bas-relief carvings** on the separate Yún Tái (Cloud Platform) built in 1342. If the kids are up for some more vigorous Wall hiking, go to **Jìnshānlíng** (© **86/10/8402-4628**), 130km (81 miles) northeast of Beijing (you'll need to hire a minivan from Mìyún). The hike from here to the Mìyún Reservoir is roughly 10km (6¼ miles) and takes 3 to 4 hours. The middle portion of the hike, where the number of fellow hikers begins to dwindle and you reach authentically crumbling parts of the Wall, can be truly sublime.

Many tour operators run day trips out to these Wall destinations, though you can also take a city-sponsored tourist bus or even a taxi.

ⓘ www.thegreatwall.com.cn.

✈ Capital Airport, Beijing.

🛏 $$$ **Grand Hyatt,** 1 East Chang An Ave. (© **800/633-7313** in the U.S. and Canada, 86/0845/888-1226 in the U.K., or 86/10/8518-1234; http://beijing.grand. hyatt.com). $$ **Days Inn Joiest Beijing,** 14 E. Ave. Zhushikou Dongdajie (© **86/10/ 6707-7799;** www.daysinn.cn).

WHY THEY'LL THANK YOU: Peering through the arrow slits, imagining the Mongol hordes.

Fortresses **204**

Acre
Israel's Crusader City
Ages 8 & up • Akko, Israel

For 2 centuries in the Middle Ages, armies of Christian knights from Europe streamed eastward to "free" the Holy Land from Muslim rule. Fueled by a strange mix of religious faith, chauvinism, and military aggression, these knights traveled impossibly far from their home countries for years at a time; they needed a safe town of their own in the eastern Mediterranean. Washing up in the ancient seaport of Acre, they transformed it into Crusade City.

Acre had been ruled by everybody at one time or another—the Phoenicians, King David, Alexander the Great, the Ptolemaic kings of Egypt. When the first Crusaders arrived in 1104, they renamed it Saint Jean d'Acre, built a great sandstone fortress, and founded what would become the greatest Crusader city of the Holy Land, eventually reaching a population of 40,000. Acre was a strategic prize, and it fell into Saladin's hands for 4 years, until Richard the Lion-Hearted of England heroically took it back in 1191. The Crusaders hung on until 1291, when they were driven out by the Mamelukes, the final blow that crushed their hopes of ruling the Holy Land. During the Ottoman empire, the Turks built a entire new city on top of the Crusader city, wiping it from view.

Modern Acre is an industrial town, just down the coast from Haifa; it does boast a fine walled **Old City,** but it looks totally Arab, with romantic minarets and palm trees against the sky. You'll want to stroll around its Arab bazaar and visit its beautiful mosques. But the ghost of that Crusader past is still there—you just have to go underground to find it. Since the 1950s, the knights' city has been gradually excavated

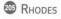

from beneath the walls of Acre Citadel, a former Ottoman prison. A replica of the Crusaders' **Enchanted Garden** blooms beside the visitor center for this **Subterranean Crusader City** (El-Jezzar St.; ✆ **972/4/981-3651**), the old Hospitallers' Fortress, headquarters of the powerful Crusader order, the Knights Hospitallers. Four wings surround a central courtyard; the first hall is a clear example of the double construction—the bottom shows the Crusaders' arches, the top the Ottomans'. Two wings have vaulted Gothic ceremonial halls with pointed arches and massive banded columns (picture them hung with banners and coats of arms), while others have smaller rooms that were probably barracks and storerooms—a medieval toilet was even uncovered.

Kids always love secret passageways, so don't miss the **Templars' Tunnel,** in the southeastern part of the Old City, on Haganah Street, a 350m-long (1,148-ft.) tunnel carved out of rock from the fortress to the port. Once you've meandered around these echoing chambers, climb up onto the broad city walls—built on the base of the old Crusader fortress—for a sweeping view of the bay. Imagine ancient Crusaders standing here, gazing back toward Europe and the homes they'd left behind, so long ago.

ⓘ **Tourist Information,** El-Jezzar St. (✆ **972/4/991-1764;** www.akko.org.il).

✈ Haifa, 22km (14 miles).

🛏 $$$ **Le Meridien Haifa,** 10 David Elazar St. (✆ **972/3/511-0050** or 972/4/850-8888; www.fattal-hotels-israel.com). $$$ **Palm Beach Hotel,** Acre Beach (✆ **972/4/987-7777;** www.palmbeach.co.il).

WHY THEY'LL THANK YOU: The medieval toilet.

Rhodes

Stopping Point on the Crusade Trail

Ages 8 & up • Rhodes, Greece

When the Crusades ended in 1270, the Knights Hospitaller—a military religious order also called the Order of St. John—didn't return home from the Holy Land like the other knights. Buoyed by the wealth they'd accumulated, they declared they would go on defending Christianity. Conquering the eastern Greek island of Rhodes, they set up their own sovereign state, where they maintained a powerful fleet to protect the Eastern Mediterranean from Muslim encroachment.

That turbulent medieval era is evoked today in **Rhodes' Old Town,** a superbly preserved historic quarter girded by a magnificent 4km (2½-mile) set of walls. Walk down cobblestoned Ippoton, also called the **Street of the Knights,** and

you'll pass a continuous series of abrupt stone facades, the "inns" where various nations' Knights took meals and lodged guests. Subtle details echo the architecture of their countries; ask the kids to see how many times they can spot the eight-pointed cross that symbolizes the order. At the bottom of the hill, **Spanish House** sits next door to the **Inn of the Order of the Language of Italy** (see the shield above the door). Then comes the **Palace of the Villiers of the Isle of Adam,** the ornate **Inn of France** with its fleur-de-lis shield, and across the street the **Hospital of the Knights,** now the **Archaeological Museum** (entrance on Museum Square). Across from the Archaeological Museum, the **Byzantine Museum** is housed in the

7 Super City Squares

Marienplatz in Munich.

Plaza, piazza, platz, ploshschad—whatever the local word might be, every great medieval city had one: a central square where markets were held, proclamations read, and historic events celebrated. Here the town hall generally stood, and often the city's main church; wealthy citizens lavished their fortunes on showy mansions, and the most powerful guilds erected opulent headquarters. Stand with the children in any of these grand historic squares and you'll feel their special magic, lighting up the heart of the city that gave birth to them.

206 Marienplatz, Munich, Germany The centerpiece of Munich's Altstadt, or Old City, is this picturesque flagstoned square, dominated by the Gothic Revival Neues Rathaus, the "new city hall" (notice the much plainer Gothic tower on the older hall, the **Altes Rathaus,** to its right). Crowds gather here every morning to see 32 enameled copper figures whirr around in the ornate stone tower, while a carillon plays jaunty music; the top "stage" features knights jousting in a tourna-ment, while at the bottom delirious townsfolk dance. Climb the 55 steps to the top of the **Rathaus tower** (an elevator is also available) for a lovely panorama of this prosperous Bavarian capital. See Deutsches Museum **284** and Neuschwanstein **367**.

207 Grand-Place: Brussels, Belgium Full of gilded facades and gold-filigreed rooftop sculptures, the Grand-Place is a dazzling sight indeed. As you circle the car-free square, paved with sparkly stone blocks, imagine the Renaissance guildsmen vying to establish their power by building the most richly embellished guild halls—the butcher's at No. 9, the brewers at No. 10, and so on. Count the 19 busts of Brabant dukes on nos. 13 to 19. The square's masterpiece is the **Hôtel de Ville (Town Hall)**—you could stand here all day, studying the dozens of little sculptures on its busy gray facade, from drunken monks to St. Michael slaying a female devil. Note that the tower is just slightly off-center—legend has it that when the architect discovered his mistake, he jumped from the tower to his death.

208 Plaza Mayor, Madrid, Spain Walk through an archway into peaceful stone-paved Plaza Mayor, and you'll sense the courtly essence of Spain's capital, so often lost in the commercial bustle of Madrid's other landmark squares. Imagine all that this enclosed plaza has witnessed since it was first laid out in medieval times: bullfights, knightly tournaments, even heretics being burned at the stake. A statue of Habsburg king Philip II on horseback prances at the center, ringed by an elegant 18th-century ensemble of red townhouses with neatly lined-up white windows and ground-floor colonnades. Most of them today contain cafes where you can sip a cool drink on summer nights, enjoying street musicians and watching Madrileños out for their nightly stroll. See Museo del Prado **337**.

209 Staroměstské nám, Prague, Czech Republic For baroque ornamentation, you can't beat the grand pastel-colored buildings that surround Prague's broad Old

Town Square, punctuated by the spiky towers of Tyn Church and the brooding Gothic Town Hall (make sure the kids check out the town hall's fabulously ornate astronomical clock). A major marketplace since the early Middle Ages, it's still lively with craftspeople, cafes, and street performers. The compelling bronze statue in the center commemorates 15th-century religious martyr Jan Hus, a champion of Czech independence. See The Jewish Quarter of Prague **200**.

210 **Red Square, Moscow, Russia** Originally called Trading Square, the name was changed in the 1660s to Krasnaya Ploshchad, probably meaning "beautiful square"— although krasnaya also mean "red," a name that took on extra significance in the Communist era when Soviet tanks draped in red flags rattled menacingly across its cobblestones. Dominated by the dazzling multidomed St. Basil's Cathedral, Red Square still has a sweeping majesty that somehow epitomizes Mother Russia. Come here at sunrise or sunset, especially in summer, and watch the sun's rays make the surrounding buildings rosier than ever. See the Kremlin **213** and St. Basil's Cathedral **327**.

211 **Rome, Italy** Rome is peppered with lovely piazzas, each with its own distinctive flair, and our family had to hit them all—Michelangelo's classically proportioned **Piazza del Campidoglio,** baroque **Piazza Navona** with Bernini's splendid **Fountain of the Four Rivers,** crowded **Piazza di Trevi** with its huge fountain full of wishing coins, the resplendent outdoor arena of **St. Peter's Square,** or traffic-crazed **Piazza Barberini** with its oh-so-wadeable Triton fountain. In the end our favorite, though, was **Piazza di Spagna**—not for the square itself as much as its long flower-banked flight of stairs, aka the **Spanish Steps,** the most romantic meeting place in Rome. It doesn't hurt that it leads directly to the posh shopping of Via Condotti, and to one of our favorite gelato shops. See the Catacombs of Rome **63**, the Colosseum **167**, the Pantheon **168**, and the Vatican **313**.

Rome's famous Spanish Steps.

212 **Piazza San Marco, Venice, Italy** Whether you arrive by gondola from the Grand Canal, or burst into it from any of the narrow side streets, your first view of **Piazza San Marco** is bound to be magical. It's arguably the loveliest public space in the world, lined with graceful loggias on either side, leading to the Byzantine glory of gold-domed **St. Mark's Basilica** at the upper end. Symmetry is beside the point—just off to the side, like an afterthought, is a perfect russet brick bell tower, with the exotic **Doge's Palace** tucked away beside it; to the other side is a baroque clock tower where two mechanical Moors (think *Othello*) chime the hour. Set the kids on a treasure hunt to count all the square's winged lions, the symbol of St. Mark, and now of Venice as well. See the Doge's Palace **365** and the Gondolas of Venice **303**.

Church of Our Lady of the Castle, the Roman Catholic Cathedral of the Knights. The church farther on the right, **Ayia Triada,** played no favorites, displaying three coats-of-arms: those of France, England, and the pope. Past the arch that spans the street, still on the right, is the **Inn of the Language of Provence,** and on the left is the traditionally Gothic **Inn of the Language of Spain,** with vertical columns and a lovely garden in the back. Though you can't enter most of these inns, which are privately owned, you can get an idea of their luxe accommodations at the **Hospice of St. Catherine,** at the opposite corner of Old Town on the Square of the Jewish Martyrs. Built in the late 14th century by the Knights to house guests, it has beautiful sea-pebble and mosaic floors, carved and intricately painted wooden ceilings, and a grand hall and lavish bedchamber.

The Order of St. John is long gone from Rhodes—Sultan Suleiman the Magnificent drove them out in 1523—after which the Holy Roman Emperor took pity and gave them the island of Malta, their international base ever since (hence their other name, the Knights of Malta). The Order still exists, defending Christianity and helping the sick around the world—a centuries-old tradition.

ⓘ **Tourist Office,** Etharhou Makariou St. (✆ **30/22410/44-330;** www.rhodes.gr).

✈ Rhodes.

🛏 $$ **Hotel Mediterranean,** 35 Kos St. (✆ **30/22410/24-661;** www.mediterranean. gr). $ **Hotel Andreas,** 28D Omirou (✆ **30/ 22410/34-156;** www.hotelandreas.com).

WHY THEY'LL THANK YOU: Where does a knight go after the Crusades?

Fortresses **213**

The Kremlin
Moscow's Red Fortress
Ages 8 & up • Moscow, Russia

When I was a kid, the name "the Kremlin" stood for the Soviet Union, in all its Cold War menace. The image of the fortress's tightly guarded gates, bristling towers, and crenellated outer walls—made of bright red brick, the very color associated with Communism—epitomized a closed totalitarian society. What a revelation, then, to discover that this 53-hectare (130-acre) compound is full of charming palaces and churches and Czarist-era treasures. Curiosities like the world's largest bell, the 200-ton **Czar Bell** (which was never rung), and the 40-ton **Czar Cannon** (which was never fired) express the ambition and excess of these Russian princes. To visit the Kremlin is to sense the full operatic sweep of Russian history.

Here's the Kremlin story in a nutshell: It began as a palisaded wooden encampment in the 12th century; white stone walls went up in the 1360s, but then it was sacked by the Mongol Tatars in 1382; Ivan the Great defied the Mongols, declared Moscow's independence in 1480, and built the red-brick walls in the 1490s. During an uprising here, young Peter the Great watched his relatives impaled; he fled Moscow in 1710 to found a new capital in the swamps of St. Petersburg. Power did not return to the Kremlin until the Soviets settled in 1918.

At the heart of the complex is tranquil **Cathedral Square** (Sobornaya Ploshchad), dominated by the gilt-domed **Ivan the Great Bell Tower,** at 80m (262 ft.) the tallest building in Russia. The square comes by its name honestly, because it's packed with churches. The imposing white limestone **Cathedral of the Assumption,** with its chunky golden domes, was where the czars were crowned, the seat of the Russian Orthodox Church. Czars were christened and married in the **Cathedral of the Annunciation,** with its quintessentially Russian silhouette of tented gables; next to it is the **Red Staircase,** which czars traditionally mounted after coronation. Within the somber **Cathedral of the Archangel Michael,** you can see the tombs of Russia's rulers from 1328 to 1696. Behind the small **Church of the Deposition of the Robe** rises the 11-domed roofline of the **Terem Palace** (not open to visitors), where the czars lived.

Besides the churches, as you roam around these cobbled streets and squares—the Kremlin's almost like its own minicity—visit the 17th-century **Patriarch's Palace,** built for the head of the Russian Orthodox Church (think of it as Moscow's version of the Vatican); nowadays it holds a dazzling collection of 17th- and 18th-century religious icons, embroidered robes, illuminated Bibles, and the patriarch's jewel-like private chapel. And don't miss the **Armory Museum** (© **7/495/621-4720**), which, despite its name, holds much more than guns—things like Boris Godunov's armor, Peter the Great's gold brocade robes, the jeweled Fabergé eggs of Czar Nicholas II and Empress Alexandra, and the Russian crown jewels (yes, the Russian state has hung onto those symbols of imperial decadence).

ⓘ Ticket kiosks at Kutafya Tower and the Alexandrovsky Gardens (© **7/495/695-4146;** www.kreml.ru).

✈ Moscow.

🛏 $$ **Cosmos,** 150 Prospekt Mira (© **7/495/234-1000;** www.hotelcosmos.ru). $$$ **Sheraton Palace,** 19 1st Tverskaya-Yamskaya Ulitsa (© **7/495/931-9700;** www.sheratonpalace.ru).

WHY THEY'LL THANK YOU: The Fabergé eggs.

8 War & Peace

The cenotaph at the Alamo

1066 & All That
The Battle of Hastings
Ages 10 & up • Battle, England

Few historical battles were as pivotal as the Battle of Hastings in 1066, a date engraved in English memory. When the duke of Normandy landed on the Sussex coast that autumn with a crack French fighting force, he was just another raider from across the sea. King Harold of the Saxons hurried south with his own valiant army, confident of repelling the Normans as he had the Danes. But by the end of one fatal day—October 14, 1066—Harold was dead (legend claims he was killed by an arrow through the eye, and his body dismembered, though careful studies of the **Bayeux Tapestry** ❿ suggest his death wasn't quite that dramatic.) William the Invader had become William the Conqueror.

The Battle of Hastings is somewhat of a misnomer—while the Normans used the town of Hastings, 101km (63 miles) southeast of London, as their base of operations, the actual battle occurred 10km (6¼ miles) inland, where the aptly-named town of Battle stands today. You may want to stop off at **Hastings Castle** (Castle Hill Rd., Hastings, ℂ **44/1424/444-412;** www. discoverhastings.co.uk), which offers a 20-minute audiovisual presentation on the Conquest, but otherwise Battle is your destination.

At the top of Battle's main street, you'll find the ruins of Battle Abbey, which William ordered built as an act of penance in 1070, using stone shipped from his lands at Caen in northern France. Medieval parts of the abbey still stand—notably the towered gatehouse—but very little is left of the Norman parts. The church's altar was supposedly set on the very spot where Harold died; today it's marked by a plaque on the ground, along with a nearby monument to Harold presented by the people of Normandy in 1903. Even more interesting is the stretch of parkland behind the **Abbey ruins,** where the battle was fought. Be sure to pick up the free interactive **audio tour,** which re-creates the sounds of the battle as you stand where the Saxon army was positioned, atop Senlac Hill, blocking the road to London. (The ground, unfortunately, was leveled when the abbey was built; you'll have to imagine the original steep slope.) The two armies were equal in number, about 8,000 each. The Saxon defense rested on a seemingly impregnable wall of shields, but the cunning Normans—who had greater numbers of archers and cavalry—pretended to flee, tempting the Saxons to charge prematurely, leaving gaps in the shield wall. The Normans poured into the breach, and by nightfall victory was theirs.

Tour the exhibits in the abbey first to get background on the battle; there's also a themed play area. At the other end of High Street, the **Battle Museum of Local History** (ℂ **44/1424/775-955;** www.battle museum.org.uk) displays the only battleaxe ever excavated from the battlefield.

ⓘ **Battle Abbey,** south end of High St. (ℂ **44/1424/775-705;** www.1066country. com).

🚆 Hastings, 1½–2 hr. from London.

🛏 $$$ **Powder Mills Hotel,** Powdermill Lane (ℂ **44/1424/775-511;** www. powdermillshotel.com).

BEST TIME: Mid-Oct, when costumed re-enactors commemorate the anniversary of the battle.

WHY THEY'LL THANK YOU: A peaceful spot to contemplate a fateful day.

Bayeux Tapestry

Telling the Tale of the Norman Conquest

Ages 10 & up • Bayeux, France

These days, we commemorate a historical event with a documentary film or massive monument. Back in the 11th century, an anonymous crew of artists—usually women—celebrated historic milestones in the medium they knew best: embroidery. This elaborately wrought tapestry has survived for nearly a millennium; when you gaze upon its detailed panels, so faithfully recording events that shook their world, you come face to face with the Dark Ages.

The Bayeaux Tapestry is actually embroidery, on a strip of linen 70m (230 ft.) long, depicting some **50 scenes.** Given the limited number of dyes available in that era, only eight colors of thread were used—still enough to illustrate every episode. The tale told is the conquest of Britain by William the Conqueror, the local Norman hero who crossed the Channel and vanquished the Anglo-Saxon army at the **Battle of Hastings 214**. Legend has it that the Bayeux Tapestry was made by Queen Mathilda, the Conqueror's wife, and it's an appealing notion—but most likely false. Commissioned across the Channel in Kent, probably by William's half-brother Bishop Odo of Bayeux, the tapestry was completed a mere 10 years after the Battle of Hastings by a team of needleworkers doggedly stitching day in and day out.

The tapestry is housed in a long climate-controlled Plexiglas case; stroll along its length to find scenes such as the coronation of Harold as the Saxon king of England,

Harold returning from a visit to Normandy, Harold learning of an ill-omened comet, William donning his war armor, and the gruesome death of Harold. The end of the strip, showing the final episodes, was somehow cut off long ago. Stitched **captions** are in Medieval Latin, and the soldiers' armor and weapons are so realistic, historians speculate that ex-soldiers must have helped design it. A key element in William's victory was his cavalry, and hundreds of powerful embroidered horses almost seem to spring from the cloth.

Remember that this was made by Norman craftspeople—some find it flagrant propaganda, justifying William's naked aggression against another nation; yet others point to scenes of Norman brutality to show the artists' sympathy for the vanquished Saxons. Don't let the kids rush past the panels—the more you study the tapestry, the more you enter its stylized and yet vividly familiar world.

ⓘ **Centre Guillaume-le-Conquérant,** 13 rue de Nesmond (✆ **33/2/31-51-25-50;** www.tapisserie-bayeux.fr).

🚄 Bayeux, 2¹⁄₂ hr. from Paris.

🛏 $$$ **Hôtel d' Argouges,** 21 rue St-Patrice, Bayeux (✆ **33/2/31-92-88-86;** www.hotel-dargouges.com). $$ **Hôtel Le Bayeux,** 9 rue Tardif, Bayeux (✆ **33/2/31-92-70-08;** www.lebayeux.com).

WHY THEY'LL THANK YOU: The art of war via the art of needlepoint.

Where Napoleon Met His Waterloo
Ages 8 & up • South of Waterloo, Belgium

So why was the famous battle called Waterloo when it really took place in Mont-St-Jean, a farm village 20 minutes south of Brussels? Well, the Brussels suburb of Waterloo was where the Duke of Wellington was staying (in a coaching inn that's now the **Musée Wellington,** chaussée de Bruxelles 147) on June 18, 1815, when he sent home his momentous announcement: Napoleon Bonaparte, the upstart French emperor who had harassed Europe for the past 12 years, was finally vanquished for good.

Approaching the battlefield, you can't help but notice the immense grassy cone rising from the rolling countryside, topped off with a cast-iron lion, a traditional symbol of victory. This **Lion Mound** was created after the battle to provide a view of the hallowed plain, with 226 steps running like a zipper straight up the slope to its summit. Stop at the visitor center before climbing the mound; a sound-and-light narration and a big-screen film shown inside will help the kids picture early-19th-century combat, when brightly uniformed troops marched in straight ranks toward the enemy line, only to be mowed down by bullets, cannon fire, and the slashing swords of swift-galloping cavalrymen. Some 350,000 soldiers marched onto this battlefield that fateful June day; 9,500 of them never left, and another 32,000 were wounded.

Climb the mound to visualize the layout of the battle, with Napoleon's forces, outnumbered two to one, caught in a pincer between Wellington's army and General Blücher's Prussian troops. Down the Brussels–Charleroi road you can spot La Haie-Stainte, a farmhouse that providentially shielded Wellington's center from direct attack; 135 monuments to various heroes and regiments punctuate the plain. Follow the signposted trail from the mound to nearby **Hougoumont Farm,** which describes one crucial phase of the fighting in detail. You also can drive 5km (3 miles) south to the village of Le Vieux Genappe to see **Le Caillou Farm,** chaussée de Bruxelles 66, Napoleon's quarters, where he planned the battle the night before—you'll see his spartan camp bed and the playing cards with which he whiled away his last night as the scourge of Europe.

On July and August weekends, costumed re-enactors hold rifle and artillery demonstrations. Beside the visitor center are two other attractions, a rather tired **waxwork museum** and a painted 360-degree **panorama** of the battle, which was evidently quite a sensation in the days before moving pictures (battle sound effects have been added to try to give it more pizzazz for today's tourists). I like these reminders that Waterloo has been a tourist site for a long time—generations have come here to contemplate how one day changed the course of European history.

ⓘ Route de Lion 315 (✆ **32/2/385-19-12;** www.waterloo1815.be).

✈ Brussels National, 24km (15 miles).

🛏 $$ **Arlequin,** rue de la Fourche 17–19, Brussels (✆ **32/2/522-33-22** or 32/2/548-98-38; www.arlequin.be). $ **De Boeck's,** rue Veydt 40, Brussels (✆ **32/2/537-40-33;** www.hotel-deboecks.be).

WHY THEY'LL THANK YOU: Reaching the top of the Lion Mound.

Culloden Battlefield
Bonnie Prince Charlie's Last Stand
Ages 6 & up • Inverness, Scotland

At Culloden Battlefield, the last of Scotland's royal blood, Charles Stuart, aka Bonnie Prince Charlie, and his rebel army were finally crushed on April 16, 1746. Pick a gray and gloomy day to visit this windswept plain where Scotland's dream of regaining the throne died a poignant death.

Before you go, brush up on the complicated politics that led up to Culloden. In 1603, England and Scotland joined their crowns when James Stuart became king of England, but over the next century, Scotland was treated more and more shabbily by the powers-that-were in London. In 1715, the son of England's deposed King James II—James Stuart, often called the Old Pretender—led the first Jacobite rebellion, so called because they were trying to restore James Stuart to the joint throne. Though that was quickly crushed, his son Charles, called (what else?) the Young Pretender, instigated a second and more persuasive Jacobite rebellion in 1745.

Prince Charlie's dashing personality at first won many supporters, but none of them made good on their promises. His gallant army of 5,000 faced down an English force 9,000 strong, led by the brutal duke of Cumberland, and in a mere 40 minutes the battle was lost. Prince Charlie escaped and eventually fled to France. With typical contrariness, the Scots have ever since revered this humiliating defeat for its romantic (and anti-English) associations.

The smart new visitor center's dramatic interactive exhibits set the stage, culminating in a 4-minute 360-degree film that recreates the clash and roar of battle. A rooftop viewing area gives you a panoramic perspective before you head off on the footpath around the battlefield, with its several marked sites. (Rent the excellent portable audio guide for detailed narration of your walking tour.) The **Field of the English** is a graveyard for English soldiers; a much more affecting sight is the **Graves of the Clans,** where Scottish fighters are interred under a few simple stones that indicate communal burying places for the dead of each clan. (The Jacobites lost 1,200 men, nearly a quarter of their number, while only 300 English died, a mere 3.3% of their ranks.) You can also see the huge **Cumberland Stone,** where "Butcher" Cumberland is said to have stood watching his bloody victory. The great memorial cairn was finally erected years later, in 1881.

Culloden.

Culloden Moor, on the B9006, 10km (6¹/₄ miles) SE of Inverness (℄ **44/844/493-2159;** www.nts.org.uk/Culloden).

Inverness, 3 hr. from Edinburgh or Glasgow.

$$ **Priory Hotel,** the Square, Beauly, A862 19km (12 miles) east of Inverness

(℄ **44/1463/78-23-09;** www.priory-hotel.com). $$ **Glen Mhor Hotel,** 9–12 Ness Bank, Inverness (℄ **44/1463/23-43-08;** www.glen-mhor.com).

WHY THEY'LL THANK YOU: The valiant last stand of a lost cause.

---

218 Battles for Independence

Fort Ticonderoga
New England's Pivotal Outpost
Ages 6 & up • Ticonderoga, New York, USA

Military history buffs will be in heaven at this 18th-century fort set on a bluff overlooking Lake Champlain at the eastern edge of New York State's Adirondack Mountains. There was a tug of war over this strategic location during not one but two wars—the French and Indian War and its sequel, the American Revolution—and it was occupied at different times by a shifting cast of French, English, or American troops (along with their various Native American allies). Few sites give a better sense of the turbulence of those 20 or so years when the American nation was forged.

Everybody, it seems, wanted a piece of this lonely little outpost. Built by the French in 1755, Fort Carillon (as it was then named) protected a key strategic point—the portage connecting Lake Champlain and Lake George. During the French and Indian War, French forces lost the fort to British attackers in 1758, and British general Lord Jeffrey Amherst renamed it Fort Ticonderoga. Sixteen years later, at the outset of the American Revolution, Ethan Allen made a daring raid with his Green Mountain Boys from Vermont, capturing the fort from the British (communications being what they were in those days, they hadn't yet heard that war had broken out at Lexington and Concord, Massachusetts). The British recaptured it from its

commander Benedict Arnold in early 1777 but set it on fire and fled after the Battle of Saratoga later that year. Tourists began to visit the ruins in the 1790s, and it's been a tourist attraction ever since.

Your **guided tour** of the fort is led by a costumed re-enactor, who could be French or British or American or Native American, depending on who's working that day. The **collection** is anything but dry, with nearly 1,000 muskets, bayonets, pistols, and swords on display, as well as a unique collection of uniforms. You'll see everything from Ethan Allen's blunderbuss to the handwritten note an American private left in his backpack to tell his ancestors why he fought in the American Revolution. There are musketry and cannon-firing **demonstrations,** and a fife-and-drum corps plays throughout the day. But what really got through to my kids—and what I most remembered from visiting as a kid myself—was the sense of how lonely life must have been for the small garrison stationed here, valiantly hanging onto their foothold in the wilderness.

On Rte. 74, Lake Champlain (℄ **518/585-2821;** www.fort-ticonderoga.org).

Burlington, VT, 56 miles.

🛏 $$ **Best Western Ticonderoga Inn & Suites,** 260 Burgoyne Rd. (📞 **877/578-2378** or 518/585-2378; www.bestticonderogahotel.com). $$ **Lake Champlain Inn,** 428 County Rte. 3, Putnam Station (📞 **518/547-9942;** www.tlcinn.com).

BEST TIME: Fort open mid-May to mid-Oct.

WHY THEY'LL THANK YOU: Gives the concept of "holding down the fort" a whole new meaning.

Battles for Independence 219

Lexington & Concord
The Shot Heard 'Round the World
Ages 6 & up • Concord, Lexington & Lincoln, Massachusetts, USA

The opening salvos of the American Revolution—the so-called Shot Heard 'Round the World—were fired in the villages of Lexington and Concord, Massachusetts, on April 19, 1775. No need to memorize the date; you'll hear it everywhere when you visit **Minute Man National Historical Park.** After I read my favorite childhood book, *Johnny Tremain,* to my kids, we just had to come here to see where the climactic battle really happened—and they loved it.

To take things in chronological order, begin in Lexington, where two messengers from Boston, Paul Revere and William Dawes, raised the alarm late on the night of April 18. The **visitor center** on the town common—or Battle Green, as they call it—has a diorama of the early-morning skirmish between local militia, known as "Minutemen" for their ability to assemble quickly, and a large force of British troops. The statue on the green depicts Capt. John Parker, who commanded the militia. At

The North Bridge in Concord.

the **Hancock-Clarke House,** 36 Hancock St., patriot leaders John Hancock and Samuel Adams were awakened by Revere and Dawes. You can also tour **Buckman Tavern,** 1 Bedford St. (✆ **781/862-1703**), on the green, where the Minutemen assembled at dawn. Ordered to disperse, the ragtag (and no doubt sleepy) band of colonists stood their ground—fewer than 100 poorly armed colonists versus some 700 red-coated British soldiers. Nobody knows who started the shooting, but when it was over, 8 militia members lay dead, including a drummer boy, and 10 were wounded.

Next move on to Concord, where the British proceeded in search of stockpiled arms (which militia members had already moved). Begin at the **North Bridge Visitor Center,** 174 Liberty St., with its diorama and video program, then proceed down Monument Street to the **Minute Man National Historical Park** (✆ **978/369-6993;** www.nps. gov/mima). A path leads from the parking lot to the one don't-miss sight, **North Bridge,** where a much larger force of Minutemen massed to attack British regulars and set off the war's first full-fledged battle. Narrative plaques and audio presentations along the path describe the onset of the battle; Daniel Chester French's famous Minuteman statue stands nobly poised by the bridge.

Drive east on Lexington Road to the next park section, where you can follow the **Battle Road Trail,** a 5.5-mile interpretive path (wheelchair, stroller, and bicycle accessible) tracing the route of the defeated British troops straggling back toward Boston. (In summer, ask at the visitor centers about ranger-led guided tours along Battle Rd.) At the Lexington end of the park, the **Minute Man Visitor Center,** off Route 2A, has a fascinating multimedia program about the Revolution and a 40-foot mural illustrating the battle.

ⓘ **Lexington Visitor Center,** 1875 Massachusetts Ave., Lexington (✆ **781/862-2480;** www.lexingtonchamber.org). **Concord Visitor Center,** 58 Main St., Concord (www. concordchamberofcommerce.org).

✈ Boston, 18 miles.

🛏 $$ **Doubletree Guest Suites,** 400 Soldiers Field Rd. (✆ **800/222-TREE** or 617/ 783-0090; www.doubletree.com). $ **The MidTown Hotel,** 220 Huntington Ave. (✆ **800/343-1177** or 617/262-1000; www. midtownhotel.com).

WHY THEY'LL THANK YOU: Listen my children, and you shall hear . . .

220 **Battles for Independence**

Valley Forge
The Winter That Saved America
Ages 6 & up • Valley Forge, Pennsylvania, USA

Battlefields tell one kind of war story; Valley Forge tells another—a victory not of weapons but of perseverance and will. Here, in the bitter-cold winter of 1777–78, George Washington really earned the nickname Father of His Country. It's the essential sequel to visiting **Independence Square,** and an easy day trip from Philadelphia, only 30 miles by today's highways, though quite a march away in those

pre-automobile days. When the ragtag Continental Army straggled into winter camp 18 miles up the Schuylkill River from Philadelphia, they had just lost two major battles, at Brandywine and Germantown. With Philadelphia captured by the British—the Liberty Bell smuggled out of town, the Continental Congress on the run—the battle of American independence was on the verge of being lost.

Washington's Valley Forge Headquarters.

Come to this patch of Pennsylvania farmland to find out how George Washington saved the day.

Arriving at Valley Forge, the Continental Army—some 12,000 hungry, homesick men and boys—found the British had already destroyed the gristmill and sawmill they'd hoped would provide food and shelter. There were 6 inches of snow on the ground, the rivers had iced up, and things looked bleak indeed. Privately, Washington despaired "that unless some great and capital change suddenly takes place . . . this Army must inevitably . . . starve, dissolve, or disperse." Almost 2,000 troops died that winter, and many others deserted. Yet with his almost-mystical leadership quality, Washington somehow kept the army going. He challenged the soldiers to build 12-man log huts, offering cash to those who finished first. Others dug earthworks to defend the camp, hoping to keep the British bottled up in Philly. On the one hand, Washington invigorated the troops' spirits; on the other, he browbeat Congress into sending supplies. On the hard-packed parade ground, Washington's training master, Prussian veteran Baron von Steuben, drilled this rabble of farmers and backwoodsmen in military skills. By springtime, the revamped Continental Army, against all odds, became a force to fear, and the tide of the war soon turned.

Walking around the rolling fields today, you can see replicas of the **soldiers' huts** (with costumed interpreters in high season), the grassy mounds of their old defenses, farmhouses the officers used as lodgings, the **parade ground,** and a sprinkling of **memorials.** An excellent 15-minute film at the visitor center explains the encampment in detail; the center also displays Washington's own tent and cases of artifacts—cooking utensils, blankets, chamber pots, bullets. For an extra admission fee, you can tour the **Isaac Potts House,** a fieldstone farmhouse that Washington used as his headquarters. With most historic sites, summer is the best time to visit, but we came here during winter break and it was perfect weather for grasping the true drama of Valley Forge.

ⓘ PA 23 and N. Gulph Rd. (© **610/783-1077;** www.nps.gov/vafo).

✈ Philadelphia International.

🛏 $$ **Best Western Independence Park Inn,** 235 Chestnut St. (© **800/624-2988** or 215/922-4443; www.independence parkhotel.com). $$$ **Rittenhouse Hotel,** 210 W. Rittenhouse Sq. (© **800/635-1042** or 215/546-9000; www.rittenhousehotel. com).

WHY THEY'LL THANK YOU: Feeling the wind whistle through the barracks' ramshackle log walls.

Fort McHenry
Oh, Say Can You See . . .
All ages • Baltimore, Maryland, USA

The kids may have learned the "Star-Spangled Banner" in school, but do they really know what those words they've memorized are all about? Maybe not—but after a trip to Baltimore, the national anthem will be charged with new meaning. True, most of today Baltimore's Inner Harbor—still a working deep-water port—has been slickly transformed, with the touristy Harborplace shopping mall, the National Aquarium, a lineup of restored vintage ships, and a host of other venues (a Hard Rock Cafe, an ESPN Zone, you know the drill). But gaze out across the water to the south and you'll get the same vista Francis Scott Key saw one heroic morning in 1812: a star-shaped fort on a hilly point overlooking Chesapeake Bay, still flying the American flag proudly over its ramparts.

The immense flag that flies over Fort McHenry today is not the one Key saw (the ragged original is now in the Smithsonian's National Museum of American History in Washington, D.C.). The original, however, was equally huge—30 feet high by 42 feet long—specially ordered by the fort's commander, Major George Armistead, soon after the U.S. declared war on England in 1812. Knowing that the British navy was bound to attack this prime harbor and ship-building center, he wanted a flag big enough that the British couldn't miss it. On September 13, the expected attack came, but after a night of fierce bombardment (as in "the rockets' red glare, the bombs bursting in air"), that gigantic flag signaled that the scrappy Americans had held the fort.

A water taxi from the Inner Harbor (**Ed Kane's Water Taxi;** © 800/658-8947 or 410/563-3901; Apr–Oct only) is the best way to approach Fort McHenry. Note how the fort's pentagonal shape—a popular design of that era—is echoed in the earthen banks surrounding the walls, those famous "ramparts" that the flag flew over. The green slopes around the fort, with their splendid water views, are popular picnic spots for Baltimoreans, but keep climbing uphill to enter the red-brick fort itself. The restored two-level barracks tucked inside the walls have been set up to re-create the enlisted men's cramped quarters, the slightly more comfortable junior officers' digs, and the commanding officer's apartment. Uniforms and weapons are displayed, and you can check out the powder magazine where ammunition was kept. Summer weekends are a great time to come, when costumed re-enactors do living history presentations, and the volunteer Fort McHenry Guard fires off muskets and cannons (always a hit with my sons).

Afterward the kids may want to visit those historic ships, though they date back to more recent eras. (Our favorite was the Civil-War-era **USS Constellation,** a triple-masted sloop-of-war.) Top your visit off with a Baltimore Orioles game at Camden Yard—Orioles fans always sing the National Anthem with extra gusto, and now you'll know why.

ⓘ **Fort McHenry National Monument,** 2400 East Fort Ave. (© **410/962-4290;** www.nps.gov/fomc).

✈ Baltimore-Washington International, 10 miles.

🛏 $$$ **Baltimore Marriott Waterfront Hotel,** 700 Aliceanna St., Inner Harbor East (© **410/385-3000;** www.baltimoremarriottwaterfront.com). $$ **Brookshire Suites,** 120 E. Lombard St. (© **866/583-4162** or 410/625-1300; www.harbormagic.com).

WHY THEY'LL THANK YOU: That star-spangled banner yet waves.

Remembering the Alamo

Ages 4 & up • San Antonio, Texas, USA

Visiting San Antonio without going to the Alamo is like visiting London and not seeing Big Ben: You can do it, but it would be wrong.

Expect the kids to be let down at first. The Alamo looks downright dinky, set smack in the heart of downtown San Antonio, surrounded by skyscrapers and traffic. But the whole point of the Alamo is that it *was* such a tiny fort, and the valiant Texan volunteers never had a ghost of a chance of escaping the Mexican army's siege—and still they fought, they fought to the death. That's heroism, Texas style.

There were only 188 Texans defending the Alamo in February 1836, facing the 4,000-strong army of General Santa Anna, who was bent on squashing the Texas territory's bid for independence from the new Mexican Republic. The Texans held out doggedly for 13 days, waiting for reinforcements that never arrived, until all the men—every last one of them, including pioneer heroes Davy Crockett and Jim Bowie—were killed in a crushing dawn attack on March 6. But a month later, when Sam Houston was leading another troop of Texans into the battle of San Jacinto, he fired them up with the cry, "Remember the Alamo!" With that heroic example to live up to, the Texans fought like demons, and this time they won, becoming the independent Republic of Texas. (It didn't join the U.S. until 1846.)

What you see today isn't much of a fort—in 1836 the fortified compound was a bit larger, its outer walls ringing much of what is today Alamo Plaza (look for foundation stones near the steps down to River Walk). After the defeat at San Jacinto, the retreating Mexican forces pulled down much of the Alamo fort to prevent the Texans from refortifying it. Only two original buildings remain. First is the gabled stone **mission church**—now officially a shrine, so show respect by removing hats and taking no photos—which was built in 1756 for the Mission San Antonio de Valero, founded in 1718 to convert local Native American tribes. By the end of the 18th century, the mission was turned over to a Spanish cavalry unit, which renamed it the Alamo (Spanish for "cottonwood") after their Mexican hometown. Besides the church, you can visit the **Long Barracks,** originally the missionaries' living quarters and later used as the cavalry's barracks; today it includes exhibits on **Texas history,** with an emphasis on the Alamo battle.

For kids, however, it's the **artifacts** displayed in the church that will be most compelling: things like a Bowie knife, Crockett's buckskin jacket, and one of the antiquated flintlock rifles the Texans used to defend the fort. Several cannons from the battle are set around the courtyard, mute witnesses to that day of incredible valor.

ⓘ 300 Alamo Plaza (② **210/225-1391;** www.thealamo.org).

✈ San Antonio International, 13 miles.

🛏 $$ **Crockett Hotel,** 320 Bonham St. (② **800/292-1050** or 210/225-6500; www.crocketthotel.com).

WHY THEY'LL THANK YOU: Heroes against all odds.

Gettysburg National Park
Blood & Sorrow in the Civil War
Ages 6 & up • Gettysburg, Pennsylvania, USA

"Awesome" doesn't begin to do justice to this vast battleground, where thousands of Union and Confederate soldiers clashed for three sultry July days in 1863. As Abraham Lincoln himself said in his famous 1864 speech here, this land has been consecrated by blood—over 50,000 deaths—and an almost-eerie atmosphere hangs over this tranquil patch of rolling farmland, now peppered with war monuments.

The park visitor center has several excellent exhibits that will help you get oriented—after all, the battle raged over a large patch of country in the course of 4 days, and there's a lot to keep straight. Don't miss the historic "Battle of Gettysburg" **cyclorama painting,** an incredibly detailed 360-degree depiction of Pickett's Charge which was painted in 1883—it's just the sort of pre-video-era special effect I love. At the tour desk, you can buy CDs for self-guided driving tours around the 250-acre battle site, but we found that this was one place where it paid to invest in a personal guide, who drove us in our station wagon around the battlefield for 2 hours (reserve at least 3 days in advance). Gettysburg's guides are gold mines of Civil War information, tailoring the tour to your particular interests; there wasn't a question we lobbed at him that he couldn't handle, whether biographies of the commanders or the physics of cannon fusillades.

We were completely engrossed by **Seminary Ridge,** where the main Confederate forces were camped; we could look down the hillside where the heroes of Pickett's Last Charge plunged to their gallant end. But we were most moved by **Little Round Top,** where a plucky band of Northern soldiers held the high ground against a furious Confederate onslaught surging up out of the boulder-strewn hollow called

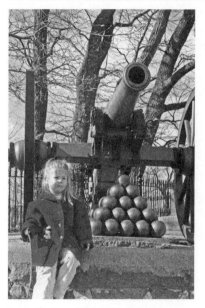

Copse of trees and High Water Mark Monument at Gettysburg.

Devil's Den. Observation towers near Seminary Ridge give you a great aerial overview, but walking around the landscape is the only way to appreciate how hard-won every inch of ground was.

In the town of Gettysburg itself, we enjoyed the **American Civil War Museum,** 297 Steinwehr Ave. (© **717/334-6245;** www.gettysburgmuseum.com), which tells the full Civil War history in waxwork dioramas; normally I find wax figures hokey or creepy but this was actually tasteful and informative. The most special part of our visit, though, was seeing the costumed re-enactors—many of them amateur Civil War buffs here for the fun of it—roaming around the town and the park, socializing around campfires or demonstrating their rifle skills. For a flicker of a moment we traveled through time, feeling the Gettysburg tragedy in our bones.

(i) **Visitor Center,** 1195 Baltimore Pike (✆ **717/334-1124;** www.nps.gov/gett). **Advance tickets,** call ✆ **877/874-2478** (www.gettysburgfoundation.org).

✈ Baltimore-Washington International, 60 miles.

🛏 $$$ **Holiday Inn Battlefield,** 516 Baltimore St. (✆ **717/334-6211;** www.ichotelsgroup.com). $$ **Quality Inn,** 380 Steinwehr Ave. (✆ **800/228-5151** or 717/334-1103; www.gettysburgqualityinn.com).

WHY THEY'LL THANK YOU: Brother fought brother on this bloody ground.

Bloody Battlegrounds 224

Vicksburg
Dixie's Darkest Day
All ages • Vicksburg, Mississippi, USA

My family still watches grainy home movies of my childhood trip to Vicksburg, Mississippi. I remember the sweltering Delta heat, abated by lazy breezes off the Mississippi River; I remember the hilly green landscape; I remember clambering over fat black cannons. I've just realized that this must have planted in me a lifelong love of visiting battlefields—vast outdoor spaces where kids can run off steam while adults somberly ponder the nature of war.

In war, topography is destiny. Vicksburg—known as the Gibraltar of the Confederacy—protected a strategic strait along the Mississippi River. The Union needed to gain control of the Mississippi, not only to reclaim this vital shipping route but also to sever the South in two. Union commander Ulysses S. Grant waged a bitter campaign across central Mississippi in the spring of 1863. He headed relentlessly toward Vicksburg, but realized when he neared the city that its hilly landscape made it nearly impossible to assault. The wily general then switched tactics, laying siege to the city instead. His troops starving, reinforcements cut off, Confederate commander John C. Pemberton finally surrendered to Grant on July 3, 1863, after 47 brutal days.

A 16-mile **driving trail** winds through the park, past cannon emplacements, grassy foundations of old forts, and the trenches Grant ordered dug to set mines beneath Confederate redoubts. Every state that fought in the campaign has its own memorial; our favorite was the Illinois monument, a domed neoclassical structure set on a hill up two long rippling flights of steps where we hopped around for a full half-hour.

The first half of the tour follows the Union siege lines. You'll pass the simple white house where the Shirley family huddled fearfully throughout the Union advance; near Grant's headquarters, a circle of bronze tablets details the other battles in Grant's long Mississippi campaign. The USS *Cairo*, a 13-gun ironclad gunboat, is on display, the first ship in history to be sunk by an electronically deployed torpedo. Halfway through the drive, you'll visit the Vicksburg cemetery, containing the graves of 17,000 Union soldiers (the 5,000 Confederate graves are at the Vicksburg City Cemetery). Then you begin to trace the Confederate lines, starting with the grassy site of Fort Hill, on a riverside bluff where gunners could strafe the Union ships down on the river below. Eventually

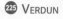

you reach the site where Pemberton surrendered to Grant on July 3—in a grim coincidence, the very same day another arm of the Confederate army lost the Battle of Gettysburg.

ⓘ 3201 Clay St. (✆ **601/636-0583;** www.nps.gov/vick).

✈ Jackson, MS, 40 miles.

🛏 $$ **Annabelle,** 501 Speed St. (✆ **800/791-2000** or 601/638-2000; www.annabellebnb.com). $ **Battlefield Inn,** 4137 I-20 Frontage Rd. (✆ **800/359-9363** or 601/638-5811; www.battlefieldinn.org).

WHY THEY'LL THANK YOU: Grant's cunning, the South's downfall.

Verdun
World War I's Bloodiest Battleground
Ages 10 & up • Verdun, France

Verdun is France's Gettysburg. Nearly 700,000 soldiers died here, in World War I's longest and bloodiest battle; it lasted an incredible 10 months, one continuous stretch of fighting from February to December of 1916. You'll need a car to tour the vast battlefield, but it's a site you'll never forget.

Left untouched by development, the Verdun battlefield still wears its battle scars—a bomb-cratered landscape littered with tangled barbed wire, rusty bullets, shards of shrapnel, and even in some cases unexploded shells and grenades (warn the children to step carefully and not to touch anything on the ground). Peering down into a warren of trenches and imagining the doughboys, living there day and night under a continual barrage of shellfire, vividly brings home the true horrors of World War I.

The fortress of Verdun—a military garrison town since Roman times—became a symbol of French toughness in the Franco-Prussian War (1870–71), which is precisely why the Germans chose to launch a major assault here, for its psychological value. Nearly a million German troops faced 200,000 French defenders in the first attack on February 21, 1916. By summer, all seemed lost, but French military leader Marshall Pétain staunchly declared, "They shall not pass!"—and the Allies held out. When the battle ended on December 18, the Allies had won, but the cost in human lives was staggering, all to gain a few yards of ground.

A 32km (20-mile) signposted **driving tour** follows routes D913 and D112 on the Meuse's right bank. To get an overview of the battle, stop first at the **Mémorial de Verdun,** 1 av. du Corps Européen, Fleury-Devant-Douaumont (✆ **33/3/29-84-35-34;** www.memorial-de-verdun.fr; closed Jan), which displays weapons, uniforms, and photographs. You can visit two important fortifications, both huddled largely underground, which fell to the Germans in the summer but were recaptured in the fall by the French. **Fort Vaux** is where French commander Raynal staged such a heroic defense that even the Germans paid tribute to him; the larger **Fort de Douaumont** is where the fiercest German assault, the "hell of Verdun," was unleashed. Stand on the roof of the fort and look out at a vast field of corroded tops of "pillboxes," bunkered gun emplacements. Near Douaumont are the sobering **Ossuaire de Douaumont,** a memorial tower embedded with the unidentifiable bones of those blown to bits, and the equally grim **Tranchée des Baïonettes (Trench of Bayonets),** a restored concrete trench dedicated to French troops killed by a shell explosion, their bayonets left sticking out of the earth. On the road back to Verdun lies a **French cemetery** of 16,000 graves—this seemingly endless field of crosses is more eloquent than any words.

ⓘ Along D913, 4km (2¹/₂ miles) east of Verdun (✆ **33/3/29-84-18-85;** www. verdun-tourisme.com).

🚆 Verdun, 261km (162 miles) from Paris.

🛏 $$$ **Château des Monthairons,** Rte. D34, Dieue-sur-Meuse (✆ **33/3/29-87-78-55;** www.chateaudesmonthairons.fr). $$ **Hostellerie de Coq-Hardi,** Av. de la Victoire, Verdun (✆ **33/3/29-86-36-36;** www.coq-hardi.com).

WHY THEY'LL THANK YOU: Trench warfare at its most tragic.

Ypres
The Poppies of World War I
Ages 10 & up • Ieper, Belgium

"In Flanders fields the poppies blow / Between the crosses, row on row . . ." The most famous poem about World War I was written by Canadian surgeon Maj. John McCrae in anguished response to what he saw at Ypres—or "Bloody Wipers," as the English servicemen called it. Bright red poppies grow wild here—you can still see them blooming every spring around this gentle Belgian hill country, like drops of blood on the ravaged landscape. They get me every time.

Wedged between France and Germany, Belgium always got caught in the crossfire in Europe's wars, but World War I hit it worst. Ypres sat squarely on the battle front that slashed across the face of Europe like a livid dueling scar; though there were only two official battles here, the area was bombarded almost continually for the entire 4 years of the war, from 1914 to 1917. Afterward there was pretty much nothing left of the town—a fact that's hard to believe when you visit it today. Ieper (the Flemish spelling) was rebuilt after the armistice, brick by brick, and though it looks charmingly medieval,

look closer and you'll see that those aren't timeworn stones; the gabled guild houses and patrician mansions around the Grote Markt are stage-set perfect.

At the west end of the Grote Markt, in the extravagantly Gothic Lakenhalle, your one essential stop in town is **In Flanders Field** (✆ **32/57/23-92-20;** www.inflanders fields.be; closed Jan), a museum designed for emotional effect as much as for conveying information. Each visitor gets an ID card of an ordinary soldier or citizen, which you insert in slots at various kiosks to discover what "you" would have experienced during the war. Toward the end, you enter a dark room full of disorienting smoke and horrid noises and acrid smells—just a sample of what the soldiers endured day after surreal day. After that, driving around the battlefield has a much keener impact. Local companies run minibus tours, or you can drive an 80km (50-mile) route on signposted roads past all the main sights. With the kids, however, it'll be enough to drive out N8 to Canadalaan, to **Sanctuary Wood,** a preserved stretch of muddy trenches complete with shell holes and shattered trees. Just imagine a giant network of such trenches snaking over the countryside as far as the eye can see—that was Ypres.

No fewer than 185 military cemeteries surround Ieper—those "crosses, row on row"—and back in town, war memorials are tucked into every spare corner. The most poignant one to me is the **Missing Memorial,** a marble arch inscribed with the names of 54,896 British troops who died here; the adjacent **Australian Memorial** commemorates the 43,000 Aussies who gave their lives. Those numbers just boggle my mind—an entire generation of men wiped out. Every evening at 8pm, traffic is halted here while Ypres firefighters play *The Last Post* on silver bugles. I dare you not to feel a chill.

ⓘ **Toerisme Leper,** Stadhuis Grote Markt (✆ **32/57/23-92-00;** www.ieper.be).

✈ Brussels National, 113km (70 miles).

⊨ $$ **Hotel Regina,** Grote Markt 45 (✆ **32/57/21-88-88;** www.hotelregina.be).

WHY THEY'LL THANK YOU: Knowing why this was called "the war to end all wars."

Bringing the Blitz to Life
Imperial War Museum & the Cabinet War Rooms
Ages 8 & up • London, England

For the first several years of World War II, with France occupied and the U.S. refusing to declare war, Great Britain fought almost single-handedly against the Axis powers, the lone dogged champion of freedom. It's an incredibly moving story, and nowhere is it told more poignantly than at London's Imperial War Museum and its satellite installation, the Cabinet War Rooms.

Among the equipment displayed at the museum are a Mark V tank, a Battle of Britain Spitfire, and a German one-man sub. In the **Documents Room** you can read the infamous "peace in our time" agreement that Prime Minister Neville Chamberlain signed in 1938 to appease Hitler. But what most brings the war alive for children is the exhibit on the **Home Front,** September 1940 to late spring 1941, when the British people's famous pluck was tested to the utmost by food and petrol rationing, conscription of men and even women, and a staggering influx of refugees and foreign servicemen. Many English children were sent to live away from their families, in some cases for years. The **Blitz Experience** reconstructs an air-raid shelter and a blitzed street, with evocative sights, sounds, and smells to capture the sensation of being caught in the bombing. A sobering exhibit on the Holocaust occupies two other floors; espionage and clandestine warfare are the themes of the Secret War Exhibition.

The perfect complement to this history lies across the river, near the government buildings of Whitehall, in the Cabinet War Rooms. This is no reconstruction but the actual secret warren of bombproof rooms abandoned by Prime Minister Winston Churchill and the British government at the end of World War II. Churchill directed Britain's valiant war effort from this underground lair, working here for months at a time. Look for the BBC microphone in his tiny bedroom, from which he broadcast radio speeches that galvanized the British

Imperial War Museum.

under the beds—there were no flush toilets down here. And don't miss the cramped closet called the **Transatlantic Telephone Room,** where a special scrambler phone allowed Churchill to hold secure phone conversations with President Franklin Roosevelt, finally convincing the Americans to join the effort and turn the course of the war.

ⓘ **Imperial War Museum,** Lambeth Rd. (✆ **44/20/7416-5000;** www.iwm.org.uk). **Cabinet War Rooms,** King Charles St. (✆ **44/20/7930-6961;** www.iwm.org.uk).

✈ Heathrow.

🛏 $$$ **London Bridge Hotel,** 8–18 London Bridge St. 9 (✆ **44/20/7855-2200;** www.londonbridgehotel.com). $$ **Vicarage Private Hotel,** 10 Vicarage Gate, South Kensington (✆ **44/20/7229-4030;** www.londonvicaragehotel.com).

WHY THEY'LL THANK YOU: Those who cannot learn from history are doomed to repeat it.

nation. In the **Map Room,** see the pinholes peppering the Atlantic Ocean, each pin representing the location of a convoy of ships. Notice, too, the chamber pots

World War II & the Cold War 228

The Nazi Invasion of England
Ages 6 & up • Jersey & Guernsey, England

Physically closer to France than to Great Britain, Jersey and Guernsey have nevertheless been part of the English kingdom ever since William the Conqueror—except for the period from 1940 to 1945, when, as part of Hitler's Atlantic Wall defense, German soldiers occupied the islands. Today the Channel Islands are popular vacation spots, with beautiful beaches and cliff-top walks, but wartime gun emplacements, secret tunnels, and concrete bunkers can still be found around both islands, if you know where to look.

On Jersey, the most intriguing site is the **Jersey War Tunnels,** Meadowbank, Les Charrieres, Malorey (✆ **44/1534/860808;** www.jerseywartunnels.com), where former Nazi hospital tunnels have been fitted

out with videos, digital effects, and dioramas, as well as glass cases full of artifacts. Aboveground, a War Trail has been laid out, taking in remnants of German defenses. The **Channel Island Military Museum,** 5 Mile Rd., St. Ouen (✆ **44/7797/732072;** summer only), is also worth a stop. Do a circuit of the island to find all the bunkers and gun emplacements set on various headlands, which can be visited at limited hours (schedules at www.cios jersey.org.uk). One of the most chilling is the slitted concrete observation tower on **Noirmont Point** (✆ **44/1534/746795;** Sun Apr–Oct only), which almost looks as if it is leering evilly out to sea. Before you leave the island, stop in the harbor town of St. Helier at the **Maritime Museum** on

New North Quay (© **44/1534/833300;** www.jerseyheritagetrust.org), where you can see the **Occupation Tapestry,** a 24m-long (79-ft.) tapestry embroidered by volunteers from every Jersey parish, recounting the story of the occupation—think of it as a 20th-century version of the Bayeux Tapestry.

In the center of the island of Guernsey are three fascinating sites. The **German Military Underground Hospital,** La Vassalerie, St. Andrews parish (© **44/1481/239100**), is a labyrinthine complex of concrete tunnels built over 3¹/₂ years by compulsory labor (Nazi captives from France, Spain, Morocco, Algeria, Belgium, Holland, Poland, and Russia, often working with their bare hands). The only bits that are visible aboveground are the entrances and the square holes of escape shafts. The **German Occupation Museum,** Les Houards, Forest (© **44/1481/238205;** www.festungguernsey.supanet.com; Apr–Oct only), has more tunnels, as well as a re-created street showing life in Nazi-occupied Guernsey. Another restored bunker just outside St. Peter Port, on the grounds of La Collinette Hotel, St. Jacques (© **44/1481/710331;** www.lacollinette.com) was once the **Germans' Naval Signals Headquarters.** As on Jersey, guns, casemates, and observation towers dotted around the Guernsey coast have been restored by local enthusiasts; they are open limited hours, usually on weekends.

ⓘ Jersey (www.jersey.com). Guernsey (© **44/1481/723552;** www.visitguernsey.com).

✈ Jersey and Guernsey, served from many U.K. airports.

FERRY: St. Helier or St. Peter Port. **Condor Ferries** (© **44/845/609-1026;** www.condorferries.com). **HD Ferries** (© **44/870/460-0231;** www.hdferries.com).

🛏 $$ **Les Charrieres Country Hotel,** St. Peter, Jersey (© **44/1534/481480;** www.lescharriereshotel.co.uk). $$ **Le Friquet Country Hotel,** rue de Friquet, Castel, Guernsey (© **44/1481/256509;** www.lefriquethotel.com).

BEST TIME: Apr–Oct.

WHY THEY'LL THANK YOU: Tunnels, bunkers, and towers—a hidden tale of war.

---

229 World War II & the Cold War

Pearl Harbor
Day of Infamy
Ages 8 & up • Honolulu, Hawaii, USA

Today Hawaii is so synonymous with leis, luaus, and tropical suntans, it's weird to realize that most Americans had barely heard of this South Pacific U.S. possession before December 7, 1941, when the horrifying news came over the radio: Japanese bombers had attacked U.S. ships at Pearl Harbor, Honolulu. Hawaii wasn't even a state, but it was still American soil, which was under attack for the first time since the War of 1812. President Franklin D. Roosevelt called it "a day that will live in infamy"; after years of pretending that World War II wasn't our fight, we realized it was.

Pearl Harbor is a site that inspires reflection on war and peace and our place in the global community. The **USS *Arizona* Memorial** at Pearl Harbor is a truly special monument. Just 6 feet below the surface of the sea, you can see the deck of the 608-foot battleship USS *Arizona,* which sank in a swift 9 minutes, killing 1,177 of its men, more than half the total casualties that tragic day. Oil still oozes up from its engine room to stain the harbor's calm blue water—some say the ship's still weeping for its lost crew. Moored a short distance from shore, the memorial is a stark white rectangle with a scooped-out roof that spans the hull of the ruined ship; on its walkways you can ponder over the ship's bell, dredged up from the wreckage, and a shrine room with the inscribed names of the dead. The gallant flagpole overhead is attached to the mainmast of the sunken ship. You'll ride out to the memorial on Navy launches from the visitor center; go early if you can, because you'll wait 2 to 3 hours at midday. A 20-minute film and exhibits at the center fill in the history for the kids while you're waiting for your assigned ship time.

Two other ships in the harbor tell the rest of the World War II story, so you're not left on a tragic note. Next to the *Arizona*, you can board a World War II submarine, the **USS Bowfin** (✆ **808/423-1341;** www. bowfin.org), nicknamed the "Pearl Harbor Avenger" for the way it harried the Japanese throughout the rest of the war. This is a great place to see how submariners lived

in their cramped underwater quarters. From the *Bowfin's* visitor center you can also visit the **USS Missouri** (✆ **877/ MIGHTYMO** [644-4896]; www.ussmissouri. com), a 58,000-ton battleship that fought at Tokyo, Iwo Jima, and Okinawa. Fittingly, the Japanese surrender was signed on September 2, 1945, on the deck of the *Missouri*. The guided tour, complete with 1940s music played on the shuttles to the ship, is a fascinating look at a massive seagoing vessel.

ⓘ Pearl Harbor (✆ **808/422-0561;** www. nps.gov/usar).

✈ Honolulu International.

🛏 $ **Hawaiiana Hotel,** 260 Beach Walk (✆ **800/367-5122** or 808/923-3811; www.hawaiianahotelatwaikiki.com). $$$ **Outrigger Waikiki on the Beach,** 2335 Kalakaua Ave. (✆ **800/OUTRIGGER** [688-7444] or 808/923-0711; www.out rigger.com).

WHY THEY'LL THANK YOU: Staring through the waves at a watery grave.

World War II & the Cold War 230

The D-Day Beaches of Normandy

Ages 6 & up • Arromanches-les-Bains to Grandcamps-les-Bains, France

Even without a veteran in the family, 21st-century youngsters—who grew up in the shadows of two Gulf Wars—can relate to the Normandy Invasion. The tale has been told in films from *The Longest Day* to *Saving Private Ryan* and *Band of Brothers*, but nothing beats standing where it actually happened.

The Allied invasion of occupied France was swift, sudden, and a complete surprise to Hitler's formidable "Atlantic wall." In June 1944, the greatest armada ever—soldiers and sailors, warships, landing craft, tugboats, jeeps—assembled along the southern coast of England. At 9:15pm on June 5, the French Resistance got a

signal to start dynamiting railways in Normandy; around midnight, Allied planes began bombing the coast; by 1:30am paratroopers dropped onto French soil to cut off roads and isolate Nazi forces. At 6:30am, the Americans began landing on the beaches, code-named Utah and Omaha, followed an hour later by British and Canadian forces at Juno, Gold, and Sword.

I recommend starting in Caen, at the emotionally charged **Caen Memorial,** Esplanade Eisenhower (✆ **33/2/31-06-06-45;** www. memorial-caen.fr), perhaps Europe's best museum on World War II and its aftermath. In Bayeux, the **Normandy Battle Memorial**

Museum, boulevard Fabian Ware (✆ **33/ 2/31-51-46-90**), has maps, models, and stirring eyewitness accounts of the battle. In Merville, **Batterie de Merville,** place de 9me Battalion (✆ **33/2/31-91-47-53;** www.batterie-merville.com), lets kids tour a renovated Germany artillery bunker and casemates, to understand the scope of the defenses that the invading Allies faced.

But the main thing is to visit the beaches themselves, where the story is told through narrative plaques (many in English), stark monuments, and the occasional war debris intentionally left in place—snarls of barbed wire, crumpled concrete bunkers, and rusted vehicles stranded on the flat sands. At **Arromanches-les-Bains,** the **Musée du Débarquement,** place de 6-juin (✆ **33/2/31-22-34-31;** www.musee-arromanches.fr; closed Jan), tells the story of the mammoth movable port (nicknamed Winston, after Churchill) that was towed across the Channel and installed to supply successive waves of Allied troops. The remains of this prefab harbor can still be seen. Moving west, **Omaha Beach** has been obscured by tourist development, but the section near Colleville-sur-Mer is still evocative, especially the nearly 10,000 marble crosses and Stars of David at the **Normandy American Cemetery** (✆ **33/2/31-51-62-00**). There's also a Canadian cemetery

at Reviers, a British one in Bayeux, and a German one at LaCambe, but the American cemetery is by far the largest, for the simple, tragic reason that the heaviest fighting was on Omaha and Utah beaches.

Farther west, see the jagged lime cliffs of **Pointe du Hoc,** where daring American Rangers scaled the cliffs to capture gun emplacements on top (ironically, the guns had already been moved); its cliff-top terrain scooped out by bomb craters vividly summons up images of the battle. Farther along the Cotentin Peninsula are **Utah Beach,** where the 4th U.S. Infantry Division landed, and the hamlet of **Ste-Mère-Eglise,** where the 101st Airborne parachuted into enemy territory—look for the statue of a paratrooper dangling on the spire of the village church.

ⓘ **Caen Tourist Board,** place Saint Pierre (✆ **33/2/31-27-14-14;** www.tour isme.caen.fr). Also visit www.normandie memoire.com.

🚃 Bayeux, 2½ hr. from Paris.

🛏 $$$ **Hôtel d' Argouges,** 21 rue St-Patrice, Bayeux (✆ **33/2/31-92-88-86;** www.hotel-dargouges.com). $$ **Hôtel Le Bayeux,** 9 rue Tardif, Bayeux (✆ **33/2/31-92-70-08;** www.lebayeux.com).

WHY THEY'LL THANK YOU: The tide of World War II turned here.

Jewish Museum Berlin

Ages 8 & up • Berlin, Germany

Europe's largest Jewish museum, the **Judisches Museum Berlin** covers the entire panorama of German-Jewish history, from the arrival of Jewish merchants to trade with Roman legions, through the medieval Ashkenazi period, and on through centuries of assimilation. But what makes its presence in Berlin especially powerful is the

inevitable chapter on the Holocaust, that horrific era when the Nazi regime systemically exterminated at least 6 million Jews, some 200,000 of them from Germany. Berlin, as Germany's center of commerce and intellectual life, had always had a prominent Jewish population, which was decimated by the Nazis. The opening of this museum marks an important step in laying the ghosts of the Holocaust to rest.

A fair amount of the material on display was resurrected from an older Jewish museum, which opened in Berlin in 1933—not the best timing, for shortly thereafter Hitler rose to power, and by 1938 the Gestapo had shut down the museum, confiscating its collection of art and Judaica. Only recently, after reunification, could it be reassembled here in this striking new site. Called "the silver lightning bolt," the museum was designed by architect Daniel Libeskind. To some viewers, its footprint suggests a shattered Star of David, an impression underscored by the scarring in the zinc-plated facade, and the odd-shaped windows haphazardly embedded in the outer walls. Inside, spaces have intentionally been designed to make the visitor uneasy and disoriented, simulating the feeling of those who were exiled. A vast hollow cuts through the museum to mark what is gone. When the exhibits reach the period of the Third Reich, the hall's walls, ceiling, and floor begin to close in. Perhaps the most chilling effect of all is in the hollow **Holocaust Void,** a dark, windowless chamber.

At the corner of Lewetzov and Jagow streets—where a synagogue once stood, which was destroyed by the Nazis—a poignant **Jewish War Memorial** commemorates the many Berliners who were deported, mostly to their deaths, from 1941 until the end of the war in 1945. Its centerpiece is a life-size sculpture of a freight car from one of the notorious "death trains," with victims being dragged into it. Even more sobering is the **Memorial to the Murdered Jews of Europe,** Stresemannstrasse 90 (✆ **49/30/26394336;** www.holocaust-mahnmal.de), just south of the Brandenburg Gate in the former East Berlin. On its vast sloping plaza, 2,711 irregular dark gray stone slabs have been set off-kilter like neglected gravestones. Follow the maze of twisting pathways through the sharp-edged stones, a claustrophobic experience that definitely inspires reflection.

ⓘ Lindenstrasse 9–14 (✆ **49/30/259933;** www.jmberlin.de).

✈ Berlin-Tagel.

🛏 $$ **Sorat Ambassador Berlin,** Bayreuther Strasse 42 (✆ **49/30/219020;** www.sorat-hotels.com). $$ **Myers Hotel Berlin,** Metzer Strasse 26 (✆ **49/30/440140;** www.myershotel.de).

WHY THEY'LL THANK YOU: Journeying through 2,000 years of German-Jewish history.

Dachau Concentration Camp Memorial Site

Ages 12 & up • Dachau, Germany

Only 16km (10 miles) from Munich, what was once a quiet little artists' community became, in the course of 12 years, a notorious symbol of Nazi atrocities. It's an easy side trip from the city in terms of travel time, but the emotional impact of visiting Dachau can be shattering. Make sure your children are old enough to handle it—and if they are, don't miss the opportunity to bring them here.

In 1933, shortly after Adolf Hitler became chancellor of Germany, Heinrich Himmler and his SS replaced a former ammunitions factory in Dachau with the first German concentration camp. Its list of prisoners—identified as enemies of the

Third Reich—eventually included everyone from communists and Social Democrats to Jews, homosexuals, gypsies, Jehovah's Witnesses, clergymen, political opponents, and certain trade union members. More than 206,000 such prisoners from 30 countries were imprisoned at Dachau. Some were forced into slave labor, building roads or manufacturing Nazi armaments. SS doctors conducted grotesque medical experiments on others. Eventually Dachau became a laboratory for systematic mass murder: Starvation, illness, beatings, and torture killed thousands who were not otherwise hanged, shot by firing squads, or lethally injected. Official records admit to at least 30,000 deaths at Dachau between 1933 and 1945, but thousands of others simply weren't recorded. The SS abandoned the camp on April 28, 1945; the U.S. Army took charge the following day, liberating some 67,000 prisoners—all on the verge of death.

Entering the camp, you pass through a wrought-iron gate with the iniquitous slogan *Arbeit macht frei* (Work sets you free). In a vast graveled central yard, prisoners lined up for daily roll calls, a long, exhausting, and often humiliating procedure (even the dead had to show up for roll call). In the concrete shower rooms, new arrivals were stripped, disinfected, shaved, and given uniforms; in the bunker prison, punishments and torture were carried out in tiny cells. The main camp road, today lined with graceful poplars, back then was flanked by 32 barracks, each housing 208 prisoners (more in the overcrowded last year of the war). Two barracks have been rebuilt to show visitors the horrible conditions the prisoners endured. A large building that once contained the kitchen and laundry has been converted into a museum, where photographs and documents explicate the rise of the Nazi regime and the persecution of prisoners. Three memorial chapels—Catholic, Protestant, and Jewish—offer condolence at the far end of the road. Outside the camp walls is a brick crematorium, where the dead were reduced to ashes (a gas chamber was built here but never put into service). Words fail to convey the impact of this haunted— and haunting—place.

ⓘ **KZ-Gedenkstätte Dachau,** Alte-Roemar-Strasse 75 (☏ **49/8131/669970;** www.kz-gedenkstaette-dachau.de; closed Mon).

🚃 Dachau, 16km (10 miles) from Munich.

✈ Munich International.

🛏 $ **Hotel Jedermann,** Bayerstrasse 95 (☏ **49/89/543240;** www.hotel-jedermann.de). $$ **Hotel Splendid-Dollmann im Lehel,** Thierschstrasse 49 (☏ **49/89/238080;** www.hotel-splendid-dollmann.de).

WHY THEY'LL THANK YOU: Some horrors can only be understood by going there.

233 **World War II & the Cold War**

Hiroshima
The Original Ground Zero
Ages 10 & up • Hiroshima, Japan

This modern city in southern Honshu, Japan's main island, has one tragic claim to fame: It was the first city ever destroyed by an atomic bomb, on August 6, 1945, at 8:15 in the morning. Kids have been taught about this tragic chapter in world history, but the full impact of it can only be felt here, at the first Ground Zero.

The A-Bomb Dome at Hiroshima.

Peace Memorial Park (Heiwa Koen) lies in the center of Hiroshima. Among the memorials you'll see are the **A-Bomb Dome,** the skeletal ruins of the former Industrial Promotion Hall; the **Atomic Bomb Memorial Mound,** which contains the ashes of 70,000 unidentified victims; the **Memorial Cenotaph,** with the names of all of those killed by the bomb; the **Peace Flame,** which will burn until all atomic weapons vanish from the earth; and **Hiroshima National Peace Memorial Hall for the Atomic Bomb Victims,** with its panorama of the bombed city, made of 140,000 tiles (one for every Hiroshiman who died by the end of 1945). The memorial kids will be most affected by is the Children's Peace Monument—a statue of a girl with outstretched arms, and rising above her a crane, a traditional Japanese symbol of happiness and longevity. Streamers of paper cranes from school kids all over Japan flutter in the breeze around her. The statue is based on a real-life girl who suffered from the effects of radiation after the bombing. Believing that if she could fold 1,000 paper cranes she would become well again, she folded 1,300 cranes—but still died of leukemia.

The main focus of the park is the **Peace Memorial Museum.** Its East Building tells of Hiroshima before and after the bomb, and rather than presenting the city as a blameless victim, as was done for years, these exhibits own up to Hiroshima's militaristic past. The museum also documents Hiroshima's current dedication to abolishing nuclear weapons. Be prepared to self-edit your walk-through of the Main Building, for many of its images of the bomb's effects are too graphic for young children—photographs of burned and seared skin, charred remains of bodies, and people with open wounds. There's a bronze Buddha that was half-melted in the blast; some granite steps show a dark shadow that suggests someone had been sitting there at the time of the explosion—the shadow is all that remains.

Visiting Peace Memorial Park is a sobering experience, but perhaps a necessary one. What was dropped on Hiroshima is small compared to the bombs of today. The decision whether or not to use them will someday be in the hands of our children—let's make sure they know what chaos they could be unleashing.

ⓘ **Peace Memorial Park,** 1–2 Nakajima-cho, Naku-ku (✆ **81/82/241-4004;** www.pcf.city.hiroshima.jp).

🚄 Hiroshima, 5 hr. from Tokyo by bullet train.

🛏 $$ **Hotel Sunroute,** 3–3–1 Ote-machi, Naka-ku (✆ **81/82/249-3600;** www.sunroute.jp). $$$ **Rihga Royal Hiroshima,** 6–78 Motomachi, Naka-ku (✆ **81/82/502-1121;** www.rihga.com).

WHY THEY'LL THANK YOU: They may not.

A City Once Divided
The Shadow of the Berlin Wall
Ages 8 & up • Berlin, Germany

History has a way of slipping past; it's startling to realize that most kids today were born after the fall of the Berlin Wall. Those of us who grew up with it may not realize how bizarre this chapter of history seems to a youngster. But visiting Berlin, I still find its shadow cast over the city, and the children listen with mouths agape to the story.

It was weird enough, how Berlin, the capital of vanquished Germany, was divvied up by the victors at the end of World War II; but then escalating Cold War tensions made the Soviet Union shut off East Germans from the western sectors. In 1948–49, Soviet and American tanks faced off on Frederickstrasse, as the Soviets tried to cut off access to West Berlin. The Allies had to coordinate airlifts to get supplies to West Berliners, until the Soviets finally eased their blockade. But from 1948 to 1961, as some 2.5 million East Germans eventually defected to the West, the Soviets tightened the border between East

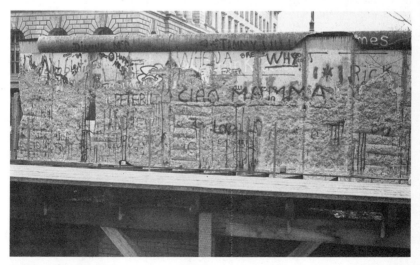

A segment of the Berlin Wall.

7 Super Ships

Exploring, raiding, carrying precious cargo, fighting pitched battles at sea—throughout the ages, oceangoing vessels have shaped human history. In our age of jet travel and concrete highways, the allure of sail and oar is more romantic than ever. Standing on the decks of these historic ships—whether they're still seaworthy or not—kids can't help but be swept up into their watery story.

235 The *Kon-Tiki*, Bygdøy Peninsula, Norway Tempt your young Viking fans to make the quick ferry ride south from Oslo to see the ancient Viking funeral ships resurrected from the Oslofjord, on display at the **Vikingskiphuset.** But the youngsters may wind up even more fascinated with another famous craft displayed nearby: the **Kon-Tiki Museum.** In 1947, young Norwegian scientist Thor Heyerdahl and five comrades sailed this primitive-looking 14m-long (45-ft.) balsa-wood raft, with its one large sail lashed to a mangrove pole, 6,880km (4,275 miles) across the Pacific, to prove that prehistoric South Americans could have settled Polynesia. Several of Heyerdahl's other intriguing seacraft are displayed as well. *Vikingskiphuset: Huk Aveny 35. ℰ 46/22/135280; www.khm.uio.no. Kon-Tiki Museum: Bygdøynesveien 36. ℰ 46/23/086767; www.kon-tiki.no.*

236 The *Golden Hinde*, London, England Moored at the old dock of St. Mary Overie, right in the middle of London, it's amazing to find an exact full-scale replica of The *Golden Hinde,* the Tudor galleon in which Sir Francis Drake made the first sea voyage that completely circled the globe, in 1577–80. Tiny as it looks, this modern replica—its square white sails boldly decorated with red crosses—has itself sailed around the world some two dozen times (call ahead to make sure the ship is actually in port.) Costumed actors chat with visitors, and the kids may even be allowed to turn the capstan, raise the anchor, or help fire one of the 22 sea cannons. See Hyde Park **55**, the Tower Bridge **94**, the British Museum's World of Treasure **176**, the Tower of London **190**, the Imperial War Museum **227**, the *Cutty Sark* **240**, Science museums **281**, Hampton Court Palace **360**, Shakespeare's Globe Theatre **352**, Wimbledon **463**, and the London Eye **485**. *St. Mary Overie dock, Cathedral St. ℰ 44/8700/118-700 or 44/2074/030-123; www.goldenhinde.org.*

237 *Vasamuseet*, Stockholm, Sweden The number-one tourist attraction in Sweden is an old boat—*the oldest* complete boat in the world, in fact, hauled up from the floor of Stockholm Harbor in 1961 and gloriously resurrected. Built in 1628, the warship *Vasa* was designed to intimidate opposing navies, with 64 powerful guns, two gun decks, and some 700 painted and gilded sculptures bristling from its decks. Tragically, it sank the day it was launched, overbalanced by those massive guns. In 1961, it was meticulously hauled to the surface and restored, along with a trove of **17th-century objects found on board; it rests today** in its own high-raftered ship hall on Stockholm's museum island, Djurgården. *Galärvarvsvägen 14 ℰ 46/8/5195-4800; www.vasamuseet.se.*

238 HMS *Victory*, Portsmouth, England Among the many ships on display in this historic English naval base, the star of the show is the **HMS *Victory,*** the flagship of Admiral Nelson's fleet during the Napoleonic wars. Launched May 7, 1765, this 104-gun ship is the oldest commissioned warship in the world. On October 21, 1805, it led the Royal Navy to a decisive victory at the Battle of Trafalgar, though a bullet claimed Nelson's life. Next to the *Victory,* the **Royal Naval Museum** houses relics of Nelson, as well as ship models, figureheads, medals, uniforms, weapons, and other memorabilia. Victory Gate, Queen and Hard sts. (*© 44/23/9286-1512; www.historicdockyard.co.uk.*

239 *Old Ironsides*, Charlestown, Massachusetts The final stop on Boston's Freedom Trail is the frigate **USS *Constitution*,** fondly known as Old Ironsides—a hero of the War of 1812. Built in 1794–97 (many of its fittings were forged in the foundry of Paul Revere), this hardy warship never lost a battle in its 18 years of active service; it participated in no fewer than 40 engagements and captured 20 of His Majesty's vessels. It won its nickname on August 19, 1812, when shots from HMS

HMS *Victory.*

Guerriere bounced off its thick oak hull as if it were iron. Today, active-duty sailors lead tours on deck, wearing 1812-vintage dress uniforms. See Boston Common **59**, Lexington & Concord **219**, Black Heritage Trail **266**, the New England Aquarium **116**, Orchard House **380**, and Fenway Park **453**. *1 Constitution Rd. (© 617/242-5670; www.oldironsides.com.*

240 *The Cutty Sark*, Greenwich, England A short boat ride east of London on the Thames, at Greenwich Pier lies the ultimate word in sail power: the sleek black three-masted *Cutty Sark,* the greatest of the clipper ships that dominated the late 19th-century tea trade from China. The youngsters will gawk at its 43 sails, 11 miles of webbed rigging, and towering 46m-high (152-ft.) mainmast, ingeniously designed to catch every breath of wind on the ocean. Launched in Scotland in 1869, the **Cutty Sark** shattered speed records for its era, traveling up to 584km (363 miles) in 24 hours. A massive restoration project is due to be completed by summer 2010; until then, you can view restorers at work through a window in the souvenir shop. See Hyde Park **55**, the Tower Bridge **94**, the British Museum's World of Treasure **176**, the Tower of London **190**, War Museum **227**, the *Golden Hinde* **236**, Science & Natural History Museums **281**, Hampton Court Palace **360**, Shakespeare's Globe Theatre **352**, Wimbledon **468**, and the London Eye **485**. *King William Walk © 44/20/8858-2698; www.cuttysark.org.uk.*

241 *The Intrepid*, New York, New York This vast gray aircraft carrier—nicknamed "The Ghost Ship" because it survived 7 bombings, 5 kamikaze raids, and one torpedo hit—sits moored today in New York City, its decks holding a rambling military museum. On the wind-whipped landing deck, children can scamper around stealth bombers, fighter jets, and choppers; below, on the cavernous hangar deck, exhibits celebrate all branches of the armed services. While some areas re-create day-to-day life on board a carrier—the dormlike Marine berths, the mess deck—others display uniforms, weapons, equipment, vintage aircraft, and memorabilia. Moored across the pier are even more craft to explore: the **nuclear missile submarine *Growler*** and the retired supersonic jet **Concorde.** See Empire State Building/Top of the Rock **27**, Central Park **58**, the Brooklyn Bridge **95**, the Bronx Zoo **127**, Statue of Liberty & Ellis Island **252**, American Museum of Natural History **273**, the Metropolitan Museum of Art **340**, American Museum of the Moving Image **354**, and the Cyclone **487**. *Pier 86, Hudson River and W. 46th St. © 212/245-0072; www.intrepidmuseum.org.*

and West Germany—and Berlin was its most vulnerable point. On August 13, 1961, the Soviets sprang into action, abruptly throwing a barbed wire barrier around the western sectors (they called it, euphemistically, an *"antifaschisti-scher Schutzwall,"* or anti-fascist protection wall). Eventually replaced by a hulking wall of concrete, covered with colorful political graffiti (on the west face only), it stretched east and north from Potsdamer Platz, absorbing one of Berlin's loveliest landmarks, the neoclassical triumphal arch of the **Brandenburger Tor,** Unter den Linden. Today, a Room of Silence in one of the restored arch's guardhouses lets visitors reflect on Germany's recent past.

The final version of the Berlin Wall was two parallel walls with a booby-trapped no man's land in between them; it was searchlit at night so armed Soviet guards could shoot escapees. Desperate East Germans did everything they could to get to freedom. Some 5,000 succeeded, but Soviet guards fatally shot at least 192 East German citizens in mid-escape. All this is commemorated at the small **Museum Haus am Checkpoint Charlie,** Friedrichstrasse 44 (© **49/30/253-7250**).

Then, miraculously, the Soviet Union fell apart—almost overnight, it seemed—and on November 9, 1989, the Wall came tumbling down, with jubilant Germans on both sides cheering on the bulldozers and snatching souvenir chunks of the infamous stone. But lest we forget, the reunified German government reconstructed on Ackerstrasse, at Bernauer Strasse, a 70m (230-ft.) stretch of the wall, the **Berlin Wall Memorial**—two stainless-steel walls embedded with fragments of the original wall. Visitors are free to peer through slits in the wall at the other side of the city, once so achingly out of reach. Starting at Bornholmer Strasse at Bösebrücke, you can hike with the kids along the signposted **Berlin Wall History Mile,** marked by a double row of cobblestones and metal plaques through central Berlin.

ⓘ **Berlin Tourist Information,** Europa-Center (www.berlin.de).

✈ Berlin-Tagel.

🛏 $$ **Sorat Ambassador Berlin,** Bayreuther Strasse 42 (© **49/30/219020;** www.sorat-hotels.com). $$ **Myers Hotel Berlin,** Metzer Strasse 26 (© **49/30/440140;** www.myershotel.de).

WHY THEY'LL THANK YOU: Daring escapes and tragic shots in the night.

The International Spy Museum
Combat under Cover
Ages 6 & up • Washington, D.C., USA

Leaving behind all of D.C.'s worthy Mall museums and sneaking up to F Street to see the Spy Museum seemed like a guilty pleasure. But the parents in our group all grew up in the era of *Goldfinger, I Spy,* and *The Man From U.N.C.L.E.,* and we were hot to see it, however schlocky. The kids trailed along, expecting some sort of *Get Smart*–ish romp. But what impressed me most was that this smartly packaged attraction is also plenty educational—a little science here, a little history there, lots of geography—we didn't have to feel guilty at all.

The entryway to the museum has a certain clandestine allure, as you pass

This shoe with a heel transmitter was used by the KGB during the Cold War.

through a blue-neon-lit tunnel and step into a very secure-looking elevator. We could have stayed forever in the **School for Spies** section, devoted to the trade-craft of espionage—everything from but-tonhole cameras and invisible ink to microdots and disguised weapons. Sev-eral interactive kiosks let the kids hone their own skills, from detecting the bug-ging devices in a room to spotting covert activity in a seemingly harmless videoed street scene. The movie connection runs strong here, with a gadget-laden Bond car and a display of disguise techniques devel-oped by Hollywood makeup artists. The kids were visibly getting drawn in.

The next gallery traces **intelligence gathering** through the ages, proving that the modern age has no monopoly on para-noia and secrecy—even leaders such as Moses and George Washington used secret agents, and don't get me started on the spying that went on in Tudor England (that's how Sir Walter Raleigh ended up in the Tower of London). I hadn't before thought of the Underground Railroad as a spy network, but what else was it, with all its secret codes and furtive activity?

The **World War II** section was espe-cially gripping, partly because so many artifacts still exist (all declassified now,

evidently). Hindsight is 20/20, they say, but it was shocking to learn how the U.S. government ignored spy warnings of Japan's imminent attack on Pearl Harbor (reminiscent of the unheeded FBI warn-ings before 9/11), and how the super-secret technology behind the first atom bomb slipped into the wrong hands. The section on **Bletchley Park,** where British code breakers feverishly worked to break Germany's famed Enigma code, engrossed me so much, the kids literally had to pull me away. Then we turned a corner and the **Cold War** was upon us, the great face-off between the CIA and the KGB that made paranoids of all us baby boomers. I loved this section, especially the reconstruction of an East Berlin street corner, on top of the CIA's high-tech surveillance tunnel beneath the Soviet Embassy. Classic John LeCarre territory.

Coming out 2 hours later, the kids pep-pered us with questions: what was the Cold War all about, and who was this Car-dinal Richelieu, and was the guy who wrote *Chitty Chitty Bang Bang* really a spy? Forget the PlayStation they were longing to get back to. . . .

ⓘ 800 F St. NW (ⓒ **202/393-7798;** www.spymuseum.org).

✈ Ronald Reagan Washington National, 5 miles. Dulles International, 26 miles. Bal-timore-Washington International, 30 miles.

🛏 $$ **Embassy Suites Hotel Down-town,** 1250 22nd St. NW (ⓒ **800/EMBASSY** [362-2779] or 202/857-3388; www.embassysuites.com). $$ **Georgetown Suites,** 1000 29th St. & 1111 30th St. NW, Georgetown (ⓒ **800/348-7203** or 202/298-7800; www.georgetownsuites.com).

WHY THEY'LL THANK YOU: Being Bond for an afternoon.

9 Settling America

Haying in Sturbridge Village.

Salt River Bay
Columbus's American Landing

Ages 6 & up • St. Croix, U.S. Virgin Islands

It must have looked inviting—the lush north coast of this 28-mile-long Antilles Caribbean island, the largest island in this cluster that is today the U.S. Virgin Islands. Cruising off shore on his second New World expedition, Christopher Columbus promptly christened it Santa Cruz (Holy Cross), anchored his fleet of 17 ships, and sent some men ashore to the village to find fresh water. Naturally, along the way the crewmen decided to pick up a couple of the native Taínos for slaves. But they didn't expect the Carib Indians—themselves aggressive invaders who'd only recently taken over the island—to come at them with spears and arrows. By the time the Europeans sailed away, one Carib and one Spaniard lay dead. And so began the history of European settlement in the United States.

The site of Columbus's first and only U.S. landing—recorded in the ship's log as November 14, 1493—was declared a national park in 1993, to coincide with the 500th anniversary of Columbus's landing. When you bring the kids here, don't expect a lot of hyped-up tourist facilities, beyond the handsome hilltop white plantation house that is being converted into a visitor center. Obviously, that sugar plantation wasn't here when Columbus landed, but if you hike along the bay's western shore, you can see remnants of things that were here in 1493, including vestiges of a prehistoric settlement and the remains of a ceremonial Taíno ballcourt. You can also see the ruins of a 17th-century Dutch colonial fort, for St. Croix passed through many hands in its motley history.

The lack of development, though, makes this relatively neglected historic site a fine place for kids to imagine what Columbus saw. Located on St. Croix's north shore, close to the port town of Christiansted and many of the big resorts, the refuge nevertheless has preserved one of the last of the large mangrove forests that originally fringed all these islands, and its turquoise waters are so clear, the bay's underwater coral canyon is rated as a choice site for divers. Come here via kayak (contact **Caribbean Adventure Tours;** ✆ **340/778-1522;** www.stcroix kayak.com; out of Salt River Marina) and you can almost imagine yourselves as the ancient Caribs or Taínos paddling their canoes to shore. Nighttime kayaking excursions are particularly intriguing, where you can explore the bioluminescent waters of the bay glowing at night.

ⓘ **Salt River Bay National Historical Park,** Rte. 75 to Rte. 80, Christiansted (✆ **340/773-1460;** www.nps.gov/sari; Nov–June only).

✈ Henry E. Rohlsen Airport, Estate Mannings Bay, 10 miles.

🛏 $$$ **The Buccaneer,** Gallows Bay (✆ **800/255-3881** or 340/712-2100, www.thebuccaneer.com). $$ **Chenay Bay Beach Resort,** 5000 Estate Chenay Bay, Rte. 82, East End (✆ **800/548-4457** in North America, or 340/773-2918; www.chenaybay.com).

WHY THEY'LL THANK YOU: In the footsteps of Columbus.

San Juan Fortress
New World Outpost
All ages • San Juan, Puerto Rico

As usual, we were feeling antsy 2 days into our beach vacation, yearning for some proper sightseeing. As we drove through Old San Juan, the Caribbean's biggest historic district, the boys leaned eagerly out the taxi windows, wondering what lay at the end of those thick city walls barricading the Atlantic seacoast. Then we came to the end of Calle Noragaray and saw it: El Morro, the staunch old fort commanding the rocky point at the entrance to San Juan Bay. A sweep of smooth green lawn (perfect for kite flying) sets it apart from the historic town it was built to protect; beyond the ramparts lies one of the most dramatic views in the Caribbean. Now *there* is a *fort*.

El Morro (the name means "headland") was built by Spanish colonists in 1540,

long before any English settlers showed up in North America. Of course, it wasn't this big at first: Originally it was just one stout round tower, now encased in the seaward core of the fort. More walls and cannon-firing positions were added over the years, until by 1787 the citadel had filled out to the current plan, an intriguing labyrinth of dungeons, barracks, vaults, lookouts, iron grates, and bulwarks. Over the main entrance, as you cross a bridge over a dry grassed-in moat, notice the Spanish royal coat of arms carved in stone. The upper plaza, where soldiers drilled and officers were quartered, faces the city to defend the fort from land; go down a long, steep ramp, designed for moving wheeled cannons, to the lower plaza and you're facing out to sea. (The enlisted men

El Morro, the fortress at the entrance of San Juan Bay.

lived here, in cramped barracks.) Starting with an attack from Sir Francis Drake in 1595, this Spanish stronghold withstood many onslaughts over the centuries from both the English and the Dutch. The United States bombarded it in 1898 during the Spanish-American War—and by the end of that war, Puerto Rico had become a U.S. possession.

Although there are historical exhibits set up around the fort, little has been done to furnish its rooms—nothing to distract from the massive, impregnable battlements of sand-colored stone, and that's what my sons most remember about it. Nowadays it's run by the National Park Service as part of the **San Juan National Historic Site,** combining El Morro with Fort San Cristóbal, the newer (1634) and larger fort a mile to the east. The combined visitor center has a film and historic exhibits, set in a World War II strategic military base that's connected to San Cristóbal by tunnels.

ⓘ Calle Norzagaray (✆ **787/729-6777**).

✈ San Juan International.

🛏 $$ **Comfort Inn,** Calle Clemenceau 6, Condado (✆ **877/424-6423** or 787/721-0170; www.comfortinn.com). $$$ **Ritz-Carlton San Juan,** Av. de los Gobernadores 6961, Isla Verde (✆ **800/542-8680** or 787/253-1700; www.ritzcarlton.com).

WHY THEY'LL THANK YOU: Standing on the mighty ramparts, looking out across the blue Caribbean.

---

245 In the Beginning

Roanoke Island
The Lost Colony
Ages 4 & up • Near Manteo, North Carolina, USA

The story has a certain Twilight Zone creepiness that kids adore. In 1587, on Roanoke Island, between the Outer Banks and the North Carolina mainland, an expedition of 120 men, women, and children landed to settle England's first permanent New World colony. Virginia Dare—granddaughter of their governor, John White—was born that year, the first child of English parents born in America. When White sailed back to England, he intended to return within the year.

But a war with Spain kept White away from Roanoke for 3 years; what he found on his return in 1590 was a mystery. The rudimentary houses that he had helped build were dismantled, the entire area enclosed by a high fortlike palisade. At the entrance, crude letters hacked on a post spelled out the word croatoan. With no evidence of violence, White concluded that the settlers had joined the friendly neighboring Croatoan tribe—but circumstances forced him to sail for England before a search could be made. No trace of the "Lost Colony" was ever found.

The visitor center at the **Fort Raleigh National Historic Site,** at the northern tip of the island, tells the colony's baffling story in exhibits and film; an oak-paneled replica of an Elizabethan room sets the historic era. Outdoors, all that's left of the fort is a silent mound of dirt, which I like—a reconstruction might have spoiled the site's sense of mystery. At the park's amphitheater, a replica of the palisade stands as a stage set for Paul Green's *The Lost Colony,* presented every night except Sunday from June through late August. This symphonic drama has been running since 1937; for tickets contact the **Waterside Theater,** 1409 National Park Dr., Manteo, NC 27954 (✆ **252/473-3414;** www.thelostcolony.org).

Evocative as the actual site is, you'll also want to flesh out the story by visiting the more commercial **Roanoke Island Festival Park** (© **252/475-1500;** www.roanoke island.com), mid-island in Manteo. A 69-foot-long three-masted bark, the *Elizabeth II,* lies moored across from the waterfront—a composite 16th-century ship built for the 400th anniversary of Sir Walter Raleigh's first exploratory voyage to Roanoke in 1584. There's also a re-creation of the camp where the first English explorers stayed. In the summer, living-history interpreters around the park portray colonists and mariners; kids can putter around the hands-on exhibits in the on-site museum,

learning about Raleigh's voyages to Roanoke, Outer Banks pirates, and the freed slaves who lived here during the Civil War.

(i) © **252/473-5772;** www.nps.gov/fora.

✈ Norfolk International, 80 miles.

🛏 $$ **Cahoons Cottages,** 7213 S. Virginia Dare Trail, Nags Head (© **252/441-5358;** www.cahoonscottages.com). $$$ **The Tranquil House Inn,** 405 Queen Elizabeth St., Manteo (© **800/458-7069** or 252/473-1404; www.tranquilinn.com).

WHY THEY'LL THANK YOU: Whatever happened to Virginia Dare?

In the Beginning **246**

Plimoth Plantation
The Pilgrims' Progress
All ages • Plymouth, Massachusetts, USA

Every American schoolchild knows about Plymouth—about how a band of English pilgrims, fleeing religious persecution, left Europe on the *Mayflower* and set up a settlement at Plymouth in December 1620. What you won't know until you visit is how small everything was, from the perilously tiny *Mayflower* to the landing point at Plymouth Rock. But rather than feel disappointed, children may be awed to realize just how difficult this venture was, and how brave the settlers were to attempt what they did.

The logical place to begin (good luck talking kids out of it) is at **Plymouth Rock.** This landing place of the *Mayflower* passengers was originally 15 feet long and 3 feet wide, though it has eroded over the centuries and been moved many times. The 1920 portico that protects that much-dwindled rock makes it even harder to imagine Pilgrims springing off the boat onto shore, but thankfully the rock is complemented by the

Mayflower II, a Plimoth Plantation attraction berthed beside Plymouth Rock. It's a full-scale replica of the type of ship that brought the Pilgrims to America in 1620; you'll be amazed that 102 voyagers survived a transatlantic voyage on a wooden vessel only 107 feet long. Costumed guides give first-person accounts of the voyage, and alongside the ship museum shops provide a stage set of early Pilgrim dwellings.

Having landed, now you're ready for the big attraction: **Plimoth Plantation,** an extensive re-creation of the 1627 Pilgrim village. Enter by the hilltop fort that protected the village and walk down to the farm area, visiting homes and gardens constructed with careful attention to historic detail. Plimoth has some of the most convincing costumed reenactors in the country, who chat with visitors while going about daily tasks as they were done in the 1600s. Sometimes you can join the activities—perhaps planting, harvesting, witnessing a trial, or visiting

The *Mayflower II* at Plimoth Plantation.

a wedding party. Though the Pilgrims enjoyed friendly relations with the native Wampanoags (nearby **Hobbamock's Homesite** re-creates their village), the plantation's Pilgrims still conduct daily militia drills with matchlock muskets, no doubt because boys like my sons so adore weapons demonstrations. Your ticket (buy a combination ticket with the *Mayflower II*) is good for 2 days' admission, so no need to rush through the site—there's too much to see.

Two non-Plantation sites in town are worth a stop: **Pilgrim Hall Museum,** 75 Court St. (© **508/746-1620;** www.pilgrim hall.org), which displays original artifacts like Myles Standish's sword and Governor Bradford's Bible; and **Plymouth National Wax Museum,** 16 Carver St. (© **508/ 746-6468**), where more than 180 life-size

figures in dioramas depict episodes in the Pilgrim story. On the hill outside is the gravesite of the Pilgrims who died that first winter—more or less half the original group, a sobering statistic indeed.

ⓘ 137 Warren Ave. (© **508/746-1622;** www.plimoth.org).

✈ Boston, 40 miles.

🛏 $$ **John Carver Inn,** 25 Summer St. (© **800/274-1620** or 508/746-7100; www. johncarverinn.com).

BEST TIME: Open Apr–Nov.

WHY THEY'LL THANK YOU: Makes Thanksgiving more than just a turkey dinner.

Charles Towne Landing
Carolina's Great Colonial Port
All ages • Charleston, South Carolina, USA

In some ways all of Charleston, South Carolina, is a historic re-creation, full of stately homes and gardens and drawling Old South decorum. Like any city, however, it started as a village, and its humble beginnings are reconstructed today at Charles Towne Landing. It's refreshingly modest, with the real feel of a struggling settlement in a raw new territory.

Carolina was originally named for King Charles of England, who in 1663, strapped for funds, gave eight of his most generous supporters a huge chunk of North America (encompassing most of present-day North Carolina, South Carolina, and Georgia). These so-called Lords Proprietors had no interest in living there, but they recruited a crew of rice growers from Barbados to farm the land, who arrived on the banks of the Ashley River in 1670. Within a decade they had established Charles Towne—again named for the king—at the fine natural harbor where the Ashley and Cooper rivers meet. Bumper crops of rice and indigo (produced by slave labor, of course) soon made South Carolina the wealthiest of England's American colonies, and Charleston remained America's busiest seaport until well into the 19th century.

Today, 663 acres at the site of that first settlement has been turned into charming Charles Towne Landing. Exhibits explaining the colony's history have been tucked underground, so as not to spoil the aboveground illusion: a re-creation of a small village, a full-scale reproduction of the 17th-century trading vessel *Adventure* (overseas trade was a key factor in Charles Towne's boom), and a replica of a 17th-century crop garden where the rice, indigo, and cotton were grown. There's no flashy theme-park atmosphere here: What you see as you walk under huge old oaks, past freshwater lagoons, and through the Animal Forest (with the same species that lived here in 1670, from bears to bison) is just what those early settlers saw. Costumed interpreters conduct hands-on learning projects, and you can rent a bike to explore 80 acres of gardens along the marsh and lagoons.

After touring the open-air park, you may also want to visit several of Charleston's historic homes, including the **Heyward-Washington House,** 87 Church St. (© **843/722-2996;** www.charlestonmuseum.org), built in 1772 by the "rice king" Daniel Heyward, with its authentic 18th-century kitchen; and **Magnolia Plantation,** 3550 Ashley River Rd. (© **800/367-3517** or 843/571-1266; www.magnoliaplantation.com), where the Drayton family have lived since the 1670s, with its simple pre-Revolutionary house (not the original, but an authentic substitute).

ⓘ 1500 Old Towne Rd. (© **843/852-4200;** www.southcarolinaparks.com).

✈ Charleston International.

⊨ $$$ **Ansonborough Inn,** 21 Hasell St. (© **800/522-2073** or 843/723-1655; www.ansonboroughinn.com). $ **Best Western King Charles Inn,** 237 Meeting St. (© **866/546-4700** or 843/723-7451; www.kingcharlesinn.com).

WHY THEY'LL THANK YOU: Wandering the old-fashioned forest.

Old Town State Historic Park
Spanish Village of Old California
All ages • San Diego, California, USA

In California, colonial history moves south to north—it was down in San Diego that the first Spanish missionary, Father Junipero Serra, came from Mexico in 1769 to begin converting the Native Americans, and he steadily moved north from there (see California Mission Trail 249). While the mission building was soon moved up the hill, this scatter of adobe buildings was the nucleus of the original town of San Diego.

Old Town's buildings have been furnished to re-create the early life of the city as it was from around 1821 to 1872. This is where San Diego's Mexican heritage shines brightest—the stars and stripes weren't raised over Old Town until 1846. In the 1820s, the town's commercial center moved closer to the waterfront, giving rise eventually to the Victorian-era **Gaslamp Quarter** (which has also been outfitted as a tourist destination, with more commercial wallop); this area was no longer prime real estate, and thus escaped redevelopment. Seven of the park's 20 structures are original; the others were constructed to supplement them in the 1930s. Among the sites are an unbelievably tiny schoolhouse; a newspaper office; La Casa de Estudillo, a mansion built around a typical central courtyard, which depicts the living conditions of a wealthy family in 1872; and the high-raftered barn of Seeley Stables, named after A. L. Seeley, who ran the stagecoach and mail service in these parts from 1867 to 1871. Pick up a map at Park Headquarters, and while you're there check out the displayed model of Old Town as it looked in 1872.

What our family liked about Old Town was its lack of preciousness—it isn't walled off from the surrounding city, and its dusty wide main street feels like a lonely Wild West outpost. When you're here, it's hard to believe that something as slick as Sea World is only a few miles away. There isn't a nonstop program of stage activities, the way there is at Williamsburg, although on Wednesday and Saturday costumed park volunteers reenact life in the 1800s with cooking and crafts demonstrations, a working blacksmith, and parlor singing. Every day there's a free 1-hour **walking tour;** but it's entirely possible to explore the site on your own, and it won't exhaust you. All around the historic complex are restaurants, some Mexican, some not. It's a relaxed, small-scale place, no hustle, no bustle—which, come to think of it, was probably just what that early settlement was like, too.

ⓘ Entrance at San Diego Ave. and Twiggs St. (ⓒ **619/220-5422;** www.oldtownsan diego.org).

✈ San Diego.

🛏 $$$ **Catamaran Resort Hotel,** 3999 Mission Blvd. (ⓒ **800/422-8386,** 877/646-3726, or 858/488-1081; www.catamaran-resort.com). $$ **Park Manor Suites,** 525 Spruce St. (ⓒ **800/874-2649** or 619/291-0999; www.parkmanorsuites.com).

WHY THEY'LL THANK YOU: Settling America with a Spanish accent.

California Mission Trail
The Priests Who Won the West

Ages 4 & up • San Diego to Sonoma, California, USA

When California fourth-graders study state history, acres of poster board get turned into maps showing **21 Franciscan missions** strung along the coast from San Diego to Sonoma—that's how well the Spanish padres saturated old California. Founded from 1769 to 1823, the missions were built to convert Native Americans to Christianity, and though they've endured fires, earthquakes, and secularization, amazingly every site is still preserved. Driving the spectacular Pacific Coast Highway up the California coast from San Diego to San Francisco, you'll already be on the Spanish settlers' El Camino Real (Royal Road). The valiant old missions make natural stopping places en route, just as they did then.

Begin in San Diego at **Mission Basilica San Diego de Alcala,** 10818 San Diego Mission Rd. (© **619/281-8449**), the first mission, founded by Spanish missionary Junipero Serra in 1769, though it was soon moved from its original site in Old Town to escape the corrupting influence of the local garrison. Next up the coast is **San Juan Capistrano,** 26801 Ortega Hwy. (CA 74) (© **949/234-1300**), known as the "Jewel of the Missions" for its beautiful gardens. The legendary swallows are said to return here to nest each March 19 (in reality, you'll see the well-fed birds here all year round).

North of Los Angeles, the **Santa Barbara Mission,** 2201 Laguna St., Santa Barbara (© **805/682-4151**), the "Queen of the Missions" with its graceful twin bell towers, sits on a hilltop overlooking the town of Santa Barbara and the Channel Islands. Farther up the Central Coast, **Mission San Luis Obispo,** 751 Palm St., San Luis Obispo

(© **805/781-8220**), was built of adobe by native Chumash laborers; when hostile natives shot burning arrows into its thatched roof, Serra doggedly replaced it with California's first clay roof tiles.

San Carlos Borromeo de Carmelo in Carmel, 3080 Rio Rd. (© **831/624-1271**), with its magnificent stone church, was Serra's sentimental favorite—he is even buried here. Northeast of Carmel, **Mission San Juan Bautista,** 2nd and Mariposa streets, San Juan Bautista (© **831/623-4526**), is supplemented today by an entire city plaza of restored historic buildings. Despite straddling the San Andreas fault, this mission's church—the largest in the chain—has been in continuous service since 1797.

On up the coast, **Mission Santa Cruz,** Mission Plaza, Santa Cruz (© **831/425-5849**), was known as the "bad luck" mission. It has survived fires, earthquakes—even a pirate attack. Its museum has excellent exhibits on the Native Americans it served.

Mission Dolores, 3321 16th St. (© **415/621-8203**), formerly Mission San Francisco de Asis, is the oldest building in San Francisco. In the 1840s, it was a gambling den; Alfred Hitchcock used its graveyard as a location for *Vertigo*. It even survived the 1906 San Francisco earthquake—perhaps Father Serra was protecting it from heaven.

ⓘ www.ca-missions.org.

✈ San Diego, Los Angeles International, or San Francisco International.

🛏 $$ **Best Western Cavalier Ocean-front Resort,** 9415 Hearst Dr., San Simeon (✆ **800/826-8168** or 805/927-4688; www.cavalierresort.com). $$ **Larkspur Hotel,** 524 Sutter St. (✆ **800/919-9799** or 415/421-2865; www.larkspurhotelunionsquare.com).

$$ **Park Manor Suites,** 525 Spruce St., San Diego (✆ **800/874-2649** or 619/291-0999; www.parkmanorsuites.com).

WHY THEY'LL THANK YOU: One way the West was won.

Williamsburg, Jamestown & Yorktown
Virginia's Colonial Past
All ages • Virginia, USA

One of our best family vacations ever was a 3-day getaway to Colonial Williamsburg, one of those summer trips we'd postponed for years, waiting until all three kids were old enough to make sense of its history. The weather was sweltering hot, then pouring rain—and none of that mattered. Williamsburg works on so many levels, it's a slam-dunk. The kids learned a lot, but they also had more fun than we ever expected.

It's also a relative bargain, considering how much Williamsburg offers for the money. Rockefeller money underwrites the 301-acre site of Virginia's colonial capital, sprucely maintaining its 88 original buildings (houses, shops, offices, inns, courthouse, jail, armory, Capitol, the works) and hiring a top-notch staff to run things so graciously, 21st-century hassles seem to disappear. We bought a package pass that admitted us to three Historic Triangle sites, which we visited in chronological order: Jamestown, Williamsburg, Yorktown (our pass also threw in nearby Busch Gardens and Water Country USA). Staying on **Colonial Williamsburg** property, we could walk in and out of the historic area, and at check-in we booked as many extras as we could from a crowded activity schedule. We had dinner in one of the taverns on-site (for reservations call ✆ **800/TAVERNS** [828-3767]), eating surprisingly delicious authentic dishes by candlelight with live minstrels strolling

around. We watched an actor channel Patrick Henry for an hour, deftly answering the audience's every question. All the costumed interpreters stationed around the site are amazingly well-informed; some of them refuse to admit they aren't living in 1770 (almost a running joke with the visitors watching them), but others are more relaxed, like the cabinetmaker who jokingly asked us to bring him some Dunkin' Donuts. Even he had PhD-level knowledge of his era—not just cabinetry but agriculture, the colonial economy, and pre-Revolutionary politics. We were fascinated by our half-hour chat while he turned chair legs on his lathe.

Jamestown, the first permanent English settlement in the New World, was a great surprise: You can drive around the actual site, with ruins of the original buildings, but the kids got more out of the Jamestown Settlement reconstruction—they could really see the alarmingly tiny ships that brought the settlers from England in 1607, and the primitive stockaded settlement, scarcely more sophisticated than the replica Powhatan Indian village nearby. At **Yorktown,** where Washington won the final victory of the American Revolution in 1781, we drove around the battlefield route and explored a replica army camp. Next time we'll skip Busch Gardens, but **Water Country USA** was a marvelous surprise, the perfect goofy way to end our history-packed 3 days.

(i) **Williamsburg Visitor Center,** VA 132, south of U.S. 60 bypass (ⓒ **800/HIS-TORY** [447-8679] or 757/229-1000; www.colonialwilliamsburg.com).

✈ Newport News, 14 miles.

🛏 $$ Crowne Plaza **Fort Magruder Hotel,** 6545 Pocahontas Trail (U.S. 60; ⓒ **800/496-7621** or 757/220-2250). $$ **Williamsburg Woodlands Hotel & Suites,** 105 Visitors Center Dr. (ⓒ **800/ HISTORY** [447-8679] or 757/220-7960; www.colonialwilliamsburg.com).

WHY THEY'LL THANK YOU: Being extras in a history movie.

Philadelphia

Cradle of Liberty

All ages • Pennsylvania, USA

It's no exaggeration to call this the most historic square mile in America, the very place where the Declaration of Independence was signed and the Constitution of the United States hammered out. The look is tidy and stereotypical, steepled red-brick buildings with neat white porticos. Yet there's nothing tidy about what happened here—it took enormous courage for these British colonists to leap off this cliff—and when you see your child's eyes light up, realizing that these were real people and not just Faces on the Money, that's when you'll be glad you came to Philadelphia.

The focal point of Independence National Historical Park is **Independence Hall,** Chestnut Street between 5th and 6th streets, where in a chamber known as the Pennsylvania Assembly Room, the Second Continental Congress convened in May 1775. Virginian Thomas Jefferson was assigned to write a document setting forth the colonists' grievances (Jefferson worked on it while boarding at **Graff House,** nearby at 7th and Market sts.), and by July 4, 1776, the Declaration of Independence was ready to be signed by the Congress— in Independence Hall you can even see the silver inkwell they used. You can also see the Rising Sun Chair that George Washington sat in 11 years later to preside over the Constitutional Convention, as President of the new United States. In a glass pavilion next door rests the 2,000-pound **Liberty Bell,** which was rung in 1776 at the first public reading of the Declaration; circle around it to find the famous crack up its side, which has been there since it was cast in 1751. At the northern end of grassy Independence Mall, the modern **National Constitution Center,** 525 Arch St., is so darn interactive, the children may not even notice how educational it is—you can take your own Presidential Oath of Office or try on a Supreme Court robe. In Signers Hall, bronze life-size statues depict the delegates who signed the Declaration—putting faces to those famous signatures was enormously satisfying.

And while you're here, follow Arch Street a few blocks east from the mall to the tiny **Betsy Ross House,** 239 Arch St. (ⓒ **215/686-1252;** www.betsyrosshouse. org), where a widowed Quaker seamstress supposedly sewed the first American flag. No one knows for sure if she really sewed it, or if this was even her house, but it makes a great story; and the house is so quaint, you'll want to believe it.

(i) **Visitor Center,** 6th and Market sts. (ⓒ **800/537-7676** or 215/965-7676; www.independencevisitorcenter.com).

✈ Philadelphia International.

$$ **Best Western Independence Park Inn,** 235 Chestnut St. (© **800/624-2988** or 215/922-4443; www.independence parkhotel.com). $$$ **Rittenhouse Hotel,** 210 W. Rittenhouse Sq. (© **800/635-1042**

or 215/546-9000; www.rittenhousehotel. com).

WHY THEY'LL THANK YOU: Imagine John Hancock, dipping his quill pen in that inkwell.

252 Forging a Nation

The Statue of Liberty & Ellis Island
Gateway to America
Ages 6 & up • New York, New York, US

The icon to end all icons, New York City's awe-inspiring Statue of Liberty is recognizable around the world as the symbol of American freedom. What's more, this is the city's greatest two-for-one deal: The same ferryboat takes you to the Ellis Island Immigration Museum, which turns out to be the real kid pleaser of the pair.

The **Statue of Liberty** (or, as she is officially known, Liberty Enlightening the World) is impressive enough from across the harbor, but close up—man, this chick is BIG. Don't be surprised if your young ones feel overwhelmed; even adults can get vertigo staring up her stately toga-clad physique. Lady Liberty weighs in at 225 tons of hammered copper, oxidized as planned to a delicate pale green, and her nose alone is 4½ feet long. Given to the United States by France, she has presided over the harbor since 1886 as a symbol of America's stature as a nation of immigrants. At present, visitors cannot climb up inside the statue, but **ranger-led tours** (© **866/782-8834,** or 212/269-5755 from outside U.S.); explore the promenade or go to the 10th-floor observatory for fascinating historic exhibits and a peek through a glass ceiling into her ingenious steel skeleton—designed by Gustave Eiffel, of Eiffel Tower fame. Even if you don't have a tour reservation, it's worth the trip to stroll around Liberty Island and gaze out over the harbor.

From the mountain of ragtag luggage stacked right inside the front doors,

upstairs to the cramped dormitories and medical examination rooms (cough the wrong way and you could be sent right back to Europe), to glass cases crammed with the family heirlooms immigrants brought with them, the **Ellis Island Immigration Museum** brings history to life. From 1892 to 1954, this was America's main immigration port of entry, where successive waves of new Americans first set foot on the soil of their new homeland. Prepare to be awed by the second-floor Registry Hall, its soaring vaulted ceiling faced with white tile, where new arrivals shuffled along in tediously long lines to be interviewed by immigration officials. (Cue up the theme from *The Godfather, Part II*.) On the Wall of Honor outside, some 420,000 immigrants' names are inscribed in steel. There are hands-on exhibits, films, live plays, computer stations where you can examine ship manifests—2 hours is barely enough to do this place justice.

Both sights are free, though you'll have to pay for the boat over. Ferryboats make frequent trips, running a 35-minute loop from Battery Park to Liberty Island to Ellis Island and back to Battery Park (from New Jersey you can board ferries in Liberty State Park).

ⓘ **Statue of Liberty,** Liberty Island (© **212/363-3200;** www.nps.gov/stli). **Ellis Island** (© **212/363-3200;** www.ellis island.org). **Ferry** (© **212/269-5755;** www.statuecruises.com).

✈ John F. Kennedy International, Newark Liberty International, LaGuardia.

🛏 $$ **Excelsior Hotel,** 45 W. 81st St. (© **800/368-4575** or 212/362-9200; www.excelsiorhotelny.com). $$$ **Le Parker**

Meridien, 118 W. 57th St. (© **800/543-4300** or 212/245-5000; www.parker meridien.com).

WHY THEY'LL THANK YOU: America's beacon to the world still shines here.

Old Sturbridge Village
Portrait of Young America
All ages • Sturbridge, Massachusetts, USA

Let's be honest: Old Sturbridge Village is a fabricated tourist attraction, a village composed of early-19th-century buildings moved here from other locations. The costumed docents around the site are only pretending to follow the pursuits of 170 years past. But Sturbridge Village is a careful, thoughtful re-creation, and my family was immediately engrossed in its depiction of an ordinary farm village, illustrating a period of time they haven't studied to death.

Kidstory, a learning gallery for children at Sturbridge Village.

Only 1 of the more than **40 restored structures** in the complex stands on its original site—the Oliver Wight House, now part of the Old Sturbridge Village Motor Lodges (see below). The rest were transported here from as far away as Maine. But all are authentic buildings and they represent the living quarters and places of trade and commerce of a rural settlement of the 1830s. What struck us, in comparison to other historic re-creations, was that by the 1830s a more diversified economy was beginning to emerge; not only are there shops for such traditional trades as blacksmithing and printing and coopering, but there are a shoe shop and a tinsmith's shop (tin ware had become a popular commodity by the era). At the edge of the village sits an industrial area with a gristmill, a sawmill, even a carding mill for the nascent textile industry. A professional class is starting to emerge by this time, too, with a lawyer setting up his tiny white frame office downtown and a country bank that issued its own currency to farmers, replacing the old barter system for local transactions. There's both a Quaker meetinghouse and a regular Congregational meetinghouse, showing the growth of religious diversity.

It's also a very kid-oriented attraction: Some of the village's "residents" include children who roll hoops and play games true to the period, and there's a **children's museum** where kids 3 to 7 can dress up in costumes and use their imaginations in a pretend farm kitchen and one-room school.

As opposed to Williamsburg and Plimoth, Sturbridge is not a place where historic events took place—it's just an ordinary hometown. At Sturbridge you can look down the town common and, for a split second, imagine you really do live in the 1830s.

ⓘ **Old Sturbridge Village,** 1 Old Sturbridge Village Rd. (✆ **508/347-3362;** www.osv.org).

✈ Bradley International, 42 miles.

🛏 **$$ Country Motor Lodge,** 277 Main St. (✆ **800/PUBLICK** [782-5425] or 508/347-3313; www.publickhouse.com).

WHY THEY'LL THANK YOU: Everyday life is history, too.

Amish Country
The Plain People of Pennsylvania
All ages • Lancaster, Pennsylvania, USA

Rolling hills, winding creeks, neatly cultivated farms, covered bridges—Lancaster County, Pennsylvania, has a bucolic beauty that would attract visitors anyway. But most tourists come here to see the Amish, dressed in their old-fashioned black clothes and driving buggies at a slow clip-clop along country roads. Yet these folks are not actors, they are real working people, and their strict customs are meant to separate them from the modern world, not to draw attention from it. The challenge of coming here with children is to discover the essence of the Amish community without falling into the tourist trap.

Begin in quaintly named Intercourse, Pennsylvania, at **The People's Place,** 3513 Old Philadelphia Pike (✆ **800/390-8436;** closed Sun), an interpretive center that will teach kids the subtle distinctions between three local sects: the Amish, the Mennonites, and the Brethren, who settled here in the early 18th century, drawn by William Penn's promise of religious tolerance. The children will learn, for example, not to take photos of the Amish; why Amish children attend one-room schoolhouses; and why they paint hex designs on their barns. Avoiding Intercourse's gaggle of Pennsylvania-Dutch–themed shops, head west to Bird-in-Hand (another quirky name) for a 20-minute jaunt in a horse-drawn buggy at **Abe's Buggy Ride,** 2596 Old Philadelphia Pike (✆ **717/392-1794;** closed Sun)—maybe this will help youngsters appreciate the slow pace of Amish life. Stop east of Lancaster for a guided tour of the 10-room **Amish Farm and House,** 2395 Lincoln Hwy. (✆ **717/394-6185**). Wind up at the **Central Market** downtown (just off Penn Sq., Tues and Fri–Sat only), the oldest farmers' market in the U.S., with its swirling fans, 1860-vintage tiles, and hitching posts.

In summer, tourists clog the main roads around Lancaster, and horse-drawn vehicles can cause bottlenecks; get a good area map so you can venture onto quiet back roads, where you have a better chance of seeing Amish farmers in their daily rounds. Stop at local farm stands to buy their excellent produce, and you'll have a natural opportunity to exchange a few words. Perhaps the best way to get the flavor of Amish life is to stay with a farm family: Contact the **Pennsylvania**

Dutch Convention & Visitors Bureau (see below) for a list of working farms that take guests. Expect simple lodgings, hall bathrooms, and filling family-style breakfasts.

ⓘ **Pennsylvania Dutch CVB,** 501 Greenfield Rd. (ⓒ **800/PA-DUTCH** [723-8824] or 717/299-8901; www.padutchcountry.com). **Mennonite Information Center,** 2208 Millstream Rd. (ⓒ **800/858-8320** or 717/299-0954).

✈ Philadelphia, 57 miles.

🛏 $$ **Country Inn of Lancaster,** 2133 Lincoln Hwy. E. (ⓒ **717/393-3413;** www.countryinnoflancaster.com). $$$ **Willow Valley Family Resort,** 2416 Willow St. Pike (ⓒ **800/444-1714** or 717/464-2711; www.willowvalley.com).

BEST TIME: Many Amish attractions are closed Sun.

WHY THEY'LL THANK YOU: Discovering that the Plain People are human too.

Forging a Nation 255

Mystic Seaport
Salty Thrill of a Vintage Shipyard
Ages 6 & up • Mystic, Connecticut, USA

Nowadays, the idea of killing a whale would be shocking—yet for many years of the 19th century, when whales were much more plentiful, whale oil was an important commodity (not to mention whalebone for ladies' corsets), and towns all along the New England coast prospered on the whaling industry. That's the sliver of history preserved at this open-air village in Mystic, Connecticut. Standing on the Seaport's re-created waterfront, we gazed out across the wide estuary of the Mystic River and found it just about impossible not to feel the lure of the open sea.

The heart of the Seaport's collection is an ever-growing cache of some 500 ships, 2 centuries' worth of seagoing vessels, powered by everything from oars and sails to steam paddle-wheels and engines. Rather than adhering to one historic period, Mystic Seaport adheres to its nautical theme. Yes, there are the requisite print ship, cooperage, schoolhouse, general store, and tavern, but the 17-acre site also features a ropewalk, a boat shed, a sail loft, a rigging loft, a lifesaving station, even shops for ship carvers and makers of nautical instruments. Staff members working in these shops aren't dressed in costumes and they aren't actors; they are real experts in the crafts they demonstrate, and delighted to share their knowledge with visitors. Somehow this makes the site feel more authentic, not less.

The most important ships in the collection have been designated national landmarks: the three-masted square-rigged whaler *Charles W. Morgan* (1841); the 1866 sloop smack *Emma C. Berry,* a graceful wood-hulled fishing boat; the 1908 paddle-wheeled excursion steamer *Sabino;* and the 1921 two-masted fishing schooner *L. A. Dunton.* But the one that my kids found most fascinating to climb aboard was the replica of the impossibly cramped slave trade schooner *Amistad,* which was re-created right here in the Seaport's restoration workshops. Museum buildings on-site display extensive collections of things like scrimshaw and ship models and figureheads. A variety of boat trips are offered; inquire at the desk when you arrive, because once you've wandered around the site for a while, the urge to get out on the water becomes pretty strong. When you exit for the day, ask the gatekeeper to validate your ticket so you can come back the next day for free.

Mystic Seaport.

ⓘ 75 Greenmanville Ave. (Rte. 27; ℂ **888/ 973-2767** or 860/572-5315; www.mystic seaport.org).

✈ Providence, 45 miles.

🛏 $$ **Hilton Mystic,** 20 Coogan Blvd. (ℂ **800/445-8667** or 860/572-0731; www. hiltonmystic.com).

WHY THEY'LL THANK YOU: Going down to the sea in ships.

256 Westward Ho

Conner Prairie Farm
Frontier Homesteads
All ages • Fishers, Indiana, USA

All right, time for a very embarrassing admission: I grew up in Indianapolis and yet I have never gone to Conner Prairie Farm. My old friends in Indy find this hard to believe; they are always going out there with their kids, on school field trips, Scout troop outings, and family Sunday excursions. I'm writing this book now so you don't put off the Conner Prairie Farm excursions in your own children's lives.

Conner Prairie Farm occupies 1,400 beautiful big-horizon acres nestled in a bend of the White River just north of Indianapolis, where in 1802 pioneer farmer John Conner snatched up a fertile patch of treeless prairie land to raise corn, rye, and oats. In 1934, pharmaceutical magnate Eli Lilly turned it into a model farm to investigate scientific agricultural methods; then in the late 1960s, it became a time capsule of **19th-century pioneer life.**

Conner Prairie Farm.

From my friends' accounts, the site is much more thoroughly developed now than it was when we were kids; there are five areas, each devoted to a different era, with costumed interpreters and authentic buildings moved here from all over Indiana. A fun place to start is with the 1859 Balloon Voyage, replicating an early aviation experiment in nearby Lafayette, Indiana; visitors even get to go up in a gas-filled balloon to get a bird's-eye view of the surrounding farmland. Then stroll back in time to 1816 with the wigwams and trading post of the original settlers, the Lenape Indians. Past that you can visit the Conner home, built in 1823, perhaps the first brick house in Indiana; it's the center of a prosperous working farmstead with two barns, a loom house, spring house, and garden. From there you proceed to 1836, a prairie crossroads village with scattered cabins, a general store, a blacksmith shop, and a one-room schoolhouse. Cross a red covered bridge to reach an 1886 small Indiana town, with a one-room schoolhouse and a Quaker meetinghouse.

There are plenty of craft demonstrations everywhere, but kids won't have to watch costumed interpreters have all the fun—they can get their own hands busy churning butter, dipping candles, carding wool, milking a cow, and building a split-rail fence. This was the part of pioneer life that appealed to me most as a kid—the fact that youngsters could be so useful with their hands—and I long to give my own kids that experience.

The best time to come is in summer, when on selected evenings you can take a picnic blanket and basket and listen to the excellent **Indianapolis Symphony Orchestra** play under the stars. We are so there next summer.

ⓘ 13400 Allisonville Rd. (© **800/966-1836** or 317/776-6000; www.conner prairie.org).

✈ Indianapolis International.

🛏 $$ **Doubletree Guest Suites,** 11355 North Meridian St., Carmel (© **800/695-8284** or 317/844-7994; www.double tree.com). $$ **Staybridge Suites,** 9780 Crosspoint Blvd., Fishers (© **800/931-4660** or 800/718-8466; www.ichotels group.com).

WHY THEY'LL THANK YOU: Communities where every child mattered.

The Amana Colonies
Communal Living on the Iowa Plains
Ages 4 & up • Amana, Iowa, USA

Who were the Inspirationists? No, not a doo-wop group from the '50s; they were a German religious sect that emigrated to the United States and in 1855 settled along the Iowa River. The original colonists' descendants still live in the seven towns they founded—Amana, East Amana, Middle Amana, West Amana, High Amana, South Amana, and Homestead. Although they voted to dissolve their strict communal lifestyle in 1932, the community they created still stands virtually intact, a landmarked district of tidy brick houses, white rail fences, and gray wooden barns set amid rolling green hills. Today's Amana folk dress just like we do—don't expect Amish-style get-ups—but there's still an appealing small-town tranquillity to these seven hamlets, even when tour buses line up outside the gift shops.

The Community of True Inspiration, to give them their full name, chose this sparsely populated area not only for the fertile farmland but also for its distance from corrupting influences (the word *amana,* from the Bible, means "to remain faithful"). Like the Amish, they had strict rules about clothing and lifestyle (11 church services a week!), but the Inspirationists also had a firm utopian plan: All land and buildings were owned by the community, with families living in assigned quarters and every person over 14 assigned a job. In a 19th-century model of town planning, every village was provided with a store, a school, a bakery, a dairy, and a church; barns and agricultural buildings were clustered at the edge, homes in the middle, and craft workshops and factories in the core.

Whereas the Amish were chiefly farmers, the Amana folk shrewdly diversified with crafts and manufacturing, becoming known for woolens, furniture, and appliances. (Heard of Amana refrigerators? They're still made here.) The **Amana Heritage Museum** in Amana (4310 220th Trail; ✆ **319/622-3567;** www.amana heritage.org) displays all sorts of crafts at which the community excelled, from tinsmithing to basket weaving. Children are most fascinated by the museum's intricate dollhouses, made by community craftspeople to amuse youngsters. Similarly, the **Mini-Americana Barn Museum,** in South Amana (✆ **319/622-3058**), is full of elaborate wooden miniatures made by woodworker Henry Moore. Also in South Amana,

Simple white stone markers in Amana's cemeteries indicate that everyone is equal in God's eyes.

the **Communal Agriculture Museum** (505 P St.) shows 19th-century farm techniques; in Middle Amana, you can visit an old **Communal Kitchen** (1003 26th Ave.), where assigned cooks put together group meals for several households. There's also a **Store Museum** in Homestead (4430 V St.), the radically simple **Community Church** in Homestead (4210 V St.), and **Opa's Tractor Barn Museum** (© 319/622-3529) in West Amana.

A fun way to explore the Colonies is on the **GPS Adventure Tour:** Starting from the Amana Heritage Museum, you drive from one set of GPS coordinates to another, picking up a series of messages that lead to a prize at the end. With a treasure hunt to follow, the kids may be happy to spend all day exploring this bucolic utopia.

ⓘ **Welcome Center,** 622 46th Ave., Amana (© **800/579-2644** or 319/622-7622; www.amanacolonies.com).

✈ Cedar Rapids/Iowa City, 25–30 miles.

🛏 $$ **Amana Holiday Inn & Water Park,** 211 U Ave., Williamsburg (© **800/344-7128** or 319/668-1175; www.ic hotelsgroup.com). $$ **Zuber's Homestead Hotel,** 2206 44th Ave., Homestead (© **888/623-3911** or 319/622-3911; www. zubershomesteadhotel.com).

BEST TIME: Open May–Oct.

WHY THEY'LL THANK YOU: Community meant something here.

Westward Ho **258**

Stockyards National Historic District
Where Cowpokes Cut Loose
All ages • Fort Worth, Texas, USA

Fort Worth sure does put the "cow" in "cowboys." When this town boomed in the 1890s, it was because it had the Southwest's biggest livestock market, where millions of cattle—as well as horses, mules, hogs, and sheep—were shipped north along the Chisholm Trail. That's how Fort Worth got the nickname "Cowtown," and the Stockyards are where the city's Old West heritage burns brightest.

Two miles north of downtown Fort Worth, the 125-acre Stockyards District, with its Spanish-flavored architecture, is still a lively place to hang out—only now it's tourists, not cattlemen, thronging the sidewalks along Exchange Street. Commercial it may be, but its robust Western vibe is infectious. Twice a day, at 11:30am and 4pm, duded-up cowhands drive about 15 head of longhorn steers down the redbrick street past the Stockyards. Former hog and sheep pens have been turned into **Stockyards Station,** a festival mall of Western-themed shops and restaurants, where the city's most authentic boots and Stetson hats are for sale. The old horse and mule barns have been turned into the **Texas Cowboy Hall of Fame,** 128 E. Exchange Ave. (© **817/626-7131;** www. texascowboyhalloffame.com), a magnet for rodeo fans. Inside the **Livestock Exchange Building,** 131 E. Exchange Ave., the nerve center of the old livestock business, the small **Stockyards Museum** (© **817/625-5087**) displays artifacts such as guns, barbed wire, furniture, and clothing. Western music and movie stars, such as Gene Autry, Dale Evans, Roy Rogers, and Bob Wills, are honored in bronze along Exchange Avenue's **Trail of Fame.**

Keeping the kids busy around here is no problemo. Across from Stockyards Station, they can get lost in the **Cowtown Cattle Maze,** 145 E. Exchange Ave.

The stock show at the Fort Worth Stockyards.

(☎ **817/624-6666**), a wooden labyrinth built to look like cattle pens. The **Grapevine Vintage Railroad** (☎ **817/410-3123;** www.gvrr.com) runs two different daily routes from the Stockyards, one to downtown Fort Worth, the other out to Grapevine, Texas. The Stockyards' **Arena & Livery,** 128 E. Exchange (☎ **817/624-3446**), offers guided horseback rides out along the Trinity River. On most weekend nights, there's rodeo action at the **Cowtown Coliseum,** 121 E. Exchange. (☎ **817/625-1025;** www.cowtown coliseum.com), the world's first indoor rodeo arena. **Billy Bob's Texas,** 2520 Rodeo Plaza (☎ **817/624-7117**), known as the world's largest honky-tonk, offers families line-dancing lessons every Thursday evening.

ⓘ 130 E. Exchange Ave. (☎ **817/625-9715;** www.fortworthstockyards.org).

✈ Dallas–Fort Worth International.

🛏 $ **Residence Inn Fort Worth University,** 1701 S. University Dr., Ft. Worth (☎ **817/870-1011;** www.marriott.com/hotels/travel/dfwrp). $$$ **Stockyards Hotel,** 109 W. Exchange Ave., Ft. Worth (☎ **800/423-8471** or 817/625-6427; www.stockyardshotel.com).

WHY THEY'LL THANK YOU: Yee-HAW! That durn cattle drive.

259   Westward Ho

Wild West Relics
Tombstone & Bisbee
Ages 8 & up • Tombstone & Bisbee, Arizona, USA

Tombstone, "the town too tough to die," is a classic tourist trap kids love—especially when actors reenact the famous Gunfight at the O.K. Corral. But only 25 miles south is the much more authentic Bisbee, one of the best-preserved historic towns in Arizona. Within day-trip distance from Tucson, Tombstone's hokey attractions make a tempting lure for the kids; swing on down to Bisbee for the real deal.

Between 1880 and 1887, an estimated $37-million worth of silver was mined in Tombstone, and the town's historic district has several imposing buildings among the gussied-up saloons and former bordellos lining the main drag, Allen Street. Narrated tours, including several by stagecoach, can be picked up around here. Daily at 2pm, there's a reenactment of the famous gun battle at the former livery stable known as the **O.K. Corral**, 308 E. Allen St. (© **520/ 457-3456**), the very spot where on one fateful October day in 1881, Virgil, Morgan, and Wyatt Earp and their friend Doc Holliday took on the outlaws Ike Clanton and Frank and Tom McLaury. It's a totally kitschy (and sometimes downright rude) attraction that also includes **Tombstone's Historama**, a multimedia affair narrated by Vincent Price that rehashes Tombstone's "bad old days." Staged gunfights, gold panning, a mock mine shaft and shooting gallery, and arcade games carry on the Wild West theme at **Helldorado Town,** 4th and Toughnut sts. (© **520/457-9035**); it's cheesy, sure, but that's Tombstone for you.

More authentic sites are the **Wyatt Earp House,** a simple adobe cottage containing an art gallery at 102 E. Fremont St. (© **520/457-3111**), and the **Boot Hill Graveyard,** Hwy. 80, north of downtown (© **520/457-3300**), where you can see the graves of Clanton and the McLaury brothers, who were killed in the shootout; the kids will get a kick out of reading epitaphs like "Here lies Lester Moore, 4 slugs from a 44, No Les, no more." Gallows still stand in the courtyard of **Tombstone Courthouse State Park,** 219 Toughnut St. (© **520/457- 3311**), which also displays artifacts and photos of Tombstone's past.

Built into the steep slopes of Tombstone Canyon on the south side of the Mule Mountains, Tombstone's neighbor Bisbee got rich on copper mining. Bisbee never became a bona fide ghost town, but it still looks like a slice of the past. Old Victorian buildings line narrow winding streets, and miners' shacks perch on the steep hillsides above downtown. (The town has more than 1,000 public stairs, built to scale those slopes.) Get an overview at the **Bisbee Mining & Historical Museum,** 5 Copper Queen Plaza (© **520/ 432-7071**), a Smithsonian affiliate with interactive exhibits, a re-created mine tunnel, and dioramas depicting Bisbee in its boomtown days. The kids will love the **Queen Mine Tour,** Hwy. 80 Interchange (© **866/432-2071** or 520/432-2071; www. queenminetour.com), which head underground into one of the old copper mines. Though Bisbee has been colonized by funky artists and boutique owners these days, on weekends when bikers rumble onto the downtown streets, the West still seems satisfyingly Wild.

(i) **Tombstone Visitor Center,** Allen and 4th sts. (© **520/457-3929**; www.tombstone web.com). **Bisbee Visitor Center,** 2 Copper Queen Plaza (© **866/2-BISBEE** [224- 7233] or 520/432-3554; www.discover bisbee.com).

✈ Tucson.

🛏 $$ **Canyon Rose Suites,** 21 Subway, Bisbee (© **866/296-7673** or 520/432- 5098; www.canyonrose.com). $$$ **Loews Ventana Canyon Resort,** 7000 N. Resort Dr., Tucson (© **800/234-5117** or 520/299- 2020; www.loewshotels.com). $$ **San Pedro River Inn,** 8326 S. Hereford Rd., Hereford (© **877/366-5532** or 520/366- 5532; www.sanpedroriverinn.com).

WHY THEY'LL THANK YOU: The Wild West, clichés and all.

California Gold Rush Country
Land of the Forty-Niners
Ages 6 & up • Hwy. 49 from Nevada City to Angels Camp, California

In a cavern, in a canyon, excavating for a mine / Lived a miner, forty-niner . . . Rarely do state highway numbers have historical significance, but California state highway 49 does. Winding through the hills west of Sacramento, **Hwy. 49** is the main road through a string of Wild West towns that sprang up overnight in the California Gold Rush of 1849. As if frozen in time, their Main streets still have raised wooden sidewalks, buildings with double porches, saloons, and Victorian storefronts. Touring the Gold Country, the kids will feel transplanted to a movie western (hundreds of films have been shot here), to a time when the promise of an easy fortune lured thousands of adventurers to risk their all in a raw new territory. Soon enough the boom went bust—but not before it had jump-started the settlement of the whole West Coast.

It's about 100 miles along Hwy. 49 from Nevada City in the north to Angels Camp in the south; visiting the whole area could take several days. Here are the highlights: Start where the Gold Rush itself began—just north of Placerville in quiet, pretty **Coloma** at the **Marshall Gold Discovery State Historic Park** (© 530/622-3470; www.coloma.com/gold). Here, on the south fork of the American River, on January 24, 1848, carpenter James Marshall was building John Sutter's sawmill when he chanced upon a gold nugget. On Main Street, the largest building in town is a replica of the sawmill; exhibits at the **Gold Discovery Museum** lay out the story of the frenzy that ensued once the news got out. Notice the number of Chinese stores on Main Street, the remnants of a once-sizable community of Chinese who immigrated here to provide labor for the mines. Some 40 miles south of here, you can tour the **Sutter Gold Mine,** 13660 Hwy. 49, Amador City (© 866/762-2837 or 209/736-2708; www.suttergold.com). You'll wear a hard hat, ride on a mining shuttle, and "tag in" just like a miner. Down in the shaft, you may be able to spot gemstones and gold deposits still embedded in the quartz of the Comet Vein. The other face of the Gold Rush shows at two nearby ghost towns—**Mokelumne Hill,** nowadays one street overlooking a valley with a few old buildings, and decrepit **Volcano,** which looks almost haunted with the dark rock and blind window frames of a few backless, ivy-covered buildings. Once it had a population of 8,000; today, it's more like 100. That's what happens when a boom goes bust.

Another 30 miles farther south, Gold Rush country's most popular site, **Columbia State Historic Park,** 22708 Broadway, Columbia (© 209/532-4301; www.columbiacalifornia.com), re-creates a boom town at its lively height. Kids love roaming around its dusty car-free streets, where they can take stagecoach rides or visit a newspaper office, a blacksmith's forge, a Wells Fargo express office, or a Victorian-era saloon.

ⓘ www.historichwy49.com.

✈ Sacramento, 55 miles from Placerville.

🛏 $$ **City Hotel,** Main St., Columbia State Park (© 800/532-1479 or 209/532-1479; www.cityhotel.com). $$ **Imperial Hotel,** 14202 Hwy. 49 (Main St.), Amador City (© 209/267-9172; www.imperial amador.com).

WHY THEY'LL THANK YOU: Gold fever and ghost towns.

National Museum of the American Indian

Ages 6 & up • Washington, D.C., USA

Among the stately white stone palaces lining the National Mall, this Smithsonian branch really stands out: A burnt sand-colored exterior of kasota limestone wraps around undulating walls, echoing the pueblos and hogans of the Southwest tribes. With its bands of reflective windows peering out like eagle eyes, it reminds me of some sort of Northwest tribal totem. Inside, a huge rotunda lobby is filled with celestial references, from the equinoxes and solstices mapped on the floor to the sky visible in the oculus dome, 120 feet overhead, and nature is brought in throughout the galleries—wonderfully appropriate for a museum celebrating Native peoples.

As one of the Smithsonian's newest branches, the American Indian museum shakes off the dusty approaches of the past, and has so much more than just exhibits in glass cases. Of course, it has an amazing number of artifacts to display, with its core collection of 800,000 **Native American artifacts**—wood and stone carvings, masks, pottery, feather bonnets, and so on, representing some 1,000 Native communities through North and South America. Children can be lost for minutes, studying some of these intricate hand-made objects. While there are many fine museums showcasing one tribal group or another, this one includes all the native populations of the Western Hemisphere, and many of the exhibits are organized around cross-cultural themes. (Never before had I noticed so many connections between North and South American tribes.)

The museum's designers also purposely made this a "living" museum, with Native peoples performing, storytelling, and

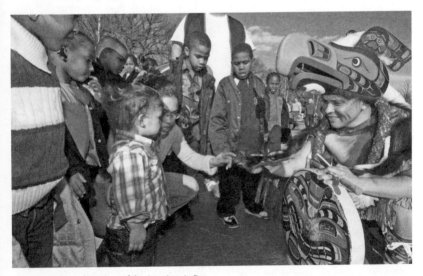

The National Museum of the American Indian.

displaying their own art alongside the historic exhibits—that fabulous atrium entrance turns out to be perfect for **ceremonial dances.** Workshops include **demonstrations** of traditional arts such as weaving or basket making; a roster of **films** includes a number of animated shorts that retell nature legends and creation myths. Almost every exhibit, it seems, has a video of some tribe member explaining the significance of this or that custom—a much easier way for kids to learn than reading blocks of text mounted on a wall. Again, how appropriate for a Native American museum to honor oral tradition.

Some of the exhibit themes are a bit too anthropological, or too politically complex, for children to follow, but just looking at the precious objects can be enough. A pair of traditional beaded moccasins alongside red high-top sneakers hand-painted with tribal motifs—that's the sort of thing kids intuitively get.

ⓘ 4th St. and Independence Ave. SW (ⓒ **202/633-1000;** www.nmai.si.edu).

✈ Ronald Reagan Washington National, 5 miles. Dulles International, 26 miles. Baltimore-Washington International, 30 miles.

🛏 $$ **Embassy Suites Hotel Downtown,** 1250 22nd St. NW (ⓒ **800/EMBASSY** [362-2779] or 202/857-3388; www.embassysuites.com). $$ **Georgetown Suites,** 1000 29th St. & 1111 30th St. NW, Georgetown (ⓒ **800/348-7203** or 202/298-7800; www.georgetownsuites.com).

WHY THEY'LL THANK YOU: Seeing what life's like for children of the tribe.

---

262 Native Americans

Mashantucket Pequot Museum
A Forgotten Tribe's History Lesson
All ages • Mashantucket, Connecticut, USA

In 1992, a nearly extinct Native American tribe—the Mashantucket Pequots, only 520 individuals—was granted permission to open a gambling casino on their ancestral lands deep in the southeastern Connecticut woods. What began as a bingo parlor grew to a casino, which then needed a hotel, and—presto!—within 3 years they had the world's most profitable gaming operation, Foxwoods, on their hands. With their newfound wealth, the tribe poured $139 million into a museum dedicated to Native American arts and culture, opened in 1998. Whatever the locals think about their gazillionaire Indian neighbors, all agree on one thing: They sure got a fabulous museum for their money.

Thoughtful, not glitzy, the Mashantucket Pequot Museum delves into **Native American history** in 3-D—instead of tired beads and feathers pinned behind a glass case, you can look at models, dioramas, and films; listen to oral histories (many in native languages, including the Pequots' Passamaquoddy tongue); and use interactive consoles. Beautiful murals have been painted by Native American artists (and not just Pequots—with so much money on hand, the tribe has done some significant reaching out to other less fortunate tribes).

These exhibits go way back in time, all the way to the Ice Age, as you descend into a re-created glacial crevasse, frigid temperatures, dripping water, and all. There's also a diorama of an **ancient caribou hunt.** To me, the most absorbing exhibit was the extensive life-size **Pequot Village re-creation,** which you can walk through: Sounds and even smells are wafted through the air as you pass wigwams, canoes, and fake campfires where costumed figures go about their daily business, fishing, hunting, cooking, butchering animals, basket weaving, and pottery making. We loved the newlyweds building their first wigwam together. My teenage nephew appreciated the museum's frank discussion of conflicts between the Pequots and new Dutch and English settlers, culminating in a reconstruction of the 17th-century Pequot fort at Mystic, which was attacked in 1637 by European settlers. But the story doesn't end there; you see how Pequots lived on, fitting into the Connecticut community (a 2-acre outdoor farmstead is open spring through fall). The last display is a trailer home, marking a sad chapter in a proud tribe's history. Of course we know that wasn't the end for the Pequots—just take a look down the road at Foxwoods.

ⓘ 110 Pequot Trail (𝒞 **800/411-9671;** www.pequotmuseum.org).

✈ Providence, 45 miles.

🛏 $$ **Two Trees Inn,** 240 Indiantown Rd., Ledyard (𝒞 **800/369-9663** or 860/312-3000; www.foxwoods.com).

WHY THEY'LL THANK YOU: A culture resurrected.

Native Americans **263**

The Hopi Reservations
Secret Ceremonies from Ancient Times
Ages 6 & up • Arizona, USA

For the Hopi people, this remote Arizona landscape of flat-topped mesas and barren plains is the center of the universe. They have lived for nearly 1,000 years on this grouping of mesas, completely encircled today by the Navajo Reservation. Here the Hopi preserve their complex ancient customs, including the famous masked kachina dances (Jan–July) and death-defying Snake Dances (Aug–Dec). Though these are generally closed to non-Hopis, you may be able to view social dances, held August through February—ask when you're on the reservation, and you might get lucky. Hopiland is not theme-park perfect—most villages on the reservation are straggles of modern homes scattered along roughly 20 miles of Ariz. 264—but that's one of the things I like about it.

At the top of First Mesa, tiny historic **Walpi** is the best place for visitors to learn more about life in the Hopi villages—you can visit only with 1-hour guided tours, offered daily (sign up at the **Ponsi Hall Visitor Center;** 𝒞 **928/737-2262**). Small stone houses seem to grow directly from the rock of the mesa top, and ladders jut from the roofs of kivas; the view stretches for hundreds of miles. On Second Mesa, you'll find the **Hopi Cultural Center** (𝒞 **928/734-2401**), a combination museum, motel, and restaurant. On the Third Mesa, the Hopi claim **Oraibi** is the oldest continuously occupied town in the United States—it dates from 1150. Today, Oraibi is a mix of old stone houses and modern cinder-block ones.

Across the reservation, small shops sell crafts and jewelry, including kachina dolls and some beautiful coil and wicker plaque baskets. The **Monongya Gallery** (𝒞 **928/734-2344**), on Ariz. 264 outside of Oraibi, has one of the largest selections of kachina dolls. Kachinas, either as dolls or as masked dancers, represent spirits of everything from plants and animals to ancestors and sacred places. According to legend, the kachinas lived with the Hopi long ago, but the Hopi people made them angry and the spirits left—after passing on how to perform their ceremonies. These ceremonies are believed to bring rain to water the all-important corn crop, but they also ensure health, happiness, long life, and harmony in the universe. As part of the kachina ceremonies, dancers often bring carved wooden kachina dolls to village children.

When visiting the Hopi pueblos, respect all posted signs; remember that photographing, sketching, and recording are prohibited in the villages and at ceremonies. Kivas (ceremonial rooms) and ruins are off-limits.

ⓘ **Hopi Office of Public Relations,** Kykotsmovi (℀ **928/734-3283**). **Hopi Cultural Preservation Office** (℀ **928/734-3612;** www.nau.edu/~hcpo-p).

✈ Flagstaff, 150 miles.

🛏 $$ **Hopi Cultural Center Restaurant & Inn,** Second Mesa (℀ **928/734-2401;** www.hopiculturalcenter.com). $$$ **Quality Inn Navajo Nation,** Main St. and Moenave Ave., Tuba City (℀ **800/644-8383** or 928/283-4545; www.qualityinn tubacity.com).

WHY THEY'LL THANK YOU: The kachinas.

264 Native Americans

Taos Pueblo
Following the Old Ways
All ages • Taos, New Mexico, USA

It's amazing that in our frenetic world, some 150 Taos Pueblo residents still live much as their Tiwa ancestors did 1,000 years ago, without electricity and running water. Their two main buildings—**Hlauuma** (north house) and **Hlaukwima** (south house)—are a rambling series of rooms piled on top of each other, built of straw and mud with distinctive flowing rooflines that echo the shape of Taos Mountain to the northeast. The adobe exterior blends in with the surrounding land; bright blue doors are the same shade as the sky that frames the brown buildings. The kids will intuitively feel these people's connection to the natural world.

The village looks much the same today as it did when a regiment from the Spanish explorer Coronado's expedition first came upon it in 1540. Though the Tiwa were essentially a peaceful agrarian people, in 1680 they spearheaded the only successful revolt by Native Americans in history, driving the Spanish from Santa Fe until 1692 and from Taos until 1698—you can still see

the old church ruined in that uprising. The Pueblo today is actually several individual homes built side by side with common walls. Some 1,800 other Tiwas live in conventional homes on the pueblo's 95,000 acres, but though 90% of them are practicing Roman Catholics, they often still practice ancestral rituals. The center of their world is nature; women use *hornos* to bake their traditional bread, and most still drink water from the sacred Blue Lake nearby.

As you explore the pueblo, you can visit the residents' **studios,** sample homemade bread, look into the **San Geronimo Chapel,** and wander past the ruins of the **old church** and **cemetery.** Ask permission from individuals before taking their photos; some will request a small payment. Do not trespass into kivas (ceremonial rooms), private homes, and other areas marked as restricted. You can buy traditional fried and oven-baked bread for the kids to sample, as well as a variety of arts and crafts like moccasins, pottery, and jewelry. To try traditional feast-day meals, stop by the **Tiwa Kitchen,** near the entrance to the pueblo. Close to Tiwa Kitchen, the **Oo-oonah Children's Art Center** displays the creative works of pueblo children.

ⓘ Veterans Hwy. (✆ **505/758-1028;** www.taospueblo.com).

✈ Santa Fe, 72 miles. Albuquerque, 140 miles.

🛏 $$ **El Rey Inn,** 1862 Cerrillos Rd., Santa Fe (✆ **800/521-1349** or 505/982-1931; www.elreyinnsantafe.com). $$ **Old Santa Fe Inn,** 320 Galisteo St., Santa Fe (✆ **800/734-9910** or 505/995-0800; www.oldsantafeinn.com).

BEST TIME: Closed 10 weeks late winter or early spring (call ahead).

WHY THEY'LL THANK YOU: Real people, living ancient lives.

Native Americans **265**

British Columbia's Native Peoples
Getting to Know the First Nations
Ages 8 & up • Vancouver & Victoria, Canada

There's nothing like a good totem pole to grab a kid's interest. They're gargantuan, for one thing, with those huge-eyed beaky faces stacked atop each other, often with ghastly leering expressions. Then there's that air of ancient wisdom that hangs about them. You can't help but want to know more about the Native American people—referred to as the First Nations—who made these giant woodcarvings. But there's so much more to the First Nations than totem poles, as you'll learn at two top-notch museums in British Columbia.

Vancouver's **Museum of Anthropology** is a stunning building to begin with, echoing in concrete and glass the traditional post-and-beam buildings of the First Nations people. You enter through majestic doors that resemble a giant carved bent-cedar box. Artifacts from various coastal communities flank the ramp leading to the Great Hall's overwhelming series of great **totem poles,** with dramatic floor-to-ceiling windows behind them revealing a backdrop of the North Shore mountains and English Bay. Although this anthropology museum mainly focuses on the aboriginal culture of British Columbian natives, the First Nations are by no means extinct, and tribute is also paid to **contemporary**

Native artists who carry on the traditions. Kids can caress the cedar bear and sea-wolf sculptures at the Cross Roads by Haida artist Bill Reid; everyone seems to be enraptured by Reid's huge yellow cedar carving *The Raven and the First Men,* relating a creation myth in which the trickster god Raven coaxes humanity out of its birthplace in a clamshell. The kids will have fun pulling out the glass-topped drawers in the Multiversity **Gallery,** where more than 15,000 artifacts—spears, native ornaments, utensils, toys, and games—are tucked away. And don't forget to walk around the grounds behind the museum, where two Haida longhouses stand, positioned authentically on a north–south axis, with 10 hand-carved totem poles alongside.

If you're up for a ferry ride—and I'd take any excuse to enjoy the 95-minute ferry ride to Vancouver Island—head over to Victoria (also covered in the **Seattle-Victoria Ferry**) to visit the **Royal British Columbia Museum.** It's a general-interest museum, with excellent natural history and modern history exhibits, but the showpiece of the museum is its outstanding **First Peoples Gallery** on the third floor. The artifacts displayed here include a full-size re-creation of a longhouse and a hauntingly wonderful gallery of totem poles and masks. The fun continues outside, in Thunderbird Park beside the museum, where you can watch a team of Native carvers working on new totem poles in a cedar longhouse.

ⓘ **Museum of Anthropology,** 6393 NW Marine Dr., Vancouver (✆ **604/822-3825;** www.moa.ubc.ca). **Royal British Columbia Museum,** 675 Belleville St., Victoria (✆ **888/447-7977** or 250/356-7226; www.royalbcmuseum.bc.ca).

✈ Vancouver International.

🛏 $$ **Granville Island Hotel,** 1253 Johnston St., Granville Island (✆ **800/663-1840** or 604/683-7373; www.granvilleislandhotel.com). $$ **Robsonstrasse Hotel,** 1394 Robson St. (✆ **888/667-8877** or 604/687-1674; www.robsonstrassehotel.com).

WHY THEY'LL THANK YOU: Those inscrutable totem poles.

Black Heritage Trail
All ages • Boston, Massachusetts, USA

Many tourists don't realize that Boston has not one but two Freedom Trails—the Revolutionary War trail, and the Black Heritage Trail, which celebrates Boston's antislavery movement. The latter runs 1.6 miles, through Beacon Hill, the center of the free black community in the years leading up to the Civil War. Walking around this neighborhood, you get a sense of how a close-knit black community gathered, gradually developing political savvy and spreading radical new ideas. The seeds of the Emancipation Proclamation were sown here on Beacon Hill. Walking the Trail is a great way to explore an era of American history that all too often takes a back seat in Revolutionary War–obsessed New England.

The 15 marked points on the trail start at the **Robert Gould Shaw Memorial** on Beacon Street across from the State House. Shaw was the white officer who led the 54th Massachusetts Regiment, the Union's first black regiment, celebrated in the 1989 film *Glory,* and this bas-relief sculpture by Augustus St. Gaudens is incredibly affecting. Other buildings you'll pass include the homes of George Middleton, an African-American Revolutionary War soldier; successful barber John J. Smith, a free black

who hosted antislavery debates both at his shop and in his home; and Lewis Heyden, a freed slave whose boardinghouse was an early Underground Railroad stop. You'll see the Baptist church where church desegregation efforts began in the 1830s (years later, after the Civil War, the same church building became Boston's first African Methodist Episcopal church).

From Memorial Day to Labor Day, National Park Service rangers lead free 2-hour **guided tours** daily along the route; the rest of the year, contact the Park Service to arrange a tour. To go at your own pace without the commentary, pick up a brochure outlining the tour at the Boston Common and State Street visitor kiosks, or from the **Museum of Afro-American History,** 46 Joy St. (✆ **617/725-0022;** www.afroammuseum.org), which is where the Trail ends. The museum's site occupies the restored **Abiel Smith School** (1834), the first American public grammar school for African-American children, and the **African Meeting House** (1806), the oldest standing black church in the United States. William Lloyd Garrison founded the New England Anti-Slavery Society in this building, where Frederick Douglass made some of his great abolitionist speeches. Once known as the "Black Faneuil Hall," it also schedules lectures, concerts, and church meetings. The museum's displays employ art, artifacts, documents, historic photographs, and other objects—including many family heirlooms. Children enjoy the interactive touch-screen displays and multimedia presentations, and the patient, enthusiastic staff helps them put the exhibits in context.

(i) (C) **617/742-5415;** www.nps.gov/boaf.

✈ Boston's Logan Airport.

🛏 $$ **Doubletree Guest Suites,** 400 Soldiers Field Rd. (C) **800/222-TREE** [222-8733] or 617/783-0090; www.doubletree. com). $ **The MidTown Hotel,** 220 Huntington Ave. (C) **800/343-1177** or 617/262-1000; www.midtownhotel.com).

WHY THEY'LL THANK YOU: A second Freedom Trail, just as important as the first.

African-American History 267

National Underground Railroad Freedom Center

Ages 4 & up • Cincinnati, Ohio, USA

It wasn't underground and it wasn't a railroad—don't let the kids come here expecting to see a subway museum. What is celebrated here is even more important: an organized secret network of homes, churches, and stores willing to harbor runaway black slaves on their desperate flight from Southern plantations to the North. It's fitting that Cincinnati, lying right across the Ohio River from Kentucky, should be the site of this museum, for once you had crossed that river you were technically free at last.

The Freedom Center sits handily between the Bengals stadium and the Reds's ballpark, but while it may share parking lots with those two venues, this is a much more serious attraction, a daringly inventive exhibit designed to change people's minds as much as to convey information. The focal point of the sleek modern lobby is a startlingly ramshackle gray wood building once used to warehouse slaves— human beings, penned like cattle—before shipping them down to plantations farther south. From there visitors are directed

along a winding route (winding like the Ohio River) through various multimedia experiences. The film theaters here don't just show films, they barrage you with images and sounds from all directions. One reason for coming here with children is so you have an excuse to participate actively in the **Freedom Seekers** section, where storytelling and role-playing exercises put kids in the shoes of runaway slaves; a warmly lit brick housefront beckons with a cellar door left ajar for secret nighttime visitors to slip in. The **From Slavery to Freedom** section tackles a wider chunk of history, with walkthrough life-size dioramas exploring New World history from the first arrivals of African slaves (and slavery was here from the get-go), through the Revolutionary War, tortuous constitutional debates, and the rise of abolitionism in the 19th century.

In the **Everyday Freedom Heroes** gallery, interactive kiosks allow visitors to learn the inspiring stories of many individuals, not just African Americans, who fought for social freedom. And once

A slave pen at the Underground Railroad Freedom Center.

you've passed through all the exhibits, the two final rooms encourage visitors to gather together to discuss what they've just seen, and its implications for the world they live in. Somewhat like the Jewish Museum Berlin, this is by no means a special-interest museum; we are all implicated in this struggle for freedom, and the message is one we can all respond to.

ⓘ 50 E. Freedom Way (ⓒ **877/648-4838** or 513/333-7500; www.freedomcenter. org).

✈ Cincinnati/Northern Kentucky International.

🛏 $$ **Millennium Hotel Cincinnati,** 150 W. 5th St. (ⓒ **866/449-9746** or 513/352-2100; www.millenniumhotels. com). $$$ **Westin Cincinnati,** 21 E. 5th St. (ⓒ **513/621-7700**; www.westin.com/ cincinnati).

WHY THEY'LL THANK YOU: Imagining the courage it took, for the runaways and for their protectors.

Dr. King's Legacy
Ages 6 & up • Atlanta, Georgia, USA

The civil rights leader Martin Luther King, Jr., is by any measure a great man. In his hometown of Atlanta, Georgia, the 10-block area around Auburn Avenue is one of the city's most-visited sites, encompassing King's boyhood home and the Baptist church where King, his father, and his grandfather were all ministers. While other civil rights sites may illuminate the issues of that tumultuous era better, this is the place where you'll really get a feeling for this complex, gifted man who dared to change history.

To me the real heart of the site is the historic buildings associated with King. Start out at the gracefully landscaped visitor center, where you can book tours of the sites (get here early in the day, at least in summer, because tickets do run out) and get up to speed on King's life and times with audiovisual programs and exhibits. First off is **the Birth Home of Martin Luther King, Jr.,** 501 Auburn Ave. (ⓒ **404/331-6922**), the modest Queen Anne–style house where Martin Luther King, Jr., was born on January 15, 1929, and lived until he was 12. The house has been restored to its appearance when young Martin lived here—even the linoleum is an authentic reproduction, and a

good deal of King memorabilia is displayed. His father (Martin Luther King, Sr., obviously) was a Baptist minister and pastor of the **Ebenezer Baptist Church** down the street at 407 Auburn Ave. (ⓒ **404/688-7300**), a Gothic Revival–style church founded in 1886 and completed in 1922. Years later, from 1960 to 1968—at the height of the civil rights struggle— Martin Luther King, Jr., served as his father's co-pastor here, the two actively using their pulpit to press for social change. The National Park Service operates it as a living museum, with guided weekday tours, periodic church services, and a monthly choir performance. In nearby **Freedom Plaza** rests Dr. King's white marble crypt, surrounded by a five-tiered reflecting pool.

The district is somewhat dominated by the hulking modern **King Center,** 449 Auburn Ave. (ⓒ **404/526-8900**; www. thekingcenter.org), a memorial and educational center directed by King's son. It has a huge library and archives on the civil rights movement, including Dr. King's personal papers, but many visitors are most interested in the exhibition hall, where selected memorabilia of King and the civil rights movement are displayed. You can see his Bible and clerical robe and a hand-written sermon; on a grim note, there's the suit King was wearing when a deranged woman stabbed him in New York City, as well as the key to his room at the Lorraine Motel in Memphis, Tennessee, where he was assassinated (see the **National Civil Rights Museum 270**). The best reason to come here is to settle down in the Screening Room to watch videos of Dr. King's most stirring sermons and speeches, including "I Have a Dream." The man's words still move us.

ⓘ **MLK, JR., National Historic Site,** 4509 Auburn Ave. NE (© **404/331-6922;** www.nps.gov/malu).

✈ Atlanta.

🛏 $$$ **The Georgian Terrace Hotel,** 659 Peachtree St., Atlanta (© **800/651-2316** or 404/897-1991; www.thegeorgian terrace.com). $$ **Marriott Stone Mountain Park Inn,** 1058 Robert E. Lee Dr. (© **770/469-3311;** www.marriott.com).

WHY THEY'LL THANK YOU: The "I Have a Dream" speech.

African-American History **269**

Alabama's Civil Rights Trail

Ages 8 & up • Montgomery, Birmingham & Selma, Alabama, USA

What seems like yesterday's headlines to us grown-ups is in fact the foggy past to our kids. Take, for example, that afternoon in 1955 when a black seamstress named Rosa Parks was arrested for not yielding her seat to a white man on a Montgomery, Alabama, public bus. A controversial bus boycott followed (led by a young Rev. Martin Luther King, Jr.), one of the first skirmishes in the civil rights battle of the 1960s. We refer to it so casually, as if everyone should know about this tumultuous era, but it's all new to the kids—and even adults may find they didn't know as much as they thought.

That 1955 street scene is re-created at Montgomery's **Rosa Parks Library and Museum,** 252 Montgomery St. (© **334/241-8661;** http://montgomery. troy.edu/museum), with a replica of the bus Parks rode, video images, and a multimedia tableau. Wonderful interactive displays throughout the museum engage children in Parks's inspiring life as an activist. King's role, of course, was pivotal, as you'll learn on the twice-daily guided tours of the neat

Dexter Avenue King Memorial Baptist Church, 454 Dexter Ave. (© **334/263-3970;** www.dexterkingmemorial.org), where King used his pulpit to press for social change. Even more evocative is the **Dexter Parsonage Museum,** 309 S. Jackson St. (© **334/261-3270;** www.dakmf.org), a simple white bungalow that's been furnished as it was in the 1950s, when King and his family lived here: You can see the study where he wrote his sermons, the dining room where activists met to plan the boycott, and a front window shattered by a bomb meant to scare King off his campaign. Downtown, the black granite **Civil Rights Memorial,** 400 Washington Ave., designed by Maya Lin, pays tribute to those who fought for racial equality.

You have to credit Alabama for embracing this anguished chapter of its past. Birmingham, 90 miles north of Montgomery, has an entire downtown district memorializing civil rights events: engrossing displays (segregated water

Statue of Rosa Parks in Alabama.

fountains, a bombed-out bus, King's jail cell) in the **Birmingham Civil Rights Institute,** 520 16th St. N. (© **205/328-9696;** www.bcri.org); the historic **16th St. Baptist Church,** 1530 6th Ave. N. (© **205/251-9402**), where a 1963 bombing by the Ku Klux Klan killed four adolescent girls; and outdoor **Kelly Ingram Park,** where a paved Freedom Path recounts crucial events with plaques and sculptures. An hour's drive west of Montgomery in Selma, you can see the **Edmund Pettis Bridge,** site of the 1965 "Bloody Sunday" riot, where a voting-rights protest march met brutal resistance from police and local vigilantes, then stop in the **National Voting Rights Museum,** 1012 Water Ave. (© **334/418-0800**), which displays artifacts about voter-registration campaigns—just one phase of the war for civil rights in America.

ⓘ **Sweet Home Alabama** (www.touralabama.org).

✈ Birmingham, 90 miles to Montgomery.

🛏 $$ **Embassy Suites Hotel Montgomery,** 300 Tallapoosa St., Montgomery (© **334/269-5055;** www.embassysuites.com). $$$ **The Redmont,** 2101 Fifth Ave. N., Birmingham (© **877/536-2085;** www.theredmont.com).

WHY THEY'LL THANK YOU: Dr. King had a dream.

---

270 African-American History

National Civil Rights Museum
How Racial Equality Became Reality
Ages 8 & up • Memphis, Tennessee, USA

Thank goodness our children's generation isn't familiar with some of these sights: the segregated lunch counter from which black students in 1960 were evicted; a public bus where in 1955 black people were expected to yield their seats to whites; the burned shell of a Greyhound bus upon which Freedom Riders were attacked in 1961. But the most sobering artifact of all in this comprehensive Memphis, Tennessee, museum is a standard 1960s-era motel room in the attached building, formerly the Lorraine Motel. The Rev. Martin Luther King, Jr., stepped out onto this balcony on the night of April 4, 1968, only to meet the gunfire of a man named James Earl Ray, lying in wait in a rooming house across the street. This historic motel, rescued in the nick of time from demolition, became the starting point for the National Civil Rights Museum, a tribute to Americans of all races who waged the battle for social justice.

Tracing roughly a century of hard-won progress, the museum begins with the Civil War and ends with that tragic night in 1968 (a new annex was recently opened to cover post-1968 developments). While the earlier galleries in the chronological story are a bit static, relying mostly on historical photos and documents, the displays become more engrossing as they deal with the so-called **"Jim Crow laws"** that institutionalized racial segregation in the United States: You'll see a chillingly anonymous Ku Klux Klan white robe and pointed hood, and a sign pointing out "white" and "colored" restrooms. By the time you get to the **school integration struggle**—an issue that really hits home with youngsters—more modern media such as video footage and taped oral histories are available to tell the story. Dioramas present landmark civil disobedience acts in Montgomery, Greensboro, Birmingham, and Memphis, with video footage in

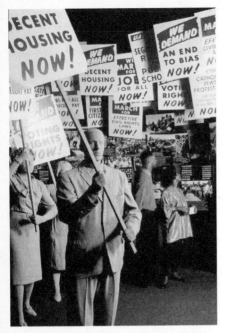

the background. (Provocatively, all figures in these tableaus are rendered in the same blank white plaster, whether the original actors were black or white.) The scene depicting the 1968 March on Washington conveys the immense crowds of that day with a blizzard of protest placards.

While bits and pieces of this story may be told more powerfully at their own sites, covered elsewhere in this section, this is the one museum that tries to make sense of the whole continuous story, and of that it does a pretty darn good job.

(i) 450 Mulberry St. (© **901/521-9699**; www.civilrightsmuseum.org).

✈ Memphis International.

🛏 $$ **Homewood Suites,** 5811 Poplar Ave. (© **800/CALL-HOME** [225-5466] or 901/763-0500; www.homewoodsuites. com). $$$ **The Peabody Memphis,** 149 Union Ave. (© **901/529-4000**; www. peabodymemphis.com).

WHY THEY'LL THANK YOU: A century of struggle, thoughtfully told.

The National Civil Rights Museum in Memphis.

African-American History 271

Brown v. Board of Education
School Segregation Stops Here
Ages 8 & up • Topeka, Kansas, USA

From the outside, the **Monroe School** in Topeka, Kansas, looks like any other mid-20th-century American public school, a solid two-story building of red brick faced with limestone. It was a perfectly acceptable modern school when it opened in 1926, but there was one catch: Only African-American students could go there—and even if they wanted to attend a school closer to their homes, they couldn't. The legal challenge to this segregated school system went all the way to the Supreme Court, resulting in a landmark 1954 decision that forever changed American public

education. If you want the kids to understand what the civil rights movement was all about, here's a great place to start, in a place where racial prejudice affected children their age.

Entering the school building, you won't see classrooms full of desks and dusty chalkboards (declining enrollment shut down Monroe Elementary in 1975). What you will see is a stark sign showing **separate entrances** for blacks and whites. True, there was never such a sign here, because whites didn't come here at all, but the sign is a graphic statement of the "separate but equal" approach to education that prevailed in 1950. A dramatic 25-minute film in the old school auditorium puts the school desegregation fight into the larger context of race in America; you'll then pass through three galleries of **interactive exhibits**—videos, sound clips, touch screens, pull-out drawers, and light-up buttons—that deconstruct the *Brown v. Board of Education* case and the importance of education in the struggle for racial equality.

Brown v. Board of Education wasn't just some local school squabble; 13 Topeka parents, with the support of the National Association for the Advancement of Colored People (NAACP), brought the suit in the summer of 1950 after they tried to enroll their children at various white schools nearer their homes; their class action suit was consolidated with four similar cases from around the country in the final Supreme Court decision. Only three of the children involved went to Monroe, one of them being little Linda Brown, whose father, Oliver, was the first named plaintiff in the case. But the exhibits at Monroe

Elementary don't just narrate one incident at one school, they tell the story of a systematic pattern of exclusion at many schools, born out of a racial discrimination woven into the fabric of American society.

The final gallery you'll pass through is the one that feels most like a classroom, the old **kindergarten room,** where visitors are asked to write, discuss, and reflect on what they've learned today. Now's the time to ask the children if the schools they know are truly different from the ones in Linda Brown's day—and why.

ⓘ 1515 S.E. Monroe St. (Ⓒ **785/354-4273;** www.nps.gov/brvb).

✈ Kansas City, 70 miles.

🛏 $$ **Capitol Plaza Hotel,** 1717 S.W. Topeka Blvd. (Ⓒ **800/579-7937** or 785/431-7200; www.capitolplazahoteltopeka.com). $$ **Ramada Inn Downtown,** 420 E. 6th Ave. (Ⓒ **800/272-6232** or 785/234-5400; www.ramada.com).

WHY THEY'LL THANK YOU: Where you go to school makes a difference.

---

272 African-American History

Little Rock Central High School
Passing the Integration Test
Ages 10 & up • Little Rock, Arkansas, USA

Imagine the courage it took for nine African American teenagers to walk into Central High School in September 1957, ready for the new school year. Central was an all-white school, and a prestigious one at that—an imposing Collegiate Gothic beauty with a turreted roofline and sweeping front staircase. It had 100 classrooms, a field house, a football stadium, and many other luxuries unheard-of at Dunbar High, the black school a few blocks away. But there were plenty of folks in town who were determined not to let those black students through those school doors.

The ink was still fresh on the Supreme Court's ruling in *Brown v. Board of Education*—now all that was needed was a test case, and civil rights leaders were prepared to give the nation one. *Brown v. Board of Education* was mostly waged in the courts; in Little Rock, it was waged by nine courageous teenagers risking physical danger, under constant scrutiny from newspaper reporters and television news cameras.

Because Central High is still a working high school, you can't just walk in and gawk at the places where all this happened. Half-hour **ranger-led tours** are permitted

African-American students escorted by the military at Little Rock Central High School.

inside the school building, but only six a week, limited to 10 people (reserve well in advance). Before taking the tour, help the kids understand the scope of this historic episode by spending some time in the spiffy **new visitor center** across the street, which was dedicated in September 2007, on the 50th anniversary of the Little Rock crisis.

At the center, videos, taped oral histories, and photographic displays tell the story of that fateful September. On the first day of the new school year, Arkansas's governor was all ready for the black students: Defying federal desegregation orders, he had the Arkansas National Guard turn them away. Three weeks later, the Nine finally entered the building to start classes, but an incensed crowd of protesters outside made the scene so dangerous, Little Rock police had to escort the kids out again. The next morning, the 101st Airborne showed up, on orders from President Eisenhower, to usher the black students safely inside, while TV news cameras whirred.

As the school year wore on, the troops and TV cameras stopped hovering outside, but opponents of integration kept tempers at a boiling point inside Central— "If parents would just go home and let us alone, we'll be all right," one white student remarked. One of the Nine, tired of continual harassment, quit school and moved to New York City. Another, Ernest Green, graduated in spring, commenting wryly, "It's been an interesting year." Yes, but a year that changed history.

ⓘ 2125 Daisy Bates Dr. (✆ **501/374-1957;** www.nps.gov/chsc).

✈ Little Rock National.

🛏 $$$ **Doubletree Hotel Little Rock,** 424 W. Markham (✆ **800/222-TREE** or 501/372-4371; www.doubletreelr.com). $$ **La Quinta Inn & Suites,** 617 S. Broadway (✆ **800/753-3757** or 501/374-9000; www.lq.com).

WHY THEY'LL THANK YOU: And they think their high school sucks?

10 For Budding Scientists

Wright Brothers National Memorial.

American Museum of Natural History
Discovering Dinosaurs
All ages • New York, New York, USA

How many children have fallen in love with dinosaurs in the echoing galleries of this world-class New York City museum? And the dinosaurs are only the tip of the iceberg: Over the years, Holden Caulfield brooded over its collection of Northwest Indian totem poles in *The Catcher in the Rye;* in the planetarium, Woody Allen wooed Diane Keaton in the 1979 film *Manhattan;* and curious scientists plunked Darryl Hannah's mermaid into a tank to examine her in the 1984 movie *Splash.* It's one of America's great museums, and invariably engrossing for children.

The Hall of African Mammals at the American Museum of Natural History.

When you enter the magnificent rotunda at the top of the Central Park West steps—named for Theodore Roosevelt, the outdoors-loving President who helped found the museum—a rearing skeleton of a mommy dinosaur protecting her baby from a small, fierce predator clues you in that the dazzling interactive fourth-floor dinosaur halls are the perennial star attraction. But our favorite sights are the superb dioramas in the **North American Mammals**—the grizzly bear raking open a freshly caught salmon, majestic elks lifting their massive antlers, wolves loping through eerie nighttime snow—or, on the floor above, the bi-level **African Mammals Hall,** where you can circle around a lumbering herd of perfectly preserved elephants or check out the giraffes browsing by their water hole. In the dimly lit **Ocean Life** room, a gargantuan model of a blue whale swims overhead while dolphins arc through plastic waves. Around the corner, the less-well-visited **North American Forest** dioramas are our family secret—a peaceful part of the museum where you can hunt for blue jays in oak trees and rattlesnakes behind the cactus. Haunting music playing in the **African** and **Asian peoples** sections lull you into studying precisely detailed displays of cultural artifacts: a Chinese bride's ornate sedan chair, a pygmy's blow darts, a re-creation of a Siberian shaman healing rite, a Yoruba ceremonial costume made of red snail shells.

The stunning **Rose Center for Earth and Space,** a 95-foot-high glass cube, includes an interactive exhibit on the nature of the universe, where you can step on a scale that shows your weight on Saturn, see an eerie phosphorescent model of the expanding universe, and touch cosmic debris. There are an IMAX theater, a space show, and always at least a couple of traveling exhibitions (my only quibble with the museum is the substantial extra fees charged for these, on top of an already hefty admission price). But there's enough to do here that you don't need to go for the extras. Wander at will, keeping your eyes open and your imagination at the ready. It's a magical place.

(i) Central Park West and 79th St. ((C) **212/769-5100;** www.amnh.org).

✈ John F. Kennedy International, 15 miles. Newark Liberty International, 16 miles. LaGuardia, 8 miles.

🛏 $$ **Excelsior Hotel,** 45 W. 81st St. ((C) **800/368-4575** or 212/362-9200; www.excelsiorhotelny.com). $$$ **Le Parker Meridien,** 118 W. 57th St. ((C) **800/543-4300** or 212/245-5000; www.parkermeridien.com).

WHY THEY'LL THANK YOU: The dioramas and the dinosaurs.

---

274 Science Museums

The Field Museum
Visiting Sue & Friends
All ages • Chicago, Illinois, USA

The minute you walk in here and gape up at the world's largest, most complete *Tyrannosaurus rex* **skeleton**—named Sue for the paleontologist who dug it up in 1990 in South Dakota—you know you're in a world-class science museum. This beloved Chicago museum is so jam-packed with bones, rocks, stuffed critters, and dioramas, it's no wonder Steven Spielberg made it home turf for his adventure hero Indiana Jones. Members of the video-game generation can learn a lot from a little chill time here, where it's not all about punching buttons and guiding cursors, but about using your eyes and your imagination to enter different habitats.

Animals, even dead ones propped into permanent poses, are always a natural draw for kids—call it the taxidermy version of a zoo—and the Field has some dramatic ones, notably the **lowland gorilla Bushman** (formerly of the Lincoln Park Zoo), and a notorious 19th-century pair of **man-eating lions** from East Africa. But there's another side to natural history, and the Field does an especially good job with the anthropological side of things, in

exhibits like the **Pawnee Earth lodge,** the scenes of South Pacific island cultures, or the continent-hopping **African peoples** gallery, which ends up on a slave ship to the Americas (just in case you needed that bit of political history underlined). Best of all in this vein is the downstairs **Egyptian exhibit,** which doesn't just set out artifacts in glass cases but re-creates scenes of day-to-day life in ancient Egypt, from a burial rite to a teeming daily marketplace to a royal barge trip down the Nile (complete with locks). Inspired by the excavated tomb of Unis-ankh in Saqqara, this classic exhibit has been perked up with touch-screens and kid-friendly activities, such as making parchment from real papyrus plants plucked from the gallery's living marsh.

The dinosaur galleries here, while not as extensive as the ones at the American Museum of Natural History in New York, have been incorporated into **Evolving Planet,** a huge new exhibit that's heavy on the interactives, which covers a 4-billion-year continuum of life on Earth (a bold move, opting to support Darwin despite the current culture wars). And then there's **Underground Adventure,** a very popular "total immersion environment," where super-sized mechanized replicas of subterranean creatures—earwigs, centipedes, wolf spiders—will terrorize your children for an extra admission fee. The kids will probably beg to try this out, and who can blame them?

(i) Roosevelt Rd. and Lake Shore Dr. (© **312/922-9410;** www.fieldmuseum. org). **Tourist office** (© **877/CHICAGO** [244-2246] or 312/744-2400; www.cityof chicago.org).

✈ O'Hare International, 15 miles.

🛏 $$ **Homewood Suites,** 40 E. Grand St. (© **800/CALL-HOME** [225-5466] or 312/644-2222; www.homewoodsuites chicago.com). $$ **Hotel Allegro Chicago,** 171 N. Randolph St. (© **800/643-1500** or 312/236-0123; www.allegrochicago.com).

WHY THEY'LL THANK YOU: Taking enough time to let each kid find his or her favorite spot.

Science Museums 275

National Museum of Natural History
Science Central
All ages • Washington, D.C., USA

Whereas its rivals in Chicago and New York (see The Field Museum 274 and American Museum of Natural History 273 above) hit visitors with a dinosaur skeleton right by the entrance, this Smithsonian museum in Washington, D.C., plays its hand more casually, starting out with a huge African bush elephant in the rotunda, where you first enter from the Mall. But that doesn't mean there aren't dinosaurs here—there are, literally tons of them, as well as one of the world's oldest fossils and a 70-million-year-old dinosaur egg. This is in fact the largest natural history museum in the world, with 125 million artifacts and specimens—nearly 90% of the Smithsonian's total holdings! And this being a Smithsonian museum, admission is free, which makes it all the easier to cruise in even if you only have a couple hours to spare. Given all the history stuff you'll probably be seeing in Washington, this place is a breath of fresh (and very kid-friendly) air.

With so much to see, the challenge is to navigate wisely. Here are the exhibits my children enjoyed most: The **Insect Zoo,** where toddlers can crawl through a model of an African termite mound; **Life in the Ancient Seas,** where you can walk around a diorama of a 230-million-year-old coral reef teeming with models of weird primitive fish; and the **Hall of Mammals,** right off the rotunda, where up-to-date lighting and sound make the dioramas of 274 taxidermied mammals completely interactive. Every once in a while, the hall erupts with animal sounds, all part of the exhibit wizardry that makes this a lifelike experience. Similar interactive techniques have jazzed up the **Hall of Geology, Gems, and Minerals,** on the second floor, which really gives a "big picture" story of earth's evolution. The huge new **Ocean Hall** was still under construction when we visited, but by all accounts it should be a knockout when it's finished. Being regular visitors to New York's Natural History Museum, my kids are hard to impress when it comes to dinosaur halls, and the one in D.C. is slated for an overhaul; it does have some amazing specimens, though, including a pterosaur with a 40-foot wingspan, and the jaw of a monstrous ancient shark, the *Carcharodon megalodon,* with teeth 5 to 6 inches long.

We also loved the outdoor **butterfly garden,** which is open year-round, with four habitats—wetland, meadow, wood's edge, an urban garden. My city kids really responded to this little slice of nature in the middle of the nation's capital. Sometimes it's the little things that grab them—you just can't predict it.

ⓘ Constitution Ave. btw. 9th and 12th sts. (Ⓒ **202/633-1000;** www.mnh.si.edu).

✈ Ronald Reagan Washington National, 5 miles. Dulles International, 26 miles. Baltimore-Washington International, 30 miles.

🛏 $$ **Embassy Suites Hotel Downtown,** 1250 22nd St. NW (Ⓒ **800/EMBASSY** [362-2779] or 202/857-3388; www.embassysuitesdcmetro.com). $$$ **Hilton Washington,** 1919 Connecticut Ave. NW (Ⓒ **800/HILTONS** [445-8667] or 202/483-3000; www.washington.hilton.com).

WHY THEY'LL THANK YOU: When the lions start to roar in the Hall of Mammals.

276 Science Museums

Franklin Institute
In the Spirit of Old Ben Himself
Ages 4 & up • Philadelphia, Pennsylvania, USA

Let's never forget that Benjamin Franklin was a scientist as well as a statesman, publisher, and philosopher: The Franklin stove and bifocal glasses were just two contraptions he invented, and of course there's that whole experiment with the kite in the thunderstorm. It warms my heart to visit the Franklin Institute in Philadelphia, which pays homage to the quirkiest of our Founding Fathers. At the core of this museum is the **Franklin National Memorial,** with a 30-ton statue of its namesake and an evocative hands-on gallery on Franklin's inventions and the scientists he inspired. While it looks all stately and neoclassical on the outside, however, this place wouldn't reflect the spirit of Franklin if it didn't have a fascinating clutter of other exhibits that simply encourage kids to putter around.

Hands-on is the watchword at the Franklin Institute; pick up a schedule of the museum staff's frequent **daily demonstrations** so you won't miss the fun stuff. The collection of science- and technology-oriented exhibits ranges from a gigantic walk-through heart to the Train Factory, where you can play engineer for a 350-ton locomotive, to a Van de Graaff generator that'll make your hair stand on end at the Electricity gallery. Kid Science, on the lower level, uses a dramatic anime-like storyline to teach basic science concepts to children ages 5 to 8. On the third floor, Sir Isaac's Loft demonstrates the principles of Newtonian physics with Rube Goldberg–ian machines, noisemakers, and light shows. The Sports Challenge section was intriguing, looking at the science behind popular sports like surfing and rock climbing, and we couldn't resist the Skybike, which you can ride along a 1-inch cable three stories above the atrium floor. The whole museum is all about curiosity, and it's one of the best embodiments of the scientific method you'll ever play in.

In the warmer months, a great **high-tech playground** sprouts out on the lawn, where young kids can really mess around with science concepts—the step-on organ is a crowd pleaser, as are the maze and the high-wire tandem bicycle. If your kids like this kind of stuff, you'll probably also want to devote some time to the nearby **Please Touch Museum,** 210 N. 21st St. (© **215/963-0667;** www.please touchmuseum.org).

ⓘ Logan Circle, 20th St. and Benjamin Franklin Pkwy. (© **215/448-1200;** www.fi. edu).

✈ Philadelphia International.

🛏 $$$ **Best Western Independence Park Inn,** 235 Chestnut St. (© **800/624-2988** or 215/922-4443; www.independence parkhotel.com). $$$ **Rittenhouse Hotel,** 210 W. Rittenhouse Sq. (© **800/635-1042** or 215/546-9000; www.rittenhousehotel. com).

WHY THEY'LL THANK YOU: Playing with electricity at Ben Franklin's museum.

Science Museums 277

Museum of Science and Industry
You Can't Beat the Classics
All ages • Chicago, Illinois, USA

The Museum of Science and Industry.

My sentimental favorite among the world's great science museums, Chicago's Museum of Science and Industry was a wonderland to me when I visited it as a kid—and if anything, its appeal has only grown through the years, with a slew of great new exhibits to involve kids in learning. This place has both cool historic things to look at *and* lots of Exploratorium-type activities to play with—the best of both worlds. It doesn't even matter that it's way the other end of Lake Shore Drive from Chicago's other great science museums, **The Field Museum 274** and the **Shedd Aquarium 117**; this place deserves a full day to itself.

There were three iconic exhibits I absolutely had to make my children see, greatest hits from my own childhood: the **U-505,** a German submarine captured in 1944; the full-scale **Coal Mine,** which simulates a trip down into a dark, mysterious mine shaft; and the giant walk-through **model of the human heart.** (Another reason to make a full day of this museum—you want to get there early to beat the long lines for these three crowd favorites.)

The train lovers in my family had to be dragged away from the refurbished **Burlington Pioneer Zephyr train,** where you can climb on board and fiddle with loads of interactive thingies, but there was no rushing past the massive model train lay-out called **The Great Train Story,** which re-creates a train's journey from Seattle across the Rockies and the Great Plains to Chicago. In the **Transportation Zone,** every 7 minutes a full-size 727 airplane revs up its engines and plays voice record-ings to simulate a "flight" from San Fran-cisco to Chicago; nearby we could gape at a real lunar exploration module, a Mercury space capsule, and an Apollo command module. The fantastic collection of famous **ship models** includes a mock-up of the quarterdeck of a 19th-century tall ship where you can give the wheel a spin. We all giggled with delight at **Out to Lunch,** a gargantuan collection of fast-food give-away toys (including several I remembered prying out of our car seats). **Toymaker 3000** is a captivating interactive gallery that shows how industrial robots perform simple tasks.

Last but certainly not least, it did my heart good to see my daughter entranced by **Colleen Moore's Fairy Castle,** a story-book miniature palace filled with priceless treasures (check out the chandeliers—they sparkle with real pearls and dia-monds). Gee, I felt the same way when I was her age.

ⓘ 57th St. and Lake Shore Dr. (ℂ **800/468-6674** or 773/684-1414; www.msichicago.org).

✈ O'Hare International, 15 miles.

🛏 $$ **Homewood Suites,** 40 E. Grand St. (ℂ **800/CALL-HOME** [225-5466] or 312/644-2222; www.homewoodsuiteschicago.com). $$ **Hotel Allegro Chicago,** 171 N. Randolph St. (ℂ **800/643-1500** or 312/236-0123; www.allegrochicago.com).

WHY THEY'LL THANK YOU: Happily exhausted by 5pm.

---

278 **Science Museums**

The Exploratorium
The Ultimate Hands-On Museum
All ages • San Francisco, California, USA

"The best science museum in the world" is what *Scientific American* magazine once called this San Francisco attraction, right by the waterfront parks of the Marina Dis-trict. Set in a sprawling former airplane hangar, every bit of floor space is taken up with inventive activity stations and dis-plays that just cry out for youngsters to press, jiggle, squeeze, fiddle, poke, and manipulate to their heart's content. I've been there with toddlers and I've been there with teens, and everyone has always been totally absorbed. They don't seem to care that they're also learning scientific concepts, in a way that will really stick.

The Exploratorium staff is constantly engaged in dreaming up new exhibits, so there's no guarantee that the stuff we loved won't have been replaced by some-thing even cooler by the time you get there. The giant soap-bubble maker is perennially popular, as is the shadow wall, the visual distortion room, and machines that make sand patterns with sound waves. The **Tactile Dome** is an amazing experience for older kids, where they grope their way around in complete dark-ness, dependent on senses other than sight. Across Marina Boulevard, at the end of the Marina breakwater, you'll find one of the Exploratorium's most intriguing inventions: the **Wave Organ,** a hunk of concrete embedded with listening tubes that lead underwater to translate the ebb

The Exploratorium.

and flow of ocean currents into strange gurgles and humming sounds.

There's a handmade quality to many of the displays that I find very appealing—clearly they've been bolted and knocked together out of plywood, wires, PVC pipes, whatever is on hand, and I can't help but think this encourages kids to become putterers and inventors themselves. As my kids get older, their interests change; the last time we were there, they gravitated to exhibits on principles of light, optics, and perception, whereas in years past they were engrossed in the simple physics concepts demonstrated in the section on matter. Biology and electricity sections on the mezzanine are fascinating too. (There's a **play area** for under-4s, a godsend if you need to entertain a toddler while your older kid works the exhibits.) On our most recent visit, I watched my continually squabbling son and daughter sit for 15 minutes on either side of a mirrored pane of glass, watching their grinning faces blend together as lighting levels were gradually raised and lowered—so much for hating your siblings.

You'll find local youngsters here, not just tourists and bored school groups. It's a noisy, high-raftered, under-lit space and eventually we hit overload and have to bail out. But we never leave because we've run out of things to do.

ⓘ 3601 Lyon St. (✆ **415/397-5673;** www.exploratorium.org). **San Francisco Municipal Railway** (✆ **415/673-6864;** www.sfmuni.com). **Convention & Visitors' Bureau,** 900 Market St. (✆ **415/391-2000;** www.onlyinsanfrancisco.com).

✈ San Francisco International.

🛏 $$$ **The Argonaut,** 495 Jefferson St. (✆ **866/415-0704** or 415/563-0800; www.argonauthotel.com). $$ **Larkspur Hotel,** 524 Sutter St. (✆ **800/919-9779** or 415/421-2865; www.larkspurhotelunion square.com).

WHY THEY'LL THANK YOU: Hands-on = brains on.

The Montreal Biodôme, Botanical Garden and Insectarium

It's Only Natural

All ages • Montreal Canada

What if your kids could look for monkeys in a tropical forest and see penguins in a polar setting, all in one day? They can if you take them to the Montreal Biodôme, a series of four environments that re-creates four eco-systems of the Americas. In between the tropic and polar worlds you'll find the seasonal Lauerentian forest, home to beavers, otters, and lynx as well as the Saint Lawerence shore-line which showcases underwater plant life and a vast bird population. The Biodôme is just a few minutes away from downtown Montreal, but you might as well be in another world as you take in the plant and animal life along the pathways to each dome. While kids are sure to love the monkeys and penguins, they'll also delight in jewel-toned hummingbirds hovering overhead. The Biodôme is, in fact, home to 4,800 animals and 750 plant species. And while it is sure to delight the entire family, there are special, interactive activities for kids ages 6 to 12.

Besides being a fun place to learn about the natural world, the Biodôme studies at-risk species by breeding them in captivity. In 2008, they joined forces with zoos, aquariums, and botanical gardens to breed amphibians in order to create a population for researchers working on survival solutions for threatened species. This work can play a vital role in introducing kids to the importance of conservation. Other programs bring the environmental message home such as the 17th International Contest featuring Toys Made of Reused Materials. Adjacent to the Biodôme are the Insectarium and the Montreal Botanical Garden, both splendid spots to resume your exploration of nature. **The Montreal**

Botanical Garden, 4101 Sherbrooke Est (℃ **514/872-1400;** http://www2.ville. montreal.qc.ca/jardin/jardin), is one of the largest of its kind, providing visitors with a riot of color and scent. This fragrant paradise offers a dizzying array of plants and flowers in large greenhouses each with a different theme, including orchids, begonias, and plants from the rainforest. You can wander serenely through the Chinese garden, designed to mimic a garden from the Ming Dynasty or watch a tea ceremony performed in a the Japanese garden. Kids old enough to have studied Native American culture may especially enjoy **The First Nations Garden,** which highlights the importance the plant world played in Inuit and Native American life. Be sure to bring binoculars for a good view of the beautiful avians attracted by the plants.

A short walk away brings you to the **Montreal Insectarium,** 4581 Sherbrooke Est, (℃ **514/872-1400;** www2.ville. montreal.qc.ca/insectarium/), which houses live and mounted insects of all kinds, including scorpions, tarantulas, hissing cockroaches, and praying mantises. Tour guides are available to shed light on what they refer to as these "strange and misunderstood" creatures, while the kids enjoy the ick factor. If you visit in summer, you can take a break from the creepy crawlies by visiting the butterfly house, full of fluttering beauties hovering near plants and flowers. Hey, butterflies are insects, too!

ⓘ 4777 Av. Pierre-de-Coubertin (℃ **514/ 868-3000;** www2.ville.montreal.qc.ca/ biodome).

289

Montréal-Pierre-Elliott-Trudeau International, 23km (14 miles).

$$ **Delta Centre-Ville,** 777 rue University (© **800/268-1133** or 514/879-1370; www.deltahotels.com). $$$ **Fairmont Le**

Reine Elizabeth, 900 bd. René-Lévesque Oust (© **800/441-1414** or 514/861-3511; www.fairmont.com).

WHY THEY'LL THANK YOU: Monkeys, penguins, and creepy, crawly bugs.

Science Museums 280

Powerhouse Museum
Where Sydney Gets Interactive
All ages • Sydney, Australia

Australia's largest museum looks so sleek and interactive, it's surprising to learn that it began more than a century ago, in 1880, as an outgrowth of the 1879 international Garden Palace Exhibition in Sydney. Like the Smithsonian in Washington, D.C., it has a sort of "nation's attic" collection, with some 385,000 objects spanning a number of fields: science, technology, engineering, transport, Australian history, and the decorative arts.

Here are just a few of the coolest things in the 22 permanent exhibitions: a priceless Boult & Watt rotative steam engine; a Catalina flying boat; a steam locomotive; a reconstructed 1930s Art Deco cinema; a re-created 19th-century sheep farmers' rural store; a Russian spacesuit; an 1880s bush-hut kitchen; a 1920s "germ-free" kitchen. What's more, the accompanying text and touch-screens aren't full of geeky technical explanations—they emphasize the role of human curiosity and creativity, hoping to inspire tomorrow's innovators. Kids will probably gravitate to the **hands-on displays** in the computer, science, and technology exhibits, which allow them to learn scientific concepts by conducting their own mini-experiments. Then there are the **media labs,** SoundHouse and

VectorLab, where kids can sign up for workshops in digital graphics and music production. The under-8s have their own section, **Kids Interactive Discovery Spaces,** where simpler hands-on activities are set up in primary-colored play areas.

The Powerhouse also owns the historic **Sydney Observatory,** Watson Road, Observatory Hill, The Rocks (© **61/2/9241-3767;** www.sydneyobservatory.com); light pollution in the metropolitan area has made its stargazing days a thing of the past, but as a museum of astronomy it's still got some cool old telescopes and exhibits, not to mention a 3-D Space Theatre.

ⓘ 500 Harris St., Ultimo (near Darling Harbour; © **61/2/9217-0111;** www.power housemuseum.com).

✈ Sydney International.

$$$ **Radisson Plaza Hotel Sydney,** 27 O'Connell St. (© **800/333/3333** in the U.S. or 61/2/8214/0000; www.radisson. com). $$$ **The Stafford,** 75 Harrington St., The Rocks (© **61/2/9251-6711;** www. rendezvoushotels.com).

WHY THEY'LL THANK YOU: Each visitor finds his or her own moment of wonder.

The Science & Natural History Museums

All ages • London, England

Here's London's knockout one-two punch: two world-class science museums, on adjacent sites in South Kensington, and both of them free. It's quite tempting to do them both in 1 day, but be forewarned: Their collections are so huge, and so engrossing, that it may be hard to move your kids on from one to the other.

The **Science Museum** is a place of hands-on galleries, working models, and video displays galore, all tracing the development of science and industry and—especially important for kids—showing their influence on everyday life. Marvelous interactive consoles placed strategically throughout the museum help you plot your visit according to your special interests. You'll see Stephenson's original rocket and the tiny prototype railroad engine; you can also see Whittle's original jet engine and the Apollo 10 space module. The King George III Collection of scientific instruments is the highlight of a gallery on science in the 18th century, an era when a gifted assortment of British scientists, many of them brilliant amateurs, led a Golden Age of scientific discoveries. In a newer wing, exhibits explore such cutting-edge topics as genetics, digital technology, and artificial intelligence—learn how engineers observe sea life with robotic submarines, or how DNA was used to identify living relatives of the Bleadon Man, a 2,000-year-old Iron Age Man.

Science of a more organic nature reigns at the **Natural History Museum.** The Science Museum's exhibits may be more exciting, but I must admit I'm a sucker for the exotic Victorian architecture of the Natural History Museum's main hall. While not quite as amazing as the New York and Washington, D.C., natural history museums, London's is a don't-miss for dinosaur

lovers, and there are magnificent specimens of all sorts of living and fossil plants, animals, and minerals. The geological history of our planet is dramatically illustrated in the exhibit "Earth Today and Tomorrow"—it truly puts the Bang in the Big Bang.

ⓘ **Science Museum,** Exhibition Rd. (✆ **44/ 870/870-4868;** www.sciencemuseum. org.uk). **Natural History Museum,** Cromwell Rd. (✆ **44/20/7942-5000;** www.nhm. ac.uk).

A diplodocus skeleton at the Natural History Museum in London.

✈ Heathrow.

🛏 $$$ **London Bridge Hotel,** 8–18 London Bridge St. 9 (© **44/20/7855-2200;** www.londonbridgehotel.co.uk), $$ **Vicarage Private Hotel,** 10 Vicarage Gate,

South Kensington (© **44/20/7229-4030;** www.londonvicaragehotel.com).

WHY THEY'LL THANK YOU: Science is their future.

Science Museums 282

Glasgow Science Centre
High-Tech Revolution for the New Millennium
All ages • Glasgow, Scotland, UK

Adults may put Glasgow on their travel itineraries because they want to see the mind-boggling art in the Burrell Collection, but for the kids, it's all about the dynamic Glasgow Science Centre.

You'll spot the Science Centre from a long way off, its gleaming titanium-clad crescent shape reflected in the river. The crescent is punctuated by the slender aerodynamic **Glasgow Tower,** which rotates 360 degrees (the whole thing rotates from the ground up, not just a platform at the top—it's the world's only structure to spin like this); a quick zip upward in an elevator and you have a panoramic view of the city, along with multimedia displays on Glasgow's history and future. The center also has a planetarium and IMAX screen (the only one in Scotland). The exhibits do emphasize Scottish scientists and inventors, specifically Glaswegians, but for good reason: Glasgow boomed during the Industrial Revolution, with great ironworks and steelworks and a huge shipbuilding industry, and engineers and designers were a vital part of all that. This is no stuffy historical display, however: Following the pattern

of such successful American museums as the Exploratorium 278, the Glasgow Science Centre explains technology in such an entertaining, interactive way that kids are completely drawn in. They'll be able to make their own soundtrack and animation, star in their own digital video, or do a 3-D head scan and then rearrange their facial features. At special shows and workshops, you'll see a glass smashed by sound, "catch" shadows, experience a million volts of indoor lightning, see liquid nitrogen, view the bacteria that lurk on you, and build a lie detector.

ⓘ 50 Pacific Quay (© **44/871/540-1000;** www.gsc.org.uk).

✈ Glasgow, 16km (10 miles) west of the city.

🛏 $$$ **Hilton Glasgow Hotel,** 1 William St. (© **800/445-8667** in the U.S., or 44/141/204-5555; http://beta.hilton.co.uk/glasgow).

WHY THEY'LL THANK YOU: Futuristic outside, geeky fun inside.

Cité des Sciences et de l'Industrie

All ages • Paris, France

As part of an ambitious urban-renewal scheme for northeastern Paris, the French government completely gutted a vacant slaughterhouse, sheathed it with a sleek new facade, surrounded it with a moat, and crowned it with a huge reflective geodesic dome—*voilà!* La Cité des Sciences et de l'Industrie was born. Opened in 1986, to coincide with the most recent flyby of Halley's Comet, La Cité was worth the $642-million price tag, drawing crowds (and not just children) to the long Métro ride out to Parc La Villette's leisurely green expanse. It's popular enough that you should call ahead to reserve timed-entrance tickets, although agreeably whiling away an hour or two in the surrounding park is no problem either.

La Cité may seem overwhelming at first but most families know to head straight for **La Cité des Enfants,** where a couple hundred hands-on activity stations painlessly educate children. Divided into two sections, one for ages 3 to 5 and another for ages 6 to 12, it features incredibly cool stuff like seeing an "x-ray" of your body breathing or racing a skeleton on a bicycle to see which bones and muscles move.

The top three floors of the museum are devoted to the Explora, geared for adults as well as children, laymen and scientists alike: Its displays are organized to relate to four themes—the universe, life, matter, and communication. These well-lit, handsomely mounted exhibits, which are continually updated and replaced, stretch the length of the building, so don't even try to see them all—stroll along and sample what appeals to you (like a recent one titled **Grossology**—what child could pass that up?). We appreciated the peculiarly Gallic sense of humor, such as the demonstration of seismographic activity presented as the comic-strip adventures of a

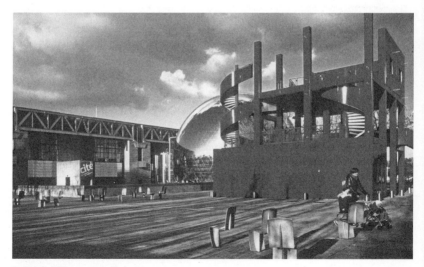

La Cité des Sciences et de l'Industrie.

jungle explorer. Visitors can also climb aboard the *Argonaut,* a diesel submarine originally built in 1905 that's like something out of Jules Verne's science fiction, a prophetic prototype for the giant nuclear subs of the later 20th century.

It's almost de rigueur for a museum of this sort to have an IMAX-style theater, but the one here, the Géode, is a doozy, occupying that striking 34m (112-ft.) silver-skinned dome that's the focal point of the complex. There's a planetarium too, and a simulator ride—no feature of such science museums has been left out. You could

easily spend a full day here, making that long subway ride more than worth it.

ⓘ 30 av. Corentine-Cariou, La Villette (ⓒ **33/1/40-05-80-00;** www.cite-sciences.fr).

🛏 $$$ **Hotel de Fleurie,** 32–34 rue Grégoire-de-Tours (ⓒ **33/1/53-73-70-00;** www.hotel-de-fleurie.tm.fr). $$ **Residence Lord Byron,** 5 rue de Chateaubriand (ⓒ **33/1/43-59-89-98;** www.escapade-paris. com).

WHY THEY'LL THANK YOU: A welcome antidote to the history overload in Paris.

Science Museums **284**

Deutsches Museum

All ages • Munich, Germany

My kids are convinced that Germans are the world's finest scientists and engineers, and I have a sneaking suspicion that that impression was riveted into their brains by visiting the German Museum of Science and Technology. It's a knockout attraction, the world's largest technology museum, set prominently on an island in the middle of the river Isar as it flows through Munich.

I instantly felt at home here, harking back to my childhood days at Chicago's Museum of Science and Industry, but the more I explored, the more I marveled at the historic nature of this collection, with so many one-of-a-kind artifacts and priceless originals. Yes, most of the important **inventions** highlighted here are German-made, but that's because Germans were at the forefront of so many scientific developments in the 19th century. You'll see the first electric dynamo (built by Siemens in 1866), the first automobile (built by Benz in 1886), the first diesel engine (Diesel, 1897), and the laboratory bench at which the atom was first split (Hahn and Strassmann, 1938). I was astonished to see an x-ray machine from 1895 and the first truly powerful refracting telescope, which

discovered Neptune in 1846. There's as much history as science here—an 1806 Jacquard loom, championed by Napoleon, that revolutionized the textile industry (thus replacing a cottage industry with factories), or the ciphering machines used in World War II to translate messages into the long-unbroken Enigma code.

Even children too young to appreciate these ground-breaking inventions will enjoy the **hands-on exhibits,** with hundreds of buttons to push, levers to crank, and gears to turn. Lots of knowledgeable staff (excellent English speakers, generally) hang around to answer questions and demonstrate the scientific principles that make steam engines and pumps work.

Don't get hung up on seeing everything; get a museum guide and head for the areas your family is most interested in, whether it be airplanes, bikes, clocks, cars, or computers. We loved the agriculture section's detailed scale models of farms throughout the ages. The electrical power hall is also intriguing, with high-voltage displays that actually produce lightning. My husband, the amateur astronomer, made sure we spent time in the astronomy exhibit—the largest in Europe—complete with a planetarium and a two-domed observatory with a solar telescope. World-class in every way.

ℹ️ Museumsinsel 1 (✆ **49/89/21791**; www.deutsches-museum.de).

✈️ Munich International, 27km (17 miles).

🛏️ $ **Hotel Jedermann,** Bayerstrasse 95 (✆ **49/89/543240**; www.hotel-jedermann.de). $$ **Hotel Splendid-Dollmann im Lehel,** Thierschstrasse 49 (✆ **49/89/238080**; www.hotel-splendid-dollmann.de).

WHY THEY'LL THANK YOU: From the Gutenberg Bible to the Helios space probe and everything in between.

Kitty Hawk
The Wright Brothers Learn to Fly
Ages 4 & up • Kill Devil Hills, North Carolina, USA

The name Kitty Hawk is forever associated with Orville and Wilbur Wright—it says so right on North Carolina's license plates. That's the place where, on December 17, 1903, this brother-brother team from Dayton, Ohio, achieved the world's first sustained, controlled, heavier-than-air powered flight. (You need all those adjectives to distinguish the Wrights' flight from a mere glider or hot-air balloon flight.) But you could score big trivia points for knowing that the Wrights didn't take off from the town of Kitty Hawk, but from a nearby 90-foot-high dune called **Kill Devil Hill** on the Outer Banks, a bony finger of land that separates the Atlantic Ocean from the inner sounds and estuaries of North Carolina's coast. Ask the kids: If you were flying

A glider at the Wright Brothers National Memorial.

295

an experimental aircraft into the teeth of gusting Atlantic winds, would you really want to launch from a place called Kill Devil Hill?

Desperate to get home to Dayton in time for Christmas, Orville and Wilbur did get the Wright Flyer off the ground that windy December day in 1903, keeping it aloft for 59 seconds and flying a distance of 852 feet. Their feat is commemorated at the **Wright Brothers National Memorial,** an imposing 60-foot-high pylon of white North Carolina granite, erected in 1932 on Kill Devil Hill. In fact, the Wrights made four successful flights that day, of increasing lengths; numbered markers on the long slopes show how far they made it each time, until on the fourth go the Wright Flyer crash-landed. The visitor center features a replica of that **Wright Flyer,** plus a glider they flew here in 1902, along with a few exhibits telling the Wright Brothers' story; park rangers lead twice-daily tours, present talks at the visitor center, and run afternoon family activities such as kite flying or paper-airplane building. You can explore reconstructions of the hangar Orville and Wilbur built for their plane and their workshop/living quarters. The main thing, though, is to stand on the big grassy dune and feel the breezes rise off the water; it suddenly becomes clear why the Wright brothers traveled all the way to North Carolina to get their spidery winged craft aloft.

Not far away, at the highest sand dune on the East Coast, 138-foot-high Jockey's Ridge, you can try out those Outer Banks winds yourself by taking a hang-gliding lesson from the world's largest hang-gliding school, **Kitty Hawk Kites,** near the visitor center of Jockey's Ridge State Park (milepost 12 off U.S. 158 Bypass; ✆ **252/ 441-7132**). Beginning, intermediate, and advanced instruction is provided; for reservations, call **877/359-8447** or 252/ 441-4124; or go to www.kittyhawk.com.

ⓘ Milepost 8, U.S. 158 Bypass (✆ **252/ 441-7430;** www.nps.gov/wrbr).

✈ Norfolk International, 80 miles.

🛏 $$ **Cahoons Cottages,** 7213 S. Virginia Dare Trail, Nags Head (✆ **252/441-5538;** www.cahoonscottages.com). $$$ **The Tranquil House Inn,** 405 Queen Elizabeth St., Manteo (✆ **800/458-7069** or 252/473-1404; www.tranquilinn.com).

WHY THEY'LL THANK YOU: Feeling the wind beneath their wings.

The History of Flight **286**

Dayton Aviation Heritage Park
The Wright Stuff
Ages 6 & up • Dayton, Ohio, USA

When Orville and Wilbur Wright returned home from Kitty Hawk, North Carolina, in December 1903, they weren't national heroes. Sure, they had flown their frail contraption on the strong air currents gusting off the Outer Banks, but they still hadn't invented a practical means of powered flight. That job was still ahead of them—and Dayton, Ohio, was where they made it happen.

The Dayton Aviation Heritage Park celebrates the next 2 years of the Wright brothers saga. The core of the park is the replica **Wright Brothers Cycle Company,** a pleasant brick corner shop where the Wrights had made bicycles since 1892. (The original shop, and the Wright brothers' Dayton home, were moved to Greenfield Village). Back in their workshop, the brothers ignored their bicycle business— itself a newfangled technology then—to focus on their fledgling airplanes. The **visitor center** at 30 S. Williams occupies a site that was once the brothers' printing business, another sideline that financed the aviation obsession.

A SPAD XIII at the National Museum of the United Sates Air Force.

East of town, on the grounds of Wright-Patterson Air Force Base, is **Huffman Prairie Flying Field,** 2380 Memorial Rd. (📞 937/425-0008), an open pasture which the brothers used for test flights. You can see a replica of their hangar, plus a catapult tower they built to launch the pesky Wright Flyer II. The ultimate outcome was the 1905 Wright Flyer III, which could reliably take off, land, turn in midair, and fly as long as it had fuel in the gas tank. The Wright Flyer III can be seen at **Carillon Park,** 1000 Carillon Blvd. (📞 937/293-2841; www.daytonhistory.org), a 65-acre open-air history park with 25 exhibit buildings; from April to October, the Wright Brothers Aviation Center here displays the plane, three original Wright Bros. bicycles, and other Wright artifacts.

While you're out at Wright-Patterson Air Force Base, aviation geeks could spend at least half a day at the **National Museum**

of the United States Air Force, 1000 Spaatz St. (📞 937/255-3284; www.wpafb.af.mil/museum), and the neighboring **National Aviation Hall of Fame,** which honors famous flyers.

By a cool coincidence, the famous black poet **Paul Laurence Dunbar** was a schoolmate of Orville's and friend of the Wrights, who published his poetry in their printing shop. You can tour his house at 219 Paul Laurence Dunbar St. (📞 937/224-7061) on weekends April and September, Wednesday to Sunday from May to August.

ⓘ 22 S. Williams St. (📞 937/225-7705; www.nps.gov/daav).

✈ Dayton International.

🛏 $$$ **Crowne Plaza,** 33 E. 5th St. (📞 877/2-CROWNE [227-6963] or 937/224-0080; www.ichotelsgroup.com). $ **Days Inn Wright-Patterson,** 1891 Harshman Rd. (📞 937/236-8083; www.daysinn.com).

BEST TIME: May–Sept.

WHY THEY'LL THANK YOU: Getting off the ground was just the beginning . . .

---

287 The History of Flight

National Air and Space Museum
Plane Fantastic
All ages • Washington, D.C., USA

The one do-not-miss stop for families visiting our nation's capital, Air and Space is pretty much the star player on the Smithsonian museum team, at least as far as kids are concerned. I still catch my breath when I walk into its sleek entrance hall off

the Mall and see all those **historic aircraft** dangling from the ceiling—the Wright brothers' historic 1903 Wright Flyer, Charles Lindbergh's *Spirit of St. Louis,* the *Enola Gay* bomber that devastated Hiroshima, the *Friendship 7* capsule that took

John Glenn into space. Jaded as I am by IMAX movies, I made a point of having my kids sit through the classic *To Fly*, still my favorite of the genre; we spent another afternoon out in Virginia at the satellite location so we could see the space shuttle *Enterprise*. Whether you come here for the history, the science, or just the techno-thrill of seeing so much heavy metal, Air and Space delivers the goods.

Air and Space holds the largest collection of historic aircraft and spacecraft in the world; only about 10% of what it owns is actually on display, even with the annex out in Virginia. Besides gawking at the famous planes hanging out in the lobby, kids love to walk through the **Skylab orbital workshop;** other galleries highlight the solar system, U.S. manned spaceflights, and aviation during both world wars. You can sneak in some hard science education with **How Things Fly,** an interactive exhibit that demonstrates principles of flight and aerodynamics (the wind and smoke tunnels are especially fun), and get into some heady astrophysics with **Explore the Universe,** which probes theories about how the universe took shape. But this big, noisy, kid-packed museum isn't the sort of place where you want to be serious and thoughtful; besides the IMAX movie we wanted to do all the pumped-up extras like the **flight simulators** and the **space show** at the planetarium—admission to the museum is free, but very few families get away without buying a ticket for one of these add-ons.

The second part of the museum is out near Dulles Airport in Chantilly, Virginia, at 14390 Air and Space Museum Pkwy., where two gigantic hangars—one for aviation artifacts, the other for space artifacts—accompany a 164-foot-tall **observation tower** for watching planes land and take off at Dulles. The **space hangar** is the length of three football fields—it has to be in order to house such huge artifacts as the space shuttle, rocket boosters, spacewalk capsules, and a full-scale prototype of the Mars Pathfinder lander. The scale of this technology is awesome, and you just can't appreciate it unless you stand right next to these babies and crane your neck upward.

(i) Independence Ave. SW, btw. 4th and 7th sts. (© **202/633-1000;** www.nasm.si.edu).

✈ Ronald Reagan Washington National, 5 miles. Dulles International, 26 miles. Baltimore-Washington International, 30 miles.

🛏 $$ **Embassy Suites Hotel Downtown,** 1250 22nd St. NW (© **800/EMBASSY** [362-2779] or 202/857-3388; www.embassysuitesdcmetro.com). $$$ **Hilton Washington,** 1919 Connecticut Ave. NW (© **800/HILTONS** [445-8667] or 202/483-3000; www.washington.hilton.com).

WHY THEY'LL THANK YOU: Historic flying machines soaring in the lobby.

The History of Flight **288**

Kennedy Space Center
10 . . . 9 . . . 8 . . .

Ages 4 & up • Titusville, Florida, USA

Spaceflight has lost so much of its glamour that it can be hard for kids to comprehend how exciting it once was to watch a mighty

booster rocket blast off from the launch pad at Cape Canaveral. So pop in a DVD of *The Right Stuff* or *Apollo 13* before your

The Kennedy Space Center.

trip to the Space Coast. Make them see how being an astronaut was once the coolest job a kid could aspire to.

You don't have to be a space buff to be awed by the sheer grandeur of the facilities at NASA's primary space-launch facility. Begin your visit at the **Kennedy Space Center Visitor Complex**—though it's a bit theme-park-slick, it does outline the history of space exploration well, and there are real NASA rockets on display, as well as (the coolest thing to me) the actual Mercury Mission Control Room from the 1960s. Hands-on activities, a daily "encounter" with an astronaut, and an IMAX theater make this place where kids will want to hang out. The **Astronaut Hall of Fame,** a separate attraction at the center, pays tribute to the Mercury, Gemini, and Apollo space jockeys, along with even more vintage spacecraft—a Mercury 7 capsule, a Gemini training capsule, and an Apollo 14 command module—and several space-y simulator rides. Plan ahead (✆ **321/ 449-4400** for a reservation) to snag a **lunch with an astronaut**—even such greats as John Glenn, Jim Lovell, Walt

Cunningham, and Jon McBride have taken their turns in this daily event.

Narrated **bus tours** depart every 10 minutes to explore the sprawling space-center grounds. Stops include the LC-39 Observation Gantry, with a dramatic 360-degree view over launch pads; the International Space Station Center, where scientists and engineers prepare additions to the space station now in orbit; and the Apollo/Saturn V Center, which includes artifacts (a moon rock to touch!), films, interactive exhibits, and the 363-foot-tall Saturn V, the most powerful U.S. rocket ever launched. It's not all Disney-fied, which in my opinion is a plus, but if the kids get restless (especially given the typical Florida heat), you can hop on the next bus and move on.

The real thrill, of course, is to see a **shuttle launch;** call ✆ **321/867-5000** or check www.ksc.nasa.gov for a schedule of upcoming takeoffs (always an iffy thing, depending on weather or equipment problems), then buy tickets at the visitor complex or online at www.ksctickets.com. Or view shuttle launches the way the locals do: from the causeways leading to the islands and on U.S. 1 as it skirts the waterfront in Titusville.

(i) NASA Pkwy. (Fla. 405; (C) **321/449-4444** for info, 321/449-4444 for reservations; www.kennedyspacecenter.com).

✈ Melbourne International, 22 miles. Orlando International, 35 miles.

🛏 $$$ **DoubleTree Hotel Cocoa Beach Oceanfront,** 2080 N. Atlantic Ave., Cocoa Beach ((C) **800/552-3224** or 321/783-9222; www.cocoabeachdoubletree.com). $$ **Riverview Hotel,** 103 Flagler Ave., New Smyrna Beach ((C) **800/945-7416** or 386/428-5858; www.riverview hotel.com).

WHY THEY'LL THANK YOU: Huge rockets up close.

Space Center Houston
The Face of Flight Control
Ages 6 & up • Clear Lake, Texas, USA

Once NASA spacecraft take off from the Kennedy Space Center at Cape Canaveral, during flight they are monitored from the Johnson Space Center in Houston, hence the famous quote from *Apollo 13*—"Houston, we have a problem." Like its Florida sibling, the Houston Space Center has turned its visitor center into an exciting **interactive exhibit hall** that makes the tram tours of the actual facility almost beside the point. In fact, the folks in Houston upstaged their Florida colleagues by bringing in Disney Imagineering to help design its exhibits—but having real access to the NASA goods makes this so much more than a theme-park attraction.

Inside the Space Center, for example, you can take a virtual visit to the hottest project in space, the 16-nation 361-foot-long **International Space Station,** via computer console in a gallery that simulates outer-space weightlessness. The **Feel of Space** gallery explores what life is like for astronauts aboard the space station, with a Mission Briefing Officer who shows how everyday tasks, such as showering and eating, are complicated by a microgravity environment. After this entertaining presentation, you're free to

enter a training module loaded up with sophisticated computer technology to try your hand at landing a lunar orbiter, retrieving a satellite, or exploring a shuttle system. Artifacts in the **Starship Gallery** include the Mercury Atlas *Faith 7* capsule flown by Gordon Cooper, the Gemini V Spacecraft piloted by Pete Conrad and Gordon Cooper, a Lunar Roving Vehicle Trainer, the Apollo 17 Command Module, the giant Skylab Trainer, and the Apollo-Soyuz Trainer. The **Kids Space Place** is a playgroundlike area where kids can try out for themselves various tasks an astronaut must master. In *Blastoff!* a film audience is treated to the sensation of liftoff before getting an update on current flight missions by a live NASA information officer. And that's not to mention the largest IMAX in Texas . . .

For a direct experience of NASA you can take the 1½-hour **tram tour** that takes you to, among other places, the **International Space Station Assembly Building** and the **Historic Mission Control Center.** This is still a working facility, so expect the precise tour route to change according to what projects are in high gear at the time; but you do get to see things as they happen, especially interesting if there's a shuttle mission in progress. Look for astronauts in midtraining—someday it could be one of your kids.

ⓘ 1601 NASA Rd. 1 (© **281/244-2100;** www.spacecenter.org).

✈ George Bush Intercontinental, 37 miles.

🛏 $$$ **Hilton University of Houston,** 4800 Calhoun Rd. (© **800/HOTELUH** [468-3584] or 713/741-2447; www.hilton.com).

WHY THEY'LL THANK YOU: Zero gravity.

---

290 Inventions & Industry

The Windmills of Kinderdijk

All ages • Kinderdijk, the Netherlands

The tidy Dutch village of Kinderdijk offers a chance to show the kids a picture postcard view that they'll never forget: 19 historic windmills—most dating from around 1740—set in a windmill park along a branching canal.

The milling complex itself is a series of eight stone windmills built in 1738, eight thatched windmills built in 1740, and two stone windmills built in 1760. One windmill dating from 1521 burned down in 1997, but has since been restored. Their powerful mill sails (each about 14m/46 ft. long) harnesses the force of the wind to turn large paddlewheels, which pick up water and sluice it into canals, draining into a reservoir and then the nearby River Lek. One windmill has been fitted with period furnishings; a miller is on hand to operate the mill and explain its technology. They're turned on for effect in July and August, but were officially retired after World War II, when diesel-driven pumping engines built in the 1920s took over the job. In 1997, they were placed on the list of UNESCO World Heritage sites.

The village is close to Rotterdam, which makes a good home base. Along with admiring the windmills, you can take a half-hour canal cruise from April to September, but you'll get an ever better view by cycling the canal paths, laid out along the absolutely flat polder embankments. It's an evocative sight, worthy of the Dutch masters, with the flat North Sea sunlight shimmering on the polder's vivid green grass under a mackerel-colored sky.

Although the view here is lovely, it is an ecosystem in transition. The windmills were meant to pump excess water from the land the Dutch had reclaimed from the sea, but the ocean still threatens the low country of the Netherlands. Although the Netherlands has the world's most sophisticated flood control system, the nation is particularly vulnerable to rising sea levels due to global warming and 65% of its land is already below sea level. As every schoolchild knows, ever since the Middle Ages, dikes have been built here to turn costal marshes into arable land. Once the Dutch began to play with nature, an inevitable cycle of events began to play out. As the land was drained, the layers of boggy peat would eventually compress and the ground level drop even further, requiring future drainage—making the underlying peat compress even more. While children will no doubt enjoy the iconic windmills, the area stands as a good environmental lesson.

Kinderijk remains peaceful, rural, and traditional, making it an ideal spot for leisurely exploration. Be sure to go in the summer when the windmills are turning.

ⓘ www.kinderdijk.org/route.shtml.

✈ Rotterdam.

🛏 $$$$ **Westin Rotterdam,** Weena 686, Rotterdam (© **31/10/430-2000;**

www.westin.com). $ **Hotel Kinderdijk,** West Kinderdijk 361, Alblasserdam (© **31/ 78/691-2425**). $ **Het Wapen van**

Alblasserdam, Dam 24, Alblasserdam (© **31/78/691-4711**).

WHY THEY'LL THANK YOU: Slowly turning windmills.

Inventions & Industry **291**

Ironbridge Gorge

Ages 6 & up • Telford, England

The 19th-century Industrial Revolution, as taught in most schools, can be a dull and dreary subject. Not so here, at this complex of historic museums in the English Midlands, just north of Birmingham. The Ironbridge Gorge Museums vibrantly bring to life how this 19th-century burst of technology changed the world.

The iron-rich Severn Valley was like the Silicon Valley of its time. In 1709 a Quaker ironmaster named Abraham Darby invented a new iron-smelting process, marking the beginning of new transportation and engineering innovations that started the area buzzing. The most impressive feature of the

site is the famous **Iron Bridge** across the River Severn, cast in 1779 by Abraham Darby III. An engineering marvel of its time, its great arch drew tourists from all over the world; the original tollhouse, at the southern end, has exhibits about its history. At the **Museum of the Gorge,** a Gothic-style riverside warehouse from 1834, exhibits detail the history of the Gorge, including a 12m (40-ft.) scale model of the river valley as it was in 1796. In the **Coalbrookdale Museum of Iron** and **Darby Houses** you can tour the first modern ironworks, with its vast water-power system and great blast furnace, and peer into the ironmasters'

Ironbridge Gorge Museums.

houses, workers' cottages, chapels, and church. There are even more historic recreations at the **Blists Hill Open Air Museum,** which presents an entire small Victorian town complete with bank, grocer's shop, chemist, printing shop, bakery, and sweet shop; the back streets are busy with small offices, works, and factories including a working foundry and iron rolling mill, all explicated by costumed staff. Lots of ancillary industries sprang up around the ironworks, and these sites offer lots of hands-on activities for children: the **Jackfield Tile Museum,** with its wealth of decorative tiles and ceramics; the **Coalport China Museum,** in a restored china factory; and the **Broseley Pipeworks,** a wonderfully preserved example of an ancient local industry, the manufacture of clay tobacco pipes. Of course, abundant natural resources made all this manufacture possible, a fact underscored when you visit the underground **Tar Tunnel,** where natural bitumen oozes freely from the walls.

The site's newest and most high-tech attraction, **Enginuity,** is an interactive museum full of gadgets; kids can pull a locomotive, harness water power to generate electricity, or compete against a robot.

ⓘ **Ironbridge Gorge Museums** (✆ **44/ 1952/433522** [Mon–Fri] or 44/1952/432166 [Sat–Sun]; www.ironbridge.org.uk).

🚃 Telford, 3 hr. from London.

🛏 $ **Library House,** 11 Severn Bank, Ironbridge (✆ **44/1952/432299;** www. libraryhouse.com). $$ **The Valley Hotel,** Ironbridge (✆ **800/528-1234** in the U.S., or 44/1952/432247; www.thevalleyhotel. co.uk).

BEST TIME: Easter to early Nov (some sites closed mid-Nov–Mar).

WHY THEY'LL THANK YOU: It puts the Revolution back into the Industrial Revolution.

292 Inventions & Industry

National Coal Museum
Going Down the Big Pit
Ages 8 & up • Blaenafon, Wales

Before my Welsh ancestors moved to America to work in the coal mines of West Virginia, they learned their wearying trade here, going "down the mines": in the coal-rich district of Wales. That personal connection makes it especially chilling for me to go down a 300-foot (90m) deep mine shaft at this refurbished mining site on the outskirts of Blaenafon, a short drive northeast from Cardiff.

It's not an experience for claustrophobes, that's for sure, but the kids will feel like real adventurers, "kitting up" with their helmet lamps, surrendering modern items like mobile phones and cameras, and making the heart-sinking descent down the mineshaft in a clanking pit cage.

(Children have to be at least 1m/3 ft. tall to go down the pit; there's a simulated mine tour up top for those who can't take the real tour.) The whitewashed plaster colliery buildings have also been outfitted with some fascinating interpretive displays, including the Pithead Baths, where miners went after their shifts to scrub off the black coal dust that inevitably coated them head to toe by the end of the day. (Don't worry, moms, they've cleaned up the tunnels since then—the kids won't come out totally grimy.) For my kids, it was sobering indeed to realize how hard a miner's life was—working underground day after day for pittance wages, living with the threat of deadly cave-ins, straining at this physically demanding labor—and even more sobering to realize that for many Welsh communities, mining was the only job option, and mine owners virtually controlled their lives. The museum displays are surprisingly upbeat, emphasizing the technological and safety improvements over the years, but I came away with nothing but admiration for the endurance of my tough Welsh forebears.

While you're in the Cardiff, don't miss **St. Fagan's** (St. Fagan's Rd., 7km/4 miles west of Cardiff city centre, just off the A432; © **44/29/2057-3500**), a fascinating open-air museum where more than 40 historic buildings have been set around the 40-hectare (100-acre) parklands of a 16th-century manor house. It's a great way to help kids understand how coal mining fits into (some would say disrupted) traditional Welsh history and culture. And if a trip to north Wales is also on your itinerary, another fascinating stop is the

National Slate Museum in tiny Llanberis (© **44/1286/870-630**), an evocative relic of Wales' other great 19th-century industry, slate quarrying. Not only will you see the massive works that stripped these mountains on the slate surfaces, you'll step into a series of workers' cottages furnished in different historic eras, a wonderful slice of social history.

ⓘ **National Coal Museum,** Blaenafon (© **44/1495/790-311;** www.museumwales. ac.uk/en/bigpit).

✈ Cardiff.

🛏 $$ **Park Plaza Hotel Cardiff,** Greyfriars Rd., Cardiff, CF10 3AL (© **44/29/ 2011-1111**). $ **The Big Sleep Hotel,** Bute Terrace, Cardiff CF10 2FE (© **44/29/2063-6363;** www.thebigsleephotel.com).

WHY THEY'LL THANK YOU: Going down a mine wearing lighted helmets; just like real miners.

National Museum of Emerging Science
Engaging Their Minds
Ages 8 & up • Odaiba Tokyo

What kid wouldn't like to play with robots? It sounds unlikely, but at the National Museum of Emerging Science, it's an everyday occurrence. Situated on Odaiba, a large artificial island in Tokyo, the museum focuses on science and technology; with hands-on exhibits, virtual reality rides, and, a state-of-the-art planetarium.

Kids no doubt will want to see robots, and they will have come to the right place; Japan leads the world in robot development and the exhibit includes industrial robots as well as humanoid and rescue robots, such as the snakelike robot Souryu. The star attraction is ASIMO, the world's most famous intelligent robot. Demonstrations illustrate the various movements of

humanoid robots and rescue methods used by the rescue robots.

The **"Innovation and the Future"** exhibit features micromachines, machines almost too small to be seen with the naked eye. There's a hands-on area where children can fiddle with the machines themselves, which they've been dying to do all along.

The Life Science exhibit includes a display illustrating the role of a genome, the genetic information passed on from parents to their children. In this area, kids can observe living organisms and cells and learn about cellular science through videos, graphic panels, and games.

Earth, Environment and Me features a digital "zone" where environmental issues are looked at from the perspective of science and technology. Visitors are encouraged to think about the fate of the earth as it relates to economy, politics, and daily life. After engaging in this process, there is an area where kids can voice their thoughts on the environment, making for a lively learning experience.

Adjacent to the museum are two other attractions that aren't educational, but are sure to be a hit with the kids. The first is **Megaweb**, 1 Aomi, Kotu-ku, Odaiba (✆ **81/3/3599-0808;** www.megaweb.gr.jp), a sprawling amusement park, which is actually a Toyota showroom—but the kids won't care. They'll be distracted by the virtual thrill rides, driving simulators, a 3-D motion theater, and driverless electric commuter cars. (Some of the rides do have height restrictions.) Inside of Megaweb are the Toyota City Showcase which includes hybrids and racing cars, and the Universal Design Showcase, featuring cars for people with disabilities. Outside is a tantalizingly large Ferris wheel that takes 16 minutes to make a complete turn.

You can top off the day at **Joypolis Sega,** Tokyo's most sophisticated virtual amusement arcade, brought to you—by you guessed it—Sega. Kids can enjoy the latest in video games and virtual reality attractions. There are virtual reality video games where players use high-tech equipment to get the sense that they are engaged in a variety of exciting activities, including bobsledding. The 3-D sightseeing tour has seats that move to the action on the screen. This is a place even jaded teens can enjoy. Joypolis Sega, Tokyo Decks, 3rd Floor, Odaiba (✆ **81/3/5500-1801**).

ⓘ **The National Museum of Emerging Science,** 2–41 Aomi, Koto-ku, Odaiba, (✆ **81/3/3570-9151;** www.miraikan.jst. go.jp).

✈ Narita Airport.

🛏 $$$ **Hotel Nikko,** 1–9–1 Daiba, (✆ **800/645-5687** in the U.S. and Canada, or 81/3/5500-5500; www.hnt.co.jp/index_ en.html). $$$ **The New Otani Tokyo** (✆ **81/3/3265-1111;** www.newotani.co. jp/en/tokyo/index.html).

WHY THEY'LL THANK YOU: Those fascinating robots.

Edison Historic Site
The Light Bulbs Go On
Ages 6 & up • West Orange, New Jersey, USA

"I always invented to obtain money to go on inventing," Thomas Edison once said. The romantic notion of a genius tinkering alone at night over a breakthrough invention? That wasn't Edison. Yes, he was a gifted chemist and visionary, but he was also a shrewd businessman who amassed a fortune. Touring the Edison Laboratories is a fascinating look at one of the most efficient R & D operations in history.

Though Edison's first lab was in Menlo Park, New Jersey, this larger West Orange complex was in operation for over 40 years and accounted for over half of his patents. Notice how closely the ivy-covered red-brick buildings are set together—Edison designed it this way so he wouldn't waste too much time scurrying from chemistry lab to machine shop to drafting room. The kids may be surprised to learn that, of the 1,093 patents credited to Edison—the most any American has ever obtained—many were actually invented by other scientists who worked for him. Walking around the restored lab complex, you can visualize his team of some 200

Edison National Historic Site.

researchers, hired to refine and improve existing inventions. There were light bulbs before Edison's, but his was more reliable, long-lasting, and easy to manufacture; the telegraph, the phonograph, the stock ticker, the movie camera, and projector were all devices that other scientists pursued at the same time, but Edison's versions *worked better*. Another 10,000 workers in the attached factory (not part of the historic site) then mass-produced these inventions for commercial sale—he controlled the entire cycle. Accessories, too—there's a music recording studio you can peek into, where Edison engineers made sure phonograph customers would have something to play on their new machines.

One mile from the lab complex, you can see the fruits of Edison's labors in **Glenmont,** a 29-room red Queen Anne–style mansion in Llewellyn Park which Edison bought for his second wife, Mina. All the original furnishings are here, reflecting the formal Victorian style of the era, with lots of ornate carved wood, damask wall coverings, and stained-glass windows; things get comfier upstairs in the family living room, where Edison's children sometimes helped him look up scientific references in shelves full of books. One thing's for sure: This was probably the first house in the neighborhood with a phonograph, let alone the Home Projecting Kinetoscope—the Edison children must have been very in demand for play dates.

ⓘ Main St. and Lakeside Ave. (© **973/736-0550;** www.nps.gov/edis).

✈ Liberty International, Newark, NJ, 15 miles.

🛏 $$ **Excelsior Hotel,** 45 W. 81st St. (© **800/368-4575** or 212/362-9200; www. excelsiorhotelny.com). $$$ **Le Parker Meridien,** 118 W. 57th St. (© **800/543-4300** or 212/245-5000; www.parkermeridien.com).

WHY THEY'LL THANK YOU: One percent inspiration, 99% perspiration.

Greenfield Village
Henry Ford's History Lesson
All ages • Dearborn, Michigan, USA

Automobile magnate Henry Ford had two passions: cars and history. No, make that three passions: cars, history, and philanthropy. (Plus he was really into clocks.) Once the phenomenal success of his Model T made him a multimillionaire, he could indulge all these passions by building a 90-acre indoor-outdoor museum complex. And Ford couldn't have spent his money any better.

Greenfield Village is more than just another historic re-creation; it's a glorious hodgepodge of actual homes transported here from around the United States (and even a few from Europe), most of them associated with specific individuals Ford admired. With money-is-no-object largesse, Ford acquired the home and bicycle shop of the Wright brothers, the farm where tire maker Harvey Firestone grew up, the workshop of botanist Luther Burbank, a courthouse where country lawyer Abraham Lincoln tried cases, the boyhood home where H. J. Heinz first bottled horseradish sauce. He snapped up the homes of poet Robert Frost and dictionary author Noah Webster, and a schoolhouse where educator William McGuffey taught. Ford's own birthplace is here, too. If he couldn't get the original, Ford had a meticulous replica made, as he did with George Washington Carver's log cabin birthplace **382** and Thomas Edison's New Jersey invention complex, above. Keeping these homes company are everything from a Cotswold stone cottage to a Cape Cod windmill to a set of Georgia slave quarters to a London clockmaker's mechanical glockenspiel to a fanciful 1913 carousel. You won't be able to imagine yourself into any single era, but you'll sure pick up vivid snippets of the past.

Once you've done Greenfield Village, there's yet more to see at the **Henry Ford Museum** next door, a 12-acre repository of Americana. With the same sort of acquisitive curiosity, Ford's staff assembled collections of historic airplanes (including the Fokker that Admiral Byrd used to explore the Arctic) and of course cars—everything from a 1901 Model T to one of the few existing '48 Tuckers to the limousine in which President John F. Kennedy was shot. My favorite things here are an original neon McDonald's sign, an unsolicited testimonial scrawled by bank robber Clyde Barrow ("I have drove Fords exclusively when I could get away with one"), and Buckminster Fuller's 1946 house of the future. From here, you can also take a tour of the famous **Ford Rouge Plant,** where you can see in action the factory assembly line process that made Ford's fortune. Two days is not enough time to see everything here.

ⓘ 20900 Oakwood Blvd. (✆ **313/271-1620;** www.hfmgv.org).

✈ Detroit Metropolitan, 10 miles.

🛏 $$$ **Dearborn Inn,** 20301 Oakwood Blvd. (✆ **800/228-9290** or 313/271-2700; www.marriotthotels.com). $ **Econo Lodge Dearborn,** 23730 Michigan Ave. (✆ **313/565-7250;** www.choicehotels. com).

WHY THEY'LL THANK YOU: History is made by individuals.

Hoover Dam
Concrete Colossus of the Southwest
Ages 6 & up • Boulder City, Nevada, USA

U.S. 93, which runs between Las Vegas, Nevada, and Kingman, Arizona, lays its ribbon of concrete right across one of the great engineering wonders of the world, Hoover Dam. Built between 1931 and 1935, this behemoth Depression-era project redrew the map of America: If it hadn't been for Hoover Dam, Arizona and California would never have had enough electricity and water to sustain their subsequent population boom. And yes, the dam also created the largest artificial lake in the United States, 110-mile-long **Lake Mead.** Driving across Hoover Dam, traffic crawls as motorists gape at the view, with smooth Lake Mead on one hand and a plummeting gorge on the other. But why let the kids be content with a mere view, when you can go inside the belly of the beast?

Going face to face with this much concrete is an awesome experience. Hoover Dam stands 726 feet tall from bedrock to the roadway atop it. At the top, it's 45 feet thick, which is stout enough, but it widens the farther down you go, until at the base it's a whopping 660 feet thick. The dam was named after Herbert Hoover, not just because he was president when the bill was signed to build it, but because the Boulder Canyon dam was in many ways his idea—as Secretary of Commerce in the early 1920s, Hoover, a civil engineer himself, first urged the southwestern states to consider such an undertaking.

While much of the Hoover Dam story is told via **historic photographs** in interpretive galleries, the part kids really remember is taking **elevators** 500 feet down into the wall of Black Canyon, then walking down a 250-foot-long tunnel to look at the guts of the power plant, with its eight huge generators. At the end of the tour, don't miss going up to the observation deck to get that **panoramic view** of Lake Mead and the Colorado basin. Functional as it is in many ways, the dam still has a streamlined Art Deco flair—check out the sculptured panels decorating the central two elevator towers rising from the top of the dam, the Nevada one celebrating the dam's benefits—flood control, navigation, irrigation, water supply, and power—the Arizona one paying tribute to Indian tribes that once lived here.

Hoover Dam makes a handy day trip from Las Vegas, 30 miles away, though I'd recommend combining a Hoover Dam visit with a stay on Lake Mead in a **houseboat** (contact **Seven Crown Resorts,** Box 16247, Irvine, CA; ℂ **800/752-9669;** www.sevencrown.com). Another fun way to visit the dam is on a **paddle-wheeler cruise** from **Lake Mead Cruises** (ℂ **702/293-6180;** www.lakemeadcruises.com).

ⓘ U.S. 93 (ℂ **866/291-TOUR** [291-8687] or 702/294-3517; www.usbr.gov/lc/hooverdam).

✈ McCarran International.

⌫ $$ **Mandalay Bay,** 3950 Las Vegas Blvd. S. (ℂ **877/632-7000** or 702/632-7000; www.mandalaybay.com). $$ **MGM Grand,** 3799 Las Vegas Blvd. S. (ℂ **800/929-1111** or 702/891-7777; www.mgmgrand.com).

WHY THEY'LL THANK YOU: Feeling the power of those generators.

Greenwich
Where Time Begins
Ages 8 & up • England

It's one of those classic photo ops: Standing astride the **Greenwich Line,** 0° 0' 0" longitude, the point from which, since 1884, all terrestrial longitudes around the globe are calculated. Tell your children they're standing on the dividing line between the Eastern and Western hemispheres; if they were here at the stroke of midnight, they could have one foot in 2 different days, for by official world decree a new day begins at the Greenwich Line.

The redbrick house on the hill was designed by a then-unknown architect, Sir Christopher Wren (himself a passionate amateur astronomer), who won the commission from Charles II in 1675. The king's motives were quite practical: Improvements in astronomy would lead to better navigation techniques, which would help Britain dominate the seven seas. (And, no surprise, it worked out exactly the way he'd hoped.) Wren's elegant **Octagon Room** was the observatory used by the first Astronomer Royal, John Flamsteed; unfortunately, because it wasn't properly aligned with celestial meridians, it was useless for observation—a fact no one bothered to tell the king—and telescopes were surreptitiously installed in a shed in the garden instead. As the years passed, uniform timekeeping became more and more important, especially to regulate railway schedules. The synchronized clocks of Victorian England eventually became a model for the rest of the world, and just as all distances were calculated from Greenwich, so was Greenwich Time established as the world standard. In this respect at least, England will always remain the center of the world.

Although the **Royal Observatory** is no longer a working observatory—light pollution from the metropolis forced a move in the 1940s—it does have galleries full of historic stargazing and timekeeping instruments (including England's largest refracting telescope, a 28-in. lens, and a rare camera obscura), which children will find of varying interest. But be sure to go out onto the roof, where there is a spectacular panorama of London, especially the nearby skyscrapers of Canary Wharf. Look up to see the red **Time Ball,** which slides down its mast every day at 13.00 hours—the world's first public time-indicating device.

Frequent ferryboats from either Charing Cross Pier or Tower Pier run every half-hour or so to Greenwich, taking about an hour; the train trip from Waterloo Station is faster, about 15 minutes, but less atmospheric.

ⓘ **The Royal Observatory,** Greenwich Park (✆ **44/20/8312-6608;** www.nmm. ac.uk).

✈ Heathrow.

🛏 $$$ **London Bridge Hotel,** 8–18 London Bridge St. 9 (✆ **44/20/7855-2200;** www.londonbridgehotel.co.uk). $$ **Vicarage Private Hotel,** 10 Vicarage Gate, South Kensington (✆ **44/20/7229-4030;** www.londonvicaragehotel.com).

WHY THEY'LL THANK YOU: Every time they look at a clock, they'll remember where the day begins and ends.

Stargazing on Nantucket

Ages 6 & up • Massachusetts, USA

Though her fame has sadly faded, Nantucket native **Maria Mitchell** (1818–89) was quite possibly the most famous American scientist of the 19th century, man or woman. In October 1847, on the rooftop of her family home, this self-educated 29-year-old trained her telescope on the night sky and became the first person ever to record a sighting of a comet that was invisible to the naked eye, an accomplishment that vaulted her to international honor.

On Nantucket, Mitchell is remembered at a complex of science centers. Your first stop should be on the southwest edge of Nantucket Town at Maria's birthplace, the **Mitchell House,** 1 Vestal St. (© **508/228-2896**), a modest Quaker home built in 1790. It was turned into a museum soon after Mitchell's death by her former students and colleagues and contains many family artifacts, including her own telescope. Take time to wander through its wildflower and herb gardens. The nearby **Hinchman House Natural Science Museum,** 7 Milk St. (© **508/228-0898**), expands Mitchell's passion for observation beyond astronomy; yes, there are exhibits about Nantucket flora and fauna, but there's also a raft of activities, such as bird-watching, wildflower walks, and hands-on discovery classes for children and adults alike. Dissecting an owl pellet can be fascinating. Over on the harborfront, the Maria Mitchell Association's **aquarium,** 28 Washington St. (© **508/228-5387**), is small but very kid-friendly, focusing on the local marine ecology.

It's only fitting that, because of Maria Mitchell, this tiny island has not one but two observatories, and if the night sky is clear, don't pass up the opportunity to stargaze here, far from the light pollution that frustrates astronomers in big cities. Out on a hill south of town, **Loines Observatory,** 59 Milk St. Extension (© **508/228-8690**), is open to the public every clear Monday, Wednesday, and Friday night in summer at 9pm (rest of the year Fri 8pm); if there's an interesting sky event, like the close orbit of Mars the summer we visited, the line may be out the door. The **Vestal Street Observatory** in town at 3 Vestal St. (© **508/228-9273**), where Maria and her astronomer father swept the skies in the 19th century, is too close to town for nighttime stargazing, but tours every day at 11am show off a good exhibit on the science of astronomy. Don't miss the outdoor scale model of the solar system.

ⓘ **Maria Mitchell Association,** 4 Vestal St. (© **508/228-9198;** www.mmo.org).

✈ Nantucket Airport.

🛏 $$ **Jared Coffin House,** 29 Broad St., Nantucket (© **800/248-2405** or 508/228-2400; www.jaredcoffinhouse. com).

BEST TIME: Early June to late Aug.

WHY THEY'LL THANK YOU: A great place to start peering through telescopes.

Griffith Observatory
Planetarium Hollywood
Ages 6 & up • Los Angeles, California, USA

Film buffs instantly recognize this stream-lined **Art Deco observatory** in L.A.'s rambling Griffith Park from the climactic scenes of the 1955 James Dean classic film *Rebel Without a Cause*. My kids, however, know it from the climactic scenes of the 1999 Steve Martin/Eddie Murphy comedy *Bowfinger*. But so what if they don't get the *Rebel Without a Cause* reference? Who could fail to dig this white stucco complex with its three bronze domes, slung into the south side of Mount Hollywood with a killer panorama of Los Angeles spread out below? In the daytime, the lawn of the observatory is one of the best places in the city to view the famous Hollywood sign; on warm nights, with the lights twink-ling below, the Griffith Observatory's wide terrace is one of the most romantic places in L.A. And if you manage to steer the children inside to do a little stargazing while you're up there at night, you're ahead of the game.

This Hollywood Hills landmark was built in 1935 in the vaguely Mediterranean style studio moguls of that era favored, and underwent a major renovation during 2003–06. A white obelisk in front honors six great astronomers of the past: Hipparchus, Copernicus, Galileo, Kepler, Newton, and Herschel. The large central dome houses a state-of-the-art **planetarium,** where nar-rated projectors display the stars and plan-ets that are nearly impossible to observe outdoors, what with all the smog and light pollution of the L.A. metro sprawl. Like most planetariums, it also screens various multimedia shows of varying scientific seri-ousness. We generally skip the planetar-ium, however, and head straight into the adjacent **Hall of Science,** which holds exhibits on galaxies, meteorites, and other

The Griffith Observatory in Los Angeles.

astronomical subjects—cool objects such as a mechanical orrery, a Tesla coil, and scales where you can check your weight on different planets. A Foucault pendulum mesmerized my boys as it methodically swung in the main rotunda, demonstrating the earth's rotation, and detailed 6-foot topographical models of the earth and the moon provide focal points in the side galleries.

The observatory's two flanking domes each house a telescope—in the west one, a triple-beamed **solar telescope** trained on the sun for daytime visitors, in the east one a 12-inch **refracting telescope.** On clear nights visitors can climb to the roof and wait their turn to gaze through it at the moon and planets. This is, after all, an observatory, and although it has never had the astronomical prestige of its California neighbor **Mount Palomar,** it does attend to sky matters.

ⓘ 2800 E. Observatory Rd., Griffith Park (✆ **323/664-1191;** www.griffithobs.org).

✈ Los Angeles International.

🛏 $$$ **Beverly Garland's Holiday Inn,** 4222 Vineland Ave., North Hollywood (✆ **800/BEVERLY** [238-3759] or 818/980-8000; www.beverlygarland.com). $$ **Roosevelt Hotel,** Hollywood, 7000 Hollywood Blvd. (✆ **800/950-7667** or 323/466-7000; www.hollywoodroosevelt.com).

WHY THEY'LL THANK YOU: A chance to study the other Hollywood stars.

Stargazing 300

Mount Palomar
Where Stars Shine over the Desert
Ages 8 & up • Mount Palomar, California, USA

In July 2005, the world was startled to learn that a 10th planet had been found orbiting our sun (just after my sixth grader got an A for his model of the solar system—a model that's now obsolete). And where was that astonishing observation made? At Mount Palomar, California, where Cal Tech astronomers have been making scientific headlines since 1949.

This mountaintop in San Diego County was purchased in 1934 because light pollution from the fast-growing Los Angeles metropolis had become a problem for Cal Tech's former observatory, atop Mount Wilson in Pasadena. For the new site, Mount Wilson's 100-inch telescope—through which Edwin Hubble had studied distant galaxies to prove the universe is expanding—was to be outdone with a **200-inch reflecting telescope.** A Depression-era American public eagerly tracked the progress of this grandiose plan. At first, no one could build a stable lens that big—until the Corning Glass company made one using its new heat-resistant Pyrex glass. The immense glass blank was carefully shipped cross-country, ground, and polished for a couple of years. Meanwhile, other parts for the telescope had to be made in shipyards, the only workshops geared to manufacture parts that big (which explains the battleship-gray hue of the scope's housings). After a 5-year hiatus during World War II, the telescope was finally ready to assemble in 1947.

Dedicated in 1948, the Mount Palomar telescope was the world's largest until 1976 (when an even-larger Soviet model debuted). Today, visitors can stand on the gallery surrounding the 200-inch Hale telescope to see the big instrument, but be prepared—the dome is kept at a steady temperature calibrated to nighttime temperatures on this mountain, so you'll need a sweatshirt or jacket even in summer. To get the full scoop, come on a Saturday for an hour-long explanatory **tour** (book a week ahead). **Astronomical photos** and other exhibits are displayed in an outer gallery, but nothing as extensive as the ones at **Griffith Observatory** down in Los Angeles.

My kids were baffled by the back-roads trek it took to get here, until we explained that isolation is *good* for astronomy. They were surprised when they saw the small, simple facility beneath that serene-looking dome in a mountain meadow. But the size of the Hale telescope, and the quiet hum of serious science going on, gradually began to impress them. They no longer felt like tourists—they felt like hardy explorers in pursuit of knowledge.

ⓘ 35899 Canfield Rd. (✆ **626/395-4033;** www.astro.caltech.edu/palomarnew).

✈ San Diego.

🛏 $$$ **Catamaran Resort Hotel,** 3999 Mission Blvd. (✆ **800/422-8386** or 858/488-1081; www.catamaranresort.com). $$ **Park Manor Suites,** 525 Spruce St. (✆ **800/874-2649** or 619/291-0999; www.parkmanorsuites.com).

WHY THEY'LL THANK YOU: Big scope, bigger sky.

301 **Stargazing**

Mauna Kea
Stargazing at the Top of the World
Ages 13 & up (summit), 10 & up (visitor center) • Mauna Kea, Hawaii, USA

The snowcapped summit of Mauna Kea—the world's tallest mountain, if measured from its base on the ocean floor—is the best place on earth for astronomical observation. It's not just the height, it's also its location near the equator, where clear, pollution-free skies give way to pitch-black nights undisturbed by urban light. That's why Mauna Kea is home to no fewer than 13 world-class telescopes, including the **Keck Telescope,** the world's largest. Even with the naked eye, the stargazing from here is fantastic.

Many tours that go to the summit won't take anyone under 16 or any pregnant women, due to the high altitude. If you opt not to go up, it's still cool to view the model of the Keck Telescope down in Waimea, 65-1120 Mamalahoa Hwy. (✆ **808/885-7887;** www.keckobservatory.org). Developed by the University of California and the California Institute of Technology, the Keck is an infrared telescope eight stories high, weighing 150 tons, and with a 33-foot-diameter mirror made of 36 perfectly attuned hexagon mirrors—like a fly's eye—rather than one conventional lens.

You'll need a four-wheel-drive vehicle if you do drive up the mountain. **The Onizuka Visitor Center,** named after a Hawaiian astronaut who died in the *Challenger* explosion, is an hour's drive from Hilo or Waimea; from Hwy. 190, take the narrow, rutted Saddle Road (Hwy. 200) 28 miles, then turn onto unmarked Summit Road and go another 6¹⁄₄ miles to the visitor center. At this point you're already 9,000 feet up, so stop for half an hour to acclimate. With younger kids, this may be your endpoint, so time your visit to join the nighttime **stargazing sessions,** 6 to 10pm, which include a lecture, a video, and the chance to peer through 11-inch, 14-inch, and 16-inch telescopes.

It's 6 miles from here to the summit, but it can take 45 minutes to drive this rough, unpaved, winding road, in low gear all the way—a climb of another 4,200 feet—to 13,796-foot-high **Observatory Hill.** Dress warmly and drink lots of liquid; wear dark

The observatory at Mauna Kea.

glasses to avoid snow blindness, and use plenty of sunscreen. At the top, 11 nations, including the U.S., Japan, the U.K., France, and Australia, have set up 13 powerful infrared telescopes to look into deep space. On this bare peak, their bulbous pale domes sprout around a loop of road like alien spacecraft plopped down on the moon. Visitors can't use those telescopes, of course, though you can look at a couple (including the Keck) from galleries. (They won't be active until night, anyway.) If you take a narrow footpath past the observatories, however, there's a cairn of rocks where you can sit and contemplate an incredible 360-degree view across the Pacific. Even if you're socked in by clouds, it's a true top-of-the-world view, with the summits of Mauna Loa and Maui's Haleakala poking through the puffy white cumulus clouds beneath your feet.

ⓘ ℂ **808/961-2180;** www.ifa.hawaii.edu/info/vis.

✈ Hilo, 29 miles.

🛏 $$ **Killauea Lodge,** Old Volcano Rd., off Hwy. 11 (ℂ **808/967-7366;** www.kilauealodge.com). $ **Volcano House,** inside Hawaii Volcanoes National Park (ℂ **808/967-7321;** www.volcanohouse hotel.com).

WHY THEY'LL THANK YOU: That monster telescope, that killer view.

Polar Nights & Northern Lights

Ages 6 & up • Tromsø, Norway

Just about every attraction in Tromsø, Norway, bills itself as the "world's northernmost" this or that—the northernmost university, the northernmost cathedral, the northernmost golf course, the northernmost brewery. What else would you expect of a city 400km (250 miles) north of the Arctic Circle? But for sky watchers, Tromsø's extreme location means great opportunities year-round to observe all sorts of unique phenomena, from the comforts of a city so cosmopolitan it's been nicknamed the Paris of the North.

Let's start with the rarest phenomenon: The Northern Lights, or **aurora borealis,** created by stray particles from storms on the sun's surface eddying around that big magnet known as the North Pole. On dark, clear nights from about 6pm to 2am, you can see their energy released in wonderful shimmering curtains of light—in Tromsø, one of the few towns on Earth where the

Lights are visible, you can see them even from the city center nightly from October through April. Green is the prevailing color up here, though on good nights the whole spectrum glows. And you do get a lot of nighttime from November 21 to January 21, when the sun never rises above the horizon. Scandinavians put a positive spin on this by calling it **Polar Nights,** and having star-spangled skies 24/7 truly isn't all bad, especially not when the aurora borealis kicks in. Tromsø is blessed with a surprisingly mild climate, even in winter, so you can get outdoors and enjoy those winter skies; several local tour operators take groups out into the countryside to see them at their most spectacular.

You can't see the Northern Lights from May through August, though, for the simple reason that the sun is always in the way: May 21 to July 21 is the season of the Midnight Sun. It sounds simple, but if

This photo of Tromsø was taken at 1am in the summer.

Public Transportation Systems

The old Buick jingle asserted that half the fun in life is getting there. Most kids don't agree; let's face it, we've all heard the refrain "are we there yet?" more often than we can count. But kids will love to ride on these novel forms of transportation; in fact, it may be the highlight of their day.

Gondolas on Venice's Grand Canal.

303 The Gondolas of Venice While other cities have canals, Venice outdoes them all—it has only canals (more than 150 of them) and no streets, just walkways. Cars are useless; and the anachronistic black gondolas are still in use as ferries over the Grand Hotel, and remain enormously popular with tourists. The kids will welcome the sight of the gondolier, standing at the bow of the boat in traditional costume. Best yet is the ride itself; water lapping against a stone, the faint scent of decay, and a certain softness in the air. It all adds up to an unforgettable memory of an ancient city. See the Piazza San Marco **212** and the Doge's Palace **365**.

304 Canal Boats of Amsterdam While Venice's canals seem designed to get you lost, the canals of Amsterdam are much more user-friendly, laid out in a tidy pattern that suits the trim gabled houses that line them. There are different boats to choose from, but the **tour boats** found in front of the Central Station are a good introduction. You can also rent beat-up bikes called *omafiets*, or "grandmother bikes." Another great option is catching a Canal bus, which allows you to hop on and off at many of the city's most famous sites. See Museumplein Masterpieces **338** and the Anne Frank House **379**.

305 Trams of Marseilles The first tramway in Marseilles was horse drawn, but today the city boasts a thoroughly modern light rail system that has over two dozen stations serving as connecting points. Be sure to point out the nautical appearance of the new tramway cars to the kids—the exterior resembles the hull of a ship, while the driver's cabin looks like the bow. It's a nod to Marseille's status as the largest seaport in the country. While most of the stations are plain, some feature themes like Notre-Dame du Mont, decorated with huge vegetables on the walls to promote a nearby market.

306 Tokyo Monorail Kids will gasp when they see the elevated view from their train car on Tokyo's Monorail, which travels swiftly at a speed of 80 mph along the coast of Tokyo Bay. The line connects Haneda Airport in Ota, Tokyo to Hamamatsucho

Station in Minato Tokyo, with 9 stops in between. Be prepared for crowds, however; this is known for being the busiest monorail line in the world, carrying over 300,000 passengers a day on 500 plus trains. Although busy, it was designed to handle travelers and features a roomy interior with plenty of room for carry on luggage. See Ueno Park ❺, Edo-Tokyo ❼, Emerging Science ㉓, and Ghibli museums ㉟. *www.tokyomonorail.co.jp/english/*

㍘ Wellington Cable Car, New Zealand   What could be more appealing than arriving to your destination by cable car? Many of the locals use the cars for work commutes, but visitors have made the Wellington Cable Car one of the city's most popular tourist attractions. Cars run from Lambton Quay in the business district and end at the top entrance of the breathtaking Wellington Botanic gardens. There are other attractions from the top station including the kid-pleasing Cable Car Museum (www.cablecarmuseum.co.nz). ℭ *64/4/472-2199; www.wellingtoncablecar.co.nz.*

㍘ New Orleans Streetcars   When Hurricane Katrina hit, it temporarily stopped the most beloved of the city's three operating streetcar lines. Happily, you can now hear the St. Charles Avenue car clanging away along with the Riverfront and Canal Street lines. Long loved by residents and tourists alike, the cars are an important part of the Big Easy's transportation system, carrying commuters to their destinations every day. Although the Desire line, which inspired Tennessee Williams' "A Streetcar Named Desire" was discontinued in the '50s, there is plenty of fun to be had riding the remaining lines. See New Orleans Aboveground Cemeteries ❼. ℭ *504/248-3900; www.norta.com.*

㍘ Cable Cars of San Francisco   I still get a thrill when I hear the clang-clang of a San Francisco cable car. These beloved wooden icons are the only moving landmark in the National Register of Historic places. Although they were nearly torn up on the grounds of impracticality, public outcry saved the last remaining three lines. Now, they are one of San Francisco's biggest tourist attractions, the big mustdo for every visitor. What kid (or grown-up, for that matter) could resist riding up and down the city's steep hills on one of these historic cars? See Escape to Alcatraz ❼, the Golden Gate Bridge ❾, and the Exploratorium ㉗. *www.sfcablecar.com.*

Wellington Cable Car.

you've ever experienced it, it's truly magical, to feel the world kissed with sunshine around the clock. Summertime in Tromsø also offers whale-watching (℅ **47/77-62-44-40**) or roaming around the open-air **historic museum,** Kvaløyveien 55 (℅ **47/77-60-19-10**), and the university's large **Alpine Botanic Garden,** full of rare Arctic flora. If you do come here in summer—which, given school vacations, may well be your time frame—you don't have to miss the Northern Lights entirely: The **Northern Lights Theatre,** Prostneset (℅ **47/92-84-27-13**), shows a film of the aurora all summer, and the University Museum of Tromsø has what it calls a **Northern Lights Machine** to simulate the experience.

ⓘ **Tourist information office,** Storgaten 61–63 (℅ **47/77-61-00-00;** www.destinasjontromso.no).

✈ Tromsø.

🛏 $$$ **Clarion Hotel Bryggen,** Sjøgata 19–21 (℅ **47/77-78-11-00;** www.choicehotels.no). $$ **Grand Nordic Hotel Tromsø,** Storgaten 44 (℅ **47/77-75-37-77;** www.rica-hotels.com).

WHY THEY'LL THANK YOU: Continuous sun or stars.

Stargazing 310

Warrumbungle National Park/ Coonabaran Observatory
Starstruck in Australia
Ages 7 & up • New South Wales, Australia

Even kids who are afraid of the dark won't mind being outside at night in Warrumbungle National Park. It's far enough from civilization that the night skies here simply dazzle with bright stars, more than most people ever get to see at night. A night being under these stars could make the most jaded kid an astronomy buff, and if they're already junior astronomers, there's even more reason to come—especially if you come from the northern hemisphere, for the night sky is completely different in the southern hemisphere. For example, the moon is seen from a different vantage point—what you see in Canada is flipped in Australia; you are down under, after all.

Warrumbungle was shaped by an ancient volcano, which left behind wonderful spires that draw rock climbers. It's also popular with hikers (the local fauna include kangaroos, koalas, emus, and a vast array of Australia's bird life), though

it's big enough that it doesn't get overrun with tourists. If your kids don't mind roughing it a bit (be aware that winter nights—which begin here in June—can be very cold), camping out in the park gives you a chance to stare at those constellations all night long. If you are bringing your own telescope, there are open areas near Camp Blackman where your kids can set up and gaze to their heart's content.

After a night under the stars the kids may clamor for a trip to nearby **Coonabaran,** known as the astronomy capital of Australia. There you'll find the **Skywatch Observatory** where you can peer through telescopes at the stars and planets through a 310mm telescope inside a geodesic dome. Featured is **"Pathway to Stars,"** a display that lets you look at ancient skies, while offering hands-on exhibits featuring computers, microscopes, and plasma balls. During the day, you can visit the planetarium, where kids can see views of the solar system and deep space slides. Night visits afford a chance to look through telescopes on an outside observation deck. Guides are on hand to offer background on what's being viewed. In the car park is a **Radio Heliograph Antenna** with a dish 13m (42 ft.) in diameter. It was once part of the antenna array used in Narribi to track the sun. For a touch of kitsch, take in 18 holes of putt-putt golf on the astronomy themed minigolf course.

If that isn't enough to sate your stargazers, take them to **Siding Spring Observatory,** located 20 minutes from Coonabaran on the National Park Road. The observatory is renowned for infrared and optical astronomy. It also features the world-famous 3.9m Anglo-Australian telescope. An elevator takes you inside the visitor's gallery, where you can view the mammoth telescope.

ⓘ **Warrumbungle National Park** (✆ 61/2/6825-4364; www.nationalparks.nsw.gov.au/parks.nsf).

✈ Sydney Airport.

🛏 $ **All Travellers Motor Inn,** Newell/Oxley Hwy., Coonabaran (✆ 61/2/6842-1133; www.alltravellers.com.au). $ **Matthew Flinders Motor Inn,** Newell Hwy., Coonabaran (✆ 61/2/6842-1766; www.matthewflindersmotorinn.com.au).

WHY THEY'LL THANK YOU: Kangaroos by day, the heavens by night.

11 Holy Places

Western Wall Plaza in Jerusalem.

311

The Temple Mount/The Church of the Holy Sepulcher/Mount of Olives

Ages 6 & up • Jerusalem, Israel

For centuries, Jerusalem has been tugged to and fro. King Solomon erected the first great Jewish temple here in 957 B.C.; Nebuchadnezzar destroyed it 4 centuries later. In 34 B.C., King Herod built the greatest religious complex in the eastern Roman Empire—which the Romans leveled in A.D. 70. (At Temple Mount's foot, a surviving fragment of Herod's wall is known as the **Wailing Wall** because, for centuries, Jews have crowded here to mourn the loss of their temple.) The prayer section of the Western Wall is an unforgettable sight, the unmortared cracks of its chalky yellow-white stone stuffed with prayers scrawled on bits of paper; Orthodox Jews stand alongside, chanting and swaying. After the Muslim conquest of A.D. 638, Temple Mount was rebuilt with Islamic holy places. **El Aksa Mosque** here is the third holiest Muslim place of prayer after Mecca and Medina, and the dazzling **Dome of the Rock** protects a rock revered by Muslims as the spot where Prophet Muhammad viewed paradise. To Jews, however, it's the rock where Abraham proved his faith by nearly sacrificing his son Isaac.

As a political compromise, the walled Old City was divided into five sections: Temple Mount, the Muslim Quarter, the Jewish Quarter, the Christian Quarter, and the Armenian Quarter. But even there, factions compete: The dour sandstone **Church of the Holy Sepulcher** in the Christian quarter is a site so holy that Roman Catholics, Armenian Orthodox, Greek Orthodox, Egyptian Coptics, Ethiopians, and Syrian Orthodox all claim it. Founded by Constantine, the first Christian emperor of Rome, it enshrines what tradition claims is the tomb of Jesus Christ (it once also held the cross that Jesus was crucified on, but the Persians stole that

centuries ago). Three incredibly **holy relics** are encompassed in this one cluttered church: the rocky outcropping of **Mount Calvary,** traditionally the site where Jesus was crucified (the huge crucifix in this chapel is particularly gruesome); the **Stone of Unction,** believed to be the same marble slab where Christ's broken corpse was prepared for burial; and, underground, a primitive stone cave traditionally accepted as the **tomb** where Jesus was buried for 3 days, before miraculously rising from the dead. After years of fire, earthquakes, and ransacking, the church was more or less razed, although its holy shrines were saved. The facade you see today dates

Church of the Holy Sepulchre.

321

from the 12th century, when the Crusaders had conquered Jerusalem and reclaimed its churches.

Outside of the Old City, the **Mount of Olives** contains one of the oldest, perhaps the holiest, Jewish cemeteries in the world, as well as the spot where Jesus ascended to heaven, the spot where Jesus taught his disciples the Lord's Prayer, and the courtyard where Jesus supposedly prayed the night before his arrest, each sanctified with its own church. With a legacy this

rich, no wonder everybody's fighting over Jerusalem.

✈ Jerusalem.

🛏 $$$ **Jerusalem Sheraton Plaza,** 47 King George St. (© **800/325-3535** or 972/2/629-8666; www.sheraton.com). $$ **King Solomon Hotel,** 32 King David St. (© **972/2/569-5555**).

WHY THEY'LL THANK YOU: The holiest of holy cities.

312

Church of the Nativity
Bethlehem's Original Crèche
Ages 8 & up • Bethlehem, Israel

For more than 17 centuries, Christian pilgrims have flocked to the city of Bethlehem to see the birthplace of Jesus Christ. Though it's only 8km (5 miles) south of Jerusalem, Bethlehem is in the West Bank, that political tinderbox torn between Israel and Palestine, so I'd opt for a guided day trip from Jerusalem. Let a tour guide sort out the hassles so you can focus on sorting out Jesus' humble birth from the chaos of busy, modern Bethlehem.

Join the faithful crowds at Manger Square, site of the ancient **Church of the Nativity.** Built in A.D. 326 by the Roman emperor Constantine, it was rebuilt 200 years later by Emperor Justinian and again by 12th-century Crusaders (blame them for its fortresslike facade). Point out to the kids the different priests walking about, all protecting their sects' claim to this sacred site—Franciscan priests in brown robes, Armenians in purple and cream-colored robes, and bearded Greeks in black robes with long hair tied into a bun. After being fought over for centuries, it's no surprise the church looks clunky and dilapidated. The stately Corinthian pillars that line the basilica's naves bear faded paintings of

apostles, bishops, saints, and kings; gilded lamps hang from the oak ceiling, and trapdoors in the stone-and-wood floor give mere glimpses of old Byzantine mosaic glories beneath.

On either side of the ornate gold-and-silver main altar, narrow staircases lead down to a marble grotto, draped in tapestries. Ancient tradition claims Mary gave birth to Jesus in this shallow cave, as was the custom of those times; altars mark nearby spots where the manger stood and where the Magi bowed to the baby Jesus. Historically accurate or not, after centuries of adoration this hushed grotto is full of spiritual aura. For a more authentic-looking relic, go to the grand **Franciscan church** just north of the Church of the Nativity; a stair from the back of its nave leads to an underground maze of rock-hewn rooms and chambers that supposedly includes the stable where Joseph and Mary stayed the night of Jesus' birth.

Your group may also take a 2-hour walk to the **Shepherds' Fields,** where tradition says angels proclaimed Jesus' birth to simple shepherds. There are two competing Shepherds' Fields, one Roman Catholic and the other Greek Orthodox—whichever you visit, you'll see real shepherds still tending their flocks on this rocky landscape. And that makes the story come real.

✈ Jerusalem.

🛏 $$$ **Jerusalem Sheraton Plaza,** 47 King George St. (✆ **800/325-3535** or 972/2/629-8666; www.sheraton.com). $$ **King Solomon Hotel,** 32 King David St. (✆ **972/2/569-5555**).

ⓘ **Guided Tours: Egged Tours** (✆ **972/3/694-8888**). **United Tours** (✆ **972/2/625-2187**).

WHY THEY'LL THANK YOU: Away in a manger.

313

The Vatican
Michelangelo's Masterpiece
Ages 6 & up • Rome, Italy

Whether or not you're a practicing Catholic, the Vatican—the world's second-smallest sovereign independent state—is a must-see when you're in Rome, if only for its enormous art collection. In truth, it has more art than most children (or most adults) can appreciate, so keep your focus narrow: Tell the kids you're here to see the work of one great artist, Michelangelo. Everything else is icing on the cake.

You enter Vatican City through grand colonnaded **St. Peter's Square,** where the Pope himself appears on a balcony at noon every Sunday (except mid-July to mid-Sept) to bless the gathered multitudes. Straight ahead is the massive facade of **St. Peter's Basilica,** Piazza San Pietro (✆ **39/6/69881662**), topped by a majestic dome designed by Michelangelo. (**Note:** The basilica has a strict dress code:

The Vatican.

no shorts, no skirts above the knee, and no bare shoulders and arms.) St. Peter was allegedly buried here in A.D. 64; this is the second basilica on the site, mostly completed in the 1500s and 1600s. Don't be surprised if the riot of gilt, marble, and mosaic inside overwhelms you all—that's what it was designed to do. Steer the kids into the first nave on the right to see (sadly, behind reinforced glass) a young Michelangelo's exquisite sculpture of the **Pietà,** with a tender Virgin Mary cradling the crucified body of her son Jesus. Pass through the grottoes, getting a peek at St. Peter's tomb, then wait in line to climb to the dome (separate ticket). You can walk up all 491 steps or take an elevator and walk only 320 steps (only!); at the top you'll have an astounding view over the rooftops of Rome.

Next you visit the **Vatican Museums** (yet another ticket line), housed in a section of the papal palaces, a labyrinthine series of lavish apartments and galleries. This collection of treasures from antiquity and the Renaissance is so big that visitors are given a choice of four partial tours—all of them ending in the **Sistine Chapel.** Among much else, you may choose to see the **Borgia Apartments,** with their frescoes of biblical scenes, or the **Raphael Rooms,** decorated by Raphael and his workshop for Pope Julius II (the highlight is the second room's scene of the Greek philosophers, who are actually portraits of great Renaissance artists). Eventually you'll reach the **Sistine Chapel,** Michelangelo's command performance for Pope Julius II. It took the artist 4 taxing years in his 30s to complete the nine panels on the ceiling, whose themes are taken from the pages of Genesis. The most famous are Adam and Eve being expelled from the Garden of Eden and the Creation of Man— bring binoculars so the kids can see the details, especially God's outstretched finger giving the divine spark of life to Adam. On the altar wall is a late Michelangelo painting, the *Last Judgment,* wherein some of the doomed sinners resemble Michelangelo's enemies. Hey, even great artists can be petty.

ⓘ (✆ **39/06/6982;** www.vatican.va).

✈ Leonardo da Vinci International Airport.

🛏 $$$ **Hotel de Russie,** Via del Babuino 9 (✆ **800/323-7500** in North America, or 39/6-28881; www.roccoforte hotels.com). $ **Hotel Grifo,** Via del Boschetto 144 (✆ **39/6-4871395**).

WHY THEY'LL THANK YOU: Michelangelo's genius.

Notre-Dame de Paris
Flying Buttresses & Gothic Gargoyles
Ages 6 & up • Paris, France

Chances are the children only know Paris's Notre-Dame cathedral from *The Hunchback of Notre Dame*—and I mean the animated Disney movie, not the classic horror film (let alone the Victor Hugo novel upon which they were based). Still, that'll get them interested, and once they see it in person, this magnificent Gothic cathedral will win them over.

In the heart of old Paris, **Notre-Dame** crowns the island in the middle of the Seine (Ile de la Cité) where the city first grew. It was the focal point of medieval Paris. Start out across the Seine, on the

Notre-Dame.

Left Bank quay, where you can view it as a glorious whole, bristling with gargoyles and flying buttresses. Then cross the bridge and stand in the front courtyard to gaze upon the trio of **13th-century sculpted portals.** Notre Dame means Our Lady, and the church is dedicated to the Virgin Mary, who is celebrated in the left- and right-hand portals (the theme of the central one is the Last Judgment and Christ's Resurrection). Go inside and turn around to admire the **rose window** over the central portal, a marvel in stained glass showcasing a statue of the Virgin and Child. There are two other beautiful round windows inside; the north rose window in the transept, from the mid–13th century, is particularly spectacular.

A perfect place for an architecture lesson, Notre-Dame is a classic example of **Gothic style** with slender, graceful columns soaring to a high cross-vaulted ceiling. Its floor plan resembles a huge cross, with the altar at the intersection; numerous small chapels devoted to various saints are tucked around the outer edges. Like most medieval cathedrals, it was decorated with images that educated a largely illiterate congregation—for example, the Biblical scenes carved on the elaborate

stone screen separating the choir from the long nave. To visit the **gargoyles** where Quasimodo lurked, you can scale steps leading to the twin square towers, 68m (223 ft.) high. Once here, you can inspect those devils (some sticking out their tongues), hobgoblins, and birds of prey.

For a study in contrasts, take a short walk to the nearby royal chapel of **Ste-Chapelle,** tucked away in the Palais de Justice, 4 bd. du Palais (✆ **33/1/53-73-78-50;** www.monum.fr). Between them, they illustrate the class divide of the Middle Ages: Ste-Chapelle is as intimate and aristocratic as Notre-Dame is monumental and all-encompassing. Save it for a sunny day so you can see its stained-glass windows at their most brilliant—with reds so red that Parisians often use the phrase "wine the color of Ste-Chapelle's windows." Delicate as lace, Ste-Chapelle's 15 windows take up most of its walls, depicting Bible scenes.

ⓘ 6 place du parvis Notre-Dame (✆ **33/ 1/42-34-56-10;** www.paris.org/Monuments/ NDame).

✈ De Gaulle.

$$$ **Hotel de Fleurie,** 32–34 rue Grégoire-de-Tours (© **33/1/53-73-70-00;** www.hotel-de-fleurie.tm.fr). $$ **Residence Lord Byron,** 5 rue de Chateaubriand (© **33/1/43-59-89-98;** www.escapade-paris.com).

WHY THEY'LL THANK YOU: Rose windows for beauty, gargoyles for the beast.

315

Mont-St-Michel
The Fortress Abbey of Normandy
Ages 6 & up • Mont-St-Michel, France

Set upon a massive rock just off the Normandy coast, the great Gothic abbey church of Mont-St-Michel is often called the Marvel of the West. Approaching across the coastal flatlands, I get chills when I see its Gothic splendor triumphantly piercing the sky, usually cloaked in dramatic fog. Legend claims it is protected by the archangel Michael, but the abbey is guarded by earthly elements as well—powerful tides churn around the tiny island, and massive rampart walls circle the abbey itself. Think of the engineering required to build on this sheer outcrop—it's a marvel it has stood this long, yet it does, a magnificent pile rising to a spire with a gilded statue of St. Michael.

In the Middle Ages, this was a popular pilgrimage site, founded in the 8th century by St. Aubert, the bishop of Avranches, upon the divine orders of St. Michael (the bishop procrastinated at first, but he came around once the angel burned a hole in his skull, so the story goes). Nowadays the

The Gothic abbey church of Mont-St-Michel.

island is connected to shore by a causeway, but medieval pilgrims could get here only at low tide, walking across treacherous tidal sands. (The kids eyed that causeway with respect, wondering if the next high tide would wash over it and strand us on the island.) In the 10th century the oratory was upgraded to a Benedictine monastery, and the monks continued to build and renovate over the next 6 centuries, as various parts burned down or toppled over. Bristling with spires as it climbs the steep slopes, the abbey looks more like a fortress than a holy retreat—a fact that served it well in the Hundred Years' War (1337–1453), when it almost miraculously resisted capture by the English. The rampant walls also made it easy to convert to a prison, after the monks were disbanded, in the days of the French Revolution. It's been a national monument since the late 19th century, and recently some new monks have settled in as well.

Warn the kids that there'll be a lot of climbing: It's a steep walk to the abbey up Grande Rue, lined with half-timbered 15th- and 16th-century houses, and inside the abbey walls are more staircases. Secreted

within the abbey are some lovely Gothic interiors, most notably the **Salle des Chevaliers (Hall of the Knights)** and graceful **cloisters** with pink granite columns. Crowning the summit is the splendid abbey church, begun in the 11th century—note the round Romanesque arches in the nave and transept, whereas the pointy arches of Flamboyant Gothic were in fashion when the choir was rebuilt in the 15th century. In the summer, you can even visit the church at night—not a bad idea if you want to avoid those modern pilgrim hordes on day-tripping coach tours.

ⓘ **Mont-St-Michel** (✆ **33/02/33-89-80-00**). **Office de Tourisme,** Corps de Garde des Bourgeois (✆ **33/02/33-60-14-30**; www.baie-mont-saint-michel.fr).

🚆 Rennes, 2½ hr. from Paris.

🛏 $$ **Les Terrasses Poulard,** Grande Rue (✆ **33/02/33-89-02-02**; www.mere-poulard.fr).

WHY THEY'LL THANK YOU: Built by faith, against all logic.

Westminster Abbey
Honoring Kings, Queens & Poets
Ages 8 & up • London, England

Compared to other great places of worship, Westminster Abbey isn't marked by a holy, mystical vibe. It's not even the head church of England (that honor is reserved for Canterbury Cathedral ③⑰). But this fascinating jumble of early English Gothic architecture is such a rich repository of British history, the kids can't help but be enthralled.

When you first enter its dark recesses, don't be intimidated by the crowds; pick up a pamphlet near the door so you can work your way methodically through the

abbey, identifying all the tombs and memorials, whether they lie among the worn stones underfoot or are mounted on the side walls. Though the central nave may be reserved for worship services, find a vantage point on one of the aisles to drink in the soaring fan-vaulted space with its intricately carved choir stalls, familiar from such famous events as Princess Diana's funeral.

Founded by the saintly king Edward the Confessor in 1065, this church started out as a Benedictine abbey; in 1066 it was immediately pressed into service for not one but two coronations—the Anglo-Saxon king Harold who succeeded Edward in January, followed by the Norman invader William the Conqueror in December. Since then, nearly every English sovereign has been crowned here, and many are also buried in the Abbey. My daughter was mesmerized by the tomb that contained both Catholic Mary I and her half-sister, the Protestant queen Elizabeth (not to mention Mary Queen of Scots on the other side of the same chapel). Near the tomb of Henry V (my sons gaped in awe at his detailed armor) is the Coronation Chair, made at the command of Edward 1 in 1300 to display the sacred Stone of Scone, upon which Scottish kings were crowned (it has since been returned to Scotland).

As if all the royal tombs weren't enough, Westminster Abbey also has a unique don't-miss feature—the side nave known as **Poet's Corner** where the ashes of famous writers from Chaucer to Dickens are interred; there are also monuments to Shakespeare, Milton, Keats, and a host of other literary figures. When my kids were younger, this corner didn't mean so much to them, but on our last trip, the older two had finally read enough literature that they wandered around simply awestruck.

Note that on Sundays the Abbey is open for worship only; no tourists are allowed.

Right across the street sit the **Houses of Parliament,** housed in a splendid 19th-century building designed to echo the Gothic arches of the Abbey. You'll instantly recognize its landmark clock tower, which most tourists know as Big Ben (fun trivia: Big Ben is actually not the tower, or the clock, but the largest bell inside the tower). Just make sure not to confuse Westminster Abbey with nearby Westminster Cathedral, an impressive Roman Catholic church in its own right—but it's nowhere near as fascinating as the Abbey.

ⓘ ✆ **44/20/7222-5152;** www.westminster-abbey.org.

✈ Heathrow.

🛏 $$$ **London Bridge Hotel,** 8–18 London Bridge St. 9 (✆ **44/20/7855-2200;** www.londonbridgehotel.com). $$ **Vicarage Private Hotel,** 10 Vicarage Gate, South Kensington (✆ **44/20/7229-4030;** www.londonvicaragehotel.com).

WHY THEY'LL THANK YOU: The Poet's Corner.

Canterbury Cathedral: Holy Survivor

All ages • Canterbury, England

Four things make this cathedral a must-see destination: its Gothic architecture; its status as the Church of England's mother church; its starring role in the English language's first masterpiece, *The Canterbury Tales;* and the treacherous murder of Thomas à Becket in 1170. The first three factors may not grab your kids, but the fourth will.

Canterbury is one of those places where layers of history pile atop each other. Britain's earliest settlements flourished in this southeast corner, the closest area to the European continent, and there was a town here well before the birth of Christ. When the Romans came to Britain, this became a major center, Durovernum Cantiacorum. When Pope Gregory I sent St. Augustine to Britain to convert the pagan Saxons to Christianity, Augustine built his abbey here. But what really established Canterbury as England's religious capital was the murder of **Thomas à Becket,** archbishop of Canterbury, who was killed on December 29,

Canterbury Cathedral.

1170, by four knights who thought King Henry II wanted him out of the way. Henry denied he ever issued such orders, and even if he did, the scheme backfired—Becket's tomb immediately became a shrine, visited by faithful worshipers from all over, and the murder victim was named a Catholic saint.

Four years after the murder, a mysterious fire leveled the monastic church. It was replaced by the magnificent early **Gothic choir** section, England's first major example of that architectural style. Like most medieval cathedrals, Canterbury was a work in progress that spanned centuries; the nave, the long main body of the church, wasn't completed until the 1300s.

By 1388, when Geoffrey Chaucer portrayed a motley crew of pilgrims in his **Canterbury Tales,** this was England's major tourist destination. The cathedral has several noteworthy **medieval tombs,** including those of King Henry IV and the renowned warrior Edward the Black Prince (loaded down with armor and weapons).

When Henry VIII decided to split England from the Roman Catholic Church, in 1538 he had Becket's shrine destroyed and its treasures carted off to line his own coffers. As a result, the interior looks remarkably restrained and pure, with pale stone surfaces, pointed arches, soaring spires, high ceilings, subtle gargoyles, and exterior supporting arches (called flying buttresses). One thing Henry left was the lovely stained-glass windows. In 1941, when Nazi Germany began bombing Great Britain, Canterbury's officials removed the precious glass for safekeeping. During a German air raid in 1942, the replacement windows were blown to bits. The originals were safely put back after the war and you can see them here today.

Elsewhere in Canterbury, you can walk along what remains of the medieval **city walls,** explore such quaint medieval-relic streets as **Mercery Lane,** and perhaps visit the **Museum of Canterbury** on Stour Street or the excavated **Canterbury Roman Museum** on Butchery Lane.

ⓘ 11 The Precincts (✆ **44/1227/762862;** www.canterbury-cathedral.org).

🚌 Canterbury, 1½ hr. from London.

🛏 $$ **The Swallow Chaucer Hotel,** 63 Ivy Lane (✆ **44/01227/464-427;** www. swallow-hotels.com).

WHY THEY'LL THANK YOU: A real-life crime scene, in dramatic Gothic surroundings.

Lutherstadt Wittenberg
Nailed to the Wall
Ages 7 & up • Wittenberg, Germany

Most history books make Martin Luther sound like a stiff wooden figure, but a trip to his home base will help kids relate to him as a firebrand and a rebel—he did, after all, split with the Catholic faith to found the Protestant Reformation. What's more, he created scandal and outrage by renouncing celibacy to marry his wife, a former nun.

The town is now officially known as Lutherstadt. The name change is no doubt a post-reunification effort to attract tourism to this East German town, where it's now possible to trace many of the key places in Luther's life. Most of the sights are clustered in the historic center, away from the industrial clutter of the modern town. Look for the round, crown-topped tower of the **Schlosskirche**, at Friedrichstrasse 1 A, where he nailed his radical 95 Theses to the door in 1517 (the brass doors there today are a 19th century addition, engraved with his theses—in church Latin, of course). Luther's affectingly simple tomb is inside.

Luther preached most of his dangerously dissident sermons, however, at the twin towered Gothic parish church of **Stadtkirche St. Marien,** Jundster 35, where he also married his wife. He's even depicted in the great altarpiece painted by Lucas Cranach the Elder (you can see Cranach's house on the Marksplatz). The Luthers settled at the **Lutherhalle,** Collegienstrasse 54—a former Augustinian monastery, disbanded at the start of the Reformation. It has been turned into a **museum** displaying Luther's desk, his pulpit, first editions of his books, and the wood paneled lecture hall where he taught up to 400 students at a time. The towering **Luthereiche (Luther's Oak),** at the end of Collegienstrasse, outside the Elster gate, commemorates the spot where Luther, in 1520, defiantly burned the papal edict that excommunicated him.

Look for **statues** of Luther and his Humanist friend Philip Melancthon, which have been erected in the cobbled city square in front of the big white city hall (Rathuas). Wittenberg lies 100 km (62 miles) from Berlin, making it an easy day trip, if that is your base. For a more leisurely tour, there are places to stay within the historic town.

ⓘ **Sacred Destinations** (www.sacred-destinations.com/germany/wittenberg.htm).

✈ Berlin.

🚃 Wittenberg.

🛏 $$ **Hotel Grune Tanne,** Am Teich 1, (✆ **49/34/916290**). $ **Hotel-Pension Am Schwanenteich** (✆ **49/3491/402807;** www.wittenberg-schwanenteich.de).

WHY THEY'LL THANK YOU: That famous door.

319

Clonmacnois
Mystical Ruin of the Irish Monks
All ages • Shannonbridge, Ireland

Resting silently on the east bank of the Shannon, Clonmacnois is one of Ireland's most profound ancient sites. You'll have to follow a twisting series of country roads to get to this remote, peaceful place, and when the kids see it's just a bunch of ruins, they may wonder at first why you bothered—until they've wandered around and let the gray stones work their mystical spell.

Standing here today, it's amazing to imagine this as one of Europe's great centers of learning and culture. But back in the Dark Ages, monasteries were vital repositories of knowledge, and ancient Ireland revered its monks. **St. Ciaran** founded a monastic community here in A.D. 548 because it was where the road between Dublin and Galway crossed the Shannon River (its modern equivalent, the N6 highway, passes a few miles north), and Clonmacnois flourished for the next 1,000 years under the patronage of numerous Irish kings. The last high king, Rory O'Conor, was buried here in 1198. In the course of time, however, Clonmacnois was raided repeatedly, first by native chiefs, then by Danish Vikings, then by Anglo-Norman invaders, until it was finally abandoned in 1552 when the monasteries had lost their power. The exhibits in the visitor center tell the story well, so don't rush past them.

When you come outdoors from the visitor center, all that you'll see are the foundations of a **cathedral,** a **castle,** and **eight churches;** a few wall fragments and arched doorways still rise, as well as two round towers you can peek into. Wander about and let the great monastery take shape in your mind's eye. Conjure up for yourselves those old robed monks, pacing meditatively from church to church. My children were particularly fascinated by the **three high crosses,** their intricate surface sculptures worn down by the elements but still telling their runic stories. More than 200 monumental slabs are laid out in a vast graveyard; plaques mark several important figures buried here. Beyond low stone walls, the ground slopes down to the gentle, marshy banks of the river. Cows graze placidly in an adjacent meadow, and even on an overcast day, the grass glows a vivid emerald-green. It's magical.

ⓘ R357, 6km (3¾ miles) north of Shannonbridge (☏ **353/90/967-4195**).

✈ Shannon, 113km (70 miles).

🛏 $ **Brosna Lodge Hotel,** Main St., Banagher (☏ **353/509/ 51350;** www.brosnalodge. com). $$$ **Wineport Lodge,** Glasson, Athlone (☏ **353/90/ 643-9010;** www.wineport. ie).

WHY THEY'LL THANK YOU: A holy place for contemplation.

Clonmacnois.

320

The Sacred Isle of Iona

Ages 6 & up • Iona, the Hebrides, Scotland

Remote, treeless Iona, just off the south-western coast of Mull in Scotland's Hebrides islands, has been a place of spiritual pilgrimage for centuries. The first Christian settlement in Scotland was founded here, its monks becoming the stalwart guardians of ancient learning throughout the Dark Ages. Some 1,000 visitors a week step off the ferry in summer, and yet somehow the island's atmosphere remains tranquil. It helps that most visitors are contemplative sorts, interested in the other-worldly values of a Benedictine abbey and relics of old saints.

You arrive by passenger ferry from the Isle of Mull, itself a 45-minute ferry trip from Oban (**Caledonian MacBrayne ferries;** ✆ **44/1688/302017**), leaving your car behind and trusting to your own two feet to get around—not too hard, because the island is only 5.6km (3½ miles) long by 1.6km (1 mile) wide. Walk off among the sheep and cows that wander freely everywhere; climb to the top of **Dun-I,** a small gray mountain, to contemplate the ocean and the landscape around you.

St. Columba arrived in A.D. 563 with a dozen companions, using this as their base for converting Scotland to Christianity. Nothing remains of the original monastery, which Norse invaders destroyed. The present-day abbey site encompasses the **ruins** of a Norman-era nunnery, the 11th-century **St. Oran's Chapel,** and square-towered **Iona Cathedral,** with its Norman arches and short round pillars. Built in spurts, the church is a jumble of styles from the 12th to the 16th centuries—but really, architectural splendor is beside the point. It's simply an incredibly holy place.

The monks of Iona played one other role: maintaining the eternal resting place of the kings of Scotland (its remoteness was an advantage; rival chieftains could not get here to desecrate their remains). Tradition claims that **St. Oran's Cemetery** holds the mossy graves of 48 Scottish kings, including Macbeth and his rival Duncan, along with assorted Irish, Norwegian, and French kings and church dignitaries.

Owned by the dukes of Argyll since 1695, Iona was recently sold to Sir Hugh Fraser, who ensured that National Trust money would be turned over to the trustees of the abbey, the **Iona Community.** This ecumenical religious group lives communally on the grounds, and interested visitors are welcome to join them for a night or two. If the spirit of this place gets to you, a stay with the Community could be a very special experience.

(i) ✆ **44/1681/700404.**

🚌 Oban, 3 hr. from Glasgow.

🛏 **Argyll Hotel** (✆ **44/1681/700334;** www.argyllhoteliona.co.uk).

WHY THEY'LL THANK YOU: A chance to get in touch with their spiritual side.

Gamla Uppsala, Sweden
Where the Vikings Worshiped
Ages 8 & up • Sweden

Kids can't help but to be intrigued by the history of Gamla Uppsala, the site where Vikings made human and animal sacrifices to Norse gods and buried their royalty. These three large 6th-century **burial mounds** lie in what was once the Capital of the Svea Kingdom.

The settlement was also home to royal castles, and Swedish kings and their families were given lavish funerals when it was their time to go to Valhalla, the Norse afterlife. In order to reach this paradise, they believed that burning the body along with all worldly possessions was essential. It was believed that the god Odin decreed it; and along with Thor and Freyr, he is represented by a wooden statue inside of the temple. The temple itself was quite grand: A golden chain hung across its gables and the interior was also decorated with gold. During the festival of Frobolt, which occurred at winter solstice every ninth year, nine people were sacrificed by hanging from trees. Their bodies were left to decay because it was believed that it would make the trees sacred. Sacrifices were performed at other times when priests decided that it would be for the good of the people. In addition to the main mounds, there is a **sprawling grave field** that at one time accommodated 2,000 to 3,000 mounds. There, you can also see the remains of the grand houses of Viking royalty.

Gamla Uppsala is just 5km (3 miles) north of the city center. Visitors come primarily to see the Royal Mounds, but you may want to visit the **Gamla Upsala**

Museum, Disa Road, 75440 Uppsala, (✆ **46/18-9300**), so the kids can get some background before they explore. The exhibit "Myth, Might, and Man" looks at the history of the area starting from the 20th century, working back to the earliest depictions of Gamla Uppsala in 11th century A.D. The museum has the period artifacts you might expect, such as rune stone copies, as well as items recovered by archaeologists, but the kids might prefer the "Viking Journey" presented on the museum's computers. During the warm months, Viking duels are staged outside.

As you walk around the burial mounds, pay particular attention to the **Eastern Mound,** which housed the grave of a young adult along with carved bronze panels and expensive weapons, and an illustration of the status of the people who were buried here. You may want to ask the kids what they think about all those treasures being buried underground.

ⓘ **Gamla Uppsala Information and Tourism** (www.uppsala.world-guides.com).

✈ Stockholm-Arlanda Airport.

🛏 $$ **Hotel Gillet Uppsala,** Dragarbrunnsg 23 753 20, (✆ **46/18/68-1800;** www.clarionhotelgillet.se). $$ **Luther-Hotel Wittenberg,** Luther-Hotel Wittenberg (✆ **49/3491-4580;** www.luther-hotel-wittenberg.de).

WHY THEY'LL THANK YOU: Buried treasure.

322

Cathedral of the Three Kings

Ages 4 & up • Cologne, Germany

"We Three Kings" is our family's favorite Christmas hymn, so we looked forward to visiting Cologne Cathedral, where a precious chest houses the mortal remains (supposedly) of the Magi. We weren't prepared, though, for the magnificence of this Gothic church. In a city heavily damaged by Allied bombing in World War II, the cathedral miraculously survived—partly because its soaring towers made a handy landmark for bomber crews, but also because in the end they could not bring themselves to destroy such an architectural marvel.

Cologne ("Köln" in German) means "colony," and this was a Roman town starting in 38 B.C. A temple was built on this site as soon as Emperor Constantine permitted open Christian worship. In 1164, Holy Roman Emperor Frederick Barbarossa acquired the holy bones of the Magi and put their shrine in Cologne, where it became a popular pilgrimage site. In 1248, work began on a suitably grand church for the relics, designed in High Gothic style. In the stop-and-go manner of medieval cathedral building, its chancel, south tower, and north-side aisles were completed by 1560, then, as the Reformation disrupted Europe, work halted for nearly 3 centuries. But in 1823, the Prussian court, inspired by the Romantic movement's veneration of all things medieval, revived the project, digging up the original plans to ensure it was completed in authentic Gothic style.

Outside, stand back from the south transept for a sweeping overall view of the huge cathedral. Note that there are no important horizontal lines—everything is vertical. The west side (front) is dominated by two towering spires, making this the **tallest Gothic structure in the world.** Entering the church, your eye is inevitably drawn upward—to God, its designers intended—by the nave's soaring arches. The medieval/Victorian mix is exemplified by the glowing windows high in the side walls: 16th-century stained glass on the north, 19th-century Bavarian glass on the south. Behind the high altar, in the chancel, is the **Shrine of the Three Magi,** shaped like a minicathedral of gold and silver. In its high-security trappings, you can't see much of the elaborate sculpted figures covering its surface, but the effect is still awesome. Admire the richly carved oak choir stalls, dating from 1310. Among the outlying chapels, the **Chapel of the Cross,** beneath the organ loft, shelters a painted wooden crucifix that is the oldest full-size cross in northern Europe; in **Our Lady's Chapel,** a famous 15th-century triptych over the altar opens up to a beautiful painting of the Three Kings worshiping the infant Jesus in the manger. Cue it: "We three kings of Orient are. . . ."

ⓘ Dompropstei Margarethenkloster 5 (ℂ **49/221/1794-0100;** www.koelnerdom. de).

✈ Köln/Bonn, 23km (14 miles).

🛏 $$ **Hopper Hotel et cetera,** Brüsselerstrasse 26 (ℂ **49/221/924400;** www. hopper.de).

WHY THEY'LL THANK YOU: A cathedral beautiful enough to survive a world war.

Catedral de León (Santa María de Regla)
Inside a Stained-Glass Kaleidoscope
Ages 4 & up • León, Spain

In the church-building sweepstakes of the Middle Ages, every Gothic cathedral vied to distinguish itself with some superlative trait. Milan Cathedral was the biggest, Chartres had the most inspiring stained-glass pictures, Palma de Majorca had the largest rose window, and so on. But León—at the time the leading city of Christian Spain—set the record for the highest proportion of window space. Its **stained-glass windows** occupy 1,672 sq. m (18,000 sq. ft.), or almost all the space where you'd expect the walls to be; they soar 34m (112 ft.) to the vaulted ceiling, framed by the slenderest of columns. It's a wondrous feat of engineering—but all your kids will notice is that the interior glows with color, like no place else on earth.

The cathedral's 13th-century architects, Juan Pérez and Maestro Enrique, were, in effect, precursors of Mies van der Rohe, with one hitch—they didn't have steel girders to support their glass walls. And while it has stood for 7 centuries, the cathedral contains some 125 original stained-glass windows, plus 57 oculi, and their weight strains the walls. The job of supporting the roof (its delicate vaulting was added in the Renaissance) was taken over by flying buttresses on the exterior; the walls have all they can do just to hold the glass.

An air of dignified calm pervades the cathedral's cloisters, full of faded frescoes and Romanesque and Gothic tombs; a short walk northwest of the cathedral you can visit a splendidly decorated Romanesque church, **Pantéon y Museos de San Isidoro,** Plaza San Isidoro 4 (✆ **34/98/787-6161**), which contains the tombs of 23 Leónese kings. Surrounding the two churches, León's historic quarter is also worth exploring, as you're already here. But the reason to come is those glorious windows; everything else in town literally pales in comparison.

ⓘ Plaza de Regla (✆ **34/987-57-70**).

🚄 León's Estación del Norte, 4–5 hr. from Madrid.

🛏 $$$ **Hotel Alfonso V,** Padre Isla 1 (✆ **34/98/722-0900;** www.hotelalfonsov. com).

WHY THEY'LL THANK YOU: Like being inside a kaleidoscope.

Gaudí Days in Barcelona
Ages 4 & up • Barcelona, Spain

Traveling around Europe, it's easy for kids to get Gothicked-out, bopping from palace to cathedral to fortress—enough! Yes, there is a Gothic **cathedral** in Barcelona,

quite a lovely one, begun at the end of the 13th century and mostly completed by the mid–15th century, with an especially charming cloister surrounding a garden of magnolias, medlars, and palm trees. Look for it at Plaça de la Seu s/n (🕾 **34/93/315-1554**). But the church that children most remember from Barcelona is the exuberantly un-gothic **La Sagrada Família,** the crowning achievement of the great 20th-century architect Antoni Gaudí.

You don't need to be an art historian to see that La Sagrada Família, or the Church of the Holy Family, is a bizarre wonder. Begun in 1882 and incomplete at the architect's death in 1926, this languid, amorphous structure embodies the essence of Gaudí's signature style: ***modernismo,*** a romantic, voluptuous Catalonian offshoot of Art Nouveau that flourished from about 1890 to 1910. Modernismo emulated forms found in nature; symmetry was out, handcrafted decoration was in. Gaudí loved drooping masses, melting horizontal lines, and giddy spirals. This cathedral erupts skyward with clusters of honeycombed spires, looking more like encrusted stalagmites than like traditional Gothic towers; its arches are neither pointed Gothic nor rounded Romanesque, but tapering curves with a certain *Star Trek*–ish flair. (Gaudí's versions of flying buttresses are more Space Age struts.) Sculpted figures seem to grow organically out of its portals and arches, with variegated color lent by several different types of stone. La Sagrada Família's **rose windows** really do look like roses, its fluted columns like flower stalks, rising to a vaulted ceiling pattern that made us think of a field spangled with daisies.

Two facades have been finished, with the central nave, still under construction, standing open to the sky. Bitten by the Gaudí bug, our family trooped around Barcelona looking for more modernismo, and enjoyed the wavy balconies of **Casa Batlló,** Passeig de Gràcia 43 (🕾 **34/93/488-0666**), and the sculpted vegetable and fruit shapes bedecking the apartment complex **La Pedrera,** Passeig de Gràcia 92 (🕾 **34/93/484-5900,** 34/93/484-5900, or 34/93/484-5995), with its phantasmagoric chimneys. The Espai Gaudí (Gaudí Space) in the attic has an intriguing multimedia display of the controversial artist's work.

ⓘ Carrer de Sardenya or Carrer de la Marina (🕾 **34/93/207-3031;** www.sagradafamilia.org).

✈ Barcelona.

🛏 $$ **Duques de Bergara,** Bergara 11 (🕾 **34/93/301-5151;** www.hoteles-catalonia.com). $$$ **Hotel Hesperia Sarriá,** Los Vergós 20 (**34/93/204-5551**).

WHY THEY'LL THANK YOU: Gaudí designed the kinds of buildings children draw themselves.

Where Constantinople Meets Istanbul
Mosques, Mosaics & Minarets
All ages • Sultanahmet, Istanbul, Turkey

Istanbul, formerly Constantinople, is a city with a foot in both Europe and Asia, and its religious heritage is equal parts Islam and Christianity (even its Christian history is half Roman Catholic, half Greek Orthodox). The kids may not always be able to keep all these elements straight, but one thing they'll remember about the Turkish capital: the exquisite mosaics and domes of its great houses of worship.

The masterpiece is **Ayasofya,** which for almost a thousand years was the largest Christian church in the world (the Statue of Liberty's torch would barely graze the top). Built by the Emperor Justinian in A.D. 537, it became the majestic symbol of Byzantine power. Its history has been turbulent; for one thing, in this earthquake-prone region, clunky flying buttresses had to be added to support its red-tinted outer walls. In 1204, the Crusaders stripped the church of its relics, a sacrilege that caused the Greek Orthodox Church to split from the Roman Catholic Church. Then, in 1453, Mehmet II took over the city (look for his stone cannonballs along the path in the inner courtyard), and his first official act was to declare the great church a mosque. Frescoes and mosaics were covered up, as Islam forbids the representation of figures; slim pointed minarets were erected; the altar was shifted to accommodate a *mihrab* (a niche pointing toward Mecca); and an ablution fountain was plunked down in the courtyard. In 1935, when Atatürk converted it to a museum, its hidden mosaics and icons were restored.

If you've never seen a **Byzantine church** before, this one will astound you, with some 1.6 hectares (4 acres) of mosaics covering the interior. The glistening narthex, or inner vestibule, is just the prelude; the 15-story-high main dome is crowned with 40 windows to filter light onto its dazzling gold mosaics. Point out to the kids that, per Islamic tradition, many mosaics have calligraphy or abstract motifs; go up in the southern gallery to find the really old ones with pictures.

When Sultan Ahmet I built his namesake mosque in 1609, the beauty of Ayasofya

so galled him, he set out to surpass it. The result is the **Blue Mosque,** a grand bubble of masonry that's a defining feature of Istanbul's skyline, with its cluster of domes and minidomes and its six gold minarets (the mosque in Mecca had to add a seventh minaret to top it). You enter through a door off the Hippodrome (remove your shoes!), beneath a symbolic chain that required even the sultan to bow his head when he arrived on horseback. The kids will be awed by the girth of the enormous "elephant foot" pillars supporting the series of domes overhead. As the sun pours in through 260 windows, the lofty space swirls with colors from the exquisite decorative tiles—mostly blues and greens, of course, hence the name. Ah, but does it surpass Ayasofya, as Ahmet hoped? There's your dinner-table discussion tonight.

(i) **Ayasofya Museum** (© **90/212/522-1750**).

✈ Atatürk International, Istanbul.

🛏 $$$ **Çiragăn Palace Hotel Kempinski Istanbul,** Çiragăn Caddesi 32. (© **800/426-3135** in the U.S., 90/212/326-46-46 in Istanbul; www.ciraganpalace.com). $$ **Blue House Hotel (Mavi Ev),** Dalbasti Sokak 14 (© **90/212/638-9010;** www.blue house.com.tr).

WHY THEY'LL THANK YOU: Imagine how many tiles it took to line those domes.

326

The Painted Churches of Moldavia
Ages 4 & up • West of Suceava, Romania

When most of the congregation is illiterate, how does a church teach Biblical lore? In medieval northern Europe, they depicted the stories in grand Gothic windows of stained glass; in Greece and other Orthodox countries, intricate mosaics were the medium. But only in northern

Romania, in a kingdom once known as Moldavia, were churches—even simple country churches—painted inside and out with vivid, dramatic narrative murals, in the iconic Byzantine style common in Eastern Rite churches. Only about a dozen of these painted churches remain today, and

A painted church in Moldavia.

often they are too poor to properly restore and preserve these treasures. The sooner you get here the better.

While Moldavia struggled against the Ottoman invaders sweeping northward from Constantinople (today's Istanbul) toward Vienna, from 1522 to 1547 a handful of artists moved around this mountainous countryside painting frescoes on church after church, all in the distinctive architecture of the region—with round towers and apses, octagonal steeples set on a star-shaped base, and wide-eaved roofs like brimmed hats clapped on top. These itinerant artists used simple paints, plus household ingredients such as charcoal, egg, vinegar, and honey to preserve the color, which evidently worked—they have withstood the rugged Carpathian climate for over 450 years. No doubt it helped that they were in small out-of-the-way towns, near the Ukrainian border, situated only a few miles from one another along narrow roads and mountain passes.

If you can only see one, make it **Voroneţ,** with its amazing Last Judgment on one large west wall. I'm also partial to

Humor because of all the daring political references its artist slipped in—look for turbaned Turkish enemies in many of his murals. Green is the dominant color at charming little **Arbore,** which has a detailed painting of the story of Genesis. **Sucevita** is not just one church but an entire fortified monastery compound, with thousands of pictures—notice the one blank wall, which was left unfinished, the story goes, when the painter fell off his scaffolding to his death. **Moldoviţa** has a particularly panoramic depiction of the Siege of Constantinople, a major event for the Greek Orthodox Church. All five can be visited in a few hours, on a loop of back roads west of Suceava.

✈ Suceava, 24–32km (15–20 miles).

🛏 $$ **Hotel Balada,** Str. Mitropoliei 3, Suceava (© **40/230/522146;** www.balada. ro). $$$ **Best Western Hotel Bucovina,** 4 Bucovina Ave., Gura Humorului (© **40/ 230/207000;** www.bestwestern.com).

WHY THEY'LL THANK YOU: Literally, storybook churches.

St. Basil's Cathedral
Ivan the Terrible's Moscow Fantasy
Ages 6 & up • Moscow, Russia

On the nightly news, whenever reporters broadcast stories from Moscow, this is where they stand: on **Red Square,** the city's central plaza, with St. Basil's Cathedral in the background, a gaudy riot of exotic bulbous domes and towers. Along with the solid red-brick wall of the Kremlin and the gray cobblestones of Red Square, on TV it looks like a psychedelic stage set. Who would ever build such a crazy candy-colored building? But that's just what makes it appealing to children.

St. Basil's is essentially a union of nine different Byzantine churches, topped with nine distinct roofs (count them), arranged in an eight-pointed star, an important symbol in medieval Christian iconography. This "tented" style of architecture was typically Russian; note that the eight smaller domes are onion-shaped, a common silhouette in Orthodox churches, clustered around one central unifying spire of a more European design. It's like a visual reminder that Russia is as much Asian as it is European. Yet even the onion domes have subtle differences in design, accentuated by their contrasting bold color schemes. Bring a sketch pad with you and let the kids have a go at drawing the domes.

St. Basil's—in Russian, Khram Vasiliya Blazhennogo—was originally built under Ivan the Terrible to honor Russia's victory over Mongol Tatars in 1555. Moscow already had several beautiful cathedrals in the **Kremlin** across the Square, but Ivan wanted to surpass them: Legend says he had the architect's eyes poked out afterward to keep him from ever again making anything to rival Moscow's "stone flower." Inside, the cathedral has a much more dour character than you'd expect. Ivan's idea was to make a separate chapel for each saint upon whose feast day he had won a battle, so instead of one main nave, like the Gothic cathedrals of western Europe, St. Basil's houses several dim and chilly sanctuaries, which you can only reach via narrow, winding passages and treacherously worn stairs. There aren't a lot of brochures or plaques around to help you sort it out, though stalls do sell icons and souvenirs. Surrender to its irrational charm and wander around, soaking up the dank medieval atmosphere. From the upper-floor windows, you get a close-up of those fantastic pilasters and a broad view of the Moscow River.

ⓘ **Moscow Hotels and City Guides** (✆ **74/95/298-3304**).

✈ Moscow.

🛏 $$ **Cosmos,** 150 Prospekt Mira (✆ **74/95/234-1000;** www.hotelcosmos.ru).

$$$ **Sheraton Palace,** 19 1st Tverskaya-Yamskaya Ulitsa (✆ **74/95/931-9700;** www.sheratonpalace.ru).

WHY THEY'LL THANK YOU: Outlining the domes, then coloring them in.

328

The Golden Temple

Ages 8 & up • Amritsar, Punjab, India

In the northern Punjabi city of Amritsar rests India's most dazzling sacred site, the Golden Temple, begun in 1574 but constantly embellished and adorned over the years since. It's not only an architectural landmark, but it's also the holiest of holies for the Sikh religion, a faith that actively preaches unity and equality among all religions. All visitors are welcome to share the temple experience. Before entering you must leave your shoes at the entrance, cover your head (bandanas are provided), wash your feet in the shallow pool by the doorway—and prepare for a very moving sight.

It's not just that the temple is spectacular, although it is that. The heart of the complex, the **Hari Mandir** (Divine Temple) is a gold-plated building with copper cupolas and jewel-encrusted marble walls that almost seems to float serenely in the surrounding pool of water. (Some 100 kilograms of gold were used to coat its inverted lotus-shaped dome.) But the complex is laid out so that the process of getting there is a ritual in itself—a clockwise walk around the sacred pool, past several smaller shrines, through a magnificent silver gate and over the long **Guru's Bridge**—meant to symbolize the soul's journey after death. Then once you're in the Hari Mandir, you take in a trancelike scene of worship, usually being broadcast live to Sikhs around India. Scriptures are chanted from a Holy Book, a ceremonial whisk is flicked over its pages, musical instruments play, and lines of devotees (you can recognize male Sikhs by their turbans, beards, and steel wrist bangles)

circulate clockwise, touching their heads in a trancelike rhythm to the temple floor and walls. In another hall, the **Guru-ka-Langar,** around 35,000 worshipers are fed every day by temple volunteers; anyone and everyone is accepted at the table, in the egalitarian spirit of Sikhism.

The majority of India's Sikhs live in the Punjab. For more background on this faith, you can stop in the **Central Sikh Museum** at the main entrance, but be forewarned: It includes some graphic portraits of gurus being tortured and executed in terrifying ways.

The best time to visit is in the evening for the **Palki Sahib,** or Night Ceremony, when the Holy Book is carried on a palanquin from the Hari Mandir to the sanctum where it rests overnight. Men line up and shift the palanquin forward from shoulder to shoulder, as if moving it along a human conveyor belt. Joining in the common task, every individual seems merged in one collective motion, the many becoming one. We can all learn from this.

ⓘ ✆ **91/183/255-3954.**

✈ Amritsar.

🛏 $ **Mrs. Bhandari's Guesthouse,** No.10, Cantonment (✆ **91/183/222-8509;** www.india9.com/i9show/Mrs.-Bhandari's-Guesthouse-32543.htm). $$ **Ritz Plaza Hotel,** 45 Mall Rd. (✆ **91/183/2562836-39;** www.ritzhotel.in).

WHY THEY'LL THANK YOU: Getting caught up in the spirit.

The Cave Temples of Ajanta & Ellora

Ages 10 & up • Near Augangabad, India

It's quite a proposition, getting to the ancient cave temples of Ellora and Ajanta, in far-flung Maharashtra, India, about 388km (241 miles) east of Mumbai. What really makes it worth the trip is not the beauty of these two worship sites—though they certain are beautiful—it's the fact that they were built at all, chiseled patiently out of the hillsides, chip by chip, using nothing but hand-held tools. The faith that inspired such an undertaking must have been powerful indeed—and it still seems to animate the stone with spiritual grace.

Ajanta is by far the older of the two complexes, begun in the 2nd century B.C. and carved out over the next 700 years by Buddhist monks. Rediscovered by a British soldier in 1819, this horseshoe of 29 caves is packed with **sculptures** and **colorful murals** of astonishing detail, telling the story of Buddhism. Some caves are chaityas, or shrines, and others are viharas, or monasteries; the pictures were meant to inspire spiritual contemplation on the life and teachings of Buddha. As you walk through with the kids, don't linger too long in any one cave: Simply imagine the long-ago monks tending to their devotions. The most brilliantly painted is **Cave 17,** where maidens float overhead, accompanied by celestial musicians, lotus petals, and scrollwork. The great mandala, or sacred meditative design, on the ceiling of **Cave 2** is also awesome.

The 34 Ellora caves are much newer—if you can imagine thinking of the 4th to 11th centuries A.D. as recent times. Located on a major trade route, Ellora was never "lost" as Ajanta was; parts were used for worship as recently as the 19th century.

What I find fascinating about Ellora is that it isn't strictly Buddhist, but a combination of 12 Buddhist, 17 Hindu, and 5 Jain temples, where you can compare the symbols and stories of the three religions. All the entrances face west, so try to visit in the afternoon, when the sunlight pours in. Be sure to see the huge **Buddha** of Cave 10 and the monks' **rock beds** in Cave 12. The showpiece of Ellora is Cave 16, the **Kailashanath Temple,** the world's largest monolithic structure. It took 800 artisans 150 years to whittle one massive piece of rock into this Hindu shrine, designed to resemble Mount Kailash, the mythical home of Shiva in the Himalayas. In general, the sculpture at Ellora isn't as fine as Ajanta's, and it doesn't have those vibrant paintings; but as a feat of architecture it's incredible—many of these temples are two or three stories high and so intricate that you'll need to remind yourself that they were cut out of the mountainside, not built as freestanding structures.

ⓘ **Maharashtra Tourism Development,** Holiday Resort, Station Rd., Aurangabad (✆ **91/240/233-1513;** www. maharashtratourism.gov.in).

✈ Aurangabad, 107km (66 miles) to Ajanta, 26km (16 miles) to Ellora.

🛏 $$ **The Ambassador Ajanta,** Jalna Rd., Aurangabad (✆ **91/240/248-5211;** www.ambassadorindia.com). $$ **Quality Inn The Meadows,** Gat nos. 135 and 136, Village Mitmita, Aurangabad (✆ **91/240/267-7412**).

WHY THEY'LL THANK YOU: Imagine the monks carving away.

330

The Great Stupa of Sanchi
Enfolding the Peace of Buddha
Ages 4 & up • Sanchi, India

There's something hugely appealing about the Great Stupa of Sanchi, a plump domed Buddhist monument of rough-dressed stone, tucked away in the landlocked state of Madhya Pradesh. The stupa may once have held some ashes of the Buddha, who died in 483 B.C. (smaller stupas alongside, like satellites around a mother ship, contain ashes of his disciples). Set on a squat hill with lovely views of the surrounding countryside, this time-weathered religious complex doesn't overwhelm the worshiper—it's a low-rise site of gentle domes and spaces for contemplation. The peace of the centuries seems to settle upon it like the folds of a sari.

India's finest example of **ancient Buddhist architecture,** the Great Stupa complex was founded in the 3rd century B.C. by the Mauryan emperor Ashoka, who converted to Buddhism after massacring thousands in his military campaigns. Ashoka's wife was a devout Buddhist from nearby Vidisha, and the city's prosperous merchants became patrons as well. Isolated Sanchi thrived in its serene way for centuries, until a resurgence of Hinduism in the 13th century A.D., along with rising Islamic militancy, made Buddhism wither. The site lay deserted for more than 500 years until 1818, when—a typical story for India—a British military adventurer stumbled upon the ruins. Excavations have gone on for nearly 200 years, unearthing about 55 temples, pillars, stupas, and monasteries (check out **Monastery 51,** with its tiny sleeping cells for monks). The more they uncovered, the more excited the archaeologists grew, for Sanchi has proven to be a textbook of evolving Buddhist architectural styles, an unbroken continuum with every era gloriously represented.

The proportions of the Great Stupa are so harmonious that you're surprised when you get up close to see how big it actually is. At 17m (55 ft.) high, nearly eight stories, it anchors the center of the complex like a massive beehive, or maybe a flying saucer. Originally it was a smaller brick hemisphere; in the 2nd century B.C., a balustrade was added (notice its bamboolike pattern) and the brick dome was enlarged considerably with a casing of unevenly cut sandstone. Four intricately carved **gateways** of finer-grained sandstone were added circa 25 B.C., facing the four points of the compass—urge the kids to try to "read" their story panels from the life of Buddha. (At that era, the Buddha was never pictured as a human—look for him instead as a lotus, a wheel, a bodhi tree, or a pair of feet.) Originally the dome and the plinth it sits on were coated with white lime concrete, the railways and gateway painted red, and the surface of the stupa painted with swags and garlands; the antennalike spire on top would have been gilded. It must have been grand in its heyday.

ⓘ **Madhya Pradesh Tourism** (www.mptourism.com).

✈ Bhopal, 45km (28 miles).

🛏 $$ **Jehan Numa Palace,** 157 Shamla Hill, Bhopal (✆ **91/755/266-1100;** www.hoteljehanumapalace.com).

WHY THEY'LL THANK YOU: In harmony with the spirit of Buddha.

Nikko

Buddhist Serenity in the Mountains of Japan

All ages • Nikko City, Japan

You might want to come here to see one of Japan's great mountain Buddhist retreats. Or you might want to pay homage to Tokugawa Ieyasu, the model for James Clavell's novel *Shogun*. But if you want the kids to enjoy this expedition from Tokyo, tell them you're on safari, looking for **animal images** in this magnificent 17th-century Japanese shrine.

On the edge of town, walk onto the vermilion-painted **Sacred Bridge (Shinkyo),** built in 1636; in the past, only shoguns and their emissaries were allowed to cross it. Up the stone steps is the 8th century **Rinnoji** Temple, housing the "gods of Nikko," three 8.4m-high (28-ft.) gold-plated wooden images of Buddha. Today the gods are taking prayers for world peace. Through a grove of ancient Japanese cedars, you come to the showpiece of Nikko, **Toshogu Shrine,** built in the 1630s by Tokugawa's grandson. No expense was too great in creating the monument: Some 15,000 craftspeople were brought from all over Japan, and after 2 years' work, they completed a cluster of buildings more elaborate than any other Japanese temple or shrine, gilded with a dazzling 2.4 million sheets of gold leaf. Go up the stairs through a huge stone torii gateway; on your left is a five-story pagoda. (Pagodas are normally found at Buddhist temples, not Shinto shrines, but the two mingle happily here.) Up more stairs to your first animal image: the **Sacred Stable,** which houses a sacred white horse (horses have long

been held sacred to Shinto gods). Above the stable door is my personal favorite carving at Nikko—three monkeys enacting "see no evil, hear no evil, speak no evil"; they're the guardians of the sacred horse. Across from the stable is **Kami-Jinko,** with a famous painting of two elephants—pretty accurate, considering that the artist had read about elephants but had never actually seen one. Up the next flight of stairs, to the left is **Yakushido,** known for its dragon painting on the ceiling. Tell the kids to clap their hands under it; the resulting echo sounds like a dragon's roar. The shrine's most stunning feature is **Yomeimon Gate,** often called the Twilight Gate because it could take you all day (until twilight) to see everything on it. Painted in red, blue, and green and decorated with gilt and lacquerwork, this gate has about 400 carvings of flowers, dragons, birds, and other animals. To the right of the main hall, look for the beloved carving of a sleeping cat above the entrance to **Tokugawa Ieyasu's mausoleum.** Beyond that, stone steps lead past cedars to Tokugawa's strikingly simple tomb.

Directly to the west of Toshogu Shrine is Futarasan Shrine (1617), where the kids should look for the **ghost lantern,** enclosed in a small wooden structure. According to legend, it used to come alive at night and sweep around Nikko in the form of a ghost, scaring one guard so much that he struck it with his sword 70 times—you can still see the marks on the lamp's rim. Spooky.

See no evil, hear no evil, speak no evil.

ⓘ **Nikko Information Center** (📞 **81/288/54-2496;** www.nikko-jp.org).

🚆 Nikko, 2 hr. from Tokyo.

🛏 $ **Annex Turtle Hotori-An,** 8–28 Takumi-cho (📞 **81/288/53-3663;** www.turtle-nikko.com).

WHY THEY'LL THANK YOU: The monkeys.

Angkor Wat
Glory in the Jungle
Ages 8 & up • North of Siem Reap, Cambodia

When French naturalist Henri Mouhot, hacking his way through the Cambodian jungle in 1861, first stumbled upon the ruins of the ancient city of Angkor Wat, I wonder what he thought. Lying before him, shrouded in roots and vines, was the largest religious monument ever constructed, a mysterious collection of hulking laterite and sandstone blocks. When it was cleared, the temple complex—capital of the Khmer kingdom from 802 until 1295—proved to cover 98 sq. km (38 sq. miles). Today it's Cambodia's chief tourism attraction, and definitely one of the great marvels of the world.

You'll probably need more than 1 day to visit Angkor Wat, to let the magic of its timeless stones begin to work their spell. This is one place where it's worthwhile to hire a guide, to illuminate this welter of crumbling stones, carvings, and columns with background information on Buddhism, Hinduism, and Khmer history. Besides, a guide will help you catch the priceless photo ops, such as a temple's perfect reflection in a pool at sunset.

The resplendent **main temple,** also called Angkor Wat, is only the beginning, though its four-spired profile is the one you'll recognize (it has virtually become the symbol of Cambodia). Dating from the 12th century, it stands 213m (669 ft.) high from its base to the tip of its highest lotus-shaped tower. The whole Angkor complex is full of storytelling bas-reliefs, which will intrigue the kids, but on the first level is one of the most famous, narrating a Hindu legend in which various gods stir the oceans to extract the elixir of immortality. Scholars have worked out that this sandstone temple's symmetry mirrors the timeline of the Hindu ages, like a map or calendar of the universe. (See why you'll need a guide?) Approaching from the main road over a *baray,* or reservoir, you climb up three levels to the inner sanctum; the steps can be tricky, but you'll soon be high up for an inspiring view.

The name Angkor Thom means "great city" in Khmer, and this other sprawling temple complex is dotted with many temples—don't miss the **bas-reliefs** on the Terrace of the Leper King and the Terrace of Elephants. The central temple, the **Bayon,** is the most fantastic. Though this is a Buddhist temple, built slightly after Angkor Wat in 1190, it also alludes to Hindu cosmology. Gaze upon its four huge stone faces, each aligned with a compass point (the same is true of each of its 51 small towers)—the expression on the face, possibly the image of the king who built the temple, is as enigmatic as that of the *Mona Lisa.*

To get an idea of what this site looked like when Mouhot found it, visit the **Ta Prohm temple,** which has been left entangled in the jungle foliage, the roots

Angkor Wat.

of fig, banyan, and kapok trees cleaving its massive stones and growing over the top of temple ramparts.

(i) **Siem Reap Tourism Office** (© 855/12/630-066; www.mot.gov.kh).

✈ Siem Reap.

🛏 $ **La Noria,** off Rte. 6, northeast of Siem Reap (© **855/63/964-242**). $$$ **Sofitel Royal Angkor,** Vithei Charles de Gaulle (© **855/63/964-600;** www.accor.com).

WHY THEY'LL THANK YOU: A great secret hidden in the jungle.

Borobudur
A Buddhist Climb to Paradise
Ages 6 & up • South of Magelang, Central Java, Indonesia

Set on a smooth green plain on the gardenlike Indonesian island of Java, Borobudur is not only the largest Buddhist monument in the world, but also quite simply one of the most stunning architectural creations you'll ever see. Some two million blocks of lava rock completed the original pyramidlike design, though some have been lost over the centuries. Seen from the ground, it looks like a mountain,

bristling with odd little spires; seen from above, it looks like an open lotus blossom, the sacred expression of Buddhism. Any kid who's ever played with Legos will get the compulsive beauty of its symmetry.

But the true brilliance of Borobudur can only be understood if you walk around it. Like the labyrinths in medieval Christian cathedrals, the **walkways** around each level of this stepped pyramid are an exercise in meditation; you'll see saffron-robed Buddhist priests pacing along, chanting as they wind around the 3km-long (1³/₄-mile) route to the top. The first six levels (plus another underground to stabilize the pyramid) are rectangular in shape, decorated with sculpted bas-relief panels, 1,460 in all. Seen in order, the panels are more or less a spiritual textbook, depicting the life and lessons of Buddha. Each ascending level represents a higher stage of man's spiritual journey. The top three levels, however, are circular terraces with no ornamentation, for Buddhism considers plainness and simplicity more virtuous than decoration. Instead of carved panels, these upper levels hold a regimented series of beehivelike stone **stupas,** their bricks set in perforated checkerboard patterns, almost as if to let in air for the **stone Buddhas** tucked inside. Each inscrutable Buddha sits cross-legged, making a hand gesture that signifies one of five spiritual attainments. At the top, one large central stupa crowns the pyramid, empty inside—scholars debate whether it once contained a bigger Buddha, or whether its emptiness symbolizes the blessed state of nirvana.

One of the many mysteries of Borobudur is why it was abandoned. When Sir Thomas Stanford Raffles discovered it in 1814, Borobudur was buried under layers of ash from nearby Mount Merapi. Perhaps it was buried Pompeii-style; or maybe a series of eruptions brought famine to the region, causing the population to move away. Either way, Borobudur lay forgotten for centuries. It's now a UNESCO World Heritage Site, and perhaps Java's most admired tourist destination. Antiquities officials, worried that tourist footprints are wearing down the ancient stone, are pressing to have the terraced walkways closed to visitors. Go now before you lose your chance.

ⓘ **Central Java Tourism** (www.central-java-tourism.com) or www.borobudurpark.com.

✈ Yogvakarta, 40km (25 miles).

🛏 $$ **Manohara Hotel,** Borobudur Archaeological Park, Magelang (ⓒ **62/293/718813;** www.baliwww.com). $$$ **Sheraton Mustika,** JL Laksda Adisucipto, Yogyakarta (ⓒ **62/274/488588;** www.sheraton.com).

WHY THEY'LL THANK YOU: Walking the circuit, reading the walls.

12 A Dose of Culture

The Louvre.

The Uffizi Gallery
Pearl of the Italian Renaissance
Ages 6 & up • Florence, Italy

Let's face it: Renaissance art can be a hard sell to kids. But my husband and I didn't want to miss the Uffizi Gallery, unquestionably one of the world's great museums, a treasure-trove of—you guessed it—Italian Renaissance art. (What else would you expect inside a former Medici palace in Florence?) Fortunately, we found a strategy that clicked: We made our visit to the Uffizi into a treasure hunt.

Here's how it worked: In the earlier rooms, you'll see painting after painting of the classic Madonna and Child pose, each artist giving his own distinctive take. We asked our youngsters to study them all (kids like looking at pictures of kids anyway) to see how through the ages the babies began to look more realistic. We also pointed out the flat, stylized backgrounds of the earlier paintings so that they could see how the scenes became deeper and more natural as painters developed the art of perspective.

A new theme starts in rooms 10 to 14, the **Botticelli rooms**—the highlight of the Uffizi for most visitors, me included. In the mid-1400s, classical mythology had become a popular subject, and so we looked for pictures of Venus, the goddess of beauty—which pointed us straight to the Uffizi's ultimate masterpiece, Botticelli's *Birth of Venus*. (Consider whether or not you want to tell them its nickname, "Venus on the Half Shell," because once you tell them they won't ever think of it as anything else.) We found ourselves even more engrossed by Botticelli's *Allegory of Spring*, or *Primavera*, which depicts Venus

Outside the Uffizi Gallery.

in a citrus grove with Cupid hovering suggestively over her head. Outside the room, look for Botticelli's *Adoration of the Magi,* in which many figures are Medici portraits (the man in the yellow robe at the far right is Botticelli); compare it to Leonardo da Vinci's unfinished *Adoration* in room 15. To carry on the Venus theme, check out the Greek statue *Venus of the Medici* in beautiful room 18 with its dome of pearl shells, and a couple of voluptuous Titian Venuses in room 28.

In rooms 23 to 25, get the kids to notice how art began to embrace storytelling by looking for episodes in the life of Jesus—Correggio's *Rest on the Flight to Egypt;* Andrea Mantagna's *Epiphany, Circumcision,* and *Ascension;* and, in room 25, Michelangelo's magnificent *Holy Family.*

Speaking of Michelangelo, it's too bad you have to pay another admission fee (and wait in line) to enter the **Galleria dell'Accademia,** Via Ricasoll 60 (✆ **39/55/2388609**), where the only thing the kids will want to see is Michelangelo's

colossal statue of **David.** We cut our losses, looked instead at the inferior copy outdoors in the Piazza della Signoria, and then headed out to **St. Mark's Museum,** Museo di San Marco; Piazza San Marco 1 (✆ **39/55/294883**). Originally a Dominican convent, its bleak, bare cells are decorated with frescoes by the mystical **Fra Angelico,** one of Europe's greatest 15th-century painters. You've been telling the kids for years not to write on the walls, but oh, if they could create scenes like these, you'd let them paint their hearts out.

ⓘ Piazzale degli Uffizi 6 (✆ **39/55/23885;** www.uffizi.firenze.it).

🚆 Florence, 2–3 hr. from Rome.

🛏 $$$ **Grand Hotel Villa Medici,** Via il Prato 42 (✆ **39/55/277171;** www.villa medicihotel.com). $ **Hotel Casci,** Via Cavour 13 (✆ **39/55/211686;** www.hotel casci.com).

WHY THEY'LL THANK YOU: The Botticelli Venuses.

---

335 Masterpieces of Art

The Last Supper
On the da Vinci Trail in Milan
Ages 8 & up • Milan, Italy

Though born in Florence, Leonardo da Vinci spent many years in Milan (1482–99 and 1506–13), under the patronage of the dukes of Milan. The finicky artist produced endless studies and sketches for projects he never finished; one he did complete, however, was a mural that Duke Ludovico commissioned for the convent of Santa Marie delle Grazie church. It just may be the master's greatest painting—but its condition is endangered. Get your kids here now, because it may not exist when they've grown up.

Set above a doorway in what was once a dining hall, **The Last Supper** *(Il Cenacolo Vinciano)* is a huge artwork—8.5m

wide and 4.6m tall (28 ft.×15 ft.)—depicting one of the most famous meals of all time: Christ's last Passover Seder in Jerusalem, shortly before his arrest. There's nothing static about this scene: Jesus, hands outspread (as if to display his future wounds) has just announced that one of his followers will betray him, and the disciples all lean away, aghast, each in his own manner protesting his fidelity. Ask the kids to pick out Judas—he's the one with his face in shadow, already clutching the bag of money he was paid to betray Jesus. Christ's sorrowful figure is isolated, the curved pediment of a doorway over his head suggesting a halo; light streams in from the windows behind him, while darkness looms behind the disciples. It's a masterpiece of composition, both technical and dramatic, and no matter how often it's parodied (Mel Brooks, Monty Python, and George Carlin have all had a go at it), the original still takes your breath away.

The kids may be shocked to see how fragile the mural looks, but to me that adds human dimension to da Vinci's artistic achievement. The painting began to disintegrate almost as soon as Leonardo finished it, for he had experimented with risky new paints and application techniques. But it is so clearly a work of genius that over the centuries artists and restorers felt drawn to save it, repainting it in the 1700s, the 1800s, and again quite recently. It's been said that all that's left of the original *Last Supper* is a "few isolated streaks of fading color"—everything else was layered on by later hands. So what are we looking at here, and why? If you can get

your kids to discuss this paradox, you'll really expand their minds.

Only 25 viewers are admitted at a time (be prepared to wait in line), and you must pass through antipollutant chambers before you get your allotted 15 minutes in front of the painting. A lot to go through, but *The Last Supper* is worth it.

(i) 758 Piazza Santa Maria delle Grazie, off Corso Magenta (© **39/2/89421146**). Reservations required; closed Mon.

✈ Milan's Aeroporto di Linate (internal European flights). Aeroporto Malpensa (transatlantic flights).

🛏 $$ **Antica Locanda Leonardo,** Corso Magenta 78 (© **39/2/48014197;** www.leoloc.com). $$$ **Four Seasons Hotel Milano,** Via Gesú 8 (© **39/0277088;** www.fourseasons.com).

WHY THEY'LL THANK YOU: The da Vinci mystique hovers here.

Masterpieces of Art **336**

Paris for Art Lovers
Ages 10 & up • Paris, France

The **Musée du Louvre** just may be the world's most impressive art museum—to go to Paris and *not* visit it would almost be absurd. Yet the collection is so staggeringly huge, you simply can't see everything. And if your adult mind soon starts to whirl, just imagine how children feel.

Don't miss the Louvre, but be smart about it: Avoid the long line at the glass pyramid entrance by using the automatic ticket machines, or order tickets in advance by credit card (© **33/8/92-68-46-94**). Skip the 90-minute guided tours; they're pitched over kids' heads, and they make every room they enter instantly crowded. Once you're through the doors, simply pick up a museum map and plan your own visit to loop past the Big Three Masterpieces: da Vinci's *La Giaconda* (better known as the

Mona Lisa), the armless classical sculpture *Venus de Milo,* and the ancient headless statue *Winged Victory.* Everybody else is trying to see them too, so expect to be jostled; the *Mona Lisa* in particular is a letdown, a small, dark painting you can't get close to. Once you've seen it, hunt for other da Vincis in the surrounding galleries, then cut over to the superb **ancient Egypt collection,** which the Louvre has been amassing since Napoleon occupied Egypt in 1798. Then spend 40 minutes or so wandering around the **Richelieu Wing,** which houses northern European and French art; my favorite bit here is the grand salons of Napoleon III.

Now you've done it, you've visited the Louvre—the children can say they saw the *Mona Lisa* in person. And, having successfully avoided an art over-dose, you've got a shot at steering them into three other Paris art museums they'll enjoy more. Across the Seine, the **Musée d'Orsay,** 1 rue de Bellechasse (✆ **33/1/40-49-48-14;** www. musee-orsay.fr), set in a trans-formed neoclassical train station, focuses on 1848–1914, which means it has lots of impression-ists, pointillists, and realists—painters such as van Gogh, Manet, Monet, Degas, and Renoir. Masterpieces include Renoir's *Moulin de la Galette,* van Gogh's *Starry Night,* James McNeill Whistler's *Arrangement in Gray and Black: Portrait of the Painter's Mother,* and Manet's *Déje-uner sur l'herbe,* with its shock-ing-for-its-time nude woman picnicking.

The **Musée National Auguste Rodin,** Hôtel Biron, 77 rue de Varenne (✆ **33/1/44-18-61-10;** www.musee-rodin.fr), is set in the great 19th-century sculptor's own mansion, with splendid rose gardens. Stand next to *The Thinker* and

Venus de Milo at the Louvre.

you'll understand how marble comes to life in the hands of a genius.

Musée Picasso, Hôtel Salé, 5 rue de Thorigny (✆ **33/1/42-71-25-21;** www. paris.org/Musees/Picasso), displays the world's greatest Picasso collec-tion, including his fabled gaunt blue figures and harlequins, a career-span-ning range of the Spanish artist's paintings and sculptures in a lovely restored mansion. It was my kids' favorite art museum in all of France—we were glad we saved it for last.

ⓘ **Musée du Louvre,** 34–36 quai du Louvre, 1er (✆ **33/1/40-20-53-17;** www.louvre.fr).

✈ De Gaulle, Orly.

🛏 $$$ **Hotel de Fleurie,** 32–34 rue Grégoire-de-Tours (✆ **33/1/53-73-70-00;** www.hotel defleurie.tm.fr). $$ **Residence Lord Byron,** 5 rue de Chateaubri-and (✆ **33/1/43-59-89-98;** www. escapade-paris.com).

WHY THEY'LL THANK YOU: The *Mona Lisa,* *Whistler's Mother,* and *The Thinker*—a trifecta of great art.

---

337 Masterpieces of Art

Museo del Prado
Where Three Old Masters Reign in Spain
Ages 6 & up • Madrid, Spain

With more than 7,000 paintings, **the Prado** is one of the most important repos-itories of art in the world, based on a royal collection fattened over the years by the wealth of the Habsburgs and the Bour-bons. Don't make the kids see everything; on your first visit, concentrate on the three great Spanish masters—Velázquez, Goya, and El Greco, who can be appreciated here as nowhere else.

One picture they must see: *Las Meni-nas* by **Diego Velázquez** (1599–1660). The figure of a small Spanish infanta in her splendid satin gown is the focal point, her self-possessed gaze as quixotic as the Mona Lisa's. Two figures in the painting look directly at the viewer: the princess and that dark-clothed figure behind her painting the royal family, a self-portrait of Velázquez. The faces of the queen and king are merely reflected in a mirror on a back wall. Then there's that departing figure on the stairs in the back—Velázquez's virtuoso technique is one thing, but this painting is so dramatically composed, we could barely drag ourselves away.

We love the work of his older contemporary **El Greco** (ca. 1541–1614), a Crete-born artist who lived much of his life in Toledo. His huge canvases look astonishingly modern, with their impressionistic lights and shadows. The Prado displays several of his rapturous saints, Madonnas, and Holy Families, even a ghostly John the Baptist.

It's also fascinating to see the work of **Francisco de Goya** (1746–1828)—note the contrast between his portraits of Charles IV and his family (so unflattering, you wonder why they continued their patronage) and politically charged paintings, such as the **Third of May** (1808), and sketches depicting the decay of 18th-century Spain. One pair of canvases, **The Clothed Maja** and **The Naked Maja,** make a brilliant contrast—almost identical portraits, except that in one the woman is clothed and in the other she's nude.

My teenagers also got into Hieronymus Bosch's The Garden of Earthly Delights, The Seven Deadly Sins, and his triptych The Hay Wagon, along with the ghoulish The Triumph of Death, by Pieter Breughel the Elder. But we only had 1 day, and we needed to scoot over to the **Museo Nacional Centro de Arte Reina Sofía,** Santa Isabel 52 (✆ **34/91/467-5062** or 91-468-3002; www.museoreinasofia.es), the Prado's modern-art sequel, where Pablo Picasso's antiwar masterpiece **Guernica** is the star, alongside works by Juan Gris, Joan Miro, and Salvador Dalí.

ⓘ Paseo del Prado (✆ **34/91/330-2800;** www.museoprado.es).

✈ Madrid, 14km (8²/₃ miles).

🛏 $ **Hotel Best Western Cortezo,** Doctor Cortezo 3 (✆ **34/91/369-0101;** www.hotelcortezo.com). $$$ **Hotel Preciados,** Preciados 37 (✆ **34/91/454-4400;** www.preciadoshotel.com).

WHY THEY'LL THANK YOU: That enigmatic, unforgettable infanta.

Masterpieces of Art **338**

Amsterdam's Museumplein Masterpieces
Dutch Masters & Then Some
Ages 6 & up • Amsterdam, the Netherlands

Maybe it has something to do with the austere northern slant of light, but from Rembrandt van Rijn to Vincent van Gogh, there's a tradition of Dutch painting that other nations can only envy. Realistic scenes of middle-class domestic life, moody polder landscapes with cloud-scudding skies, arresting portraits of shrewd burghers—it's the sort of art that looks you straight in the face and holds a conversation, and I personally love it. Now I had to turn my kids on to it, too.

The **Golden Age** of Dutch painting came in the 17th century, the high point of Holland's international power and wealth, and naturally the **Rijksmuseum,** Holland's national museum, has a rich collection of those Dutch masters. My favorites are the **Vermeers,** those almost photographic household scenes, bathed in natural light. Compared to his delicately frozen moments, the robust paintings of Jan Steen and Frans Hals look downright jolly. Crowds flock around Rembrandt's immense *Nightwatch,*

The van Gogh Museum in Amsterdam.

a dramatically lit group portrait of a cadre of militiamen checking their weapons before going out on patrol. Even more than *Nightwatch,* our favorite Rembrandt group portrait was the iconic *The Sampling Officials,* a cluster of guildsmen in almost identical black suits, square white collars, and brimmed black hats. Rembrandt painted each man staring outward with an arresting gaze that cuts through the centuries like a knife.

We felt a bit let down by the **Museum Het Rembrandthuis** (Rembrandt House Museum), Jodenbreestraat 4–6 (✆ **31/20/ 520-0400;** www.rembrandthuis.nl). It was interesting to see inside a 17th-century house, but there weren't many personal possessions—and Rembrandt himself, so good at revealing the personalities of others in his paintings, remained tantalizingly mysterious, like one of his shadowy self-portraits.

The raw emotion of Vincent van Gogh's painting flares like a comet at the **van Gogh Museum,** a short walk down Museumplein from the Rijksmuseum. Few painters deserve a solo museum more than

van Gogh, whose saturated colors and bold sinuous outlines make neighboring canvases look pallid. More than 200 van Gogh paintings are hung here—landscapes, portraits, still lifes—and as we moved through the galleries, arranged in chronological order, we got an eerie sense of the meteoric development in this artist's brief career (1880–90). From the early, brooding *Potato Eaters* to the vivid late *Sunflowers,* the evolution was startling enough to bowl over the kids. Mission accomplished.

ⓘ **Rijksmuseum,** Jan Luikenstraat 1 (✆ **31/ 20/647-7000;** www.rijksmuseum.nl). **Van Gogh Museum,** Paulus Potterstraat 7 (✆ **31/20/570-5200;** www.vangogh museum.nl).

🛏 $ **Amstel Botel,** Oosterdokskade 2–4 (✆ **34/20/626-4247;** www.amstel botel.com). $$ **Estheréa,** Singel 303–309 (✆ **34/20/624-5146;** www.estherea.nl).

WHY THEY'LL THANK YOU: From Vermeer's Delft kitchen to van Gogh's Arles bedroom.

The Hermitage
Art Treasures of the Czars
Ages 8 & up • St. Petersburg, Russia

One thing you have to say about the Russian czars—they collected some great art over the centuries, especially Catherine II and her grandson Nicholas I. Determined to prove that they were enlightened European monarchs, they spent their imperial fortunes recklessly on paintings and statues, as well as on coins, antiquities, and jewelry. And then, of course, in 1917 the Russian revolution came along, and the czars were history. Except for their art—the savvy Bolsheviks hung onto that all right.

The ghosts of that czarist era still linger in St. Petersburg, nowhere more so than at elegant **Palace Square** (Dvortsovaya Ploshchad). Standing under the Alexander Column—a 600-ton monolith topped by a cross-carrying angel—imagine all that this asymmetrical plaza has seen, from royal coaches pulling up to the baroque **Winter Palace** on one side, to Communist solidarity marches in front of the long curved **General Staff Building.** Through the grand courtyard of the Winter Palace today, you enter the State Hermitage Museum, where, in the absence of the czars, the art has finally taken over. In these extravagantly decorated salons, with their marble columns and parquet floors and dazzling chandeliers, it seems as if every inch of the red walls is covered with artworks in fussy gold frames. And yet, believe it or not, this is only a fraction of the collection.

The Hermitage has an incredible catalog of **Renaissance Italian art,** including two rare da Vinci Madonnas, and loads of **Dutch and Flemish masters** (look for Rembrandt's *Return of the Prodigal Son* and *Old Man in Red*). Among its **Spanish masterpieces** are one of my favorite El Grecos, *The Apostles Peter and Paul,* and Velázquez's arresting portrait of Count Olivares. The Hermitage has so many French artworks—more than any museum outside of France—that my personal favorites, the **French impressionists** and two rooms of early **Picasso,** have been crowded up to plainer rooms on the third floor, which can be stuffy and crowded in summer. Crowds are thinner in the **Antiquities halls** on the ground floor, which displays relics from the Greeks, Romans, and Egyptians.

Many visitors are so busy squinting at the pictures, they forget to look around them—and that's missing the point of this great Fabergé egg of a museum. The czars longed so desperately to impress the world with how cultured they were, they probably overdid it. But after the Revolution, did anyone ever again build a place as beautiful as this?

ⓘ 1 Palace Sq. (ⓒ **7/812/110-9079;** www.hermitagemuseum.org; Tues–Sat only).

✈ Pulkovo-2 International Airport (16km, 10 miles).

🛏 $$$ **Corinthia Nevsky Palace,** 57 Nevsky Prospekt (ⓒ **7/812/380-2001;** www.corinthia.ru). $$ **Pulford Apartments,** 6 Moika Embankment (ⓒ **7/812/325-6277;** www.pulford.com).

WHY THEY'LL THANK YOU: Remembering to look up at the ceilings.

The Metropolitan Museum of Art
Manhattan's Treasure Trove
All ages • New York, New York, USA

The echoing marble-clad Great Hall tells you as you enter that this is a Serious Art Museum. But don't let that put you off—New York City's number-one tourist attraction can be a lot of fun for children, even toddlers. Make a beeline for the areas kids really love: **Arms & Armor** (first floor), the extensive **Egyptian rooms** (also on the first floor—don't miss the glorious mummies), **musical instruments** (second floor, off the American Wing's courtyard), the **Costume Institute** (ground floor—rotating installations will often be of interest to kids), and the **European and American furniture rooms** (all over the place—any kid who's read *From the Mixed-Up Files of Mrs. Basil E. Frankweiler*, about a brother and sister who hide out for weeks in the Met, will adore these). On the first floor of the American Wing, a side gallery displays vintage baseball cards,

and a whole gallery of grandfather clocks ticks away on the second floor. Older kids who are beginning to appreciate art may go for the **impressionist gallery** (second floor), full of Monets and van Goghs they'll instantly recognize, or the **Lehman Pavilion,** set up like the town house of a wealthy collector—it's art in small enough doses that it doesn't overwhelm.

Our favorite corner, hands down, is the **courtyard of the American Wing,** a light-filled open space with plantings, benches, and statues kids can actually relate to (a mountain lion and her cubs, a pensive Indian brave). Back in the corner is an entire Frank Lloyd Wright room—all dark wood and low-slung right angles—that our family could move into at a moment's notice. Bring lots of small change for kids to throw into the American Wing reflecting pool and in the pool in

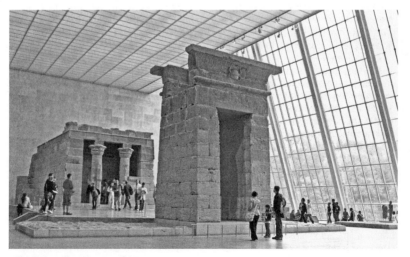

The Metropolitan Museum of Art.

front of the Egyptian Wing's serene **Temple of Dendur.** In the Japanese galleries, find the room overlooking the Temple of Dendur; off the musical instruments gallery, find the balcony overlooking the mounted knights in armor. Get the idea? Wander around this immense museum, keep your eyes open, and be willing to walk away from anything that doesn't interest your children.

The huge museum gift shop has a lot of good stuff for kids, and there are plenty of free children's programs.

ⓘ Fifth Ave. and 82nd St. (ⓒ **212/535-7710;** www.metmuseum.org).

✈ John F. Kennedy International.

🛏 $$ **Excelsior Hotel,** 45 W. 81st St. (ⓒ **800/368-4575** or 212/362-9200; www.excelsiorhotelny.com). $$$ **Le Parker Meridien,** 118 W. 57th St. (ⓒ **800/543-4300** or 212/245-5000; www.parkermeridien.com).

WHY THEY'LL THANK YOU: Great art is great art.

Masterpieces of Art 341

The Art Institute of Chicago
Hitting Art's Highlights in the Loop
Ages 4 & up • Chicago, Illinois, USA

My kids are great fans of the movie *Ferris Bueller's Day Off,* the greatest Chicago travelogue ever made, in my opinion. What Ferris (Matthew Broderick) and his two pals do in Chicago while playing hooky from their nice North Shore high school is our dream itinerary for a day in the Windy City: a Cubs game, a parade—and a stroll through the Art Institute of Chicago. If it was fun enough for Ferris, my kids figured, it would be fun enough for them.

Of course we were compelled to begin, like Ferris, with the immense pointillist canvas by George Seurat, **Sunday Afternoon on the Island of La Grande Jatte.** Like every other visitor there, we alternated standing up close to see the individual dots, then standing way back until the dots blur into a busy panorama of springtime in the park. But like the Seurat painting, the Art Institute has so many individual pieces of art, you can lose the big picture. The trick is to steer kids to see the things they'd love before they hit Museum Overdose. After *La Grande Jatte,* we wandered dreamily through the rest of the **impressionists,** a collection so rich in

Renoirs and Monets that we almost felt a sugar high; we hunted down the van Gogh self-portrait and then Picasso's blue-period *The Old Guitarist* and felt very satisfied.

Going from the hazy impressionists to sharply detailed 20th-century American paintings was a bracing contrast. We homed in on two masterpieces: the iconic **American Gothic** by Grant Wood, which they've seen spoofed so often, and Edward Hopper's evocative late-night diner scene **Nighthawks.** Then off we went to my favorite nook in the museum: the reconstructed turn-of-the-20th century **Chicago Stock Exchange trading room,** a dazzling Louis Sullivan showpiece with art-glass insets and stenciled decorations and molded plaster capitals—a perfect expression of Gilded Age tycoonery.

From there, we zigzagged back to the **Thorne Miniature Rooms,** filled with tiny reproductions of furnished interiors from European and American history (heaven for my dollhouse-loving daughter) and then rewarded the boys for their patience with a browse through the great hall of **European arms and armor,** where more than 1,500 objects range from horse armor to maces to poleaxes.

We missed the world-famous collection of glass paperweights; we missed the splendid Japanese wood block prints—who cared? We didn't even worry about plotting a logical course through the museum, since scuttling back and forth allowed us to pass Marc Chagall's jewel-toned **stained-glass windows** more than once, always a good thing.

ⓘ 111 S. Michigan Ave. (✆ **312/443-3600;** www.artic.edu).

✈ O'Hare International (15 miles).

🛏 $$ **Homewood Suites,** 40 E. Grand St. (✆ **800/CALL-HOME** [225-5466] or 312/644-2222; www.homewoodsuites chicago.com). $$ **Hotel Allegro Chicago,** 171 W. Randolph St. (✆ **800/643-1500** or 312/236-0123; www.allegrochicago.com).

WHY THEY'LL THANK YOU: Connecting the dots.

---

342 Masterpieces of Art

Huntington Library
Pasadena's Great Portrait Gallery
Ages 6 & up • San Marino, California, USA

The word "library" in the name may make the kids wince—why visit a musty old library on vacation? Well, even if they wanted to, they couldn't flip through the rare items in Henry E. Huntington's book collection. What they can see, though, is his terrific **art collection** in a stately Italianate mansion on a 207-acre hilltop estate.

As a girl, I was captivated by one pair of paintings here: Thomas Gainsborough's **The Blue Boy** and Thomas Lawrence's **Pinkie,** a long-haired boy in blue satin and a slim, dark-haired girl in a filmy white gown and pink bonnet, warily eyeing each other from facing walls of a wood-paneled salon. These life-size paintings capture the moodiness of adolescence so perfectly, you almost expect the kids to step out of those frames and start dissing each other. Blue Boy—aka Jonathan Buttall, son of a wealthy hardware merchant—peers guardedly at us, left hand cockily set on his hip. My sons thought his lace-collared outfit was "kinda sissy"; I explained that it wasn't the style of his time, but an homage to Flemish painter Anthony Van Dyck. Pinkie—in real life Sarah Barrett Moulton, an aunt to the Victorian poet Elizabeth

Barrett Browning—stands poised on tip-toe, the satin ribbons of her askew bonnet fluttering, one hand raised defensively. Stormy skies boil behind both subjects,

The Blue Boy, a modern interpretation.

357

mirroring their defiant teenage expressions. *Pinkie* was painted 25 years after *Blue Boy*, and there was no specific connection between the two—until Henry Huntington bought them both and set them here, a sort of blind date for eternity.

It's always interesting to see great art in a private home setting (if nothing else, it's less intimidating for children than a big formal Art Museum), but it's particularly apt for 18th-century English portraits, which were originally commissioned by aristocrats to decorate their own country manors. The Huntington's main gallery presents the best assemblage anywhere of **full-figure English portraits,** with work by Romney and Reynolds as well as Gainsborough and Lawrence—the Fab Four of late-18th-century portraiture. And the Huntington adds the final touch by serving daily **high tea** (or at any rate what Americans think of as high tea, with pastries and finger sandwiches) in a tearoom overlooking a fabulous rose garden. (Call

☎ **626/683-8131** for reservations, at least 2 weeks in advance.) For locals, the **botanical gardens** are the Huntington's main draw—an exotic cactus garden, a lush jungle garden, soothing lily ponds, and a Japanese garden with open-air house, koi-filled stream, and Zen garden. The gardens are lovely indeed, but *Blue Boy* and *Pinkie* are what make us return.

ⓘ 1151 Oxford Rd. (☎ **626/405-2100;** www.huntington.org).

✈ Los Angeles International.

🛏 $$ **Beverly Garland's Holiday Inn,** 4222 Vineland Ave., North Hollywood (☎ **800/BEVERLY** [238-3759] or 818/980-8000; www.beverlygarland.com). $$ **Roosevelt Hotel,** Hollywood, 7000 Hollywood Blvd. (☎ **800/950-7667** or 323/466-7000; www.hollywoodroosevelt.com).

WHY THEY'LL THANK YOU: Blue Boy and Pinkie, sitting in a tree . . .

Music 343

Salzburg
Mozart's Hometown
Ages 6 & up • Austria

Here's a dirty little secret: Wolfgang Amadeus Mozart didn't even like Salzburg—he couldn't wait to leave his provincial hometown and get to Vienna, where the real action was. Salzburg audiences didn't appreciate him, he complained. Well, the rest of the world didn't either; he died a pauper at age 35, buried (in Vienna) in an unmarked grave. But today Salzburg appreciates him all right—Mozart is Salzburg's main tourism draw, with a huge Mozart festival every summer, a Mozart Week in January, and frequent concerts at the town's premier concert hall, the (you guessed it) Mozarteum. Better late than never, I guess.

A statue of Mozart was erected in 1842 in the center of town, in a cafe-lined plaza renamed, naturally, Mozartplatz, a charming place to feel the pulse of what is still a bourgeois provincial town, like a time warp of mustard-colored baroque architecture. Head through the narrow shop-lined streets of the historic district to the composer's birthplace, the **Mozart Geburthaus,** where the Mozart family lived until he was 17. As a child prodigy propelled by an ambitious father, he was constantly on tour, but when he came home it was to this cramped apartment; his boyhood violin, his concert violin, and his viola, fortepiano, and clavichord are on display. As a child, Mozart often trooped from these drab quarters to perform at the **Residenz,** Residenzplatz 1 (☎ **43/662/80422690**), the grand baroque palace of the prince-archbishop of Salzburg; a tour of its lavish staterooms is quite a contrast to the Mozart digs. In 1773, the family moved across the river to the roomier **Mozart Wohnhaus,** which was badly bombed in World War II. Rebuilt as a Mozart museum in 1996, it has comprehensive exhibits on his poignant life and glorious music.

Should you take the kids to the Mozart Festival? Only if they adore classical music, because it's an expensive crush of high-profile music lovers who snare every hotel room in town. (Try your luck with the **Salzburg Festival box office,** Hofstallgasse 1, A-5020 Salzburg; ☎ **43/662/8045-500;** www.salzburgfestival.at.)

You can hear Mozart's music in more relaxed circumstances around town all year, not to mention seeing kid-friendly shows at the **Salzburger Marionetten Theater,** Schwarzstrasse 24 (☎ **43/662/872406;** www.marionetten.at).

ⓘ **Mozart Birthplace,** Getreidegasse 9 (☎ **43/662/844313**). **Mozart Residence,** Makartplatz 8 (☎ **43/662/844313**).

✈ Salzburg-Mozart Regional.

🛏 $ **Altstadthotel Wolf-Dietrich,** Wolf-Dietrich-Strasse 7 (☎ **43/662/871275;** www.salzburg-hotel.at). $$ **Hotel Mozart,** Franz-Josef-Strasse 27 (☎ **43/662/872274;** www.hotel-mozart.at).

WHY THEY'LL THANK YOU: Realizing that Mozart wrote *Twinkle, Twinkle, Little Star*—among other tunes.

344 Music

The Paris Opera
Where the Phantom Lurked
Ages 8 & up • Paris, France

Whether the Andrew Lloyd Webber musical or the scarifying Lon Chaney silent movie is their reference point, most kids have heard of the *Phantom of the Opera.* Perhaps they'll be disappointed to learn such a tragic fellow never existed, but was merely a literary creation from a 1910 novel by Gaston Leroux. However, the building he haunted absolutely does exist, and a **guided tour** lives up to all weird and wonderful expectations.

Officially called the Opéra de Paris Garnier, it was designed by 19th-century architect Charles Garnier for Emperor Napoleon III. Napoleon III's reign was known as the Second Empire and prized a highly decorated aesthetic style, as if the reinstated monarchy was determined to outdo the old regime's Sun

King opulence—to out-Versailles Versailles. There is no better example of Second Empire luxury than the **Paris Opera.** Topped by a green copper dome and heavily ornamented pediment, the facade is a crazy excess of rose marble columns, friezes, massed sculptures, and gilded statues. Things only get more lavish once you venture inside the lobby, with an immense marble grand staircase and a grand foyer with tons of chandeliers and Venetian mosaics all over the ceiling. Inside the actual auditorium, everything is upholstered in red velvet, with plaster cherubs capering over walls and ceilings and gold-leaf accents glinting on every possible surface. The luminous ceiling painting by Marc Chagall is stunning, though not precisely fitting the period. But

The Paris Opera.

when an underground lake—again, just as in the Phantom story—was discovered beneath the site. (It's still there.) Finally completed in 1875, the grandiose Opera became Paris's premier opera house. But your kids don't have to worry—you can't drag them to watch an opera, chiefly because the modern Opéra de Paris Bastille opened in 1989, relegating the Opéra Garnier to host mainly ballet. Wonder what the Phantom would think of that?

(i) **Place de l'Opera** (© **34/1/40-01-22-63,** or 34/1/40-01-19-70 for tours).

✈ De Gaulle, Orly.

🛏 $$$ **Hotel de Fleurie,** 32–34 rue Grégoire-de-Tours (© **33/1/53-73-70-00;** www.hotel-de-fleurie.tm.fr). $$ **Residence Lord Byron,** 5 rue de Chateaubriand (© **33/1/43-59-89-98;** www.escapade-paris.com).

WHY THEY'LL THANK YOU: A theater so grand, it deserves a phantom.

oh, that **chandelier,** just as in the musical's climactic scene—six tons of sparkling crystal suspended over the orchestra seats. The term *pièce de résistance* was coined to describe just this sort of show-stopping beauty.

Although workers started building the Opera in 1862, work halted for some time

Music

Doolin
The Haunting Keen of Irish Folk Music
Ages 8 & up • Doolin, County Clare, Ireland

So you're here in County Clare, Ireland, and you've seen the spectacular Cliffs of Moher and the Burren. What do you do at night? Head to the secluded fishing village of Doolin, where you'll get a taste of another side of Irish life—the **traditional music** of fiddle and flute, harp and bodhran drum, performed live in atmospheric pubs strung along one steep village street.

True, **pubs**—short for "public houses," which have a license to sell alcoholic beverages—are more or less bars; but in Ireland they are also community gathering places, so don't hesitate to take kids there for an evening, especially not when music,

rather than drinking, is the pub's chief attraction. Simple bar food is served, sawdust litters the floor, and seating is often on hard benches (some nights it's standing room only). Don't worry if you can't get a good view of the musicians; you'll hear them all right. Traditional music, usually referred to simply as **"trad,"** is a vital part of contemporary Irish culture, not relegated to secondary folk-music status, and it often shades into acoustic rock, with many musicians writing their own trad-style songs as well as performing the folk classics. Listen to a couple of albums by the Chieftains or Cherish the Ladies or the Clancy Brothers before you go so the kids will recognize beloved tunes like "Carrick-fergus" and "Foggy Dew" and "Raglan Road" when they break out—everyone else in the pub is sure to clap in recognition when they hear the first strains.

The best-known place in town is **Gus O'Connor's,** Fisher Street (© **353/65/707-4168**), situated in a row of thatched fishermen's cottages near the pier; it's been around since 1832, so expect those rafters to be weathered with years of smoke. But it's popular with tourists and often crowded. Up on Lisdoonvarna Road, at **McGann's** (© **353/65/707-4133**) or **McDermott's** (© **353/65/707-4328**), the

music is just as good and the audience more local. Besides the advertised performers, these pubs are magnets for musicians from all over the world, who are quite likely to join in an impromptu jam.

ⓘ www.doolin-tourism.com.

✈ Shannon International.

🛏 $$ **Aran View House,** Doolin (**353/65/707-4061;** Apr–Oct only).

WHY THEY'LL THANK YOU: Skirling fiddles, thumping bodhrans, heart-piercing tin whistles—no music lover can resist.

---

346 Music

Liverpool Beatles Tour
Ages 8 & up • England

It was more than 40 years ago today—1962, as a matter of fact—that a quartet of hungry young musicians from this grimy port city rocketed to the top of the pop charts, not only in the U.K. but around the world. Their sound was so fresh, so original, and so exciting, that in some respects music would never again be the same. If your kids aren't already Beatlemaniacs, a visit to their birthplace should change things.

Liverpool, grimy no more, has had a serious face-lift since the 1960s; the spruced-up waterfront around Albert Dock now has boutiques in converted warehouses, a branch of the Tate Art Museum, and of course the slick **The Beatles Story,** Britannia Pavilion, Albert Dock (© **44/ 151/709-1963;** www.beatlesstory.com), an audiovisual "experience" housing Beatles memorabilia, including a yellow submarine with live fish swimming past the portholes. Cheesy it may be, but my kids loved it. But for a deeper insight, contact the **National Trust** (© **44/870/900-0256;** www.nationaltrust.org.uk) to book tours of Paul McCartney's and John Lennon's boyhood homes, meticulously restored to

their 1950s appearance. Here you'll see the lumpy brown sofa where Paul and John scribbled their first songs, and John's tiny bedroom, with its Elvis Presley and Brigitte Bardot posters on the walls. You'll get the point that musical genius raised these two from humble roots indeed.

You can also stop by the **Cavern Club,** downtown at 8–10 Mathew St. (© **44/ 151/236-1965;** www.cavernclub.org), a replica of the venue where the Beatles were virtually the house band, playing 292

Beatles Story at the Britannia Pavilion.

gigs between 1961 and 1963; it was here that their future manager, Brian Epstein, first heard them on November 9, 1961. The Cavern hands out maps for a walking tour of pertinent Beatle sites in the city center and operates a 2-hour Magical Mystery bus tour, which takes in Beatles-related sites such as the bustling Penny Lane intersection and the Salvation Army children's home Strawberry Fields.

There's a **Beatles** shop at 31 Mathew St., and the Beatles-themed **Hard Day's Night** hotel is around the corner on North John Street. And even though the song "Ferry Cross the Mersey" was by fellow Liverpudlians Gerry & the Pacemakers, not the Beatles, kids will enjoy taking a

boat from Pier Head to Woodside for a sweeping view of the port. Contact **Mersey Ferries** (© **44/151/330-1444;** www.merseyferries.co.uk).

ⓘ **Liverpool Tourist Information Centre,** Maritime Museum, Albert Dock (© **44/151/707-0729;** www.visitliverpool.com).

🚆 Liverpool, 3 hr. from London, 45 min. from Manchester.

🛏 $$ **The Feathers Hotel,** 117–125 Mt. Pleasant (© **44/151/709-9655;** www.feathers.uk.com).

WHY THEY'LL THANK YOU: The Fab Four forever.

Music 347

Graceland

Memphis Music Mecca

Ages 6 & up • Memphis, Tennessee, USA

To many music fans, Memphis, Tennessee, means one thing: the world's greatest Elvis shrine, Graceland. But chances are your kids know more about tacky Elvis impersonators than they do about the King himself. So when you come to Memphis, show them the whole story—the amazing music heritage that first drew the shy teenager from Tupelo, Mississippi, to this Tennessee river city. Begin on **Beale Street,** the nerve center of the South's most vital post–Civil War black community. W. C. Handy brought the blues sound up Hwy. 61 from Mississippi at the turn of the century and it caught fire in the clubs of Beale Street; later, such legends as B. B. King, Muddy Waters, and Howlin' Wolf added their voices. Stroll along the street, read the historic markers, and check out who's playing at the nightclubs between Second and Fourth streets. Visit the **W. C. Handy House Museum,** 352 Beale St. (© **901/527-3427**), and the Smithsonian's **Rock 'n' Soul Museum,** 191 Beale St. (© **901/205-2533**), with photos,

recordings, and artifacts, from a satin Elvis Presley suit to Ike Turner's piano.

In 1950, in a tiny brick corner storefront, recording engineer Sam Phillips opened **Sun Records Studio,** 706 Union Ave. (© **901/521-0664;** http://sunstudio.com), where then-unknowns Carl Perkins, Roy Orbison, Jerry Lee Lewis, Johnny Cash, and Elvis Presley took the blues sound, mixed it with country and bluegrass, and came up with a new sound: rock 'n' roll. You can tour Sun Studio's surprisingly Spartan setup; records are still made here by such current artists as U2 and Bonnie Raitt.

Yet another sound was born in Memphis in 1959, when Stax Records began recording such soul-music greats as Isaac Hayes, Otis Redding, and Wilson Pickett. The **Stax Museum of American Soul Music,** 926 E. McLemore Ave. (© **901/942-SOUL** [942-7685]), has such evocative exhibits as a re-created gospel church and the dance floor from the TV show *Soul Train.*

Elvis in front of his home, Graceland.

Now that you've placed Elvis in music history, head out Elvis Presley Boulevard to **Graceland,** the colonial-style mansion Elvis bought in the late 1950s for the then-huge price of $100,000. As the King's fame grew, 14-acre Graceland became his refuge, and eventually his retreat from reality. Touring the mansion, you'll get a glimpse of the lavish lifestyle the poor Delta boy chose once he hit the big time: carpeted wall-to-wall in white, with gold accents and satin drapes everywhere. Walls covered with gold record plaques, mannequin after mannequin sporting Elvis's stage outfits—it's an assault on the senses. Don't miss the flower-laden memorial garden where Elvis is buried alongside his parents. It completes the whole arc of Elvis's career, from raw young rockabilly to hip-swiveling teen heartthrob to sequin-jumpsuited mega-star. As you drive away, play a mixtape of Elvis hits from *That's All Right Now Mama* and *All Shook Up* to *Love Me Tender* and *Suspicious Minds*. Now the kids *know* who Elvis is.

ⓘ 3734 Elvis Presley Blvd. (© **800/238-2000** or 901/332-3322; www.elvis.com).

✈ Memphis International.

🛏 $$ **Homewood Suites,** 5811 Poplar Ave. (© **800/CALL-HOME** [225-5466] or 901/763-0500; www.homewoodsuites.com). $$$ **The Peabody Memphis,** 149 Union Ave. (© **800/PEABODY** [732-2639] or 901/529-4000; www.peabodymemphis.com).

WHY THEY'LL THANK YOU: Elvis never left *this* building.

The Nashville Music Scene
Country Music's Capital
Ages 8 & up • Nashville, Tennessee, USA

Nashville: The very name is synonymous with music, specifically the brand of country music played on the Grand Ole Opry radio show, broadcast from here since 1927. To perform on the Grand Ole Opry is to officially "make it" in country music, and thus it's a town buzzing with music-biz execs, state-of-the-art studios, and happening clubs, with a surprising amount of jazz and rock going down as well. I love Nashville, and even though I'm no country-music aficionado, it only takes a couple hours here to get hooked on its twangy energy.

A music pilgrimage to Nashville centers on three areas: downtown near Ryman auditorium, the original home of the Opry; in the West End along 16th Avenue, known as Music Row, where you can often spot music stars going in and out of the studios; and east of town at the vast Opryland complex where the Opry relocated in 1974. Out at Opryland, the current **Grand Ole Opry House,** 2802 Opryland Dr. (© **615/889-6611;** www.opry.com), produces three live TV shows a week, April to December—order your tickets well in advance. Exhibits at the **Grand Ole Opry Museum** next door, at 2804 Opryland Dr., celebrate Opry stars past and present. For a more rounded idea of country music, though, head downtown for the **Country Music Hall of Fame and Museum,** 222 Fifth Ave. (© **800/852-6437** or 615/416-2001; www.countrymusichalloffame.com). From sequin-spangled costumes to historic guitars to over-the-top custom cars (a crucial status symbol in country music culture), it's an impressive roundup

of artifacts, and the kids really get into the video and audio clips, interactive jukeboxes, and touch-screen computer kiosks, exploring the differences between intertwined musical genres—bluegrass, cowboy music, rockabilly, Cajun, honky-tonk, country swing. Once you're grounded in the music, walk 2 blocks to the **Ryman Auditorium,** 116 Fifth Ave. (© **615/254-1445;** www.ryman.com), aka the Mother Church of Country Music (built as a church in 1892, it still has stained-glass windows). Dowdy as it looks outside, inside it's a finely restored arenalike theater with top acoustics. By day, it offers memorabilia exhibits, a backstage dressing room tour, and a booth where you can record your own live CD; by night, it has a full roster of live concerts. Then take in an early-evening show at the **Bluebird Cafe,** 4104 Hillsboro Rd. (© **615/383-1461;** www.bluebirdcafe.com), to hear today's up-and-coming singer-songwriters.

ⓘ **Nashville Visitor Information Center,** Gaylord Entertainment Center, 501 Broadway (© **615/259-4747;** www.nashville cvb.com).

✈ Nashville International (8 miles).

🛏 $$ **Courtyard Marriott Nashville Vanderbilt/West End,** 1901 West End Ave. (© **800/245-1959** or 615/327-9900; www.marriott.com). $$–$$$ **Opryland Hotel,** 2800 Opryland Dr. (© **615/883-2211;** www.gaylordhotels.com).

WHY THEY'LL THANK YOU: When their boots start a-tapping.

Rock 'n' Roll Hall of Fame
Cleveland Rocks
Ages 6 & up • Ohio, USA

Why Cleveland? Why not? This is the town where DJ Alan Freed first coined the term *rock 'n' roll,* where Chuck Berry played his first public gig; it's the hometown of musicians from Phil Ochs to Chrissie Hynde to Trent Reznor. And what's more, it's within a day's drive of 50% of the U.S. population, so this high-profile shrine can be visited by as many music lovers as possible.

Designed by I. M. Pei, the museum building is an all-shook-up mass of porcelain-tiled geometric shapes, piled up like a guitar and amps in the back of a roadie's van, with a glass pyramid jutting out from one side over Lake Erie. Inside is a cool collection of **pop-culture memorabilia** to browse through. Even if you and the kids don't listen to the same artists, there's plenty here for everyone to groove on. Exhibits display programs, posters, photos, instruments (from Junior Walker's lovingly shined saxophone to a smashed guitar from Paul Simonton of the Clash), and stage costumes (James Brown's red rhinestone-studded tuxedo coat, Neil Young's fringed leather jacket). But what really grabs kids are the artifacts from rock stars' childhoods—things like Jimi Hendrix's baby picture, Jim Morrison's Cub Scout uniform, John Lennon's report card, Joe Walsh's high-school football jersey. Not to ignore current chart toppers, on the plaza level a rotating exhibit features today's artists, from Destiny's Child to Rage Against the Machine. For those of us who actually remember the 1950s, the **Rave On exhibit** displays mementos from such rock 'n' rollers as Eddie Cochran, Buddy Holly, and the Everly Brothers on a curved wall evoking a chrome-and-neon diner.

Still, rock 'n' roll isn't about artifacts, it's about performance, which is why it's stirring to watch the filmed Hendrix performance in the **Jimi Hendrix Surround Sound Theater.** Up in the **Hall of Fame,** a video collage of all the 200-plus inductees is mesmerizing. The Hall of Fame includes mostly musicians (eligible 25 years after their first record release), as well as a few producers, DJs, and journalists. Though displays near the entrance focus on the most recent class of inductees, huge "virtual jukebox" stations let you access just about any song recorded by any Hall of Famer; their autographs are etched in glass on a great wall projecting over the lake. As with all such ventures, the list of who's in and who's not is controversial, but then that makes for great dinner-table arguments.

ⓘ 1 Key Plaza (ⓒ **888/764-ROCK** [764-7625] or 216/781-7625; www.rockhall.com).

✈ Cleveland International (10 miles).

🛏 $$ **Cleveland Marriott Downtown,** 127 Public Sq. (ⓒ **800/228-9290** or 216/696-9200; www.marriott.com). $$ **Holiday Inn-City Center Lakeside,** 1111 Lakeside Ave. (ⓒ **888/425-3835** or 216/241-5100; www.ichotelsgroup.com).

> **WHY THEY'LL THANK YOU:** It's only rock 'n' roll, but they'll like it.

Rock 'n' Roll Hall of Fame.

Experience Music Project (EMP)

Ages 6 & up • Seattle, Washington, USA

Gliding on the monorail from downtown Seattle to the Space Needle, Seattle's flying-saucer-ish landmark from the 1962 World's Fair, you'll roll right past an angular multicolored jumble of architecture—Frank Gehry's controversial home for the Experience Music Project. While our local friends complained that the Experience Music Project was too pricey for what it is, I beg to disagree. Pricey it is, but we spent hours at the EMP, loving every minute of it, and if your kids are at all into rock music they will too.

The brainchild of Microsoft co-founder Paul Allen, this museum was originally intended as a tribute to Seattle native son Jimi Hendrix, and the **Hendrix gallery** is wonderfully comprehensive, from mementos of his childhood to stage costumes to a mixing board he used. But the collection grew to encompass a great deal more, from the early Northwest rock scene (bands like the Ventures, the Fleetwoods, and the Kingsmen, notorious for "Louie, Louie") all the way to Nirvana, Pearl Jam, Soundgarden, and the incredibly fertile grunge scene of the 1990s. Special exhibits feature current trends in music, and the dramatically lit specimens in the guitar gallery show the whole family tree of today's electric guitars. The exhibits are somewhat text-heavy, although videos play everywhere, giving some kids their first taste of the magic of great performers of the past (the Bob Dylan exhibit we saw was especially good at setting the 1960s folk-music context out of which Dylan grew). Eventually, of course, it's not enough just to hear music, you want to make some of your own, and as you'd expect from a high-tech guru's pet project, there are extensive **sound labs** where you can try your hand at different instruments and studio production techniques. It seems like someone's always hogging the console you want, unfortunately, but patience is rewarded.

Connected to the EMP, the somewhat smaller **Science Fiction Museum** is offered as a possible add-on. While we were disappointed in it, hard-core sci-fi fans may feel differently.

(i) 325 Fifth Ave. N. (© **877/EMPLIVE** [367-5483] or 206/EMPLIVE [367-5483]; www.empsfm.org).

✈ Seattle-Tacoma International (14 miles).

🛏 $$ **Comfort Suites Downtown/Seattle Center,** 601 Roy St. (© **800/517-4000** or 206/282-2600; www.comfort suites.com). $$$ **Westin Seattle,** 1900 Fifth Ave. (© **800/WESTIN-1** [937-8461] or 206/728-1000; www.westin.com/seattle).

WHY THEY'LL THANK YOU: Learning the real lyrics to "Louie, Louie."

The Ancient Theatre of Epidaurus
Greek Drama under the Stars
All ages • Peloponnese, Greece

Whereas many ancient sites were pillaged for building blocks, the Theatre of Epidaurus is just far enough off the beaten track that it was left more or less alone—it's the best-preserved of all ancient Greek theaters, where simply robed actors first brought heroic dramas to life. Even when it was new, it was known for its miraculous acoustics: Though it is an open-air amphitheater that seats 14,000, a whisper can be heard all the way from the stage to the top rows of seats. Every ham in the family will want to run down and give it a try.

The theater is only the most famous part of the **Sanctuary of Asklepios,** an important healing center attached to a cult worshipping Asklepios, the healer god and son of Apollo. Along with lodgings for patients and other guests, it had bathhouses, a gymnasium, and several temples and shrines; little is left but foundation stones, which you can walk around, imagining the bustling site in its prime. As the Sanctuary grew in wealth and fame it added attractions such as a stadium, where games were held every 4 years (much like Olympia), and poetry and music performances. In the 4th century, the celebrated architect Polykeitos was hired to design a full-scale theater, and what a triumph it was. The audience area, or *theaton* (meaning "seeing place"), originally had 34 rows of seats; 21 upper rows were added in the 2nd century B.C., under the Romans. The stage area—the "orchestra"—is a full circle, which is rare (the Romans changed most theaters' orchestras to the semicircle they preferred). The low building behind it, the *skene,* was where actors kept costume changes and props; its roof was sometimes used as a second stage level. Nowadays the *skene* has tumbled down, revealing a glorious valley view that makes a stunning backdrop for performances. Every summer ancient Greek tragedies and comedies (usually in modern Greek translations) are performed here on weekend nights. The theater's stark grandeur is a brilliant venue for the stripped-down theatrics of Aeschylus and Sophocles. Packages that include bus service are available in Athens from the **Greek National Tourism Organization** (✆ 30/210/327-1300); the **Hellenic Festival Office,** 39 Panepistimiou (✆ 30/210/322-1459); and the **Rex Theater** box office, Panepistimiou (✆ 30/210/330-1881). You can sometimes get tickets at the theater itself just before a performance.

One word of warning: A nearby town is called Ancient Epidaurus, and just to add to the confusion, it also has a small ancient amphitheater. Be careful which signs you follow!

ⓘ Lygourio (✆ 27530/22-009).

✈ Athens, 177km (110 miles).

🛏 $$ **Hotel Agamemnon,** 3 Akti Miaouli, Nafplion (✆ 27520/28-021).

WHY THEY'LL THANK YOU: Whispering on that stage.

Shakespeare's Globe Theatre

Ages 10 & up • London, England

It was probably the most important public theater ever built, the place where such masterpieces as *Julius Caesar, Hamlet, Othello,* and *King Lear* premiered, all written by the resident playwright, William Shakespeare. While a visit to Stratford-upon-Avon is useful for filling in the sketchy details of Shakespeare's life, Shakespeare is remembered today for what he achieved while living in London, and the Globe Theatre really brings this to life.

This circular half-timbered open-air theater is a meticulous reconstruction of the original Globe Theatre, built in 1599 as a playhouse for Shakespeare's theatrical troupe, the King's Men, and located on the Thames's disreputable South Bank along with the rest of London's theaters. (The original Globe was torn down in 1644, during the Reformation, when all theaters were closed.) The late American filmmaker Sam Wanamaker worked for some 20 years to raise funds to re-create the theater as it existed in Elizabethan times, thatched roof and all. He was able to acquire a site only 200 yards from the original, near where another Elizabethan theater, The Rose, had already been excavated. The Globe you'll see today re-creates the typical floor plan of the period, based on the designs of Roman amphitheaters (remember, the Romans once occupied Britain, and the remains of a Roman amphitheater can still be seen up in Chester). A raised two-level stage thrusts out in the audience, triple-decked galleries seat wealthier patrons, and the ground floor area right in front of the stage is where the so-called "groundlings" stand. If it rains, everyone in the galleries stay nice and dry, but the groundlings had better wear hoods or hats.

Part of Wanamaker's vision was to make this an operating theater, and some half-dozen **plays** (most, but not all, by Shakespeare) are produced here May through September. Scenery is minimal, costumes elaborate; all music is live and the actors wear no mics. If you can't take in a play, you can still visit the attached **exhibit** (a tour of the theater is included if there's no play in progress), which many children will enjoy more than a performance. The exhibits include live demonstrations of sword fighting and costumes, musical instruments, and printing presses, as well as touch-screen terminals explaining how the Elizabethans pulled off such special effects as Lear's thunder, Lady Macbeth's bloody hands, and Puck's flying.

Julius Caesar, Hamlet, Othello, and *King Lear* all premiered at the Globe Theatre.

ⓘ 21 New Globe Walk (📞 **44/20/7902-1400**; www.shakespeares-globe.org).

✈ Heathrow.

🛏 $$$ **London Bridge Hotel,** 8–18 London Bridge St. 9 (📞 **44/20/7855-2200**; www.londonbridgehotel.com). $$ **Vicarage Private Hotel,** 10 Vicarage Gate, South Kensington (📞 **44/20/7229-4030**; www.londonvicaragehotel.com).

WHY THEY'LL THANK YOU: The play's the thing.

Stratford-upon-Avon
Birthplace of the Bard
All ages • England

This charming Warwickshire market town on the banks of the river Avon has one claim to fame, but it's a biggie: William Shakespeare was born here, grew up here, and retired here. From Victorian times on, Shakespeare worshipers made sure that many of Stratford's Tudor/Jacobean buildings were preserved. What you see today gives you a pretty good idea of an Elizabethan-era provincial town.

Stratford feeds upon Shakespeare's legend, and thousands of tourists flood through each year (summers are especially crowded). Along with souvenir shops and Shakespeare-themed eateries, there are several historical sights in town, all charging brisk admission fees. The one exception is **Holy Trinity Church,** where Shakespeare was baptized and buried; admission is free, and there's only a small charge to visit his tomb (alongside those of his wife, Anne Hathaway, and daughter Susanna). The Shakespeare Trust sells a five-in-one ticket to five main sights:

Shakespeare's birthplace.

Shakespeare's Birthplace on Henley Street, in the center of town, a modest half-timbered home, suitable for a middle-class craftsman's family (Shakespeare's father was a glove maker); **New Place/Nash's House** on Chapel Street, the 16th-century home of Shakespeare's grand-daughter, adjoining the garden of the torn-down house where Shakespeare moved in 1610; **Hall's Croft** in Old Town, near Trinity Church, a fine Tudor town house where Shakespeare's daughter Susanna lived with her physician husband; **Anne Hathaway's Cottage,** the thatched farmstead where Shakespeare's wife grew up, a mile's walk outside of town in Shottery; and **Mary Arden's House,** a farmhouse even farther out of town (in Wilmcote) that pretends to be, but isn't, the girlhood home of Shakespeare's mother. If you only have time for one, Shakespeare's Birthplace is the most impressive, and exhibits in the attached **Shakespeare Centre** tell the story of the Bard's life in vivid detail.

These days, a Stratford boy wouldn't need to leave town to have a major theater career, because the prestigious **Royal Shakespeare Company** (launched in 1960, out of the seeds of a company started in 1875) built a sprawling brick complex of performance spaces on the banks of the Avon. The RSC presents five plays a season, which lasts April to October. (For tickets, call the box office at ✆ **0870/609-1110** in the U.K. or 44/17/89-40-34-34.) Guided backstage tours are conducted a couple times a day; call ✆ **44/17/89-40-34-03** for schedules.

ⓘ **Shakespeare Centre** (✆ **44/17/89-20-40-16;** www.shakespeare.org.uk).

🚆 Stratford-upon-Avon, 2 hr. from London.

🛏 $$ **Alveston Manor,** Clopton Bridge, off B4066 (✆ **800/225-5843** in the U.S. or Canada or 0870/400-8181; www.macdonaldhotels.co.uk). $ **Victoria Spa Lodge,** Bishopton Lane (✆ **44/17/89-26-79-85;** www.victoriaspa.co.uk).

WHY THEY'LL THANK YOU: It turns Shakespeare from a literary god into a human being.

Theater & the Movies **354**

American Museum of the Moving Image
New York on Film

Ages 6 & up • Astoria, Queens, New York, USA

Don't tell Hollywood, but New York City is really the home of the American movie industry—it's where Thomas Edison screened his first moving pictures and the early talkies were all shot, many of them in Paramount's 13-building studio complex in Astoria, Queens, just a hop, skip, and a jump over the 59th Street Bridge from Manhattan. And if you're not convinced, you will be after visiting the American Museum of the Moving Image, an in-depth museum for TV and movie fans housed in one of those Astoria studio buildings.

Many of the historic artifacts on display—a 1910 wooden Pathé camera, a 1959 Philco TV set—will mean little or nothing to youngsters, but the extensive **costume gallery** should grab them, with such items as Robin Williams' padded house-dress from *Mrs. Doubtfire*. Famous props exhibited range from Charlton Heston's chariot from the classic film *Ben-Hur* to a

American Museum of the Moving Image.

Yoda puppet constructed for the 1980 film *The Empire Strikes Back.* The Monk's Coffee Shop set from *Seinfeld* is re-created here, and there's a fun display of tie-in toys and lunchboxes promoting TV shows from *Howdy Doody* to *The Simpsons.*

What really fascinates kids, however, are the hands-on exhibits demonstrating the moviemaking process. While it may be demonstrated with more flash at Universal Studios, here the kids get more involved in the process and really learn how it's done. At interactive workstations you can fiddle with sound effects, dub in new dialogue, call up different soundtracks, and even add your face (a la Woody Allen's *Zelig*) to classic movie scenes. Sit in front of a camera and make a series of wacky expressions and, presto! They're reproduced in your own flipbook, which you can take home. At the digital animation stands, you can move cardboard cutouts around to create your own animated short. The makeup exhibition, too, has more than enough ghoulish masks to satisfy young horror movie fans, with staffers on hand to demonstrate how they were made.

While in New York, media mavens should also take in the **Museum of Television and Radio** in Manhattan, 25 E. 52nd St., at Fifth Avenue (© **212/621-6600;** www.mtr.org).

ⓘ 35th Ave. and 36th St. (© **718/784-0077;** www.ammi.org).

✈ John F. Kennedy International, Newark Liberty International, LaGuardia.

🛏 $$ **Excelsior Hotel,** 45 W. 81st St. (© **800/368-4575** or 212/362-9200; www. excelsiorhotelny.com). $$$ **Le Parker Meridien,** 118 W. 57th St. (© **800/543-4300** or 212/245-5000; www.parker meridien.com).

WHY THEY'LL THANK YOU: Taking part in the magic of moviemaking.

Hooray for Hollywood
Movie Mecca
Ages 8 & up • Hollywood, California, USA

The name Hollywood may be synonymous with moviemaking, but many tourists are disappointed by how shabby the town itself is. I relish its seedy, down-at-heels aura, but my kids were not impressed—until they got an eyeful of **Grauman's Chinese Theatre,** 6925 Hollywood Blvd. (✆ **323/464-MANN** [464-6266]), still one of the world's great movie palaces, with over-the-top Chinese embellishments and an entry court where such stars as Elizabeth Taylor have set their signatures and hand- and footprints in cement. So what if the kids didn't recognize most of the names? Nearby is the relatively recently built **Kodak Theatre,** 6834 Hollywood Blvd., where they give out the Oscars every year; we also marveled at the refurbished **Egyptian Theatre,** 6712 Hollywood Blvd., and the Art Deco **Pantages Theatre,** 6233 Hollywood Blvd., for a *Sunset Boulevard* taste of 1920s glamour. Stars who couldn't get a spot at Grauman's were honored with bronze medallions in the pavement along the **Hollywood Walk of Fame,** Hollywood Boulevard between Gower Street and La Brea Avenue; and Vine Street, between Yucca Street and Sunset Boulevard (✆ **323/469-8311;** www.hollywoodchamber.net). John Lennon, Elvis Presley, and Eddie Murphy, those were medallions worth a snapshot or two.

But why settle for sidewalk plaques when you can see films really being made? A quick prefab version is the hour-long tram tour at **Universal Studios Hollywood,** Hollywood Freeway, Universal Center Drive or Lankershim Boulevard exits, Universal City (✆ **818/662-3801;** www.universalstudioshollywood.com); but these days, thrill rides are more Universal's raison d'être. We'd rather walk around the wardrobe and prop departments, back lots, and active sets of a real working studio. These walking tours run Monday through Friday and last 2 hours or more; advance reservations are essential. Here are your options: **Paramount Pictures,** 5555 Melrose Ave. (✆ 323/956-1777); **Warner Brothers Studios,** WB Studio Gate 3, 4301 W. Olive Ave., Burbank (✆ 818/972-TOUR [972-8687]; www.wbstudiotour.com; ages 9 and up); **Sony Pictures,** 10202 W. Washington Blvd., Culver City (✆ 323/520-TOUR [520-8687]; www.sonypicturesstudios.com; ages 12 and up); and **NBC Studios,** 3000 W. Alameda Ave., Burbank (✆ 818/840-3537; www.studioaudiences.com).

Or you can get free tickets to join the studio audience for a sitcom or talk show taping (however, many shows don't admit children under the age of 10 or even 18). For these, contact well in advance: **Audiences Unlimited, Inc.** (✆ 818/753-3470; www.tvtickets.com); **TVTIX.COM** (✆ 323/653-4105; www.tvtix.com); **CBS Television City,** 7800 Beverly Blvd. (✆ 323/575-2458); **NBC Studios,** 3000 W. Alameda Ave., Burbank (✆ 818/840-3537); **Paramount Studios** (✆ 323/956-1777); or **Universal Studios** (✆ 800/UNIVERSAL [864-8377]; www.universalstudios.com).

ⓘ **Hollywood Visitor Information Center,** 6801 Hollywood Blvd. (✆ **323/467-6412;** www.discoverlosangeles.com).

✈ Los Angeles International.

🛏 $$$ **Beverly Garland's Holiday Inn,** 4222 Vineland Ave., North Hollywood (✆ **800/BEVERLY** [238-3759] or 818/980-8000; www.beverlygarland.com). $$ **Roosevelt Hotel,** Hollywood, 7000 Hollywood Blvd. (✆ **800/950-7667** or 323/466-7000; www.hollywoodroosevelt.com).

WHY THEY'LL THANK YOU: Seeing stars.

Ghibli Museum
The Genius of Animation
All ages • Tokyo, Japan

Anime addicts—you know who you are—just may find this idiosyncratic museum the highlight of their trip to Japan. It's not so much that it pays homage to the animated films of **Hayao Miyazaki,** it's that Miyazaki himself was so involved in developing this museum that his wondrous sensibility is written all over it.

Miyazaki and his fellow animator Isao Takahata are the talents behind **Studio Ghibli.** Miyazaki—the genius behind such classics as *Princess Mononoke, Spirited Away,* and *Howl's Moving Castle*—makes optimistic films with children in mind, because, he has said, he wants them to develop a positive view of the world. His heroines are usually plucky girls, with mysterious animals and otherworldly creatures drifting in and out of their lives almost at random. The animation is so detailed and lifelike, the stories told with such lyrical emotion, that they are truly spellbinding.

It does take a bit of effort to visit the Ghibli Museum. **Tickets** must be bought in advance, up to 3 months ahead, either through the museum's website, through Japan Tourist Bureau offices in Japan or abroad, or at Lawson convenience stores in Japan. When you buy your tickets, you commit to a specific date and time. The museum is not conveniently located, set on the outskirts of Tokyo (a 30-min. train ride from Shinjuku station, followed by a 5-min. bus ride or 15-min. walk along a river). But once you're there, you enter a whimsical flight of imagination.

Even from the outside, the dreamlike quality of Miyazaki's animation is expressed in the rounded stucco buildings, softened by flowers and foliage. Inside, the floor plan is delightfully random, with catwalks and spiral staircases shooting off in all directions, and many of the exhibits are waist-high, speaking directly to children. A ground floor exhibit explains how animation works, using strobe lights and spinning plaster figures from Ghibli films; on the second floor, reproductions of animators' studios demonstrate the filmmaking process, from storyboard to cel painting—you can almost feel the creative energies at work, with a flurry of sketches tacked up over the artist's desk and books piled everywhere. Children can scamper on top of a **giant stuffed kitten bus** like the one from *Totoro* (my children have longed to climb onto that bus ever since they first saw that movie), or scurry up a spiral staircase to the rooftop garden with a metal sculpture of the giant robot from *Laputa: The Castle in the Sky.* A fancifully painted theater shows animated shorts made exclusively for the museum. **Note:** The text accompanying displays is only in Japanese, so hang onto the English-language guide you're handed when you enter.

ⓘ 1–1–83 Shimorenjaku, Mitaka City (✆ **81/442/40-2233;** www.ghibli-museum.jp).

✈ Narita International.

🛏 $$$ **Imperial Hotel,** 1–1–1 Uchisaiwaicho, Chiyoda-ku (✆ **800/223-6800** in the U.S. and Canada, or 81/03/3504-1111; www.imperialhotel.co.jp). $ **Sakura Ryokan,** 2–6–2 Iriya, Taito-ku (✆ **81/03/3876-8118;** www.sakura-ryokan.com).

WHY THEY'LL THANK YOU: The kitten bus.

13 Historic Homes

Monticello, Thomas Jefferson's home.

Hadrian's Villa
A Roman Emperor's Fantasy Hideaway
Ages 6 & up • Tivoli, Italy

In the 2nd century A.D., globe-trotting Roman emperor Hadrian retired to one of the greatest estates ever built, in the resort town of Tibur (now Tivoli) about 28km (17 miles) east of Rome. Somewhat like that other compulsive collector William Randolph Hearst (see Hearst Castle **370**), Hadrian had filled acre after acre with examples of the **architectural wonders** he'd encountered on his travels. A patron of the arts, a lover of beauty, and even something of an architect, Hadrian was creating much more than a villa: It was his own Xanadu, a self-contained world for his huge royal entourage and the hundreds of servants and guards they required to protect, feed, and bathe them, and satisfy their libidos.

Born in Spain, Hadrian was named emperor of Rome by his predecessor, Trajan, but even while in Rome, Hadrian preferred to retreat outside the city, accompanied by trusted cronies. Tivoli was ideal because its marble quarries could provide tons of travertine for columns, statues, and terraces, as well as water sources to feed the ornamental pools, fountains, canals, and baths artfully laid out around the grounds. Built for pleasure, the villa was a marvel of landscape design, with cunning perspectives and garden panoramas. Hadrian filled the palaces and temples with sculptures, some of which now rest in the museums of Rome.

In later centuries, barbarians, popes, and cardinals, as well as anyone who needed a slab of marble, carted off much that made the villa so spectacular. Still, enough remains for us to piece together the story. (For a glimpse of what the villa used to be, see the plastic reconstruction at the entrance.) The most outstanding remnant is the **Canopus,** a re-creation of the Egyptian town of Canope and its famous Temple of the Serapis. In the main residential palace, the rectangular ruins of **Piazza d'Oro** (the Golden Court) are surrounded by a double portico, and the **Sala dei pilastri dorici** (Doric Pillared Hall) still has pilasters with Doric bases and capitals holding up a Doric architrave. The ruins of the **Baths** reveal rectangular rooms with concave walls. Only the north wall remains of the **Pecile,** or Poikile, which Hadrian discovered in Athens and had reproduced here. Don't miss the **Teatro Marittimo,** the ruins of a circular maritime theater with a central building ringed by a canal spanned by small swing bridges. It'll take time to wander these vast grounds, but that's the point.

ⓘ Via di Villa Adriana (✆ **39/774/530203**).

✈ Leonardo da Vinci International Airport.

🛏 $$$ **Hotel de Russie,** Via del Babuino 9 (✆ **800/323-7500** in North America, or 39/06/328881; www.romeby.com/derussie/pages/reach.htm). $ **Hotel Grifo,** Via del Boschetto 144 (✆ **39/06/4871395;** www.hotelgrifo.com).

WHY THEY'LL THANK YOU: Emperor or frustrated architect? You decide.

Elsinore
Prince Hamlet's Come Home
Ages 8 & up • Kronborg, Denmark

Scholars say there really was a Prince Hamlet of Denmark, and there really is a royal palace in Elsinore (Helsingør in Danish)—the trouble is, that particular Hamlet lived a long time before this palace was built in 1574. Yes, the palace existed when Shakespeare wrote his great tragedy *Hamlet,* but he certainly never visited it. In typical Shakespeare fashion, he made the whole thing up. All the same, when you walk around the corridors of **Kronborg Castle,** full of secret passages and casemates, the brooding spirit of the Danish prince is undeniably present. No wonder so many famous productions of *Hamlet* have been performed here—the castle is a born stage set. Once the kids have visited Elsinore, Shakespeare's greatest tragedy will be so much more to them than just words on a page.

Here, for example, looking out over the Øserund waters, above the battlements is a **waterfront platform,** backed by massive bronze guns—exactly the spot where Hamlet would have seen the ghost of his father. Inside, the **Ballroom** (the largest hall in northern Europe) could have hosted the court banquet where Hamlet staged a cunning little play to "catch the conscience of the king"; down the corridor the **Councillor's Hall** is hung with seven rare tapestries, portraits of Danish kings, any of which snooping Polonius could have been hiding behind when Hamlet mistakenly ran him through with his sword.

A 50-minute train ride north from Copenhagen, the town of **Helsingør** has its own quiet medieval charm, with a handful of 15th-century churches worth a look. Kronborg Castle is less than a kilometer (about half a mile) from the train station, a steeply gabled sandstone pile set on a jutting peninsula guarding the strategic strait between Denmark and its rival Sweden. Cross the moat on a wooden bridge and circle around to the main courtyard, from which you can visit the **royal apartments** (the Danish Mari-time Museum also occupies some of the castle). Not much of its former splendor remains, but the spare rooms only add to Elsinore's bleak, austere personality. It doesn't matter if Shakespeare ever saw this place—Kronborg Castle *is* Hamlet's Elsinore, from the tip of its dreaming spires to the bottom of its dank moat.

ⓘ ℂ **45/33-92-63-00;** www.kronborg castle.com.

✈ Copenhagen's Kastrup Airport, 53km (33 miles).

🛏 $ **Hotel Ansgar,** Colbjørnsensgade 18–20 (ℂ **45/33-13-19-13;** www.ansgar-hotel.dk). $$$ **Sofitel Copenhagen,** Bernstorffsgade 4 (ℂ **800/221-4542** in the U.S., or 45/33-14-92-62; www.sofitel.com).

WHY THEY'LL THANK YOU: Finding the statue of Holger Dansk in the basement.

Elsinore Castle.

Going Batty at Count Dracula's Castle

Ages 6 & up • Bran, Romania

His name was Vlad Tepes—Vlad the Impaler—but this Romanian prince (1431–76) often signed his name "Dracul," or the Devil, no doubt to unnerve his enemies. Bram Stoker's 1897 novel *Dracula* wasn't really based on Vlad Tepes: No matter how vicious Vlad was, no one ever accused him of being a vampire. Still, the creepy association clings to this castle in the heart of the Carpathian Mountains. This Gothic stronghold on a rocky outcrop in the Romanian village of Bran is full of secret passageways, hidden courtyards, overhanging balconies, and steep stone staircases where—you never know—a vampire just might lurk after all.

Bran Castle is a stop on every package tour of Romania, and a cluster of souvenir stands in the village below push the Dracula connection a bit too hard. Historians are quite clear on one point: Vlad Tepes never owned Bran Castle. His grandfather was born here, and Vlad hid out here in 1462 while fleeing the Turks, but only briefly. In those turbulent years, the ruthless warrior Vlad—a Wallachian king, not a Transylvanian count—was one of the Hungarian empire's best hopes for driving out the hated Turk invaders; he was a national hero, not a reviled bloodsucker. (All right, Vlad liked to behead mice, was fond of bats, and tortured his prisoners by impaling them on a spear, but nobody's perfect.)

This fortress was a defensive stronghold, not a royal residence, as you can see from its thick double walls and impregnable-looking gate tower. Guarding the strategic pass between Wallachia and Transylvania, it was fortified specifically to protect the trading city of Brasov, 28km (17 miles) northeast, from the Turks. The castle itself, mostly built in the late 14th century, with its white-plastered stone buildings, four fairy-tale turrets, and jaunty red tile roofs looks more *Heidi* than *Dracula*, but be wary—that fountain in the

Dracula's Castle in Romania.

half-timbered inner courtyard leads to an underground labyrinth of secret passages, perfect for clandestine escapes.

Inside, the furnishings reflect another, more recent, resident: the enormously popular Queen Marie of Romania, who made it her summer home from 1920 to 1938. Some of her vast art collection is displayed in the castle's clean and cozy-looking interiors. The most arresting object in the castle to me is the elaborately carved 18th-century bedstead in her bedroom, its wood stained almost black over the centuries—a bed you can almost imagine Count Dracula occupying.

(i) **Bran Castle,** 498 Traian Mosoiu St. ((C) **40/268/238332;** www.romaniatourism. com/dracula.html).

✈ Otopeni, Bucharest 140km (87 miles).

🛏 $$$ **Hotel Aro,** 27 Eroilor, Brasov ((C) **40/268/142840**). $$ **Hotel Capitol,** 19 Eroilor, Brasov ((C) **40/268/418920**).

WHY THEY'LL THANK YOU: Dracula or Vlad the Impaler, he was still one scary dude.

Hampton Court Palace
Henry VIII's Playground
All ages • Hampton Court, England

The 16th-century palace of Cardinal Wolsey serves as a useful lesson: Don't try to outdo your boss, particularly if he happens to be Henry VIII. The rich cardinal did just that, and he lost his fortune, power, and prestige, finally giving his lavish palace to the Tudor monarch. Once Henry took over, of course, he even outdid Wolsey in embellishing this fine redbrick palace, making it the ultimate weekend house of its time.

Hampton Court, 21km (13 miles) west of London, is a great day trip from the city; you can easily get here by car, train, or, best of all, excursion boat. Although the palace enjoyed prestige and pomp in Elizabethan days, it owes much of its present look to the great architect Sir Christopher Wren, who at the behest of the monarchs William and Mary designed the Northern or **Lion Gates,** intended to be the main entrance to the new parts of the palace.

You can parade through the apartments, filled with period porcelain, furniture, paintings, and tapestries. The **King's Dressing Room** is graced with some of the best art, mainly paintings by old masters on loan from Queen Elizabeth II. Tudor additions included the **Anne Boleyn gateway,** with its 16th-century astronomical clock that tells the high-water mark at London Bridge, and one of Henry's major contributions, the aptly named **Great Hall,** with its hammer-beam ceiling. Be sure to inspect the **royal chapel** (Wolsey wouldn't recognize it). Hampton Court had quite a retinue to feed, as you can see from the **Great Kitchen.**

Other amenities added by Henry were the **Tiltyard** (where jousting competitions were held) and a **tennis court.** What most children remember best, however, is getting lost in the serpentine **shrubbery maze** in the garden (another Wren design), which was a popular source of courtiers' entertainment in those pre-Xbox days. The **formal gardens** here are justly famous, demonstrating examples of garden methods and designs from several important periods of history. If you don't want to pay to enter the palace itself, you can still roam the delightful gardens for free (except for the Privy Garden).

(i) North bank of the Thames (© **44/870/752-7777**; www.hrp.org.uk).

✈ Heathrow.

🛏 $$$ **London Bridge Hotel,** 8–18 London Bridge St. 9 (© **44/20/7855-2200**; www.londonbridgehotel.com). $$ **Vicarage Private Hotel,** 10 Vicarage Gate, South Kensington (© **44/20/7229-4030;** www.londonvicaragehotel.com).

WHY THEY'LL THANK YOU: The amazing maze.

Scotland's Royal Castles
Where Mary Queen of Scots Slept
Ages 4 & up • Edinburgh, Linlithgow & Stirling, Scotland

A cluster of Scottish castles, all of them either in or near Edinburgh, traces the life of one of history's most tragic figures—Mary Queen of Scots. Don't expect richly furnished apartments like the royal homes in England or France; Scotland's kings lost their crown a long time ago, and the shabby fate of their great palaces is a tale in itself.

Start in Edinburgh, Scotland's capital, where two palaces stand at either end of the **Royal Mile,** a grand street lined with ancient churches, shops, and houses. At its upper end, dour **Edinburgh Castle** (© **44/131/225-9846**) perches on a rocky summit. Founded in the 11th century by Malcolm III, this seat of Scottish kings was demoted to a mere military garrison for the past couple of centuries. A set of State Apartments has been fitted out for visitors, however, and in Queen Mary's Bedroom, you'll see where Mary Queen of Scots gave birth to her son, James VI of Scotland (later James I of England). Don't miss the Crown Chamber, housing the Honours of Scotland (Scotland's Crown Jewels, but hardly in the same class as England's).

Meander the length of the Royal Mile to the **Palace of Holyroodhouse** (© **44/131/556-7371**), which looks much more royal—no surprise, as most of it was built in the 1660s by the English king Charles II

after Scotland and England were united. (It's still a royal residence, and if the Queen's in town you can't go in.) In a surviving old wing, Mary Queen of Scots once lived in King James Tower; her husband, Lord Darnley, had his own rooms on the floor below. Here, in 1566, a jealous Darnley and his accomplices stabbed Queen Mary's Italian secretary, David Rizzio, 56 times before her eyes.

Eighteen miles west of Edinburgh is **Linlithgow Castle,** on A706 in Linlithgow (© **44/150/684-2896**), where Mary Queen of Scots was born in 1542—6 days before her father, James V, died, making her Queen of Scotland. Beloved by the Stuart kings, who built it in stages from 1425 to 1624 (the last of them, Bonnie Prince Charlie, stayed here in 1745), it met its doom in 1746, when English troops, under the Duke of Cumberland camped here, leaving it in flames as they departed—heading north to defeat Charlie at **Culloden.** It's one of the country's most affecting ruins, its pink-ocher buttressed walls soaring to the open sky. From the scale of the rooms, you can guess how grand they were once.

Another day trip from Edinburgh (60 km/ 37 miles northwest), **Stirling Castle,** Stirling (© **44/1786/450000**), looms high on a basalt rock over the river Forth, a strategic position between the Highlands

379

and Lowlands. Within those forbidding walls are some handsome 15th- and 16th-century residences, only now being restored to their former glory. James V died while building its lavish main palace to impress his new French wife; their daughter, the new Queen Mary, spent the innocent first 4 years of her star-crossed life here.

ⓘ **Edinburgh and Scotland Information Centre,** 3 Princes St., Edinburgh (✆ **44/845/ 225-5121;** www.edinburgh.org).

✈ Edinburgh.

🛏 $$$ **Carlton Highland Hotel,** 19 North Bridge, Edinburgh (✆ **44/ 131/472-3000;** www.paramount-hotels. co.uk). $ **Thrums Private Hotel,** 14–15 Minto St., Edinburgh (✆ **44/131/667-5545;** www.thrumshotel.com).

WHY THEY'LL THANK YOU: Poignant castles for a poignant queen.

Castles & Mansions **362**

The Forbidden City
The Chinese Emperor's Little Hideaway
Ages 8 & up • Beijing, China

The most spectacular palace in China, **Gù Gōng** (to give it its Chinese name), is truly something to see, an immense layout of red-walled buildings topped with glazed vermilion tile and ringed by a vast moat. It was home to 24 emperors over half a millennium, from 1420 to 1923. Although many parts may be closed when you visit, thanks to a massive renovation lasting through 2020(!), there's more than enough left to explore. It isn't any one structure you've come to see, it's the scale and harmony of the whole, an irrefutable statement of Chinese imperial might.

An army of workers began construction in 1406, taking only 14 years to complete the complex. Given various ransackings and fires, though, most of what we see today was built in the Qīng dynasty (1626–1912) rather than the earlier Ming era. Point out to the kids the blue and green tiles trimming several of the up-curled roofs—the Qīngs were Manchus, and it's said this color reminded them of their native grasslands.

You enter through the **Meridian Gate,** but before you go farther, check out the largest gate, the **Gate of Heavenly Peace,** where Mao Tse Tung made his dramatic announcement founding the People's Republic in October 1949. You can't miss it—it's the gate with the giant portrait of Mao hanging above the central door, flanked by sonorous inscriptions. The **Gate of Supreme Harmony** leads into the perfectly symmetrical outer court, with its three grand ceremonial halls, where the emperor conducted official business. Just as Islamic temples always face toward Mecca, in the Imperial City most major halls open to the south, the direction associated with imperial rule.

It's the **inner court**—the emperor's private residence—that makes this truly the Forbidden City, for only the imperial family (which included concubines and as many as 1,500 eunuchs) were allowed here. Three palaces, mirroring the three halls in the outer court, are set in the inner court, and at its rear is a marvelous garden of ancient conifers, rockeries, and pavilions, an oasis largely unchanged since the Ming era.

The Forbidden City.

If you really want the kids to get the point of the Forbidden City, though, go beyond the central axis, where all the tourists mass; explore the quieter maze of pavilions, gardens, courtyards, and theaters on the eastern side. (You have to giggle at the useless over-shoe slippers you're required to buy along with this section's extra admission fee.) The **Hall of Clocks** (Zhōngbiǎo Guǎn) is worth tracking down, as is the **Well of the Pearl Concubine** (Zhēnfēi Jǐng), a narrow hole covered by a large circle of stone. Here, a 25-year-old favorite was stuffed down the well as the imperial family fled the aftermath of the Boxer Rebellion; she'd dared to suggest that the emperor stay to face the mobs, as he'd supported the Boxers in the first place. Defying the emperor? *Not* a good idea.

ⓘ North side of Tiān'ān Mén Square, across Cháng'ān Dàjiē (✆ **86/10/6513-2255,** ext. 615).

✈ Capital Airport, Beijing.

🛏 $$$ **Grand Hyatt,** Dōng Cháng'ān Jiē 1, Dōngchéng District (✆ **86/10/8518-1234;** http://beijing.grand.hyatt.com). $$ **Red House,** Chūnxiù Lù 10, Cháoyáng District (✆ **86/10/6416-7810**).

WHY THEY'LL THANK YOU: Discovering a forbidden world.

363

Fontainebleau
Refuge of Kings
Ages 8 & up • Fontainebleau, France

If **Versailles** is all about formal gardens and gilt-encrusted furnishings, the other royal residence within day-trip distance from the capital, Fontainebleau, is all about its ancient forests and grand Renaissance paintings. It has a more impressive history, having been built a century earlier by François I, and remained in use later. Less crowded, and therefore more peaceful, than Versailles, Fontainebleau may appeal to your children even more than its over-the-top cousin.

François I, like Louis XIV after him, sent to Italy for artists to decorate his royal digs. What came to be called the School of Fontainebleau arose, led by the painters Rosso, Fiorentino, and Primaticcio. Their handiwork adorns one of the most outstanding rooms at Fontainebleau: the **Gallery of François I,** where stucco-framed panels on every hand depict such scenes as Jupiter abducting Europa, the Nymph of Fontainebleau (with a lecherous dog peering through the reeds), and the king holding a pomegranate, a symbol of unity.

As you go through the palace, have the kids hunt for the oft-repeated figure of a salamander, symbol of the Chevalier King, François I. In the **Ballroom,** peer at the splendid decorations to find the interlaced monograms H & D, which stand for François's successor, Henri II, and the woman he loved, Diane de Poitiers. Reminders of Napoleon include his throne room, the room where he abdicated (the abdication document displayed is a copy), his offices, his bedroom (look for his symbol, a bee), and his bathroom.

French kings originally came to Fontainebleau because it offered great hunting, and the surrounding forest is still verdant and inviting—Parisians flock here not only to visit the château but for horseback riding, picnicking, and hiking. Stand on the back terrace and imagine a misty 17th-century morning, with huntsman's horns trumpeting and hounds baying as the king and his boon companions set off into the dusky woods for a day's hunt. Then set off on foot along hiking trails made by French kings through the forest—that's when history comes alive.

ⓘ Place du Général-de-Gaulle, Avon (✆ **33/01/60-71-50-70**).

✈ De Gaulle, Orly.

🛏 $$$ **Hotel de Fleurie,** 32–34 rue Grégoire-de-Tours (✆ **33/01/53-73-70-00;** www.hotel-de-fleurie.tm.fr). $$ **Residence Lord Byron,** 5 rue de Chateaubriand (✆ **33/01/43-59-89-98;** www.escapade-paris.com).

WHY THEY'LL THANK YOU: Even Napoleon needed a place to chill out.

Versailles

Palace of the Sun King

Ages 8 & up • Versailles, France

When your nickname is the Sun King, you need a resplendent palace to live up to your image, and Louis XIV of France sought just that in 1661 when he undertook renovations on his father's hunting lodge at Versailles. It took 50 years, but the end result was a royal residence so fabulous that its very name has become synonymous with luxury living. Yes, it's good to be the king.

Under Louis XIV and his equally extravagant great-grandson Louis XV, Versailles typically hosted some 3,000 courtiers and their retinues at a time. Given the constant entertainment and lavish banquets, few turned down the chance to join the glittering throng—to gossip, dance, plot, and flirt away while the peasants on their estates sowed the seeds of the Revolution. It all caught up with the next monarchs, well-intentioned but weak Louis XVI and his frivolous queen, Marie Antoinette, who were eating cake at Versailles on October 6, 1789, when they learned that citizen mobs were converging on the palace. Versailles became a museum under Louis-Philippe (1830–48) and has remained so ever since.

Visitors can tour the **State Apartments,** loaded with ornate furniture, paintings, tapestries, vases, chandeliers, and sculpture; it seems as if every inch on every wall has been gilded or plastered in

A glimpse of the extravagance of Versailles.

some baroque design. The most dazzling room—a long arcade called the **Hall of Mirrors,** with windows along one wall and 357 beveled mirrors along the other—is where the **Treaty of Versailles,** officially ending World War I, was signed in 1919. In the **Queen's Apartments,** Marie Antoinette played the harpsichord for guests; in the **Clock Room,** 7-year-old Mozart performed for the court; and the gold-and-white **Royal Chapel** is where Louis XVI married Marie Antoinette in 1770. You won't visit all 700 rooms in the palace, but you'll glimpse a *Dangerous Liaisons*–type lifestyle of wealth, power, and decadence.

The **Gardens of Versailles** are the ultimate in French formal garden design, with geometrical flower beds, terraces, pools, topiary, statuary, lakes, and canals. The kids will enjoy these vast gardens even more if you time your visit to coincide with the summer spectacles—weekend daytime programs where classical music is piped in and all 50 fountains are turned on full blast, or nighttime shows of illuminated fountains, fireworks, and costumed actors portraying Louis XVI and his court. Call ☎ **33/01/30-83-78-88** for information.

A walk across the park will take you to two outlying residences: the pink-and-white-marble **Grand Trianon,** still used today as a VIP lodging, and the **Petit Trianon,** where Louis XV held trysts with Madame du Barry. The **Queen's Hamlet,** nearby, is a rustic set of half-timbered buildings where Marie Antoinette and her chums dressed like shepherdesses and lived "humbly."

ⓘ ☎ **33/01/30-83-78-00;** www.chateau-versailles.fr.

✈ De Gaulle, Orly.

🛏 $$$ **Hotel de Fleurie,** 32–34 rue Grégoire-de-Tours (☎ **33/01/53-73-70-00;** www.hotel-de-fleurie.tm.fr). $$ **Residence Lord Byron,** 5 rue de Chateaubriand (☎ **33/01/43-59-89-98;** www.escapade-paris.com).

WHY THEY'LL THANK YOU: Conspicuous consumption to the max.

Castles & Mansions 365

The Doge's Palace
Ages 6 & up • Venice, Italy

Other cities were reigned over by kings, emperors, or mayors—but ever-exotic Venice couldn't have something as ordinary as one of those. No, the guy in charge there was the *Doge* ("duke" in Renaissance Italian), an all-powerful autocrat who lived just off St. Mark's Square, with his own gondola landing off the Grand Canal. For around 1,000 years, a succession of elected-for-life doges ruled over this wealthy city-state from this stunning palace, designed not so much for a life of luxury as for power and intrigue.

One of Europe's most distinctive palaces, the **Palazzo Ducale** was first built in the 14th century, but it looks weirdly futuristic, with its pale, blank rectangular facade, perforated by a pattern of tiny apertures, resting on a base of slender white lozenge-topped columns that look oddly like lollipops. There are no windows, no towers, no grand entrance, though if you slip through the courtyard (through the so-called Paper Gate, where decrees were officially read to the public), you'll find one relentlessly long main staircase known as the **Scala dei Gigantes,** or Stairway of the Giants. Ordinary citizens were never permitted to walk up these stairs—ask the kids to imagine how intimidating they must have looked to visitors, hoping to beg a favor from the imperious doge. By the time you got to the top, you'd be shaking in your boots.

Sure, the kids will enjoy trooping through all the **ceremonial salons,** where the doge's mighty council and even-more-powerful inner senate convened. The extraordinary detail of the painted ceilings, the gilded and cushioned seating, will no doubt impress—that's what they were designed for, to overwhelm foreign visitors to this maritime republic, which depended upon a cosmopolitan trade network with a vast range of other nations. The epitome is the immense **Great Council Hall,** which contains a painting by Veronese that's believed to be the world's largest oil painting, *The Triumph of Venice.* There's a conspiratorial air still hanging around the courtrooms where the doge's security force, the **Council of Ten,** dispensed a harsh, murky sort of justice.

But the part of the palace that most intrigued my kids was—you guessed it—the adjacent **prison.** Ceaseless political maneuvering was essential for any doge to hang onto his position, and those cells were occupied by prisoners from the writer Casanova to the humblest traitor; you can still see the plaintive graffiti scratched onto the walls of the grim little cells. In order to reach the cells, you cross over an arched windowed bridge linking the two buildings; the famous **Bridge of Sighs,** so named because prisoners sighed grievously as they were led away to captivity. For the best insider's account of palace intrigues, book a **Secret Itineraries tour**—it may take a little longer, but it's worth it for the extra color your kids will get.

ⓘ **Venice Tourist Board,** Piazza San Marco 1-30124 (☎ **39/4127/15911;** www.museicivicivceneziani.it).

✈ Aeroporto Marco Polo.

🛏 $$$ **Locanda Ai Santi Apostoli,** Strada Nuova, Cannaregio (☎ **39/4152/12612;** www.locandasantiapostoli.com). $$ **Pensione Accademia,** Fondamenta Bollani, Dorsoduro (☎ **39/4152/37846;** www.pensioneaccademia.it).

WHY THEY'LL THANK YOU: Walking the Stairway of the Giants.

366 Castles & Mansions

Topkapi Palace
Relaxing with the Sultans in Istanbul
Ages 8 & up • Istanbul, Turkey

Nothing says "lap of luxury" like magnificent Topkapi Palace, built in the 1450s by Mehmet the Conqueror on Istanbul's best real estate, at the tip of a peninsula commanding the Bosporus Strait. For almost 400 years, Ottoman sultans reigned here over their legendary empire. It's an exotic marvel of brilliant-colored ceramic tiles, inlaid ivory, and ornate friezes and mosaics—but it's the elements of cruelty, lust, and political intrigue that will fascinate the kids.

As you enter through the **Gate of Augustus** (aka the Bab-i Hümayün Gate), look up to see where the decapitated heads of uncooperative officials or rebels were displayed as a public warning. The first courtyard, the **Court of the Janissaries,** is a shady public garden; just inside is the Istanbul Archaeology Museum (a bore for most kids). Only the sultan could pass through the **Gate of Salutation,** flanked by two octagonal prison towers; after beheadings, the executioner washed the blood off his hands in the fountain to the right.

In the second courtyard, you'll see the enormous **Palace Kitchens,** where more than 1,000 servants worked day and night to serve 5,000 residents (the palace's amazing porcelain collection is on display here now), and the **Imperial Armory,** featuring the swords of Mehmet the Conqueror and Süleyman the Magnificent. The sultan's private quarters began past the **Gate of Felicity** (decapitated heads were impaled above this gate as well). Within that gate, the **Palace Clothing Exhibition** shows off the sultan's absurdly baggy costumes of silk, brocade, and gold-threaded fabrics, while the **Treasury** displays the awesome spoils of 400 years of Ottoman rule. In room no. 1, check out the priceless **ceremonial thrones;** room no. 4 holds the Treasury's pièce de résistance, the famous **Topkapi Dagger,** as well as the 86-carat **Kaşikdi Diamond.** At the far corner of the third courtyard is the always-crowded **Holy Relic Section.** It contains the first copy of the Koran, personal belongings of the Prophet Mohammed, and even the staff of Moses.

You'll need a separate admission ticket for a half-hour tour of the **Harem** (buy them near the Carriage Gate in the second courtyard). It may sound sexy and lurid—the word *harem* is Arabic for "forbidden"—but these living quarters were really a deluxe prison. There are three main sections: the cell-like quarters of the Black Eunuchs, the Harem's guards; the claustrophobic inner courtyard where up to 800 concubines lived in cramped cubicles; and, in stark contrast, the lavish seaview apartments reserved for the sultan, his mother, favorite concubines, and heirs to the throne. And, oh yeah, don't miss the **Golden Cage,** where brothers of the sultan were kept under house arrest so they wouldn't take over the throne. Those sultans, they took no chances.

ⓘ At the end of Babuhümayun Cadissi., Sultanahmet (✆ **90/212/512-0480**).

✈ Atatürk International, Istanbul.

🛏 $$$ **Çirağan Palace Hotel Kempinski Istanbul,** Çirağan Cad. 84 (✆ **800/426-3135** in the U.S., 90/212/258-3377 in Istanbul; www.ciraganpalace.com). $$ **Blue House** (Mavi Ev), Dalbasti Sok. 14 (✆ **90/212/638-9010;** www.bluehouse.com.tr).

WHY THEY'LL THANK YOU: The sultan's rap-star wardrobe.

---

367 Castles & Mansions

Neuschwanstein
Mad King Ludwig's Castle
Ages 6 & up • Hohenschwangau, Germany

Approaching the castle of Neuschwanstein, children get a shock of déjà vu—where have they seen this before? Disneyland, of course—Walt Disney had this Bavarian fantasy castle in mind when he designed the Cinderella castle in 1955. It's madly popular (be prepared to wait in line for hours in summer), but the kids will remember it always, not just for its fairytale facade, but also for the tragic life story behind it.

Ludwig II was a handsome 18-year-old when he became king of Bavaria. A loner who never married, as time passed Ludwig became more and more enmeshed in his own extravagant fantasies—closeting himself away with an indulgent entourage; mounting full-fledged productions of operas by his favorite composer, Richard Wagner, with himself as the only audience; and last but not least, building three lavish castles: Herrenchiemsee, Linderhof, and Neuschwanstein, this ethereally pale, multiturreted medieval folly on a crag high above the little town of Hohenswangau. Finally, Ludwig's extravagance and bizarre behavior drove his advisors to have him declared insane in 1886 at age 41. Three days later, he was found drowned in a lake on the outskirts of Munich—whether murder or suicide, we may never know. When Ludwig died, construction on Neuschwanstein—which had been puttering on for 17 years—stopped abruptly, and there's an eerie sense of abandonment about it today. Ludwig lived here for a total of only about 6 months.

Neuschwanstein is literally a storybook castle, with **wall paintings** everywhere depicting scenes from Nordic legends—Tannhäuser in his gold-and-silver silk-lined study, Tristan and Isolde in his elaborately carved bedroom, Parsifal in the grand fourth-floor Singer's Hall. In the **throne room,** kids are entranced by a Byzantine-style floor mosaic showing the animals of the world—but also notice a hauntingly empty space where Ludwig's throne was to have been placed.

The same parking lot serves both this and Hohenschwangau Castle, built by Ludwig's father, Maximilian I; be prepared for a steep 1km (half-mile) walk up to Neuschwanstein—that mountaintop site was not chosen for its convenience. You'll visit the castle on a 35-minute **guided tour** (offered in English), which plays up the dramatic ironies of Ludwig's memorable life. Afterward, hike up to the **Marienbrücke** (the trail is signposted), for a splendid view of Mad King Ludwig's fantasy castle.

ⓘ Neuschwansteinstrasse 20 (✆ **49/8362/939880;** www.neuschwanstein.de).

✈ Munich, 116km (72 miles).

🛏 $$ **Hotel Lisl and Jägerhaus,** Neuschwansteinstrasse (✆**49/8362/8870;** www.neuschwanstein-hotels.de). $$ **Hotel Müller Hohenschwangau,** Alpseestrasse (✆ **49/8362/81990;** www. hotel-mueller.de).

WHY THEY'LL THANK YOU: More beautiful than the Disney rip-off—and a better back story.

Newport's Mansions
The Gilded Age Elite's Summer "Cottages"
Ages 7 & up • Newport, Rhode Island, USA

Driving around Newport, Rhode Island, you can't help but gawp at the turn-of-the-20th-century mansions—Italianate *palazzi,* Tudor-style manors, faux French château, all set in elegant formal landscaping, with imposing gates or walls to keep out the hoi polloi (for example, *you*). It's incredible to imagine the sort of wealth that built these homes, even more incredible to realize that these were just these families' summer houses (offhandedly referred to as mere "cottages").

While many of these houses are still private property, nine are open to the public for guided tours, popular with tourists year-round (though not all are open daily in winter). Don't cram too many into 1 day—the sheer opulence of these interiors can soon bring on sensory overload. The most popular is **The Breakers,** Ochre Point Avenue (✆ **401/847-1000**), a 70-room 1895 mansion designed for Commodore Vanderbilt by Richard Morris Hunt. Patterned after Renaissance Florentine *palazzi,* it has a stunning great hall, an ornate 50-foot cube sheathed in marble. The Breakers even has bathrooms (very high-tech for the time) where both fresh and salt water come out of the taps. Stanford White modeled **Rosecliff,** Bellevue

387

The Breakers in Newport.

Avenue (ℂ **401/847-1000**), after the Grand Trianon at Versailles. Built in 1902 for an heiress of the Comstock Lode mining fortune, it has only 40 rooms (how sad), but it also has Newport's largest ballroom and a heart-shaped grand staircase. **Beechwood,** 580 Bellevue Ave. (ℂ **401/846-3772**), was built for the famous Mrs. Astor, who personally maintained a list of who counted and who didn't in New York

and Newport society. Kids will especially like this house because actors in period dress are on hand to tell anecdotes about late Victorian high society.

Two other Bellevue Avenue houses belonged to the same woman—named Alva Vanderbilt when she was mistress of **Marble House,** 596 Bellevue Ave. (ℂ **401/ 847-1000**), so called because it shows off just about every type of marble there is. Its ballroom is literally dazzling, with three kinds of gold encrusting its walls. Alva divorced her Vanderbilt husband and promptly married his best friend, who was a Belmont and lived down the street at **Belcourt Castle,** 657 Bellevue Ave. (ℂ **401/ 846-0669**). My daughter couldn't get over the luxurious stables. The Breakers may have had bathrooms, but Belcourt Castle had electricity, designed by Thomas Edison, no less. Tell the kids to look for the 14 secret doors.

ⓘ **Preservation Society of Newport,** 424 Bellevue Ave. (ℂ **401/847-1000;** www.newportmansions.org).

✈ Providence, 28 miles.

🛏 $$$ **Hyatt Regency Newport,** 1 Goat Island (ℂ **800/233-1234** or 401/851-1234; www.hyatt.com). $$ **Mill Street Inn,** 75 Mill St. (ℂ **800/392-1316** or 401/849-9500; www.millstreetinn.com).

BEST TIME: Dec, when the houses are decorated for the holidays.

WHY THEY'LL THANK YOU: Imagine sliding down these banisters.

Castles & Mansions **369**

The Biltmore Estate
The Vanderbilts' Mountain Cabin
Ages 6 & up • Asheville, North Carolina, USA

If the Gilded Age mansions in Newport, Rhode Island, were "cottages," what would you call this French Renaissance–

style château that George Washington Vanderbilt built in 1895? With 250 rooms, it's the largest private residence in the

United States (although open to the public for years, it's still owned by Vanderbilt descendants), covering no less than 4 acres under one sharp-peaked slate roof. It's imposing all right, yet surprisingly airy and light, a gracefully proportioned expanse of warm pale stone. Grand as it is, Biltmore somehow felt like a place I could live.

G. W. Vanderbilt journeyed through Europe and Asia buying up paintings, porcelains, bronzes, carpets, and other antiques. As a result, Biltmore is like a miniseminar in the history of decorative arts, with each successive room a fresh surprise. He picked up, for example, exquisite pieces of 18th-century furniture by Chippendale and Sheraton, and he also became a patron of late-19th-century artists, acquiring canvases by Renoir, Sargent, and Whistler when they were still alive to reap the profits. The oak-paneled billiards room looks like an exclusive men's club; the tapestry-hung dining hall has a baronial stone fireplace and 70-foot-high ceilings. Each guest bedroom has a strikingly different decor, inspired by a particular work of art. There are 65 fireplaces, a 23,000-volume library, an indoor pool, a bowling alley, a glass-roofed winter garden full of lush palms and ferns. On and on and on.

If the Biltmore house is rivaled by anything in Asheville, it's by its own **gardens,** a breathtaking layout by Frederick Law Olmstead (the designer of New York's Central Park). French-style formal plots with statuary and pools counterbalance naturalistic English-style areas (the Spring Glade is particularly charming). Capitalizing on the mountain climate, Olmstead went azalea-crazy, planting more than 200 varieties, which are at their most spectacular in late April and May. After exploring that immense house, let the kids romp through the gardens to let off steam.

(i) 1 Approach Rd. (U.S. 25; (C) **800/624-1575** or 828/225-1333; www.biltmore.com).

✈ Asheville.

🛏 $$$ **Grove Park Inn Resort,** 290 Macon Ave. ((C) **800/438-5800** or 828/252-2711; www.groveparkinn.com). $$ **Richmond Hill Inn,** 87 Richmond Hill Dr. ((C) **828/252-7313;** www.richmondhillinn.com).

WHY THEY'LL THANK YOU: It's what you would build if you had the money.

Castles & Mansions

370

Hearst Castle
California Palace in the Sky
Ages 8 & up • San Simeon, California, USA

It's not entirely true that the hilltop California estate of publishing magnate William Randolph Hearst is a 20th-century replica of an Old World manor. True, it was built from 1919 to 1947, but the bits and pieces are nearly all authentic—400-year-old Spanish and Italian ceilings, 500-year-old mantels, 16th-century Florentine bedsteads, Renaissance paintings, Flemish tapestries, and innumerable other European treasures, which Hearst compulsively acquired for years.

Each week, railroad cars carrying fragments of Roman temples, carved doors from Italian monasteries, hastily rolled canvases by the old masters, ancient Persian rugs, and antique French furniture arrived—5 tons at a time—in San Simeon. Orson Welles's 1941 masterpiece *Citizen Kane*, a thinly disguised fictional biography of Hearst, has an unforgettable shot of priceless antiques warehoused in dusty piles, stretching as far as the eye can see.

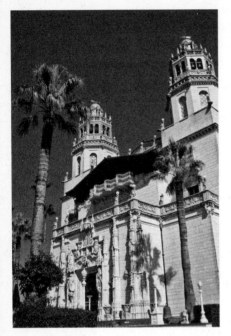

Hearst Castle.

screened first-run films. They longed to jump into the fabulous swimming pools—a Roman-inspired indoor pool with intricate mosaics, and the breathtaking outdoor Greco-Roman Neptune pool, flanked by marble colonnades that frame the distant sea.

Book your **guided tour** in advance if possible—there's not much else around this stretch of California coast, so Hearst Castle doesn't cater to drop-in business (everybody staying at our motel had either been there that day or was going tomorrow). You'll park down at the visitor center and take a bus uphill to the compound. Four different daytime tours visit various parts of the estate, with very little overlap; they last about 2 hours. Tour 1 covered all the essentials my kids wanted, but I regretted not seeing Hearst's private library and Gothic bedroom, which were on Tour 2. Too bad the **evening tours** were full when we booked—for those, costumed docents portray Hearst's celebrity house party guests. Thanks to Hearst's mistress, actress Marion Davies, the estate was a playground for the Hollywood crowd.

Only a fraction of what Hearst bought was ever installed in the estate.

Despite this patchwork approach, this sprawling Mediterranean Revival–style compound has a unified look, no doubt because one architect (and a woman at that, Julia Morgan) directed its entire 28-year creation. The main house, **Casa Grande,** alone has more than 100 rooms of baronial splendor. My kids lusted after the red-velvet-padded private movie theater where Hearst (also a movie mogul)

ⓘ U.S. 1 (© **805/927-2020,** or 800/444-4445 for tour reservations; www.hearst castle.org).

✈ Monterey Peninsula, 94 miles.

⊨ $$ **Best Western Cavalier Oceanfront Resort,** 9415 Hearst Dr. (© **800/826-8168** or 805/927-4688; www.cavalier resort.com).

WHY THEY'LL THANK YOU: Versailles-scale opulence for an American Sun King.

Sherwood Forest

Ages 4 & up • Nottingham, England

Every schoolchild knows the legend of Robin Hood and his Merry Band, but few can say that they have stood in Sherwood Forest, the purported home of Robin. While the jury is out on whether or not Robin really existed, it doesn't stop families from flocking to Edwinstowe every year, especially in summer, when the week-long annual **Robin Hood Festival** gets underway, featuring jugglers, jousters, jesters, and troubadours aplenty. The whole affair culminates in a parade of all things Robin (✆ **44/8449-80-80-80**).

The site of all this revelry was never really pure forest. Even in Robin's day, it was a mixed landscape of heath, pasture-land, and wooded glades, with a few scattered hamlets. This royal hunting ground covered 40,500 hectares (100,000 acres), running 32km (20 miles) long and 13km (8 miles) wide. Only the king or his subjects could hunt here, but peasants were allowed to gather acorns, collect firewood, make charcoal, or graze sheep and cattle. (Of course, a rebel like Robin wouldn't have observed such rules).

Today, Sherwood Forest is a 182-hectare (450-acre) park surrounding the village of Edwinstowe, squeezed between the urban areas of Nottingham and Sheffield; but it remains an essential part of the nation's heritage and around 1,000 of its stout oak trees survive. The most famous, the **Major Oak**—touted as Robin Hood's tree still stands, albeit with a little help from props and cables. This is understandable for a tree this old, although recent bark analysis suggest it might be younger than the 13th century. But the kids won't worry about the details when the story is this good and the atmosphere this fun. Although they might be drawn to the kitschy models of Robin and his Merry Men, pull them away long enough to check out the exhibition at **Ollerton Tourist Information Center** (next to Sherwood Heath; ✆ **44/1623/863887**), where you'll find a wall-size mural of summer flora and fauna along with a visual timeline of the forest's people.

ⓘ **Sherwood Forest Trust** (✆ **44/1623/ 758231;** www.sherwoodforest.org.uk).

✈ Heathrow, 2¹/₂ hr. drive.

🚅 Via Lincoln, 45 min.

🛏 $$ **Park Inn Nottingham,** 296 Mansfield Rd. (✆ **44/1159/359988;** www. parkinn.com). $$$ **Strathdon Hotel,** 44 Derby Rd. (✆ **44/1159/418501;** www. strathdon-hotel-nottingham.com).

WHY THEY'LL THANK YOU: Walking in Robin's forest.

Joan of Arc

Ages 8 & up • Rouen, France

There aren't too many female military heroes, but Joan of Arc looms large—many towns in France clamor to be associated with her larger than life story.

Her birthplace, **Maison Natle de Jeanne d'Arc,** in Domremy la Pucelle, 2 rue de la Basilique (✆ **33/3/29-06-95-86**), is a popular tourist site. It was here that she first heard the voices of saints and archangels. The original house with its steeply slanted roof is still standing, and has been restored to its original state. The house is plain—but large—with four rooms on the first floor. Despite its size, the lack of decoration and small windows suggest the home of a peasant family. Only the first floor is open for viewing, but you can see Joan's birth chamber, and a free museum devoted to her is just a short walk away.

I feel Joan's spirit is most alive in northwest France. In **Orléans** in 1429, 119km (74 miles) southwest of Paris, a 17-year-old Joan led a French army to free the besieged city from English attackers. Models and exhibits tell her story at the **Maison Jeanne-d'Arc,** 3 place de Gaulle, Orléans (✆ **33/2/38-52-99-89**), a reproduction of the half-timbered house where she stayed during the siege. The original house was destroyed by bombing in the '40s, but it has been faithfully re-created, with rough white plaster walls and simple wood beamed ceilings. The first floor is devoted to temporary exhibits, while the second and third floors feature dioramas, costumes, and weapons of the time, including a petite suit of armor. Be sure to see the **famous statue** of Joan on horseback in town at place de Mortroi.

The tragic final chapter of Joan's story is told in **Rouen,** 135km (84 miles) northwest of Paris. After someone at court eventually betrayed her, she was captured by the English in 1430 and brought to this English stronghold in Normandy. Corrupt clergy put her on trial, first on a charge of witchcraft, then of heresy (for wearing male clothing into battle). The **Musee Jeanne-d'Arc,** 33 place du Vieux-Marché, Rouen (✆ **33/2/35-88-02-70**), vividly lays out the details of her life with dioramas, waxworks, and exhibits; right outside its door is **place du Vieux-Marché,** where Joan was burned at the stake in 1431, the exact spot marked by a bronze cross.

Down the rue du Gros-Horloge, behind Rouen's Notre-Dame Cathedral, stand the ruins of the **Archbishop's Palace,** where Joan's mockery of a trial was held. Many English soldiers wept on the day this sincere, passionate young woman was burned at the stake, and her ashes were lovingly gathered up and scattered into the Seine.

ⓘ **Rouen Tourist Office,** 25 place de la Cathedrale, Rouen (✆ **33/2/32-08-32-40;** www.rouentourisme.com). **Orléans Tourist Office,** 8 rue d'Escures, Orléans (✆ **33/2/38-78-04-04;** www.tourismeloiret.com or www.tourisme.fr).

🚆 Orléans, 50 min. from Paris. Rouen, 70 min. from Paris.

🛏 $$ **Hotel Mercure Orléans,** 44–46 quai Barentin, Orléans (✆ **33/2/38-62-17-39**). $$ **Mercure Centre,** rue de la Croix-de-Fer, Rouen (✆ **33/2/35-52-69-52**).

WHY THEY'LL THANK YOU: Joan of Arc proved what a girl could do.

Verona
Romeo & Juliet's Hometown
Ages 6 & up • Italy

The most famous love story in the English language, Shakespeare's *Romeo and Juliet* was set in Verona, Italy, and though the Bard never set foot here—he "borrowed" the story ready-made from a 1562 version by one Arthur Brooke—Verona is quite happy to trade on the association. Whether Romeo or Juliet ever existed, Veronese entrepreneurs have dreamed up Capulet and Montague sites to snare tourists, making a useful hook to entice our children on a day trip from Venice to this lovely northern Italian city. Authentic or not, anything that makes them think about Shakespeare is okay by me.

The so-called **Juliet's House,** Via Cappello 23 (✆ **39/45/8034303**), has no proven connection to any family named Capulet (locals claim that in the 19th century it was a bordello), but this small,

sparely furnished home, with its stone balcony and tidy courtyard, fits the image—you can just imagine Romeo saying, "But, soft! What light through yonder window breaks?" The right breast on a bronze statue of Juliet is brightly polished from visitors giving it a traditional good-luck rub, and a blizzard of hopeful love letters are posted outside. A few blocks away, **Romeo's House,** Casa di Romeo, Via Arche Scaligeri 2, at least may have been home to the Montecchi family, the model for Shakespeare's Montagues; it's now an atmospheric restaurant, the **Osteria dal Duca** (✆ **39/45/594474**).

The nearby **Piazza delle Erbe,** once a Roman-era forum and today a lively open-air food market, is where I imagine Romeo, Mercutio, and Tybalt having their fatal street brawl. The kids decided the Roman

Whether or not she existed, it's fun to imagine Juliet on her balcony.

statue in the center, called *The Virgin of Verona,* was Juliet—who was I to argue? As for the play's church scenes, we envisioned them set in **Basilica San Zeno Maggiore,** Piazza San Zeno (© **39/45/8006120**), a near-perfect Romanesque church and campanile built between the 9th and 12th centuries west of the river Adige. Coming back along the riverbank, we pictured **Castelvecchio,** Corso Castelvecchio 2 (© **39/45/594734**), built in the 14th century for the ruling Della Scalla family, as the home of the play's Prince Escalus, its crenellated battlements like a perfect Lego castle. We stopped at the wonderfully intact **Roman arena,** dating from the 1st century A.D., then swung south to a Franciscan monastery that

claims to hold **Juliet's Tomb,** Via del Pontiere 5 (© **39/45/8000361**).

If you're here in July and August, get tickets for the Shakespearean festival—nothing beats seeing *Romeo and Juliet* or *Two Gentlemen of Verona* in this setting.

ⓘ **Tourist Office,** Via degli Alpini 9 (© **39/45/8068680**; www.tourism.verona.it).

🚊 Verona, 2 hr. from Venice.

🛏 $$ **Colomba d'Oro,** Via C. Cattaneo 10 (© **39/45/595300**; www.colombahotel.com). $$$ **Hotel Gabbia d'Oro,** Corso Porta Borsari 4A (© **39/45/8003060**; www.hotelgabbiadoro.it).

WHY THEY'LL THANK YOU: "In fair Verona, where we lay our scene . . ."

Famous Homesteads **374**

Brontë Parsonage Museum

Ages 8 & up • Haworth, England

The most-visited literary shrine in England after Shakespeare's hometown of Stratford-upon-Avon, this modest parsonage amid the bleak Yorkshire dales was home to not one but three gifted novelists—Charlotte, Emily, and Anne Brontë. Whether your favorite Brontë heroine is mousy governess Jane Eyre or passionate Catherine Earnshaw of *Wuthering Heights,* the spell of this remote, obscure Yorkshire home is captivating.

The village of **Haworth,** though overrun in summer by Brontë worshipers, still seems to hang precariously onto the edge of the Yorkshire moors. Try to screen out the crowds as you walk its steep, cobbled main street, where you can visit a pub called the Black Bull, which was frequented by the writers' dissolute artist brother, Branwell. Stop by the very post office where in 1847 the sisters mailed their manuscripts hopefully to London publishers.

At the top of the village on Church Street stands the square, stone-sided

Georgian **parsonage** where the Brontë family lived, granted for life to Patrick Brontë, curate of the local Church of St. Michaels. The Brontë children knew tragedy early—their mother and two sisters died when they were young—and though the shy, odd Brontë sisters ventured away for school or teaching jobs, they always fled back to this haven. The sparely furnished house has been preserved complete with personal treasures, pictures, books, original manuscripts, a huge collection of family letters, and the authentic family furniture (some bought with proceeds from Charlotte's literary success). Look at the dining room, where the sisters sat side by side writing their novels at the dining table, and the nursery, where they scribbled on the wall in their tiny, spidery handwriting. The walled garden has been laid out to resemble the one cultivated by the Brontës. Note that the museum tends to be extremely crowded in July and August, and is closed in January.

Charlotte and Emily are buried in Haworth in the family vault under the Church of St. Michael (the one standing here today is not the original church, which was torn down and rebuilt in 1879). Be sure to allow time to walk out onto the nearby moors, where the spirit of *Wuthering Heights* still sighs in the wind.

ⓘ ✆ **44/1535/642323;** www.bronte.org. uk.

🚂 Keighley, 3 hr. from London.

🛏 $$ **Old White Lion Hotel,** 6–10 West Lane (✆ **44/1535/642313;** www. oldwhitelionhotel.com).

WHY THEY'LL THANK YOU: Proof that genius can flourish anywhere.

---

375 Famous Homesteads

The Fairy-Tale Road
In the Boot Steps of the Brothers Grimm
All ages • Hanau to Hameln, Germany

Children have loved the aptly named Grimm's fairy tales ever since these real-life brothers first published their children's stories in 1812. Central Germany is Grimm country, and the so-called **Fairy-Tale Road** (Märchenstrasse) rolls right through it, past half-timbered villages, towered castles, and gnarled forests where many a poor woodcutter toiled. From Hanau to Hameln, it's a 400km (250-mile) drive. While a few sites are worth a stop, the main thing is to gaze out the window at the *Shrek*-like landscape where Snow White or Rumpelstiltskin could dance out into the road at any moment.

The official starting point is a monument to the Grimms, at Neustadter Marktplatz, in **Hanau,** a suburb 20km (12 miles) east of Frankfurt. Jakob Grimm was born here in 1785, his brother Wilhelm a year later, but there's little 18th-century charm left in Hanau; for that, head north on B43 to **Steinau an der Strasse,** where the Grimm brothers spent their youth. A memorial fountain honors them in the main cobblestone square, and on weekends puppet shows enact fairy tales at the **Steinauer Marionettentheater,** Kumpen 2 (✆ **49/6663/245**). Continue north on B40, then B254 and along the Schwalm River, which the Germans call *Rotkäppchenland,* or Little

Red Riding Hood country. Quaint towns, such as Fulda, Lauterbach, and Alsberg, set the fairy-tale scene; Neustadt has a circular tower where Rapunzel could have let down her golden tresses. A good stop for the night is **Kassel,** where the Grimms lived from 1798 to 1830; the **Bruder Grimm Museum,** at Schone Aussicht 2, contains letters, portraits, and mementos.

After Kassel, go north on B3 and Rte. 80, following signs to Sababurg, where **Dornröschenschloss Sababurg,** in Hofgeismar (✆ **49/5671/8080**), was the setting of the Sleeping Beauty legend. Briar roses still bloom in the courtyard of this turreted Italianate castle, which is set in an old zoological garden and encircled by a wilderness of ancient oak and beech trees. North on Rte. 80, then 83, **Bodenwerder** was the birthplace of Lügen Baron von Münchhausen (1720–97), known as the "Liar Baron" because he told the biggest whoppers in Germany; his tall tales became a popular children's book. In the Rathaus, or town hall, the **Münchhausen-Erinnerungszimmer** (Münchhausen Memorial Room) displays mementos of his life (Apr–Oct only).

Then it's northwest on Rte. 83 to picturesque **Hameln,** site of the Pied Piper legend. When the stingy citizens refused to pay an itinerant rat-catcher who rid the town of rats, he played a bewitching tune on his flute and lured Hameln's children out of town, never to be seen again. Frescoes in the restaurant of **Rattenfängerhaus** (Rat-Catcher's House), Osterstrasse 28 (© **49/5151/3888**), illustrate the legend; Hameln shops sell rat figures of every conceivable material, including candy.

ⓘ **Hameln Tourist Office,** Deisterallee 1 (© **49/5151/957823;** www.hameln.com).

✈ Frankfurt.

🛏 $$$ **Mercure Hotel Hameln,** 164er Ring 3, Hameln (© **49/5151/7920;** www.dorint.com). $$ **Schloss Hotel Wilhelmshöhe,** Schlosspark 8, Kassel (© **49/5613/0880** or 49/5613/088428).

WHY THEY'LL THANK YOU: Rapunzel's tower, Sleeping Beauty's castle, and a rat for the Pied Piper.

Famous Homesteads **376**

Hans Christian Andersen House
Denmark's Storyteller Supreme
All ages • Odense, Denmark

Though the children may not recognize the name Hans Christian Andersen, they know his stories all right: *The Emperor's New Clothes, The Princess and the Pea, The Ugly Duckling,* or *The Little Mermaid* (yes, the story existed before Disney), immortalized in the famous statue in Copenhagen harbor. Like most gifted writers for children, Andersen tapped into the terrors and humiliations and stubborn yearnings of his own childhood. How better to understand those stories than to get a picture of the boy Andersen was?

Begin at the **Hans Christian Andersen Museum,** a major museum documenting Andersen's life, times, and works. Films, touch-screens, and listening posts bring the writer into focus; a tall, clumsy, ugly man who, beneath his sophisticated manners, remained at heart a poor kid with a chip on his shoulder. You can see a re-creation of the study where he wrote, the bed where he died, and such memorabilia as a lock of his hair, his trademark walking stick, a top hat, a battered portmanteau, and letters to his dear friends the Swedish opera singer Jenny Lind and fellow writer Charles Dickens. Next door is his **birthplace,** a tiny yellow house on a corner

where five poor families lived, including Andersen's grandparents and parents, at his birth in 1805. Andersen's father was a shoemaker, his mother a drunken washerwoman, and Andersen himself grew up a shy, somewhat dorky kid, susceptible to the folk tales and superstitions he heard around him. A few blocks away, the **H.C. Andersens Barndomshjem** (Childhood Home), Munkeøllestraede 3, is the humble half-timbered house where he lived from age 2 until 14—when, dazzled by a traveling theater troupe, young Hans ran off to Copenhagen to become an actor.

The city of Odense has created a **walking tour** around the downtown area that passes several historic buildings Andersen would have known. Look for granite squares in the sidewalk, decorated with a cheery sun face of Andersen's own design. Try your best to take in the Andersen **plays** performed mid-July to mid-August at 4pm outdoors in **Funen Village,** Sejerskovvej 20 (© **45/14-88-14;** closed Mon), the open-air cultural museum with reassembled historic buildings from around the island. It's a site worth visiting even if you don't attend a play, a good place to recapture the 19th-century lifestyle of

Andersen's time. Even though the plays are in Danish, it'll be easy for the kids to follow the visuals—these simple, timeless stories speak a universal language.

ⓘ Bangs Boder 29 (✆ **45/66-14-88-14**; www.odense.dk).

🚃 Odense, 3 hr. from Copenhagen.

🛏 $$ **Clarion Hotel Plaza Odense,** Østre Stationsvej 24 (✆ **45/877/424-6423** in the U.S., or 45/66-11-77-45; www.hotel-plaza.dk). $$$ **Radisson SAS H.C. Andersen Hotel,** Claus Bergs Gade 7 (✆ **800/333-3333** in the U.S., or 45/66-14-78-00; www.odense.radissonsas.com).

WHY THEY'LL THANK YOU: Discovering the ugly duckling behind the famous writer.

The Hans Christian Andersen Theatre performs *The Emperor's New Clothes*.

377 Famous Homesteads

Beatrix Potter Country

All ages • The Lake District, England

Though she was born down in Suffolk, Beatrix Potter—author and illustrator of beloved children's stories like *The Tale of Peter Rabbit*—fell in love with England's stunning Lake District as a teenager when her family summered here, and as soon as she won literary fame she bought a farm near Lake Windermere and spent most of the rest of her life here. It's one of the U.K.'s most evocative (and popular) literary pilgrimages, for adults as well as children.

The logical place to begin is in the Victorian lakeside tourist town Bowness-on-Windermere, at the blatantly commercial **World of Beatrix Potter,** The Old Laundry (✆ **44/1539/488444**; www.hop-skip-jump.com), a 3-D "experience" where children can cavort around replica figures of Tom Kitten, Jemima Puddleduck, Benjamin Bunny, and other classic Potter animal

characters. It does a good job, though, of telling how this nature-loving Londoner happened to turn her detailed drawings into pocket-size children's books, and went on to become a successful Cumbrian farmer and conservationist.

To reach Potter's home, either drive west around the lake or, better yet, follow an 11km (6.8-mile) walking route (get details from the World of Beatrix Potter). The car ferry across Lake Windermere gives you an excuse for taking in glorious water views of the District's dramatic mountain peaks. Proceed to Sawrey, at the southeast end of Esthwaite Water, to visit **Hill Top,** the 17th-century gray stone farmhouse where Potter lived when she wrote some of her most famous stories. Due to the site's enormous popularity, visitors are issued timed-entry tickets (book ahead if you can); there's an atmospheric pub next door where you can have refreshments while you wait your turn. The deep-windowed, wainscoted interiors appeared in many of her illustrations (such as my favorites from *The Roly-Poly Pudding*) and the splendid cottage garden looks endearingly familiar—you almost expect Mrs. Tiggy-Winkle or the Flopsy Bunnies to pop out of the shrubbery at any moment.

Your next stop is in Hawkshead, at the **Beatrix Potter Gallery**, Main Street (ⓒ **44/15394/36355**), where a rotating selection of Potter's original drawings is displayed in the office once used by her lawyer husband, William Heelis, whom she married at age 47 (you may recognize the office as Tabitha Twitchit's shop in *The Pie and the Patty Pan*). There's a shuttle bus back to Bowness from Hawkshead.

ⓘ **Beatrix Potter Home,** Hill Top, near Sawrey (ⓒ **44/15394/36269;** www.nationaltrust.org.uk).

🚃 Windermere, 3¾ hr. from London.

🛏 $$ **Lindeth Howe,** Longtail Hill, Storrs Park, Bowness-on-Windermere (ⓒ **44/15394/45759;** www.lindeth-howe.co.uk). $$$ **Rothay Manor,** Rothay Bridge, Ambleside (ⓒ **44/15394/33605;** www.rothaymanor.co.uk).

WHY THEY'LL THANK YOU: Childhood images coming vividly to life.

Famous Homesteads **378**

The Anne Frank House
Life in the Secret Annex
Ages 8 & up • Amsterdam, The Netherlands

Teens and preteens in particular connect with the spirit of Anne Frank, not because she was anything special, but precisely because she wasn't. She was a mixed-up kid like themselves—only she happened to be a mixed-up kid fleeing the Nazi terror, living pent up for more than 2 years in a secret set of rooms in Amsterdam with seven other people. We know about her only because she poured out her heart in a startlingly frank diary, which now every school kid eventually reads. In summer you may have to queue for an hour or more to get in, but nobody should miss seeing this house, where Anne Frank waited out the darkest days of World War II. Even if they haven't yet read the book, this is the place where kids really get the tragedy of the Holocaust.

The hiding place Anne's father, Otto Frank, prepared for his family and friends was a back section of a house, consisting of four rooms and a tiny damp attic, connected to his office and warehouse. It's a typical Amsterdam canal house, with very steep interior stairs; the entrance to it from the office was hidden by a movable bookcase. Their existence protected by four trusted employees, they remained safe until close to the end of the war—after the landings at Normandy Beach spelled hope for the war to end—when suddenly, tragically, the secret annex was raided by Nazi forces. All eight of the *onderduikers* (divers or hiders) were deported to concentration camps. Anne herself died, with her sister Margot, at Bergen-Belsen; only Otto survived to see the secret annex again.

The rooms of the hiding place look surprisingly bare, for all the furniture was confiscated after the arrest; at one time it was refurnished to replicate its appearance from July 1942 to August 1944, but today it is stark and empty and utterly moving. Among the few things left in place are photos Anne pinned up of her favorite actress, Deanna Durbin, and the young English princesses Elizabeth and Margaret, along with a map upon which Otto Frank hopefully charted the progress of the war. The canal side of the house, where the helpers worked, has been restored to its authentic appearance, based on references in Anne's diary. **Personal items** belonging to each of the eight fugitives have been put on display in the building next door, along with the **original manuscript** of Anne's diary, which helper Miep Gies found scattered on the annex floor after the Franks were dragged away. The red-and-white autograph album in which Anne began her diary lies in a glass case, looking so innocent and childish—it makes her tragedy especially poignant.

(i) Prinsengracht 263 (© **31/20/556-7105;** www.annefrank.nl).

✈ Amsterdam Schipohl, 13km (8 miles).

🛏 $ **Amstel Botel,** Oosterdokskade 2–4 (© **31/20/626-4247;** www.amstelbotel.com). $$ **Estheréa,** Singel 303–309 (© **31/20/624-5146;** www.estherea.nl).

WHY THEY'LL THANK YOU: An ordinary teenager, living in extraordinary time.

379 Famous Homesteads

The Paul Revere House
Starting the Midnight Ride
Ages 6 & up • Boston, Massachusetts, USA

Kids love to play connect-the-dots—so how cool it is to play it on a life-sized scale, by walking **Boston's Freedom Trail** (© **617/357-8300;** www.thefreedomtrail.org). Starting at the Boston Common, this 3-mile walking route hits all the high spots of Revolutionary War history, following a red line painted on the sidewalk; even stroller-bound toddlers get the point of following that line. And, to my mind, the climax of the whole hike is the Paul Revere House, home of the famous silversmith and patriot who rode out to Lexington and Concord on April 18, 1775, to rouse the colonial forces before the first battle of the war for independence.

My favorite book as a kid was Esther Forbes' *Johnny Tremain,* a wonderful historical fiction covering those anxious months in the Massachusetts Bay colony from the Boston Tea Party to the battles of Lexington and Concord. Revere was a prominent character in that novel, and on my first Boston trip seeing this cramped steep-gabled house of nearly black weathered wood, with its tiny diamond-paned windows and brick-paved courtyard, was like visiting a shrine for me. Revere had 16 children (he called them "my lambs"), eight with each of his two wives, although given the size of these living quarters, you'll be relieved to know that not all lived here at the same time. He supported this large family with a thriving silversmith's trade, becoming one of the colony's most respected artisans. On the self-guided tour, you can linger over typical 18th-century household furnishings, the incendiary political cartoons Revere engraved for local newspapers, or the classically simple silver pieces that earned Revere his fame. From the huge brick fireplaces to the narrow rope-mattress beds, these rough-beamed and raftered rooms offer an intriguing glimpse into daily life from more than two centuries ago.

The oldest house in downtown Boston, it was built around 1680, bought by Revere in 1770, and put to a number of uses before being turned into a museum in 1908. Across the courtyard is the home of Revere's Hichborn cousins, the **Pierce/ Hichborn House,** built in 1711 and a rare surviving example of 18th-century middle-class architecture—(shown only by guided tour; call ahead for reservations at © **617/ 523-2338**).

North Square is the heart of the North End, which eventually became an atmospheric Italian neighborhood—it's a great place for lunch after walking the Trail. If you're short on time, you may cut to the chase and just visit the Revere House on its own, but personally I think that would be a pity—Revere's house means even more if you've already seen the spire of **Old North Church,** where the signal lanterns were hung to tell Revere which route

the Redcoats would be taking. (For the record, they went "by sea," ferried across the Charles River). Freedom Trail maps are available at the visitor information booth on Tremont Street; a hard-core history fiend could easily spend 4 hours along the trail, but a family with restless children can easily do it in less.

ⓘ 19 North Square (© **617/523-2338;** www.paulreverehouse.org).

✈ Boston's Logan Airport.

🛏 $$ **Doubletree Guest Suites,** 400 Soldiers Rd. (© **800/222-TREE** [222-8733] or 617/738-0090; www.doubletree.com). $$ **The Midtown Hotel,** 220 Huntington Ave. (© **800/343-1177** or 617/262-1000).

WHY THEY'LL THANK YOU: One if by land, two if by sea.

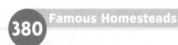

380   Famous Homesteads

Orchard House
The Little Women House
Ages 6 & up • Concord, Massachusetts, USA

Even girls who haven't read Louisa May Alcott's 1868 classic novel *Little Women* know the story from its many film versions and the Broadway musical. The story of its author, Louisa May Alcott—Jo in the novel—is even more powerful when you consider that she was one of the first women to earn a living as a writer. My daughter and I were thrilled to feel her presence hovering in every room of **Orchard House.**

The Alcott family lived from 1858 to 1877 in this saltbox-style frame house. Not only was *Little Women* set here, but it also was written here by the adult Louisa, at a shelf desk her father built between two windows in her bedroom. Although Louisa was 26 when they moved into Orchard House, she modeled the March's family's house on it.

Other family members were the models for the characters in *Little Women:* Anna ("Meg"), the eldest, an amateur actress; Elizabeth ("Beth"), a gifted musician who died before the family moved to this house; and May ("Amy"), a talented artist who went to study in Europe on Louisa's profits from *Little Women.* Their mother, the social activist Abigail May Alcott, frequently assumed the role of family breadwinner—her father, Louisa wrote in her journal, had "no gift for money making." Louisa herself, who never married, also helped support the family when she began to publish her short stories at age 22.

Visitors are guided through the modestly furnished house, which features many authentic heirlooms—the family china is laid out on the dining room table, props and

Inside Orchard House, the home of *Little Women* author Louisa May Alcott.

costumes await their amateur theatricals, half-finished needleworks lie on side tables, and some of May's drawings are still scribbled on her bedroom walls. Anna's wedding was held in the parlor here, just as Meg's was, and all the sisters took turns cooking in the spartan kitchen.

Also in Concord is **The Wayside,** 455 Lexington Rd. (© **978/369-6975;** May–Oct only), the Alcotts' prior home (the girls called it "the yellow house"), where Nathaniel Hawthorne later lived, from 1852 until his death in 1864.

ⓘ 399 Lexington Rd. (© **978/369-4118;** www.louisamayalcott.org).

✈ Boston, 18 miles.

🛏 $$ **Doubletree Guest Suites,** 400 Soldiers Field Rd. (© **800/222-TREE** [222-8733] or 617/783-0090; www.doubletree.com). $ **The MidTown Hotel,** 220 Huntington Ave. (© **800/343-1177** or 617/262-1000).

WHY THEY'LL THANK YOU: Meg, Jo, Beth, and Amy live on here.

Booker T. Washington Birthplace
A Slave Boy, a Free Man
All ages • Hardy, Virginia, USA

It's easy to imagine that every plantation in the Old South was straight out of *Gone With the Wind*. The tobacco plantation where Booker T. Washington, Jr., was born in 1856, however, followed a different model: With only 207 acres and 10 slaves, owner James Burroughs and his sons worked in the fields right alongside their slaves. It does seem amazing that a boy born into slavery should become a college president and the country's foremost black leader (in the eyes of whites at least—some blacks chafed at Washington's pragmatic stance on such issues as lynching and voting rights). But walking around the Burroughs plantation, it becomes clear how the man Booker T. Washington grew out of this Virginia slave boy.

Although no original buildings are left from Washington's childhood, several **reconstructions** show visitors a typical Piedmont farm of this era: a smokehouse, blacksmith shed, corncrib, horse barn, chicken lot, and the tobacco barn where harvested leaves were hung to dry. Made authentically of hewn logs chinked with clay, these buildings show a hardscrabble farm very different from the King Cotton plantations of the Deep South. The reconstructed kitchen cabin replicates the one where Washington, whose mother was the plantation's cook, was born. Stone outlines in the grass show the actual location of the original kitchen cabin and the "big house"—a mere five rooms—where the owner's family lived (with 14 children, they outnumbered the slaves). Only about 5 acres were actually planted with tobacco, the farm's sole cash crop; other crops and livestock fed and clothed the family, a model of self-sufficiency that underlay Washington's lifelong commitment to making African Americans economically self-reliant. All children on the farm worked (hard work was another of Washington's lifelong ideals) and one of Booker's jobs was to fan flies from the Burroughs's dinner table, where he overheard mealtime conversations that informed his view of the world. His familiarity with the white owners may have made it easier for him as an adult to cultivate white philanthropists to underwrite his projects, notably Tuskegee Institute in Alabama. Young Booker became passionate about education, begging his father to let him attend a local black school, doing extra chores to earn money to go at age 16 to Hampton Institute. Slaves were freed by then, but education was Washington's key to escaping farm drudgery, and he devoted the rest of his life to ensuring education for other African Americans.

A 1.3-mile-long **nature trail** through the adjoining woods shows where slaves foraged, fished, and chased the family's free-ranging hogs. Walking in these cool, lovely woods along a crystalline brook, you can imagine a slave boy slipping away here to dream of making something of himself.

ⓘ 12130 Booker T. Washington Hwy. (VA 122; ✆ **540/721-2094;** www.nps.gov/bowa).

✈ Roanoke, 25 miles.

🛏 $ **Colony House Motor Lodge,** 3560 Franklin Rd., Roanoke (✆ **866/203-5850** or 540/345-0411). $$$ **Hotel Roanoke,** 110 Shenandoah Ave., Roanoke (✆ **800/222-TREE** [222-8733] or 540/985-5900; www.hotelroanoke.com).

WHY THEY'LL THANK YOU: Preaching the gospel of hard work.

George Washington Carver's Birthplace
Nature's Laboratory
All ages • Diamond, Missouri, USA

Kids often get George Washington Carver confused with Booker T. Washington, and not just because they both had "Washington" in their names (though Carver added it later in life): Both were born into slavery, worked hard to get an education, and won fame at Tuskegee Institute in Alabama. But they were two quite different sorts of men, one a savvy political leader, the other a gentle scientific genius. Following the walking trail through the Missouri farm where George Washington Carver was born, you begin to see how nature inspired him, even as a boy: This farm was a perfect nature laboratory.

The Carver homestead was not large, only 240 acres, and owner Moses Carver and his wife, Susan, were by all accounts kind to their few slaves. But they were extra close to young George and his brother Jim: When he was an infant, George and his mother had been kidnapped by Civil War bushwhackers, and when the boy was finally returned, half-dead, Mr. and Mrs. Carver adopted orphan George and his brother and raised them as their own. Because George was frail, he was only given light domestic chores, which left him plenty of time to wander outdoors, observing flowers and trees and experimenting to see what made them grow. He soon became known in the area as the "plant doctor," with amazing self-taught botanical skills. The **interpretive trail** at the historic site leads you past a natural spring, a teeming pond, a fertile patch of deciduous forest, a persimmon grove, a stand of walnut trees, and several acres of the sort of tallgrass prairie that once covered much of the Great Plains; signs along the path point out

George Washington Carver National Monument.

nature details that we're usually too distracted to notice. George Carver noticed them, and his boundless curiosity led him to wonder *why* plants grew as they did—and then to find the answers for himself.

Though the tiny cabin where he was born was blown away by a tornado years ago, a set of low walls outlines its location; farther on the trail you can go inside **Moses Carver's home,** not much more than a cabin itself, to see how a Missouri farm family lived in the 1860s. George left this farm at age 11 to attend a black school in nearby Neosho. Over the next 19 years, while patiently supporting himself with menial household labor, he eventually earned a master's degree and was hired by Booker T. Washington to teach agricultural chemistry at Tuskegee. Beyond his famous work with peanuts, he made so many scientific discoveries that he became known as the Wizard of Tuskegee. Generations of African-American students have been inspired by him.

ⓘ Carver Rd. 9 (✆ **417/325-4151;** www.nps.gov/gwca).

✈ Joplin, 15 miles.

🛏 $ **Best Western Oasis Inn,** 3508 S. Range Line Rd., Joplin (✆ **800/780-7234** or 417/781-6776; www.bestwestern.com). $$ **Holiday Inn,** 3615 S. Range Line Rd., Joplin (✆ **800/315-2621** or 417/782-1000; www.holiday-inn.com).

WHY THEY'LL THANK YOU: How a natural genius saw nature.

Robert Louis Stevenson's Treasured Island

Ages 6 & up • Saranac Lake, New York, USA

Look at the houses around Saranac Lake and you'll notice many share one architectural peculiarity—sleeping porches on the second story. That's because 19th-century Saranac Lake centered on a famous sanitarium, the Trudeau Clinic, where patients with tuberculosis came to be cured in the cool, dry Adirondack forest air. Modern medicine has nearly wiped out tuberculosis, and no one comes to Saranac anymore for "the cure." But on the edge of town there is one relic of those days—the cottage where one of Dr. Edward Trudeau's most famous patients, the writer Robert Louis Stevenson, fought for his life.

The **Stevenson cottage** isn't well advertised; its hours are limited, and you'll have to ring the doorbell hoping the caretaker/curator will come out and let you in. But for Stevenson fans like my kids, that made the experience all the more special. This quiet white frame cottage is absolutely crammed to the gills with Stevenson **memorabilia,** and the curator (who grew up here—his grandparents were caretakers before him) knows just about everything that's worth knowing about the author of such classics as *Treasure Island, Kidnapped,* and *Dr. Jekyll and Mr. Hyde.* While there are other Stevenson museums around the world, each with its own cache of manuscripts, letters, and clippings, this was the first (founded in 1915) and it's the one most evocative of the great writer's life.

The threadbare Victorian furniture here is all original, and dusty glass cases display such treasures as a lock of his hair, his velvet smoking jacket (a sprig of heather in its buttonhole), the old-fashioned ice skates he wore to skate on the local pond, even burn marks in the mantelpiece from his cigarettes. I fell in love with this place myself as a child and was astounded to find, 40 years later, that it was exactly the same. And having read so many Stevenson books to my kids, I was thrilled to see them fall under its delicate, musty spell, too.

ⓘ 11 Stevenson Lane (✆ **518/891-1462;** www.adirondacks.com/robertlstevenson. html).

✈ Saranac Lake.

🛏 $$ **Hotel Saranac,** 101 Main St., Saranac Lake (✆ **800/937-0211** or 518/891-2200; www.hotelsaranac.com).

BEST TIME: Open July to mid-Sept; rest of year, call curator for appt.

WHY THEY'LL THANK YOU: The legend of a great storyteller burns bravely on.

Huck Finn Meets Uncle Tom

Ages 6 & up • Hartford, Connecticut, USA

Tom Sawyer, Huckleberry Finn, The Connecticut Yankee in King Arthur's Court: Mark Twain's books are some of the few that make kids laugh out loud when they read them in school. His image is instantly recognizable even today—a white-suited man with wild white hair, an even wilder white moustache, and eyes glinting with sarcastic humor. Twain was in some ways a perpetual kid himself, which is why even young visitors get into the spirit of his house.

Mark Twain was already a successful author in 1874 when he built this 19-room mansion in "Picturesque Gothic" style, with a profusion of steeply peaked gables and patterned painted-brick walls. Inside there's lots of elaborate woodworking and stenciled wallpapers, very Victorian and yet somehow expressive of Twain's own restless, wide-ranging mind. On the hour-long **guided tour,** you get a sense of his enthusiasm for newfangled gadgets—*Life*

on the Mississippi is said to be the first novel written on a typewriter—and we were surprised to see such modern touches as flush toilets and the primitive telephone installed in the entrance hall. On the top floor we visited his main workroom, a large space dominated by a billiard table. The chief impression I got from the tour was of Twain's mercurial nature—his egotism and insecurity, his irascible temper, an imperfectly stifled romantic streak, and his emotional attachments to his children. All in all, a complex and fascinating man.

It's no coincidence that one of Twain's next-door neighbors was another famous writer—**Harriet Beecher Stowe,** whose sensationally melodramatic 1852 antislavery novel, *Uncle Tom's Cabin,* was one of the 19th century's biggest bestsellers. (Abraham Lincoln himself believed the book responsible for touching off the Civil

Mark Twain's home in Hartford.

War.) This hilltop parcel of land was **Nook Farm,** an enclave for arty progressive types, so both Twain and Stowe fit right in. Throughout the tour of Stowe's modestly furnished small house, however, I kept wondering how this dowdy theologian's wife (her father and brothers were also clergymen) got along with her outrageous cigar-chomping neighbor. We would never have made a trip solely to visit Harriet Beecher Stowe's house, but the contrast with Twain's was pure serendipity.

(i) **Twain House,** 351 Farmington Ave. (© **860/247-0998;** www.marktwainhouse. org). **Stowe house,** 77 Forest St. (© **860/ 522-9258;** www.harrietbeecherstowe center.org).

✈ Bradley International, 12 miles.

🛏 $$$ **Hilton Hartford Hotel,** 315 Trumbull St. (© **800/445-8667** or 860/728-5151; www.hartford.hilton.com).

WHY THEY'LL THANK YOU: Twain's irrepressible spirit, embodied in bricks and mortar.

The Mark Twain Home
Tom Sawyer's Stomping Grounds
Ages 6 & up • Hannibal, Missouri, USA

When you roll into this laid-back river town, about 130 miles up the scenic Mississippi river road from St. Louis, you may get a nagging feeling that you've been here before. Well, you have—if you've read *The Adventures of Tom Sawyer.* Every scene in that book was based on affectionate memories of the town where a boy named Sam Clemens grew up, long before he became Mark Twain. Sometimes Hannibal leans on the association a bit too much—every third restaurant or shop seems to be named after a Tom Sawyer character—but the historic heart of town really does have a remarkable connection to this beloved American writer.

Eight properties around town, packaged under the name The Mark Twain Museum, have rock-solid associations with Sam Clemens. The main one is the small white frame house at 208 Hill St., where the Clemens family lived from 1844 to 1853; the parlor, the dining room, the kitchen, and the three upstairs bedrooms are all furnished in the period. You can almost imagine Sam climbing out the window of the back bedroom he shared with

his brother Henry, sneaking off to nighttime escapades. Across the street is the much more prosperous house of the Hawkins family, whose daughter Laura—Twain's lifelong friend—was the model for Becky Thatcher. The law office of Sam's father, John Clemens, has been moved to the same street; its tiny front courtroom was the setting for Muff Potter's trial in *Tom Sawyer.* After a shift in the family fortunes, the Clemenses moved to cramped quarters above the old-fashioned pharmacy run by Dr. Orville Grant, over on Main Street. The last stop on this historic trail may not be authentic, but it could be the kids' favorite: the **Museum Gallery,** set in an old department store on Main Street, where interactive displays on *Tom Sawyer* allow children to whitewash a fence, hide in a spooky graveyard, and get lost in a cave, just like Tom and Huck and Becky did.

Of all the peripheral attractions in town, the one that has the most true Tom-'n'-Huck flavor is the **Mark Twain Cave,** a mile south of town on U.S. 79. Whether or not Sam Clemens actually got lost during a school picnic in either of these two caves, it's easy to imagine him making mischief down here, and the guides on the 1-hour tour are sure to work in references to the book.

Sleepy as Hannibal seems most of the year, it crackles to life during the **National Tom Sawyer Days,** the long weekend around July 4. All sorts of Twain-themed activities are held outdoors, from fence painting to frog jumping, and it's just generally the sort of whoop-de-do that Sam Clemens—or Tom Sawyer—would have loved.

ⓘ 208 Hill St. (✆ **573/221-7975;** www.marktwainmuseum.org).

✈ Lambert-St. Louis International, 125 miles.

🛏 $ **Hannibal Travelodge,** 500 Mark Twain Ave. (✆ **800/578-7878** or 573/222-4100).. $$ **Hotel Clemens,** 401 Third St. (✆ **573/248-1150;** www.hotelclemens.us).

WHY THEY'LL THANK YOU: Channeling an idyllic small-town childhood.

---

386 **Famous Homesteads**

Laura Ingalls Wilder's Homes
Little Houses on the Prairie
Ages 4 & up • Multiple sites, USA

Laura Ingalls Wilder's books about her frontier childhood are such an indelible part of the American girl zeitgeist that just about every little girl I know has had a "Little House" phase, even if she didn't get through the entire series. Because the Ingalls family was always on the move, each book recalls a different childhood home of Laura's; today each of those towns tries to claim its own piece of the Little House tourism market. What's a Little House fan to do?

If you're really ambitious, you could probably make a pilgrimage to all the Little House sites in a week or so. The upper Mississippi river town of **Pepin,** Wisconsin, was Laura's birthplace, where a replica log cabin 7 miles north of town re-creates the environment of what she later called the *Little House in the Big Woods.* Another reconstructed log cabin down in southeastern Kansas, just southwest of **Independence, Kansas,** claims to be the *Little House on the Prairie,* Wilder's second book. The Ingallses then hauled back north to **Walnut Grove, Minnesota,** to the home depicted in *On the Banks of Plum Creek;* today the site is

merely a well-marked depression in the grassland outside of town, but back in town a cluster of typical late-19th-century buildings—depot, school chapel, a striking onion-domed house—has been fashioned into the thoroughly satisfying **Laura Ingalls Wilder Museum.** This museum snapped up several mementos from the popular 1970s TV series, which supplement the few real pioneer items on display; it does have a quilt Wilder sewed, her family Bible, and lots of letters and photos. The collection of 250 antique dolls has nothing to do with the Little House books, but girls will eat it up. A little over 100 miles west on U.S. 14 was the Ingallses' fourth frontier home, in **DeSmet, South Dakota.** You can take a walking tour of several period buildings here, including a one-room wood schoolhouse like the one where Laura had her first teaching job.

The only true Little House you can visit is another long drive south in **Mansfield, Missouri**—the lovely white farmhouse in the Ozark hills where the adult Wilder and her husband moved in 1894. Here at **Rocky Ridge Farm,** Wilder in 1932 sat down to write her memoirs of frontier life;

407

7 Presidential Homesteads

Presidential homesteads are a great way to illustrate to kids that history is made by real people, just like them. Here are seven homes where giants of history lived; but seeing their surroundings suddenly makes them human.

387 Mount Vernon Standing majestically atop a lawn sloping down to the Potomac River, the white columned colonial home of George and Martha Washington is one of America's most visited shrines. A quick 15-mile drive from Washington, D.C., Mount Vernon is a popular day trip, but don't let this deter you: Mount Vernon reveals the real George Washington. It's clearly the home of a country gentleman; prosperous but not ostentatious. See the Washington Monument **28**, the International Spy Museum **242**, the National Museum of the American Indian **261**, the National Museum of Natural History **275**, and the National Air and Space Museum **287**. *℗ 703/780-2000; www.mountvernon.org.*

388 Monticello Jefferson wasn't just a politician, he was a Renaissance man—statesman, agricultural reformer, philosopher, inventor, and last but not least, architect, and his home in Charlottesville, Virginia, stands as his crowning architectural achievement. As befit the author of the Declaration of Independence, Jefferson was fiercely anti-British; when be began to design this home in 1769, he rejected the popular Georgian style and went for the 16th-century Italian style of Andrea Palladio. The kids will instantly recognize its exterior from the back of the U.S. nickel. *℗ 434/984-9822; www.monticello.org.*

389 The Hermitage His face stares out at us from the $20 bill, a restless looking man with a mane of wild hair and a high cravat. Our first frontier president was a passionate man of the people who made his home in Nashville, Tennessee. At first the wide verandas and thick white columns of the hermitage look too dignified for a man like Jackson, but then we learned that the neoclassical portico was a later addition; the core is a square, plain eight-room brick house, which replaced a log farmhouse only after Jackson had a war-hero image to burnish. See the Nashville Music Scene **348**. *℗ 615/889-2941; www.thehermitage.com.*

390 Lincoln Trail Driving the part of Lincoln trail that covers Lincoln's early years will allow your kids to discover the backwoods boy behind the great president. The first stop is Hodgenville, Kentucky, at the **Lincoln Birthplace National Historic site,** where a neoclassical memorial encloses a tiny log cabin, reportedly where Lincoln was born. Lincoln's humble origins are evident 7 miles north at **Lincoln's Boyhood Home,** a reconstruction of the cabin he lived in from ages 2 to 7. Drive 135 miles, and you'll find yourself in Lincoln City, Indiana—home of **The Lincoln Boyhood National Memorial,** a living history farm that recreates early-19th-century farm life. *Abraham Lincoln Birthplace Historical Site: ℗ 502/358-3874. Lincoln Boyhood National Memorial: ℗ 812/937-4541.*

The Hermitage, Andrew Jackson's home in Nashville, Tennessee.

391 FDR Hyde Park   Franklin D. Roosevelt's lifelong home, Springwood, was a modest farmhouse when FDR's father built it. Franklin expanded it in an eclectic Dutch colonial style. He entertained Winston Churchill, King George VI, Queen Elizabeth of England, and many other dignitaries here. He also designed his own presidential library, the nation's first. A wooded trail leads from Springwood to their pair of private cottages where FDR and Eleanor could escape the pressures of political life. They are buried in the rose garden on the grounds. ✆ *845/229-8144; www.nps.gov/hofr.*

392 Truman Home   The house that Harry S. Truman shared with Bess in Independence, Missouri, is a testament to his reputation as a man of the people. They were small town folks and their summer White House Home was simply Bess' gabled family home. Inside you'll see the kitchen where Harry and Bess ate breakfast, and the book-lined study that was Truman's favorite retreat. Get tickets early, because they do sell out—the house can only be seen on a guided tour and tours are limited to eight people because the rooms are fairly small. ✆ *816/254-9929; www.nps.gov/hstr.*

393 LBJ Homestead   Stonewall, Texas, is the site of the sprawling limestone-and-wood ranch house LBJ bought from his aunt and uncle in 1951. Overlooking the Pedernales River, it was the centerpiece of a working ranch (still in operation). World leaders often gathered in lawn chairs under the spreading live oak in the front yard. The Johnsons retired to the ranch in 1969, where 4 years later Johnson died of a heart attack; his gravesite is nearby, in the Johnson family cemetery. See the Guadalupe River **435** and the Alamo **222**. ✆ *830/868-7128; www.nps.gov/lyjo.*

you can see her study, the lap desk upon which she wrote, and several cherished family mementos she had kept, including Pa Ingalls' old fiddle. Somehow I feel closest to little Laura here, where the grown-up Laura plunged back into her memories to create her timeless stories.

ⓘ **Laura Ingalls Wilder Museum,** 330 8th St., Walnut Grove, MN (✆ **800/528-7280;** www.walnutgrove.org). **Rocky Ridge Farm,** 3068 Hwy. A, Mansfield, MO (✆ **417/924-3626;** www.lauraingallswilderhome.com).

✈ Minnesota/St. Paul International (for Pepin, Walnut Grove, DeSmet). Kansas City International (for Independence, Mansfield).

🛏 $$ **Oasis Inn,** 2550 N. Glenstone, Springfield, MO (✆ **417/866-5253**).

WHY THEY'LL THANK YOU: Imagine covering the distances between these homes in a covered wagon, with no super-highways.

Anne of Green Gables Country

Ages 8 & up • Cavendish, Prince Edward Island, Canada

Sometimes I wonder what Prince Edward Island would have done to attract tourism if Lucy Maud Montgomery hadn't written the *Anne of Green Gables* books. Lush and bucolic, blessed with red-sand beaches on the relatively warm Gulf of St. Lawrence, PEI can be enchanting—but you wouldn't necessarily know that without having been

drawn here by this wholesome, century-old book series about a red-haired orphan girl.

Start out in Charlottetown with ***Anne of Green Gables—The Musical,*** which plays every summer at the downtown arts center at 145 Richmond St. (✆ **800/565-0278** or 902/566-12670). Chirpy and well performed, it's a quick refresher course in the book's plot and main characters.

Then head for the center part of the island's north coast, where the town of Cavendish is Green Gables Central. Bypass the tourist traps and head to **Green Gables,** a solid white mid-19th-century farmhouse with green shutters (and, naturally, green gable points) that belonged to Montgomery's cousins. In her imagination this tidy farm with its precise white rail fences became the Cuthbert farmstead, where spunky orphan Anne Shirley arrives from Nova Scotia to live with dour Matthew and Marilla Cuthbert. Parks Canada owns the site and has meticulously furnished the rooms according to descriptions in the books. Getting outdoors is essential for falling under the Anne of Green Gables spell, and walking trails from the house lead to settings from the novel such as **Lover's Lane** and the **Haunted**

Green Gables.

Woods. Although Montgomery spent most of her adult life with her clergyman husband in Ontario, she remained so attached to her native PEI **landscape** that she asked to be buried in the nearby Cavendish Cemetery.

Amid a stretch of tacky amusement parks and motels, **Avonlea,** Rte. 6 (✆ **902/963-3050;** www.avonleavillage.com), has a bit more class than its neighbors: Among the faux vintage buildings of its "village center" (Avonlea being Montgomery's fictional name for Cavendish) are a few real historic structures imported from elsewhere in the region, including a schoolhouse in which Montgomery once taught and a church she attended. The costumed staff moves along various kinds of jollity, including hayrides, games, cow milking, and oyster shucking. Commercial, yes, and a little hokey, but younger children especially will find it engaging.

To connect with the rural vibe, head for nearby **Prince Edward Island National Park,** a lovely swath of sand beaches, placid inlets, vast salt marshes, and wind-sculpted dunes topped with marram grass. Pastoral peace and quiet—that's the gift of *Anne of Green Gables.*

ⓘ 2 Palmers Lane (✆ **902/963-7874;** www.gov.pe.ca/greengables).

✈ Charlottetown, Prince Edward Island, 40km (25 miles).

🛏 $$ **Red Road Country Inn,** Rte. 6, Clinton (✆ **800/249-1344**). $$$ **Shaw's Hotel,** Rte. 15, Brackley Beach (✆ **902/672-2022;** www.shawshotel.ca).

WHY THEY'LL THANK YOU: Getting hooked on the books.

14 Out & About

Rock climbing in Yosemite National Park

Yosemite
Rock-Climbing Heaven
Ages 8 & up • Yosemite, California, USA

Most folks visiting Yosemite National Park don't seem to realize that there's more to it than Yosemite Valley, where crowds of cars and RVs inch along the roads while their passengers stare at the 3,000-foot-high glacier-carved granite walls and the waterfalls that drop down them. Yes, you should drive past the awesome 7,549-foot-high sheer rock face called El Capitan; you should pull off the road to take the easy half-mile trails to view Bridalveil Fall or Lower Yosemite Falls. But don't stop there—go up into the high country, where you can explore wilderness without the crowds.

The eastern half of 39-mile-long **Tioga Road** is open only in summer and fall, and the developed area around **Tuolumne Meadows** is much less crowded than Yosemite Valley; there's even a grove of sequoias, where you can enjoy the gigantic trees in much greater peace than you'll have at larger Mariposa Grove, near the park's south entrance. Coming from the west, Tioga Road rises up through towering pines and then breaks out on solid granite highlands dramatically furrowed by glaciers. Around Olmsted Point, the views become really dramatic—look at a cliff jutting up in the distance, and you'll realize that the ants scaling it are actually rock climbers. Yosemite is the most popular rock-climbing destination in the United States, thanks largely to the **Yosemite Mountaineering School** (✆ **209/372-8344;** www.yosemitemountaineering.com). The climbing school runs beginner classes daily out of its base in popular Curry Village, but in summer you can also take classes at Tuolumne Meadows. Kids as young as 14 are accepted, and the instructors will soon have your teenagers inching up the granite walls to heights of 60 feet.

Even children who are too young to scale a sheer rock face can get a little climbing experience in Yosemite's high country. From Tuolumne Meadows Lodge, a 4.2-mile trail leads to the top of **Lembert Dome** (take a shuttle bus back to the lodge from the trail's other end). Another option is off of Glacier Point Road, south of the Yosemite Valley loop. You'll want to drive this road anyway to get to that great Glacier Point overlook, the top of a 3,200-foot vertical cliff. But stop partway along Glacier Point Road at mile 13.2, where a trail head leads 2.2 miles round-trip to **Sentinel Dome,** one of many granite domes in the park whose rounded shapes were formed by glaciers moving over them. It's 8,122 feet high, the second-highest viewpoint into the valley. **Taft Point** is the same distance the other way from the trail head; it has weird and scary cracks as well as cliff-overhang views. The hike itself isn't threatening, but hold hands near the end.

ⓘ Entrances on CA 41, CA 120, and CA 140 (✆ **209/372-0200;** www.nps.gov/yose).

✈ Fresno-Yosemite International, 90 miles.

🛏 $$$ **The Ahwanee,** Yosemite Valley (✆ **801/559-5000**). $ **Tuolumne Meadows Campground** (✆ **800/436-7275;** www.recreation.gov).

WHY THEY'LL THANK YOU: Being on those peaks, not just looking at them.

Joshua Tree

Praying Trees in the California Desert

Ages 4 & up • Twentynine Palms, California, USA

In the winter, when it gets too cold in Yosemite, the rock climbers of California flock to this bizarre desert landscape near Palm Springs. If you think a desert is just one big sandbox, Joshua Tree's extremes will soon set you straight. Part mountainous Mojave Desert, part cactus-studded Colorado Desert lowlands, this national park is a mixture of lush fan palm oases and trackless sand dunes. Come spring, the arid landscape puts on a surprising **wildflower display,** including pale yellow blooms on the twisted yucca for which the park is named. **Rock climbing** is a brilliant way to engage with the tortured rockscape of this fragile ecosystem.

Eight million years ago, this landscape was rolling grasslands, where horses, camels, and mastodons grazed, preyed upon by saber-tooth cats and wild dogs. But then came years of climate change, volcanic eruption, savage floods, and shifting tectonic plates, and the land was wrenched into jagged cliffs, boulders, and tilting rock piles—sensational opportunities for climbers. The first climbing routes were laid out in the 1950s, and the sport really took off in the 1960s. Today Joshua Tree offers some 4,000 climbing routes, ranging from the easiest of bouldering to truly difficult climbs. November through May is the prime season. Beginners can learn the ropes, so to speak, at the

Rocks like melted candle wax in Joshua Tree National Park.

Joshua Tree Rock Climbing School (📞 **800/890-4745** or 760/366-4745; www. rockclimbingschool.com). Bring loads of water with you—there are few places to buy it, and you can get dehydrated quickly in the desert.

If climbing's your focus, stay in the northwest part of the park, where popular features include **Jumbo Rocks,** with its array of rock formations, Joshua tree forest, and yucca-dotted desert; **Wonderland of Rocks,** 12 square miles of massive jumbled granite; and mile-high **Keys View,** on the crest of the Little San Bernardino mountains. Climbers congregate in the Cap Rock area; even if you're not planning to climb, you can follow the short paved **Cap Rock Nature Trail** and test your footing on the rocks.

One thing I especially like about Joshua Tree is its many kid-friendly nature trails. From Jumbo Rocks, a 1.5-mile trail leads to **Skull Rock,** one of many rocks in the area that eerily resemble humans, dinosaurs, or monsters—children get a kick out of spotting these. Near Hidden Valley, the **Barker Dam** trail visits a small lake tucked deep in the Wonderland of Rocks; kids can scramble atop the old dam and hunt for Native American petroglyphs on the base of cliffs. Down Pinto Basin Road, the **Cholla Cactus Garden** trail leads you through dense clusters of the fluffy-looking "teddy bear cactus" with its deceptively barbed needles—look but don't touch!

ⓘ **Oasis Visitor Center** (📞 **760/367-5500;** www.nps.gov/jotr or www.joshua tree.org).

✈ Palm Springs, 40 miles.

🛏 $$ **Holiday Inn Express Hotel and Suites,** 71809 Twentynine Palms Hwy. (📞 **800/344-7128** or 760/361-4009; www. ichotelsgroup.com). $$$ **29 Palms Inn,** 73950 Inn Ave. (📞 **760/367-3505;** www. 29palmsinn.com).

WHY THEY'LL THANK YOU: Scaling rocks like a lizard in the desert sun.

---

397 **Hiking & Backpacking**

Climbing Ben Nevis
The Crown of the Highlands
Ages 10 & up • Near Fort William, Scotland

In the middle of the Scottish Highlands, **Ben Nevis,** at 1,342m (4,403 ft.), is the tallest mountain in Britain. Even if you've tackled higher peaks, don't sell Ben Nevis short: The 16km (10-mile) climb is a difficult 8 hours to the summit even along the most popular route, a pony track. The final 300m (984 ft.) is really steep terrain, but having gone this far, few can resist the challenge of going all the way. For a much rougher but more scenic trail, come up out of lovely Glen Nevis, with its clear rivers and cascading waterfalls, soft meadows and moorlands. The summit is flat and covered with loose stones, sloping off gently to the south, but a series of jagged rock precipices plunge down the northeast side, a challenge suitable for only the most expert rock climbers.

Before going, check in with the staff at the **Fort William tourist office,** 6km (3¾ miles) northwest of the mountain; they can give you advice as well as maps, and they'll pinpoint the best starting places. Note that the unpredictable Scottish weather adds to the challenge: Dress in layers and bring along a waterproof jacket (stout-soled shoes are essential). The mean monthly temperature of Ben Nevis falls below freezing; snow has been reported at all times of year, even during the hottest months of July and August. Howling winds are frequent.

Hikers head up expecting a panoramic view, but that same fickle weather means they're often disappointed—be prepared to appreciate the beauty of whatever you see up there, even if it's a dramatic cloak of swirling mist. If you're so lucky as to have clear weather, you can see the Irish foothills some 193km (120 miles) to the southwest, the Hebridean Isle of Rhum 148km (92 miles) to the west, the Glencoe peaks directly south, and the Cairngorm peaks to the east. If some members of your party vote against climbing, they can still get a pretty darn stunning view by taking the cable car to a panoramic viewing area about halfway up.

ⓘ **Fort William Tourist Information,** Cameron Square, Fort William (✆ **44/1845/ 22-55-121;** www.visit-fortwilliam.co.uk).

🚃 Fort William, 4 hr. from Glasgow.

🛏 $$ **The Alexandra Hotel,** The Parade, Fort William (✆ **44/1397/702-241;** www.strathmorehotels.com). $$ **The Moorings,** Banavie (✆ **44/1397/772-797;** www.moorings-fortwilliam.co.uk).

WHY THEY'LL THANK YOU: An eagle's-eye view of the wild and wooly Highlands.

Hiking & Backpacking **398**

Mount Kilimanjaro
Africa's Great White Mountain
Ages 12 & up • Kilimanjaro National Park, Tanzania

It's an unforgettable sight—the snowy plateau of Mount Kilimanjaro, rising above the Tanzanian plains, just south of Kenya. Named Oldoinyo Oibor, or "white mountain," by the Masai tribesmen and Kilima Njaro, or "shining mountain," in Swahili, it's Africa's highest mountain and one of the world's largest free-standing peaks, a triple volcano thrusting out of equatorial jungle and moorland. As world-class peaks go, it's a relatively easy climb—the lower slopes are downright gentle—but you don't need to go all the way to the summit to get the Hemmingway-esque thrill of exploring Kilimanjaro.

Ascending, you pass through four radically different climate zones. First comes the lush, steamy Kilimanjaro Forest Reserve surrounding the base; then the grassy moorlands of the shouldering slopes; above 13,000 feet, the mountain suddenly becomes steeper and more barren, with rocky scree underfoot. Last of all, you hit glacial ice fields, dazzling in the reflected African sun. It's not a technical climb, but it's a strenuous steep hike, and the extreme altitude makes it physically challenging if your body hasn't acclimated properly.

Enter at the **Marangu Park Gate**—you should already have obtained park permits and hut reservations (available through a licensed tour operator or local hotels in Moshi), but at the park gate you'll hire a guide, and possibly a porter (you won't be allowed on the mountain without a guide). Park fees are substantial, but they include hut accommodation on the mountain; guides and porters ask ridiculously low wages, hoping for generous tips on top. If you book with a tour operator (which I recommend), most of this, along with a cook to prepare all meals en route, will be included in your package.

It takes 5 to 7 days round-trip to reach the summit, staying in mountain huts all the way. With kids, though, you may be content to abbreviate this trek, going only partway up the well-traveled **Marangu Trail.** You'll spend your first night on the mountain in the wooden A-frame huts at Mandara, a 3- to 4-hour 12km (7.5-mile) walk from the gate through misty, mossy rainforest. On your second day, hike across grassland to the gardenlike Maundi Crater; scramble up to the rim for panoramic views of the barren highlands towering above you. If you're not gung-ho mountaineers, head back down from here, or go on to Hotombo Hut that night and Kibo Hut the third night before turning around.

ⓘ **Kilimanjaro National Park** (www.tanzaniaparks.com/kili.html).

✈ Kilimanjaro International, 56km (35 miles).

TOURS: Destination Africa Tours, Pretoria, South Africa (✆ **27/12/333-7110;** www.climbingkilimanjaro.com); **Roy Safaris,** Arusha, Tanzania (✆ **255/27/250-2115;** www.roysafaris.com); and **Tanzania Adventure,** Arusha, Tanzania (✆ **255/73/297-5210;** www.tanzania-adventure.com).

WHY THEY'LL THANK YOU: Towering above Africa.

Mount Fuji
Scaling the Symbol of Japan
Ages 8 & up • Fuji-Hakone-Izu National Park, Japan

The Japanese call it "Fuji-san," as if it were a dear old friend. It's not only the tallest mountain in Japan—an almost perfect cone 3,776m (12,388 ft.) high, its majestic peak usually swathed in clouds—it symbolizes the very spirit of their country. Today, about 600,000 people climb Fuji-san every year, mostly on July and August weekends. It's not like climbing Everest, a challenge for the expert mountaineer; you'll see everyone from grandmothers to children wending their way up those level slopes. It's the quintessential Japanese experience.

You don't need climbing experience to ascend Mount Fuji, just stamina and a good pair of walking shoes. Six well-established trails lead to the summit; another six lead back down. Each is divided into 10 stages, with the actual climb beginning around the fifth stage. From Tokyo, which is only about 100 km (62 miles) from Fuji, **Kawaguchiko Trail** is the least steep and easiest to get to. Take a shortcut directly to Kawaguchiko's Fifth Stage by **bus** from Tokyo's Shinjuku Station (be sure to book in advance); the trip takes about 2¹/₂ hours.

From this starting point, it's about a 6-hour climb to the summit, with another 3 hours to make the descent; at the top, a 1-hour hiking trail circles the crater.

Mount Fuji.

The highlight of the classic Fuji climb is to watch the sunrise from the peak, which in summer means being there by 4:30am. There are three ways to accomplish this: Take a morning bus, start climbing in early afternoon, spend the night near the summit in a mountain hut, and get up in time to arrive at the peak at sunrise; or alternatively, take in the sunrise from your hut—that still counts, honest!—and then climb to the top. Then there are the night climbers, who get off the bus at the Fifth Stage late in the evening and climb through the night using flashlights, timing it to hit the summit at sunrise. The mountain huts have futons for as many as 500 hikers each and serve simple Japanese meals (dried fish, rice, soup) if you aren't carrying your own grub; they're open July to August only and you must book early. One of the most popular with foreigners is the **Fujisan Hotel 2** (✆ **81/555/22-0237**) at stage 8.

It may be disconcerting to get off the bus at the Fifth Stage and see a crush of souvenir shops, blaring loudspeakers, and tour bus hordes—hardly the atmosphere for a purifying ritual. But don't worry, most of those tourists aren't here for the climb. You'll soon find yourself on a steep rocky path, surrounded only by scrub brush and a few intent hikers below and above you. Settle into your stride, and after a couple hours you'll find yourself above the roily clouds—as if you are on an island, barren and rocky, in the middle of an ocean. Ah, there's your spiritual high.

ⓘ **Fujiyoshida City Tourist Office** (✆ **81/555/24-1236;** www.city.fujiyoshida. yamanashi.jp).

✈ Narita International, 48km (30 miles).

🛏 For help with booking huts, call the **Japanese Inn Union of Mount Fuji** (✆ **81/555/22-1944**).

TOUR: Mt. Fuji Mountaineering School GoRiki (✆ **81/555/24-1032;** www.fujitozan. jp/english).

BEST TIME: Mid-July to Aug 31.

WHY THEY'LL THANK YOU: As the old Japanese saying goes, "Everyone should climb Mount Fuji once (only a fool would climb it twice)."

Hiking & Backpacking **400**

Mount Cook
Alps Down Under
Ages 8 & up • South Island, New Zealand

If you're mountain-climber Edmund Hillary, training to be the first man ever to climb Mount Everest, where do you go? Hillary chose New Zealand's highest mountain, an awesome snow-capped peak on the South Island, named after the same Captain James Cook who charted so much of the South Pacific. (The Maori people already had their own name for it: Aoraki.) Today it's a national park known as a mecca for thrill-seekers—skiers, mountaineers, and kayakers with a yen for paddling around glaciers.

An awful lot of mist and rain rolls through Mount Cook's range of mountains, frustrating many a traveler who drove all the way here just to view a famous peak. So why settle for just the car window view? Get onto the slopes of the mountain itself and your views can't fail to be interesting. From the park entrance at Mount Cook Village, there's an easy 45-minute loop through beech forest, populated with keas, those nervy olive-green mountain parrots that are Mount Cook's unofficial mascots. From the Hooker Valley campground, an hour-long walk to Kea Point and back gives you great close-up views of Mueller Glacier and more distant panoramas of the Mount Cook peak. For kids with a little more walking experience, try the half-day ramble from the campground on the Hooker Valley trail, where you'll cross two swinging bridges over gorges, pass two pristine lakes, cross a boardwalk over boggy tussocks, and wind up right at the frosty face of a glacier.

Although more than a third of the park lies under permanent snow and ice, the kids will be amazed to see how the remaining steep, thin-soiled slopes are carpeted with alpine wildflowers, many of them found only in New Zealand. The rarest species is the Mount Cook Lilly, a giant buttercup that can grow up to 1m (3 ft.) tall with flowers 5 to 8 cm (2–4 in.) across, flaunting a double layer of dazzling white petals and conspicuous bright yellow stamens. You'll have a hard time convincing the kids that this is a rare flower, though— not when they're staring at thousands of Mount Cook lilies, covering the slopes like a blizzard, throughout the New Zealand summer (Nov–Jan). Alongside that giant buttercup you'll see mountain daisies, snow gentians, mountain flax, fierce spikes of golden Spaniard, loose clusters of the petite Alpine avens, and tiny-flowered South Island edelweiss. You'd never see *that* from a car window.

ⓘ **Aoraki/Mount Cook National Park,** 1 Larch Grove, Mount Cook Village (✆ **64/3/435-1186;** www.doc.govt.nz).

✈ Mount Cook Village.

🛏 $$$ **Hermitage Hotel,** Terrace Rd., Mount Cook Village (✆ **64/3/435-1809;** www.mount-cook.com). $$ **Glencoe Lodge,** Terrace Rd., Mount Cook Village (✆ **64/3/435-1809;** www.mount-cook.com).

WHY THEY'LL THANK YOU: Alps with parrots.

401 Hiking & Backpacking

Walking the Appalachian Trail
Ages 8 & up • White Mountains, New Hampshire, USA

For the ultimate family bonding adventure, nothing quite equals a hike along the Appalachian Trail. No, I'm not suggesting you do the whole rugged 2,100 miles of the Trail, which runs from Maine to Georgia. But you can conquer a segment of it, and one I'd recommend runs 56 miles through the White Mountain National Forest, where the nonprofit **Appalachian Mountain Club (AMC)** runs a unique network of eight huts, each a day's walk apart. Providing food and bedding, they let you travel light, reduced to backpacking essentials: some warm clothes, foul-weather gear, water, snacks. You'll be amid some of the most spectacular scenery in the East—no trash, trailers, or loud music (the curse of overcrowded national park campgrounds), just room for kids to explore the world with new friends, kicking dust, balancing on fallen trees, and learning that when it rains you can't always change the channel.

My personal favorite family hike is a 3-day excursion up **Mount Lafayette.** Begin on the Franconia Notch Parkway (Rte. 93), about 7¹/₂ miles north of Lincoln, New Hampshire, where you'll find the signpost for the Old Bridle Path trail head. It's a sometimes-steep 2.9-mile hike from the road to the Greenleaf Hut, just above timberline at 4,200 feet, a warm, friendly place on Lafayette's west slope. When we last visited, the cook banged a pot with a

The White Mountains of New Hampshire.

heavy metal spoon at 6pm sharp, and we joined about 25 others—a lively mingling of singles, couples, and families—at long wooden tables for a very honest chicken-and-vegetable stew, with homemade bread and a mysterious pudding. After dinner, we sat on a rocky ledge and watched the evening mist flow through the valley below.

Next morning is your main hiking day: Climb 1.1 miles to the rocky, often wind-swept summit of Mount Lafayette. The payoff, on clear days, is the 1.7-mile (1-hr.) walk from Lafayette along a narrow ridge, with the whole Franconia range stretched below you, to Little Haystack. Retrace your steps to the Greenleaf Hut for your second night. On the morning of the third day, return to your car, an easy 2-hour downhill hike.

Other AMC huts that are popular with families are at **Zealand Falls,** a 2.8-mile walk to a choice four-season spot near waterfalls, perfect for moose spotting; and the even more accessible **Lonesome Lake Hut,** a painless 1.7-mile hike to a lake. Guided hut-to-hut trips can also be arranged.

ⓘ ☏ **603/528-8721;** www.fs.fed.us/r9/forests/white_mountain.

✈ Logan Airport, Boston, MA.

🚃 Contact **Appalachian Mountain Club** (☏ **603/466-2727;** www.outdoors.org).

WHY THEY'LL THANK YOU: The joy of reaching the summit—together.

The Great Smoky Mountains
Backpacking in the Misty Forest
Ages 4 & up • Near Gatlinburg, Tennessee, USA

Wilderness is all too rare in the Eastern United States, so it's a blessing to find a huge protected swath of it—let alone a huge swath as gorgeous as Great Smoky Mountains National Park. Roughly 60 miles by 20 miles, Great Smoky is a thickly forested sweep of the southern Appalachians—the oldest mountains in the world—where you can hike through dense old-growth forest groves, past brightly flowering rhododendron, wildflower meadows, crystalline waterfalls, and chattering mountain streams. During all seasons, seeing the mist trailing poetically in the folds of the mountains, you'll suddenly get it—oh, so *that's* why they're called the Smokies.

Some 10 million people visit this park every year, 70% of them doing no more than driving **Newfound Gap Road,** a scenic 32-mile route that snakes across the back of the mountains from Cherokee, North Carolina, to Gatlinburg, Tennessee. Most of those who do get out of their cars take the same few short trail hikes, mostly to gape at waterfalls. So it doesn't take much to escape the crowds and have the wilderness to yourselves. There's an astonishing variety of trees for kids to identify here (bring field guides), ranging from the lower elevations' hickories, yellow poplars, dogwood, and shaggy ancient hemlocks, to the midlevel beech and yellow birch forests, to the evergreens of the higher slopes, chiefly Fraser firs and red spruce. Check out the **Smoky Mountain Field School** (✆ **865/974-0150;** www.outreach.utk.edu/smoky), for naturalist-led outdoor expeditions on summer weekends specifically designed for families.

If your family has never tried backpacking, Great Smoky is an ideal place to start. There are about **100 backcountry campsites,** many of them quite close to each other, so you can plan short hikes from one to the next. The park's trails include many loops, so you can plan a trip that returns to your car without covering the same trail twice. It's rarely cold at night in summer, and although climbing a mountain with a backpack on a hot summer day is sweaty work, you can usually stop and dunk yourself in a creek to cool off. In any season, expect rain and mist—that's what makes the Smokies smoky.

Hiking in the Smokies.

ⓘ **Great Smoky Mountains Association,** 115 Park Headquarters Rd., Gatlinburg, TN (✆ **888/898-9102** or 865/436-7318; www.smokiesstore.org). **Great Smoky Mountains National Park,** visitor center on U.S. 441 (✆ **865/436-1200;** www.nps.gov/grsm).

Knoxville, 48 miles.

📧 **Backcountry campsite reservations** (📞 865/436-1231). **National Parks Resort Lodge,** 2385 Parkway, Pigeon

Forge (📞 **800/843-6686** or 865/453-4106; www.nprlodge.com).

WHY THEY'LL THANK YOU: A sleepover in the woods.

Hiking & Backpacking **403**

Getting Past the Crowds in Yellowstone

All ages • Entrances at Gardiner & West Yellowstone Montana & Jackson & Cody Wyoming, USA

Every visitor to Yellowstone National Park wants to see the park's signature attraction, the Old Faithful geyser, which erupts about every 90 minutes. You can drive to Old Faithful on the Lower Loop Road from the park's west entrance and join the crowds of tourists sitting on benches waiting for this baby to blow. Another popular drive-up sight is the limestone terraces of **Mammoth Hot Springs,** near the north entrance, where masses of bacteria and algae in the thermal water turn the rocks orange, pink, yellow, green, and brown. But these two sights only scratch the surface

of Yellowstone's geothermal features, if you're willing to get out and do some hiking to see them.

You'll have the geysers practically to yourself if you head for the **Shoshone Geyser Basin,** which begins a mile west of Shoshone Lake (find a trail head for Delacey Creek Trail on the road 8 miles east of Old Faithful; it leads 3 miles to Shoshone Lake). The **North Shoshone Trail** passes 26 campsites as it winds through a lodgepole-pine forest. The **Bechler Meadows Trail** in the park's southwest corner is rich in waterfalls, cascades, and thermal

Yellowstone National Park.

areas. If it's wildlife you're after, try the **Sportsman Lake Trail,** which passes through sagebrush plateaus full of elk and a meadow popular with moose.

Yellowstone is also one of the country's best places for families to go backpacking. Some beautiful campsites are just a couple miles off the road, and it only takes a walk of 20 minutes or so before you feel gloriously alone with the bison, elk, and other wildlife. Some great family trails for day hikes include these: at Mammoth, the 5-mile **Beaver Ponds Loop** from the hot springs at Liberty Cap (go in the evening or early morning to see the beavers); the 6-mile round-trip hike up **Mount Washburn,** an alpine trail leading to a 10,243-foot-high view over much of Yellowstone (watch for bighorn sheep); and the **Clear Lake trail** from the Wapiti trail head, which wanders through beautiful rolling meadows to a strange body of water fed by hot springs.

The backcountry season here is short—mid-June through the end of August, when the snow has finally melted off and streams drop to fordable levels—so it's wise to make a campsite reservation way in advance.

ⓘ ✆ **307/344-7381;** www.nps.gov/yell. **Yellowstone Backcountry Office** (✆ **307/344-2160**).

✈ West Yellowstone Airport, 2 miles. Yellowstone Regional Airport, Cody, WY, 52 miles.

🛏 $ **Madison Hotel,** 139 Yellowstone Ave., West Yellowstone (✆ **800/838-7745** or 406/646-7745; www.madisonhotelmotel. com). $$ **Mammoth Hot Springs Hotel** (✆ **866/439-7375** or 307/344-7311; www. travelyellowstone.com).

BEST TIME: June–Sept.

WHY THEY'LL THANK YOU: Learning to tell an elk from a moose.

---

404 Hiking & Backpacking

Bryce Canyon National Park
Doing the Hoodoo Voodoo
Ages 4 & up • Bryce Canyon, Utah, USA

Even preschoolers enjoy Bryce Canyon National Park: They may be too young to absorb overwhelming panoramas like the Grand Canyon, but they completely get the point of Bryce's cliffs of weird colored stone and the crazy stone pillars known as hoodoos.

Most park visitors stick to driving the 18-mile-long park road north-to-south, tracing the course of the Pink Cliffs, but don't be content to merely drive by: Hop out and start walking. At the northern end, **Bryce Amphitheater** makes an impressive dent in the cliff, with four stunning overlooks—Sunset Point, Sunrise Point, Inspiration Point, and Bryce Point, where you can look down into the amphitheater's hundreds of pink, red, orange, and brown

hoodoos. The 5-mile **Rim Trail** connects the four overlooks, with a paved half-mile between Sunset and Sunrise points that's stroller accessible. It's a great after-dinner walk in summer, when you can watch the changing evening light on the rosy rocks below.

Even getting down into the canyon is totally doable for kids; there's a 3-mile loop combining the **Navajo Loop** (trail head at Sunset Point) with the **Queen's Garden Trail** (trail head at Sunrise Point). Along the **Navajo Loop,** with its dramatic series of graveled switchbacks, you'll pass Thor's Hammer (hard to imagine why it hasn't fallen), and ponder the towering skyscrapers of Wall Street. Turning onto the **Queen's Garden Trail,** you'll see

423

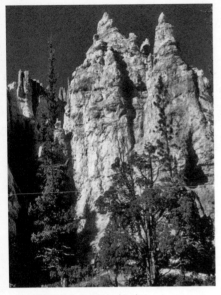

Bryce Canyon National Park.

highest point, leads to an 1,800-year-old bristlecone pine, believed to be the oldest living thing at Bryce Canyon.

If your kids are good hikers, when you return to the park's north end you may want to try the little-used 8-mile-long **Fairyland Loop Trail,** which descends 900 feet into a small canyon full of strange rock shapes. You'll meet a challenging ascent back to the top of the canyon to Sunrise Point, where you pick up a continuation of the Rim Trail, through a fragrant forest of pinyon and juniper back to Fairyland. Really, in the end, all of Bryce Canyon is Fairyland.

some of the park's most fanciful formations, including majestic Queen Victoria, for whom the trail is named, plus the Queen's Castle and Gulliver's Castle. Farther south along the park drive, a short loop trail from **Rainbow Point,** the park's

ⓘ Rte. 63 south of Rte. 12 (✆ **435/834-5322;** www.nps.gov/brca).

✈ Cedar City, 87 miles.

🛏 $$ **Bryce Canyon Lodge,** Bryce Canyon rim (✆ **888/297-2757** or 435/834-8700; www.brycecanyonlodge.com). $ **North Campground,** across from visitor center (✆ **877/444-6777;** www.recreation. gov).

BEST TIME: Apr–Oct.

WHY THEY'LL THANK YOU: Walking from one hoodoo to the next, they'll never notice how far they're hiking.

Hiking & Backpacking 405

Dune Walking in the Sahara

Ages 6 & up • Ksar Ghilane, Tunisia

Some 4.5 million Europeans, mostly French, vacation each year in Tunisia, offering their oiled bodies to the sun on the powdery white sands of Djerba. This sybaritic North African island has some of the most spectacular beaches in the world—but it's a pity that few tourists bother to travel on to the fantastic desert landscapes to the south. They're missing the thrill of setting foot on the waving dunes of the Sahara, crossing the shifting sands to an abandoned fort. And for kids,

there's even a movie tie-in: exploring towns that helped inspire the *Star Wars* movies.

Granted, it's a long, thankless drive—3¹/₂ hours from Djerba to **Ksar Ghilane,** an oasis at the very edge of the Grand Erg Oriental, one of the Sahara's two great sand seas, and it's best to hire a driver so you don't lose your way on these deceptive desert tracks. But when you arrive, the kids will immediately get the concept of an oasis: Rising up out of the desert, a hot

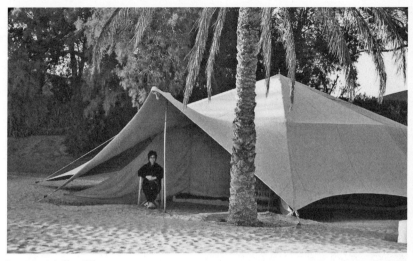

Luxury tents in Ksar Ghilane.

spring here feeds a swimming hole and a greenness of tamarisk trees. As befits the desert, you'll stay in **tents,** although quite luxurious tents, air-conditioned and with a private bathroom—it certainly beats a Motel 6. The highlight of your stay in the oasis is a 2km (1.2-mile) walk through the shifting dunes, as smooth and clean as a toddler's cheek, following a trail of camel turds to an **abandoned fort** worthy of Lawrence of Arabia. Kids will understand the importance of turbans here, which they'll need to wear against the blowing sands. (If they're young, you can arrange for an all-terrain vehicle to meet you and drive you back; doing the trek on a camel is a more exotic option.)

Tour packages often combine the Ksar Ghilane expedition with a trip around the amazing **Ksour district** to the east. "Ksour" is the plural for "ksar," a traditional mud-and-stone structure built by the ancient Berber people—communal granaries, where every family in a village had its own chamber for storing grain. In later times, the villagers turned these granaries into forts against foreign invaders. Most of these ksour are crumbling and abandoned, haunting relics left in the desert when their inhabitants moved to modern towns. You can visit several ksours in

the course of a day's desert drive around the modern town of **Tataouine**—a name borrowed by George Lucas for an entire planet in *Star Wars.* The nearby village of **Ksar Haddada** (on C207) was the setting for Luke Skywalker's hometown in the first *Star Wars* movie, *A New Hope;* head up north to Matmata (at the juncture of C104 and C107), where scenes from both *A New Hope* and *Attack of the Clones* were filmed: It's a village full of troglodyte cave dwellings, carved out of the desert rock, where people still live—some have even been turned into hotels, cramped and dank and utterly exotic. Scoring an overnight stay in Luke Skywalker's house—now that's a parenting coup.

ⓘ **Tunisia Tourism** (www.tourismtunisia. com).

✈ Djerba, 3½ hr.

🛏 $$ **Pansea Ksar Ghilane,** Ksar Ghilane (☎ 216/75/759-330; www.pansea. com). $ **Hotel Sidi Driss,** Matmata (☎ 216/ 75/240-005).

TOUR: TunisUSA (☎ 800/474-5502 or 484/754-0086; www.tunisusa.com).

WHY THEY'LL THANK YOU: Strolling through the vast golden Sahara.

Landmannalaugar
World of Fire & Ice
Ages 8 & up • Iceland

Traveling around the central highlands of Iceland is a trip to a world that is still being created—a world of shapes and colors most kids have only seen in dreams. The earth steams and bubbles; conical volcanoes rise like islands in a sea of black sand. Twisted lava, cracked and cooled in a thousand grotesque shapes, seems to have eyes that follow you wherever you go. It's a landscape so lunar, NASA astronauts trained here in preparation for landing on the moon. And of the many awesome spots in Iceland's unearthly interior, none is more spectacular than the geothermal hotbed of Landmannalaugar.

One-day bus trips come out from Reykjavík in summer to the hot springs at Landmannalaugar, quickie excursions that leave time for nothing but a look around and a brief dip in the bathtub-warm natural thermal pools, sunk into a boggy lowland. (Bring bathing suits, but you'll find Americans are the only ones who bother to wear them.) Yet one look at the nearby mountains, undulating like folds of silk and tinted with rare mineral colors—blues, yellows, bright reds, even shocking pink—will make the kids itch for more time to explore them. So spend a night or two at one of the mountain huts here, run by the **Iceland Touring Association** (Ferda–félag Islands), to give yourselves time to

hike into those bewitching mountains along the marked trails of the surrounding Fjallabak Nature Reserve. The huts are usually booked up in July and August, so reserve in advance, or arrange to sleep in a tent. Horseback riding is also available from a stable at the site.

If you're ambitious, the premier walk in Iceland is the 3- to 4-day hike from Landmannalaugar to Thórsmörk, through a stark terrain of snow, ice, and rock, sleeping in a series of mountain huts along the way. Any decently fit person 12 years old or older should be able to backpack for the full route, either independently or in a group led by a guide. At the far end of the hike, **Thórsmörk** is another designated nature reserve, a somewhat softer landscape with woods and grass nestling among mountains and glaciers. If you make it all the way to Thórsmörk, you can take a bus back to Reykjavík.

ⓘ **Icelandic Tourist Board** (✆ 212/885-9700 in the U.S.; www.visiticeland.com).

✈ Reykjavík, 4¹⁄₂ hr.

🛏 **Ferdafélag Islands** (✆ 354/568-2533; www.fi.is/en/huts).

WHY THEY'LL THANK YOU: Like walking on the moon.

Traipsing through the English Cotswolds

Ages 4 & up (Ramble), 10 & up (Cotswold Way) • England

Known for its picturesque villages of golden-stone cottages, England's charming Cotswolds hills are popular with motorists keen on gardens and antiques. But the best way to explore this rolling countryside is on foot, following a meandering 167km (104-mile) path called the **Cotswold Way** that cuts across farms, streams, cottage backyards, and swaths of forest. The payoff is spectacular panoramas and a time-warp sense of being back in medieval England.

The path stretches from Chipping Campden, at the northern edge of the Cotswolds, to Bath, and is easy to follow thanks to bright yellow signs at every intersection. The southbound route (Chipping Campden to Bath) involves slightly less uphill climbing and is less well traveled, so you won't find yourself in pedestrian "traffic jams." Regardless of the direction you follow, it's a significant undertaking to do the whole route: Tourist officials in Chipping Campden report that most participants take between 7 and 8 days to walk the entire path, often emerging blistered, sunburned, rain-drenched, and exhausted. (Of course, with kids you may opt to do only a section of the route.) Bring a raincoat and sturdy shoes.

Most of the route avoids traffic arteries completely, guiding you through **forests and fields** and along rocky escarpments where views sweep out over medieval wool villages. At least a dozen **historic towns** en route can be visited via short detours. Every tourist office in the Cotswolds carries the Ordnance Maps and specialized walking tour guides you'll need to locate the Cotswold Way, and local souvenir shops eagerly provide mementos like Cotswold Way T-shirts and an

The English Cotswolds.

official-looking certificate announcing the direction you've walked the path.

For less intrepid hikers, another option is the **Great Cotswold Ramble,** a 4km (2.5-mile) mostly paved walk from the car park in Upper Slaughter to the village green at Bourton-on-the-Water, along the course of the River Eye. (Once you're at Bourton, you'll find several kid-friendly attractions—a motor museum, model railway exhibit, model village, and birds-only zoo called **Birdland.**) Follow signs for the Warden's Way; from Lower Slaughter on south, the Warden's Way follows the route of the Fosse Way, an ancient Roman footpath.

ⓘ www.nationaltrail.co.uk/Cotswold.

🚂 Moreton-in-Marsh, 2 hr. from London. Cheltenham, 2¼ hr. from London.

🛏 $$$ **Calcot Manor,** Calcot, 6km (3¾ miles) west of Tetbury (ⓒ **44/1666/890-391;** www.calcotmanor.co.uk). $$ **Chester House Hotel,** Victoria St., Bourton-on-the-Water (ⓒ **44/1451/820-286;** www.chesterhousehotel.com).

TOURS: For guided group walks, contact **The Ramblers' Association** (✆ 44/20/ 7339-8500; www.ramblers.org.uk) or the **Cotswold Voluntary Wardens Service** (✆ **44/1451/862-000;** www.cotswolds aonb.org.uk).

WHY THEY'LL THANK YOU: Getting inside the postcard views.

Hiking & Backpacking 408

Snowdonia National Park
Rambling the Rugged Welsh Mountains
All ages • North Wales

Mountain peaks and steep wooded slopes, spectacular estuaries and rugged cliffs brooding over secluded coves, valleys with tiny towns looking as if they were carved out of granite—all these join to make up Snowdonia National Park, which sprawls across much of north Wales.

The park takes its name from **Snowdon,** at 1,085m (3,560 ft.) the highest peak in Wales and England; Sir Edmund Hilary trained here before he climbed Mt. Everest. Many visitors to the park are focused on climbing Snowdon, which takes about 5 hours up and back. The view from the top is spectacular, but it's also possible to get to that spectacular view by taking the **cog railway** to the summit (See The Mountain Railways of North Wales 41). And there's so much more to this park— lakes, moorlands, river rapids, sprawling estuaries, farms, charming towns—that our family skipped the mountain climbing entirely in favor of hiking, cycling, and pony trekking.

Hiking around Snowdonia holds special charms for children. For one thing, you're likely to encounter wild ponies and free-ranging sheep, who don't seem surprised

Snowdonia National Park.

at all to meet hikers. Then there's the peculiar walking surface, a funny combination of springy turf and gravelly scree—it takes some getting used to (be sure to watch your footing), but before long it just made us giggle.

A highlight of our trip was the almost unbearably picturesque town of **Betws-y-Coed** (pronounced Bet-us-ee-Coyd), set in the lush Gwydyr Forest along a tumbling river. No less than eight bridges span the river along the short main street. One of the most popular walks here is a steep 4km (2.5-mile) route starting in town from behind St. Mary's church and going up to a small mountain lake, Llyn Elsi, passing en route the breathtaking Swallow Falls, a series of waterfalls robed in swirling mist.

Dolgellau is another good base; a couple of interesting short walks here are the 3km (1.75-mile) Torrent Walk along a dramatic ravine, or the 6.4km (4-mile) Precipice Walk around the flanks of Moel Cynwch. The **Mawddach Valley Nature Reserve,** 3km (1³/₄ miles) west of town, is a superb place for bird-watching and has a couple of short trails; here you can also pick up the last 12km (7.5 miles) of the Mawddach Trail along the spreading waters and wetlands of the Mawddach river's estuary, walking over a high railway bridge and ending up at the coast in Barmouth. North of Dolgellau, **Coed Y Brenin Forest Park** (✆ 44/1341/440-747; www.snowdoniaguide.com/coed_y_brenin.html) is a mountain-biking mecca with miles of cycling trails, including some designed for families.

ⓘ **Snowdonia National Park** (✆ 44/1766/770-274; www.eryri-npa.co.uk). **Betws-y-Coed Tourist Office,** Royal Oak Stables (✆ 44/1690/710-426; www.betws-y-coed.co.uk).

🚋 Betws-y-Coed, 3¹/₂ hr. from London.

🛏 $$ **Ty Gwyn,** Holyhead Rd., Betws-y-Coed (✆ 44/1690/710-383; www.tygwynhotel.co.uk). $$ **Bridge View B&B,** Old Church Rd., Betws-y-Coed (✆ 44/1690/710-127; www.betwsguesthouse.co.uk).

WHY THEY'LL THANK YOU: Coming face-to-face with a wild pony.

409 Hiking & Backpacking

Grindelwald
Glacier Hiking through the Swiss Alps
Ages 8 & up • Switzerland

It's one thing to hike through a valley sculpted by long-ago glaciers, quite another to hike where the glaciers are still carving their way between peaks, a colossal river of slow-moving ancient ice. But that's just what you'll see in the Swiss Alps at Grindelwald, a popular ski resort surrounded by chalet-studded hamlets. In summer, the skiers may disappear, but that just leaves the mountain free for hikers and mountain climbers.

Even relatively short and easy hikes from Grindelwald will get you and the kids up on those mighty glaciers. A guided 1-day hiking tour organized by the **Bergsteigerzentrum** mountaineering organization (✆ 41/33/853-5200) begins with a scenic mountain train ride from Grindelwald to Eiglergletscher (*gletscher* is the German word for "glacier"). A local mountain guide leads you to Bergsteigerzentrum, Grindelwald's husky-breeding center (always a hit with kids), then along the foot of the north wall of Mount Eiger. You'll end up in Alpiglen for lunch and then take a train back to Grindelwald.

Another hike, which takes only half a day, goes from Grindelwald along the Milchbach, a river so named because melting

Junfraubahn.

glacial ice runs off in a stream that's milk-colored from all the gravel sediment it's carrying. It's an hour's easy climb from Grindelwald to the base of the Upper Grindelwald Glacier; another 45 minutes' walk goes up 850 steps above the Milchbach to the nose of the glacier, where the kids may want to visit the **Blue Ice Grotto,** a chamber carved out of ice. There are some dramatic walking trails from here, leading right along the edge of the glacier. Catch a postal bus back down from the grotto to Grindelwald.

Hikes can only go so far, though; cap off your glacier touring with a trip on the rack-and-pinion railway to Kleine Scheidegg, where you switch to the **Jungfraubahn** (© **41/33/828-7233;** www.jungfraubahn. ch), the highest rack railway in Europe. This train climbs up 9.6km (6 miles), mostly through a tunnel carved in the mountain (at the Eismeer stop, view the sea of ice from windows in the rock), to the Jungfrau-joch terminus. Take a few minutes to

adjust to the altitude, then board the elevator behind the post office up to the **Eispalast** (Ice Palace), a dazzling series of chambers carved 20m (65 ft.) below the glacier's surface, with everything inside sculpted out of ice, including full-size replicas of vintage cars and caricatures of local clergymen.

(i) **Tourist Office,** at the Sportszentrum on Hauptstrasse (© **41/33/854-1212;** www.grindelwald.com).

Interlaken, 2 hr. from Zurich, 40 minutes from Bern.

$$ **Hotel Jungfrau Lodge,** Grindelwald (© **41/33/854-4141;** www.jungfrau lodge.ch). $$$ **Romantik Hotel Schweizerhof,** Grindelwald (© **41/33/854-5858;** www.hotel-schweizerhof.com).

WHY THEY'LL THANK YOU: Seeing just how massive this river of ice truly is.

Wunderhiking in the Black Forest

Ages 6 & up • Triberg, Germany

One of the richest timberlands in the world lies in southwestern Germany, where the mountains are thickly planted with conifers, their arrow-straight trunks so close together that sunlight barely penetrates to the woodland floor. This is the famous Black Forest, home of traditional woodcarving, cuckoo clocks, and dense chocolate cake, and its fairy-tale atmosphere is irresistible. You can sample its beauty by driving the 144km (89-mile) scenic **Schwarzwald Hochstrasse** (Black Forest High Rd., Rte. B500) north–south from the fashionable 19th-century spa of Baden-Baden to Waldshut on the Rhine. But hiking is the best way to explore its forested heart. On a village-to-village walk, you pass through sunny panoramic pastures and deep, fragrant pine woods, where you almost expect Bambi and Thumper to spring out of the next glade.

Clearly marked signs guide you across this easy trail, which starts at Triberg, traditionally the birthplace of the cuckoo clock. A series of hotels, beginning with the **Parkhotel Wehrle** (see below), have coordinated to map out a route and convey your luggage for you, so you can hike with only a small rucksack. You can hike from 1 or 2 to 10 days, even more if you have the time. Distances between hotels range from 20 to 27km (12–17 miles), and restaurants and farmhouses offer food and refreshment en route.

If you only want a day hike, climb up to the highest waterfall in Germany, **Wasserfelle Gutach,** just outside of Triberg. This lovely cascade drops some 160m (525 ft.), spilling downhill in seven misty and poetically evocative stages. They're only accessible on foot, and only from April through November. Park your car in designated lots in the town center, near the Gutach Bridge, then follow a signposted trail that, round-trip, requires about an hour of moderately difficult hill climbing. Even if you don't make it to the top, there are some very satisfying waterfall vistas partway up.

Triberg can be crowded and touristy, another good reason to get out and hike instead of wandering around town. Being in cuckoo-clock country, however, it may be hard to resist three Triberg-area attractions that promote this trade as well as related crafts such as woodcarving and music boxes: the **Schwarzwald-Museum of Triberg,** Wallfahrtstrasse 4 (© **49/7722/4434;** www.schwarzwaldmuseum.de); the world's largest cuckoo clock at the shop **Eble Uhren-Park,** Schonachbach 27, Schonach (on the B33, btw. Triberg and Hornberg; © **49/7722/96-220;** www.uhren-park.de); and the **Deutsches Uhrenmuseum** (German Clock Museum), 10 miles south on B500 at Gerwigstrasse 11, Furtwangen (© **49/7723/920-2800;** www.deutsches-uhrenmuseum.de).

ⓘ **Tourist Information,** Wallfahrtstrasse 4 (© **49/7722/86-6490;** www.dasferienland.de).

🚋 Triberg, 4¹/₂ hr. from Munich, 3 hr. from Frankfurt.

🛏 $$$ **Romantik Parkhotel Wehrle,** Gartenstrasse 24 (© **49/7722/860-20;** www.parkhotel-wehrle.de). $ **Römischer Kaiser,** Sommerauerstrasse 35 (© **49/7722/96-940;** www.roemischer-kaiser.com).

WHY THEY'LL THANK YOU: Hearing a cuckoo in the woods.

Bicycling on Nantucket

All ages • Nantucket, Massachusetts, USA

Bringing a car to Nantucket, the tiny Massachusetts island 30 miles off Cape Cod, can be an incredible hassle in summer—there are only six pokey car ferries per day from Hyannis, and they book up months in advance. Day visitors generally choose to come on foot (which frees you to opt for a high-speed ferry), but then they don't explore any farther than tourist-mobbed Nantucket Town. Your solution? Rent bikes. Flat, sandy Nantucket is heaven for beginning bicyclists, with paved paths leading all over. Bring helmets with you (they're required for children under 12) or rent them along with bikes in Nantucket Town at shops right by the wharf. Nothing could be easier, or more fun.

Bicycling the trails on Nantucket.

Here's the lay of the land: Three major bike routes radiate out from Nantucket Town, one heading west to Madaket, 6¼ miles, one south to Surfside 3½ miles, and the longest one a 17-mile loop out to Siasconset Beach ('Sconset to locals) and Sankaty Head lighthouse. It's classic beachy terrain, with few trees, wide skies, and swaths of tall dune grass on both sides. The pedaling is easy, and the island's small scale makes you feel you're really getting somewhere, especially when you hit the bluffs and get that Atlantic panorama. Picnic benches and water fountains are conveniently provided at strategic points along all the paths, which you'll appreciate if you're towing really young ones in a bike trailer.

Madaket is picturesque, especially at sunset, but has strong surf; with kids, you're better off turning right on Eel Point Road and swimming at gentler Dionis Beach. Popular **Surfside** beach is your best bet with young children, not only because the ride is shorter but also because there's a snack bar. My favorite, though, is the ride to **'Sconset,** even though it is the most demanding, longer and with a few hills. 'Sconset is rarely, if ever, crowded, perhaps because of the water's strong sideways tow. Lifeguards are usually on duty, but the closest facilities (restrooms, grocery store, and cafe) are back in the center of the village, which is lovely and worth a stop anyway. From 'Sconset, head north along the coastal path on Polpis Road, stopping off to snap Nantucket photos in front of the classic lighthouse at Sankaty Head. If you've planned ahead, though, you've booked an unforgettable naturalist-led tour (offered June–Oct) of the barrier beaches with the **Coskata-Coatue Wildlife Refuge** (© **508/228-6799;** reservations required); detour up Wauwinet Road to the Wauwinet Inn to meet the tour. By the time you pedal back into Nantucket Town and get back on the ferry, you'll have spent a day in the sun you won't soon forget.

(i) **Nantucket Visitor Services,** 25 Federal St. (☎ **508/228-0925;** www.nantucket-ma.gov).

🛏 $$ **Jared Coffin House,** 29 Broad St., Nantucket (☎ **800/248-2405** or 508/228-2400; www.jaredcoffinhouse.com).

WHY THEY'LL THANK YOU: A first taste of bike touring that'll leave them wanting more.

412 Cycling

Mackinac Island
Not a Car in Sight
All ages • Straits of Mackinac, Michigan, USA

You pronounce it "*Mack*-i-naw," like the raincoat (the mainland town where the ferries operate from is spelled Mackinaw City, just so out-of-towners get it straight). Cropping out of the Straits of Mackinac, which separate the Upper and Lower peninsulas of Michigan at their closest point, this summer resort island is a Victorian period piece of white frame houses and trim gardens. The only way to reach it is by private plane or ferry; and since you can't bring a car you have three options

Mackinac Island.

for getting around the island: on foot, by horse-drawn carriage, and on a bike. Pedaling happily along the limestone cliffs overlooking the straits, you may wonder why the automobile was ever invented.

A complete circuit of the island on traffic-free **Lake Shore Road** only takes 8 miles, doable even with fairly young riders (rental bikes in town also offer child seats and trailers if that's a better option for you). You'll have to stop along the way, of course, to drink in the views—don't miss Arch Rock on the east coast, a boulder pierced with a gaping 30- by 40-foot hole gouged by waves and glaciers, or Sunset Rock on the west bluff above town. Most of the island is covered by **Mackinac Island State Park** (✆ **906/436-4100;** www.mackinacparks.com), with 70 miles of paved roads and trails where cyclists can explore the cedar- and birch-forested interior. Above the town, you can also cycle up to **Fort Mackinac** (7127 Huron Rd.), built by British soldiers during the American Revolution to defend the link between Lakes Michigan and Huron, vital to the lucrative fur trade. Fourteen buildings, mostly from the 1880s, are still intact, and costumed interpreters do military reenactments; shoot off rifles and cannons; lead children's games; and perform bugle, fife-and-drum, and bagpipe music. The cliff-top site was chosen specifically for sentries to watch over the lakes, so you can just imagine how fantastic the views are.

Of course, if you'd rather take in the scenery from a rocking chair, you can always plunk yourself down on the white colonnaded veranda—the world's longest front porch—of the landmark **Grand Hotel** (see below), built in 1887. Even if you're not staying here, you can tour the historic hotel. In the center of town, a few neat low white buildings recall the days of the early-18th-century fur traders, along with a bark chapel built by the original Huron natives.

ⓘ **Mackinac Island Chamber of Commerce** (✆ **877/847-0086;** www.mackinacisland.org).

✈ Mackinaw City, 12 miles from ferry docks.

🛏 $$$ **Grand Hotel,** West Bluff Rd. (✆ **800/33-GRAND** [334-7263] or 906/847-3331; www.grandhotel.com). $$ **Mission Point,** 6633 Main St. (✆ **800/833-7711** or 906/847-3312; www.missionpoint.com).

BEST TIME: May–Oct.

WHY THEY'LL THANK YOU: Overtaking a carriage, your bikes will be the fastest things on the road.

Cycling **413**

Montréal
Riding Les Pistes Cyclables
Ages 8 & up • Montréal, Québec, Canada

Long country bike rides attract the Lance Armstrongs among us, but younger riders quickly get bored—they need something to look at as they cycle. Well, they won't get bored bicycling around Montréal—according to *Bicycling Magazine,* it's the number-one bicycling city in North America, with 349km (217 miles) of urban bike paths, or as they say in French-speaking Montréal, *pistes cyclables.*

One of the city's main tourist magnets, the restored harborfront **Vieux-Port** area, has bike paths running along its 2km (1¼-mile) promenade—the kids may beg you to rent one of those four-wheeled Q-cycles they'll see trundling along, a welcome option for families with toddlers. At the eastern end of the port, park your bikes to visit the 1922 clock tower, Le Tour de l'Horloge, with 192 steps climbing past exposed clockwork gears to three observation decks.

Perhaps the city's most popular bike route is the flat 11km (6.75-mile) path to Lac St-Louis along the spruced-up **Lachine Canal,** which begins just west of the Vieux-Port. Stop en route at the open-air **Atwater Market,** 138 Atwater St., to pick up freshly baked bread, gourmet cheese, and fruit for a picnic along the canal. Montréal is named after the towering hill in the middle of **Parc Mont-Royal**—start from the top and you'll coast 4km (2.5 miles) downhill through woods and grassy expanses. A more ambitious route goes west 16km (10 miles) from the **St-Lambert Lock** to the suburb of Côte Ste-Catherine.

Montréal taxis have bike racks, and the superclean and efficient Métro system will let you take bikes on its subway trains (enter the last car); so it's easy to zip out from downtown to various start points. Take your bikes on the Métro west to Angrigon station to pedal around the 6.4km (4-mile) bike circuit in **Angrigon Park.** Go east to Pie-IX station to ride around the lushly landscaped **Botanic**

Garden before you visit the **Biodôme de Montréal** ㉗, which was originally built for the 1976 Olympics as—fittingly enough—a velodrome for bike races.

To rent bikes, check out **CaRoule** in the Vieux-Port, 27 rue de la Commune est (✆ **877/866-0633** or 514/866-0633; www.caroulemontreal.com), or **Vélo Montréal** near the Botanic Garden, 3880 rue Rachel est (✆ **514/259-7272;** www.velomontreal. com). At 1251 Rachel St., the headquarters of **Vélo Québec** has a cycling boutique and the **Bicicletta Café,** modeled after Italian bicyclists' cafes.

ⓘ **Vélo Québec,** 1251 Rachel St. (✆ **800/ 567-8356** or 514/521-8356; www.velo. qc.ca).

✈ Montréal-Pierre-Elliott-Trudeau International.

🛏 $$ **Delta Centre-Ville,** 777 rue University (✆ **800/268-1133** or 514/879-1370; www.deltahotels.com). $$ **Fairmont Le Reine Elizabeth,** 900 bd. René-Lévesque oust (✆ **800/441-1414** or 514/861-3511; www.fairmont.com).

WHY THEY'LL THANK YOU: Like your own Tour de France.

---

414 Cycling

Cycling the Rim Road
Crater Lake
Ages 8 & up • Crater Lake, Oregon, USA

The story begins with a volcanic explosion so fearsome—scientists estimate it was 42 times as powerful as Mount St. Helens—that it left behind a phenomenally deep crater, which in time filled with water to become America's deepest lake. But this version of events doesn't prepare you for the sight of Crater Lake, for the intense sapphire blue of its cold spring-fed waters reflecting the sheer forested cliffs that

encircle it. It's simply breathtaking, a panorama of supreme serenity that belies its violent origins. It takes about 2 hours to drive around Crater Lake—which, unfortunately, is all most park visitors do, rolling along the asphalt, narcotized by the pretty scenery. Trade in those four wheels for two, though, and you'll really feel the transforming power of this volcanic landscape.

The 33-mile **Rim Drive,** open only in summer, has 30 overlooks where you can gaze at these pristine waters cupped in their rocky chalice. Travel clockwise, wear bright clothing so motorists can spot you, and if possible sleep in the park the night before so you can hit the narrow road early before the traffic gets heavy (as it inevitably will). The Rim Drive may look like an easy pedal, but don't underestimate it—it can be demanding, especially on the east side of the lake, where there are more hills (hills you'd scarcely notice if you were just driving). On the other hand, the east side of the lake has more panoramic views, providing good excuses to catch your breath. The **Cloudcap Overlook** is 2,000 feet high, with vistas that stretch as far as Mount Shasta. Another cool turnoff overlooks the **Phantom Ship,** a jagged basalt formation jutting up out of the lake.

An alternative ride goes from the Rim Village visitor center north to the **Cleetwood Cove Trailhead** and back, 21 miles total, on the flatter west rim. Cleetwood Cove is the sole trail that goes down to the lake's edge; it may only be 2.2 miles round-trip, but the way back is strenuous, like climbing 65 flights of stairs. My advice: Save your strength for the cycling.

No matter which of the park's entrances you come in, you'll drive a few miles to get to the Rim Drive, where you can park your car and get the bikes off your rack. If you've got more than one driver in your party, consider taking turns driving the car to meet the cyclists at each overlook—it'll give the kids the option of pooping out if necessary. (Blame it on the high altitude.) There are no bike rentals in the park, but you can rent them at **Diamond Lake Resort,** 5 miles from the park's north entrance on S.R. 138.

ⓘ Along OR 62 (☏ **541/594-3000;** www.nps.gov/crla).

✈ Rogue Valley International, Medford, OR, 71 miles.

🛏 $$$ **Crater Lake Lodge,** Rim Rd. (☏ **541/830-8700;** www.craterlakelodges.com). $ **Mazama Village Campground,** in the park, off OR 62 (www.craterlakelodges.com/Mazama-Village-Campground-815.html).

BEST TIME: Late June–Sept.

WHY THEY'LL THANK YOU: Discovering how rugged this pretty place really is.

Cycling **415**

Circling Arran Island on a Bike
Ages 10 & up • Isle of Arran, Scotland

At the mouth of the Firth of Clyde, the Isle of Arran is often described as "Scotland in miniature" because of its varied scenery. The coast road circles the island in a 97km (60-mile) circuit—you could do it in 1 day if you're ambitious, or in 2 days with a stay overnight on the west coast. Several intriguing stops en route (many associated with the 14th-century hero Robert the Bruce) will keep kids distracted enough to forget their aching calves.

The ferry arrives at Brodick, where you can pick up a picnic lunch in the shops,

then rent a bicycle at **Bilsland's, Shore Rd.** (☏ **44/1770/302-272**), or **Arran Adventure,** Auchrannie Rd. (☏ **44/1770/302-244;** www.arranadventure.com). Heading clockwise around the island (go south from Brodick), you'll come to **Lamlash,** a beachy sea resort, then **King's Cross Point,** where Robert the Bruce is said to have sailed for the mainland after hiding out on Arran for months. The road climbs to **Dippin Head,** and the southern curve of the island's coast is high over the sea with great views of tiny islands and the

Ailsa Crag lighthouse. The road goes downhill toward **Sliddery,** where an overgrown mound marks the site of an old Norse keep. At **Tormore,** north of Blackwaterfoot, you can detour a mile inland to visit some standing stones. **Drumadoon Point** on the west coast has basalt columns and the remains of an old fort, and **King's Hill** has caves where Robert the Bruce hid out from his enemies for months.

At the northern end of the island, the scenery turns ever more romantic and Highlands-like, with rugged mountains towering over narrow green glens. Castle ruins at **Lochranza** were reputedly the hunting seat of Robert the Bruce. Back on the east cost, you'll pass dramatic **Glen Sannox** and the **Fallen Rocks,** huge sandstone boulders that have tumbled off the cliffs. On your right looms the island's highest mountain, **Goat Fell** ("mountain of the winds"), with its 874m-high (2,867-ft.) conical peak. At its foot are Arran's two major sights—the **Isle of Arran Heritage Museum,** a series of restored buildings tracing life on Arran from prehistoric times to the present, and the red sandstone

Brodick Castle, ancestral home of the dukes of Hamilton. The castle has fine furnishings inside, but the real attraction is its gardens, which feature plants from such far-flung habitats as Tasmania, Chile, and the Himalayas. The rhododendrons are amazing. Cycle back into Brodick, where you can return your bike and catch the ferry back to Ardrossan.

ⓘ **Tourist Information,** The Pier, Brodick (✆ **44/1770/303-774;** www.visitarran. com).

FERRY: 30 min. from Ardrossan. **Caledonian MacBrayne** ferries (✆ **44/9705/650-000;** www.calmac.co.uk).

🛏 $$$ **Auchrannie Country House Hotel,** Auchrannie Rd., Brodick (✆ **44/1770/302-234;** www.auchrannie.co.uk). $$ **Best Western Kinloch Hotel,** Blackwaterfoot (✆ **44/1770/860-444;** www. bw-kinlochhotel.co.uk).

WHY THEY'LL THANK YOU: Sparkling sea on your left, stunning scenery on your right.

416 Cycling

Holland's Haarlem
Traversing the Polders
Ages 8 & up • The Netherlands

One thing every school kid learns about the Netherlands: It's the land of dikes, those walls against the sea that the thrifty Dutch built to turn their flood-prone coastal lowlands into arable farmland. Miles and miles of reclaimed polder land stretch along the North Sea coast west of Amsterdam—no rolling hills, no dramatic seaside cliffs, just a low steady horizon and roads laid straight as arrows. What could be better for bicycling?

Our favorite day trip out of Amsterdam is to head for Haarlem. It's a lovely town

with a sedate 17th-century charm, but few sights that will interest kids. We come here for the surrounding countryside, which lives up to all the images of the Dutch landscape painters: neat patchwork farmlands with the occasional windmill, and broody gray clouds scudding against a vast scrim of silvery skies.

Rent bikes in Haarlem at **Pieters Rijwielshop,** Stationsplein 7 (✆ **31/23/531-7066**), or **Bike Planet,** Gierstraat 55–57 (✆ **31/23/534-1502;** www.bikeplanet.nl), and you can be out of town in no time. The

Grote Markt in Haarlem.

beach resort of **Zandvoort** is 7km (4¹/₃ miles) directly west of Haarlem, an easy cycle through woods, polders, and sand dunes to a seemingly endless stretch of smooth sand lined with seasonal cafes. Or branch off to the **Zuid-Kennermerland National Park,** just north of Zandvoort, a dune-edged nature reserve where you can breathe the salt tang of the North Sea air. South of Haarlem is another popular cycle, along N206 or N208, where from late January through May masses of vibrantly colored tulips fill the fields. This so-called **Bollenstreek Route** runs 60km (37 miles) all the way to Leiden, though you only need ride as far as you want.

So where are the dikes? Steam pumps did the job when the Haarlem area was reclaimed in the mid–19th century; if the kids are keen to see dikes, drive 62km (39 miles) north of Amsterdam on A7/E22 to the 30km-long (19-mile) **Afsluitdijk** (Enclosing Dike). Completed in 1932, this huge dike finally sealed off the encroaching North Sea, transforming the saltwater Zuiderzee into the freshwater IJsselmeer (and turning several fishing villages into farm towns). Haul out your bikes again, because a bike path runs along the highway as it follows the top of the dike. Expect it to be windy while you're out on this ribbon of highway, with nothing but sea on either side. Halfway across, you can turn around at the monument (with a cafe) that commemorates the workers who built this massive wall against the sea, mostly by backbreaking manual labor.

ⓘ **Tourist Office,** Stationsplein 1 (✆ **31/ 23/571-2262;** www.vvvzk.nl).

✈ Amsterdam Schipohl.

🛏 $ **Amstel Botel,** Oosterdokskade 2–4 (✆ **31/20/626-4247;** www.amstelbotel. com). $$ **Estheréa,** Singel 303–309 (✆ **31/ 20/624-5146;** www.estherea.nl).

WHY THEY'LL THANK YOU: Tulips, dikes, windmills, the whole package.

Rocky Mountain National Park
Trail Riding on the Roof of the World
Ages 6 & up • Near Estes Park, Colorado, USA

Chances are you've never been as close to the sky as you'll be at Rocky Mountain National Park, most of which is at least 8,000 feet high. Up here, the air is so thin and cool you'll feel giddy, the sun's UV rays so intense that sun block and sunglasses are a must. It's a land of ponderosa pine, gnarled alpine tundra, heathery slopes, bare granite, dizzying views, and so many elk they'll browse right up to your campground. The Continental Divide slices across the middle of this compact park—you can drive over it on Trail Ridge Road, that stretch of U.S. 34 that cuts across the park east to west—it's 48 miles of truly spectacular mountaintop views, much of it above the timberline. The park also has laid out several short nature trails that kids will enjoy—check park maps for the Moraine Park Nature Trail, the Sprague Lake Nature Trail, and the Bear Lake Trail; the Beaver Boardwalk near the beginning of Trail Ridge Road is a great place to scout out dam-building beavers.

But the best way to plunge into this wilderness is to swing into a Western saddle and take a ride on horseback. Ever since this park was founded in 1915, it's been a popular high-country riding area. While many national parks offer only a standard 1-hour circle ride, at Rocky Mountain you can take guided trail rides from 2 to 8 hours, or even book overnight pack trips; early-morning trail rides that include a cowboy breakfast are always a hit with kids. An ample network of worn dirt trails—some 260 miles of them—wind into the glacier-carved countryside past steep, craggy mountain slopes and small, round reflecting lakes. Children as young as 6 can have a horse to themselves, while younger children ride with a parent.

There are stables all over the area, several of them run by **Sombrero Ranch Stables** (www.sombrero.com). On the more developed eastern side of the park, there's one at Moraine Park (✆ **970/586-2327**), another near the Glacier Basin Campground on Sprague Lake (✆ **970/586-3244**), and one just outside the park opposite Lake Estes Dam on U.S. 34 (✆ **970/586-4577**). On the west side of

Rocky Mountain National Park.

the park, there's another just outside park boundaries in the Grand Lakes area (✆ **970/627-3514**). Also in Grand Lake, the family-oriented **Winding River Resort** (see below) offers 1- and 2-hour trail rides, plus pony rides for younger riders.

ⓘ U.S. 34 or U.S. 36 (✆ **970/586-1206;** www.nps.gov/romo).

✈ Denver International, 65 miles.

🛏 $$$ **Glacier Lodge,** 2166 CO 66, south of park entrance (✆ **800/523-3920** or 970/586-4401; www.glacierlodge.com). $$ **Winding River Resort,** 1441 C. Rd. 491, Grand Lake (✆ **800/282-5121,** 970/627-3215, or 303/623-1121; www.windingriverresort.com).

BEST TIME: Mid-May to mid-Sept.

WHY THEY'LL THANK YOU: The clip-clop of hooves echoing off the top of the world.

In the Saddle **418**

Monument Valley
The Iconic Wild West Landscape
Ages 6 & up • Kayenta, Arizona, USA

When most of us think of the American West, this is what clicks into our mental Viewmasters: A vast, flat sagebrush plain with huge sandstone spires thrusting to the sky like the fingers of ancient Mother Earth clutching for the heavens. Ever since movie director John Ford first started shooting westerns here in the 1930s, this landscape has felt familiar to millions who have never set foot here. (Just outside the park, **Goulding's Museum and Trading Post** re-creates the era in the 1920s and 1930s when the moviemakers first discovered the area.) We've all seen it on the big

Monument Valley.

screen, but oh, what a difference to see it in real life.

Because the park is on Navajo tribal lands—their name for it is Tsebii'nidzisgai, "the valley within the rocks"—there are only three ways to tour the area: driving the 17-mile Valley Drive past 11 photo-op overlooks; taking an off-road jeep tour with a Navajo guide; or on guided hikes and trail rides, which range from 1-hour loops to 8-hour excursions. The classic way to experience these dramatic scrublands, of course, is from on a Western saddle, the way John Wayne saw it. The native guides, born and bred to this barren landscape, will not only lead the ride, they'll help you appreciate the intricate beauties of this landscape, which is sacred to their tribe. One of the most comprehensive tour companies (jeeps, hikes, horses, you name it) is **Sacred Monument Tours** (✆ **435/727-3218;** www.monumentvalley. net). Many of the trail rides follow the Mittens trail, which heads north to Sentinel Mesa and then comes back along the floor of the West Mitten mesa; longer rides add on the Castle Butte, Stage Coach, or Big Indian Spire mesas. Another popular option for more experienced riders goes into backcountry, outside the official park boundaries, to visit Teardrop Arch and Horseshoe Canyon. If you possibly can,

time your visit to include sunset—as the sheer walls of these monoliths capture the light of the setting sun, they truly seem to catch fire.

Although most of the park lies in Arizona, it is right on the state border, and you enter it from Utah. The Valley drive circuit is a good way to get acclimated; be sure to get a map so the kids can learn the eccentric rock formations' names—such imaginative names as Three Sisters, Camel Butte, Elephant Butte, the Thumb, and Totem Pole. And as you stare at them, take an extra moment to imagine the forces of nature that have sculpted the soft desert stone into these incredible shapes. It's an only-in-America panorama that the kids won't ever forget.

ⓘ U.S. 163, 30 miles north of Kayenta (✆ **435/727-5870;** www.monument valleyonline.com).

✈ Flagstaff Pulliam, 200 miles.

🛏 $$ **Goulding's Lodge,** Monument Valley, UT (✆ **435/727-3231;** www. gouldings.com). $$ **Hampton Inn Kayenta,** U.S. 160, Kayenta, AZ (✆ **800/HAMPTON** [426-7866] or 928/697-3170; www.hampton-inn.com).

WHY THEY'LL THANK YOU: Just like the movies—only more so.

---

419 In the Saddle

Doing the Dude Ranch Thing

Ages 6 & up • Around Jackson, Wyoming, USA

As a horse-mad girl of 7, I was sick with jealousy when my parents went off to Wyoming for a week at a dude ranch. Don't do this to your children! Dude ranches—or, excuse me, *guest ranches* is the preferred term now—have figured out how to court families, and it's a huge bit of their business. The standard 1-week package may cost $1,500 to nearly $3,000 per person (with discounts for children), but

that covers everything—family-style meals, cozy log cabins to sleep in, and all ranch activities, such as horseback riding, fly-fishing, hiking, float trips, nature hikes, paintball, roping lessons, square dances, maybe even big-game hunting—yee-*haw!*

To me, the quintessential ranch experience is in western Wyoming, with constant views of the snow-dusted Grand Teton range and trail rides through sagebrush flats, green foothill meadows, and rocky timberline terrain. A handful of ranches close to Jackson Hole abut national parkland—not just Grand Teton National Park, but the vast Bridger-Teton and Targhee National Forests—which provides a broad choice of trails, not to mention swift sparkling rivers for those float trips and fly-fishing outings.

The **Triangle X Ranch,** in Moose (© **307/733-2183;** www.trianglex.com), is actually within the national park borders, and it's the most rustic-feeling of the lot; the laid-back **R Lazy S Ranch,** in Teton Village (© **307/733-2655;** www.rlazys.com), is right on the park border. The **Red Rock Ranch,** in Kelly (© **307/733-6288;** www.theredrockranch.com), serves up fairly gourmet dinners and even has a heated swimming pool. **Heart Six Ranch,** in Moran (© **888/543-2477;** www.heartsix.com), features modern cabins grouped around a historic log-cabin homestead; the **Gros Ventre River Ranch,** in Moose (© **307/733-4138;** www.grosventreriverranch.com), also has lodges for more hotel-like accommodations. Don't expect manicured landscaping or uniformed employees—these are all decidedly rural places, with pole fences and low-slung buildings and trophy elk heads mounted on pine-paneled walls. You'll dress casual

and be on a first-name basis with the wranglers. And you won't be watching TV at night—not when you've got a sky full of stars and a crackling campfire for toasting marshmallows.

The ranchers have large herds and can carefully match horses to the riding abilities of the guest, usually giving you "your own" horse for the entire week. Even beginners catch on quickly, given that they're riding Western saddle and following a group along a well-marked trail (usually at an easy pace). When choosing a ranch, consider how its children's program is set up—at Triangle X, Red Rock, and R Lazy S, children have their own trail rides and separate meals, which significantly reduces your bonding time; there is an optional supervised kids' program at Heart Six Ranch, but children can join the adult trail rides if their riding ability passes muster with the wranglers. At Gros Ventre River Ranch, family togetherness is the norm on trail rides, but there is a rec room kids can escape to when their parents get too embarrassing.

✈ Jackson Hole.

🛏 See individual listings in review.

WHY THEY'LL THANK YOU: Saddle sore and loving it.

In the Saddle 420

Pony Trekking in Connemara
Ages 8 & up • Western County Galway, Ireland

West of Galway City lies a land of "savage beauty," in the words of Oscar Wilde. The Atlantic coastline around here is ragged, notched with hundreds of tiny inlets; inland is a vast bog-mantled, granite moorland sown with lakes, running north to stark mountains, the Maum Turks and The Twelve Bens. It's a wild, tough, treeless countryside, sparsely populated since the famine of the 1840s—and that very wildness is what begs

for exploration. There's no better way to do so than on horseback, preferably on the native sure-footed Connemara pony.

Horses need to be sure-footed to cross Connemara's plum-colored boglands, where unexpected marshy patches can plunge you fetlock-deep into water. The land looks flat, but each twist of the track reveals hidden gorges, streams, and lakes. Up close you see how gorse and heather, rhododendrons, and wildflowers soften the harsh rock-strewn land. The Connemara pony—the only horse breed native to Ireland—is ideal for children's riding, with its great stamina and gentle temperament, and the locals are justly proud of their native steeds—the inland crossroad of Maam Cross is famous as the site of the annual Connemara pony fair, and Clifden, Connemara's chief town, has a **Connemara Pony Museum** (© 353/95/21494) set up in the old train station.

If pony trekking is the focus of your vacation, consider a weeklong horseback tour, beginning and ending in Galway City, with **Connemara and Coast Trails,** Loughrea (© **353/91/841216;** www.connemara-trails.com), for experienced and beginning riders alike. Your luggage is transported from hotel to hotel and all meals are catered. The **Aile Cross Equestrian Center** (© 353/91/843968), which provides Connemara Trails' horses, also offers hour, half-day, or daylong rides around Loughrea. The long-established **Slieve Aughty Riding Centre,** also in Loughrea (© 353/90/97-45246; www.riding-centre.com), offers 6-day riding packages that combine lessons, treks into the surrounding forest, and accommodations.

For shorter rides, the **Errislennan Riding Centre** (© 353/95/21134; www.errislannan manor.com), up in Clifden, leads some wonderful daily cross-country pony treks into the moorlands. If splashing along the Atlantic beaches is your dream, **Point Pony Trekking** in Ballyconneely (© **353/95/23685**) runs beach rides and day treks around the area, and the **Cleggan Beach Riding Centre** (© **353/95/44746;** www.clegganriding centre.com), in the seacoast village of Cleggan, organizes among other rides a 3-hour excursion at low tide across the shallow channel to Omey Island.

ⓘ **Clifden Tourist Information,** the Square (©**353/87/052-0295;** www.clifden chamber.ie).

✈ 🚌 Galway City, 80km (50 miles).

🛏 $ **Glen Valley Farm B&B,** Killary Harbour (©**353/95/42269;** www.glenvalley house.com). $$$ **Renvyle House,** Renvyle (© **353/95/43511;** www.renvyle.com).

WHY THEY'LL THANK YOU: Sturdy ponies, stunning views.

---

421 **In the Saddle**

Stalking the Loch Ness Monster

Ages 8 & up • Drumnadrochit, Scotland

The Loch Ness monster—or "Nessie," as she's fondly called—is one of the world's great mysteries. It's just about impossible to pass along the shores of this long lake in the Scottish Highlands without peering at its deep, dark waters and expecting a scaly snout or a sinuous, slimy hump to break the surface. Hwy. A82 runs along the north shore of the 39km-long (24-mile) lake, one of a string of lakes that almost sever Scotland between Fort William and Inverness—but why look out of a car window, when you could be on horseback, feeling the bracing Highland mist on your face?

Don't let monster mania distract you from the lovely scenery of this Highlands lake, where mossy Glen Urquhart runs down to Loch Ness's deep-blue waters. Even on a cloudy day—and there are plenty up here—the shifting play of light on the wild landscape is dramatic. In the bucolic village of Drumnadrochit, 1.6km (1 mile) inland from the lake and 23km (14 miles) west of Inverness, the **Highland Riding Centre** at Borlum Farm (© **44/1456/450-220**) runs 1- to 2-hour tours on horseback around a sprawling moorland

The Loch Ness Centre.

sheep farm overlooking Loch Ness. Be sure to book in advance.

In the village itself, Drumnadrochit cashes in on Nessie's myth with the multimedia **Loch Ness Monster Exhibition,** on A82 (℃ **44/1456/450-573;** www.loch ness.com), centered on what purports to be a scale model of the creature. In summer, you can even take a cruise out onto the lake with **Deepscan Passenger Cruises** (℃ **44/1456/450-218;** www.loch ness.com) to peer into those mysterious deep waters. Even if you don't spot Nessie, you'll get a fine view of ruined **Castle Urquhart,** sitting on its promontory 2.4km (1½ miles) south of the village; it's the spot where sightings have most often been reported.

The first recorded sighting of an underwater beast was by St. Columba in A.D. 565,

and they've continued unabated ever since. Is it a sole survivor from prehistoric times? A gigantic sea snake? A cosmic wanderer? Everyone has his or her own theory. A team of scientists from Massachusetts has sonar-triggered cameras and strobe lights rigged up year-round, hoping to document Nessie's existence, but so far no luck.

🚂 Inverness, 3½ hr. from Glasgow or Edinburgh.

🛏 $$ **Polmaily House Hotel,** A831, 3.2km (2 miles) west of Drumnadrochit (℃ **44/7776/190-894;** www.polmaily.co. uk). $$ **Borlum Farm** (tel) **44/1456/450-358;** www.borlum.co.uk).

WHY THEY'LL THANK YOU: This could be the day Nessie comes up for air.

The Camargue
France's Cowboy Country
Ages 8 & up • Camargue National Park, France

On a marshy delta where two branches of the Rhône empty into the Mediterranean, the Camargue is France's cattle country. Here, black bulls are raised for bullfights in nearby Arles and Nîmes. The cattle are herded by *gardians*, French cowboys who ride the range on small white horses said to have been introduced by the Saracens. This exotic corner of France, with its white-washed houses, plaited-straw roofs, roaming Gypsies, and pink flamingos, can be explored by canal barge, bike, or jeep, but the best way to plunge into its rich interior is on the back of *camarguais* **horses**—proud white steeds whose cousins you'll see running wild through the salt marshlands, and whose hoofs are so tough they don't need shoes.

Descended long ago from Arabian horses, these sturdy little horses have distinctive long manes and bushy tails, which evolved over the centuries to slap the pesky, gluttonous mosquitoes who thrive in these wetlands. Two to three dozen stables (depending on the time of year) along the highway from Arles to Stes-Maries offer expeditions into the **park** (on D570, near Camargue's capital, Stes-Maries-de-la-Mer). Given the easy temperament and sure-footedness of Camargue ponies, these rides are recommended even for those who have never been on a horse before. On horseback, you can ford the waters to penetrate deep into the interior where black bulls graze and wild birds nest.

The French cowboys of the Camargue live in thatched huts called *cabanes,* wear large felt hats, and carry long three-pronged sticks to prod the cattle. With the most fragile ecosystem in France, the alluvial plain of the Camargue has been a national park since 1970, and exotic flora and fauna abound. Besides the wild horses, the bird life here is the richest in Europe—not only colonies of **pink flamingos,** but some 400 other species, including ibises, egrets, kingfishers, owls, wild ducks, swans, and ferocious birds of prey. The best place to see flamingo colonies is the area around **Ginès,** a hamlet on N570, 5km (3 miles) north of **Stes-Maries-de-la-Mer**—a perfectly preserved medieval walled town set amidst swamps and lagoons, long ago an embarkation point for the Crusades and well worth a visit.

ⓘ **Tourist Information,** place St. Louis, Aigues-Mortes (✆ **33/4/66-53-73-00;** www.ot-aiguesmortes.fr).

🚃 Aigues-Mortes, 1 hr. from Nîmes.

🛏 $$$ **Hotel Les Templiers,** 21–23 rue de la République, Aigues-Mortes (✆ **33/4/66-53-66-56;** www.hotelles templiers.fr). $$ **Hotel d'Arlatan,** 26 rue du Sauvage, Arles (✆ **33/4/90-93-56-66;** www.hotel-arlatan.fr).

WHY THEY'LL THANK YOU: Playing cowboy with an exotic twist.

Galloping through the Brazilian Pantanal

Ages 8 & up • Southwestern Brazil

When you live on the world's largest flood plain—a flat wetlands as big as France, stretching across southwestern Brazil all the way to Paraguay—you don't bother planting crops or laying down roads. Why would you, when it's all going to lie underwater from December through March? So in the Pantanal, ranchers graze their cattle in the dry season and retreat to higher ground in the floods; and when the waters spread, they simply splash around on horseback. This fertile land, ruled by the rhythms of its waters, is simply the best place in South America to see wildlife, better even than the Amazon. To see it at its best, make like a cowpoke and get up on a horse.

And what creatures there are to see—the Pantanal is home to capybaras, caimans, jaguars, pumas, marsh deer, anacondas, giant otters, colorful Hyacinth macaws, kites, hawks, and storks; there are nearly 700 species of birds alone, and 80 species of mammals. The Transpantaeira, a gravel road that was supposed to traverse the Pantanal, is one of the few roads here. Only the northern 89 miles were ever built, though, and today the Transpantaeira functions more like a nature trail, taking visitors into the heart of north Pantanal, where its roadside ditches are favorite feeding grounds for kingfishers, egrets, jabiru storks, and more than four varieties of hawks and three different kinds of kites. Beneath the many rickety bridges are small rivers or pools where caimans lurk by the hundreds.

Now that the secret is out, ecotourism is on the rise, and many of the region's cattle ranches *(fazendas)* have created accommodations and gone into business as resorts, or at least as the Brazilian version of dude ranches. The stout Pantanal horses are accustomed to slogging through the shallow waters that engulf this treeless plain every wet season, and sitting in the comfortable Western-type saddles the local cowboys use, you can ramble far from settled areas, where the local wildlife wanders otherwise undisturbed. Rein in your mount and observe a flock of herons fishing in the rich floodwaters, then take off with a splash at a full gallop, startling alligators and snakes underfoot. While local lodges may offer short rides around their properties, you can also book entire tour packages based on exploring the flood plain by horse: Tour operators include **Pantanal Explorer,** in northern Patanal (© **51/65/3682-2800;** www.pantanalexplorer.com.br), and **Open Door,** in the south (© **55/67/3321-8303;** www.opendoortur.com.br).

✈ Cuiabá, in the north; Campo Grande, in the south.

🛏 $$$ **Araras Eco Lodge,** Transpantaneira Hwy. (© **51/65/3682-2800;** www.araraslodge.com.br). $$$ **Refugio Caiman,** near Miranda (© **51/11/3706-1800;** www.caiman.com.br).

WHY THEY'LL THANK YOU: Seeing your 20th capybara—or a first jaguar.

15 On the Water

Snorkeling on the Great Barrier Reef.

Canoeing the Everglades
Paddling through a River of Grass
Ages 6 & up • Florida City or Everglades City, Florida, USA

The Everglades is a bizarre ecosystem, when you think about it: a drawling grassy river that's rarely more than knee-deep, but spreads some 40 miles wide, harboring an exotic population of manatees, hawksbill turtles, water moccasins, coral snakes, panthers, armadillos, muskrats, opossums, river otters, herons, egrets, the roseate spoonbill, and the big black anhinga bird. It's the only place in the world where alligators and crocodiles live side by side. There's nothing like it anywhere else—and it might not be here much longer, given the encroaching development in southern Florida. Bring the kids here now, to dip a paddle into this River of Grass while it still flows.

While you can stick to dry land—driving or biking on the paved park roads, or walking short nature trails through junglelike patches of forest—the whole point of this place is that it *isn't* dry land. What you really want is to feel the sway and lap of the park's waters, the lazy grace of its fluid meander through mangroves and cypresses and sawgrass prairies. Rent canoes at the **Gulf Coast visitor center** on Hwy. 29 in Everglades City or the **Flamingo Lodge** by the Flamingo visitor center at the end of Hwy. 9336 at the southern tip of the park. In a canoe you'll be incredibly close to the water level, casually coexisting with gators and birds as if you're part of their natural environment. That just won't happen on those powered airboats that offer Everglades tours just outside park boundaries. (They aren't allowed in the park proper.)

Everglades National Park's longest "trails" are designed for canoe travel, and many are marked as clearly as walking trails. From the Gulf Coast, you can canoe 2 miles across **Chokoloskee Bay** to a mangrove island, or follow the **Turner River** 8 miles from freshwater cypress forest into saltwater mangrove swamp. From Flamingo, the **Noble Hammock Canoe Trail** is an easy 2-mile loop; the **Hell's Bay Canoe Trail** is 3 to 6 miles, depending on how far you venture. A guided canoe tour is a great idea, not only to find your way but to benefit from the guide's familiarity with the flora and fauna; contact **Everglades National Park Boat Tours** (© 239/695-2591) at the Parks Docks on Chokoloskee Causeway (Hwy. 29) in Everglades City, or **North American Canoe Tours** at the Ivey House (see below).

ⓘ **Ernest F. Coe Visitor Center,** Hwy. 9336, west of Florida City (© **305/242-7700;** www.nps.gov/ever).

✈ Miami International, 40 miles.

🛏 $$ **Best Western Gateway to the Keys,** 411 S. Krome Ave. (U.S. 1), Florida City (© **305/246-5100;** www.best western.com). $$ **Ivey House B&B,** 107 Camellia St., Everglades City (© **239/695-3299;** www.iveyhouse.com).

BEST TIME: Dry season (winter or spring).

WHY THEY'LL THANK YOU: Gliding through the glassy, grassy silence.

An Everglades frog.

Way Down upon the Swanee River
Paddling the Okefenokee Swamp
Ages 6 & up • Southeast Georgia, USA

To start with, it's got a great singsong name—Oh-kee-fee-noh-kee, like something out of a Creedence Clearwater song or a Scooby-Doo cartoon—which means, in the Creek Indian language, "land of the trembling earth." To call this huge freshwater wetlands in southeastern Georgia a swamp is too simplistic: It's a fascinating mixed terrain of wet prairies, peat marsh, pine uplands, hardwood hammocks, small lakes and "gator holes," and floating islands, covering 650 square miles of wilderness. Paddling through its faintly creepy backwaters is an experience the kids will never forget.

There are a few developed park areas around the edges, but no roads traverse the wilderness itself—for that you'll have to get into a canoe (rentals, as well as maps, are available at all the visitor centers) and strike out on marked canoe trails over the tea-colored water. **Okefenokee Swamp Park,** GA 177, Waycross (© **912/283-0583**), on the northern edge of the preserve, is an easy place to start; there is an interpretive center, a boardwalk with observation tower, and a 1½-mile steam railroad tour included with admission. The swamp looks even thicker and more jungly at the western entrance at **Stephen C. Foster State Park,** GA 177, Fargo (© **912/637-5274**), an 80-acre island park named after the 19th-century songwriter who was born in nearby Fargo. The Suwanee River of which he wrote flows through the swamp here, carrying much of its runoff. There are 225 miles of mirror-like black waterways to paddle through, delving into a sprawling forest of black gum and cypress; listen in the silence for the rat-a-tat-tat of a red-billed woodpecker or the agile slither of an otter. The

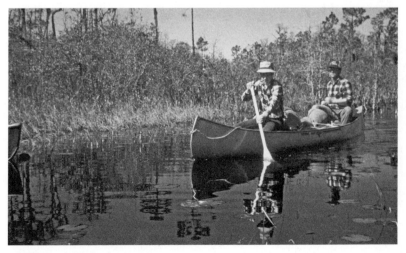

Paddling on the Okefenokee Swamp.

449

Suwanee Canal Recreation Area, GA Spur 121, Folkston (© **912/496-7156**), on the eastern fringe of the wilderness, has a good set of park amenities—visitor center exhibits, a boardwalk to an observation tower, an underwater Swamp Sub, interpretive nature trails, bike paths—and it's also the place to go for guided canoe expeditions (contact **Okefenokee Adventures,** © **866/ THE-SWAMP** [843-7926] or 912/496-7156; www.okefenokeeadventures.com). If you're really hardy and want to head out on your own, camping overnight deep in the wilderness, make **campsite reservations** 2 months in advance with the **U.S. Fish and Wildlife Service** (© **912/496-3331**). The paddling can be strenuous at times—you may have to climb out and push your canoe over peat buildups or shallow drafts—but then that's what being a backwoods explorer is all about.

ⓘ www.fws.gov/okefenokee.

✈ Jacksonville, FL, 50 miles.

🛏 $$ **Holiday Inn,** 1725 Memorial Dr., Waycross (© **888/465-4329** or 912/283-4490; www.holiday-inn.com). $ **Stephen C. Foster State Park rental cabins,** Rte. 1, Fargo (© **800/864-7275;** www.gastateparks.org).

WHY THEY'LL THANK YOU: Gliding under the cypress canopy.

Paddling Away **426**

Canoeing in the Adirondacks
Pristine Waters of a Northern Wilderness
Ages 6 & up • Saranac Lake, New York, USA

The 6 million acres of New York's Adirondack State Park enfold no fewer than 3,000 lakes and ponds, connected by 6,000 miles of rivers and streams. Nothing could be closer to a canoers' paradise. You can choose a route where you slip along quiet rivers onto forested lakes; the only sounds you may hear are birdcalls and the dip of your paddle as it slices through the glassy water. Even first-time canoers are quickly hooked.

Saranac Lake is a smart base for canoeing, not least because there are two excellent outfitters in town: **Adirondack Lakes and Trails Outfitters,** 168 Lake Flower Ave. (© **518/891-7450;** www.adirondackoutfitters.com), and **St. Regis Canoe Outfitters,** 73 Dorsey St. (© **888/ 775-2925** or 518/891-1838; www.canoe-outfitters.com). You can rent canoes (or kayaks), paddles, life jackets, and camping gear; they'll also give you detailed maps and advice, or even provide a guide or a van to transport you.

Children too young to paddle can enjoy gliding along in the belly of a canoe, watching the shore slide past. Pull up to the water's edge whenever the mood strikes for a picnic, a nature hike, a swim, or an overnight stay (free campsites are plentiful along most of these routes). You may want to set out on the **Saranac lakes,** where several half- or full-day paddles are possible; a great starter trip for young children combines an easy 2-hour canoe excursion with a ride on the **Adirondack Scenic Railroad** (© **800/819-2291** or 518/891-3238; www.adirondackrr.com), which runs between Lake Placid and Saranac Lake. Drive east on Rte. 3 to the Tupper Lake area, where there's a good continuous route along the **Raquette River,** with only one 1-mile portage. **Little Tupper Lake,** off Rte. 30 between the towns of Tupper Lake and Long Lake, is the area's largest motor-free lake.

The classic Adirondacks canoeing experience, however, is the Seven Carries

Route through the gorgeous **St. Regis Canoe Wilderness** north of Saranac Lake. It's rare to find such an extensive stretch of water reserved solely for nonmotorized boats. As the name suggests, there are seven portages along this route, as you visit all three of the St. Regis lakes and several secluded ponds. With so many miles of canoeing waters, you could easily spend 3 or 4 days up here, camping onshore every night. Closed in by woods on every side, it's possible to imagine yourselves back into the ages when Native Americans in their silent canoes were the only inhabitants of this wilderness.

ⓘ **Adirondack Park Visitor Center,** 8023 S.R. 30, Paul Smith, NY (ⓒ **518/327-3000;** www.adkvic.org). Also www.visit adirondacks.com and www.adirondack lakes.com.

✈ Saranac Lake.

🛏 $$ **Hotel Saranac,** 101 Main St., Saranac Lake (ⓒ **800/937-0211** or 518/891-2200; www.hotelsaranac.com). $ **Saranac Lake Islands campsites** (ⓒ **800/456-2267** or 518/891-3170; www. newyorkstateparks.reserveamerica.com).

WHY THEY'LL THANK YOU: Pristine waters and peaceful wilderness.

---

427 Paddling Away

Sea Kayaking in Acadia National Park
The Maine Way to Enjoy the Coast
Ages 8 & up • Mount Desert Island, Maine, USA

Maine's Mount Desert Island is home to spectacular Acadia National Park, a rich glacier-carved mound of rugged cliffs, restless ocean, and quiet woods. Mount Desert (pronounced des-*sert*) is surrounded by small bays and coast-hugging islands and nearly knifed in half by narrow, 7-mile-long Somes Sound, the only true fjord in the continental United States. Most visitors crowd onto 20-mile **Park Loop Road,** a spectacular drive that starts near the **Hulls Cove Visitor Center** and follows the rocky coast past picturesque coves, looping back inland along **Jordan Pond** and **Eagle Lake** with a detour to **Cadillac Mountain**—a sort of greatest-hits tour of the island. But why spend your time poking along in traffic, staring out at the ocean, when you could be skimming along the water's surface, skirting the coast and exploring the coves in your own light and agile sea kayak?

Frenchman's Bay, where the island's main town, **Bar Harbor,** sits, is a great place for youngsters to learn how to kayak, sitting in the front seat of a flat, stable two-person kayak with a parent paddling in back. Head south from the bay and you'll reach Atlantic waters, where popular park sights include **Thunder Hole,** a shallow cavern where the surf surges boisterously in and out, and **Otter Cliffs,** a set of 100-foot-high granite precipices capped with dense spruce that plummet down into roiling seas. From your kayak you can also enjoy open views of waterside villages and the great shingled "cottages" of the wealthy elite—Carnegies, Rockefellers, Astors, Vanderbilts—who summered here in the island's late-19th-century heyday as a resort.

Outfitters offer a variety of options, from a 2½-hour harbor tour to a 7-hour excursion. **Coastal Kayaking Tours,** 48 Cottage St., Bar Harbor (ⓒ **800/526-8615** or 207/288-9605; www.acadiafun.com), has a 4-hour outing tailored for families with children as young as 8. Experienced kayakers can set out on their own with

Kayaking in Acadia National Park.

rentals from **Loon Bay Kayaks,** Barcadia Campground, junction of routes 3 and 102 (© **888/786-0676** or 207/677-2963), or **Aquaterra Adventures,** 1 West St., Bar Harbor (© **877/386-4124** or 207/288-0007; www.aquaterra-adventures.com).

Frenchman's Bay is populated by seals, osprey, and other wildlife; in early fall, huge flocks of eider ducks can sometimes be seen floating just off the Atlantic shore. Summer boasts even more spectacular wildlife: humpback, finback, minke, and (occasionally) right whales, which migrate to cool summer waters offshore to feast on krill and plankton. For a closer look you can take an excursion with the **Bar Harbor Whale Watch Company,** 1 West St., Bar Harbor

(© **888/533-WALE** [533-9253] or 207/288-9800; www.barharborwhales.com).

ⓘ **Hulls Cove Visitor Center,** Rte. 3 (© **207/288-3338;** www.nps.gov/acad).

✈ Trenton, just across the causeway from Mount Desert Island.

🛏 $ **Bar Harbor Campground,** 409 State Hwy. 3, Salisbury Cove (© **207/288-5185**). $$$ **Harborside Hotel & Marina,** 55 West St., Bar Harbor (© **800/328-5033** or 207/288-5033; www.theharborside hotel.com).

WHY THEY'LL THANK YOU: Skimming over steel-blue seas, swift as an osprey.

Apostle Island National Park
Seeing the Great Lakes by Kayak
Ages 8 & up • Bayfield, Wisconsin, USA

The old French explorers, the original voyageurs who paddled across North America in the 1600s seeking fur-trapping riches, probably would have used sea kayaks instead of canoes if they'd only known. A closed cockpit boat like a kayak is exactly what you want in order to venture onto the cold, often rough waters of Lake Superior, the largest freshwater lake in the world. Come here in the summertime and the waters aren't quite so cold, though the waves are still unpredictable. But you're snug in your kayak and you can ride it out just fine.

Right off the northernmost tip of Wisconsin lies a scatter of 22 forested islands—on the map it almost looks as if the Bayfield Peninsula had sneezed them out into Lake Superior—and boaters have long found island-hopping in these frigid (but relatively shallow) waters an irresistible temptation. The Apostle Islands

National Park headquarters lies on the tip of the Bayfield peninsula, but that's merely an anchor point—most of the park is accessible only by boat. Let the kids look at a map and choose day-trip destinations within easy kayaking distance—historic island lighthouses, shipwreck sites, abandoned brownstone quarries, a ruined one-room schoolhouse, inviting sand beaches. Red sandstone cliffs line the otherwise woodsy shore, with sea caves in their bases that only kayaks can explore.

Local outfitters offer rentals, kayaking instruction (usually in protected bays or inland lakes rather than Superior itself), and guided excursions, both day trips and overnights—unless you're already experienced kayakers, having a guide is a huge plus, allowing you to paddle directly to the most interesting sights. (The sea caves in particular can be treacherous to visit if you don't know the waters well.) Outfitters include

Apostle Island National Park.

Living Adventure (☎ **866/779-9503** or 715/779-9503; www.livingadventure.com), **Trek and Trail** (☎ **800/354-8735;** www.trek-trail.com), and **Whitecap Kayak Excursions** (☎ **906/364-7336;** www.whitecapkayak.com).

If your kayaking skills aren't enough to get you out onto the islands, never fear—you can always go there on narrated trips run by **Apostle Islands Cruise Service** (☎ **800/323-7619** or 715/779-3925; www.apostleisland.com), departing from the Bayfield city docks.

ⓘ **Park Visitor Center,** 415 Washington Ave., Bayfield (☎ **715/779-3397;** www.nps.gov/apis).

✈ Hayward, WI, 75 miles. Bessemer, MI, 75 miles.

🛏 $$ **Bayfield Inn,** 20 Rittenhouse Ave. (☎ **715/779-3363;** www.bayfieldinn.com). $$ **Winfield Inn,** 225 E. Lynde Ave. (☎ 715/779-3252; www.winfieldinn.com).

BEST TIME: May–Sept.

WHY THEY'LL THANK YOU: Feeling like a voyager.

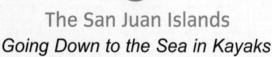

Paddling Away **429**

The San Juan Islands
Going Down to the Sea in Kayaks
Ages 6 & up • Puget Sound, Washington, USA

If you were trying to invent the perfect seascape for kayaking, you couldn't outdo the San Juan Islands. In the inland sea of Puget Sound, protected by mainland Washington State on one side and the Olympic peninsula on the other, lie hundreds of emerald islands, many of them designated wildlife refuges accessible only by private boats. Paddling around, you'll pass rocky islets where fat harbor seals nap, and reach isolated campsites no ferry passengers will ever use.

It seems odd to imagine the San Juans as ancient mountain peaks, submerged after the last Ice Age; the snowcapped Olympic mountains that loom across the Sound dwarf them nowadays. But because the Olympics cast what's called a "rain shadow" over the Sound, blocking the rainfall that soaks most of the Northwest, the San Juans are a rare mosaic of microclimates—rainforest, desert, patches of ferns and lichens, old-growth forests of cedar, hemlock, yew, and alder. The San Juans have the largest breeding population of bald eagles in the United States, and they're a magnet for

migrating wildlife—not only orcas and minke whales (whale-watching expeditions set out from all the main harbors June–Sept), but also trumpeter swans and snow geese and salmon. You're likely to spot dall porpoises, Steller sea lions, harbor seals, and brown river otters too, especially if you venture around in a kayak.

There are 175 islands in the San Juans that are big enough to be given names; another 600 or so smaller outcroppings punctuate the waters in between. Only four islands—San Juan, Orcas, Lopez, and Shaw—are served by Washington State Ferries, and only the first three have tourist accommodations; so make reservations before you arrive. To rent kayaks or join short guided paddles, in San Juan Island's main town, Friday Harbor, check out **San Juan Safaris** (☎ **800/450-6858** or 360/378-1323; www.sanjuansafaris.com) or **Outdoor Odysseys** (☎ **800/647-4621** or 360/378-3533; www.outdoorodysseys.com). Also in Friday Harbor, **Sea Quest Kayaks** (☎ **888/589-4253** or 360/378-5767; www.sea-quest-kayak.com/sanjuan.htm)

has three-person kayaks that are great if you've got younger children. **Shearwater Adventures** (© **360/376-4699;** www.shearwaterkayaks.com) operates from Orcas Island's ferry landing. On Lopez Island, **Lopez Island Sea Kayaks,** Fisherman Bay Road (© **360/468-2847;** www.lopezkayaks.com), offers a 2-hour sunset paddle that's great for families.

If the kids are up for multiday tours, try **Crystal Seas Kayaking** (© **877/732-7877** or 360/378-4223; www.crystalseas.com) or **San Juan Kayak Expeditions** (© **360/ 378-4436;** www.sanjuankayak.com).

ⓘ **Visitor Information,** 135 Spring St., Friday Harbour (© **888/468-3701** or 360/378-5240; www.travelsanjuans.com).

✈ San Juan, Orcas, and Lopez islands.

🛏 $$$ **Lakedale Resort,** 4313 Roche Harbor Rd., Friday Harbor (© **800/617-2267** or 360/378-2350; www.lakedale.com). $$ **Lopez Islander Resort,** 2864 Fisherman Bay Rd., Lopez Island (© **800/736-3434** or 360/468-2233; www.lopezislander.com).

WHY THEY'LL THANK YOU: Paddling alongside a porpoise or whale.

The Okavango Delta
A Mokoro Ride through the Floodwaters
Ages 8 & up • Okavango Delta, Botswana

Every winter—which in Botswana begins in July—the Okavango River flows south out of the uplands of Angola, its waters swollen to bursting by the rainy season. By the time it gets to this vast bowl in Botswana, it's overrun its banks, spreading out throughout the delta. Crystal-clear pools, channels, and lagoons spring up everywhere, playing host to a rich diversity of wildlife, which flock here in grateful escape from the adjacent Kalahari Desert.

Game lodges in the delta are classified as "wet" or "dry" according to whether or not they are surrounded by water during flood season, but it's not as if being surrounded is a problem—it just means you'll do all your traveling around by *mokoro*, a narrow canoelike boat propelled through the water by a human with a long pole. (Traditionally hollowed out of tree trunks, nowadays most of them are made from fiberglass.) These silent, shallow craft make it possible to get really close to birds and animals for wildlife viewing, and though they won't have the fun of poling it

themselves, the kids will still be drawn intimately into the mysteries of life on the flood plain. As you glide along, the air is filled with the sounds of birds calling, frogs trilling, and antelopes rustling in the reeds. Wildebeest, hartebeest, buffalo, and zebra roam the islands before you; elephants wade across channels guarded by hippos and crocs.

Game camps in the Okavango are generally tented affairs—operators are required to make no permanent marks on the land—but some of these are quite luxurious tents indeed. Most of the camps are set within the **Moremi Game Reserve,** in the northeastern segment of the delta. Families with children are accepted, but generally required to book their own separate vehicle for game viewing, which works out just fine—that way the safari experience can be run at a softer pace.

Given the complexities of travel within Botswana, it's best to book your lodgings as part of a package trip through a safari specialist company (see below). All of these trips are pricey, but they're once-in-a-lifetime special.

 Maun.

TOUR: Abercrombie & Kent (© **800/554-7016;** www.abercrombiekent.com). **Wilderness Safaris** (© **27/11/895-0862;** www.wilderness-safaris.com). **Okavango Tours & Safaris** (© **44/20/8343-3283;** www.okavango.com).

BEST TIME: July–Sept.

WHY THEY'LL THANK YOU: Sharing the river with the hippos.

Paddling Away **431**

Phang Nga Bay
Thailand's Secret Caverns
Ages 8 & up • Phuket, Thailand

James Bond fans in your group may recognize this stunning setting from *The Man with the Golden Gun,* which was filmed on this gorgeous bay north of the well-developed Thai resort island of Phuket. Limestone karst towers jut precariously from the water's glassy turquoise surface, creating more than 120 small islands that look like something out of a Chinese scroll painting. Kids, of course, are notorious for not appreciating beautiful scenery; what they will appreciate is the unique way you get to explore this craggy seascape—lying down in small canoes to slip inside secret caves. It lives up to every pirate fantasy they've ever had, and then some.

An arm of the Andaman Sea, its warm waters edged with white beaches, red mud banks, and tropical stands of mangrove trees, **Phang Nga Bay** is a national park 1½ hours' drive north of Phuket Town. Two-passenger kayaks, with an experienced paddle guide at the helm, dart around the bay's distinctive craggy island rocks; you'll be told to lie flat in the boat to slip through tight cave openings. Once inside, magnificent chambers open up above the internal lagoons (called *hongs,* which is Thai for "rooms"), where it's believed pirates once hid their operations—or, if you're James Bond, secret agents hid their evil devices.

Touristy as it is, it's something you've got to do, especially with kids. The **day-long tours** include transport to and from Phuket Town, a cruise to the part of the bay where the islands cluster, a paddle guide, a bright-yellow inflatable kayak, and lunch. Once you've finished the tricky maneuvering around the caves, the guide may even let you paddle a bit yourself. The

Kayaking in Thailand.

premier operator for these trips is **Sea Canoe** in Muang (✆ **66/76/528-839-40;** www.seacanoe.net).

Of course, if you want to do things the cushy way, you can just cruise around this lovely tropical bay on a restored Chinese sailing junk, the *Bahtra* (contact **Phuket Travel;** ✆ **66/81/737-0860;** www.phuket-travel.com). You won't get inside those caves, but you'll still feel plenty pirate-y.

✈ Phuket International.

🛏 $$$ **Dusit Laguna Resort,** 390 Srisoontorn Rd., Cherngtalay District (✆ **66/76/36-2999;** www.dusit.com). $$ **Karon Beach Resort,** 51 Karon Rd., Tambon Daron (✆ **66/76/330-0067;** www.katagroup.com/karonbeach).

WHY THEY'LL THANK YOU: Hoping to find pirate treasure.

---

432 Paddling Away

Torres del Paine
Kayaking on Glacial Lakes
Ages 10 & up • Puerto Natales, Chile

Ready for adventure? Then come to Patagonia, the extreme end of South America, where Chile and Argentina run side by side down the narrowing tip of the continent as if they're racing each other to the Cape of Good Hope. The most dramatic bit is Chile's Torres del Paine, a set of granite peaks and towers that soars from sea level to upward of 2,800m (9,186 ft.), but it doesn't stop there—surrounding the Paine Massif are vast glaciers and startling blue lakes (*paine* is the Tehuelche Indian word for "blue"), their waters turned milky turquoise by glacial melt. It's quite a challenge to get here—and to get around once you've arrived—but your reward will be mesmerizing glacier close-ups and an exhilarating end-of-the-earth feeling.

From Puerto Natales, the frontierlike gateway town to Torres del Paine, several boat tours head out to the glaciers, located in **Parque Nacional Bernardo O'Higgins,** but your goal is to do it yourself on sea kayaks. **Bigfoot Expeditions** (✆ **56/61/414-525;** www.bigfootpatagonia.com), the main adventure-tour packager in Punta Arenas, leads kayak day trips onto the glacial fjord Ultima Esperanza; if the weather's right you'll get a view of the Paine Massif.

Thrilling as it sounds, this is actually an easy paddle in cold but glassy protected waters. A 2-day version of this trip starts by riding the cutter *21 de Mayo* to Lake Serrano, then kayaking around Ultima Esperanza and camping overnight near Balmaceda Glacier; your second day is spent paddling

Torres del Paine.

around protruding icebergs in Lake Serrano, then returning on the *21 de Mayo* back to Puerto Natales. Just be sure the kids dress warmly, because there's a distinct deep-freeze element to this experience, even if you come in Chile's version of summer (Jan or Feb). Winters (July–Aug) can be cold but may be a better time to visit because the punishing Patagonian winds die down then.

If the view of Torres del Paine from the fjord wasn't enough, you can book a cruise on an open Zodiac boat past the glaciers Tyndall and Geike to the Torres del Paine entrance and on up the gnarly Rio Serrano to the narrow Serrano Glacier; disembark to walk upon the ice before boarding another boat for a 3½-hour ride back to Puerto Natales. **Aventour** (© **56/61/241-197;** www.aventourpatagonia.com) and **Onas** (© **56/61/614-300;** www.onaspatagonia. com) both offer this full-day expedition.

ⓘ www.torresdelpaine.com.

✈ Puerto Natales.

🛏 $$ **Hosteria Las Torres,** Torres del Paine National Park (© **888/695-2603** or 56/61/363-636; www.lastorres.com). $$$ **Hotel CostAustralis,** Pedro Montt 262, Puerto Natales (© **56/61/412-000;** www. hoteles-australis.com).

WHY THEY'LL THANK YOU: The ultimate kayaking adventure.

Paddling Away **433**

Nova Scotia
Riding the Tidal Bore
Ages 4 & up • Maitland, Nova Scotia, Canada

In the middle of the ocean, tides are no big deal—it's only when they get close to shore that you notice a difference in water levels. But when you funnel that rising water into a V-shaped bay that keeps getting narrower *and* shallower until it gets squeezed into the mouth of a river and hits the outflowing current—well, that's your recipe for an honest-to-goodness tidal bore. You can't see this natural phenomenon many places in the world, but you sure can see it up in Nova Scotia, on the eastern arm of the Bay of Fundy. And when that surge of tidal water comes rushing up the Shubenacadie River, you and the kids want to be there, to ride it like a bucking bronco.

The top outfitter is **Shubenacadie River Runners,** who have the routine down to a science. Aboard 4.8m (16-ft.) Zodiac boats, fitted with powerful outboard motors, you'll lie in wait at the mouth of the Shubenacadie, admiring the forested cliffs on either side, waiting for the precisely timed tide to arrive. As soon as the first wave swells beneath the boat— it can lift anywhere from .3 to 3.3m (1–11 ft.), depending on water conditions—the boat is whisked on the powerful surge of the tidal bore upstream for half a mile or so, as the water keeps rising and rising. Then, as the tidal bore begins to dissipate, the boat slips off of its ride for a moment. Look up in the sky and you may spot bald eagles hovering overhead, scrutinizing the goings-on. The next part of the adventure consists of chasing a series of natural sand rapids, which develop in the river only at high tide—the convoluted pattern of sandbars, which normally lie above the water's surface, create rapids when they are submerged, but they don't last for long; you've got to time things just right.

The tidal bore hits the river at different times daily—consult River Runners' tides chart to find the right time for the dates

A typical Nova Scotia view.

educational experience for children, a virtual seminar in physical science and marine biology and all that. Sure. An educational experience, and *not fun at all*. Right.

ⓘ **Shubenacadie River Runners,** 8681 Hwy. 215 (✆ **800/856-5061** or 902/261-2770; www.tidalborerafting.com).

✈ Halifax, 177km (110 miles).

🛏 $$$ **Bellavista Bed & Breakfast,** 8029 Hwy. 215 (✆ **866/506-1414** or 902/261-2626; www.bbcanada.com/samcon). $$ **Cresthaven by the Sea,** 19 Ferry Lane (✆ **866/870-2001** or 902/261-2001; www.cresthavenbythesea.com).

BEST TIME: May–Sept.

WHY THEY'LL THANK YOU: Riding nature's roller coaster.

you're looking at. You can also choose dates when the ride is expected to be wilder or tamer, according to tide conditions. Like I said, they've got it down to a science. And of course, this can be an

---

434 Paddling Away

The Delaware Water Gap
Tubing the Lazy River
Ages 6 & up • Bushkill, Pennsylvania, USA

Some people prefer their rivers lazy, and I have to confess I'm one of them. The idea of floating downstream on a slow-moving current, with the water sparkling and the sun shining, suits me just fine. Tubing down the Delaware River? That's my idea of a laid-back summer's afternoon, and a great no-hassle way to bond with my kids.

When you see the dramatic vista of the Delaware Water Gap you might expect some white-water action. But what you'll find is a relatively shallow stretch of river with just a few riffles and quiet pools parting for tiny scrubby islands and drinking in tributaries along the way. The Delaware can take its time, because it's the last undammed big river in the East, though just barely—much of the land upstream from the Gap was once cleared for a planned hydroelectric project, which accounts for the absence of houses for 40

miles of riverbank in the Delaware Water Gap National Recreation Area. The government had to do something with the land it had already appropriated—and turning it into a park was the perfect solution.

Access points have been created along the river every 4 to 10 miles, which makes it ideal for short canoeing and kayaking trips; for inner tubes, which travel even slower, a trip of 4 miles or so is ideal (considering that the river only flows around 1½ mph). Local outfitters include **Pack Shack Adventure,** 88 Broad St., Delaware Water Gap (✆ 570/424-8533; www.packshack.com), and **Chamberlain Canoes,** River Road, Minisink Acres Mall, Minisink Hills (✆ 800/422-6631; www.chamberlaincanoes.com). They'll not only provide river maps and rent you stout inner tubes (with safety handles and two air chambers, so you can still float if one is punctured), but even rent you a cargo tube to carry a cooler and towels, so you can stop off at an island or river beach for a picnic en route. Wear aqua shoes or old sneakers so you can hop out easily. They'll drive you to your access point and pick you up afterward—all you have to do is slather on the sun block and hit the water.

As you drift along, you'll have time to gaze at the forested ridges on either side, to see map turtles basking on rocks in the sun, to eyeball the bald eagles soaring overhead. A canoe or kayak may glide past you, but no jet skis will disrupt your idyll. Little sisters can keep up with their big brothers, because you can't go any faster than the river, and the river's in no hurry. Chill out.

ⓘ **Park Headquarters,** River Rd., just north of Shawnee-on-Delaware (ⓒ **570/ 426-2452;** www.nps.gov/dewa).

✈ Lehigh Valley International, Allentown, PA, 65 miles. Newark International, Newark, NJ, 70 miles.

🛏 $ **Delaware River Family Campground,** 100 Rte. 46, Delaware, NJ (ⓒ **800/ 543-0271** or 908/475-4517; www.nj camping.com/delaware). $$ **Shannon Inn,** exit 309 from I-80, E. Stroudsburg, PA (ⓒ **570/424-1951;** www.shannoninn.com).

WHY THEY'LL THANK YOU: Gliding through the Gap.

Guadalupe River
Tubing, Texas-Style
Ages 6 & up • Spring Branch, Texas, USA

Down here in the Texas Hill Country they call it "toobing," and it's a little livelier than those gentle floats on the Delaware Water Gap (433). Hill Country Texas defies most outsiders' expectations of Texas—it's hilly, green countryside between San Antonio and Austin, where the local heritage is more German than Hispanic. The Guadalupe winds a looping southeasterly course through the hills down to the Gulf, and all those loops—not to mention patches of just-gnarly-enough rapids— make the tubing plenty interesting.

The Guadalupe River is well-known as a tubing spot, but what most people think of when they picture Guadalupe River tubing is the 18-mile stretch south of the Canyon Dam, near New Braunfels, Texas. New Braunfels' River Road is lined with watersports outfitters, and on a hot summer weekend afternoon the Guadalupe becomes like one big crowded frat party,

where the tubes ride as close as bumper boats. You might as well be tubing at the New Braunfels water park, **Schlitterbahn,** 400 N. Liberty Ave. (ⓒ **830/625- 2351;** www.schlitterbahn.com), which claims to be the largest water park in the world, and I don't doubt it. Hey, we *like* water parks, but tubing on a natural river should be another thing altogether.

For families, the scene is a little calmer up above Canyon Lake, around **Guadalupe River State Park.** Along here the river is lined picturesquely with bald cypress trees, their huge roots exposed at the banks, as well as a couple of steep limestone bluffs. The kids are likely to spot deer, opossum, and armadillo browsing around the woods, and four natural rapids make intriguing hiccups in the river, all of them relatively gentle. There are no tube rentals at the park, but you can get fitted out nearby at **Big Foot**

Canoes, on the Weidner cattle ranch, FM 311, Spring Branch (℗ **830/885-7106;** www.bigfootcanoes.com); the **Bergheim Campground,** 103 White Water Rd., Boerne (℗ **830/336-2235;** www.bergheim campground.com); or **Rio Raft,** Canyon Lake (℗ **877/RIO-RAFT** [746-7238] or 830/964-3613; www.rioraft.com), all of which can arrange to drive you to your starting point and pick you up again wherever you choose to come off the river. Four miles or so should be just enough to splash off the summer heat.

ⓘ **Guadalupe River State Park,** 3350 Park Rd. 31 (℗ **830/438-2656;** www.tpwd. state.tx.us/park/guadalup).

✈ San Antonio International, 25–30 miles.

🛏 $$ **Crockett Hotel,** 320 Bonham St., San Antonio (℗ **800/292-1050** or 210/225-6500; www.crocketthotel.com). $$$ **Ye Kendall Inn,** 128 W. Blanco, Boerne (℗ **800/364-2138** or 830/249-2138; www. yekendallinn.com).

WHY THEY'LL THANK YOU: It's totally toobular.

---

436 | Paddling Away

The Snake River
White Water from Hell (Canyon)
Ages 8 & up • Enterprise, Oregon, USA

When the kids have to deliver the standard what-I-did-on-my-summer-vacation school report in September, there's an enormous coolness factor in saying, "I white-water rafted on the Snake River." It works even if all your family did was take a mild float trip along the Snake up in Grand Teton National Park. But now add this phrase: "I white-water rafted on the Snake River *through Hell's Canyon.*" Now they *own* that homeroom.

Hell's Canyon is the deepest gorge in North America, a full mile and a half deep, and it's gorgeous to boot. It curls along the border between Idaho and Oregon, as the river builds up a head of steam to pour into the Columbia River in Washington State. (One look at a map and the kids will agree they couldn't call this loopy river anything *but* the Snake.) The standard 3-day rafting trip through this steep-walled forested canyon covers about 36 miles, but it's not rapids all the way, not by any means—there are plenty of placid sections where rafters can relax and enjoy stunning views of the Seven Devils Mountains (another dynamite name) and the

Summit Ridge. Technically, in fact, it can be classified as an easy run. What makes this white water so awesome is not the wildness of the waters, but how long the rapids go on, shooting through this relatively straight stretch of the river. And while they might be scary to those paddling a kayak (which may be an option for the daredevils in your party), if you're seated in a large inflatable raft it'll be a manageable thrill. Of course you'll get splashed and soaked, but that's part of the whole whitewater experience.

When you're not rafting, there's plenty more to do along this stretch of the Snake River. Short hikes lead you away from the river to view Native American pictographs on canyon walls, or to find the abandoned cabins of early-1900s settlers. There are chances to try trout fishing, and also to swim in the surprisingly warm waters. Wildlife viewings may include bighorn sheep, elk, and eagles.

Outfitters (see below) will handle all the details—supplying equipment, guiding the rafts, directing activities, setting up a very comfortable camp each night, and shuttling you to the starting point and from the ending point.

(i) **Hell's Canyon National Recreation Area,** 88401 Hwy. 82 (© **541/426-5546;** www.fs.fed.us/hellscanyon).

✈ Lewiston, ID, 125 miles.

TOUR: Northwest Voyageurs (© **800/ 727-9977;** www.voyageurs.com). **O.A.R.S.** (© **800/346-7277;** www.oars.com). **Zoller's Outdoor Odysseys** (© **800/366-2004** or 509/493-2641; www.snakeraft.com).

WHY THEY'LL THANK YOU: Thrills, but hopefully no spills.

Swimming **437**

Swimming with a Million Tiny Lights

Ages 4 & up • Vieques, Puerto Rico

I thought Puerto Rico was an island—but how can an island have an island? Well, Puerto Rico has two, Vieques and Culebra, for years a well-kept secret among Puerto Ricans themselves, who come here to escape the tourists on the big island. Since the U.S. Navy, in 2003, closed its installation on Vieques, though, much more land is available for vacationers, and Vieques is rapidly becoming known as an ecofriendly—and still charmingly scruffy—destination.

With some 40 palm-lined white-sand beaches, and reefs of snorkel-worthy antler coral off shore, Vieques—11km (6³⁄₄ miles) off the big island's east coast, only an hour by ferry—has an obvious appeal for sun-loving families. But one of the coolest things on Vieques has nothing at all to do with the sun. Just west of the main town, Isabel Segunda, lies **Mosquito Bay,** which has been renamed Phosphorescent Bay for the way its waters glow in the dark,

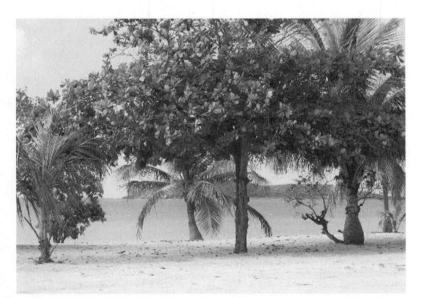

A palm-lined white sand beach in Vieques.

thanks to millions of tiny bioluminescent organisms called pyrodiniums (translation from science-speak: "whirling fire"). They're only about one-five-hundredth of an inch in size, but when these tiny swimming creatures are disturbed (by, for example, a hovering tour boat), they dart away and light up like fireflies, leaving eerie blue-white trails of phosphorescence. These pyrodiniums exist elsewhere, but not in such amazing concentrations: A gallon of water in Mosquito Bay may contain upward of three-quarters of a million such creatures. It's definitely worth letting the kids stay up late for once. Wear a bathing suit because it's possible to swim in these glowing waters, a sensation the kids will find incredibly eerie and cool.

Don't make the mistake of coming here on a full moon, however—the glow of the pyrodiniums is only discernible on a cloudy, moonless night. (***Warning:*** Some tour boats go out to the bay regardless of the full moon—and you won't get your money back if you're disappointed.)

Island Adventures (© **787/741-0720;** www.biobay.com) operates 2-hour nighttime trips in Phosphorescent Bay aboard the *Luminosa,* though not during the full moon. If the kids are into kayaking, they can get even closer to those glow-in-the-dark waters on a kayak tour offered by **Blue Caribe Kayak** (© **787/741-2522;** www.enchanted-isle.com/bluecaribe). In fact, Blue Caribe acts as a clearinghouse for all the island's watersports outfitters—it's a small island, and virtually everybody is related to everyone else. That small-town casualness is one of the things that still makes Vieques a great place for traveling families, hot spot or not.

ⓘ www.enchanted-isle.com.

FERRY: Isabel Segunda (1¼ hr. from Fajardo, P.R.)

🛏 $$ **The Crow's Nest,** Rte. 201, Barrio Florida (© **877/CROWS-NEST** [276-9763] or 787/741-0033; www.crowsnestvieques.com). $$ **Trade Winds Guesthouse,** Calle Flamboyan 107, Esperanza (© **787/741-8666;** www.enchanted-isle.com/tradewinds).

WHY THEY'LL THANK YOU: Nature's night light.

438 Swimming

Blue Lagoon
Iceland's Tropical Oasis
All ages • Iceland

Okay, so maybe it is one of the most touristy things to do when you're visiting Iceland. But the bathers who frolic in this warm-water lagoon 40 minutes outside of Reykjavik include just as many locals as tourists—everybody wants to enjoy this great outdoor bathtub. Even when the countryside is covered in snow, steam rises from this huge pool of turquoise-colored water, and the very idea that you could have such a balmy swim in a place called Iceland will be irresistible to the kids.

Several local tour operators run half-day excursions from Reykjavik to the Blue Lagoon geothermal spa; in fact, it's so close to Keflavik airport that some travelers stop by for one last iconic Icelandic experience before boarding their flight home.

The entrance fee isn't cheap (though kids do get in for half-price), but you can easily spend a couple of hours in this large pool sunk into a lava field, fringed by black-sand beaches and tumbled chunks of volcanic rock. It's not, in fact, a natural

Steam rises from the Blue Lagoon.

phenomenon but a by-product of the nearby power plant, where hot seawater is used to heat spring water, which in turn produces central heating for the houses in Reykjavik. The excess seawater is then pumped into this lagoon, for bathers to enjoy the curative powers of its salts and minerals (which do occur completely naturally). An ell of New Age-y modern buildings anchors one corner, where services such as a sauna and steam bath are offered; the sapphire lake snakes away from the building, dotted with a few scattered black rocky outcrops and topped by wispy trails of steam.

Stepping into the lagoon, you'll notice how smooth its sides are—the result of high silica content in the water—and your toes will sink into thin soft sediment on the bottom, full of blue-green algae that gives the lagoon its distinctive color (as one recent visitor describes it, the exact color of Riptide Rush Gatorade). The water maintains a temperature of about 104°F (40°C), though as you swim about you'll find all sorts of vents and heat currents that make certain areas warmer than others. And as we all know, there's nothing a kid likes better than hovering by the place where hot water rushes into a heated swimming pool—well, the Blue Lagoon has dozens of such gushers to seek out.

Adults may want to spend extra on treatments such as a facial mask made of silica mud, but for the kids, just paddling around in this immense jewel-colored hot tub will be enough. Just another weird, one-of-a-kind thing about Iceland.

ⓘ 240 Grindavik (✆ **354/420-8800;** www.bluelagoon.com).

✈ Keflavik International, 20km (12½ miles).

🛏 $$ **Hotel Bjork,** Brautarholt 22–24, Reykjavík (✆ **354/511-3777;** www.bjork hotelreykjavik.com). $$ **Hotel Vik,** Síðumúla 19, Reykjavík (✆ **354/588-5588;** www.hotelvik.is).

WHY THEY'LL THANK YOU: The mist rising off the waters.

Floating in the Dead Sea

All ages • Israel

The sensation of floating in the Dead Sea is so freaky, you keep testing it again and again—releasing your body into that incredibly saline water and popping up to the surface, as buoyant as if you were weightless. It works every time, even for a novice swimmer. Such a simple thing, and yet utterly absorbing. The kids are likely to break out in fits of giggles—and then try it again . . .

Less than an hour's drive from Jerusalem, this is *the* saltiest sea there is, by a long shot, and the richest in minerals (magnesium, calcium, bromine, potassium). Not only that, it's the lowest point on earth, a remarkable 417m (1,368 ft.) below sea level. Water flows into the Dead Sea from several sources, notably the Jordan River, but it doesn't flow out, it just evaporates—at a rate so fast, the sea is shrinking year by year, so the sooner you get here the better. The air contains 10% more oxygen than normal, so just breathing makes you feel relaxed and energized. It's hot (up to 108°F/42°C in summer) but dry, and thanks to an extra layer of atmosphere caused by evaporation, the sun's UV rays are filtered, making it a fairly safe place to sunbathe. And there's sunshine 330 days a year.

The name is a misnomer, because this inland lake isn't truly dead—granted, no fish live in this salt-saturated water, but a certain green algae does just fine, plus lots of red archaebacterium. The water looks slightly greenish, and also milky from all the minerals; at rocky coves along the shore you can see encrustations of salt from evaporation. And although the desert ridges around the sea look sand-scoured and fierce, along the lakeside highway you'll find a few lush oases, many of them with sulfur hot springs.

Two main beach areas thrive along the Israeli shore. The first is at the ancient desert oasis **Ein Gedi,** where you'll find a rather crowded public beach, a kibbutz with a good hotel and spa, and a botanic garden planted with rare trees and shrubs from all over the world. Even nonguests can pay a day-use fee to use the hotel's spa or beach, which may be the Dead Sea's best for swimming. At Ein Gedi kibbutz, you can book a desert jeep safari, a Bedouin feast in a tent, or an hourlong cruise on the Dead Sea in an eccentric wooden double-deck boat called *Lot's Wife.* Farther down the coast, you'll pass the ancient fortress of **Masada,** and then reach **Ein Bokek,** where there are several hotels and free public beaches. The water is richer in minerals down here, and therefore said to be more curative. We won't argue—not if it gives us a chance to try floating again . . .

Floating in the Dead Sea.

(i) **Ein Bokek Tourist Office** (✆ **972/8/997-5010;** www.deadsea.co.il).

✈ Jerusalem, 112km (70 miles).

🛏 $$$ **Golden Tulip Dead Sea,** Ein Bokek (✆ **972/8/668-9444;** www.goldentulipclubdeadsea.com). $$ **Ein Gedi Resort Hotel,** Ein Gedi (✆ **972/8/659-4222;** www.ngedi.com).

WHY THEY'LL THANK YOU: Doing the Dead Sea float.

The Great Barrier Reef
World's Biggest Marine Park
Ages 6 & up • Pacific Coast, Queensland, Australia

It's the only living structure on Earth visible from the moon; it's bigger than the United Kingdom; it's home to 1,500 kinds of fish, 400 species of corals, 4,000 kinds of clams and snails, and who knows how many sponges, starfish, and sea urchins. And snorkelers are in a prime position to see the Great Barrier Reef at its best—the rich colors of the coral depend on lots of light, so staying close to the surface maximizes your view of the brightest and richest marine life. Staring through your mask at green and purple clams, pink sponges, red starfish, purple sea urchins, and fish from electric blue to neon yellow to lime is truly a magical experience.

Even if the kids have never gone snorkeling before, there's no more rewarding place to start. Outfitters and resorts all

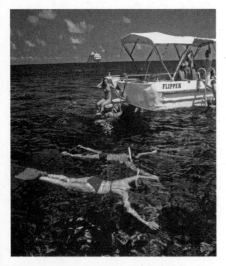

You may spot a ray or a reef shark while snorkeling on the Great Barrier Reef.

along the Reef coast make it easy for you. **Day trips** on motorized catamarans head out from Cairns, Port Douglas, Townsville, Mission Beach, and the Whitsunday mainland and islands, with snorkel gear provided and marine biologists on board to explain all about the Reef. Each boat ties up at its own private permanent pontoon, anchored to a platform reef. The pontoons have glass-bottom boats for passengers who don't want to get wet, but there's lots of instruction to ease novices into the water.

If a long boat ride puts you off, the coral cay of **Green Island** lies less than an hour from the city wharf at **Cairns,** the town with the most direct air connections. The closest Reef site off **Port Douglas,** an hour north of Cairns, is the **Low Isles,** two tiny lushly vegetated coral cays where you can wade out to the coral right from the beach. The coral is not quite as dazzling as the outer Reef's, but the fish life here is rich, there are lots of seabirds, and you may spot sea turtles. From the lovely rainforest town of **Mission Beach,** south of Cairns, it only takes an hour to get to the Outer Reef, where shallow waters full of vibrant marine life surround the sandy coral cay, **Beaver Cay.**

If you base yourselves in the **Whitsunday Islands,** of course, you're already out in the Outer Reef, on rainforested islands surrounded by the waters of the Great Barrier Reef Marine Park. Just about any Whitsunday island has fringing reef around its shores, and there are good snorkeling reefs between the islands, a quick boat ride away. Most folks' favorite is **Blue Pearl Bay,** off Hayman Island; it has loads of corals and some gorgonian fans in its gullies, and heaps of reef fish, including

Maori wrasse and sometimes even manta rays—and you can walk right in off the beach.

(i) **Cairns Tourist Information,** 51 The Esplanade (© **61/7/4051-3588;** www. tropicalaustralia.com). **Whitsundays Information Centre,** Bruce Hwy., Proserpine (© **800/801-252** in Australia, or 61/7/4945-3711; www.whitsundaytourism. com).

✈ Cairns.

🛏 $ **Mackays,** 7 Porter Promenade, Mission Beach (© **61/7/4068-7212;** www. mackaysmissionbeach.com). $$ **The Reef Retreat,** 10–14 Harpa St., Palm Cove, Cairns (© **61/7/4059-1744;** www.reef retreat.com.au).

WHY THEY'LL THANK YOU: Floating facedown in Technicolor wonder.

441 Snorkeling & Diving

Biscayne National Park
Florida's Homegrown Coral Reef
Ages 8 & up • Homestead, Florida, USA

Biscayne National Park is one of the least-crowded parks in America's national park system, probably because its main attractions are kinda difficult to reach. It's not a question of being remote—it's so close to Miami, you can do it as a day trip—but more about being hidden from view. Aboveground, you'll see only a no-big-deal strip of mangrove shoreline and 44 barrier islands, most of them mere specks off of South Florida's east coast. But beneath the surface lies the world's third-longest coral reef, an aquatic universe pulsing with multicolored life. All it takes is strapping on a snorkel and fins for kids to be able to cruise around this tropical paradise, encountering bright parrotfish and angelfish, gently rocking sea fans, and coral labyrinths.

The clear, warm waters of Biscayne National Park are packed with reef fish, rays, moray eels, jellyfish, anemones, sponges, even sea turtles and dolphins—some 512 species, all told, in this 173,000-acre expanse. Not only that, an **underwater trail** identifies five shipwrecks about 3 miles east of Elliott Key; mooring buoys point the way to the wrecks, with waterproof cards attached to

tell the kids what they're seeing. You can rent equipment at the full-service dive shop at the park's mainland entrance at Convoy Point, and if you don't have your own boat, you can take a 3-hour snorkeling or diving tour operated every afternoon by **Biscayne National Underwater Park, Inc.** (© **305/230-1100**); you'll either stick to the bay or head out to the reefs, depending on the very changeable weather. Even beginning snorkelers will get a satisfying eyeful.

The mainland entrance is 9 miles east of Homestead, off U.S. 1; a small beach and marina are nearby, but the rest of the park is accessible only by boat, either your own or the park concession's water transport (© **305/230-1100**). Few of the park's islands are even open to visitors; the two most popular are Elliott Key and Boca Chita Key, which can be reached by launch from the visitor center. Both islands have campsites (call the park ranger at © **305/230-1144** for information on permits and camping fees) and places to moor your boat; **Elliott Key** also has an interesting nature trail, and **Boca Chita,** once an exclusive haven for yachters, has some restored historic buildings.

Snorkeling in Biscayne National Park.

If you prefer not to dive, take the wimp's way out and view the underwater sights on a 3-hour **glass-bottom boat tour** offered by Biscayne National Underwater Park, Inc., departing from Convoy Point at 10am. Reservations are almost always necessary.

ⓘ **Dante Fascell Visitor Center,** at Convoy Point, 9700 SW 328th St. (✆ **305/230-7275;** www.nps.gov/bisc).

✈ Miami International, 40 miles.

🛏 $$ **Indian Creek Hotel,** 2727 Indian Creek Dr., Miami Beach (✆ **800/491-2772** or 305/531-2727; www.indiancreekhotel. com). $$$ **Ritz-Carlton Key Biscayne,** 455 Grand Dr. (✆ **305/365-4500;** www. ritzcarltonhotel.com).

WHY THEY'LL THANK YOU: Tropical colors and eerie shipwrecks.

Snorkeling & Diving 442

St. John
Snorkeling on the Trunk Bay Trail
Ages 6 & up • St. John, U.S. Virgin Islands, the Caribbean

The first place my kids ever put a mask and snorkel into the water was down here in the U.S. Virgin Islands, and I'm afraid it spoiled them for more ordinary snorkeling experiences. I still have photos of them standing on the white-sand beach at

Cinnamon Bay, along with the five kids of the other families we were traveling with, looking like an invasion party of aliens in their rented snorkeling gear—eight breathing tubes sticking up like antennae, eight pairs of flippers shifting impatiently in the sand, and their masks making them look like eight frowning Cyclopes. We deliberately took forever getting that shot, just because it made them so antsy. Enough photos already, they wanted to get out in that turquoise water and *start snorkeling.*

Their snorkeling debuts took place where so many others have started out: at Trunk Bay, where the National Park Service has set up the **National Park Underwater Trail.** This 225-yard trail follows a reef where all the underwater features are labeled with signs 5 to 15 feet under the water's surface. Snorkeling snobs wouldn't be caught dead at popular Trunk Bay doing the trail—they prefer more remote places like Watermelon Cay or Salt Pond Bay or Haulover Bay, where the snorkeling's a lot more challenging—but with children, Trunk Bay is just the thing. The signs help to focus young snorkelers' attention and keep them going, and it was extremely helpful for them to learn the difference between various coral structures, between a sea fan and an anemone. As for the bright parrotfish flitting by, well, no sign can be attached to something that elusive, but since the signs had made the kids more attentive snorkelers, they spotted the parrotfish all right. They were hoping for sea turtles—hawksbills and leatherbacks are common in these waters—but the turtles sensibly kept their distance. With kids, we were also grateful for Trunk Bay's other amenities—flush toilets, a snack bar, and lifeguards.

We also just plain fell in love with St. John—with two-thirds of it protected as Virgin Islands National Park, it's remarkably unspoiled, with lots of dense foliage and hiking trails and unruffled quiet, surrounded by expanses of clear, sparkling turquoise waters. It's what we'd always expected the Caribbean to be—and now that we had the kids hooked on snorkeling, our island-hopping days could begin.

ⓘ **Virgin Islands National Park,** Trunk Bay (*ⓒ* **340/776-6201;** www.nps.gov/viis).

✈ St. Thomas, 45–60 min. by boat.

🛏 $$ **Cinnamon Bay Campground,** Cruz Bay (*ⓒ* **340/776-6330;** www. cinnamonbay.com). $$$ **Westin St. John Resort,** Great Cruz Bay (*ⓒ* **888/627-7206** or 340/693-8000; www.westinresort stjohn.com).

WHY THEY'LL THANK YOU: Connecting the dots underwater.

St. John.

7 Super Beaches

A little laid-back beach time can be such a vacation-saver, an opportunity for the kids to run free, breathe deep, get messy, and burn off excess energy. But while we adults are often content just to acquire a tan and get lost in a paperback, kids need a little more activity at a beach, whether it be body-surfing, shell-gathering, tide-pool exploring, or burying each other in sand. You'll want a beach where the sand is clean, the surf gentle, the sea floor shallow and smooth; restrooms are another high priority, and if there are lots of other kids around to play with, so much the better. Here's a bevy of great family beaches from around the world.

443 Cape Hatteras National Seashore, Outer Banks, North Carolina North Carolina Highway 12 runs for 70 miles along this chain of four wind-scoured barrier islands—Bodie, Hatteras, Ocracoke, and Cedar Islands. Their tawny sands and dunes make it a great barefoot place for dabbling in the surf, though serious swimming and watersports require caution—throughout the Cape has been dubbed "the Graveyard of the Atlantic," for its treacherous offshore riptides and shifting shoals. **Historic lighthouses, nature trails, boogie-boarding spots,** and **fishing piers** help keep the kids entertained; summer evenings, rangers tell shipwreck and pirate stories by campfires under the stars. See Roanoke Island **245**, Kitty Hawk **285**. *www.nps.gov/caha.*

Shells on the beach of Sanibel Island.

444 Sanibel Island, Florida For young seashell hunters, there's no more rewarding spot than this charming key off Florida's west coast, on the Gulf of Mexico just south of Fort Myers. Sugary white sand, healthy stands of palm trees, low-rise beach development, and plenty of wildlife refuges are just the icing on the cake. Bring a big pail, because some **200 species of shells** lie scattered thickly on Sanibel's wide, placid beaches, especially at low tide. Just make sure the kids peer inside to check whether there are living creatures still inside. *www.sanibel-captiva.org.*

445 Santa Monica State Beach, California It's the classic Southern California experience: a wide golden-sand beach with the Pacific Ocean sparkling blue-green beyond and a gentle white-fringed surf. Restrooms, yes; tacky food stands, no (but there are nice cafes nearby in artsy, hip Santa Monica). You can even bicycle here on the paved beach path from nearby funky Venice Beach; end the day with the vintage rides and amusements at adjacent **Santa Monica Pier.** See Santa Monica Pier **483**. *Ocean Ave. at the end of Colorado Blvd.* ☏ *310/458-8900; www.santamonicapier.org.*

446 Poipu Beach, Kauai, Hawaii Even among the Hawaiian islands, Kauai is celebrated as the "garden isle," a beach lover's dream of tropical greenery, soft golden sand, majestic ocean cliffs, and purposely low-key development. The island's most popular beach is the North Coast's **Hanalei Beach** (yes, just like in "Puff, The Magic

Dragon"), but, for families, the best option is **Poipu Beach,** on Kauai's sun-soaked south shore. Head to the left of the sandbar and you find a calm, child-friendly sandy-bottom pool protected by a lava-rock jetty; head to the right and you face an open bay of vivid turquoise water that attracts swimmers, snorkelers, surfers, and boogie-boarders, a perfect place for would-be surfers to ride their first waves. *www.poipu-beach.org.*

Poipu is Kauai's most family-friendly beach.

447 Antigua Island, the Caribbean Once, the British colony of Antigua was known for its sugar plantations; today this independent nation is known for a different kind of sugar—the fine white sand of its myriad beaches. Antigua's lodgings are small, exclusive inns rather than high-rise resort complexes, and most open right onto the ocean sand. Go beach-hopping, to sample their distinct characters. Top bets for families: **Dickenson Bay,** in the northwest, with its wide strip of powder-fine sand, blissfully calm turquoise waters, and nearby **Paradise Reef** for snorkeling; the southern coast's **Carlisle Bay** beaches, where you can actually see the calm Caribbean waters meet the turbulent Atlantic; or beautiful **Half Moon Bay,** where a reef protects the waters nearer shore. *www.antigua-barbuda.com.*

448 Whitehaven Beach, Queensland, Australia Kids will really get the back-to-nature flavor of the **Outer Great Barrier Reef** at this pristine 6km-long silica-sand strand on Whitsunday Island, the largest of the 74 reef-fringed islands in the Whitsunday archipelago. It's the most-photographed beach in Australia, purposely kept unspoiled and serene. Covered with dense pine and eucalyptus forest, Whitsunday is mostly an uninhabited **wildlife refuge;** you'll have to sail here on a day cruise from Shute Harbor, just south of Airlie Beach on the mainland. Be sure to stroll up to Hill Inlet at its north end, a stunning cove with beautifully colorful waters. See Great Barrier Reef **440.** *www.whitsundaytourism.com.*

449 Cambrils, Costa Dorada, Spain Only an hour southwest of Barcelona—and, even more important for the kids, 3km (2 miles) from the blockbuster Port Aventura amusement park—this fishing town's wide, gently shelving golden sands epitomize the beaches that gave the Costa Dorada, aka Golden Coast, its name. Much more relaxed than its neighboring high-rise resort towns, Cambrils still wears the character of a traditional Spanish fishing village, with narrow cobbled streets, crumbling stone walls, street markets, and traditional fiestas. All its beaches are well equipped, but families gravitate south of the fishing port to L'Horta de Santa Maria, La Llosa, L'Ardiaca and El Mas de l'Arany beaches, relaxed spots where sunbathing and sandcastle-building take precedence over watersports. *www.cambrils-tourism.com.*

Bonaire Marine Park
Diving Deep into Paradise
Ages 6 & up • Netherlands Antilles, the Caribbean

Bonaire may be a dry, dusty island, but it's surrounded by rich coral reefs and incredibly clear water—visibility is often about 30m (100 ft.) or more. A couple of decades ago, as hotels first began cropping up along the ocean's edge, savvy Bonaire residents had the foresight to capitalize on this, their greatest tourism draw. By creating the Bonaire Marine Park, they ensured that this island would forever be known as a diver's paradise.

Stateside, you might ask someone his opinion about the best pizza place in town and spark some controversy. Here, ask a group of natives to name their favorite snorkel spots and the same sort of lively give-and-take begins. There's no consensus, but some of the more popular include Thousands Steps, Tori's Reef, Karpata (when it's calm), Andrea 1, and Windsock. The dive-shop pier by the **Divi Flamingo Beach Resort** is another starting point, relatively close to the cruise ship pier. The Marine Park plays no favorites, incorporating the entire coastline plus the tiny offshore island of Klein Bonaire. What it provides is permanent dive-site moorings (since anchoring on coral is a big no-no), rangers to police the reefs and enforce regulations, and services and facilities including a visitor center, the **Karpata Ecological Center,** at the entrance to Washington Slagbaai Park on the island's northwest end.

The reefs here are home to over 355 species, from beautiful parrotfish and damselfish to outsize groupers and tough-looking moray eels. The variety of coral formations attracts a corresponding variety of fish: At 1m (3¼ ft.) you can find brain coral; at 3m

(9¾ ft.) you begin to see staghorn and elkhorn coral and the graceful, swaying, feathery soft-coral "trees" known as gorgonians. Snorkelers only get to see the upper layers; it's divers who really get the best view of the island's 80-plus dive sites.

If the kids didn't take scuba lessons at home before you left, they can do so on the island. NAUI (www.naui.org) and PADI (www.padi.com) are the two most reliable certification organizations; both offer different levels of instruction, starting at age 5. Diving instruction takes time and commitment. Kids need to know that it's incredibly rewarding but it's also a serious endeavor. Every dive shop has slightly different offerings; some of the better ones, that also rent snorkeling equipment, include **Divi Dive Bonaire** (© 599/717-8285), **Captain Don's Habitat Dive Shop** (© 599/717-8290), and **Bonaire Dive and Adventures** (© 599/717-2227).

ⓘ **Bonaire Marine Park** (© **599/717-8444;** www.bmp.org). **Bonaire Tourist Office** (© **800/BONAIRE** [266-2473] in the U.S., or 599/717-8322; www.info bonaire.com).

✈ Bonaire.

🛏 $$ **Divi Flamingo Beach Resort,** J.A. Abraham Blvd. 40 (© **800/367-3484** in the U.S., 44/161/929-8612 in the U.K., or 599/717-8285; www.diviresorts.com). $$ **Sand Dollar Condominium Resort,** Kaya Gobernador N. Debrot 79 (© **800/288-4773** or 599/717-8738; www.sanddollar-bonaire.com).

WHY THEY'LL THANK YOU: Underwater, overwhelming.

451 Snorkeling & Diving

Feeding the Rays in Stingray City

Ages 8 & up • Grand Cayman, Cayman Islands

In the 1980s, fishermen of Grand Cayman Island cleaned their catch every evening in the shallow, sunny waters of North Sound, about 3.2km (2 miles) east of the island's northwestern tip. Over the years, stingrays began to gather to feast on the scraps. These days the fishermen have given way to snorkelers and divers, who allow these giant, gentle creatures to suck up bait up from their flat, open hands.

Grand Cayman's reputation as one of the best dive sites in the world means that you have a great number of solid, reputable dive shops to choose from, all of whom offer stops at Stingray City as part of their dive tour options. For kids who are comfortable snorkeling—and for kids who've just learned to scuba—Stingray City is a great spot, because the animals swim right over your shoulders or nudge your arms. Feeding them feels a bit like feeding a horse, except the mouths of the rays do create a fair bit of suction; it might frighten some kids if they're not forewarned. About 30 to 50 rays congregate here, in water that's about 4m (13 ft.) deep. They're as tame as any wild animal could be, and petting them is like stroking some wondrous newfangled silk-and-velvet fabric. The rays have occasionally

harmed people who have mistreated them—*never* grab a stingray by its tail—but make sure your youngsters know to show a little respect and they'll be fine.

Divers sometimes find it challenging to balance in the water here, as it's relatively shallow. The only other challenge is to avoid the little bit of fire coral that lies along the ocean bottom. Boat captains go over safety procedures, though, before letting anyone in the water. The different companies are all in communication with each other and have planned in advance who gets to approach the site at a particular time. Operators include **Don Foster's Dive Cayman** (© 345/949-5679; www.donfosters.com) and **Seven Mile Watersports** (© 345/949-0332; www.7milediver.com). You can also opt for a 4½-hour catamaran tour that includes a stop at Stingray City and lunch offered by **Red Sail Sports** (© 877/RED-SAIL [733-7245] in the U.S., or 345/945-5965; www.redsailcayman.com).

Popular snorkeling spots in the clear, warm waters of the Caymans are **Parrot's Reef** and **Smith's Cove,** south of George Town, lush reefs abounding with parrotfish, coral, sea fans, and sponges. And of course, plain old swimming and sunbathing are fabulous at **Seven Mile Beach,** one of the Caribbean's best.

ⓘ **Tourist Office** (© 345/949-0623; www.caymanislands.ky).

✈ Grand Cayman.

🛏 $$$ **The Anchorage,** Seven Mile Beach (© 800/433-3483 or 345/945-4088; www.theanchoragecayman.com). $$ **Cobalt Coast Resort,** 18 Seafan Dr. (© 888/946-5656 or 345/946-5656; www.cobaltcoast.com).

WHY THEY'LL THANK YOU: The whoosh and suck of a stingray, up close and personal.

Swimming with the rays at Stingray City.

16 Calling All Sports Fans

The Calgary Rodeo.

452

Baseball Hall of Fame

Shrine to the Great American Pastime

Ages 6 & up • Cooperstown, New York, USA

Admittedly my family is crazy for baseball, but even when I look at it objectively, I'd have to say that the Baseball Hall of Fame in Cooperstown sets the gold standard for sports museums. The very word *Cooperstown* has become synonymous with baseball history, for legend (now discredited) claims that Abner Doubleday invented baseball here. Opened in 1939, the Hall of Fame has been around long enough to amass an unparalleled collection of sports memorabilia. You don't have to be a statistic-spouting baseball fanatic to feel moved by this homage to America's pastime.

The Hall's redbrick Federal-style facade looks as all-American as the game it represents. Laid down like a giant timeline, it walks you through the **history of baseball,** starting with the various European ball-and-bat games that were its predecessors. Recent renovations have added more hands-on and interactive exhibits for kids, including a 13-minute multimedia show and a special area for toddlers and preschoolers, but it's the **memorabilia** that really tells the story, from Ty Cobb's glove to Babe Ruth's bat. You'll see the ridiculous scanty protective gear catchers used to wear behind the plate, the gradual evolution of the regulation ball and bat, a panoply of uniforms through the decades, the ever-changing look of trading cards. You'll learn about the Black Sox scandal of 1919 and how baseball survived World War II. Special galleries are devoted to

The Baseball Hall of Fame.

topics such as the Negro Leagues and the women's professional leagues. Snippets of vintage broadcasts and video footage of historic games are played at the touch of a button. Sure, my kids gravitated at first to exhibits paying tribute to today's stars and teams, set in a replica major-league locker room, but the more they saw of baseball's storied past—the actual objects, worn and discolored from play—the more they got into it. We saved a stroll through the actual Hall of Fame gallery for last, and by that time, those names on the plaques really meant something.

(i) 25 Main St. (© **888/HALL-OF-FAME** [425-5633] or 607/547-7200; www.baseball halloffame.org).

✈ Albany, 75 miles.

🚫 $ **Best Western,** 50 Commons Dr. (© **607/547-7100;** www.bwcooperstown. com). $$$ **Inn at Cooperstown,** 16 Chestnut St. (© **607/547-5756;** www. innatcooperstown.com).

WHY THEY'LL THANK YOU: Baseball is more than a game, it's a window on America.

453

Fenway Park
Where the Red Sox Rule
Ages 6 & up • Boston, Massachusetts, USA

When the **Boston Red Sox** won the 2004 World Series—ending an 86-year dry spell—they may have lost their status as one of baseball's most beloved underdogs, but I haven't heard any members of Red Sox Nation complaining. Sure, the Yankees, their perennial American League East rivals down in New York City, have a higher payroll and more world titles. None of that matters to dedicated Red Sox supporters, and their numbers are legion. The 2005 movie *Fever Pitch* didn't exaggerate anything: Sit among them in the stands and you'll definitely remember that the word "fan" comes from "fanatic." But I, for one, never mind. You're watching ball in an intensely green place that's older than your grandparents, inhaling a Fenway Frank and wishing for a home run—what could be better?

My father was a Red Sox true believer his whole life, and though my family has committed the ultimate treason of rooting for the Yankees, we still harbor a secret fondness for the Sox. So it is that from time to time, we take off our Yankees caps and visit Fenway Park.

It's a venerable stadium, though "stadium" seems almost too grand a term for this, the oldest park in the major leagues (built in 1912). Its quirks only add to the Fenway mystique: the narrow seats, the hand-operated scoreboard, the 37-foot-high left-field wall known as the **"Green Monster"** for its tendency to rob opposing hitters of their home runs. Those seats may be uncomfortable but they're gratifyingly close to the field, without the wide swaths of grass other parks have put between the fans and the players.

Compared with its modern brethren, however, Fenway is tiny, and **tickets** are both expensive and hard to get. Throughout the season, a limited number of standing-room tickets go on sale the day of the game, and fans sometimes return presold tickets (especially if a rainout causes rescheduling). It can't hurt to check. Forced to choose between seats in a low-numbered grandstand section—say, 10 or below—and those in the bleachers, go for the bleachers. They can get rowdy during night games, but the view is better from there than from the deep right-field corner.

Fenway Park.

We took a **Fenway Park tour** (conducted year-round; no tours on game days or holidays) that actually allowed us to peer inside the cramped space behind the Green Monster and walk out onto the warning track, stop in the press box, and visit the Red Sox Hall of Fame. Best of all was the guide's commentary, rich in team lore and highly entertaining.

ⓘ 4 Yawkey Way (℗ **877/REDSOX-9** [733-7699] for tickets, 617/226-6666 for tours; www.redsox.com).

✈ Boston's Logan Airport.

🛏 $$ **Doubletree Guest Suites,** 400 Soldiers Field Rd. (℗ **800/222-TREE** [222-8733] or 617/783-0090; www.double tree.com). $ **The MidTown Hotel,** 220 Huntington Ave. (℗ **800/343-1177** or 617/262-1000).

BEST TIME: Season runs Apr–Oct.

WHY THEY'LL THANK YOU: Baseball legends still matter here.

Wrigley Field
The Cubs' Den
Ages 4 & up • Chicago, Illinois, USA

The **Chicago Cubs** haven't played in the World Series since 1945 and haven't won the darn thing since 1908. When the Red Sox finally won a Series in 2004, the Cubs became undisputed holders of the crown for Most Beloved Losers. Chicagoans do love their Cubbies, champs or not, and there's no question that the team plays in one of baseball's classic venues, tiny Wrigley Field. Back in 1988, lights were finally installed for night play, but they're rarely used—the Cubs still play mostly day games. With its ivy-covered outfield walls, a hand-operated scoreboard, a view of Lake Michigan from the upper deck, and the El rattling past, it's old-fashioned

Wrigley Field.

baseball all the way, and our kids enjoyed every minute of their game there.

Built in 1914, Wrigley Field is the second-oldest venue in baseball (after Fenway Park), although the Cubs didn't move in until 1916 (a decade after their last Series victory!). Originally Weeghman Field, it was renamed in 1926 after the team's new owner, William Wrigley, Jr., the chewing-gum magnate.

No matter how the Cubs are doing in the standings, tickets go fast—most weekend and night games are sold out by Memorial Day. Your best bet is to hit a weekday game, where you'll be sitting alongside plenty of Chicagoans who called in sick to work and miraculously recovered by game time. Wrigley is small enough that every seat is a decent seat, and the place truly earns its nickname "The Friendly Confines"—every time I've been there, the fans around me were passionate, friendly, well-informed, and good-natured in the face of defeat. Riding the Red Line El to the Addison Street stop is part of the experience: You can look down into the park from the train, and hear the roar of the crowd as soon as you step onto the platform. During the regular season on non–game days, you can take a 90-minute **tour** of the vintage stadium, visiting the press box, dugouts, both visitors' and

Cubs' clubhouses, and the playing field itself; these tours are popular, so book in advance (© 773/404-CUBS).

Just some of the **traditions** we love at Wrigley: Enterprising owners of surrounding houses have built stands on their roofs where they seat their own ticket holders; ground rules declare that if a ball gets stuck in the ivy, it's a double; and a pennant is flown after every game with a big "w" or "l" to alert passersby to the outcome of the game (who needs the Internet?). When the opposing team hits a home run out of the park, somebody on the sidewalk outside picks up the offending ball and throws it back over the wall. You've gotta love a ballpark where that happens.

ⓘ W. Addison St. (© **773/404-CUBS** [404-2827]; www.cubs.mlb.com).

✈ O'Hare International, 15 miles.

🛏 $$ **Homewood Suites,** 40 E. Grand St. (© **800/CALL-HOME** [225-5466] or 312/644-2222; www.homewoodsuites chicago.com). $$ **Hotel Allegro Chicago,** 171 N. Randolph St. (© **800/643-1500** or 312/236-0123; www.allegrochicago.com).

WHY THEY'LL THANK YOU: Watching a Cubs homer sail over those ivy walls.

455

Summer Baseball on Cape Cod

All ages • Cape Cod, Massachusetts, USA

My New York–born kids have been spoiled when it comes to watching baseball, with two excellent major-league teams right in town. But sometimes the slick perfection of those pro games obscures the heart of the sport. That's when we seek out **AA or AAA teams**—or, better yet, go to Cape Cod to watch some of the nation's best college players compete as unpaid amateurs in a summer season during which they hope to be spotted by major-league scouts.

It's refreshing to watch this level of baseball: Pitchers do not dominate batters, home runs are rare events, and pop-ups and outfield flies are often dropped. Games are held on grass fields on the edge of town, where families picnic, fireflies swarm, and local kids pop wheelies on their bikes in the parking lot between innings. They're a real community gathering, and admission is free, although there's often a request for a donation as you walk in (the league runs on a nonprofit basis). It's a small-town sort of experience that reminds you why baseball is America's game.

There are 10 teams in the league, each playing in its own Cape Cod town. Over the years, we've become partial to the Cotuit **Kettleers** (so named because of the many kettle ponds in the area) and the Falmouth **Commodores** (named for Falmouth's sea-captain heritage). Few players carry over from season to season, but we do try to remember the names of the most promising athletes, just in case they show up on pro rosters in a year or two. That's not such a long shot, if you look at the names of recent Cape Cod Leaguers who made it to the majors: Nomar Garciaparra, Tino Martinez, Jeff Bagwell, John Franco, Barry Zito, J. T. Snow, Jeff Conine, Jeremy Giambi, Javy Lopez, Jeff Kent, and Jason Varitek.

Here's our routine: We warm up with a round of minigolf in the late afternoon. (Rte. 28, btw. Hyannis and Dennis, is studded with courses, but our favorite is the Cape-Cod-landmark-themed **Storyland,** 70 Center St., Hyannis (*℗* **508/778-4339**). Then we find someplace local for a quick dinner (fried clams or pizza usually hit the spot; we love **Captain Frosty's** in Dennis, 219 Rte. 6A), and get over to the ballgame; starting times range from 4:30 to 7pm. After the game, we have to stop for ice-cream cones, at either **Smitty's** in Falmouth, at 326 E. Falmouth Hwy., or **Four Seas** in Centerville, at 360 S. Main St. This is the essence of a Cape Cod summer night, and nothing could be sweeter.

ⓘ *℗* **508/432-6909;** www.capecod baseball.org.

✈ Hyannis.

🛏 $$ **Cape Codder Resort and Spa,** 1225 Iyannough Rd./Rte. 132, Hyannis (*℗* **888/297-2200** or 508/771-3000; www. capecodderresort.com). $$$ **Red Horse Inn,** 28 Falmouth Heights Rd., Falmouth (*℗* **508/548-0053;** www.redhorseinn.com).

BEST TIME: Season runs mid-June to late Aug.

WHY THEY'LL THANK YOU: Baseball gets back to its roots.

Home of the Green Bay Packers
Cheesehead Capital

Ages 6 & up • Green Bay, Wisconsin, USA

The Green Bay Packers may not be the winningest team in NFL history—though surely they've had their day, especially in the Vince Lombardi era, when they won the first two Super Bowls—but in many ways they are the purest embodiment of American football. Founded in 1919, before there even was a National Football League, they've played in Lambeau Field since 1957, which makes this the longest-tenured stadium in football. Season tickets have been sold out for 45 years straight. All other NFL franchises belong to big cities, but the Packers thrive in a salt-of-the-earth Midwestern town of 100,000 people some 2 hours north of Milwaukee—and the local community actually owns the team, not some fat cat in a skybox. Late in the season, Lambeau Field gets so cold, it's been nicknamed the Frozen Tundra, but there's no sissy roof over the stadium.

Okay, Lombardi did install soil-warming coils under the sod, but it is real dirt, holding real grass, not artificial turf. Like I said, pure football.

That's why a pilgrimage to Green Bay means something to every football fan. **Packer Fan Tours** (*©* **800/851-7225;** www.packerfantours.com) offers a range of reasonably priced packages that include tickets, Green Bay lodging, autograph sessions, tailgate parties at the Brett Favre Steakhouse, and so on. Individual tickets may also be available at **www.eventusa.com**.

Year-round, you can visit the **Packers Hall of Fame** in the atrium attached to Lambeau field, which has interactive videos, mementos, an activity area for kids, and even a replica of Vince Lombardi's office. Any non–game day, hour-long stadium tours are conducted (tickets first-come, first-served; *©* **920/569-7513**),

The Packers Hall of Fame next to Lambeau Field.

culminating in a walk through the concrete team tunnel onto the famed gridiron turf. Considering the Green Bay weather, however, you may prefer to come mid-July through mid-August, when you can watch preseason training sessions at Claire Hinkle Field, take the 1-hour Legends of Lombardi Avenue trolley tour around town (© **920/494-9507**), and enjoy the **Packers Experience** (1901 S. Oneida St.; © **920/487-5664**)—no mere video arcade, but an athletic activity gallery with such stations as a 40-yard dash, bungee run, obstacle course, passing challenge, and cheese maze. Yes, cheese—this is Wisconsin, the Dairy State, and Packers fans are nicknamed Cheeseheads. Don't be surprised if you end up wearing home an orange Styrofoam wedge strapped onto your own head.

ⓘ **Lambeau Field,** 1265 Lombardi Ave. (© **920/569-7500;** www.packers.com).

✈ Green Bay, 6 miles.

🛏 $$$ **Hilton Garden Inn,** 1015 Lombardi Ave. (© **920/405-0400;** www.hilton-gardeninn.com). $ **Microtel Inn & Suites,** 3031 Allied St. (© **920/338-9000;** www.microtelinn.com).

WHY THEY'LL THANK YOU: Being a Cheesehead for a day.

Notre Dame
The Holy Land of College Football
Ages 8 & up (Notre Dame), 6 & up (Hall of Fame) • South Bend, Indiana, USA

From Notre Dame Stadium, you can see a 132-foot-high mosaic of Jesus on the side wall of the campus library—a mosaic shrewdly placed so that Christ, with upraised hands, is centered right over the north goal post. **Touchdown Jesus** is a fitting sight for this Catholic university in northern Indiana, which has had no fewer than eight national championships, seven Heisman Trophy winners, five number-one pro draft picks, and 171 All-Americans. You don't have to be an alum to be a rabid fan of Notre Dame football—you just have to love football, like my teenage son does.

Notre Dame has had a football team since 1887 (though its famous marching band is even older, the oldest in the country, formed in 1845). The redbrick stadium is vintage, built in 1930, the last year of famed coach Knute Rockne's decade at the school. Rockne, more than anyone, is responsible for the nationwide Notre Dame fan base, for he actively sought far-flung matches and developed cross-country rivalries, with such schools as Michigan,

USC, Navy, and Boston College. Notre Dame's popularity nowadays transcends regional loyalties; they're the nation's only football team, pro or collegiate, whose entire schedule is broadcast on radio coast to coast, and since 1966 there's only been one home game that wasn't sold out. But here's the catch: All 80,000 seats at home games are allocated to season ticket holders, alumni, students, faculty, and parents of current students, although somehow they do pop up on ticket services (at inflated prices, of course). Or work your connections—find a Notre Dame alum or parent who'll buy tickets for you. Otherwise, you'll have to be content with buying merchandise at the Irish Store in Eck Hall, or taking a 1¼-hour, free, student-led **walking tour** of the beautiful rolling campus (© **574/631-5726**), which doesn't go inside the stadium.

There is, however, another reason to come to South Bend. In 1995, the **College Football Hall of Fame** moved from King's Island, Ohio, to a new state-of-the-art

The College Football Hall of Fame.

facility in downtown South Bend. Built to look like a football stadium, with a green gridiron-lined outdoor plaza, the museum has, besides the honoree exhibits, plenty of interactive kiosks, a 360-degree theater where you can stand surrounded by the noisy blur of game-day action, and sizable interactive areas for testing your skills against some of the greatest players in college football history.

(i) **Notre Dame Stadium,** University of Notre Dame (www.und.collegesports.

com). **College Football Hall of Fame, 111 S. St. Joseph St. (© 800/440-FAME** [440-3263] or 574/235-9999; www.college football.org).

✈ South Bend Regional.

🛏 $$ **Comfort Suites,** 52939 S.R. 933 (© **574/272-1500;** www.choicehotels. com). $$ **Inn at St. Mary's,** 53993 U.S. Hwy. 933 (© **574/232-4000;** www.innat saintmarys.com).

WHY THEY'LL THANK YOU: Seeing Touchdown Jesus.

458

Pro Football Hall of Fame
Gridiron Glory
Ages 6 & up • Canton, Ohio, USA

To my mind, each of the pro sports halls of fame reflects the character of its sport—the Baseball Hall of Fame has a vintage intellectual appeal, the Basketball Hall of Fame has got a more jazzed-up and high-tempo game, and the Pro Football

Hall of Fame is solid and down-to-earth, winning your interest a few dogged yards at a time. A bit off the beaten track—in Canton, Ohio, where the forerunner of the National Football League first formed in 1920—this NFL mecca caters to the true-blue gridiron fan. That's not me, but it sure is my sons.

You enter through an arena-shaped round building, with a white oblong protruding from its top like a giant football. Inside the front doors you're greeted by a bronze statue of Jim Thorpe (I won points for knowing the back story of this great Native American athlete, who was denied his Olympic medals because he had briefly played professional ball). In the rotunda, a century of **football history** is told in glass-case displays full of jerseys, balls, and scuffed cleats. There's a historical display on each of the league's 32 teams, one gallery devoted to the history of the Super Bowl, another to African-American players, another to upstart leagues that rivaled the NFL. Fans who, like my older son, devour football stats will love the cases of artifacts representing current record holders' milestones. Each Hall of Famer (and there are over 200) is honored with a bronze bust in one dazzling wall. Three to six new inductees are elected every year by a team of sportswriters who meet the day before the Super Bowl. Players are eligible only 5 years after retiring, which means that kids recognize some names—John Elway and Steve Young, not to mention ex-players such as Dan Marino and Terry Bradshaw who have found a second career as sportscasters.

Lest we forget that football is an action sport, the **GameDay Stadium** evokes the excitement of a live game in a rotating movie theater with an amazing Cinemascope screen; NFL action films are shown in another theater. And on the lower level beside the snack bar, museumgoers can get into the action themselves, with a football-passing activity, interactive trivia contests, and a Call the Play station where visitors take the role of quarterback, making snap decisions on how to run plays. Even non–football fans can't help but be engrossed by the museum by this point. I only regret that my football-fanatic dad never got a chance to take his grandsons here—that would have been the ultimate bonding experience for them.

ⓘ 2121 George Halas Dr. NW (✆ **330/456-8207;** www.profootballhof.com).

✈ Cleveland International.

🛏 $$ **Cleveland Marriott Downtown,** 127 Public Sq. (✆ **800/228-9290** or 216/696-9200; www.marriott.com). $$ **Holiday Inn-City Center Lakeside,** 1111 Lakeside Ave. (✆ **888/425-3835** or 216/241-5100; www.ichotelsgroup.com).

WHY THEY'LL THANK YOU: First down and goal to go.

Pro Football Hall of Fame.

459

The Basketball Hall of Fame
Hoop Dreams & Hardwood Heroes
All ages • Springfield, Massachusetts, USA

Its official name is the Naismith Memorial Basketball Hall of Fame in honor of Dr. James Naismith, who invented basketball right here in Springfield, Massachusetts, in 1891. You can't miss it—there's a 136-foot spire twirling a 13-foot illuminated orange basketball on its fingerlike tip, and an immense titanium sphere (a globe? A giant basketball?) that's visible from I-91.

Inside the great sphere, glass elevators glide to the top (third) level, where visitors start at the circular balcony of the **Honors Ring**, detailing the biographies of the nearly 300 figures elected to the Hall of Fame. Along with familiar names such as Walt Frazier and Wilt Chamberlain, Bill Bradley and Larry Bird, Kareem-Abdul Jabbar and Magic Johnson, illuminated panels and memorabilia cases honor players, coaches, and other figures from the more distant past and more obscure realms of the game. One of the things I love about this museum is that it weaves in the stories of the women's game, high-school and college basketball, and the evolution of racial equality—not with separate galleries but as part of the whole Big Picture.

On the second floor, more excellent displays tell the sport's history in thoughtful detail. **Memorabilia** include everything from old peach baskets like those that Naismith's first team shot into, to the red-white-and-blue balls used by the short-lived American Basketball Association; a huge case of team jerseys represents players old and new, including many current players not yet enshrined in the Hall. And here's the other thing I love about this museum, especially when you've got kids in tow: There are **interactive stations** everywhere. In the section devoted to The Players, you can compare your skills in a virtual one-on-one against various pro players; in The Coaches, you study great game plans and then test your own coaching calls in simulated court situations; in The Media, you see yourself on camera as a sports announcer. Video and audio clips run continually, adding texture to the experience.

The ground floor features the most interactive area of all: an almost-regulation-size hardwood court where frequent clinics and skill challenges are held. After listening to the echo of bouncing basketballs and overlooking the court from the top two floors, now your itchy hands can finally grab a ball and play. And, always with the youngest fans in mind, the Kids Court section has been built with hoops of varying heights. Sweet.

ⓘ 1000 W. Columbus Ave. (✆ **413/781-6500;** www.hoophall.com).

✈ Bradley International, 20 miles.

🛏 $$ **Sheraton Springfield,** 1 Monarch Place (✆ **800/426-9004** or 413/781-1010; www.Sheraton.com/springfieldma).

WHY THEY'LL THANK YOU: Hitting Center Court with a whole new sense of the game.

460

Old Trafford
Theatre of Dreams
Ages 8 & up • Manchester, England

You may not have played soccer as a kid yourself, but chances are your kids do—which brings them in step with the rest of the world, where "football" is understood to refer to a non-stop contest of skill, speed, and endurance played with a round ball (and no helmets or shoulder pads). For my young soccer players, an essential part of a trip to Manchester has to be visiting Old Trafford, the hulking redbrick home of Manchester United and one of England's most venerable football stadiums.

Man U's legendary captain Sir Bobby Charlton nicknamed this stadium the The-atre of Dreams, and its lore runs deep indeed. Despite modern refurbishments that have kept the stadium sleek and up-to-date, it still has an undeniable aura. Opened in 1910, Old Trafford was the first English stadium to surround its pitch com-pletely with a ring of stands and seating; it originally held a whopping 80,000 specta-tors, making it the second-largest arena in the country after **Wembley Stadium**. (The capacity was reduced somewhat in the 1990s when the league required all U.K. stadiums to convert to all-seat designs.) Heavily bombed in World War II, Old Trafford was stoutly rebuilt in the same shape after the war; the one feature that survived the bombing was the old players' tunnel leading from the dressing rooms to the pitch, which you can still walk through on a guided tour of the sta-dium. Standing on the famous pitch, you can gaze up at the red seats of the West Stand, aka the Stretford End, where the most hard-core Man U fans congregate.

(Chances are that's not where you'll want to sit during the game, not with kids.) On the tour, you'll also visit the players' cushy changing rooms and the dugout, and see a vintage clock stopped at the exact time when seven Manchester United players died in a tragic 1958 plane crash in Munich. Guides point out the spot near the front doors where the ashes of many die-hard fans—or Red Devils as they're known, after the team's color—have been interred; Sir Matt Dusby, Man U's famous manager in the 1950s and 1960s, is also buried here (that's his bronze statue you'll pass under at the front entrance).

The Manchester United Museum fills in the history of the club from its founding in 1878 to the present day; the Hall of Fame honors many of the players who've helped Manchester United dominate the English football league over the years, and the Trophy Room displays enough brass and silver to compete with the Crown Jewels.

ⓘ Sir Matt Busby Way, Trafford (✆ **44/161/868-8000;** www.manutd.com).

✈ Manchester International.

🛏 $$ **Jurys Inn,** 56 Great Bridgewater St. (✆ **44/161/953-8888;** www.manchester hotels.jurysinn.com). $$ **Premier Lodge Old Trafford,** Waters Reach, Trafford Park (✆ **44/870/423-6450;** www.premierlodge. com).

WHY THEY'LL THANK YOU: Football as the world plays it.

461

Lord's Cricket Grounds
The Hallowed Turf
Ages 8 & up • London, England

If baseball is the quintessential American game, then cricket is its English equivalent—a pastoral fantasy of gentlemen in white, knocking balls around a velvety-green lawn, in a leisurely match that can take days to complete. (Frequent breaks for tea seem essential.) Though many of the best cricket teams nowadays hail from far-flung parts of the former British Empire—Australia, India, the West Indies, New Zealand—their spiritual home remains here, in London, at the stately grounds of the Marylebone Cricket Club.

With its notoriously slow pace and intricate rules, cricket may be a hard sell to the Xbox generation, yet there's still an indefinable allure about sitting through a match at this fabled stadium in a posh corner of North London. (Despite cricket's supposed resemblance to baseball, my sons were a little perplexed by the match's action, but they still loved their sunny afternoon in the stands.) The resident team, Marylebone Cricket Club, is considered the official keeper of the almost sacred Laws of Cricket; MCC's teams (or "sides") play around 500 games a year, promoting cricket around the world. Even if they're not scheduled to play while you're in London, between Middlesex Cricket Club matches, international test matches, club finals, and historic rivalries such as Oxford v. Cambridge and Eton v. Harrow, there's almost always something on throughout the summer cricket season.

The first matches were played here in 1814, though the stadium's been frequently renovated over the years—the most recent addition, the **Media Centre,** is impressively futuristic, like an aluminum

Lord's Cricket Grounds.

TV set floating above the stands. The heart of the grounds is the redbrick 1890-vintage **Pavilion,** the balcony-bedecked domain of the team members during matches; luckily, you can view it on daily tours. Within it is the **MCC Museum,** the world's oldest sporting museum, founded in 1864; its collection features such treasures as the Wisden Trophy, the cricket kit of such famed players as Jack Hobbs and W.G. Grace, and a 19th-century urn called the Ashes—an artifact representing England's triumph in wresting back supremacy from Australia in an 1883 test match. A **film theater** screens clips of great moments in cricket history. The tour of Lord's includes visiting the Pavilion's Long Room, with its panoramic view of the pitch; the players' dressing rooms; the

Grand Stand and Mound Stand; and one of the last courts in the world where "real tennis"—the original form of the game—can be played (see International Tennis Hall of Fame **469**).

ⓘ St. John's Wood Rd. (✆ **44/20/7616-8595;** www.lords.org).

✈ Heathrow.

🛏 $$$ **London Bridge Hotel,** 8–18 London Bridge St. 9 (✆ **44/20/7855-2200;** www.londonbridgehotel.com). $$ **Vicarage Private Hotel,** 10 Vicarage Gate, South Kensington (✆ **44/20/7229-4030;** www.londonvicaragehotel.com).

WHY THEY'LL THANK YOU: The mystical heart of the sport.

National Sports Museum
Australia's Sporting Temple
Ages 8 & up • Melbourne, Australia

Australians are renowned for their devotion to sports—and what better place to erect a temple to this secular religion than on the grounds of the Melbourne Cricket Club? After all, this immense round arena in Yarra Park has hosted much more than just cricket matches since it opened in 1853; it's also regarded as the birthplace of Australian rules football, once hosted the 1992 World Cup finals, and was a major venue for both the 1956 Melbourne Olympic games and the 2006 Commonwealth Games.

Separate sections of the museum are devoted to various sports, beginning with the **Australia's Game gallery,** which focuses on the country's biggest spectator sport, Australian rules football (my sons were amazed to learn that there's a *third* type of football played worldwide). It's played with an oblong ball on a grassy oval, often an off-season cricket ground,

which is why the Melbourne Football Club—who codified the rules by which the sport is still played— was first founded, so that cricketers could stay in shape between seasons. The Melbourne football club has long shared the MCG with the cricket team, although given football's booming popularity, the "G" today hosts much more football than cricket. The Grand Finals—Australia's version of the Super Bowl—is usually played here, and the National Sports Museum now incorporates the Australian Football Hall of Fame.

The **Baggy Green gallery** celebrates the history of Australian cricket, epitomized by the traditional baggy green caps that Australian Test cricketers pass down from athlete to athlete. There's also a gallery on **Australia's Olympic history,** an **Australian Sports Hall of Fame,** and a **multisports gallery** that covers everything else, from basketball to tennis to golf to soccer to rugby to netball (a women's version of basketball). You'll end up in a spiffy **interactive section** where kids can swing a cricket bat, shoot a ball through a hoop, and generally test out their new knowledge.

After you've browsed the museum, it's time to take the hour-long **tour of the open-air stadium,** Australia's largest, holding an impressive 100,000 spectators. The original Victorian-era and early 20th-century stands have been replaced over the years—both the Olympics and the Commonwealth Games inspired major renovations—but the various sections retain their traditional names. Time your visit for a day when there's no game, and you can visit the changing rooms and the coaches' box, even walk on the actual pitch and visit the Long Room, where players hang out during games. Then come back to the "G" on another day to watch a match—if you're visiting in July or August (which is winter in Australia), there won't be any cricket, but there'll be plenty of football.

(i) Brunton Ave., in Yarra Park, Richmond (© **61/3/9657-8879;** www.nsm.org.au).

✈ Melbourne.

🛏 $$$ **The Como Melbourne,** 630 Chapel St., South Yarra (© **61/3/9825-2222;** www.mirvachotels.com.au). $$ **Fountain Terrace,** 28 Mary St., St. Kilda (©**61/3/9593-8123;** www.fountainterrace. com.au).

WHY THEY'LL THANK YOU: Australian rules rule.

The International Hockey Hall of Fame
Canada's Game
Ages 6 & up • Toronto, Canada

Hockey may be played around the world, but let's face it—the ice-rink version of this game belongs heart and soul to Canada. So it's fitting that the shrine to this sport should be in downtown Toronto, in a wonderfully ornate old bank building not far from the CN Tower ㉚. It won't be hard to find—just look outside for the bronze sculpture depicting a handful of eager young players, all helmeted and suited up, clutching their hockey sticks and ready to scramble over the boards onto the ice. It tells you all you need to know about the passion of hockey players and hockey fans.

There's nothing hallowed or mystical about this brash, intensely physical game, and appropriately enough, once you're inside, its Hall of Fame is an up-to-date space of slick black granite, grids of frosted glass, and bright stainless steel. **NHL Legends** is the section celebrating such great individual players of the past as Bobby Orr, Wayne Gretzky, Gordie Howe, and Mario Lemieux. They are also honored in the wood-paneled Great Hall's official Hall of Fame portraits—appropriately close to a glittering silver horde of trophies, most prominent among them being the **original Stanley Cup,** displayed in its own special steel vault. Another gallery titled the Stanley Cup Dynasties homes in on nine teams that dominated the NHL in their various eras—the Ottawa Senators of the 1920s, the Toronto Maple Leafs of the 1940s and 1960s, the early 1950s Detroit Red Wings, the Montréal Canadiens of three eras (late 1950s, 1960s, and 1970s), the New York Islanders of the early 1980s, and the Edmonton Oilers of the late 1980s. (You can't help loving the replica of an old Canadiens locker room.) Professional NHL hockey isn't the whole story of this game, either, as you'll be reminded in the Hometown Hockey

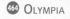

exhibit, a multimedia tribute to dozens of smaller grass-roots leagues.

Historical displays are one thing, but kids may have more fun with the museum's host of interactive exhibits—trivia kiosks, a simulated rink for virtual shootouts, broadcast booths where you can try calling various historic hockey games, two theaters showing clips of famous moments on ice, and a lounge where you can sink into a chair and listen to tapes of great broadcasts.

(i) Brookfield Place, 30 Yonge St. (© **416/360-7765;** www.hhof.com).

✈ Pearson International, Toronto.

🛏 $$ **Delta Chelsea,** 33 Gerrard St. West (© **800/890-3222** or 416/595-1975; www.deltahotels.com). $$ **Hotel Victoria,** 56 Yonge St. (© **800/363-8228** or 416/363-1666; www.toronto.com/hotelvictoria).

WHY THEY'LL THANK YOU: Having your fun on ice.

Olympia
Home of the Ancient Greek Games
Ages 6 & up • Olympia, Greece

Legend claims that Herakles (Hercules) founded the **Olympic Games:** After completing the last of his 12 labors, to celebrate he paced off 183m (600 Olympic ft.) and then ran the distance without taking a single breath. Whatever the origin, that distance became the length of the stadium at the religious sanctuary of Olympia, and for over a millennium, from 776 B.C. to A.D. 393, athletic contests were held here every 4 years.

Thousands poured into Olympia for the Games; much of the surrounding countryside was a tent city. (Women couldn't compete or even watch—any woman caught sneaking into the stadium was thrown to her death from a nearby mountain.) Events included footraces, short and long jumps, wrestling and boxing contests, chariot races, the arduous pentathlon (discus, javelin, jumping, running, and wrestling), and the vicious pankration (which combined wrestling and boxing techniques). The most prestigious event was the *stade,* or short footrace, for which the stadium was named.

Olympia's setting is magical: Pine and olive trees shade a small valley dominated by the conical Hill of Kronos. Make your first stop the **Archaeological Museum,** chock-full of statues (some of them world famous) as well as athletic paraphernalia from the ancient Games: stone and bronze weights used by jumpers, bronze and stone discuses, and even an enormous stone with a boastful inscription that a weight lifter had raised it over his head with only one hand.

The site itself is a jumble of foundation stones and toppled columns, marking various buildings around the ancient sanctuary. You'll see the ruins of **Roman baths** where athletes and spectators took hot and cold plunges; slender columns mark the site of the **gymnasium** and **palestra,** where athletes practiced foot racing and boxing. Olympia was devoted to the worship of Zeus, so there's one **temple** devoted to Hera (Zeus's wife) and an even bigger one for Zeus, which once contained an enormous gold-and-ivory statue of the all-powerful god, one of the Seven Wonders of the Ancient World. Passing through a vaulted archway to walk onto the pavement of the old stadium, which could accommodate 45,000 on its sloped sides, you can just imagine the roar of the ancient crowd. The Olympic flame is kindled here by sunlight every 2 years and then relayed by torch to the site of that year's Games.

The Museum of the History of the Olympic Games in Antiquity (© 30/26240/22-529), up a steep path from the site, has a superb collection of artifacts: chariot wheels, musical instruments, statues of athletes, and all kinds of athletic gear.

ⓘ **Tourist Office** (© 30/26240/23-100; closed Sun).

✈ Olympia (change at Pirgos), 5½ hr. from Athens.

🛏 $$$ **Grecotel Lakopetra Beach,** Kato Achaia, Achaia (© 30/26930/51-713). $ **Hotel Praxitelous,** 7 Spilliopoulou, Ancient Olympia (© 30/26240/22-592).

WHY THEY'LL THANK YOU: Lighting the torch.

Siena
The Running of the Palio
Ages 8 & up • Siena, Italy

In Siena, a city of Gothic palaces, aristocratic mansions, narrow streets, and medieval gates, walls, and towers, it's easy to feel transported back to the Middle Ages.

Be sure to see the sights, such as the Duomo, while in Siena for the Palio.

It has one of Europe's oldest universities, founded in 1240, and an unforgettable cathedral. But as soon as I stepped into its historic Piazza del Campo, designed like a sloping scallop shell, my imagination leapt to the spectacle that takes place here each July 2 and August 16: the intense, colorful **Palio delle Contrade.** Part historical pageant, part horse race, it pits each of the city's 17 wards *(contrade)* against each other in a contest held ever since the 15th century.

For the 3 days before the big race, trial races are held, with the final trial the morning of the event. Though there are 17 *contrade*, Piazza del Campo holds only 10, so the wards are chosen by lot. Young partisans, flaunting the colors of their *contrada,* roam the medieval streets in packs. Food and wine abound on the streets the eve of the race. (You're likely to be invited along by the first local you befriend, but while visitors are welcome, this event is truly for the Sienese.)

Although tickets for seats are expensive, there's no charge for standing with the throng in the middle of the square. You'll have to get to Piazza del Campo *very early,* though, and expect to be trapped there for hours in a teeming crowd. (With younger kids, I'd opt for buying tickets, or else stick to the less crowded trial-race days.) On the big day, before the actual race, there's loads of pageantry, with colorfully costumed men and banners parading up and down. But the race itself is a deadly earnest competition, with each bareback-riding jockey wearing his *contrada*'s traditional colors. There have been kidnappings of the most skilled jockeys, and bribery is commonplace. Jockeys have been known to unseat the competition, although a riderless horse is allowed to win. Horses are sometimes impaled by guardrails along the track. In theory, riders are supposed to alternate whip strokes between their mounts and their competitors, but in practice anything goes.

The horses gallop three times around Piazza del Campo, and even though the Piazza is quite large, it doesn't take long. A blur of action, and then the race is over—time to start gearing up for next year.

ⓘ **Tourist Office,** Piazza del Campo 56 (✆ **39/577/280-551;** www.terresiena.it).

🚃 Siena, 230km (143 miles) from Rome, 34km (21 miles) from Florence.

🛏 $$ **Palazzo Ravizza,** Pian dei Mantellini 34 (✆ **39/577/280-462;** www.palazzo ravizza.it).

WHY THEY'LL THANK YOU: When horse racing takes to the streets.

The Kentucky Derby
Bluegrass & Red Roses
Ages 4 & up • Louisville, Kentucky, USA

As a kid, I must admit being disappointed that the grass wasn't bright blue in Kentucky bluegrass country, although it does have a bluish cast. Legend has it that this species of grass is the best for raising Thoroughbred racehorses. It must have some effect, because more than two-thirds of the winners of the Kentucky Derby—America's premier horse race—have been bred right here on Kentucky's splendid horse farms.

Louisville's **Churchill Downs** racetrack, its huge white frame grandstand topped by a distinctive pair of slim gray spires, opened in 1875, and the Kentucky Derby—originally patterned after England's Epsom Derby—has been run every May since then. It's the first in the Triple Crown, a trio of renowned flat races for 3-year-olds, and its traditions have become famous, from the prerace singing of "My Old Kentucky Home" down to the garland of 554 red roses draped over the winning colt's neck.

Grandstand seats for the Derby must be booked months ahead and cost a fortune; a more casual option is to join the euphoric crowd picnicking in the 40-acre infield (you won't see much of the race but you'll have a fun party).

The **Kentucky Derby Museum,** open year-round just outside Gate #1 (✆ **502/ 637-1111**), has videos and hands-on exhibits (don't miss the one where you sit on a saddle in a real starting gate).

Before you hit the track, though, I suggest driving around the countryside near Lexington, 100 miles southeast of Louisville, to see where generations of Thoroughbred champions have been bred. The most famous horse farm, **Calumet Farms,** doesn't allow visitors, though you can do a drive-by with **Horse Farm Tours** (✆ **859/ 268-2906**), which then visits other working horse farms. You can tour **Claiborne Farm,** Winchester Road, Paris (✆ **859/233-4252**), where Seabiscuit was born and

Racing at Churchill Downs, home of the Kentucky Derby.

Secretariat was a longtime stud stallion (his grave is on the farm), or **Three Chimneys Farm,** Old Frankfort Parkway, Versailles (✆ **859/873-7053**), where Seattle Slew was the resident stud. The **Kentucky Horse Park,** 4089 Iron Works Pike, Lexington (✆ **800/568-8813** or 859/233-4303; www.kyhorsepark.com), has Man O' War's grave and a museum on horse history, but the real fun for kids is walking through the barns, seeing shows in the equestrian arena (mid-Mar to Oct), and taking horse and pony rides.

ⓘ 700 Central Ave. (✆ **502/636-4400;** www.churchilldowns.com).

✈ Louisville International.

⇤ $$$ **Seelbach Hilton,** 500 4th St., Louisville (✆ **502/585-3200;** www.seelbach hilton.com). $$ **Sheraton Suites,** 2601 Richmond Rd., Lexington (✆ **800/262-3774** or 859/268-0060; www.starwoodhotels.com).

WHY THEY'LL THANK YOU: And they're off!

467

Saratoga Race Course
Where Horseracing Goes High Society
All ages • Saratoga Springs, New York, USA

Saratoga Springs is not only the USA's oldest thoroughbred track, it is also the most beautiful, a place where smartly dressed socialites still quaff champagne as they cheer on the winners from their box seats.

With its sprucely painted white Victorian gingerbread and peaked green roofs, shady white-railed paddocks, and lush flower planters, Saratoga is an elegant place, where a dress code is strictly observed—forgo the jeans, shorts, and tank tops for your day at the races. During the **Spa Meet,** from the end of July through Labor Day, races are held here every day but Tuesday. There may be some seat tickets available on race day (buy at Gate A at 8am or at the Holiday Inn downtown the night before), but in general if you want a reserved seat you should book ahead (✆ **718/641-4700;** during race season, contact the racetrack directly—see below). Post time for the day's first race is 1pm; there are steeplechases as well as flat racing on either dirt or turf tracks.

Early morning before races is a great time to come out to the track. Expert commentary accompanies the thoroughbreds as they go through their morning workouts, and a buffet breakfast is served on the Clubhouse Porch from 7 to 9:30am. During the season, free tram tours are available from 8 to 9am. These include a stroll around the stables and a demonstration of the mechanized starting gate; at the interactive **Discovery Paddock exhibit,** children can dress like a jockey, "weigh in" on a scale, and hammer a mock horseshoe.

If you're here out of season, you can still visit the **National Museum of Racing and Hall of Fame,** 191 Union Ave. (✆ 518/584-0400; www.racingmuseum. org), displaying trophies, memorabilia, artworks, and film explaining not just Saratoga's story but 3 centuries of thoroughbred racing in the United States. There's a Hall of Fame for the greatest names in the sport's history—such horses as Man O' War and Seabiscuit, jockeys such as Willie Shoemaker and Eddie Arcaro, and trainers from Tom Smith to D. Wayne Lukas. Interactive screens allow visitors to relive great moments in racing.

ⓘ **Saratoga Racetrack,** 267 Union Ave. (✆ 518/584-6200). **Saratoga Convention and Tourism Bureau** (www.discover saratoga.org).

✈ Albany, 30 miles.

🛏 $$ **Adelphi Hotel,** 365 Broadway (✆ **518/587-4688;** www.adelphihotel. com). $$ **Holiday Inn,** 232 Broadway (✆ **800/465-4329;** www.spa-hi.com).

BEST TIME: Racing season is late July to Labor Day.

WHY THEY'LL THANK YOU: Glimpsing horse racing's elegant past.

The starting gates at Saratoga.

Wimbledon

A Grand Slam on Grass

Ages 6 & up • London, England

Although there are four Grand Slam tennis championships, the Wimbledon tournament is the only one still played on grass. Some of the world's best tennis players compete here over a fortnight of elimination matches, spanning roughly the last week in June to the first week in July. Watching a match at Wimbledon is a tennis player's dream (the only thing better would be to actually playing at Wimbledon—but there you're on your own).

It is possible to get **tickets** to the tournament, even one of those coveted center-court seats, which are awarded via public lottery. Send a request for an application form, along with an international reply coupon or self-addressed envelope (with U.K. stamps) to: All England Lawn Tennis & Croquet Club, Box 98, Church Road, Wimbledon SW19 5AE, England. It must be postmarked by December 15 for the next summer's tournament, and the application itself must be returned by December 31. For more information, go to www.wimbledon.org, which also explains about same-day ticket sales at the gate. You'll have to stand in line for this limited number of tickets and you may wind up disappointed; but it's worth a try, especially early in the tournament, when even the outside courts have top players competing on them. For recorded ticket information, call © **44/20/8946-2244**.

Wimbledon's home is the **All-England Lawn Tennis & Croquet Club,** founded as a croquet club in 1868. In 1873, Major Walter Clapton Wingfield invented an outdoor racquet game, which soon became known as lawn tennis; by 1877 the croquet club was already holding an annual lawn tennis tournament—which grew into the championship we know today.

Outside of tournament time, visitors can soak up tennis lore by visiting the **Wimbledon Lawn Tennis Museum** on the club grounds. Displays include videos of matches and interactive exhibits, as well as historic trophies, racquets used by famous players, a costume gallery charting a century's radical changes in women's tennis clothes, and championship trophies. Museum visitors get a look at the fabled **Centre Court;** you can also book a behind-the-scenes tour, which takes in **No. 1 Court,** the **Water Gardens,** and the **Press Interview Room,** where all those post-match interviews are filmed. A visit to this lovely suburb makes a nice break from London sightseeing; you can get here via the Underground (District Line), and the tennis club is an easy 20-minute walk from the station.

ⓘ Church Rd., Wimbledon (© **44/20/8946-6131;** www.wimbledon.org).

✈ Heathrow.

🛏 $$$ **London Bridge Hotel,** 8–18 London Bridge St. 9 (© **44/20/7855-2200;** www.londonbridgehotel.com). $$ **Vicarage Private Hotel,** 10 Vicarage Gate, South Kensington (© **44/20/7229-4030;** www.londonvicaragehotel.com).

WHY THEY'LL THANK YOU: Wimbledon scores game, set, and match.

469

International Tennis Hall of Fame
Where Newport's New Sport Became King
Ages 6 & up • Newport, Rhode Island, USA

Miffed at fellow members of Newport's exclusive Newport Reading Room club, in 1880 *New York Herald* publisher James Gordon Bennett, Jr., launched a rival club called the Newport Casino. Determined to make it bigger, better, and more fashionable, Bennett hired McKim Mead & White—favorite architects of the Gilded Age New York elite—to produce a rambling shingle-style edifice of lavish proportions, with dark-green turrets and verandas and an interior piazza for games and social events. Along with archery and lawn bowling, space was provided for a new game called lawn tennis, which quickly took root among upper-class athletes. The very next year, the newly formed United States National Lawn Tennis Association held its first national championship at the Casino's grass **Horseshoe Court.** Now known as the U.S. Open, this tournament is played today at Flushing Meadows, Queens, but the Casino still holds professional tournaments, as well as the U.S. amateur grass championship. The Horseshoe Court is a permanent grass court, one of few remaining in this hard-court age, and there's still a **walled court** for court tennis, one of only nine in the United States. And in the elegant former club rooms, the old Casino has, since 1954, housed the **International Tennis Hall of Fame.**

Even if you're not a die-hard tennis fan, it's fun to tour the Hall of Fame just to explore this landmark building. Exhibits explore how lawn tennis exploded in popularity, how professional tennis developed out of the amateur sport, and the growth of women's tennis. Honorees include American champions from Bill Tilden and Stan Smith to John McEnroe, Jimmy Connors, Billie Jean King, and Chris Evert, not to mention the African-American groundbreakers Althea Gibson and Arthur Ashe. The Hall of Fame doesn't play national favorites; you'll see plaques for such international talents as France's Rene Lacoste and Yannick Noah; Sweden's Bjorn Borg and Mats Wilander; Germany's Steffi Graf and Boris Becker; Australia's John Newcombe and Evonne Goolagong; Romania's Ilie Nastase; Argentina's Guillermo Vilas; and Czechoslovakia's Martina Navratilova. Even a kid who's just picked up a racquet can feel swept into a grand old sporting tradition here.

ⓘ 194 Bellevue Ave. (✆ **800/457-1144** or 401/849-3990; www.tennisfame.org).

✈ TF Green Airport, Providence (30 miles).

🛏 $$$ **Hyatt Regency Newport,** 1 Goat Island (✆ **800/233-1234** or 401/851-1234; www.hyatt.com). $$ **Mill Street Inn,** 75 Mill St. (✆ **800/392-1316** or 401/849-9500; www.millstreet inn.com).

WHY THEY'LL THANK YOU: How a pastime of the privileged became a sport of the people.

The International Tennis Hall of Fame.

St. Andrews
The Birthplace of Golf
Ages 8 & up • St. Andrews, Scotland

This historic sea town in northeast Fife, Scotland, was once an ecclesiastic hot spot filled with monasteries (St. Andrew is Scotland's patron saint). When Henry VIII dissolved the churches in the 1530s, St. Andrews seemed to have lost its claim to fame. What saved it was a little game invented a century-and-a-half earlier by a group of bored aristocrats knocking a stone into a rabbit hole with a driftwood club, something they called *gowff*. Though James II, III, and IV outlawed the sport, the ancient monks just kept right on playing. Today, the wind-scoured bluffs they played on are the world's most famous golf course.

The Old Course, Golf Place (© **44/1334/466666**), is a classic links course, meaning one beside the sea. Its fairways and greens have been kept emerald-green for centuries by devoted greenskeepers, but the surrounding rough shows what the local vegetation actually is—tall sharp-bladed grasses, heathery shrubs, and wind-stunted trees. Wind is always a factor when you're playing here, along with that treacherous deep rough, hidden pot bunkers, huge double greens, and devilish corrugations on deceptively flat fairways.

There are actually six golf courses in the town: the **Old Course,** the **New Course** (1896), **Jubilee Course** (1897), **Eden** (1914), **Strathtyrum** (1993), and the 9-hole **Balgrove,** laid out especially for children in 1972. Encircled by all of them is the world's most prestigious golf club, the **Royal and Ancient Golf Club** (© **44/1334/472-112**), founded in St. Andrews in 1754. You've seen its golden-stone exterior on TV, the memorable backdrop to the Old Course's 18th green, but sorry, you can't get inside to see its famous trophy room unless you know a member.

Anyone can play the New, Jubilee, Eden, and Strathtyrum courses; you can even book a tee time online at www.standrews.org.uk. It's a little trickier to get onto the Old Course, where club members have priority, but it's possible: Fill out a ballot card with the Old Course starter on Golf Place by 2pm for a chance at one of the time slots the next day, which are drawn by lottery. You must present a current handicap certificate and/or letter of introduction from a bona fide golf club. Chances are the youngsters you're with, however, aren't ready to play the Old Course; they can still get a firsthand look at those mean bunkers via a 40-minute guided walking tour (daily every hour in summer); book ahead for a more comprehensive 2-hour version. You can all drive balls at the Golf Practice Centre, overlooking the Old Course, or putt around the Himalayas putting course by the Links Clubhouse. Also by the clubhouse is the **British Golf Museum** (© **44/1334/460-046**), with glass-case exhibits on the game's history.

ⓘ © **44/1334/466-666;** www.standrews.com.

🚆 Leuchars, 1 hr. from Edinburgh.

🛏 $$$ **Rufflets Country House Hotel,** Strathkinness Low Rd. (© **44/1334/472-594;** www.rufflets.co.uk).

WHY THEY'LL THANK YOU: For golfers, this is Mecca.

The Calgary Stampede
Great Rodeo of the Great North Plains
Ages 6 & up • Calgary, Canada

Joining the Calgary Stampede is not something you do at the last minute—for 10 days every July, this big friendly city on Canada's western plains lassos in as many visitors as its hotels and restaurants can handle, so plan several months in advance. But it's worth it: Of all the big rodeo events in North America, this is the one to see, not least because it happens in summer, when the kids are out of school and the nearby Canadian Rockies are at their most glorious.

Though Calgary has acquired a sky-scrapers-and-business-suits persona since the oil boom of the 1960s, at heart it's still a good ol' cattle town, and Calgarians get back to their Old West roots during the Stampede, putting on Stetson hats and whooping and hollering. Their high spirits are infectious. Downtown is abuzz with pancake breakfasts, rope twirling, square-dancing, and horse-drawn wagon tours, but most Stampede action takes place in **Stampede Park,** a show, sports, and exhibition ground south of downtown that was built for just this purpose. Top billing goes to the rodeo events, the largest and most prestigious in North America, held in the 16,000-seat Stampede Grandstand. Over a million Canadian dollars in prize money is won by competitors from around the world, riding bucking broncos or Brahma bulls, roping calves, wrestling steers, and barrel racing. Nighttime events include the **Chuckwagon Races** and **Stampede Grandstand,** a huge outdoor

Trying to stay in the saddle at the Calgary Stampede.

extravaganza with a nightly race of old-time cook wagons thundering around the track, followed by precision kick lines, clowns, bands, and a sky full of fireworks.

Stampede Park has two other stages as well for **nightly concerts**—rock, alternative, and comedy as well as lots of country music—and the Saddledome, winter home of the Calgary Flames hockey team, hosts several indoor events day and night. Teens will gravitate to shows with stunt mountain bikers and exhibition skateboarding. A midway is set up with noisy lit-up rides whirling and swooping; you can wander around a replica Indian village or a re-created 1912 Calgary streetscape. Livestock shows, a food fair, crafts competitions, art shows, lectures, even a minicasino make Stampede Park a whirl of activity even if you don't have tickets to any rodeo events.

While you're in town, there's one essential attraction the kids will enjoy: **Fort**

Calgary Historic Park, 750 9th Ave. SE (✆ **403/290-1875;** www.fortcalgary.ab.ca), a 16-hectare (40-acre) park built around the ruins of the 1875 Canadian Mounties fort where Calgary began. Bit by bit, volunteers are building an authentic replica of the fort, and there are lots of role-playing activities for kids, along with videos and guided tours.

ⓘ Box 1060, Station M (✆ **800/661-1767;** www.calgarystampede.com).

✈ Calgary International, 16km (10 miles).

🛏 $ **Elbow River Inn,** 1919 Macleod Trail S. (✆ **800/661-1463** or 403/269-6771; www.elbowrivercasino.com). $$$ **Westin Hotel,** 320 4th Ave. SW (✆ **800/937-8461** or 403/266-1611; www.westin.com).

WHY THEY'LL THANK YOU: A place to play cowpoke all day.

472

The Highland Games
Olympics in Kilts
All ages • Various towns in Scotland

Men wear kilts, traditional flings are danced, and there's a continual skirl of bagpipes—it's the **Highland Games,** Scotland's version of the Olympics, and if these summer festivals seem more focused on clan traditions than athletic prowess, well, that just makes them more fun.

The Heavies, gigantic men who follow the circuit all summer, draw the most attention with their uncanny brawn. Athletic contests are mostly feats of strength such as tug of war, wrestling, the hammer throw, and a primitive kind of shot putting using round stones. Wellie throwing and haggis hurling are often thrown in for good measure. Perhaps the most famous and unusual events are the caber-tossing contests. A caber is a 6m-long (20-ft.) pine tree, stripped

to its bare trunk, which is flung into the air in hopes that it'll land on a straight line. If you think it's easy, just try it.

If you're not picky about which games to attend, you'll be happy to know that there's a series of them, all across Scotland, the whole summer long—contact the **Council of Scottish Clans and Associations,** www.cosca.net, for a full schedule. In June, the Bearsden and Milgnavie Highland Games (✆ **44/141/942-5177**) are held at Burnbray in the small town of **Milgnavie** (pronounced *mill*-guy), 6 miles north of Glasgow. **Inverness** holds its Highland Games in July (Highlands of Scotland Tourist Board, Castle Wynd, off Bridge St.; ✆ **44/1463/234353**). In August, it's the turn of the western Highlands city of

Oban (Oban Tourist Information Centre, Argyll Sq.; ℂ **44/1631/563122**), where pipe bands are a specialty. But the grandest of the Highland Games is the one in early September in the town of **Braemar** (Braemar Tourist Office, The Mews, Mar Rd.; ℂ **44/1339/742208**), at the eastern end of the Grampian Mountains. Braemar is conveniently near Balmoral Castle, and ever since the days of Queen Victoria these have been designated the **Royal Highland Gathering.** It's held in the Princess Royal and Duke of Fife Memorial Park, and the queen herself often attends. As a result, the whole Braemar locality is flooded with visitors, so book your lodgings at least 6 months in advance.

ⓘ www.cosca.net. Contact local tourist offices or www.visitscotland.com.

🛏 $$ **Glen Mhor Hotel,** 9–12 Ness Bank, Inverness (ℂ (**44/1463/234308; www.glen-mhor.com). $$$ **Hilton Glasgow Hotel,** 1 William St. (ℂ **800/445-8667** in the U.S., or 44/141/204-5555; http://beta.hilton.co.uk/glasgow).

BEST TIME: May–Sept.

WHY THEY'LL THANK YOU: Watching a kilted Heavy toss a caber.

NASCAR Classic
The Daytona 500
Ages 4 & up • Daytona, Florida, USA

Like much else in Florida, it all began with a beach: beautiful Daytona Beach, which runs for 24 miles along a skinny peninsula divided from the north Florida mainland by the Halifax River. In the early 1900s, when "horseless carriages" were still a novelty, automobile enthusiasts discovered that Daytona Beach's uniquely hard-packed white sand made the perfect drag strip. A century later, the town has every right to call itself "The World Center of Racing."

Auto racing in Daytona outgrew the beach long ago. In 1959, a proper 2½-mile racetrack, the **Daytona International Speedway,** was built 4 miles inland, and stock car racing's premier event, the 200-lap Daytona 500, was launched. The National Association for Stock Car Auto Racing (NASCAR) is now based in Daytona, and over a million race fans come here for 9 or 10 major events a year. Big races sell out months in advance—tickets to the Daytona 500 in February can be gone a year ahead of time (ℂ **386/253-7223** for tickets).

If you're not attending a race, you can still get a fair idea by visiting the **World Center of Racing Visitor Center** at the east end of the speedway. You can enter the stands to see the track, or take a 30-minute **guided tram tour** that visits the garage area, pit road, and so on. Speed freaks can pay a stiff fee to have the **Richard Petty Driving Experience,** run by seven-time Daytona 500 winner Richard Petty (ℂ **800/237-3889;** www.1800bepetty.com; May–Oct)—a three-lap ride around the tri-oval track in a real stock car, cruising at an average speed of, oh, say 115 mph. The kids, however, may prefer to spend your money on the phenomenally popular **DAYTONA USA** (ℂ **386/947-6404** or 386/947-6800; www.daytonausa.com), also in the visitor center, where all sorts of state-of-the-art motion simulators, interactive activities, and IMAX films re-create the adrenaline-pumping experience of racing in Daytona.

(i) 1801 W. International Speedway Blvd. (© **800/748-7467;** www.daytonaintl speedway.com).

✈ Daytona Beach International.

🛏 $ **Old Salty's Inn,** 1921 S. Atlantic Ave., Daytona Beach Shores (© **800/417-1466** or 386/252-8090). $$ **Shoreline All**

Suites Inn, 2435 S. Atlantic Ave., Daytona Beach Shores (© **800/293-0653** or 386/252-1692; www.daytonashoreline.com).

WHY THEY'LL THANK YOU: Banking the turn into the home stretch.

The Indianapolis Speedway
Home of the 500
Ages 6 & up • Speedway, Indiana, USA

The auto-racing world has many battling factions—NASCAR versus Formula One versus Grand Prix versus Indy cars—but as a native of Indianapolis, I remain true to the greatest single-day sporting event in the world: The Indianapolis 500 Mile Race. Launched in 1911, it's a classically simple race: 33 cars trying to complete 200 circuits of a 2.5-mile oval track. "How could that be interesting?" friends ask me. But it *is* interesting; it's chock-full of maneuvering and heartbreak and human valor, with

crashes and mechanical failures laying waste to the best-laid plans of even the most seasoned racing teams. I still tune into the race every Memorial Day weekend, hooked for life on the death-defying spectacle of drivers hurtling around the track at speeds over 200 mph.

Out of season, you can visit the **Indianapolis Motor Speedway Hall of Fame Museum** inside the oval, where more than 30 winning cars are displayed. The bus tour around the famous track is eye-opening,

More than 400,000 fans fill the grandstands every May in anticipation of the Indianapolis 500.

because when you see the race on TV you can't imagine how steeply banked those treacherous corner turns are, or how lonely that backstretch can feel, far from your car's mechanics in the pit area over by the grandstands. The track is nicknamed "the Brickyard" because originally it was paved in red brick; all the bricks have long been paved over with smooth asphalt, except for one yard-wide brick stripe at the starting/finishing line of the race. Here the official starter intones "Gentlemen (and ladies), start your engines" (no automatic ignition for these babies) and a black-and-white checkered flag is dropped 500 miles later as the winner whizzes past.

More than 400,000 spectators crowd into the Speedway every May to watch this race, either in the grandstands or in the big rowdy picnic of the infield area. Unlike the Kentucky Derby, another primo Midwestern sporting event, this one isn't over in a few tense minutes—you'll be here for hours, bonding with your neighbors, trying to keep track of the drivers' shifting positions, watching the field gradually whittling down to a few hardy contenders. Wear a hat and sunscreen and pack the best picnic cooler you can. Traffic to and from the track is a nightmare, and you come home begrimed with burnt rubber particles and temporarily deafened from the persistent roar of the engines— but it's an experience you'll never forget.

If you can't make it to the 500 itself, try coming one of the 2 weekends before the race for the **time trials,** during which hopeful drivers try to post competitive times for shorter circuits of the track. The drivers who post the fastest times get to start in the front rows of the race ("pole position"), which is no small advantage. My first Indy outings were on time-trial weekends, not race day, and it's still an exciting day at the track.

ⓘ 4790 W. 16th St. (ⓒ **317/481-8500;** www.brickyard.com).

✈ Indianapolis International.

🛏 $$ **Doubletree Guest Suites,** 11355 North Meridian St., Carmel (ⓒ **800/ 695-8284** or 317/844-7994; www.double tree.com). $$ **Staybridge Suites,** 9780 Crosspoint Blvd., Fishers (ⓒ **800/931-4660** or 800/718-8466; www.ichotelsgroup.com).

WHY THEY'LL THANK YOU: The whine of the engines, the gasps of the crowd.

The Grand Prix of Monaco
Ages 6 & up • Monte Carlo, Monaco

Nowhere in Europe is driving more exciting, even for the ordinary motorist, than along the French Riviera, with its precipitous climbs, breathless curves, and mountain-piercing tunnels. In such movies as *Casino Royale* and *The Bourne Identity,* jet-setters whipping around those twisty roads in low-slung sports cars are part of the Riviera mystique: It was chillingly apt that Monaco's beloved Princess Grace would die in 1982 in a crash on the same hairpin turn she took at top speed in the 1956 Hitchcock film *To Catch a Thief* (the film that brought her to Monte Carlo, where she met Prince Rainier). Perhaps the most famous road race of all is driven in Monaco every May—the **Monte Carlo Grand Prix.**

First held in 1929, the Grand Prix covers a 3.3km (2-mile) route that daringly runs right through town, hurtling up a steep hill to the Monte Carlo casino, plunging back downhill, whooshing through a waterfront tunnel, then slicing sharply around the quays. Formula 1 race cars (similar to Indy cars) whir around this hair-raising route for

78 laps, negotiating turns and jockeying fiercely for position, with the possibility of a spectacular crash always imminent. Grandstands are set up for spectators along the quays, though viewing spots are hard to secure.

This densely built-up Riviera town—congested even in the slow season—becomes a madhouse at race time. You may opt to visit Monaco another time of year and simply drive the route, imagining the race cars and protective barriers and cheering crowds for yourselves. Stop in the **Formula 1 shop,** 15 rue Grimaldi (ℭ **377/93-15-92-44**), where everything from racing helmets to specialty key chains and T-shirts celebrates the roaring, high-octane racing machines; then visit the **Collection des Voitures Anciennes de S.A.S. le Prince de Monaco,** Les Terrasses de Fontvieille (ℭ **377/92-05-28-56**), which displays more than 100 vintage autos belonging to Prince Rainier III,

including the 1925 Bugatti 35B that won the Monaco Grand Prix in 1929 and the 1956 Rolls-Royce Silver Cloud that carried Rainier and Princess Grace on their wedding day.

While in Monaco, don't miss the **Musée de l'Océanographie,** avenue St-Martin (ℭ **377/93-15-36-00**), founded by Albert I, great-grandfather of the present prince. A passionate oceanographer, he himself collected most of the exotic specimens exhibited here, many of them previously unknown.

ⓘ **Automobile Club de Monaco,** 23 bd. Albert 1er (ℭ **377/93-15-26-00**).

✈ Nice.

🛏 $$$ **Le Monte Carlo Grand Hotel,** 12 av. des Spélugues (ℭ **377/93-50-65-00;** www.montecarlograndhotel.com).

WHY THEY'LL THANK YOU: Grand Theft Auto with a lot more class.

17 Rides & Thrills

The Boulder Dash roller coaster at Lake Compounce.

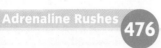
Summer Bobsledding in the Austrian Alps

Ages 14 & up • Igls, Austria

Ever since we saw *Cool Runnings,* the 1993 film about Jamaica's 1988 Olympic bobsled team, our family's been fascinated with this particular sport, one that requires daredevil athletes to strap themselves into a low-slung sleigh and hurtle at breakneck speed down a chute of preternaturally slick ice. Now I personally don't plan to do any bobsledding ever, but if you've got folks in your family who do, I can tell you where to go: Innsbruck, Austria.

Innsbruck looks just the way an Alpine town is supposed to look, with narrow medieval streets; a jumble of turrets, gables, and dormers; and horse-drawn carriages clopping over cobblestone pavements, all tucked into a narrow valley beneath forested peaks. Innsbruck has been a winter sports magnet for years, hosting not one but two Winter Olympics, in both 1964 and 1976. The facilities built for those Games are still going strong— there are gleaming ice rinks in town, and the ski slopes in outlying Igls, only 5km (3 miles) north of town, are booked solid all winter. In the summer, of course, when the snows melt, this Alpine scenery is overrun by mountain climbers and hikers instead of skiers. But the state-of-the-art **ice chute** created for bobsled, luge, and skeleton events is still active June through September, and it's quite a kick to find yourself bobsledding in the middle of summer. Granted, in summer they use a modified sled, but the adrenaline-pumping

Olympiaworld in the Austrian Alps.

effect is the same, juddering downhill at speeds of up to 100kmph (62 mph).

Experienced professional bobsledders pilot you in a four-man bob down the track, which has 14 curves, one loop-de-loop, and sides banked as steep as 7m (23 ft.) high. The track drops about 100m (328 ft.) in altitude in the course of a run some 1.25km (⁴/₅ mile) long. You must be at least 14 years old to participate; in summer this thrill is only offered Thursday and Friday afternoons from 4 to 6pm.

While it pales in comparison, if you pass on the bobsled ride you can still get a little vertigo on the **cable car** from Pätsch (the next village up the mountain from Igls) to the top of the Pätscherkofel mountain, a peak 2,241m (7,352 ft.) high with glistening panoramas of the nearby Stubai Glacier. The cable car covers a distance of 4km (2½ miles) and takes 18 minutes one way.

ⓘ **Olympic Bobsled Run,** Römerstrasse (✆ **43/512/338380;** www.olympiaworld. at).

✈ Innsbruck-Kranebitten, 8km (5 miles).

🛏 $$ **Best Western Hotel Mondschein,** Mariahilfstrasse 6, Innsbruck (✆ **43/512/22784;** www.mondschein.at). $$$ **Sporthotel Igls,** Hilberstrasse 17 (✆ **800/780-7234** or 43/512/377241; www.sporthotel-igls.com).

WHY THEY'LL THANK YOU: Speeding downhill like a demon.

---

477 Adrenaline Rushes

Soaring over Mont Blanc in a Cable Car

Ages 8 & up • Chamonix, France

Yes, it's possible to burrow under the French Alps in 20 minutes by driving through the Mont Blanc Tunnel into Italy. But why go underground when you can see more of the mountains—and get a real adrenaline rush—by going over them in a cable car?

Nestled in an alpine valley practically at the junction of France, Italy, and Switzerland, **Chamonix** is the historic capital of Alpine skiing—it was the site of the first Winter Olympic Games, in 1924—with western Europe's highest mountain, **Mont Blanc** (4,734m/15,531 ft. high), as its irrefutably dramatic backdrop. Numerous cable cars and mountain railways stretch like a spider's web from Chamonix into the surrounding mountains. The most thrilling route by far is the one that climbs to the Aiguille du Midi and on to Italy—it's a full day's journey if you go the whole way, although there are various points where you can shorten the trip.

The first section, a 9-minute run to the **Plan des Aiguilles** at an altitude of 2,263m (7,425 ft.), isn't so alarming. But the second stage, to the **Aiguille du Midi** station at 3,781meters (12,405 ft.), may make your heart leap, especially when the car rises 610m (2,000 ft.) between towers. At the summit, you'll be about 100 meters (328 ft.) from Mont Blanc's peak, with a commanding view of the aiguilles of Chamonix and Vallée Blanche, the largest glacier in Europe (15km/9⅓ miles long). From here you can gaze at the Alpine peaks of three countries: France, Switzerland, and Italy.

At this point, having survived the most precipitous climb, you can descend back to Chamonix, making it a half-day excursion. But if you have your passports ready, the next stage will take you to **Pointe Heilbronner, Italy.** Leave the tram station along a chasm-spanning narrow bridge to reach this third cable car, which swings you over the 19km (12-mile) Vallée Blanche glacier ski run and through mountain peaks, past jagged needles of rock and ice bathed in dazzling light. There's only one word for it: awesome.

From Pointe Heilbronner, which is roughly the same altitude as Aigulle de Midi, you can descend on three more cable cars to Pavillon, then Rifugio Torino, and finally to La Palud, a suburb of Chamonix's Italian counterpart, the ski resort of Courmayeur, Italy. From Courmayeur, you can catch a bus back through the **Mont Blanc Tunnel** (© **33/4/50-55-55-00**)—the way ordinary travelers cross the Alps.

If the trip up the glacier seems too scary for the children (or, admit it, for you), never fear—another cableway from Chamonix makes a more gradual 1½-hour round-trip

up to **Le Brévent,** which, at 2,485m (8,153 ft.), still offers breathtaking views of Mont Blanc and the Aiguilles de Chamonix.

ⓘ **Compagnie du Mont-Blanc,** 35 place de la Mer de Glace (© **33/4/50-53-30-80;** www.compagniedumontblanc.fr).

✈ Chamonix, 8 hr. from Paris.

🛏 $$ **Albergo del Viale,** Viale Monte Bianco, Courmayeur (© **39/165-846712;** www.hoteldelviale.com). $$ **Hotel de l'Arve,** 60 Impasse des Anémones, Chamonix (© **33/4/50-53-02-31;** www. hotelarve-chamonix.com).

BEST TIME: The route to Pointe Heilbronner operates only mid-May to mid-Oct.

WHY THEY'LL THANK YOU: Feeling like you're at the top of the world.

Adrenaline Rushes · 478

On Camel Safari in India
Roughing It in Rajasthan
Ages 10 & up • Rajasthan, India

The ancient land of the princes, Rajasthan is a sun-scorched desert province where magnificent forts and palaces once guarded trade routes of inestimable wealth—a perfect snapshot of the exotic essence of India, yet within easy striking distance of Delhi and the **Taj Mahal.** You can cross that perilous desert too, and do it the way the ancient traders did—on board a swaying camel, the traditional "ship of the desert."

While camel treks are popular in the sand-dune deserts of western Rajasthan, especially out of Jaisalmer (best known for its magnificent medieval Golden Fort), I'd recommend heading instead for **Shekhawati,** an arid semidesert area only 200km (124 miles) southwest of Delhi. Shekhawati

is fascinating to explore, with a number of towns full of painted houses and temples, their elaborate exterior murals a status symbol for wealthy merchants under the British Raj. One of the better options is a 2- to 4-day safari with **Royal Riding Holidays** (© **91/140/262-2949;** www.royal ridingholidays.com), based out of Nawalgarh. Going out for a few days allows you to explore a more varied terrain of semi-desert, forests, salt lake, marshes, and flat grasslands, and includes visits to local villages and with passing nomads. You'll sleep in colorful striped Asian-style tents with chairs, beds, mosquito nets, and a full floor covering; toilet and bath tents are provided as well, and the expedition is fortified with a cook who spreads out a

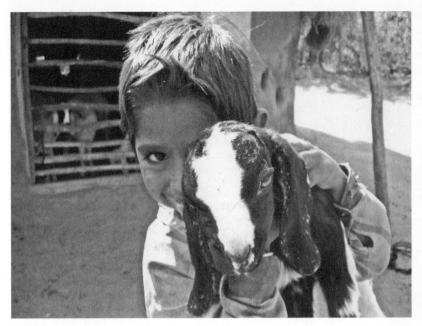

Boy and goat in Rajasthan.

desert buffet at every meal. Expect to spend 4 to 5 hours in the saddle per day, covering 25 to 40km (16–25 miles). Horseback safaris are available as well.

For kids, just perching high on the camel's elaborate saddle will be a thrill, learning to rock along with the long-legged camel's loping gait. (Hang on for dear life when the camel heaves up from its knees after you've mounted and when it kneels down again at the end of the ride!) There are a saddle in front of the hump and another behind it, and a driver will pilot the beast from the front saddle while you cling to the back seat. If someone in your group doesn't care to ride, they can follow the safari in a jeep and still have the fun of sleeping out in the desert in those maharajah-style tents. Don't expect to bond with your mounts, though—camels are *notorious* grumps.

ⓘ **Indian Visit** (www.indianvisit.com).

✈ Jaipur 160km (100 miles).

🛏 $$ **Desert Resort,** Mandawa (© **91/141/237-1194**; www.mandawahotels.com). $$ **Roop Niwas Palace,** Nawalgarh (© **91/159/422-2008**).

BEST TIME: Nov–Mar.

WHY THEY'LL THANK YOU: Sailing across the sands.

Ballooning over the Great Red Rocks

Ages 8 & up • Sedona, Arizona, USA

Hot-air ballooning is extremely popular in the Southwest—Albuquerque's annual balloon festival every October is the country's largest—and there are plenty of operators vying for your business. Beautiful as all these desert landscapes are, the one that's most thrilling to soar over, to my mind, is the red-rock country around Sedona, Arizona, with its wind-sculpted buttes and outcroppings thrusting up from the desert scrub, the rock glowing as if on fire.

These excursions are always early-morning affairs—you need still morning air to properly inflate the balloon and to ensure a stable takeoff. The entire outing may take as much as 3 hours, of which only an hour or so is actually in the air. But the kids will enjoy watching the limp silk billow into shape as burners inflate the balloon and, once you've settled back to earth, having a breakfast picnic in the desert while waiting for the "chase team" to arrive, deflate the balloon, and pack it back into its sack. Gondolas suspended below the balloons carry up to seven passengers at a time, and the ride is surprisingly steady—instead of fighting wind currents, you're going with the flow. True, the pace is often slow and majestic rather than death defying. Still, you're high up and protected only by the wicker sides of the basket, which is thrilling enough. You're also at the mercy of the elements somewhat—pilots can't steer the balloons, they

Hot-air ballooning in Sedona.

can only change altitude, but there's a certain skill in finding wind currents heading in different directions to get you where you want to go. If the winds are right they may even be able to lower the balloon onto the surface of a river, slap the water lightly with the bottom of the gondola, and then lift back up into the sky.

Three Sedona-area operators are licensed to fly over the spectacular Cocomino National Forest: **Northern Light Balloon Expeditions** (© **800/230-6222** or 928/282-2274; www.northernlightballoon. com), **Red Rock Balloon Adventures** (© **800/258-3754** or 928/284-0040; www. redrockballoons.com), and **Sky High Balloon Adventures** (© **800/551-7597** or 928/204-1395; www.skyhighballoons.com). In flight, their pilots will chat with the kids about the landscape they're flying over and about the science and art of hot-air ballooning.

ⓘ **Sedona Visitor Information,** 331 Forest Rd. (© **800/288-7336** or 928/282-7722; www.visitsedona.com).

✈ Phoenix, 116 miles.

🛏 $$ **Best Western Inn of Sedona,** 1200 W. Hwy. 89A (© **800/292-6344** or 928/282-3072; www.innofsedona.com). $$$ **Hilton Sedona Resort,** 90 Ridge Trail Dr. (© **800/HILTONS** [445-8667] or 928/284-4040; www.hiltonsedona.com).

WHY THEY'LL THANK YOU: Up, up, and away.

Adrenaline Rushes **480**

The Call of the Wild in Denali
Your Own Personal Iditarod
Ages 10 & up • Denali National Park, Alaska, USA

Alaska's Denali National Park is about as pristine a wilderness as a national park can get, and in an attempt to keep it that way, the Parks Service permits no public access by automobile—there's only one gravel road through the center of the park, which you can travel on a shuttle bus that links rest stops and campgrounds and lodges and scenic overlooks. Disembarking at various points, parkgoers can then hike into the tundra as far as they wish, though most folks seem content just to ride the bus and look out the window at those incredible Arctic views. But there's another way to get even deeper into this stunning wilderness—by racing over the snowy backcountry on a **dog sled,** just as the park rangers do.

Two outfits have been approved to run wintertime dog-sledding packages into Denali, using their own rustic lodges as home base (guests sleep in private log cabins near the lodges). Both of these lodges are just outside the park, but so close that they feature views of majestic Mount McKinley, America's biggest mountain. **Denali West Lodge,** set on the shore of Lake Minchumina, is the smaller of the two operations (only 10 guests at a time), and so remote that you'll need to fly in on a little private plane. Its mushing expeditions are mostly day trips from the lodge. You can drive via Alaska Hwy. 3 to **Earthsong Lodge,** which runs 3- to 10-day dog-sledding camp-outs (using tents or outlying cabins), although itineraries can be tailored to guests' interests. Each guest 12 and over drives his or her own sled, with teams of four to six huskies. (Younger children may simply ride along on the sled.) Earthsong even offers an option for summer visitors to get a taste of the dog-sledding experience by driving a husky team with a wheeled cart.

Guests at the Earthsong Lodge cuddle future dog-sled team members.

It may sound as if you'd need special skills, but the proprietors of both lodges are longtime mushers experienced in training first-timers. You just need to be strong enough to hold on tight as the dogs surge forward, whipping you over the snowy track. Perhaps 4 or 5 hours of the day is spent mushing, covering on average 30 miles of terrain, across the snowy tundra, around lakes, through taiga forests and glacial river valleys. You're practically guaranteed sightings of moose, caribou, Dall sheep, foxes, lynx, wolverines, and beavers; your chances of running across other human beings, however, are practically nil. Nighttime camp-outs may be lit by the Northern Lights and serenaded by nearby wolves, howling in sync with the huskies. Now *that's* getting away from it all.

ⓘ Denali Park Rd. (𝚌 **907/683-1266;** www.nps.gov/dena).

✈ Fairbanks, 125 miles. Anchorage, 236 miles.

🚂 **Alaska Railroad** (𝚌 **800/544-0552** or 907/265-2494; www.alaskarailroad.com) runs trains from Anchorage (6¹/₂ hr.) and from Fairbanks (3³/₄ hr.) summers only.

🛏 $$$ **Denali West Lodge** (𝚌 **907/674-3112;** www.denaliwestlodge.com). $$$ **Earthsong Lodge** (𝚌 **907/683-2863;** www.earthsonglodge.com).

BEST TIME: Nov–Mar.

WHY THEY'LL THANK YOU: Bonding with the huskies.

The Flying Horses

All ages • Watch Hill, Rhode Island, USA

The oldest operating carousel in the United States, dating back to 1867, is tucked away in the charming resort town of Watch Hill, the westernmost community on Rhode Island's coast. These Flying Horses really do fly, because they aren't mounted on a revolving platform—they're hung by chains from overhead sweeps, the only such merry-go-round in the country. Once the carousel gets going, they are a textbook demonstration of centrifugal force, swinging outward as you spin dizzyingly around the central post. The hand-carved wooden horses may be smaller than average, but they're real works of art, with horsehair manes and genuine leather saddles and bright agate eyes. Come here before your kids get too old, because only children under 12 can ride this landmark merry-go-round.

Watch Hill is a stunning beach town, but like many such enclaves it's more about insiders than tourists. So once we've done the carousel, we jump back into the car and head for the other end of Rhode Island (which, face it, is less than an hour's drive) to check out two more historic carousels in the Providence area, both from the 1890s. Notice advances in technology since the Flying Horses was built: These two have bigger, more elaborately carved horses mounted on poles, the majority of them prancing up and down as the platform revolves. The **Slater Memorial Park Carousel,** Armistice Boulevard in Pawtucket (✆ **401/726-1876**), throws in some more exotic animals like a camel and a giraffe and has lovely stained-glass windows in its enclosing pavilion, but the real showstopper is the **Crescent Park Carousel,** 700 Bullocks Point Ave., in East Providence (✆ **401/433-2828**), which the Looff Company designed as its showy sales piece: It glitters with beveled glass panels, glass jewels, and electric lights, and the band organ at its hub is covered with carved figures that move about in time to the music. Snazzy.

ⓘ **Flying Horses** (✆ **401/348-6007**). **Watch Hill** (www.visitwatchhill.com).

✈ Providence.

🛏 $$$ **Providence Biltmore,** 11 Dorrance St., Providence (✆ **800/294-7709** or 401/421-0700; www.providencebiltmore. com).

BEST TIME: Open mid-June to early Sept.

WHY THEY'LL THANK YOU: Developing the art of merry-go-round design.

The Flying Horses Carousel
Grabbing the Brass Ring
All ages • Oak Bluffs, Massachusetts, USA

Here in picturesque Oak Bluffs, on Martha's Vineyard, the Flying Horses is the United States's oldest working platform carousel (the Flying Horses in Watch Hill, Rhode Island, predates it but doesn't have a platform), and it does look suitably antique, almost like something out of a Grandma Moses painting. The first time we watched it, my children felt vaguely disappointed—why didn't the horses go up and down, like they do on all the merry-go-rounds they were used to? Then they looked longer and figured out the special thrill of riding this carousel: All the local kids know to stand up

Gingerbread house in Oak Bluffs on Martha's Vineyard.

in their stirrups and lean outward as they pass one point of the circuit, waving an arm wildly to swipe a metal ring from a dispensing arm. If the ring you grab is made of brass, you get a free ride.

Built in 1876 at Coney Island, and brought to Martha's Vineyard in 1884, this National Historic Landmark is now maintained by the Martha's Vineyard Preservation Trust. It's in a small seaside area of refreshment stands and arcades that preserves an old-fashioned innocence. The carousel itself is inside a building, but you can hear the joyful strains of calliope music a couple streets away. When they were little, my kids were content to glide smoothly along the painted horses, clutching their real horsehair manes, never making a risky stretch for the rings. But once you start participating in the **ring grab,** you never go back; you get obsessed. In between rides, take a moment to admire the intricate hand-carving and gaze into the horses' glass eyes for a surprise: tiny animal charms glinting within.

I have to admit, for years I used the Flying Horses to tempt my children onto the ferry from Cape Cod to Martha's Vineyard, just so I could prowl around **Oak Bluffs's Camp Meeting Grounds** afterward. This 34-acre circle with more than 300 gaily painted gingerbread cottages is a window onto the 19th-century past, when families flocked here for weeklong religious retreats; continual prayer services were held in revivalists' tents on the central green. My kids are outgrowing the carousel these days, but they still love the Camp Meeting Grounds. And someday I hope we'll be lucky enough to hit Oak Bluffs on whatever mid-August weeknight the community leaders choose (the date is kept secret beforehand) as **Illumination Night,** when today's cottagers light up their homes with Japanese lanterns all on the same evening. That would be a special memory indeed.

✈ Martha's Vineyard Airport, 5 miles.

🛏 $$ **The Dockside Inn,** 9 Circuit Ave. Extension, Oak Bluffs (✆ **800/245-5979** or 508/693-2966; www.vineyardinns.com).

BEST TIME: Mid-Apr to mid-Oct.

ⓘ 33 Circuit Ave. (✆ **508/693-9481;** www. mvpreservation.org/carousel.html).

WHY THEY'LL THANK YOU: Going for the brass ring.

Merry-Go-Round the West Coast
On the Santa Monica Pier
All ages • Santa Monica, California, USA

With so many bigger-is-better southern California attractions to give it competition, this classic wooden carousel sits comparatively neglected on the Santa Monica Pier. Photo shoots and corporate events frequently use it as a setting, but on a summer weekday you'll hardly have to stand in line to take a ride. It's an underappreciated gem, a forgotten bit of Californiana.

The open-sided building covering the carousel is itself a historic landmark, a Byzantine-Moorish-California fantasy built in 1916 by Charles I.D. Looff, one of the great artisans of the Golden Age of wooden carousel design. The carousel inside was built in 1922 in Philadelphia, its ornate hand-carved wooden horses and chariots painted by German and Italian immigrant craftsmen. Inset mirrors and strings of light bulbs keep it bright and snazzy; romantic landscape panels sweep around the parapet.

The Santa Monica Pier was one of California's hottest attractions in the 1920s, back in the days when seaside amusement piers were all the rage. Times have changed, however, and the Pier just hasn't kept up. Today it offers a handful of other attractions—a small aquarium, a games arcade, and **Pacific Park** (✆ **310/260-8744;** www.pacpark.com), which has 12 squeaky-clean amusement park rides

The Santa Monica Pier.

including a moderately thrilling roller coaster and Ferris wheel. I admire the spirit of the city's intention to avoid a honky-tonk atmosphere—this is, after all, haute Santa Monica—but there's not quite enough to make it a tourist destination, and even local families often forget it's here.

Well, finding little windows onto an earlier era is part of my mission as a parent, and finding them in L.A. is a special challenge I embrace. As we circled around on these vintage prancing ponies, with the Pacific Ocean stretching to the horizon right outside, we took deep breaths of ocean air and were grateful for a bit of shade to let our sunburned skins cool off after a morning at the beach. And we were selfishly glad to have the place to ourselves; you can only stand in line at Disneyland so long.

ⓘ **Santa Monica Pier** (✆ **310/394-8042;** www.santamonicapier.org).

✈ Los Angeles International.

🛏 $$ **Best Western Marina Pacific,** 1697 Pacific Ave., Venice (✆ **800/786-7789** or 310/452-1111; www.mphotel. com). $$$ **Hotel Oceana,** 849 Ocean Ave., Santa Monica (✆ **800/777-0758** or 310/393-0486; www.hoteloceana.com).

WHY THEY'LL THANK YOU: Nostalgic nook on the ocean.

Carousels & Ferris Wheels **484**

Wheeling around Vienna
The Prater's Classic Ride to the Top
All ages • Vienna, Austria

In the 1949 film *The Third Man,* set in a rubble-strewn post–World War II Vienna, Orson Welles and Joseph Cotten hold a clandestine meeting in the Prater, Emperor Josef II's old hunting ground and the official birthplace of the waltz (invented in 1820 by Johann Strauss, Sr., father of the "Waltz King" Johann Strauss, Jr.). And where do Welles and Cotten talk where no one can overhear them? In one of the enclosed cars of the Riesenrad, the Prater's giant Ferris wheel, where they lift high over the rooftops of Vienna, warily gazing over the ravaged city below their feet.

Talk about classics—the **Riesenrad** was built for the Universal Exhibition in 1897 (commemorating the 50th year of Franz Josef's reign) by British engineer Walter Basset. This "giant wheel" was supposed to be a temporary exhibit, but like the Eiffel Tower, which had been built for the World's Fair in Paris a decade earlier, it never closed. Heavily damaged in 1945, it was reopened in 1947 as a symbol of Vienna's rising from the ashes. At its zenith, the wheel is 67m (220 ft.) high; one revolution takes 20 minutes. Instead of sitting in small fixed cars, passengers stand in roomy wide-windowed cabins, where you can move from side to side, taking in fine aerial views of Vienna across the Danube canal.

The Riesenrad sits right near the entrance to the **Prater,** which has been Vienna's favorite outdoor gathering place since the emperor opened it to the public in 1766. The **Panorama,** an audiovisual exhibit in a set of replica Riesenrad cabins at the foot of the wheel, illustrates Vienna's history. An **amusement park** behind the wheel has typical attractions kids love—merry-go-rounds, go-karts, tilt-a-whirls, shooting galleries, and a couple of excellent roller coasters, one of them rising nearly as high as the top of the Riesenrad.

The Prater is charming at night, with tiny lights strung in the trees around open-air cafes and beer gardens, and the rides themselves decked out in colored light bulbs. From the top of the Riesenrad, the concentric rings of Vienna's city layout sparkle like strands of a diamond necklace. But we like it in the daytime too, when we can pick out Vienna's landmarks—the needlelike spire of St. Stephan's Cathedral, the massive complex of the Hofburg palace, the stately Kunsthistoriche art museum. Out here in the Prater, Vienna's sometimes-dour personality softens and relaxes into the dreamy rhythms of a waltz, and I remember why dowdy old Vienna is one of my favorite cities on earth.

(i) **Praterverband** (✆ **43/1/7295430;** www.wienerriesenrad.com).

✈ Vienna International.

🛏 $$ **Hotel am Schubertring,** Schubertring 11 (✆ **43/1/717020;** www. schubertring.at). $$$ **Hotel Römischer Kaiser,** Annagasse 16 (✆ **800/528-1234** or 43/1/512775113; www.bestwestern. com).

WHY THEY'LL THANK YOU: Spinning slowly in an old-world pleasure ground.

Vienna's Riesenrad.

The London Eye
Big Wheel, Bigger View
Ages 6 & up • London, England

As Ferris wheels go, they sure don't get any bigger than the London Eye. This is no mere amusement park ride—after all, what is there to see from the top of ordinary Ferris wheels? From the top of the Eye, you can take in a glorious view, the vast panorama of one of the world's greatest cities.

At 135m (443 ft.) in circumference, it's the world's largest observation wheel—to be precise, not a Ferris wheel at all (named after Pennsylvanian engineer George Ferris, who invented one for the 1893 Chicago Exposition; in England they just call them

"big wheels"). A Ferris wheel has swinging, open cars hanging from the wheel; an observation wheel has enclosed cars fixed on the wheel's perimeter, which, for better or worse, make the ride less scary. Passengers are carried in 32 air-conditioned "pods" that make a complete revolution every half-hour, hardly a breakneck pace—at the bottom, the pods keep moving, but so slowly that disembarking is no problem.

From the top of the wheel, in clear weather you can gaze in all directions for some 40km (25 miles) over this famously spread-out metropolis, easily spotting not

The London Eye affords spectacular views of London.

only the Gothic spires of the Houses of Parliament and Westminster Abbey across the river, but also the British Museum, St. Paul's Cathedral, Nelson's Column in Trafalgar Square, Buckingham Palace, the Tower of London, Tower Bridge, and the green necklace of parks that runs through central London.

Since the restaurant and observation deck at the top of the BT Tower were closed in the 1970s, London has had no great vantage point for tourists. Well, they've got one now, and how.

ⓘ **Millennium Jubilee Gardens** (ⓒ **44/87/0500-0600;** www.londoneye.com).

✈ Heathrow.

🛏 $$$ **London Bridge Hotel,** 8–18 London Bridge St. 9 (ⓒ **44/20/7855-2200;** www.londonbridgehotel.com). $$ **Vicarage Private Hotel,** 10 Vicarage Gate, South Kensington (ⓒ **44/20/7229-4030;** www.londonvicaragehotel.com).

WHY THEY'LL THANK YOU: This view of London isn't just for the birds.

Roller Coasters 486

Boulder Dash
An Instant Wooden Classic
Ages 8 & up • Bristol, Connecticut, USA

The nation's oldest continuously operated amusement park (opened in 1846), **Lake Compounce** has tidy New England–y landscaping and a traditional sort of family-friendly wholesomeness, but the rides are completely up-to-date. For fans of wooden roller coasters—a breed unto themselves—it's hard to choose between the two at Lake Compounce. Sure, the Wildcat is a vintage wooden coaster, built in 1927, an exciting double out-and-back with that jittery jolted-out-of-your-seat effect that wooden coasters are famous for. But the park's other wooden coaster is the one

that's been winning all the awards, even though it's only been around since 2000: Boulder Dash, the only roller coaster that's actually built into the side of a mountain.

Boulder Dash hurtles along at speeds up to 62 mph, rising up a wooded slope to its first dramatic drop of 115 feet—a drop you can't anticipate because you can't look through the mountain to see what's coming ahead. From here on, the coaster whips over a course nearly a mile long, diving in and out of woods, crashing over and around a series of boulders, down to the nearby lake and back; the ride takes

The water park at Lake Compounce.

2¹/₂ minutes. The height requirement is only 48 inches, which means this is an excellent ride for younger thrill-seekers who still need to work up to the nerve rattlers I cover below.

As you'd expect from an outdoor New England site, Lake Compounce is open only seasonally, mid-May through early September (check schedule on the website before you go). Just as the name implies, it's set on a clear little lake, nestled into the wooded hills west of Hartford. The park also has a fairly extensive **water park area,** all part of the same admission. There's a good-sized **kiddieland** to occupy younger brothers and sisters, and a **vintage 1911 carousel** with hand-carved wooden horses and the original Wurlitzer band organ. A half-hour **cable car** ride glides gently to the top of a mountain—the same mountain that you dive down from at top speed when you ride Boulder Dash.

ⓘ 822 Lake Ave. (📞 **860/583-3300;** www.lakecompounce.com).

✈ Bradley International Airport, 30 miles.

🛏 $ **Hannibal Travelodge,** 500 Mark Twain Ave. (📞 **800/578-7878** or 573/221-4100). $$ **Hotel Clemens,** 401 Third St. (📞 **573/248-1150;** www.hotelclemens.us).

BEST TIME: Mid-May to early Sept.

WHY THEY'LL THANK YOU: Going over the cliff.

The Cyclone
The Coaster That Made Coney Island Famous
Ages 8 & up • Brooklyn, New York, USA

Back in the days before air-conditioning, New York families flocked to the beach at Coney Island to cool off in summer, and it was a rite of passage to grow tall enough (54 in.) to be allowed on New York's most famous roller coaster, the Cyclone. Thrill rides may have advanced technologically since then, but this classic coaster, built in 1927, is still one of the best, plunging a heart-stopping eight stories from its highest peak.

The charms of Coney Island go well beyond the Cyclone, of course; for one thing, there's that dynamite location, right on a wide white-sand beach where Atlantic waters crash. **The New York Aquarium,** Surf Avenue and West 8th Street (© **718/265-3400;** www.nyaquarium.com),

just a short stroll up the boardwalk, features dolphins, sea lions, seals, and walruses. Also clustering along the boardwalk are a handful of small private amusement parks, each selling their own ride tickets. One of the parks, **Astroland,** closed in 2008, amid rumors that other parks would follow. For now there is still plenty to enjoy, but it is another good reason to take the kids to this great landmark soon.

At 12th Street, Demo's Wonder Wheel Park features the 1920 landmark **Wonder Wheel,** an ingenious double Ferris wheel of gargantuan proportions. For those who like to stay closer to earth, there are bumper cars, tilt-a-whirls, spinning teacups, carousels, and kiddie rides, as well as satisfyingly cheesy arcades; the area also has

Coney Island's Wonder Wheel.

mini-golf and go-kart concessions. Compared to huge plasticized theme parks such as Disney, Six Flags, and Busch Gardens, the Coney Island amusements have a grungy midway glamour that older kids will appreciate—it's the Real Thing. (With kids, it's best to visit by day—and know where your wallet is at all times.)

The beach and boardwalk have been spruced up lately, though, and the beachfront souvenir shops and food stands have acquired a post-modern hipster gloss, with Brooklyn artists decorating their side walls with retro murals. Even the local freak show, tucked up a Surf Avenue side street near the parks, has the whiff of a performance art installation. The Stillwell Avenue subway station (last stop for the D and F trains) has been refurbished to a high sheen, and along the boardwalk to the east, there's a tidy baseball stadium for a popular Mets farm team, the **Brooklyn Cyclones** (© **718/449-8497**; www.

brooklyncyclones.com). But you can still get a reliable kosher frank at Nathan's famous open-air hot dog stand on Surf Avenue—some things never change.

ⓘ Surf Ave. and 10th St. (© **718/372-0275**; www.astroland.com).

✈ John F. Kennedy International, Newark Liberty International, LaGuardia.

🛏 $$ **Excelsior Hotel,** 45 W. 81st St. (© **800/368-4575** or 212/362-9200; www.excelsiorhotelny.com). $$$ **Le Parker Meridien,** 118 W. 57th St. (© **800/543-4300** or 212/245-5000; www.parkermeridien.com).

BEST TIME: Amusement parks open daily June to Labor Day, Sat and Sun Apr to May and Sept to Oct.

WHY THEY'LL THANK YOU: Atmosphere, atmosphere, atmosphere.

---

488 Roller Coasters

Millennium Force
Cedar Point's Record Setter
Ages 10 & up • Sandusky, Ohio, USA

When it opened in 2000, the Millennium Force at Ohio's Cedar Point amusement park not only was the world's tallest roller coaster (310 ft.), but also had the longest drop (300 ft.), the steepest banked turns of any noninverted coaster (122 degrees), and traveled at the fastest speed (93 mph). It may climb up that 310-foot peak (taller than the Statue of Liberty) at a modest 45-degree angle, but when it plunges down the other side it's angled at 80 degrees. It whips through two tunnels, and covers more than a mile in length, speeding to its finish line in 2 minutes and 20 seconds, almost before you know what hit you. But no record is unbreakable. Within 3 years, the Millennium Force was

surpassed—by another roller coaster at Cedar Point, of course.

There's no question that Cedar Point prides itself on its roller coasters—it has 16 of them, the newest being the **Top Thrill Dragster,** which debuted in 2003. Top Thrill accelerates like a dragster right out of the gate, taking only 4 seconds to reach 120 mph, and then climbs *straight up,* perpendicular to the ground, to a height of 420 feet, the equivalent of a 42-story building. And what does it do next? It drops down just as steeply (again at 120 mph), throwing in a wrenching 270-degree twist. The **Wicked Twister** is another heart-in-your-mouth experience, a U-shaped suspended coaster that ping-pongs back and forth between two

The Top Thrill Dragster at Cedar Point.

others are passionate about the experience on **Magnum,** or **Raptor,** or **Gemini,** or **Blue Streak,** or any of the other innovative steel coasters at Cedar Point.

Like Lake Compounce (see Boulder Dash ⓐ), Cedar Point is a vintage park, first opening in 1870 on a peninsula jutting out into Lake Erie, about halfway between Cleveland and Toledo. Cedar Point has 68 rides in all and that's not even counting the attractions at the adjoining 18-acre water park, **Soak City;** an indoor water park, **Castaway Island,** recently opened to extend the season (outdoor areas May–early Sept only). Four resort hotels on the 364-acre property are available for those who need more than 1 day to do all the rides.

ⓘ 1 Cedar Point Dr. (✆ **419/627-2350;** www.cedarpoint.com).

✈ Cleveland International, 10 miles.

🛏 $$ **Cleveland Marriott Downtown,** 127 Public Sq. (✆ **800/228-9290** or 216/696-9200; www.marriott.com). $$ **Holiday Inn-City Center Lakeside,** 1111 Lakeside Ave. (✆ **888/425-3835** or 216/241-5100; www.ichotelsgroup.com).

BEST TIME: May to early Sept.

WHY THEY'LL THANK YOU: That moment at the peak, before the drop. Multiplied 16 times.

215-foot-high towers, corkscrewing up and down each tower, three times forward and twice backward, reaching a speed of up to 70 mph. No wonder these two have a minimum height requirement of 52 inches, whereas for Millennium Force you only need to be 48 inches. Each of these coasters has its rabid fans, while

Roller Coasters 489

Kingda Ka
Bigger Is Better in New Jersey
Ages 10 & up • Jackson, New Jersey, USA

As soon as one roller coaster sets a record, another new coaster is built to break it. Recently, the crown passed from Cedar Point to **Six Flags Great Adventure** in New Jersey, where the Kingda Ka debuted in 2005. It's almost as if a designer went down a list of stats from the previous record holder, the Top Thrill Dragster (see above), and nudged each one just a tick higher. At the time we went to press, this one held all the records.

Using hydraulic technology, the Kingda Ka launches from 0 to *128 mph* in a breathtaking 3.5 seconds, then climbs 458 feet at

El Toro at Six Flags Great Adventure.

a 90-degree angle—nearly 40 feet higher than Top Thrill. Making a neat quarter-turn at the top of its green steel track, the ride hesitates—just long enough for you to realize where you're going and wonder why you ever thought this was a good idea—then whooshes back down the whole 458 feet, torquing into a 270-degree spiral. This is followed by a fast-paced camel hump and a banked left turn, before you glide back to the start, shaken if not stirred. The whole episode lasts less than a minute—50.6 seconds, to be exact—and you probably stood in line an hour to do it. And you'll probably do it again.

For those who prefer wooden coaster action—where the heights may be less but the sensation more intense—Six Flags Great Adventure has **El Toro.** This out-and-back wood coaster drops at a record-breaking 76 degrees on its first 188-foot hill, followed by three more hills in rapid succession (112 ft., 100 ft., and 82 ft.), all at a speed of 70 mph.

As you'd expect from this homogenized theme-park franchise, the New Jersey Six Flags has an overwhelming number of top-class rides—wood coasters, steel coasters, dark rides, soak rides, free-falls and flumes, and a Ferris wheel, many of them with licensed-character tie-ins (Batman: The Ride and Superman Ultimate Flight are two of the most popular). There are a cable car, a large section of rides scaled for younger kids, and plenty of pocket-emptying food and souvenir stands. Lines are a fact of life, and it doesn't come cheap—but for East Coast roller coaster addicts, this is an essential visit.

(i) **Six Flags,** Off I-195 (© **732/928-1821;** www.sixflags.com).

✈ Newark, NJ, 67 miles. Philadelphia, PA, 60 miles.

🏨 $$ **Freehold Gardens Hotel,** 50 Gibson Place, Freehold, NJ (© **732/780-3870;** www.freeholdgardens.com). $$ **Ramada Inn,** 2373 Rte. 9, Toms River, NJ (© **800/5-HOTELS** [546-8357] or 732/905-2626; www.ramada.com).

BEST TIME: June–Aug; Sat and Sun Apr–May and Sept–Oct.

WHY THEY'LL THANK YOU: Saying they rode the biggest.

Dueling Coasters at Islands of Adventure

Ages 10 & up • Orlando, Florida, USA

For kids who've graduated to the top of the thrill-ride chain (that is, those who can pass the 54-in. height requirements), no trip to Orlando is complete without tackling **The Incredible Hulk Coaster** and **Dueling Dragons** at Islands of Adventure. Both were opened in the same year, 1999, almost as if Universal Studios Florida—the theme-park mega-corporation that's given Disney such a run for its money in Orlando—knew it was setting up a duel. Coaster addicts can't go home without riding both, investing a serious chunk of line-waiting time—no matter how early in the day you get here, you can only stand in line for one at a time, which means that by the time you hit your second coaster, the line is already snaking around the block.

Dueling Dragons was the world's first **inverted dual coaster,** running two intertwined coasters (the red Fire Dragon and the blue Ice Dragon) through loops, rolls, corkscrews, inversions, and . . . oh, yes, at each other (don't worry—you'll miss your oncoming foe by about 12 in.). As green as its comic namesake, the Hulk coaster is a steel-framed thriller that pulls the same G-forces as an F-16 fighter jet, includes **seven inversions,** hits speeds of up to 60 mph, and (much to the delight of kids) **glows at night.**

The Incredible Hulk Coaster at Islands of Adventure.

So, who wins the battle between the Hulk and the Dragons? Both rides offer good themes and preattraction queue areas: You tour Bruce Banner's lab as you wait to climb aboard the Hulk; over at Dragons, you wend your way through a medieval castle and get briefed by Merlin. The Incredible Hulk Coaster offers a more dramatic launch (from a dark tunnel out into the sunlight) and a smoother ride than Dueling Dragons, but for pure thrills, the front seat of the Fire Dragon (which tops out at 60 mph, 5 miles faster than its Ice counterpart) gets my vote as the best rush in town.

Once you've tackled both coasters, Islands of Adventure offers plenty of other adrenaline-pumping options. Take an 85-foot plunge on the amazingly detailed **Jurassic Park River Adventure** water ride; get swept up in a tangle of 3-D action and special effects on **The Amazing Adventures of Spider-Man** ride, perhaps the best themed ride in all of Orlando; or nose-dive in a log flume at 50 mph over **Dudley Do-Right's Ripsaw Falls.** Though there are rides for younger kids (especially in the delightfully whimsical **Seuss Landing**), Islands will appeal most to the over-10 set.

ⓘ ℂ **800/711-0080** or 407/363-8000; www.universalorlando.com.

✈ Orlando International, 25 miles.

🛏 $$ **AmeriSuites Universal,** 5895 Caravan Court (ℂ **800/833-1516** or 407/351-0627; www.amerisuites.com). $$$ **Royal Pacific Resort,** 6300 Hollywood Way (ℂ **800/232-7827** or 407/503-3000; www.loewshotels.com).

WHY THEY'LL THANK YOU: Action, action, and more action.

---

491 Roller Coasters

Catching Airtime Along the Strip
Las Vegas's In-House Thrill Rides
Ages 8 & up • Las Vegas, Nevada, USA

The Strip in Las Vegas already looks like a carnival midway, with hyperbolic dazzle on all sides competing for your attention. So no one should be surprised to learn that Las Vegas has its own set of roller coasters and thrill rides that dance in and out of the casinos. For me, that kitschy incongruity is exactly what makes it a sure bet for kids.

The New York–New York property uses its roller coaster almost as a decorative flourish, highlighting the fake Manhattan skyline atop the casino, and for many gamblers that's all it will ever be, a bit of scenery. But this **Manhattan Express** does in fact offer coaster hounds quite a respectable 3-minute ride, hitting speeds of up to 67 mph. It begins by climbing 203 feet, dropping 75 feet, then surprising you with a second vertical drop of 144 feet. (Somewhere in here you careen past the Statue of Liberty's torch, but who's paying attention to the scenery?) Next comes the coaster's trademark "heartline" twist, a barrel-roll inversion that hangs passengers upside down for a terrifying instant before diving under its own track again. A series of bunny hops atop the skyline repeatedly lift you off your seat, followed by a second inversion and a 540-degree spiral drop for a finale.

At the Sahara, **Speed: The Ride** is a stellar example of a shuttle coaster, that is, a ride that goes to the end of its track and then makes the return trip backward (as in not-being-able-to-see-where-you're-going backward). The ride begins in the NASCAR Café (where there are also several race-car

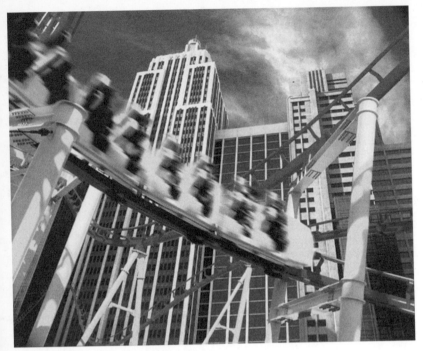

Manhattan Express roller coaster in Las Vegas.

simulators), blasts through a hole in the wall, dips through a tunnel under the Sahara's sidewalk, whirs around a vertical loop, rattles through Arabian-fantasy arches in the hotel's marquee, and shoots straight up a 224-foot tower—yep, at a 90-degree angle—where it hangs for one gravity-defying moment before crashing backward and repeating the whole course in reverse, loop and tunnel and all. You do this at 70 mph and see how wobbly your legs are when you get out of the car.

(i) **Manhattan Express,** New York–New York Hotel & Casino, 3400 Las Vegas Blvd. S. (© **702/740-6969;** www.nynyhotel casino.com). **Speed: The Ride,** Sahara Hotel & Casino, 2535 Las Vegas Blvd. S. (© **702/737-2111;** www.saharahotel casino.com).

✈ McCarran International.

🛏 $$ **Mandalay Bay,** 3950 Las Vegas Blvd. S. (© **877/632-7000** or 702/632-7000; www.mandalaybay.com). $$ **MGM Grand,** 3799 Las Vegas Blvd. S. (© **800/929-1111** or 702/891-7777; www.mgm grand.com).

WHY THEY'LL THANK YOU: Loop-de-loops over the Strip.

Playland's Retro Rides

All ages • Rye, New York, USA

Remember in the movie *Big,* when a creepy fortunetelling machine granted Tom Hanks's younger self a fateful wish to become big? That scene was shot at Playland, a nostalgic throwback of an amusement park set in a leafy seaside suburb conveniently close to New York City. This old-timey collection of rides and games is what amusement parks used to be like before they went on steroids and became big, overhyped, commercialized mega–theme parks.

But it's no mere rinky-dink midway—Playland is actually listed on the National Register of Historic Places. Playland opened in 1928, right on Long Island Sound, and has been kept up beautifully ever since, with neat landscaping, landmark Art Deco buildings, and old-fashioned charm: striped awnings, painted wooden fences enclosing the rides, and festive-looking ticket booths.

Kids 5 and under should be steered straight to **Kiddyland,** which has rides tailored to their size such as The Kiddy Whip, Kiddyland Bumper Cars, and the Demolition Derby. For older kids, the most thrilling rides (which, of course, require the longest waits in line) are probably the **Hurricane Coaster,** the **Crazy Mouse, Power Surge,** and the vintage wooden **Dragon Coaster**—tame by Busch Gardens' standards, but enough to make me lose my lunch. My favorites, however, are the more retro rides: the **Ferris Wheel,** the **Whip,** and, best of all, the one-of-a-kind **Derby Riders,** a circular track where you plunge forward on steel horses that race twice as fast as carousel nags. I'm embarrassed to tell you how many times in a row I've ridden that one. Plan on several hours here; your kids will insist on it.

To make a full day of it, in addition to the rides, Playland offers a beach, a pool, an ice rink, minigolf, and a lake for boating, which are open seasonally.

ⓘ Playland Pkwy., 1 hr. from Manhattan (✆ **914/813-7010;** www.ryeplayland.org). **MetroNorth** (✆ **800/METRO-INFO** [638-7646] or 212/532-4900; www.mta.nyc.ny. us/mnr).

✈ John F. Kennedy International, Newark Liberty International, LaGuardia.

🛏 $$ **Excelsior Hotel,** 45 W. 81st St. (✆ **800/368-4575** or 212/362-9200; www. excelsiorhotelny.com). $$$ **Le Parker Meridien,** 118 W. 57th St. (✆ **800/543-4300** or 212/245-5000; www.parker meridien.com).

BEST TIME: May–Sept.

WHY THEY'LL THANK YOU: A kinder, gentler notion of what it takes to have fun.

The Santa Cruz Boardwalk
California Classic by the Sea

All ages • Coast between Monterey & San Francisco, California, USA

One of the few old-fashioned amusement parks left in the world, the Santa Cruz Beach Boardwalk is California's answer to Rye Playland. Situated next to Santa Cruz's lovely mile-long public beach, the boardwalk is a half-mile strip of rides, shops, and restaurants, harking back to an era of seaside innocent fun. It's the sort of classic site you don't necessarily expect on the West Coast.

The park has 34 rides, two of them national landmarks. **The Carousel of Delight,** built in 1911 by Charles I.D. Looff, boasts hand-carved wooden horses, a 342-pipe organ band, and one of the few brass ring grabs left in existence; snatch the brass ring as your horse whirls past the post, then throw it into a painted clown's mouth to win a free ride. Looff's son, Arthur Looff, designed the park's other landmark, the red-and-white 1924 **Giant Dipper** roller coaster, which offers great views of Monterey Bay from its peaks—though few riders manage to take them in while being hurtled up and down at 55 mph. They have a split second longer to enjoy the views from the top of the 125-foot-tall Double Shot drop tower. A host of other thrill rides trade on speed, with such names as Hurricane, Typhoon, and Tsunami; indoor "dark rides" include the Haunted Castle and Ghost Blaster,

The Santa Cruz Boardwalk.

though I prefer the 1961-vintage **Cave Train,** where glow-in-the-dark prehistoric characters pop out. There is a section of smaller-scale rides for the under-36-inch crowd as well.

Although there's no admission fee to get onto the boardwalk, the individual ride tickets can mount up fast—an "unlimited rides" bracelet, which at first doesn't seem cheap, could end up saving you money. The beach boardwalk keeps seasonal hours, open daily from Memorial Day weekend to Labor Day but only on weekends and holidays throughout the spring and fall.

ⓘ ℰ **831/426-7433;** www.beachboardwalk.com.

✈ San Francisco International, 77 miles.

🛏 $$ **Fern River Resort,** 5250 Hwy. 9, Felton (ℰ **831/335-4412;** www.fernriver.com).

WHY THEY'LL THANK YOU: Screaming from the top of the Giant Dipper.

---

494 Theme Parks

Disneyland
The Theme Park That Started It All
All ages • Anaheim, California, USA

I was a Disneyland baby—my parents took me there the summer it opened, in 1955, when it was still surrounded by sleepy orange groves. I went again in 1967, 1989, and most recently in 2005, the amusement park's 50th anniversary year. And although I'm not a theme-park fanatic, I will always have a deep and abiding love for Disneyland. My skeptical 13-year-old, having heard it dubbed "The Happiest Place on Earth," spent his entire day in the Magic Kingdom looking for people who weren't happy—and he failed. Happily.

Smaller than Walt Disney World, Disneyland feels truer to the childlike enthusiasm of founder Walt Disney. Originally Disneyland was divided into four "lands"—Adventureland, Fantasyland, Frontierland, and Tomorrowland, symmetrically arranged around the iconic **Cinderella's castle,** where fireworks still scintillate every night. As the 1950s Wild West fad waned and Sputnik-era optimism went sour, Frontierland and Tomorrowland shrank and new areas were wedged in: Main Street USA, an old-timey-America shopping area; New Orleans Square; Critter Country; and Mickey's Toontown, a Roger Rabbit–inspired section for younger children. In the process, the park's layout has become a little more confusing; we were constantly consulting the free park map we got at the front gate.

Every kid will have different **favorite rides,** but these were my kids' (remember, this is from a teenager and two preteens): Mr. Toad's Wild Ride (Fantasyland), Pirates of the Caribbean (New Orleans Square), Tom Sawyer's Island (Frontierland), Peter Pan's Flight (Fantasyland), Davy Crockett's Canoes (Critter Country), the Jungle Cruise (Adventureland), It's a Small World (Fantasyland), and Innoventions (Tomorrowland). And what they liked about them was the storytelling—not heart-skidding vertical drops, not flashy laser light effects, just scrupulous artistic detail and wry humor. Hurtling into a cartoon hell with naughty Mr. Toad—that alone made the whole day worthwhile.

Long lines are a fact of life at Disneyland, especially on weekends and all school vacations. Don't be suckers for them—my kids decided that 5 minutes of watching huge ceramic Dumbos fly around flapping their ears was more fun than waiting 45 minutes to ride them. If you must, arrive early and make a beeline for the most popular rides, which are generally the adrenaline pumpers—the Indiana Jones Adventure, Star Tours, Big Thunder Mountain Railroad, Splash Mountain, the Haunted Mansion, and Pirates of the Caribbean. But I'm philosophical about lines: What's so bad about 30 extra minutes of unplanned conversation with a child?

ⓘ **Magic Way** (✆ **714/781-4565** or 714/ 781-7290; www.disneyland.com).

✈ Los Angeles International, 33 miles. John Wayne Airport, in Santa Ana, 15 miles.

🛏 $ **Candy Cane Inn,** 1747 S. Harbor Blvd. (✆ **800/345-7057** or 714/774-5284; www.candycaneinn.net). $$$ **Disney's Grand Californian Hotel,** 1600 S. Disneyland Dr. (✆ **714/956-MICKEY** [956-6425] or 714/635-2300; www.disneyland.com).

WHY THEY'LL THANK YOU: The one, the only, original theme park.

Theme Parks **495**

Legoland

Constructing a Fantasy, One Brick at a Time

All ages • Billund, Denmark

Every spring, the Legoland in Denmark opens its doors to enthusiastic Lego lovers the world over. The Danish Legoland is much like its cousins in Germany, England, and in California, but it is the oldest and largest park of the chain. It shares with the other parks an environment that's all primary colors, right angles, modular components and imagination.

Legoland is by no means all built of Lego blocks: the Danish park feature lush landscapes and pristine walkways along with over 50 rides, shows, and attractions. While a few coasters and rides have a higher thrill factor, these are tame compared to the Six Flagses and Bush Gardenses of this world, making Legoland and ideal place to take younger children. In fact, there is a special roller coaster just for smaller kids called the Frog Hopper.

The heart of the park in **Miniland,** where you can see cities and famous landmarks all make of Lego blocks. The obsessively accurate models of sites in the United States, Germany, Holland, Norway, Sweden, and Denmark are stupefying. To build a Washington Monument out of Legos is one thing; to make a model of Mount Rushmore is quite another, but there it stands. Young movie fans will enjoy visiting the **Lego version of Los Angeles,** where they can become movie moguls as cameras roll and actors perform on a stage wing built of 750,000 Lego bricks. For the adventurous, Miniland offers plenty of action and suspense with a canoe ride that end at a waterfall, and a safari where kids can see lions, elephants and other exotic animals—all made of Legos—of course.

Another popular feature is the **driving school,** where kids can tool around in electric cars and gain a driver's license, combining fun with lessons about traffic safety. They can further stretch their minds at the **Mindstorms Robotic Center,** which allows visitors to build their own Lego robots. Also featured is the low-tech but fun activity rooms stocked to the brim with Lego blocks.

All of the parks attractions are Lego themed and many are based on a particular line of Lego: The dragon coaster, for example, is based on the Knight's Kingdom Lego sets, so your kids will find themselves immediately—and happily—at home.

ⓘ Nordmarksvej 9, DK7190, Billund (✆ **45/75/33-13-33;** www.legoland.com).

✈ Billund Airport.

🛏 $$$ **Hotel Legoland,** Aastvej 10, DK-7190 Billund (✆ **45/75/33-12-44;** www.hotellegoland.dk). $ **Zleep Hotel Billund,** Passagerterminalen 4 (✆ **45/75/33-19-00;** www.zleep.dk).

WHY THEY'LL THANK YOU: Piecing the world together, and pulling it apart again.

Legoland.

496 Theme Parks

The Mall of America
Minnesota's Mega-Mall Amusements
All ages • Bloomington, Minnesota, USA

What nerve it took to build a shopping center in suburban Minnesota and call it The Mall of America. And yet there is something iconic about this over-the-top shrine to consumerism. Subscribing to the all-American bigger-is-better philosophy, the mall could hold seven Yankee Stadiums or 258 Statues of Liberty; walk one circuit around a level of stores and you've clocked nearly a mile. There are over 520 stores at this huge retail center 20 minutes south of downtown Minneapolis, stacked on four brightly lit levels around a central glass atrium—not only that, but 14 movie screens, a food court, 20 sit-down restaurants, half a dozen attractions, and even a wedding chapel. You've got to see it to believe it.

The main attraction is **Nickelodeon Universe,** America's largest enclosed theme park, which covers 7 ground-floor acres in the immense central atrium with 30 rides, including a kiddie roller coaster that loops around large planters full of trees. This will thrill toddlers and young grade schoolers; kids who've outgrown

Underwater Adventures Aquarium.

those tame rides will still enjoy the **Underwater Adventures Aquarium,** where 4,500 sea creatures swim around in tanks on a subterranean level. Between the virtual submarine ride and the "shark encounter"—a glass tunnel that walks you through a shark tank—it's like a mini–Sea World. At the mall.

For teens or preteens (and, admit it, adults too), the **A.C.E.S Flight Simulators** let you play virtual pilot on an F-18 Hornet jet or a World War II-era P-51 Mustang. An even bigger deal is the **NASCAR Silicon Motor Speedway,** where anyone over 52 inches tall can get behind the wheel of a rigged-up stationary stock car and spend 20 minutes stepping on the gas, banking on the turns, and stomping on the brakes (there's a passenger seat where kids age 4 and older can ride shotgun on this virtual race).

While not strictly a theme attraction (no admission charge, for one thing), the four-story **Lego store** is as good as a ride, with some 90 life-size Lego models to marvel at; the **Build-a-Bear Workshop** is another store that offers plenty of entertainment. So what if most of the other shops are the usual gang of chain stores? It's called the Mall of America, dude—so who's expecting snooty high-end retail? It's supersize, it's commercial, and it caters to the masses—and there's nothing more American than that.

ⓘ 60 E. Broadway (www.mallofamerica. com).

✈ Minneapolis/St. Paul International, 10 miles.

🛏 $ **Best Western Kelly Inn,** 161 Saint Anthony Ave., St. Paul (ⓒ 800/780-7234; www.bestwesternstpaul.com).

WHY THEY'LL THANK YOU: Flying planes and driving race cars.

Luna Park

Ages 4 & up • Sydney, Australia

No child who has ever walked into Luna Park, through the grotesque gaping grin of the Face, could fail to be wowed. First opened in 1935, and continually refurbished throughout the 1950s, Luna Park is Sydney's homegrown version of Disneyland, and while it may not have the Disney imagination going for it, it made up for that with a sturdy Aussie sense of fun.

The Sydney Harbor and Opera House serve as the stunning backdrop for this charmingly nostalgic park. Though its history from the 1970s on has been rocky—redevelopment proposals, shutdowns, safety and noise violations—adults who were hooked as children have continually risen to save the park, and it now stands as a National Heritage protected site, providing fun for a whole new generation of kids.

The entrance is still through the face, a giant, polyurethane mask nearly 9m (20 ft.) wide. Behind the mask, the midway stretches to Coney Island, the original 1930s funhouse—a cornucopia of vintage

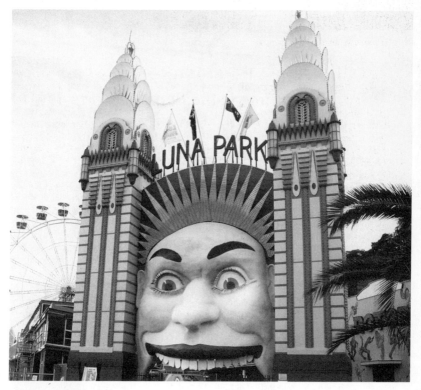

The entrance to Luna Park.

amusements like rotating barrels, moving platforms, large slides plus a bank of arcade games where your kids can try their luck. Along the midway, you'll find major rides like an **antique carousel** (the Racing Cockerels), a **Ferris wheel,** a **flying saucer ride,** and the 1960s era **Wild Mouse.** A **boardwalk** ambles along the park's seaside edge, making it a perfect place to take in the sights of both the park and Sydney Harbor.

The park's Heritage listed **Crystal Palace** has been retrofitted as a function space while an event venue called the **Luna Circus** replaces a ride called the Big Dipper—which was ruled too noisy to remain in this densely populated neighborhood. It's not a perfect restoration, but it's enough to keep the spirit of the original amusement park alive—and an experience that your kids will not forget. You can get there by taking one of the Sydney Harbor Ferries at Milson's Point—an event in itself.

ⓘ 1 Olympic Dr., Milson's Point (✆ **61/2/9922-6644;** www.lunaparksydney.com/index.html).

✈ Sydney International Airport.

🛏 $$$ **North Sydney Harbourview Hotel,** 17 Blue St., North Sydney (✆ **61/2/9955-0499,** or toll-free in Australia 300/785-453; www.viewhotels.com.au). $$ **Wattle Private Hotel,** 108 Oxford St., Darlinghurst (✆ **61/2/9332-4118;** www.thewattle.com).

WHY THEY'LL THANK YOU: Walking through the face.

Theme Parks **498**

Parc Asterix
'Toon Time in the Paris Outskirts
All ages • Plailly, France

Explain me this: Why would a family who took the trouble to fly all the way to France ever go to Disneyland Paris? You could just as easily go to a real French theme park that's just as much (if not more) fun: Parc Asterix. Families I know who've done both definitely vote for the homegrown French park—its *joie de vivre* is the real thing.

Granted, English-speaking children may not be familiar with these comic book characters. But you don't have to read *Asterix* comics to get the gist of the thing; it's enough to know that the characters are goofy Gauls living under the rule of the Roman Empire, which gives the theme park an excuse to haul out images from Roman mythology, Viking lore, even the Druids. There's definitely a sense of humor at play—when you stand underneath the giant statue of a thunderbolt-clutching Zeus that presides over the top-rated roller coaster, look up under his toga and you'll see he's been provided with spotted underpants (providing a photo op that few parkgoers pass up). Parc Asterix's autoroute ride cracks me up: Nationale 7, where children drive Model-T-style jalopies along a replica of the French highway that's famously choked with holiday traffic every summer weekend. So what if it doesn't tie into the Asterix theme—they couldn't resist the joke.

This spick-and-span, smartly conceived amusement park, open seasonally, offers some 30 rides, for all levels—everything from a tiny **kiddie carousel** to the **Towers of Zeus** (Europe's biggest wooden roller coaster) and the exhilarating **Goudurix,** a speedy coaster with no fewer than seven loop-de-loops. Themes are not just tacked on, they really enhance the rides—such as the swing ship shaped like a Viking longboat,

Parc Asterix.

the scramble ride with a many-headed Hydra dragon sprouting from the center, or the inner tube ride that swoops down the Styx river, the mythological entry to Hell. The kiddie section is designed like a Druid forest (or at least a cozy Smurf-esque Druid forest); the stage shows are in a pseudo-Roman arena, with an aquatic Poseidon's Theater added for dolphin shows.

Your vision of touring France with your family may be all about Versailles and the Louvre, but the children may eventually clamor for something more . . . well, *fun.* In that case, you can feel good about giving in to the Parc Asterix option: In its own way, it is a little slice of French culture, something you could never do back home. Yet it's about the same distance from Paris as Disneyland: 35km (22 miles) north of

Paris, easily within day-trip range (you'll need a connecting bus from the Roissy train station if you don't go by car). *Pourquoi pas?*

ⓘ Off the A1 (✆ **33/3/44-62-31-31;** www. parcasterix.fr).

✈ De Gaulle, Orly.

🛏 $$$ **Hotel de Fleurie,** 32–34 rue Grégoire-de-Tours (✆ **33/1/53-73-70-00;** www.hotel-de-fleurie.tm.fr). $$ **Residence Lord Byron,** 5 rue de Chateaubriand (✆ **33/1/43-59-89-98;** www.escapade-paris.com).

BEST TIME: May–Sept.

WHY THEY'LL THANK YOU: It takes a lot of Gaul to have this much fun with history.

Europa-Park
The Grand Tour, All in a Day
All ages • Rust, Germany

From the country that brought you the Porsche and the autobahn, you'd expect the rides at Germany's largest theme park to be high-tech and speed-obsessed. And yes indeed, Europa Park does have Europe's highest and fastest roller coaster, the **Silver Star,** which climbs to 240 feet, travels at 79 mph, and (here's a plus) delivers a ride that's a full 4 minutes long. But, though there are seven dramatic roller coasters at Europa Park, this place is not just about the rides. It's a clever **microcosm of Europe,** with shops and restaurants and shows as well as rides in miniversions of 11 different countries. Corny as it may sound, it works.

Sound familiar? Yes, Epcot in Orlando originated the pocket-nation idea, and Busch Garden Williamsburg jumped on the same bandwagon—but Europa Park covers more European countries on its 65-hectare (160-acre) site, from Scandinavia to Greece, from Portugal to Russia, and does so with an attention to architectural detail that puts the other parks' stage-set streetscapes to shame. From the replica of England's venerable Globe Theatre to one of Russia's Mir Space Station, it hits all the cultural highlights; the **Panorama Train** that circles the park lets you drink it all in for an overview, but immerse yourself in each section and you'll be engrossed. If thrill rides aren't your thing, well, Europa Park is fun, even without taking a single ride.

But when it comes to the rides, attention to creative detail again makes all the difference. The folks who designed this park

The Alpen Express at Europa-Park.

clearly have scoped out the competition—if they can't have Mad Tea Party spinning teacups, they'll put **spinning Delft coffee cups** in the Holland section; instead of a Haunted Mansion, they have a **Ghost Castle** in the Italy area; and let's just call Pirates in Batavia, in the Portugal section, an "homage" to Pirates of the Caribbean. But these aren't cheesy imitations, they are every bit as well-executed as the Disney originals, and just as much fun.

Although Europa Park isn't open year-round—that pesky German climate—they manage to have at least part of the park open most of the time, with a Halloween-themed experience in October and a December Christmas theme; even though several of the bigger outdoor rides are closed in the off season, there's still plenty to do. See the website for details.

ⓘ Europa-Park Strasse 2 (✆ **49/180/5776688;** www.europapark.de).

✈ Freiburg, 2 hr. from Frankfurt.

🛏 $$$ **Colombi-Hotel,** Ritteckring 16, Freiburg (✆ **49/761/21060;** www.colombi.de). $$ **Park Hotel Post,** Eisenbahnstrasse 37, Freiburg (✆ **49/761/385480;** www.park-hotel-post.de).

BEST TIME: May–Sept.

WHY THEY'LL THANK YOU: Fjord-rafting and splashing in the Mediterranean, all in a single park.

500 Theme Parks

Tivoli Gardens
Copenhagen's Jewel
All ages • Copenhagen, Denmark

Though it's been around forever—since 1843—and is as much a simple pleasure garden as it is a thrill-ride attraction, Copenhagen's Tivoli Gardens still regularly appears on 10-best lists of amusement parks. Profuse flower beds, fantasy pavilions, tiny twinkling lights illuminating it at night—the entire fairy-tale effect is magical, just what you'd expect from the homeland of Hans Christian Andersen. This place is as classic as it gets—and kids still love it.

Perhaps even more so than its Vienna counterpart, the Prater, Tivoli Gardens is woven into the life of its city. Tivoli is right in downtown Copenhagen, between the city hall and the central railway station. While much of Tivoli is devoted to gardens, restaurants, theaters, and a tiny lake for pleasure boating, there are **25 fanciful rides,** spangled with lights day and night. The kids can try out a merry-go-round of tiny Viking ships, a Ferris wheel with cars shaped like hot-air balloons, a set of dragon boats, and the Flying Trunk, where you wheel past wooden-doll scenes from Hans Christian Andersen stories. There are a fun house, a couple of auto-drives, and not one but two drop rides, one of them scaled for toddlers—two-thirds of the rides, in fact, are suitable for younger children. For older kids, the new steel roller coaster here, the **Demon,** is the biggest in Denmark, and though it only goes 49 mph, it does have three vertical loops; there's also an exciting wooden coaster, the **Rutschebanen.** The **Star Flyer** is Europe's tallest swing ride, bedazzled with stars and planets in tribute to the great Danish astronomer Tyco Brahe.

Between the rides, just strolling around Tivoli is delightful. An Arabian-style palace, with towers and arches, houses more than two dozen **restaurants** (including a

You'll meet all sort of interesting characters at Tivoli Gardens.

Hard Rock Cafe!) in a range of prices. Try to time your visit to coincide with the parade of the red-uniformed **Tivoli Boys Guard,** looking just like toy soldiers, on early weekend evenings (also Wed); their regimental band gives Saturday afternoon concerts on the large open-air stage at the center of the gardens, where at night you can see tumbling clowns, acrobats, and aerialists.

ⓘ Vesterbrogade 3 (℗ **45/33/15-10-01;** www.tivoligardens.com).

🛏 $ **Hotel Ansgar,** Colbjørnsensgade 18–20 (℗ **45/33/13-19-13;** www.ibsens hotel.dk). $$$ **Sofitel Copenhagen,** Bernstorffsgade 4 (℗ **800/221-4542** in the U.S., or ℗ 45/33/14-92-62; www.sofitel. com).

BEST TIME: Mid-Apr to mid-Sept.

WHY THEY'LL THANK YOU: Speaks to the child in all of us.

The United States

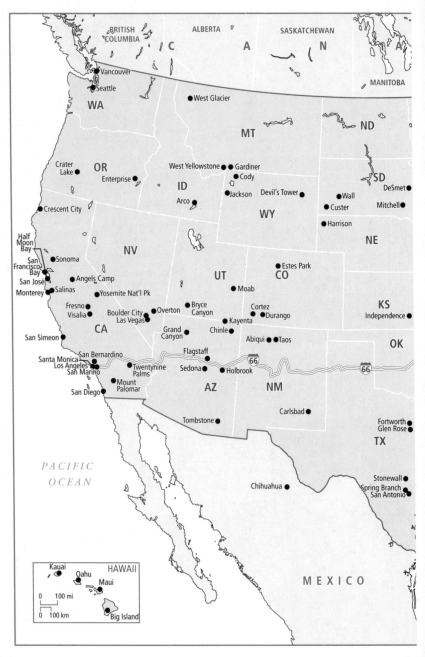

BRITISH COLUMBIA
Vancouver
Seattle
WA

ALBERTA C A N A D A SASKATCHEWAN

MANITOBA

West Glacier

MT

ND

Crater Lake
OR
Enterprise

West Yellowstone ● Gardiner
● Cody
ID
Arco ●
Jackson

Devil's Tower ●

SD
DeSmet ●

● Wall
● Custer
Mitchell ●

Crescent City

Half Moon Bay
San Francisco Bay
San José
Monterey

NV

Sonoma

Angels Camp
Salinas
Fresno
Visalia

WY

● Harrison

NE

Estes Park ●
UT
● Moab
CO

Yosemite Nat'l Pk

Boulder City ● Overton
Las Vegas

CA

Bryce Canyon ●

Grand Canyon ●

Cortez ●
● Durango
Kayenta ●

Chinle ●

Abiqui ● ● Taos

KS
Independence ●

OK

San Simeon

San Bernardino
Santa Monica
Los Angeles
San Marino

Flagstaff ●
Twentynine Palms
Sedona ●

66

66

Mount Palomar
San Diego

AZ

Holbrook

NM

Carlsbad ●

Fortworth ●
Glen Rose ●
TX

Tombstone ●

PACIFIC
OCEAN

Chihuahua ●

Stonewall ●
Spring Branch ●
San Antonio ●

Kauai ●

HAWAII

Oahu ●
Maui ●

0   100 mi

0   100 km

Big Island ●

MEXICO

300 mi
300 km

ONTARIO

QUEBEC

ME

D   A

Mount
Desert Is.

Bemidji

Bayfield   Mackinac   VT
                                              Ticonderoga   Lexington,
                                     Saranac   Concord,
MN   Lake   NH   Lincoln
                                                              Boston
            Greenbay   NY   Plymouth Rock
                 WI   MI   MA   Cape Cod
        Pepin   Cooperstown Sturbridge RI   Nantucket
Walnut   Hartford   Martha's
Grove   CT   Vineyard
                                     West   Newport
Harpers   Orange   Mashantucket
Ferry   NewYork City Mystic Seaport
        Chicago   Dearborn   Bushkill
IA   Sandusky   PA Valley Forge
        Amana   South   Cleveland Lancaster   Philadelphia
                       Bend   Canton Gettysburg NJ
                  IN   OH   Baltimore DE
            Fishers   Newark   MD
IL   Dayton   Washington D.C. Assateague Island
        Hannibal   Cincinatti   WV
66   Louisville   Williamsburg
Topeka   Collinsville Cave City   Monteo   Yorktown
Independence MO   KY   Jamestown
                     Park City   VA   Kill Devil Hills
Diamond Mansfield
66   Nashville   Gatlinburg Asheville NC
        AR Memphis   TN
Little Rock   Stone   SC
                     Birmingham Atlanta Mountain
Vicksburg   Charleston
        MS   AL   GA
              Selma Montgomery
        LA   ATLANTIC
                                    OCEAN
                          Okefenokee Swamp
Clear Lake   FL
        New Orleans   Homosassa   Daytona
                       Springs Orlando Titusville
Austwell
                       Sanibel
                       Island
                       Everglades City Homestead
        Gulf
        of
        Mexico

CUBA

539

Europe

Asia

Africa

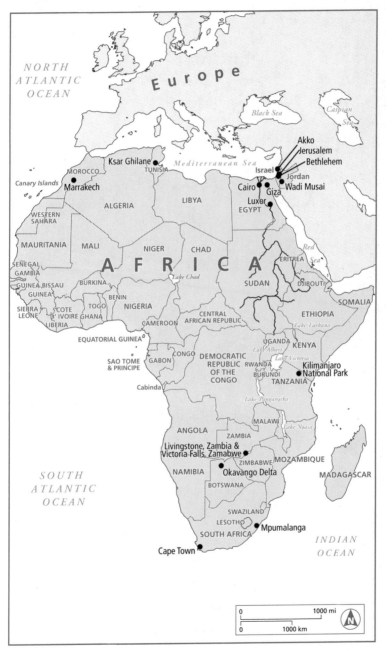

NORTH ATLANTIC OCEAN

Europe

Black Sea

Caspian Sea

Ksar Ghilane

Mediterranean Sea

Akko
Jerusalem
Bethlehem
Israel
Jordan
Wadi Musai

Cairo
Giza
Luxor
EGYPT

Canary Islands

Marrakech

MOROCCO

TUNISIA

ALGERIA

LIBYA

WESTERN SAHARA

MAURITANIA

MALI

NIGER

CHAD

A F R I C A

Lake Chad

SUDAN

ERITREA

Red Sea

SENEGAL
GAMBIA
GUINEA-BISSAU
GUINEA
SIERRA LEONE
LIBERIA
COTE D' IVOIRE

BURKINA

BENIN

TOGO

GHANA

NIGERIA

CAMEROON

CENTRAL AFRICAN REPUBLIC

DJIBOUTI

SOMALIA

ETHIOPIA

Lake Turkana

EQUATORIAL GUINEA

SAO TOME & PRINCIPE

GABON

CONGO

DEMOCRATIC REPUBLIC OF THE CONGO

UGANDA

Lake Albert

RWANDA

BURUNDI

Lake Victoria

KENYA

Kilimanjaro National Park

Cabinda

TANZANIA

Lake Tanganyika

MALAWI

Lake Nyasa

ANGOLA

ZAMBIA

Livingstone, Zambia & Victoria Falls, Zamabwe

ZIMBABWE

MOZAMBIQUE

MADAGASCAR

SOUTH ATLANTIC OCEAN

NAMIBIA

Okavango Delta

BOTSWANA

SWAZILAND

LESOTHO

SOUTH AFRICA

Mpumalanga

INDIAN OCEAN

Cape Town

0   1000 mi

0   1000 km

N

South America

Canada

Notes

Indexes

Geographical Index

Alphabetical Index

Photo Credits

p. 1: © Courtesy humboldtredwoods.org; p. 4: © Alexandra Picavet ; p. 6: © Arturo Bullard / PromPerú; p. 8: © Michael McLaughlin; p. 11: © Jack Brink; p. 12: © Lauren Etting; p. 15: © Jack Brink; p. 17: © Margot Weiss; p. 19: © Margot Weiss; p. 22: © Margot Weiss; p. 24: © Jack Brink; p. 26: © William Villalobos; p. 28: © Mui Lim; p. 31: © David Restivo, NPS; p. 33: © Jack Brink; p. 35: © Jack Brink; p. 39: © Jack Brink; p. 40: © Tourism Australia; p. 42: © Yvonne Lashmett; p. 45: © Glacier Express; p. 48: © Photo courtesy of Tourism Queensland; p. 50: © Jack Brink; p. 54: © John Troynousky ; p. 56: © Hurtigruten Image Library; p. 58: © Jack Brink; p. 60: © John Troynousky ; p. 61: © JNTO; p. 64: © Corn Palace, Mark Schilling; p. 67: © Open Stock Photography; p. 69: © Paris Tourism Bureau Photgraphe: Henri Garat; p. 70: © Courtesy www.labirintus.com; p. 72: © Jack Brink; p. 73: © Margot Weiss; p. 76: © Courtesy Alcatraz Cruises; p. 81: © Jack Brink; p. 84: © Courtesy Wigwam Motel; p. 86: © Lauren Etting; p. 93: © Gary Berdeaux of Diamond Caverns; p. 94: © NPS photo by Vickie Carson; p. 96: © Debra Hunter; p. 97: © Mohd Zaini ; p. 100: © San Diego Zoo; p. 101: © National Park Service; p. 103: © Groupe Dufour; p. 110: © Carla Reid; p. 111: © Neil Osborne / for Caribbean Conservation Corporation; p. 112: © Jack Brink; p. 114: © Alexis Lipsitz-Flippin; p. 115: © Alexis Lipsitz-Flippin; p. 119, top: © Shjan Carter; p. 119, bottom: © Sydney Aquarium; p. 122: © San Diego Zoo; p. 123: © Courtesy Toronto Zoo; p. 124: © Tourism Australia; p. 127: © Courtesy National Park Service; p. 132: © Jack Brink; p. 135: © Jack Brink; p. 137: © Jack Brink; p. 140: © Puako Petroglyphs Park; p. 145: © Jack Brink; p. 147: © Declan Masterson; p. 150: © Michael McLaughlin; p. 153: © Jack Brink; p. 155: © Jack Brink; p. 156: © Jack Brink; p. 157: © Jack Brink; p. 162: © Jack Brink; p. 163: © Greek National Tourism Organization; p. 168: © Lisa Monsees; p. 170: © Lisa Monsees; p. 174: © Peter Bobrowsky; p. 178: © Jack Brink; p. 180: © Suzanna R. Thompson; p. 183: © Mexico Tourism Board; p. 186: © Mike Spring; p. 187: © Peter Bobrowsky; p. 191: © James Horan; p. 194: © Vanessa Berberian; p. 196: © Courtesy Warwick Castle; p. 198: © Michael McLaughlin; p. 201: © Suzanna R. Thompson; p. 202: © Tourisme Brugge; p. 204: © Melinda Quintero; p. 205: © Heidelburger Kongress und Tourismus GmbH; p. 207: © Margot Weiss; p. 210: © JNTO; p. 211: © Jack Brink; p. 214: © Landeshauptstadt München Tourismusamt; p. 215: © Vanessa Berberian; p. 218: © SACVB/Michael Giordano; p. 222: © Jack Brink; p. 224: © Photo Courtesy of MOTT, Jim Higgins, photographer; p. 226: © National Park Service; p. 229: © Dell Bleekman; p. 234: © IWM; p. 240: © JNTO; p. 241: © Margot Weiss; p. 243: © Jack Brink; p. 245: © Courtesy of the International Spy Museum; p. 246: © Old Sturbridge Village photo by Thomas Neill; p. 248: © Debra Hunter ; p. 251: © Photo courtesy of MOTT; p. 258: © Old Sturbridge Village photo byErika Sidor; p. 261: © Jack Brink; p. 262: © Courtesy of Conner Prairie; p. 263: © Amana Colonies Convention and Visitors Bureau © 2005; p. 265: © Fort Worth Convention & Visitors Bureau; p. 268: © Katherine Fogden, NMAI; p. 274: © Collections of the National Underground Railroad Freedom Center; p. 276: © Alabama Bureau of Tourism & Travel/ Photographer Karim Shamsi-Basha; p. 278: © State of Tennessee; p. 280: © Courtesy Central High Museum Historical Collections/UALR Archives; p. 281: © Photo courtesy of the North Carolina Division of Tourism, Film and Sports Development; p. 282: © Margot Weiss; p. 286: © Scott Brownell, Museum of Science and Industry; p. 288: © The Exploratorium, photo credit Lily Rodriguez; p. 291: © NHM; p. 293: © Paris Toursim Bureau Photographe: Catherine Balet; p. 295: © National Park Service; p. 297: © National Museum of the United States Airforce; p. 299: © Kennedy Space Center Visitor Complex; p. 302: © Jack Brink; p. 306: © National Park Service; p. 311: © Griffith Observatory; p. 314: © Bruce Omori; p. 315: © Jack Brink; p. 316: © Jack Brink; p. 317: © Courtesy Wellington Cable Car; p. 320: © Courtesy State of Israel, Ministry of Tourism; p. 321: © Courtesy State of Israel, Ministry of Tourism; p. 323: © Jack Brink; p. 325: © William Villalobos; p. 326: © William Villalobos ; p. 329: © Barry Turner ; p. 331: © Tourism Ireland Imagery/Holger Leue; p. 338: © Mike Spring;